Praise for

THROUGH WOMEN'S EYES

"With compelling visual sources and imaginatively selected primary documents, Ellen DuBois and Lynn Dumenil draw the reader into the historical moment. On every page, history is tangible, engaging, and real. Beautifully written and cogently argued, *Through Women's Eyes* will stand as the defining text in U.S. women's history for years to come."

— VICKI RUIZ, *University of California, Irvine*

"The visual sources are delightful and the accompanying essays are critical to helping students see how to analyze such material."

— JOHN R. M. WILSON, *Vanguard University*

"I am an enthusiastic admirer of *Through Women's Eyes*. Its many resources allow for the varied learning styles of my community college students."

— MARY C. PRUITT, *Minneapolis Community & Technical College*

"Creation of a readable narrative [in women's history] has been at least thirty-five years in the making."

— SARAH H. GORDON, *Quinnipiac University*

"This text has it all—a lively, coherently organized narrative; coverage of key developments in both national and women's history; a stunning array of primary sources; and a remarkable collection of visual images. Students will be captivated by its engaging style, user-friendly organization, and riveting images, while teachers will find it extremely effective in presenting information and encouraging students to think critically."

—SUSAN HARTMANN, *The Ohio State University*

"Addressing racial, cultural, and ethnic diversity was one of my primary concerns and a reason for selecting *Through Women's Eyes*."

—LISA MILES BUNKOWSKI, *Park University*

"DuBois and Dumenil have created an excellent textbook. . . . I was very impressed with the variety of primary sources."

—DEBRA MEYERS, *Northern Kentucky University*

"The book reminds students how the points in women's history fit into the bigger picture of U.S. history."

—AMY BIX, *Iowa State University*

"The inclusion of an appendix with important documents related to both women's history and 'traditional' U.S. history makes this book particularly appealing. You could teach women's history on the moon because everything is there for you."

—KAREN MANNERS SMITH, *Emporia State University*

Second Edition

THROUGH WOMEN'S EYES

An American History

WITH DOCUMENTS

Volume One: To 1900

Second Edition

THROUGH WOMEN'S EYES

An American History
WITH DOCUMENTS

Volume One: To 1900

Ellen Carol DuBois
UNIVERSITY OF CALIFORNIA,
LOS ANGELES

Lynn Dumenil
OCCIDENTAL COLLEGE

BEDFORD/ST. MARTIN'S
Boston ◆ New York

For Bedford/St. Martin's

Publisher for History: Mary Dougherty
Director of Development for History: Jane Knetzger
Executive Editor for History: William J. Lombardo
Developmental Editor: Kathryn Abbott
Senior Production Editor: Deborah Baker
Senior Production Supervisor: Joe Ford
Executive Marketing Manager: Jenna Bookin Barry
Editorial Assistant: Alix Roy
Copyeditor: Janet Renard
Text Design: Anna Palchik
Indexer: Steve Csipke
Cover Design: Donna Lee Dennison
Cover Art: L to r: Library of Congress Prints and Photographs Division, Gladstone Collection; Worcester Art Museum, Worcester, Gift of Mr. and Mrs. Albert W. Rice; Library of Congress Prints and Photographs Division; Smithsonian American Art Museum, Washington, DC/Art Resource, NY; Susan B. Anthony House, Rochester, NY.
Composition: Pine Tree Composition, Inc.
Cartography: Mapping Specialists Ltd.
Printing and Binding: R.R. Donnelley & Sons Company

President: Joan E. Feinberg
Editorial Director: Denise B. Wydra
Director of Marketing: Karen R. Soeltz
Director of Editing, Design, and Production: Marcia Cohen
Assistant Director of Editing, Design, and Production: Elise S. Kaiser
Managing Editor: Elizabeth M. Schaaf

Library of Congress Control Number: 2008925874

Manufactured in the United States of America.

3   2   1   0   9   8
f   e   d   c   b   a

For information, write: Bedford/St. Martin's, 75 Arlington Street, Boston, MA 02116 (617-399-4000)

ISBN-10: 0-312-46887-3 (Combined edition)   ISBN-13: 978-0-312-46887-3
            0-312-46888-1 (Volume One)   978-0-312-46888-0
            0-312-46889-X (Volume Two)   978-0-312-46889-7

For Daniel Horowitz

and in memory of Lawrence W. Levine

PREFACE
FOR INSTRUCTORS

WHEN WE CONCEPTUALIZED the first edition of *Through Women's Eyes: An American History with Documents,* we were confident in our vision for an inclusive and diverse U.S. women's history that combined narrative and documents into one text. We have been thoroughly delighted that this book has resonated with instructors and students alike. We are pleased that others share our belief that U.S. women's history is U.S. history and vice versa. In constructing this textbook, we self-consciously followed the lead of Mary Ritter Beard, when she expressed the hope that her book, *America Through Women's Eyes,* first published in 1933, would "illustrate, if in a fragmentary way, the share of women in the development of American Society—their activity, their thought about their labor, and their thought about the history they have helped to make or have observed in the making."[1] In this new edition, we have drawn upon new scholarship published since the appearance of the first edition and have benefited tremendously from the insights of reviewers and adopters of the first edition of *Through Women's Eyes.*

APPROACH AND FORMAT

Through Women's Eyes: An American History with Documents challenges the separation of "women's history" from what students, in our experience, think of as "real history." We treat all central developments of American history, always through women's eyes, so that students may experience the broad sweep of the nation's past from a new and illuminating perspective. *Through Women's Eyes* combines in-depth treatment of well-known aspects of the history of women, such as the experiences of Lowell mill girls and slave women, the cult of true womanhood, and the rise of feminism, with developments in U.S. history not usually considered from the perspective of women, including the conquest of the Americas, the American Revolution, Civil War battlefields, post–World War II anti-communism, the civil rights movement, and the increasingly visible role that women have played in recent politics. Our goal of a full integration of women's history and U.S. history is pragmatic as well as principled. We recognize that the students who read *Through Women's Eyes* may have little background in U.S. history, that they will be learning the nation's history as they follow women through it.

At the same time that we broaden the conception of women's and U.S. history, we offer an inclusive view of the lives of American women. In this edition, we have

---

[1]Mary Ritter Beard, ed., *America Through Women's Eyes* (New York: Macmillan Co., 1933), 9.

strived to include more coverage of the broad range of classes, ethnicities, religions, and regions that constitute the historical experiences of U.S. women. We continue to decenter the narrative from an emphasis on white privileged women to bring ethnic and racial minorities and wage earning women from the margins to the center of our story. In providing an integrated analysis of the rich variety of women that includes ethnic and racial diversity and class, immigrant status, geographical, and sexual orientation differences, we have also explored the dynamics of relationships between women. Examples of sisterhood emerge from our pages, but so too do the hierarchical relations of class and race and other sources of tensions that erected barriers between women.

Now available in two volumes as well as the combined version.   The format of *Through Women's Eyes* elicited praise from scholars and teachers of U.S. women's history. In response to adopters' enthusiasm for the first edition of *Through Women's Eyes* and their desire to have the text more compatible with their teaching format, this book is now available in separate volumes for courses that do not cover all of women's history: Volume One, To 1900 (Chapters 1–7); and Volume Two, Since 1865 (Chapters 6–12).

In addition, the second edition includes even more written and visual primary sources. Just as many of our students hold preconceived notions of women's history as an intriguing adjunct to "real history," they often equate the historian's finished product with historical "truth." We remain determined to reveal the relationship between secondary and original sources, to show history as a dynamic process of investigation and interpretation rather than a set body of facts and figures. To this end, we divide each of our chapters into narrative text and primary-source essays. Of the essays, 20 center on written documents, providing more than 84 readings ranging from diaries, letters, and memoirs to poems, newspaper accounts, and public testimony. Our 16 visual essays collect over 130 images extending from artifacts, engravings, and portraits to photographs, cartoons, and television screen shots.

Together, the sources reveal to students the wide variety of primary evidence from which history is crafted. Our documentary and visual essays not only allow for focused treatment of many topics—for example, the experience of Native American women before and after European conquest, women on the Civil War battlefields, the Great Migration of African Americans in the World War I era, women's use of public spaces in the early twentieth century, popular culture in the 1950s, the impact of the 1960s and 1970s feminist movement on workplace practices, and the "third wave" feminist revival of the 1990s—but also provide ample guidance for students to analyze historical documents thoughtfully. Each essay offers advice about evaluating the sources presented and poses questions for analysis intended to foster students' ability to think independently and critically. Substantive headnotes to the sources and plentiful cross-references between the narrative and the essays further encourage students to appreciate the relationship between historical sources and historical writing.

NEW TO THIS EDITION

For this new edition, we have built on the strengths of the first edition of *Through Women's Eyes,* while expanding the coverage of a number of topics and offering fresh new document essays and illustrations. By adding new chapters at the beginning and end of the text, we have enhanced its global framework and chronological reach. The second edition provides new material on the experiences of African women, Native American women, and European women in the era before and after the establishment of the first European New World colonies and on the impact of modern globalization on women's work and political activism. In this edition, our treatment of recent history includes more on conservative women in the post–World War II era and on feminism in the late twentieth and early twenty-first centuries. We have also expanded our treatment of key themes such as sexuality and popular culture.

New visual sources essays include "Material Culture in Colonial America," "Depictions of Family in Colonial America," "Alice Austen: Gilded Age Photographer," and "Feminism and the Drive for Equality in the Workforce." Some visual essays from the first edition have also been significantly revised, notably "Women in the World," which devotes more attention to immigration and to women in the military. These essays, plus additional in-text visuals and maps allow for a richer understanding of U.S. women's history.

New primary documents essays include "African Women in the Slave Trade," Elizabeth Cady Stanton's articles in nineteenth-century women's rights magazines, Zitkala-Ša on Indian childhood and boarding schools, "Documents from the Women's Liberation Movement," and "Is a Working Mother a Threat to the Home?" from a 1958 forum published in the *Ladies' Home Journal.*

FEATURES AND PEDAGOGY

We are proud as well of the pedagogical features we provide to help students enter into and absorb the text. Each chapter opens with a *thematic introduction* that starts with a particular person or moment in time chosen to pique students' interest and segues into a clear statement of the central issues and ideas of the chapter. An *illustrated chapter timeline* alerts students to the main events covered in the narrative and relates women's experience to U.S. history by visually linking key developments. At the close of each narrative section, an *analytic conclusion* revisits central themes and provides a bridge to the next chapter.

Beyond the visual sources presented in the essays, *over 95 historical images and 14 maps and graphs* extend and enliven the narrative, accompanied by substantive captions that relate the illustration to the text and help students unlock the image. Also animating the narrative while complementing the documentary essays are *34 primary-source excerpts drawn from classic texts* featuring women such as Anne Hutchinson, Catharine Beecher, Sojourner Truth, Margaret Sanger, and Ella Baker. At the end of each chapter, we provide *plentiful footnotes* and *an annotated bibliography* that gives students a myriad of opportunities for reading and research beyond the boundaries of the textbook.

In addition, we open the book with an *Introduction for Students* that discusses the evolution of women's history as a field and the approach we took in capturing its exciting state today. An *extensive Appendix* includes not only tables and charts focused on U.S. women's experience over time but, in keeping with our mission to integrate women's history and American history, fundamental documents relating to U.S. history: the Declaration of Independence, the U.S. Constitution and its amendments, the Seneca Falls Declaration of Sentiments, a compendium of presidential administrations, and annotated extracts of Supreme Court cases of major relevance to U.S. history "through women's eyes."

ADDITIONAL RESOURCES

Bedford/St. Martin's has published both online and print resources relevant to the women's history course that complements our textbook.

Book Companion Site at bedfordstmartins.com/duboisdumenil Expanded and revised for this edition, the book companion site provides instructors and students with new and improved resources for teaching and learning U.S. women's history. Resources include a new online instructor's resource guide that includes revised assignment suggestions, term paper suggestions, teaching tips and lecture strategies, multiple-choice questions, and mid-term and final exam suggestions. New features of the book's companion Web site include television and film suggestions, tips on working with visual sources, and content for the classroom using i<clicker. Through Bedford/St. Martin's Make History link, the book companion site integrates maps, selected images, primary documents, links to relevant Web sites, and online research resources. The book's companion Web site also contains new and revised resources for students, including annotated chapter outlines, identification terms, focus questions, and notetaking outlines.

Trade Books Titles published by sister companies—Farrar, Straus and Giroux; Henry Holt and Company; Hill & Wang; Picador; and St. Martin's Press—are available at a 50 percent discount when packaged with Bedford/St. Martin's textbooks. For more information, visit bedfordstmartins.com/tradeup.

Bedford Series in History and Culture The more than 80 American history titles in this highly praised series include a number focused on women's history and combine first-rate scholarship, historical narrative, and important primary documents for undergraduate courses. Each book is brief, inexpensive, and focused on a specific topic or period. Package discounts are available.

ACKNOWLEDGMENTS

Textbooks are for learning, and writing this one has taught us a great deal. We have learned from each other and have enjoyed the richness of the collaborative process. But we have also benefited immensely from the opportunity to read and assess the works of literally hundreds of scholars whose research and insights have made this book possible.

We continue to be grateful to friends and colleagues who reviewed the first edition and suggested revisions for the second. For reading this edition's Chapters 1 and 2, we thank Alice Nash of the University of Massachusetts at Amherst. For reading through the entire manuscript, we thank Danielle Alexander, Napa Valley College; Amy Bix, Iowa State University; Lisa Miles Bunkowski, Park University; Mina Carson, Oregon State University; Sarah H. Gordon, Quinnipiac University; April Heaslip, Greenfield Community College; Paula Hinton, Tennessee Technological University; Rebecca Mead, Northern Michigan University; Debra Meyers, Northern Kentucky University; Mary C. Pruitt, Minneapolis Community & Technical College; Linda P. Pitelka, Maryville University; Jennifer Ritterhouse, Utah State University; Karen Manners Smith, Emporia State University; Jean A. Stuntz, Western Texas A&M University; Connie Tripp, College of the Canyons; Bari Watkins, Ohio University-Lancaster; Karol Weaver, Susquehanna University; and John R. M. Wilson, Vanguard University.

Numerous colleagues, former students, researchers, and archivists graciously answered phone and e-mail queries, helping us to find facts, quotations, images, and references. Thanks to Steve Aron, Sharla Fett, Kevin Terraciano, Ann D. Gordon, Kate Flint, Ramón Gutiérrez, Lisa Sousa, Ruth Rosen, and Sheila Tobias. Nicole Rebec provided admirable research assistance and we are also thankful for the assistance of archivists at Tamiment Library, New York University. We both want to thank Rumi Yasutake and her Japan-based team, who are preparing a Japanese-language version of *Through Women's Eyes* and in the process helped us to clarify our own text at crucial points. Lynn thanks Norman S. Cohen for his continued enthusiasm for the project.

We have a great deal of admiration for the people at Bedford/St. Martin's who worked so hard to bring both editions of this book to fruition. Former president Charles H. Christensen and current president Joan E. Feinberg have been warmly enthusiastic, as have editorial director Denise Wydra, publisher Mary Dougherty, director of development Jane Knetzger, senior marketing manager Jenna Bookin Barry, and editorial assistant Alix Roy. We appreciate the enthusiastic engagement of our developmental editor, Kathryn Abbott. Our first editor of *Through Women's Eyes*, Elizabeth Welch, has also continued to be an inspiration. Rose Corbett-Gordon did a superb job researching and clearing photo images; Sandy Schechter and Linda Winters cleared text permissions; Janet Renard copyedited the manuscript; Anna Palchik designed the interior of the book; Donna Dennison designed the cover; and Deborah Baker oversaw the production process.

We viewed the first edition of *Through Women's Eyes* as an exciting new departure, and the wide adoption and warm reception of reviewers and adopters has confirmed our aspirations. The revisions for this new edition benefited significantly from the comments of instructors who have used the textbook in their classes. We also reiterate, as we noted in the first edition, that this book would not have been possible without the dynamic developments and extraordinary output in the field of U.S. women's history since Mary Beard wrote her book. In 1933 Beard acknowledged that the "collection, editing, sifting and cataloguing of sources dealing with women's work and thought in the making of civilization" was ground as yet uncultivated.[2] We have been fortunate to reap a rich harvest from the scholarly literature of the last forty years, a literature that has allowed us to express the diversity of women's lives and to conceive of U.S. history from a gendered perspective.

Finally, we dedicate this edition of *Through Women's Eyes* to Daniel Horowitz, and to the memory of Lawrence W. Levine. They taught us as undergraduates and graduates, inspired us with a great love of U.S. history, provided models for the kind of approach that blossomed into *Through Women's Eyes,* and supported us in all of our efforts.

---

[2]Ibid.

BRIEF CONTENTS

CONTENTS

CHAPTER 2
Colonial Worlds, 1607–1750
56

CHAPTER 7
Women in an Expanding Nation: Consolidation of the West, Mass Immigration, and the Crisis of the 1890s
390

SPECIAL FEATURES

INTRODUCTION FOR STUDENTS

IN READING THIS TEXTBOOK, you will encounter a rich array of source materials and a narrative informed by a wealth of scholarship, so you may be surprised to learn that women's history is a comparatively new field. When Mary Ritter Beard, the founding mother of women's history in the United States, assembled *America Through Women's Eyes* in 1933, she argued that an accurate understanding of the nation's past required as much consideration of women's experience as of men's. But so limited were the sources available to her that she had no choice but to present the first women-centered American history as a spotty anthology of primary and secondary writings by a handful of women writers. Not until the 1970s, with the resurgence of feminism that you will read about in Chapter 11, did researchers start to give extensive attention to women's history. In that decade, history, along with other academic disciplines such as literature and sociology, underwent significant change as feminist scholars' desire to analyze as well as to protest women's unequal status fueled an extraordinary surge of investigation into women's experiences. Feminist theorists revived an obscure grammatical term, "gender," to distinguish the meaning that a particular society attaches to differences between men and women from "sex," or the unchanging biological differences between men and women. Because gender meaning varies over time and among societies, gender differences are both socially constructed and subject to change.

The concept of gender and the tools of history go together. If we are to move past the notion that what it means to be a woman never changes, we must look to the varying settings in which people assume female and male roles, with all their attendant expectations. Definitions of femininity and masculinity, family structures, what work is considered properly female or male, understandings of motherhood and of marriage, and women's involvement in public affairs all vary tremendously across time, are subject to large forces like economic development and warfare, and can themselves shape the direction of history. As historian Joan Scott forcefully argues, gender can be used as a tool of historical analysis, to explore not only how societies interpret differences between women and men but also how these distinctions can work to legitimize other hierarchical relations of power.[1]

This textbook draws on the rich theoretical and historical work of the past forty years to present a synthesis of American women's experiences. We begin Volume 1 with a discussion of the many meanings of "America" and end Volume 2 with a set of images that place women in the context of the globalized world of

---

[1] Joan Wallach Scott, "Gender: A Useful Category of Historical Analysis," *American Historical Review* 91, no. 5 (December 1986): 1067.

the twenty-first century. In between we highlight both the broad patterns of change concerning women's political, economic, and family lives and the diversity of American women's experiences.

As its title suggests, however, *Through Women's Eyes: An American History, with Documents* aims for more than an account of U.S. women's history. Beyond weaving together the wealth of scholarship available to U.S. women's historians, we seek to fulfill Mary Beard's vision of a text that covers the total range of the nation's history, placing women—their experiences, contributions, and observations—at the center. We examine major economic developments, such as the emergence of slavery as a labor system, the rise of factories in the early nineteenth century, the growth of an immigrant labor force, and the shift to corporate capitalism. We explore major political themes, from reform movements to political party realignments to the nation's many wars. We look at transformations in family and personal life, the rise of consumer and mass culture, the racial and ethnic heterogeneity of the nation's peoples, and shifting attitudes about sexuality. And we analyze international developments, beginning with the inter-relationship of the Americas, Europe, and Africa in the Atlantic world of the sixteenth and seventeenth centuries and ending with contemporary globalization. But as we do so, we analyze how women experienced these national developments and how they contributed to and shaped them.

THE HISTORY OF WOMEN'S HISTORY: FROM SEPARATE SPHERES TO MULTICULTURALISM

When the field of U.S. women's history began to take off as a scholarly endeavor in the 1970s, one particular form of gender analysis was especially influential. The "separate spheres" paradigm, as historians termed it, focused on the nineteenth-century ideology that divided social life into two mutually exclusive arenas: the private world of home and family, identified with women, and the public world of business and politics, identified with men. In a second phase, as scholarship on women of color increased, the primacy of the separate spheres interpretation gave way to a more nuanced interpretation of the diversity of women's experiences.

Separate Spheres and the Nineteenth-Century Gender System

Women's historians of the 1970s found in the nineteenth-century system of separate spheres the roots of the gender distinctions of their own time. They observed that although ideas about separate spheres had been of enormous importance in the nineteenth century, these ideas had received little to no attention in historical accounts. The approach that women's historians took was to re-vision this nineteenth-century gender system through women's eyes. They found that, although women's lives were tightly constricted by assumptions about their proper place within the family, expectations of female moral influence and a common sense of womanhood allowed women collectively to achieve a surprising degree of social authority.

The separate spheres paradigm proved a valuable approach, but it hid as much as it yielded about women's lives. Early on, historian Gerda Lerner observed that it was no coincidence that the notion of women's exclusive domesticity flourished just as factories were opening up and young women were going to work in them.[2] Because adherence to the ideology of separate spheres helped to distinguish the social standing of middle-class women from their factory-working contemporaries, Lerner urged that class relations and the growth of the female labor force be taken into account in understanding the influence that such ideas held. Subsequent historians have observed that the idealization of women within the domestic sphere coincided exactly with the decline of the economic importance of family production relative to factory production; and that just as class inequality began to challenge the nation's democratic self-understanding, American society came to define itself in terms of the separate spheres of men and women.

Additional problems emerged in the reliance on the separate spheres paradigm as the dominant basis for nineteenth-century U.S. women's history. Historian Nancy Hewitt contends that whatever sense of female community developed among nineteenth-century women rarely crossed class or race lines. On the contrary, hierarchical relationships—slave to mistress, immigrant factory worker to moneyed consumer, nanny to professional woman—have been central to the intricate tapestry of the historical female experience in America.[3] Even among the middle-class wives and mothers who did not work outside the home and whose family-based lives made them the central focus of separate spheres ideology, Linda Kerber urges historians not to confuse rhetoric with reality, ideological values with individual actions.[4] The lasting contribution of the historical exploration of separate spheres ideology is the recognition of the vital impact of gender differentiation on American history; the challenge posed by its critics is to develop a more complex set of portraits of women who lived in, around, and against these notions. As it matures, the field of women's history is able to move from appreciating the centrality of gender systems to accommodating and exploring conflicts and inequalities among women.

Toward a More Inclusive Women's History: Race and Ethnicity

The field of U.S. women's history has struggled to come to terms with the structures of racial inequality so central to the American national experience. As Peggy Pascoe observes, modern scholars have learned to think about race and gender in similar ways, no longer treating either as unchanging biological essences around which history forms but as social constructions that change meaning and content

---

[2]Gerda Lerner, "The Lady and the Mill Girl," *Midcontinent American Studies Journal* 10 (1969): 5–15.
[3]Nancy Hewitt, "Beyond the Search for Sisterhood: American Women's History in the 1990s," in Vicki Ruiz and Ellen Carol DuBois, eds., *Unequal Sisters: A Multicultural Reader in U.S. Women's History*, 3rd ed. (New York: Routledge, 2000), 1–19.
[4]Linda K. Kerber, "Separate Spheres, Female Worlds, Woman's Place: The Rhetoric of Women's History," *Journal of American History* 75, no. 1 (June 1988): 9–39.

over time and place.[5] Building on a century-long scholarly tradition in African American history, black women scholars started in the 1980s to chart new territory as they explored the interactions between systems of racial and gender inequality. Analyzing the implications of the denial to late nineteenth-century black women of the privileges granted white women, Evelyn Brooks Higginbotham observes that "gender identity is inextricably linked to and even determined by racial identity."[6]

Other scholars of color, especially Chicana feminists, advanced this thinking about racial hierarchy and its intersections with the structures of gender. They made it clear that the history of Chicanas could not be understood within the prevailing black-white model of racial interaction. The outlines of a multivocal narrative of U.S. women's history that acknowledge women's diversity in terms of race, class, ethnicity, and sexual orientation are advanced by *Unequal Sisters: A Multicultural Reader in U.S. Women's History,* coedited by Vicki Ruiz and one of the authors of this text, Ellen Carol DuBois. This anthology of pathbreaking research pays particular attention to the historical experiences of Western women, noting that "the confluence of many cultures and races in this region—Native American, Mexican, Asian, Black, and Anglo"—required "grappling with race" from a multicultural perspective.[7] By using her own southwestern experience, Gloria Anzaldúa added the influential metaphor of "borderlands" to this approach to suggest that the division between different communities and personal identities is somewhat arbitrary and sometimes shifting.[8] This new approach took the logic of the historical construction of gender, so important to the beginning of women's history, and pushed it further by emphasizing an even greater fluidity of social positioning.

APPROACHING HISTORY *THROUGH WOMEN'S EYES*

How then to bring together a historical narrative told from such diverse and at times conflicting viewpoints? All written histories rely on unifying themes to organize what is otherwise a chaotic assembly of facts, observations, incidents, and people. Traditionally, American history employed a framework of steady national progress, from the colonial revolt against England to modern times. Starting in the 1960s, the writing of American history emphasized an alternative story line of the struggles of workers, slaves, Indians, and (to some degree) women, to overcome enduring inequalities. Initially, women's history emphasized the rise and fall of the

---

[5]Peggy Pascoe, "Gender," in Richard Wightman Fox and James Kloppenberg, eds., *A Companion to American Thought* (Cambridge, MA: Blackwell, 1995), 273.

[6]Evelyn Brooks Higginbotham, "African American Women's History and the Metalanguage of Race," *Signs* 17, no. 2 (Winter 1992): 254.

[7]Ellen Carol DuBois and Vicki L. Ruiz, eds., *Unequal Sisters: A Multicultural Reader in U.S. Women's History* (New York: Routledge, 1990), xii. This reader has three later editions (1994, 2000, 2008) that include substantially different articles.

[8]Gloria Anzaldúa, *La Frontera/Borderlands: The New Mestiza* (1987; San Francisco: Aunt Lute Books, 1999).

system of separate gender spheres, the limits of which we suggest above. In organizing *Through Women's Eyes*, we employ another framework, one that emphasizes three major themes that shaped the diversity of women's lives in American history—work, politics, and family and personal life.

Work and the Sexual Division of Labor

The theme of women's work reveals both stubborn continuities and dramatic changes. Women have always labored, always contributed to the productive capacity of their communities. Throughout American history, women's work has taken three basic forms—unpaid labor within the home, chattel slavery, and paid labor. The steady growth of paid labor, from the beginning of American industrialization in the 1830s to the present day (women now constitute essentially half of America's workforce), is one of the fundamental developments in this history. As the female labor force grew, its composition changed, by age, race, ethnicity, and class. By the mid-twentieth century, the working mother had taken over where once the working girl had predominated. We have also followed the repeated efforts of wage earning women to organize collectively in order to counter the power of their employers, doing so sometimes in conjunction with male workers and sometimes on their own. Always a small percentage of union members compared to men, women exhibited unanticipated militancy and radicalism in their fight with employers over union recognition and fair wages and hours.

Most societies divide women's work from men's, and America's history has been no exception. Feminist scholars designate this gender distinction as the "sexual division of labor." Yet the content of the sexual division of labor varies from culture to culture, a point made beginning with the discussion of Native American communities in the precolonial and colonial eras and of African women's agricultural labor in their native lands. When women first began to take on paid labor in large numbers, they did so primarily as servants and seamstresses; the nature of their work thus generally followed the household sexual division of labor. The persistence of sex segregation in the workforce has had many sources of support: employers' desire to have a cheap, flexible supply of labor; male workers' control over better jobs and higher wages; and women's own assumptions about their proper place.

The division between male and female work continued, and with it the low wages and limited opportunities on the women's side of the line. This was true even as what counted as women's jobs began to expand, and teaching and secretarial labor, once securely on the male side of the line, crossed over to become "feminized" job categories. American feminism in the late twentieth century has been committed to eroding this long-standing principle that work should be divided into male and female categories. As historian Alice Kessler-Harris puts it, feminists "introduced the language of sex discrimination onto the national stage, casting a new light on seemingly natural patterns of accommodating sex difference."[9] The

---

[9]Alice Kessler-Harris, *In Pursuit of Equity: Women, Men, and the Quest for Economic Citizenship in 20th-Century America* (New York: Oxford University Press, 2001), 245–46.

degree to which the sexual division of labor has been substantially breached—whether it is half achieved or half undone — we leave to our readers, who are part of this process, to determine.

Gender and the Meaning of Politics

The theme of politics in women's historical experience presents a different sort of challenge, for it is the *exclusion* of women from formal politics that is the obvious development in U.S. women's history, at least until 1920 when the Nineteenth Amendment granting woman suffrage was ratified. While the story of women's campaign for the vote plays an important role in our historical account, we have not portrayed the suffrage movement as a monolithic effort. Rather, we have attended to the inequalities of class and race and the strategic and ideological conflicts that ran throughout the movement. We have also stressed the varying political contexts, ranging from Reconstruction in the 1860s to the Populist upsurge in the 1890s to Progressivism in the 1910s, within which women fought for their voting rights. Finally, we have traced the significance of voting in U.S. women's history after the right to it was formally secured, following women's efforts to find their place—as voters and as office holders—in the American political system.

U.S. women's historians have gone beyond the drama surrounding the vote, its denial and its uses, to a more expansive sense of the political dimension of women's historical experience. Feminist scholars have forged a definition of politics that looks beyond the formal electoral arena to other sorts of collective efforts to change society, alter the distribution of power between groups, create and govern important institutions, and shape public policy. Women's historians have given concrete substance to this broad approach to female political involvement by investigating the tremendous social activism and civic engagement that thrived among women, especially through the long period during which they lacked formal political rights. "In order to bring together the history of women and politics," writes Paula Baker, "we need a more inclusive definition of politics . . . to include any action, formal or informal, taken to affect the course or behavior of government or the community."[10]

From this perspective, the importance of women in the realm of politics reaches back to the Iroquois women who elected chiefs and participated in decisions to go to war and the European women colonists who provided the crucial support necessary to sustain pre-Revolutionary boycotts against British goods in the struggle for national independence. Just a small sampling of this rich tradition of women's civic activity through the nineteenth century includes the thousands of New England women who before the Civil War signed petitions against slavery and Indian removal; the campaign begun by Ida B. Wells against the lynching of southern blacks; the ambitious late nineteenth-century national reform agenda of Frances Willard's Woman's Christian Temperance Union; and Jane Addams's lead-

[10]Paula Baker, "The Domestication of Politics: Women and American Political Society, 1780–1920," *American Historical Review* 89 (June 1984): 622.

ership in addressing problems of the urban immigrant poor and on behalf of international peace. "Women's organizations pioneered in, accepted and polished modern methods of pressure-group politics," observes historian Nancy Cott.[11]

Indeed, this sort of extra-electoral political activism extended into the twentieth century, incorporating women's challenges to the arms race of the post–World War II era and the civil rights leadership of women such as Ella Baker of the Southern Conference Leadership Conference in the 1950s and Dolores Huerta of the United Farm Workers union in the 1960s. This inclusive sense of what constitutes "politics" has not only enriched our understanding of women's history, but it has generated a more complex understanding of the nature of political power and process within U.S. history in general.

Given the theme of politics as one of the major frames for this book, what is the place of the politics of feminism in the tale we tell? There are many definitions of feminism, but perhaps the clearest is the tradition of organized social change by which women challenge gender inequality. The term "feminism" itself arose just as the woman suffrage movement was nearing victory, but the tradition to which it refers reaches back to the women's rights movements of the nineteenth century. Historical research has unearthed a great deal of breadth and diversity in the many campaigns and protests through which women from different groups, in different times and places, dealing with different challenges, expressed their discontent with the social roles allotted to them and pursued their ambitions for wider options, more individual freedom, and greater social authority.

Feminism and women's history are mutually informing. Feminism is one of the important subjects of women's history, and history is one of feminism's best tools. Knowing what the past has been for women, doing the scholarship that Anne Firor Scott calls "making the invisible woman visible," is a necessary resource in pressing for further change.[12] But feminism is also a method by which historians examine the past in terms of women's efforts to challenge, struggle, make change, and sometimes achieve progress. Like so many of the scholars on whom the authors of this text rely, we have worked from such a perspective, and the passion we have brought to this work has its roots in a feminist commitment to highlighting—and encouraging—women's active social role and contribution to history. For us, however, a women's history informed by feminism is not a simple exercise of celebration, but a continuing and critical examination of what we choose to examine in the past and the methods we use to do so.

The Role of Family and Personal Life

The third integrating category of *Through Women's Eyes* is the theme of family and personal life. In contrast to the categories of labor and politics, which have been recognized in all narratives of the nation's past, women's historians took the

---

[11]Nancy Cott, *The Grounding of American Feminism* (New Haven: Yale University Press, 1987), 95.
[12]Anne Firor Scott, "Making the Invisible Woman Visible: An Essay Review," *Journal of Southern History* 38, no. 4 (November 1972): 629–38.

lead in bringing family and personal life into the mainstream of American history. Indeed, one of the fundamental contributions of feminist scholarship has been to demonstrate that kinship and sexuality have not been static elements of human nature but have their own complex histories. We try to make this clear by discussing the variety of family patterns evident among Native Americans, immigrants, African Americans, white middle-class Americans, and other ethnic groups.

Over the span of American history, family life has gone from the very center of political power and economic production in the seventeenth and eighteenth centuries to a privileged arena of emotional life in the early twenty-first century. As we write this introduction, family life—who can marry whom, what forms of sexuality should be tolerated, who should care for children and how—have become topics of intense public contest and political positioning. Thus concepts and experiences of family and sexual life, once viewed as the essence of women's separate sphere, are increasingly understood as a major connection between private concerns and public issues.

The histories of both motherhood and female sexuality reveal this connection. Motherhood not only has been central to women's individual family lives but also has served larger functions as well. Within slave communities, mothers taught their children how to survive within and fight against their servitude. Among middle-class women in the nineteenth and early twentieth centuries, motherhood became an effective way to claim female public authority. In the 1950s, at the start of the Cold War between the United States and the former Soviet Union, radical women subverted intense anti-Communist interrogations under the cloak of motherhood, thus trumping one of the decade's most dramatic themes with another. The social significance of motherhood has been used for conservative political purposes as well, with claims about the centrality of women's maternal role to social order providing the fuel of the anti-feminist backlash of the 1970s and through it the emergence of a new political right wing.

When it comes to the subject of sexuality, historians have proved particularly innovative in learning to read through the euphemisms and silences that obscure women's sexual lives even more than men's. They have delved into documents left by guardians of sexual propriety about prostitutes and by lascivious masters about slave women, in order to imagine how the objects of these judgments themselves experienced these encounters. When historians set aside modern attitudes toward sexuality and reexamined the lives of seemingly prudish nineteenth-century middle-class women, they found, as Linda Gordon demonstrates, the origins of the American birth control movement and all the radical changes in women's lives that flowed from it.[13] No longer content to portray the history of female sexuality as a simple move from repression to freedom, historians have examined the changing understandings of female sexuality and its shifting purposes in the twentieth century, as it played a major role in advancing new standards of consumerism, and in

---

[13]Linda Gordon, *The Moral Property of Women: A History of Birth Control Politics in America* (1976; Urbana: University of Illinois Press, 2004).

modernizing—though not necessarily making more egalitarian—relations between men and women.

Perhaps historians of women have been most creative in learning to look beyond the heterosexual relations that traditionally have defined sexuality to explore the intimate, romantic, and ambiguously sexual relations among women themselves. Carroll Smith-Rosenberg pioneered in demonstrating how common romantic friendships among women were in the nineteenth century, describing them as "an intriguing and almost alien form of human relation, [which] flourished in a different social structure and amidst different sexual norms."[14] Historical work into what has come to be called "homosociality" has deepened understandings of sexuality overall. Thus, as with the concepts of gender and race, women's history has led us to view sexuality itself as socially constructed, not as biologically prescribed.

Sexuality has been an especially important site for historians to locate the intersections of race and gender. Middle-class white women's historical prominence rested in considerable part on the contrast between their reputed sexual innocence and propriety and the supposedly disreputable (and titillating) sexuality of women of color on the margins, such as black slaves, so-called Indian squaws, and Asian prostitutes. This intersection between sexuality and race has also been investigated from the position of women who found themselves on the other side of the vice-virtue divide. As historian Paula Giddings argues, the rising up of recently freed African American women against their reputations as sexually available and that of African American men as sexually predatory helped to generate the creation of a black middle class and "a distinctive mix which underlined Black women's activism for generations to come."[15]

These and other discoveries in the field of U.S. women's history have made this textbook possible. The rich body of scholarly literature developed over the past decades has also enabled us to achieve our goal of integrating women's history into U.S. history, of showing how material once separated as "women's history" contributes to a broader understanding of the nation's history. In *America Through Women's Eyes*, Mary Beard insisted that women not be rendered as the passive objects of men's actions but as makers of history themselves; and that they not be removed from the historical flow into a separate narrative, but that their history be understood as part and parcel of the full range of national experience. This has been our guiding principle in writing this textbook—and the reason we have titled it an American history "through women's eyes."

---

[14]Carroll Smith-Rosenberg, "The Female World of Love and Ritual," *Signs* 1 (1979): 1–29.
[15]Paula Giddings, *When and Where I Enter: The Impact of Black Women on Race and Sex in America* (New York: William Morrow, 1984), 50.

Second Edition

THROUGH WOMEN'S EYES

An American History
WITH DOCUMENTS

Volume One: To 1900

1

America in the World

TO 1650

PEOPLE WHO LIVE IN THE UNITED STATES OFTEN REFER to themselves as Americans and to their nation as America. From this perspective, "America" includes the places, peoples, and economic systems that eventually became the single national entity of the United States. But there are other meanings of "America" to consider. America is the name given to the entire hemisphere by the Europeans who accidentally encountered it in the late-fifteenth and early-sixteenth centuries. "America" is also the term that eventually devolved on the northern continent of that hemisphere; there many European empires vied for control before England prevailed. The indigenous peoples of North America had many names for themselves that translated as "men" or "the people," but Europeans called them "Americans" or "American Indians." Finally, colonists of European descent came to refer to themselves as Americans, to distinguish themselves from their Old World predecessors. Modern Americans have inherited all of these meanings of "America."

To begin American history, more and more historians are looking beyond (or before) the English establishment of the thirteen Atlantic colonies. Using a multicultural lens, we can reconfigure early American history as the intersection of and conflict between several distinct histories—Native American, European, and African. In addition, each of these groups contained many different societies. With this approach, we can reach back before the traditional starting events, the first English settlements that proved to be permanent on the North American continent—Jamestown in 1607 and Plymouth in 1620—to important and shaping processes in the 1500s. These include the developments among Native peoples; the impact of the initial sixteenth-century contact between Native peoples and Europeans, including disease, trade, and conquest; the powerful Spanish empire in the New World that preceded, inspired, and competed with the later arriving English; the invention of transatlantic slavery and the plantation agriculture system that it served; and political, economic, and religious upheavals in Europe from the late Renaissance through the Protestant Reformation.

To view these beginnings of American history through women's eyes requires creativity. Although our cherished national myths emphasize the family origins of seventeenth-century New England immigration, the first century of European incursions to the western hemisphere was overwhelmingly male. So was the introduction of African slaves to the Americas in the sixteenth century, because enslaved women were held back in Africa, where they were valued, even as enslaved men were worked to death in the Americas. But Native women and European and African men encountered each other, willingly and unwillingly, across a divide of massive cultural difference that has been described as "an epochal cross-roads of gender."[1]

For much of their national history, Americans have preferred to think of their country as exceptional, different from the other nations of the world, set apart by geography, democratic traditions, and Christian heritage. In our own age of airplanes and the Internet, in a thoroughly multicultural and multireligious society, faith in American exceptionalism and superiority seems outdated. America in the twenty-first century is situated thoroughly in a global system of culture, economics, power relations, and human migration (see Visual Sources: American Women in the World, pp. 778–93).

But America was in and of the world in other periods as well. From the 1500s on, people, ideas, natural materials, and manufactured goods went back and forth between the Old World and the New, including the horse, a European animal that dramatically changed the culture of Native

1542	Bartolomé de Las Casas publishes account of the devastation of the Indies
1550–1600	Portuguese and Spanish sugar cultivation begun in Americas; first using indigenous slave labor, later using African slave labor
1558–1603	**Queen Elizabeth I's reign**
1565	Spanish establish St. Augustine, Florida
c.1581	**Birth of Nzinga, queen of Angola**
1585–1587	Roanoke colony
1586?	**Birth of Virginia Dare**
1595?	**Pocahontas born**
1598	Spanish Franciscan friars come to New Mexico
1598	Acoma rebellion in New Mexico
c.1600	Powhatan confederacy established
1607	Jamestown founded
1607	John Smith taken captive and adopted by Powhatans
1608	Samuel de Champlain founds Quebec
1614	**Pocahontas marries John Rolfe**
1616–1617	**Pocahontas travels to England; dies the next year**
1619	First record of Africans brought into British North America
1620s	**María de Jesús de Agreda, a Spanish nun, appears to indigenous people throughout New Mexico**

peoples, and the maize plant, first developed in what is now Mexico, then imported to Europe to become an important staple crop. As one historian has put it, "America was international before it was national."[2]

NATIVE AMERICAN WOMEN

With at least two hundred languages spoken in North America on the eve of European conquest, the world of Native Americans defies simple generalization. Historians usually analyze Native Americans in the context of region and economic activities. Thus, in the Southwest lived agricultural peoples, the Pueblos. In California lived hunter-gatherers, for example, the Chumash; in the Northwest, the fishing Nootkas, and in the Great Plains, hunters such as the Crows, the Sioux, and the Blackfeet. In the Great Lakes region, groups such as the Ojibwas emphasized hunting. In the eastern woodlands, the Iroquois lived inland west of the Hudson River and Algonquian-speaking peoples populated the Atlantic Coast from what is today Maine to the present Carolinas. Both the Iroquois and coastal Algonquians engaged in agriculture (see Map 1.1).

The diversity of Native peoples extended to their gender systems, which shifted from group to group. Here, as in all of the history that went into creating America, this fundamental fact stands out: the divisions between the worlds of men and the worlds of women, the distinctions that we call gender, were omnipresent but infinitely varied. In horticultural societies, where people depended on corn and other crops, lineage was generally traced by matrilineal descent, or through the mother's line. In hunter-gatherer societies, lineage was often determined by patrilineal descent, that is, through the father's line. Women's experiences after marriage depended on whether they were expected to live among their husband's people (patrilocal marriage) or whether their husbands came to live with them (matrilocal). Indigenous women's daily work varied according to where they lived and what foodstuffs were available. For example, women planted and tended corn in both the Northeast and the Southwest, but southwestern women spent more time irrigating their crops. Women also had different degrees of status and autonomy in their societies. No matter what specific tasks were included, roles related to economic activities were a powerful determinant in Native women's lives.

Indigenous Peoples before 1492

Archaeological evidence indicates that at least fourteen thousand years ago (and probably much earlier) Native Americans migrated across a land bridge that once united Siberia and Alaska. Historians believe that by the fifteenth century, between 7 and 12 million indigenous people lived in the area that is now the United States. Although popular images of Native Americans depict them primarily as hunter-gatherers or nomadic hunters, a significant number engaged in farming, along with fishing or hunting. In these agricultural communities, women fulfilled

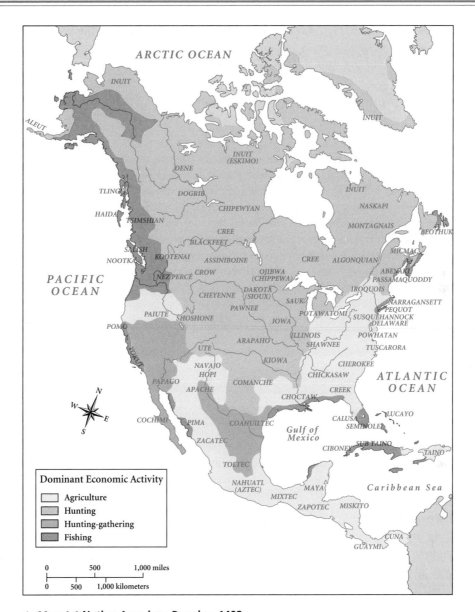

◆ **Map 1.1 Native American Peoples, 1492**

By the time of Columbus's arrival, Native American peoples populated the entire Western Hemisphere. Among those groups who practiced intensive agriculture, both men and women farmed. Among groups who practiced both hunting and agriculture, men were primarily the hunters while women did most of the farming. Among tribes engaged primarily in hunting, women hunted smaller game, gathered wild plant foods, and processed the meat and skins of the larger animals killed by men.

crucial roles in planting, harvesting, and processing food. Before the arrival of Europeans, some indigenous groups hunted bison on the Great Plains by using fires to stampede the animals over cliffs. It was not until Native groups living on the borders of the plains—like the Comanches, Arapahos, Cheyennes, and Sioux—had access to horses from Europe that significant numbers migrated to the Great Plains and became nomadic bison hunters. In all groups that emphasized hunting, men killed big game while women skinned the animals and prepared the meat.

Wherever they lived, indigenous Americans were not a static people, frozen in time waiting for Europeans to "discover" them. Historians have mapped out an amazing array of Indian trails that crisscrossed the continent. Trading in shells, furs, agricultural products, pottery, salt, copper, and slaves, Native Americans had contact with and knowledge of many other groups with whom they shared the continent. Although trade was peaceful, Native Americans sometimes warred with one another over land and resources. This violence had special meaning for women since they and children were often taken captive and integrated into the societies of their captors. Both warfare and ecological pressures such as drought prompted significant migration, the merging of communities, and the rise and fall of powerful Indian nations. Although we have virtually no documents written by the women themselves, a cautious reading of European eyewitness accounts of the communities they encountered has provided historians with insights into Native American lives. (See Visual Sources: Images of Native American Women, pp. 35–46.)

In many Indian nations, women had more power and sexual choices than most European women of their time did, albeit in the context of clear distinctions between the labor and responsibilities of men and women. In other words, in traditional native societies, relations between the sexes were characterized simultaneously by difference and by a degree of equality. The following examination of two well-documented groups reveals the diverse lives of Native American women and their cultures.

The Pueblo Peoples

Perched on cliffs in present-day New Mexico and Colorado are the remains of prehistoric dwellings of the Native people called Anasazi, who settled in the area as early as 300 B.C.E. From their distinctive multistoried, mud-plastered buildings came the generic name Pueblos, which the Spanish gave to Anasazi descendants such as the Zuñi, Hopi, Acoma, and similar peoples who were living in the American Southwest (New Mexico, Arizona, Colorado, and Utah) by 1250 C.E. When the Spanish arrived in the region in the mid-sixteenth century, there were close to 250,000 Pueblo people living in more than one hundred towns and villages. The Pueblo peoples encompassed seven language groups, and undoubtedly customs and rituals varied from tribe to tribe, despite many points of similarity. Like many other Indian peoples, the Pueblos apparently experienced much social disruption in the years preceding conquest. The hostile incursions of more nomadic Apaches from the Great Plains into their region may have been one of the causes for significant Pueblo migration and change in the region during the thirteenth and fourteenth centuries.

By the 1500s, the Pueblos were already practicing intensive agriculture, growing corn, squash, and beans. As in other societies, labor was divided by sex. Men traded goods and provided defense; they also tended the corn crop. Men collected and placed the timbers for the construction of their homes, but women plastered the walls. Women's work centered on what went on within those walls, the "inside" of the community. They created pottery, made moccasins and blankets, and, most crucially, prepared the food. Grinding the dried corn was women's work, a task that daughters and mothers shared. Women viewed their food production as something vital to their people, as something spiritual, a point reinforced by the Acoma Pueblo origin story (see box, "Two Sisters and Acoma Origins").

In addition to its association with corn and the earth's fertility, women's spirituality—and men's—was tied to their sexuality. Intercourse often held ritualistic and religious meanings. It was not only the source of life but also a means of taming bad spirits in nature and of integrating outsiders into the tribe. It helped to maintain the cosmic balance. Pueblo ideology thus recognized women's sexual power, a factor that, like women's role in food production, contributed to relatively egalitarian relationships between the sexes.

The matrilineal system, tracing ancestry and control of land through the female line, consolidated women's position in their communities. Like most Native American peoples, among the Pueblos land and households were occupied communally by particular families and, in their case, passed through the female line. Control of the land was tied to its use, not to some abstract concept of ownership. In addition to being matrilineal, Pueblos were matrilocal, meaning that men left their mothers' homes to marry and moved in with their wives' families. In Pueblo society, men and women could leave their marriages and choose new partners without stigma, an arrangement in accord with the understanding that an individual's primary identity was defined by his or her mother's identity, not a marital bond. Older women were therefore particularly influential members of the community. While men dominated the "outside" realm—trade, defense, and war—women dominated the world inside the pueblo walls they had constructed.

The Iroquois Confederacy

Far away from the southwestern Pueblos, the Iroquois Confederacy—initially consisting of the Seneca, Cayuga, Onondaga, Oneida, and Mohawk people—constructed another version of native life. In the forests of what became New York State and Ontario, Canada, an estimated twenty to thirty thousand people lived in perhaps ten villages at the turn of the seventeenth century. The Iroquois were unique among Native peoples for their Great League of Peace and Power, thought to have been founded in 1451, which linked them in an elaborate confederation. The chiefs of the Iroquois Confederacy were always men, but they were chosen by the women and could be deposed by them. The distinctive political power of Iroquois women is also reflected in how families were organized. The Iroquois matrilineal system

Two Sisters and Acoma Origins

According to the Acoma Pueblo Indians' origin story, the first women in the world were two sisters, born underneath the ground and sent above by Tsichtinako (Thought Woman). She first taught them to plant corn, tend and harvest it, grind it for food, and use fire to cook it. What follows is an excerpt from one such story told in 1928 by residents of the Acoma and Santa Ana pueblos to anthropologist Matthew W. Stirling. Native peoples' oral traditions, recorded by ethnographers, have become the source of much knowledge of Native history. What are the advantages and disadvantages of oral traditions recorded by outsiders as a source of historical knowledge? Why do you suppose corn played such an important part in the way in which Pueblo people understand their origins?

Tsichtinako spoke to them, "Now is the time you are to go out. You are able to take your baskets with you. In them you will find pollen and sacred corn meal. When you reach the top, you will wait for the sun to come up and that direction will be called ha'nami [east]. With the pollen and the sacred corn meal you will pray to the Sun. You will thank the Sun for bringing you to light, ask for a long life and happiness, and for success in the purpose for which you were created." Tsichtinako then taught them the prayers and the creation song, which they were to sing. . . .

They now prayed to the Sun as they had been taught by Tsichtinako, and sang the creation song. Their eyes hurt for they were not accustomed to the strong light. For the first time they asked Tsichtinako why they were on earth and why they were created. Tsichtinako replied, "I did not

emphasized women's importance for establishing identity and rights to the use of land in each clan. Several families lived together in longhouses, large bark-and-log dwellings, which were supervised by the clans' elder women, or matrons.

The sexual division of labor reinforced women's dominance in the village. Men prepared fields for planting, but their major duties took them to the forests, where they hunted, conducted trade, and warred with hostile tribes. Women's responsibilities centered in the village, where they raised crops (corn, beans, and squash); gathered mushrooms, berries, and nuts; prepared food; distributed the results of men's hunting; and made baskets, pottery, and other implements. They worked hard but communally. This gendered division of labor continued even after European colonization began. Mary Jemison, a British captive who married and raised a family among the Seneca in the eighteenth century, later explained: "In order to expedite their business, and at the same time enjoy each other's com-

make you. Your father, Uchtsiti made you, and it is he who has made the world, the sun which you have seen, the sky, and many other things which you will see. But Uchtsiti says the world is not yet completed, not yet satisfactory, as he wants it. This is the reason he has made you. You will rule and bring to life the rest of the things he has given you in the baskets." . . . Tsichtinako next said to them, "Now that you have your names, you will pray with your names and your clan names so that the Sun will know you and recognize you." Tsichtinako asked Nautsiti which clan she wished to belong to. Nautsiti answered, "I wish to see the sun, that is the clan I will be." The spirit told Nautsiti to ask Iatiku what clan she wanted. Iatiku thought for a long time but finally she noticed that she had the seed from which sacred meal was made in her basket and no other kind of seeds. She thought, "With this name I shall be very proud, for it has been chosen for nourishment and it is sacred." So she said, "I will be Corn clan." . . .

When they had completed their prayers to the sun, Tsichtinako said, "You have done everything well and now you are both to take up your baskets and you must look to the north, west, south, and east, for you are now to pray to the Earth to accept the things in the basket and to give them life. First you must pray to the north, at the same time lift up your baskets in that direction. You will then do the same to the west, then to the south and east." They did as they were told and did it well. And Tsichtinako, said to them, "From now on you will rule in every direction, north, west, south, and east."

SOURCE: Matthew W. Stirling, *Origin Myth of Acoma and Other Records* (Washington, D.C.: Smithsonian Institution, 1942), 3–5.

pany, they all work together in one field, or at whatever job they may have on hand." In the spring, Jemison continued, "they choose an older woman to be their driver and overseer, when at labor, for the ensuing year. She accepts the honor, and they consider themselves bound to obey her."[3]

Women also had a significant voice in religious activities. According to Jemison, Seneca women formed Chanters of the Dead, a group that interpreted dreams and participated in numerous rituals. In other ways Iroquois women influenced what might be termed the political side of life. Because they controlled food supplies—both current crops and the food they had carefully preserved and stored—they provisioned warriors and thus had a say in plans for raids and wars. They also determined adoptions into a clan—a means of integrating captives and minimizing losses due to disease and warfare—and could call for the avenging of deaths in their own families, thus initiating raids and warfare. Iroquois women's

◆ Huron Women

In 1615, Samuel de Champlain, French founder of Quebec City, lived for a time with the Hurons. He was both impressed and disturbed by Huron women's responsibilities. He wrote: "[They] till the soil, sow the Indian corn, fetch wood for the winter, strip the hemp and spin it, and with the thread make fishing-nets for catching fish, . . . have the labour of harvesting the corn, storing it, preparing food, and attending to the house." In contrast, the men "do nothing but hunt deer and other animals, fish, build lodges and go on the warpath."[4] (Figure "E" is Champlain's depiction of a Huron warrior.) Champlain also drew Huron women in several of their roles. Figure "F" is an adult woman, holding a child in one hand and a stalk of corn in the other. Figure "G" is a young girl, both provocative and modest, dressed for a ritual dance. Figure "H," wrote Champlain, depicts "how the women pound the Indian corn." *The Newberry Library.*

political power impressed European observers. Father Joseph-François Lafitau, a French Jesuit missionary in Canada, noted as late as 1724 that "nothing, however, is more real than this superiority of the women. . . . The land, the fields and their harvest all belong to them. They are the souls of the Councils, the arbiters of peace and of war. They have charge of the public treasury. To them are given the slaves. They arrange marriages. The children are their domain, and it is through their blood that the order of succession is transmitted."[5]

Native Women's Worlds

Pueblo and Iroquois women lived far apart. Their economic systems and their environments varied dramatically, as did their social structures. Iroquois women had more formal power than Pueblo women. But the similarities in their lives provide a starting point for sketching a few broad generalizations about indigenous women of North America in the era of conquest. What were their economic roles? What can we know of their sexual lives? What political and religious influence did they exert within their communities?

Women's economic significance was a common denominator most indigenous peoples shared. Starting with Christopher Columbus, who observed in 1493 that "the women seem to work more than the men," the productive role of women was an object of much commentary. European men reacted as if their own women were entirely freed from hard labor, which they certainly were not (see box, "Letter to Lord Raphael Sánchez, Treasurer to Ferdinand and Isabella").

Nonetheless, the economic centrality of Native women is worth noting. Among the coastal Algonquians, women not only tended crops but also participated in the fishing vital to their people's survival. They fashioned mats and baskets and other essential artifacts of daily life. Among the groups that emphasized hunting, like the Ojibwas of the Great Lakes region or the Apaches of the southern plains, men's role as hunters was complemented by women's labor of curing meat and dressing skins. Women also gathered feathers from birds, fashioned moccasins, and sometimes bartered in the increasingly important fur trade. In 1632, a French cleric, Paul Le Jeune, observed of the Iroquois: "The women know what they are to do, and the men also; and one never meddles with the work of the others." As one Iroquois man reported to Le Jeune, "To live among us without a wife . . . is to live without help, without home, and to be always wandering."[6]

All indigenous groups had strict moral codes within their own cultural norms. European observers tended to view Native American sexual practices though a pejorative lens, giving readers the impression that Native women were promiscuous. It is also difficult to untangle the effects of intimate relations across cultural borders, notably in fur-trading regions, on sexual mores. In some cases, European men projected their own desires onto Native women. In others, women entered into liaisons with fur traders so that these outsiders could be incorporated into the community. Europeans were also shocked by some groups' polygyny, whereby a man might have multiple wives who were often sisters. Another factor

CHRISTOPHER COLUMBUS
Letter to Lord Raphael Sánchez, Treasurer to Ferdinand and Isabella

Immediately upon returning from the first of his four voyages to the Indies in March 1493, Christopher Columbus (1451–1506) wrote an account meant for his royal patrons. He still believed he had landed on the far shore of Asia. Among his several observations about the gender arrangements of the natives, Columbus's mention of an all-woman island, probably Martinique, is particularly interesting. Much of what he saw he had anticipated seeing. Like the man-eaters Columbus was sure he had found on Charis (probably the Island of Dominica), he also was prepared by European myths to find warrior women. One possibility is that all the men had been exterminated in war and their women kept for marriage and reproduction by the Carib victors.

As far as I have learned, every man throughout these islands is united to but one wife, with the exception of the kings and princes, who are allowed to have twenty: the women seem to work more than the men. I could not clearly understand whether the people possess any private property, for I observed that one man had the charge of distributing

that seemed to give Native women more sexual freedom than their European counterparts, especially in matrilineal societies, was that women did not need to stay in unhappy marriages for economic security. According to a French observer of a group of Algonquians, "A Young Woman, say they, is Master of her own Body, and by her Natural Right of Liberty is free to do what she pleases."[7]

To early Europeans, one of the most striking aspects of Native American sexuality was the existence of individuals who crossed the gender line and lived the lives of the opposite sex. Later anthropologists used the word "berdache" for such a person. Male-to-female transgendering was present in virtually all Native American societies, but female-to-male crossing was by no means unknown. Modern feminist theory contends that the possibilities of gender extend beyond two categories, and evidence for this is striking in several traditional Native American societies. In the 1520s on Mexico's northern frontier, Cabeza de Vaca recorded, "I saw one man married to another . . . , and they go about dressed as women, and do women's tasks, and shoot with a bow, and carry great burdens . . . and they are huskier than the other men and taller."[8] The explanations, and probably the causes, of transgendering were multiple. Some men may have been responding to sexual desires to play the female role, although there is evidence of male homosexuality in Native cultures that took other forms. In some cases, the berdache was

various things to the rest, but especially meat and provisions and the like. I did not find, as some of us had expected, any cannibals amongst them, but on the contrary men of great deference and kindness. Neither are they black, like the Ethiopians: their hair is smooth and straight: for they do not dwell where the rays of the sun strike most vividly,—and the sun has intense power there, the distance from the equinoctial line being, it appears, but six-and-twenty degrees. . . . I saw no cannibals, nor did I hear of any, except in a certain island called Charis, which is the second from Hispaniola on the side towards India, where dwell a people who are considered by the neighboring islanders as most ferocious: and these feed upon human flesh. The same people have many kinds of canoes, in which they cross to all the surrounding islands and rob and plunder wherever they can; . . . These are the men who form unions with certain women, who dwell alone in the island Matenin, which lies next to Hispaniola on the side towards India; these latter employ themselves in no labour suitable to their own sex, for they use bows and javelins as I have already described their paramours as doing, and for defensive armour have plates of brass, of which metal they possess great abundance.

SOURCE: *Select Letters of Christopher Columbus*, R. H. Major, ed. and trans. (Hakluyt Society, 1847).

an especially spiritual person whose path across the gender divide was dictated by a youthful vision quest.

Despite their relative sexual freedom and the importance of their economic contributions, most Native American women held no formal political power. The Iroquois matrons were one exception; another were the few Algonquian women—like Wetamo, a sachem (chief) of the Wampanoag people of New England, or Cockacoeske, female sachem of the Pamunkey Indians of Virginia—who actually held direct authority and power. Informally, women's influence was often significant, especially in the many Native communities that emphasized consensus in decision making and allowed the voices of women, particularly older ones, to be heard. As one historian has noted, speaking of the Indians of the East Coast, "The women's power normally operated more covertly, though often no less effectively than the men's, for they were the acknowledged guardians of tradition and peace in societies whose survival depended in large measure on both."[9] In religious matters, women's access to high-status roles varied from group to group. In some groups they might be healers, crucial to the well-being of their people, while in others they were religious leaders.

Whatever their roles in their societies, Native American women, like men, faced extraordinary challenges in the wake of the European invasion. Historians often describe the interaction of the two worlds of indigenous peoples and Europeans in the context of a "Columbian exchange." Enslaved Africans and European settlers were the human part of the exchange. From the Americas, the Europeans took gold and silver, furs, fish, and crops such as corn, potatoes, and tobacco. To the Americas, they brought disease, Christianity, and new technology. The meanings of this complex process of conflict and contact varied for indigenous peoples. But overall these changes would have specific—and usually damaging—effects on Native women.

EUROPEANS ARRIVE

Europe in the sixteenth century was a continent undergoing dramatic change, not all of which constituted "progress" for European women but much of which had an impact on American history. On the one hand, this was the age of European queens, powerful, educated, politically savvy women, two of whom—Isabella of Castile and Elizabeth of England—presided over the beginnings of the two major European empires in the Americas. The Protestant Reformation, starting with Martin Luther in Germany in 1517, challenged the hierarchical control of the Catholic clergy and eventually led to important changes in women's status. Yet processes that two centuries later would lead to enhanced education and greater independence for women had the immediate impact of limiting their possibilities. Conflict between Catholics and Protestants restrained and even eliminated female religious orders that had permitted some women education, spiritual authority, and alternatives to family life. One historian has called the sixteenth century "the zenith of the patriarchal family" in Europe, as women were newly confined to wifehood and motherhood.[10] Similarly, as the foundations of modern European capitalism unfolded, women found themselves in subordinate positions, rarely controlling the production of goods for market and always earning less than men for their labors.

Early Spanish Expansion

In the century before the English settlement of America began in earnest, Spanish America flourished. As every American schoolchild knows, the Italian explorer Christopher Columbus "discovered" the Indies of the West, while traveling in search of the Indies of the East, under the sponsorship of King Ferdinand and Queen Isabella of Spain. However, the funds for Columbus's journey came not, as the story goes, from the queen's jewels, but from the confiscated wealth of the Jews, whom the royal pair was expelling from Spain and Portugal along with the Moors (Muslims), to cleanse the Iberian Peninsula of non-Christian influences. Queen Isabella was devoted to the triumph of the Catholic faith against all competitors. Her support for Columbus's oceanic adventure was also shaped by her desire to spread what she understood as the one true faith. When it became clear that the lands Columbus claimed in her name were not the East Indies but a "new" world, Isabella showed considerable concern for the souls of the indigenous peoples there, rejecting, for instance, a gift of seized Native American slaves. Her death in 1504 removed one important obstacle to Spanish conquistadores' exploitation of Native labor and the natural resources found on Native lands. Forty years later, the Spanish Dominican priest Bartolomé de Las Casas passionately pleaded the case of indigenous Americans, but by then their cause was virtually lost (see box, "On the Deaths of Caribbean Indians").

Las Casas documented the catastrophic collapse of Native populations as European diseases ran rampant through peoples with no immunity to them. The first places to be devastated were the Caribbean islands of the Columbian expeditions, Hispaniola and Cuba especially. This process of disease, death, and conquest happened over and over in the New World, with European microbes often preceding European settlement. The first Spanish incursion into Florida in 1513, for example, failed to establish a permanent settlement, but the Spaniards' brief visit spread disease and by the time the next Spanish landed there, twenty-five years later, the population had already fallen precipitously; further, the pathogens had spread all the way to the Mississippi River. Two and a half centuries later, when the Spanish finally settled northern California, the same process occurred again, as the population of Native peoples plummeted, female fertility suffering in particular, leaving the very foundations of the community and culture in tatters and the way opened for thorough occupation and conquest (see pp. 257–60). Although historians are still debating the actual numbers of human beings living in the Americas in 1500, it is likely that the population losses during the first century after Columbus, which varied from group to group, ranged from 60 to 90 percent.[11]

In the initial phases, the Spanish invaders of the Americas were almost entirely male and focused on the wealth to be gained, first from the booty of existing cultures, then from the resources of the land, and finally from the labor and tribute of the Natives, in a system known (in Spanish) as the *encomienda*. In 1519, Hernán Cortés, who had participated in the Spanish conquest in the Caribbean, made his way to the east coast of Mexico. As he moved inland, the indigenous Aztec empire he found there was notable not only for its incredible wealth but also for its high level of political organization. Cortés's success in subduing the Aztecs colored all subsequent Spanish exploration, including that into North America. Other adventurers followed rumors and legends of cities of gold and Natives easily subjugated elsewhere on the continent. But only in Peru, where silver deposits flowed into Spanish coffers, were these aspirations for wealth met.

The virtually all-male character of the first phases of the Spanish invasion resulted in patterns of intimacy between Native women and European men that shaped American history until European women began to appear later in the sixteenth century. As we shall see, this distinguished the gender relations of Spanish America from those of British America, a century later, in which official, legitimate marriages across cultural, racial, and religious barriers were frowned upon. In Spanish America, cross-cultural conjugal relationships took various forms and have been the subject of much scholarly controversy, especially turning on the role

Bartolomé de Las Casas
On the Deaths of Caribbean Indians

Bartolomé de Las Casas (1484–1566) was the first and, because his protests were so effective, one of the greatest European defenders of Native American human rights. In 1502, the young man accompanied Columbus to Hispaniola and stayed, although he traveled back to Spain on a number of occasions. His witness of the rampant mistreatments of the Arawak Indians led him to take vows as a Dominican priest and to publish The Devastation of the Indies: A Brief Account *(1542), from which this excerpt is taken. His passionate advocacy was largely responsible for the Spanish "New Laws," which mandated greater protections for the Amerindians. Las Casas's testimony helps us to understand how the near extermination of the Native peoples was effected so swiftly.*

And of all the infinite universe of humanity, these people are the most guileless, the most devoid of wickedness and duplicity, the most obedient and faithful to their native masters and to the Spanish Christians whom they serve. They are by nature the most humble, patient, and peaceable, holding no grudges, free from embroilments, neither excitable nor quarrelsome. These people are the most devoid of rancors, hatreds, or desire for vengeance of any people in the world. And because they are so weak and complaisant, they are less able to endure heavy labor and soon die of no matter what malady. . . . As to their dress, they are generally naked, with only their pudenda covered somewhat. . . . They are very clean in their persons, with alert, intelligent minds, docile and open to doctrine, very apt to receive our holy Catholic faith, to be endowed with virtuous customs, and to behave in a godly fashion. . . . Some of the secular Spaniards who have been here for many years say that the goodness

and volition of the Native women involved. Many of these relations were coercive, best described as rape and/or sexual and domestic slavery. In others, women determined that attaching themselves to European men would bring benefits to themselves, their children, and their people. No doubt, as with all such relationships, some of these connections involved genuine affection.

Many of the individual Native women whose names we know from these early years were involved in such intimate relationships, and played important diplomatic and political roles as bridges between Native and European communities of the Americas. Of these, the first and most controversial was Malintzin, known to history as Malinche. Originally one of twenty female captives given to the

of the Indians is undeniable and that if this gifted people could be brought to know the one true God they would be the most fortunate people in the world. . . .

On the Island Hispaniola . . . Christians perpetrated their first ravages and oppressions against the native peoples. This was the first land in the New World to be destroyed and depopulated by the Christians, and here they began their subjection of the women and children, taking them away from the Indians to use them and ill use them, eating the food they provided with their sweat and toil. The Spaniards did not content themselves with what the Indians gave them of their own free will, according to their ability, which was always too little to satisfy enormous appetites, for a Christian eats and consumes in one day an amount of food that would suffice to feed three houses inhabited by ten Indians for one month. . . .

After the wars and the killings had ended, when usually there survived only some boys, some women, and children, these survivors were distributed among the Christians to be slaves. . . . And the care they took was to send the men to the mines to dig for gold, which is intolerable labor, and to send the women into the fields of the big ranches to hoe and till the land, work suitable for strong men. Nor to either the men or the women did they give any food except herbs and legumes, things of little substance. The milk in the breasts of the women with infants dried up and thus in a short while the infants perished. And since men and women were separated, there could be no marital relations. And the men died in the mines and the women died on the ranches from the same causes, exhaustion and hunger. And thus was depopulated that island which had been densely populated.

SOURCE: Bartolomé de Las Casas, *The Devastation of the Indies: A Brief Account* (1542: Baltimore: Johns Hopkins University, 1992), 41–42.

Spaniards as a gift, she became Cortés's interpreter and the mother of his son. Her language skills and her residence among both the Aztecs and the Mayans aided Cortés in communicating with the Nahuatl-speaking Aztecs. She remained loyal to him even when he passed her on to his lieutenant and married a high-ranking Spanish woman. Among subsequent generations of Mexicans, Malinche has been both revered as the mother of their race and reviled as the first to betray native peoples to Europeans. In the 1970s, Chicana feminists sought to understand her, not merely as a victim of Europe and of men, but as a woman seeking to act in a swiftly changing historical environment and to find a way between cultures and to the future (see pp. 680–81). In a 1978 poem, Carmen Tafolla imagined Malinche

◆ **Malinche and Cortés**
Prior to the arrival of the Spanish, the Aztecs were already recording their culture and history in pictorial form, in volumes called codices (codex in the singular). In the colonial period, these were adapted to include Spanish words, figures, and versions of history. Many include images of Malinche (or Mariana, as she is called in Spanish) and Cortés that depict Malinche's importance in various ways. In the mid-sixteenth-century *Codex Coyoacan*, Malinche/Mariana is equal in size, though standing behind, Cortés, who is always indicated by his hat, cloak, and beard. Malinche/Mariana's clothing is Aztec, but she carries her Catholic rosary prominently. The accompanying text indicates that she helped to organize the murder of local leaders, an event also depicted in the images of the codex. *Bibliothèque Nationale de France, Paris.*

defending her actions: "I was not tricked, not screwed, not traitor / for I was not traitor to myself / I saw a dream / and I *reached* it / *Another world* / la raza."[o12]

By the middle of the sixteenth century, Spanish women in the New World were increasing in number, although they never exceeded more than a third of the immigrants in any one decade. The pressure from crown and clergy to curb the violence of womanless men and to facilitate permanent settlement in the Americas encouraged wives to come to join their husbands and unmarried daughters to marry unattached male colonials. A pattern was for women to marry men much older than themselves, making widowhood a common experience. Spanish property law (in contrast to English) allowed widows to inherit easily, and this made widows attractive candidates for remarriage. Women immigrants congregated in the great cities of Mexico City and Lima. Throughout the Spanish empire, the wealth that the Americas promised, plus the presence of Indian women as servants to do most of the domestic labor, elevated Spanish women beyond the class from which they had come. Maria de Carranza encouraged her sister-in-law in Seville to give up "the poverty and need which people suffer in Spain" and hurry to immigrate to "a land where food is plenteous."[13] Life on the northern frontier of Spanish America was more difficult for women; amid continuing warfare between colonists and Natives, the threats of kidnapping and Indian captivity shadowed their sex. Fewer women immigrated to the northern frontier voluntarily, and more were recruited to strengthen settlement.

One unusual Spanish woman in Mexico about whom we know something is Marina de San Miguel, who came to Mexico as a child in 1547. After her profli-

°**la raza:** the race.

gate father squandered his American riches, she dedicated herself to celibacy and to religious life, serving as a teacher of native girls and a sort of freelance religious adviser and spiritual counsel to her community. She earned enough from her labors to buy her own home in Mexico City. Her spiritual independence and economic success, unusual for Spanish women outside of marriage, drew her to the attention of Spanish authorities. In these years, church and royal authority combined to bestow enormous power on the Inquisition, an institution for the detection and rooting out of all forms of heresy from the true Catholic faith. In Spain, the Inquisition particularly concentrated on cleansing the faith and the country of Moors and former Jews suspected of superficial conversion to the Catholic faith. In 1601, finding Marina de San Miguel guilty of spiritual arrogance and sexual misconduct, the Mexican wing of the Spanish Inquisition subjected her to community humiliation and the termination of her vocation.

The history of these New World women points to their changing options in the context of Protestant/Catholic conflicts in Europe. Reformation-era pressures to cleanse the Catholic Church of corruption bore down particularly hard on women, whose allegedly unruly sexuality seemed to threaten religious purity. Starting in the middle of the century, the church placed religious sisterhoods under male supervision, strictly cloistered them, and prohibited their efforts in education and social service. In 1540, the first American convent, Nuestra Señora de la Concepción, opened in Mexico City under Franciscan supervision. Most of the women who lived there were Spanish and of high birth, but Native women were occasionally admitted: two of the Aztec ruler Montezuma's granddaughters, for example, became sisters of La Concepción.

In the sixteenth century, the Spanish made several incursions north, into what would eventually be the United States. These lands, much more sparsely populated than those of Mexico and Peru, offered no great Indian empires to conquer and loot. The coast of northern California was explored and mapped but not opened to settlement until the eighteenth century. In 1565, the Spanish established St. Augustine in what is now Florida; formed to protect Spanish Cuba from French marauders and pirates, it is the longest continually occupied colonial settlement in the United States, founded four decades before the English established permanent settlements to the north. None of these excursions, however, uncovered great empires or elaborate cities, stores of gold or mountains of silver. Indeed, the only valuable commodity of these early frontier efforts were the Native people, who were seized and sold as slaves. For an overwhelmingly male population of soldier-colonists, Native women were particularly valuable as sexual partners (willing or not), as mothers of their children, as laborers, and as a bridge between indigenous and colonial men.

Spain's Northern Frontier

The northern territories in which the Spanish were most active in the sixteenth century were the lands occupied by the Pueblo peoples. In 1540, a group of Spaniards from central Mexico led by Vásquez de Coronado ventured into the

La V.ᵐ Mᵃ Maria de Iesus de Agreda. Predicando á los Chichimecos del Nuebo-mexico. Antᵗ de Costoᵍ.

◆ María de Jesús de Agreda

Born in 1602, María de Jesús de Agreda, a Franciscan nun, was an important figure in the history of New Spain, although she remained cloistered in her convent in Agreda, Spain, all her adult life. Deeply mystical, she claimed to have been transported hundreds of times, while in rapturous trances, across the Atlantic to answer the call of Native people for knowledge of Christ. Hauled before the Spanish Inquisition, which was concerned about ecstatic excesses, especially among women, she held to her claims. The Jumanos in West Texas still maintain legends of a white-skinned "lady in blue," representative of the Virgin Mary, who appeared to them to bring Christianity. *Nettie Lee Benson Latin American Collection, University of Texas Libraries, University of Texas at Austin.*

land of one of these peoples, the Zuñis. Frustrated at failing to find the gold they had expected, Coronado's men seized food, blankets, and women. The Spaniards' relationship to and treatment of Native women lay at the root of this first and formative disastrous encounter on Mexico's northern frontier. Some Native men traditionally exchanged women to cement treaties with former enemies. What the Pueblos saw as the gift of a marital alliance, Spanish men saw as their patriarchal right. When the Spanish kept demanding tributes and women's bodies without offering appropriate exchanges, the Pueblos' anger mounted. The Zuñis drove Coronado back to central Mexico. Evidence of his failure to find great wealth and news of his brutal treatment of the Indians created such controversy that the Spanish made no further attempts to subdue the northern territories for another five decades.

In 1598, when the Spanish returned to the Pueblos' lands, they did so under another guise. Instead of soldiers in search of gold and tribute, Franciscan missionaries led the way, in search of souls and Christians. Less openly violent than the military men of the 1540s, Spanish Christians nonetheless wreaked their own kind of havoc on Native cultures. Franciscan friars pressured the Pueblos to participate in Catholic rites and suppressed traditional religion. The church tried to impose a more familiar patriarchal system on Native women by attempting to restructure a division of labor consistent with European notions of proper gender roles. They urged men to take over building and farming tasks that formerly had been women's work. The friars also called for Natives to enter into monogamous, lifelong marriages and for women to emulate European notions of female modesty and reserve.

To ensure that the events of the 1540s were not repeated, the friars required that the soldier-settlers that accompanied them be married men. Even so, and although their purpose was to "pacify" the Natives under Spanish and Catholic authority, violence soon broke out, as it had a half century earlier. Accounts differ. The Indian men objected to the arrogance with which the soldiers seized their women. Not recognizing the complex rules and rituals surrounding Pueblo sexuality, the soldiers believed that the women were making themselves sexually available. Modern scholars point to the very different ways in which the Natives and the soldiers conducted their sexual relations and the violent turn that these differences could take under conditions of abrupt cultural clash. What the women thought, we do not know. In 1598, in response to the rape of one of their women, Indian men killed a dozen soldiers, in retaliation for which the Spanish massacred eight hundred Natives. Most of those slaughtered must have been men, because the survivors who were rounded up and punished by enslavement were overwhelmingly women and children.

The important tasks of converting and educating Native Americans were left largely to male priests. How might the first contacts between Europeans and Native Americans have been affected if colonial women had also been representatives of the Christian faith? Would the sexual tensions surrounding conversion efforts have been defused? Would the traditional sexual/spiritual role of Pueblo women have found more room to survive? Or would colonial women have been as immune to Native American concerns as Spanish men were?

The only record of a female presence among the invading Spanish comes from a late seventeenth-century Franciscan legend, incorporated into Native oral tradition. Both claim that the Spanish nun María de Agreda made mystical trips throughout the New Mexican frontier in the 1620s, appearing as a vision more than five hundred times to convert the indigenous people.

Thus, in New Mexico, Spanish rule proceeded along two lines: the physically violent, economically exploitative, military-led version of the conquistadores and the spiritually driven, culturally and morally coercive version of the priests. Both undermined and profoundly altered Pueblo societies. At the beginning of the seventeenth century, then, European invasions had already established a century-long legacy of invasion, disease, military conflict, religious coercion, and enslavement, contributing to a precipitous decline in the numbers and integrity of Native cultures and the position of women in them.

Fish and Furs in the North

While the Spanish achieved uncontested rule over Mexico and much of South America, other European powers, eager to find their own sources of profit and global power, looked to the north. For much of the sixteenth century, the French, English, and Dutch presence in North America was informal. The crucial process was trade, and the crucial commodities were fish and fur on one side, European manufactured goods, including ironware and guns, on the other. Women were active in this process as both producers and consumers. As in Spanish America, sexual contact and disease accompanied and complicated trading relations. Permanent settlements of European men and women developed later, in the first years of the seventeenth century (see Chapter 2).

Hundreds of European ships yearly fished the waters from Newfoundland to Massachusetts, drawn by an inexhaustible supply of cod, the source of protein at the base of the Western European diet. By the middle of the sixteenth century, more than half the cod consumed in Europe came from North American waters. Men cast the nets, but in Europe, especially in the coastal cultures, women sold their catch on the streets. Fishwives, as these market women were called, came perilously close to the disreputable, all-male culture of the wharfs and the ships, and the term outlived the occupation, becoming synonymous for any foul-mouthed, quarrelsome female.

By the 1580s, fur had overtaken fish as the primary source of European wealth gained in North America. Beaver in particular was a luxury commodity, the North American equivalent of Mexican gold. It was warm and, when properly tanned, waterproof, and thus highly prized. Men were still the fashionable gender in Europe in the sixteenth century and sported most of the large, jaunty beaver hats of the age. Pocahontas was one of the few women to be pictured in such a hat (see Figure 1.12, p. 46). Most women wore lesser furs as collars and cuffs on their gowns. The French dominated the trade. Native men were the hunters, while women were responsible for the scraping, tanning, and preparing the skins. The European commodities that Native people received in exchange fell along gendered lines, as women got beads, metal needles, and iron kettles to use in fur preparation, while men received guns and knives, as well as alcohol. Both male and female Natives got and valued cloth and clothing.

The fur trade with the French affected family and gender relationships. Instead of hunting communally for larger animals such as moose and caribou, men trapped in small groups for beaver. Hunting and trapping for the market left men with less time and energy for subsistence activities. Thus, Native societies demanded more and more trade goods, including clothing and food. As the hunt for fur intensified, men had to travel farther and farther away from home to satisfy the demands of the market, intensifying intertribal warfare. Looking over this process from the perspective of the late nineteenth century, ethnologist Lewis Henry Morgan, writing about the Iroquois, hypothesized that the rise of capitalist economies was responsible for the subordination of women.

Native women played another role in the fur trade, especially in the Great Lakes region, through their marriages with European men. Although some fur traders formalized their marriages to Native women, most of these relationships were what the French called *mariage à la façon du pays* (marriage in the custom of the country, that is, without formal church recognition). Begun in the late sixteenth century, this practice flourished over the next two centuries until significant numbers of European women arrived. These so-called country marriages were markedly different from the interracial liaisons in Spanish America, because they tended to accept European men into Native culture rather than Native women into European culture. Native wives gave their French husbands, in the words of one historian, "an entrée into the cultures and communities of their own people. In this way, Indian women were the first important mediators of meaning between the cultures of two worlds."[14] The children of these liaisons formed a mixed, or métis, society along the trade routes of rivers and lakes deep, into the North American heartland.

Early British Settlements

The British were particularly slow to follow the Spanish and Portuguese in settling the Americas. During the first half of the sixteenth century, the British ignored America in favor of subduing and occupying Ireland, a promising colony much closer to home. In 1558, the half-century reign of Elizabeth I began, and England's relation to the other side of the Atlantic started to change. Elizabeth shared with Isabella of Spain considerable queenly ambition and talent, but not much else. In contrast to the highly religious Spanish queen, Elizabeth was a thoroughly worldly monarch. Following her father's lead, she abjured the Catholic Church in favor of the Church of England, which she headed and which was always more a source of political than spiritual identity and authority. She maneuvered through the difficulties of being a female monarch by refusing to marry, having no children, and maintaining a reputation for chastity despite numerous

◆ **Queen Elizabeth I**

In 1588, the Spanish navy, or armada, attempted to invade England. This epochal event was commemorated in this extraordinary portrait by George Gower. Elizabeth is encased in symbols of royal and imperial power, including pearls from the New World. The channel storm that helped the English to defeat the Spanish is depicted on the upper right as a sign of England's divine destiny. The globe in the lower left is turned to show the Americas, and Elizabeth's hand rests on the continent's northern lands, above New Spain, which were to become British North America. The defeat of the Spanish Armada helped to clear the way for England's growth as a transatlantic power. *Woburn Abbey, Bedfordshire, UK/Bridgeman Art Library.*

male "favorites." To one of these favorites, Sir Walter Raleigh, she granted dominion over the large, undefined American territory that Raleigh named Virginia to honor not the Virgin Mary but the Virgin Queen.

British colonial efforts built on, yet differed from, those of the Spanish and French. In contrast to the frontiers of inclusion that the earlier Europeans created, largely by liaisons between European men and native women, the English created "frontiers of exclusion," bringing in white women very early and generally pushing out Native Americans to make room for their own settlements. As Protestants, the English had few structures for and little interest in converting the Natives to Christianity. And while British New World efforts followed the Spanish by focusing on settlement, they concentrated on agriculture rather than on the extraction of natural wealth and human tribute.

The first effort at British settlement on the American mainland was a famous failure. In 1587 more than a hundred British men, women (including at least four single women), and children sailed across the Atlantic to the island of Roanoke, on the North Carolina coast. The symbol of British hopes for establishing a fully English society on American soil and the centrality of families to that effort was the birth, barely a month after landing, of Virginia Dare, the infant granddaughter of John White, Raleigh's representative and leader of the community. Imagining this series of events through women's eyes leads us to wonder about the experience of Virginia's mother, nineteen-year-old Eleanor White Dare, pregnant during the grueling two- to three-month transatlantic journey. Who aided her in the birth? Perhaps it was a Native American woman, recognizing the commonality of female experience with this otherwise strange being from unknown places.

◆ **Virginia Dare Stamp**

The legend of Virginia Dare looms much larger in American history than the child herself. All the English settlers of the Roanoke colony, including Virginia, disappeared sometime between 1587 and 1590. Not until the latter part of the nineteenth century did the "lost colony of Roanoke" become the basis of a legend in which Virginia was rescued and raised by kindly nearby Indians. This U.S. stamp was issued in 1937, the 450th anniversary of Dare's birth. Dare was commemorated as "the first white child born of English parents in the New World," as if the history of North America were coeval with its population by white Europeans. Excluded from this celebration were the many offspring born of white European men and Native or African women in the Americas before 1585. *The Granger Collection, New York, NY.*

John White sailed back to England, leaving his daughter, his grandchild, and most of the other colonists behind. White was an artist, and upon his return to England he published an extraordinary set of drawings, many of them focused on Native women (see Figures 1.6 and 1.8, pp. 40 and 42). In addition to providing a kind of ethnographic record of Native women's labors, these images suggest the English (men's) fascination with the physical appearance of Native women, their beauty, strength, and of course partial nudity. For reasons that are not clear, White did not return to Roanoke until 1590, only to discover that the entire settler community had disappeared. Both modern scholarship and local oral tradition suggest that as the community was unable to sustain itself, at least some of its members were absorbed, perhaps as slaves, into nearby Native societies.

Twenty years later, Raleigh attempted another settlement farther north, along the more sheltered banks of the Chesapeake Bay, naming the community after the new British monarch, James I. Jamestown survived, and 2007 marked the four hundredth anniversary of its founding. The first shipments of settlers were all male, heavily biased toward adventurous gentlemen, and singularly unprepared to provide the labor to survive. Subsequent trips increased the numbers of English women; however, they were never more than about 20 percent of the population in the early years. By the winter of 1609, the inability of the settlers to feed themselves became lethal, and more than three-quarters died.

It was the women of the surrounding peoples, the Algonquian-speaking Powhatans, who made the difference between life and death for the surviving few. As in so many Indian communities, women planted, harvested, and controlled the crops that were the core of their diet. English observers recorded with considerable astonishment and unconcealed disdain that, unlike their home cultures, here in the New World, women were the primary agriculturists. To them, women's labor in their fields made them drudges and their husbands lazy and uncivilized, and yet this female labor provided for the narrow difference between widespread and total starvation in their own lives, as Native women delivered foodstuffs regularly in the first few years.

Certainly the most well-known woman in the first years of permanent British settlement on the Virginia coast was Pocahontas (see Figures 1.11 and 1.12, pp. 45–46). She was the daughter of one of the many wives of the powerful paramount chief, Powhatan (also the name of his people) and, from a very young age, served as an intermediary between her people and the English settlers. Had she never become involved with the English settlers of Jamestown, she might have become a powerful female leader in her own right.

The legend of Pocahontas as it has come down through history follows suspiciously close to the lines of a typical European romance, with the young girl (no more than thirteen at the time) saving Jamestown leader John Smith from death at the hands of her father out of personal passion for the dashing Englishman. This version comes from Smith, who published it upon returning to England several years later. A more likely explanation is that Pocahontas was participating in a Powhatan ritual by which Smith was being absorbed into the community by some sort of adoption process, as was often the case with valuable captives of war.

Several years later, Jamestowners kidnapped Pocahontas, and she remained, apparently willingly, as part of their community for the rest of her short life. She was treated as a woman of noble birth, converted to Christianity, renamed Rebecca, and married in a church ceremony to gentleman planter John Rolfe. Several portraits of her survive because, in 1616, Pocahontas, along with her husband, her son, and a considerable Native entourage, sailed to England, where they were presented to the royal family as encouraging evidence of the future of the colonial experiment in Virginia. This is curious inasmuch marriages between English men and Native women were rare and increasingly discouraged in both Virginia and Massachusetts. Interestingly, Pocahontas's role as Indian foremother for British America brought her historical praise from her adopted people, rather than the reputation of traitor, as in the case of Malinche a century before. Pocahontas never returned to Virginia, dying in England two years later of unknown causes.

One final detail of Pocahontas's life bears emphasis: with her help, John Rolfe became Virginia's first cultivator of tobacco, the next in a long line of valuable commodities, beginning with sugar, produced in America and traded around the world. Tobacco cultivation allowed for the development of market-based plantation agriculture in Virginia, which was critical to the wealth and power of the British Empire. Tobacco cultivation also encouraged the development of African slavery in North America, and to this we now turn.

AFRICAN WOMEN AND THE ATLANTIC SLAVE TRADE

The first Africans to be recorded in Virginia arrived in 1619, forty-three years before the Virginia legislature passed the initial laws establishing African chattel slavery. Nonetheless, the origins of this institution, with its incalculable significance for American history, lie in the Atlantic slave trade developed long before British settlement of North America. In what has been called the triangle trade, Europeans brought goods to Africa to trade for slaves, slaves to the New World to trade for slave-grown agricultural commodities such as sugar and tobacco, and these commodities to Europe for consumption. The roots of North American slavery can be found in the European trade of African slaves during the fifteenth and sixteenth centuries, in the understandings that Europeans used to classify Africans as inferior, and in the development of a commercial plantation economy in the eastern Atlantic and Brazil. In each of these, the ideologies of gender roles were important dimensions.

Women in West Africa

West African women were productive, independent, sometimes truly powerful members of their societies. They were agriculturalists, with responsibilities for cultivating major foodstuffs, such as yams and rice. They produced textiles, spinning and weaving cloth. In towns and along trading routes, women were often the local traders, an economic practice that West African women have maintained to this day. Though productive and family roles were divided by gender, women could cross over into male roles under exceptional circumstances. In the internal slave trade, discussed in the following section, some African women bought female slaves so that they could have their own "wives" and through them augment their families' wealth.

As we have observed, this was a period of female monarchs in Europe. So too in Africa. In the middle of the sixteenth century, Queen Amina, a renowned warrior, ruled the Hausa Zazzau peoples in what is now northern Nigeria. More is known about Queen Nzinga. Herself the daughter of a slave, in 1623 she was allowed to become ruler in what is now Angola because of matrilineal practices

◆ Queen Nzinga

Nzinga was undoubtedly one of the most politically and diplomatically skilled monarchs of the early modern period. A kinless woman in a region that based authority on family networks and on maleness, she effectively moved through and between powerful Africans and Europeans. She converted to Catholicism to strengthen her position with the Portuguese and cemented her control over the trade in slaves within Africa for similar reasons. This 1657 image, completed six years before her death, portrays negotiations with the Portuguese governor. There is much debate among historians about whether the positioning of Nzinga's seat below that of the Portuguese governor indicates her subordination to him. Behind her is a large, imposing view of the Kongo landscape. *David Sweetman,* Women Leaders in African History, *Heinemann, Oxford, 1984.*

of inheritance, at a moment when the Portuguese were moving eastward in search of new sources of human commodities. Her strategies for consolidating her rule alternated between allying with Portuguese traders and offering refuge to runaways from the slave trade.

However, European records of fifteenth- and sixteenth-century encounters with sub-Saharan Africans record little of this. Early European slave traders dealt primarily with African men. When they did come across women, they mainly noticed their sexuality and their maternity; comments focused on their nakedness and the way they carried and breastfed their children. Writing in 1555 of his voyage to Guinea, the Englishman William Towerson was astonished that both

◆ **Thomas Herbert, *Hottentot Monster Mother***

This image, from Thomas Herbert's 1634 exploration saga, *A Relation of Some Yeares Travaile into Afrique and the Greater Asia*, demonstrates a European view of African motherhood in extreme form. Herbert, an Englishman, sailed around the southern tip of Africa on his way to Persia. In what would later become Cape Town, South Africa, he encountered the Khoikhoi people, previously nicknamed Hottentot (in imitation of their speech) by Dutch explorers. By emphasizing the woman's fierce and ugly face and showing her clutching animal entrails, Herbert renders her virtually as a wild animal. As in other illustrations of African women, she nurses her child, who clings like an insect to her back, by flinging her breast—Herbert calls it her "uberous dugg"—over her shoulder. *Beinecke Rare Book and Manuscript Library, Yale University.*

men and women went about unclothed. He particularly noticed the women's breasts—indeed, he could not take his eyes off them—yet not because he thought they were beautiful: "In the most part be they very foule and long, hanging down like the udder of a goate."[15] Such comments likening black mothers to animals may have helped to ease the consciences of slavers who often separated mothers and their children when they traded them.

The Early Slave Trade

Trading in African slaves predates the involvement of Europeans. Long-standing slaving practices in Africa allowed victors to keep captives taken in war or, more likely, sell them to trans-Saharan caravans trading them elsewhere on the continent. Within Africa, women were more desirable as slaves than men because they could provide both agricultural labor and offspring. They could be absorbed by marriage and motherhood as inferior members of the kin structures of the peoples who acquired them.

Beginning in the mid-fifteenth century, European slavers on the west coast of Africa developed working relationships with indigenous African slave traders, who supplied them with people from inland Africa. The European slave trade drew primarily from the West African coast south of the Sahara, initially from the Upper Guinea area and shifting to the region south of the mouth of the Congo River. The growing demand among Europeans for African labor drove the internal African slave trade to new heights. For all the European nations involved, the slave trade became the source of immense wealth, both because of the profit involved in buying and selling human beings and because of the fruits of their labor in the commercial enterprises of the New World.

The Iberians were the first Europeans to trade in African slaves. At first, the Spanish and Portuguese brought their black captives to their own countries, where they served as domestic and personal servants. Unused to slave trading, common people in Spain and Portugal were at first horrified, but they soon accommodated themselves to the sight of human beings sold on wharves along with other African commodities, crying children being pulled from weeping mothers, husbands and wives clutching each other as they parted. (See Documents: African Women and the Slave Trade, pp. 47–52.) By the turn of the sixteenth century, there were as many as ten thousand Africans in Lisbon and almost that number in Seville.

Within two decades, captured black Africans were being shipped off the mainland to Iberian settlers on a small group of otherwise unpopulated Atlantic islands midway between the Iberian peninsula and the Guinea coast. On Madeira, São Tomé, and the Canary and Cape Verde islands, displaced Africans formed the labor force of a new form of large-scale, commercially oriented agriculture. This was the beginning of the plantation system, which, along with chattel slavery, eventually flourished in the Americas, including the British North American colonies. On these sixteenth-century plantations, mostly male and some female African slaves cultivated and processed crops meant for sale around the known world. Sugar set the pattern later taken up by tobacco: it was a luxury product, not meant for local consumption and indeed irrelevant to the subsistence of the people who grew it, of interest instead to people far away with disposable wealth and cosmopolitan tastes.

In the late sixteenth century, sugar cultivation crossed the Atlantic, arriving in the massive Portuguese colony of Brazil and the Spanish island colonies of Hispaniola (now Haiti and the Dominican Republic) and Cuba. There, the gradual shift to an African slave-labor force in the late sixteenth century was the ironic consequence of the protests by Las Casas and others of the mistreatment and high death rates of American Native peoples. Already exposed to the diseases carried by Europeans during more than a century of trade, Africans seemed hardier than the American natives. Thus one tragedy, the near eradication of the Native population of the Americas, was compounded by a second one, the development of a brutal traffic in human beings, brought from Africa to work in the fields of America for crops to be consumed largely in Europe. By one estimate, at the end of the sixteenth century, there were 150,000 African slaves in the Spanish West Indies and 50,000 more in Portuguese Brazil (see Chart 1.1).[16]

The transatlantic slave trade was much larger and more violent than the intra-African slave trade that preceded it. Instead of domestic service, enslaved Africans were employed in a modern, commercial, globally oriented form of production. Far from home, surrounded by strangers, they had no means of escape. Unlike the intra-African slave trade, which was mostly female, the majority of Africans taken across the Atlantic to be slaves were men. And in the Americas, slaves were distinguished from their masters by the unbridgeable difference of their African blackness.

Racializing Slavery

Long before European colonists to the Americas solidified the legal status of black Africans and their offspring as lifelong slaves, skin color differentiated black Africans from other categories of unfree labor. The long history of prior slave systems rested on various sorts of difference, such as kinship, religion, or geography. The Spanish and Portuguese were particularly experienced with distinctions of religion, as they were busy cleansing their society of Jews and Moors at the same time as they were inventing the transatlantic slave trade. But these other systems of differentiating and relegating people to slavery allowed for some individuals to cross over to freedom, by conversion for instance, or by adoption and marriage.

A new, far more inescapable form of human categorization was emerging in connection with the enslavement of Africans in Europe and the Americas, that of "race." Nothing could make a black person white. The "science" of racial classification and hierarchy was not fully formed until the nineteenth century. But the idea of an ineradicable and unbridgeable difference inscribed on the face and the body of the potential slave was already beginning to appear in the sixteenth century. The profitable prospect of enslavement encouraged debasing, dehumanizing images of Africans. Europeans' contempt for black Africans as closer to animals than themselves encouraged enslavement. The two worked hand in hand.

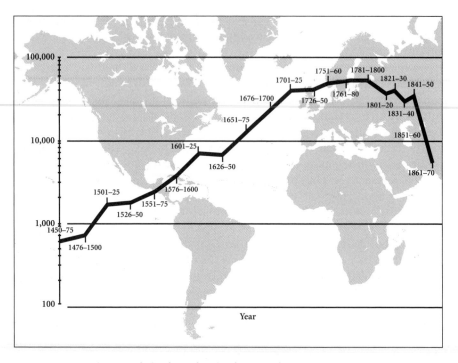

◆ **Chart 1.1 Major Trends in the Atlantic Slave Trade**
Traditionally, the numbers of Africans caught up in the transatlantic slave trade over the course of 400-plus years was estimated at 15 million. In 1969, historian Philip Curtin revised the figure to 10 million, based on a careful examination of ship manifests, colonial censuses, and port records. In this chart, based on Curtin's findings, the steep rise between 1626 and 1701 indicates the entry into slaving, first of the Dutch, and then of the British and French. The end of legally sanctioned trading by the French after the French revolution, followed by the exit of the English and Americans from the Atlantic slave trade in the early 1800s, accounts for the nineteenth-century decline. But even as late as 1870, when slavery still existed in Brazil and some of the Caribbean islands, the numbers of slaves imported annually were still higher than in 1600. These figures account for the deaths of thousands during the Atlantic "middle passage" but do not include the enormous mortality rates after arrival in the Americas. Subsequent studies have refined but not fundamentally altered Curtin's findings. *Philip D. Curtin,* The Atlantic Slave Trade, A Census *(Madison: The University of Wisconsin Press, 1969), 266.*

African women were fundamental to this development. Although sexually intrigued by the nakedness and exoticness of African women, Europeans were rarely interested in domesticating or civilizing them through marriage or conversion to Christianity—unlike their attitude toward Native Americans. On the contrary, once the idea of the inherited differentiation called "race" hardened, African women became crucial to the development of permanent and inherited enslavement. At the point that transatlantic slavery shifted away from working Africans to death and toward a system of slavery that could reproduce its own labor force, the reproductive capacity of African women's bodies was the key.

African Slavery in the Americas

By the middle of the sixteenth century, 25 percent of the people who came across the Atlantic to the New World were African. By the first half of the eighteenth century, that percentage had risen dramatically to 75 percent. With regard to gender, transatlantic slavery in its first century was the mirror image of the intra-African slave trade: it was preponderantly male. Although the great majority of Africans shipped to the pre-nineteenth-century Americas as slaves were men, African women constituted a significant majority of nonnative women there. Put another way, although men outnumbered women in the slave trade, African women outnumbered European women in early migration to the New World. Unlike virtually all other female immigrants in this period, African women were not sent to America as wives or daughters within male-headed family systems.

The position of African women on the plantations of the sugar islands of the Atlantic also differed from European patterns of gendered labor. Unlike the way that most human societies arranged their work patterns, plantation society did not distinguish African workers by gender in the labor they performed. Whereas sixteenth-century European women rarely could be found working in the fields, enslaved African women, in a perverse version of their agricultural roles in their own lands, were incorporated alongside men into gangs of workers on the sugar plantations of the Caribbean and South America. Sugar was a grueling crop to raise, cut, and process. Slave women seem to have had special responsibility for the dangerous work of feeding the freshly cut cane between millstones. According to one historian, the pace at which sugar cane was brought into the mills and ground down was so furious that, "in northeastern Brazil slave women with a missing arm were a common sight."[17]

The overwhelmingly male nature of the early Atlantic slave trade indicated the lack of any interest in creating a labor force that could reproduce itself. Thus African slaves in Brazil and the Caribbean were generally worked to death, because it was less costly to replace them than to sustain them. Once enslaved women began to arrive in significant numbers, they were, as in Africa, valued for both their productive and their reproductive labor. The arrival of African women marked the shift to permanent settlement, of persons of African descent on the North American continent.

Beginning in 1640, the entire system of plantation agriculture and African slavery was transported to British Atlantic colonies, beginning with Barbados, which rose to rival Brazil as the leading sugar producer of the world. In Barbados, the numbers of African women began to climb, but even so, the slave force was still not self-reproducing. Workers died quickly, and there is some evidence that slave women turned to native contraceptives and abortifacients to keep from giving birth to children whom they would then lose to slavery.

Not until the eighteenth century did the plantation system take off in the North American colonies. By this time, the Dutch and the British, who prided themselves in not tolerating slavery in their own countries, had overtaken the Portuguese and Spanish as the major powers in the transatlantic slave trade. African slavery as it matured in its North American form in the late eighteenth century finally became self-reproducing: more people were born into slavery in North America than were imported into the institution from abroad. The consequences of this shift became clearer over the next two centuries: even though no more than 7 percent of Africans traded into the New World ended up in North America, the United States at the end of the twentieth century was home to 30 percent of the people of African origin in the Americas.[18]

The climate of North America did not favor sugar, so other crops became the focus. In the Carolinas rice was a challenge to grow and difficult to mill, yet cheap to ship. In Africa, cultivating and milling rice were women's tasks, and numerous legends on either side of the Atlantic suggest that the first rice crops in America came from seeds that enslaved women hid in their hair, perhaps to remind themselves of their homeland, or in the hair of the children sold away from them, to make sure that they would be properly fed. But for international commerce, the crucial plantation crop grown by African slaves in British North America starting in the early seventeenth century was the Indian medicine that Pocahontas's widower, John Rolfe, was the first to cultivate: tobacco.

CONCLUSION: Many Beginnings

The beginnings of all nations are difficult to identify, even a nation as relatively young as the United States. Our cherished national narratives tell us that our roots were in the wilderness. By contrast, in this account, the beginnings of America are set in the wide world: in the diverse cultures of the Americas of course, but also in those of western sub-Saharan Africa and of Europe. The distinctions between the two American continents had not yet hardened, except that the southern one offered riches and conquests that the northern one did not. Perhaps most surprisingly, the history of the American nation reaches back at least a full century before the first permanent European settlements, not only in the British Atlantic colonies but also in Spanish incursions into Florida, the Southwest, and the lower Mississippi River valley.

Of all these conflicting and intersecting cultures, only Native American societies involved men and women from the same society in approximately equal numbers, living together in family and kin groupings, engaged in complementary productive tasks and varying political roles as determined by their communities. The others, the Europeans who came freely and the Africans who did not, were mostly men. Their women would not arrive in significant numbers for another hundred years. Thus, many of the interactions between men and women in sixteenth-century America were also between peoples largely unknown to each other, and many of the cross-cultural contacts that characterized the New World of the 1500s were accomplished via relations between men and women, the inequalities of culture intersecting with those of gender.

VISUAL SOURCES

Images of Native American Women

I N EXPLORING THE LIVES OF early Native American women, historians use two major sources: one is the archaeological record of artifacts created by indigenous groups before the European invasion; the second consists of the images and narratives produced by Europeans eager to describe the peoples they encountered in what they viewed as the New World. As this essay on images of native women suggests, both sources have their advantages and limitations in conveying women's lives accurately and clearly.

Figure 1.1, a stone effigy pipe of a woman grinding corn, dates from about 1200 and came from the Cahokia Mound area in present Madison County, Illinois. Given the information in Chapter 1 about corn cultivation and Native American women, what do you think is the significance of this type of artifact? Fortunately, historians are not totally dependent on guesswork in interpreting such images, as they can build on a wide range of archaeological evidence. The people of Cahokia were part of a large group whom historians call Mississippians. They lived in the Mississippi and Ohio rivers watersheds in North America's eastern woodlands from roughly 1000 to 1730, reaching their cultural height between 1100 and 1400. Distinguished by the large earthen mounds they built for ceremonial, political, and residential purposes, they apparently had a highly stratified social structure and complex culture. Artifacts recovered from the mounds, especially ones designed to be buried with the deceased, reveal a wide variety of artisanal crafts, including pottery and stonework. Some of these goods may have been produced by women. In addition, the mounds contained "foreign" material such as marine-shell beads and copperware that indicate a trading network among Native peoples extending to the Great Lakes in the north, Florida in the east, and the Rocky Mountains in the west.

◆ Figure 1.1 **Effigy Pipe from Cahokia Mound, Illinois (c. 1200–1400)**
Collection of Dr. Kent Westbrook. Photo by John T. Pafford.

Archaeological evidence such as food remains, human bones, and pollen indicates the centrality of maize—what Europeans called Indian corn.[19] Maize constituted 50 percent of the Mississippians' diet, and they used pottery to cook it and to store it in pits. For reasons that historians debate, such as climate change or warfare, the mound-builders had largely disappeared by the time of European contact. But the native peoples Europeans encountered in these regions continued to rely heavily on the corn produced by women. Corn became a vital staple for Europeans as well. What does this effigy pipe indicate about women's role in Mississippian societies?

Figure 1.2, a meticulously carved ceramic bottle in the shape of a nursing mother, dates from the same period and was also found in Illinois. Presumably it was not for everyday use but for ritualistic or symbolic purposes—perhaps it was placed in a grave for use in the afterlife. What insight into Mississippian women's lives and into the larger meanings of motherhood in their culture does the image offer?

Europeans' representations of Native American women tell us about European perceptions of their conquest of the Americas. However, depending on the artist, and with careful critical tools, we can also learn about the women depicted. Figure 1.3 uses allegory, a device common in western European art—employing the female form to symbolize a country or abstract qualities such as virtue or liberty. Images of America represented by an idealized Native American woman were highly popular in Europe. The illustration here, entitled *America*, is an engraving created around 1580 by Theodor Galle, based on a drawing from around 1574 by Jan van der Straet. The striking image represents Amerigo Vespucci, the Italian explorer whose name was eventually given to the land mass he first explored in 1499,° as he "awakens" America. The animal at bottom right is a sloth, and in the background naked people are roasting a human leg on a spit, indicating the widespread belief that American Natives were

◆ **Figure 1.2 Effigy Bottle, Cahokia Mound, Illinois (c. 1200–1400)**
From the Henry Whelpley Memorial Collection at the St. Louis Science Center.

°Historians dispute the exact year of Vespucci's arrival in the Americas.

◆ **Figure 1.3 Theodor Galle, *America* (c. 1580)**
Reproduced by permission of the Huntington Library, San Marino, California; Burndy Library, #78222.

uncivilized, barbaric, and cannibalistic. The engraving projects America as a bountiful land, but with savage peoples. The phrase in Latin may be translated in two ways, depending on the reader's interpretation of the word *retexit*: "Amerigo rediscovers America; he called her once and thenceforth she was always awake" or "Amerigo laid bare America; once he called her and thenceforth she was always aroused." How might these different translations elicit different interpretations of the engraving? What is the significance of Vespucci's being clothed and standing while the woman representing America is largely naked and reclining? Why would Europeans choose to depict America as a woman? What does the engraving reveal about European society and values?

More helpful to us in understanding the reality of indigenous women's lives are the illustrations and descriptions made by Europeans who encountered them in the sixteenth and seventeenth centuries. Often these accounts aimed at promoting enthusiasm and funding for exploration, colonization, or missionary activity, so they presented Native American peoples in ways that would appeal to their readers. But they also reflect ethnographic intentions to record, with more or less accuracy, the appearance and ways of strange new peoples. Publications such as Theodor de Bry's multivolume *Great Voyages* (1590) provided texts with illustrations detailing geography, information about flora and fauna, and accounts of

Native peoples. A native of Flanders, de Bry had a fervent interest in promoting the colonization schemes of Protestant nations on a continent where the Catholic French and Spanish had already established a foothold. His depiction in Figure 1.4 must be analyzed with his point of view and purpose in mind. The image is based on the work of artist Jacques Le Moyne de Morgues, who had spent time in Florida when the French had an outpost there. The drawing purports to describe the Timucua, a Muskogean-speaking people. Timucuas were a matrilineal, agricultural people who raised corn, beans, and squash. Scholars believe that details in this image such as the dress, the baskets, and the sticks used to punch holes in the ground for planting may be accurate, but the straight rows are apparently modeled after the plowed fields of Europe, and the hoes depicted are Flemish tools. The bodies of the women themselves reflect European ideas of classical beauty (female nudes were common in European painting). What does this image suggest about the Timucuas' sexual division of labor?

A much later depiction of women's work (Figure 1.5) appeared in *Moeurs des Sauvages Amériquains* (1724) by Joseph-François Lafitau, a Jesuit missionary in the region of Montreal, Canada. It is included here because there are no such depictions of Iroquois women's traditional work in the Great Lakes area from the sixteenth century. Accompanying his illustration of Canadian Iroquois women making maple sugar, Lafitau wrote, "The women are busy going to get the vessels

◆ Figure 1.4 **Indians Planting Corn, from Theodor de Bry, *Great Voyages* (1590)**
Library of Congress, LC-DIG-ppmsca-02937.

◆ **Figure 1.5 Canadian Iroquois Women Making Maple Sugar, from Joseph-François Lafitau,** *Moeurs des Sauvages Amériquains* **(1724)**
General Research Division, the New York Public Library, Astor, Lenox, and Tilden Foundations.

which are already full of the sap which drips from the trees, taking this sap and pouring it into the kettles which are on the fire. One woman is watching over the kettles while another one, seated, is kneading with her hands this sap which is thickening and in condition to be put in the shape of sugar loaves. Beyond the camp and the woods appear the fields as they look at the end of winter. We can see the women busy putting the fields into shape for the first time and sowing their corn."[20] What does this drawing and description suggest about the work patterns of these Iroquois women? What are the similarities and differences with Figure 1.4?

◆ Figure 1.6 **John White, *Theire sitting at meate* (c. 1585–1586)**
Library of Congress, LC-USZ62-570.

Undoubtedly the most comprehensive set of sixteenth-century North American drawings are those of John White, who was not only the most prolific and accomplished European artist of the New World but also governor of Roanoke, the first English attempt at settlement on the North American continent. Sir Walter Raleigh commissioned White to illustrate plant and animal life and the Native peoples encountered in the three Roanoke voyages of 1584–1590. White's extraordinary watercolors, such as Figure 1.6, appear to have been accurately drawn from his careful observations of the coastal Algonquians, who lived on the Outer Banks of today's North Carolina. Among most Algonquian peoples, men and women ate separately, although these Carolinians seem to have had different practices. Who may have made the mat on which the couple sits? "They are very sober in their eatinge, and drinkinge, and consequentlye verye longe lived because they doe not oppress nature," Thomas Harriot wrote in the accompanying text.[21] How is White's admiration for these people portrayed visually?

Theodor de Bry modified White's drawings when he published them in 1590. In White's version (Figure 1.6), the only dish the couple is eating is boiled maize. De Bry's version adds nuts, a fish, and corn; there is also a gourd, a pipe, and a

◆ **Figure 1.7** **Theodor de Bry, *Their sitting at meate* (1590), based on a drawing by John White**
Courtesy of the John Carter Brown Library at Brown University.

shell. What are the other differences between the two versions of the image *Theire sitting at meate*? Why might de Bry have changed White's original drawing?

White's detailed depiction of clothing and ornamentation is particularly valuable. Why might the English have been so interested in such details? Figure 1.8, *A Chief Lady of Pomeiooc and Her Daughter*, features the wife of the chief in an Algonquian town in what is now North Carolina. Although not clear from the drawing, the accompanying text indicates that the marks on the woman's arms and face are "pounced," or tattooed.[22] What other ways has the woman decorated herself? Her fringed skirt is made of skins and covers her front only, not her back. She is wearing a three-strand necklace, probably made of pearls and/or copper, hanging to her waist. Her daughter also wears a beaded necklace and, though it is hard to see, a skin covering of her genitals. She carries a doll—a European one, dressed in Elizabethan clothing. A caption for a similar illustration that appeared in de Bry's volume concludes with a comment concerning the doll: "They are greatley Diligted [delighted] with puppetts, and babes which wear [were] brought oute of England."[23] What is the significance of the inclusion of this European item?

Europeans such as White were struck with the participation of women in the public rituals that they observed. Why was this phenomenon worth depicting so lavishly? In *Indians Dancing Around a Circle of Posts* (Figure 1.9), also of Algonquian people, women are depicted both in the outer circle alongside men and at the center. The women can be distinguished from the men by their hair, which is tied back at the nape. Scholars have identified this as a corn festival, and the women

◆ Figure 1.8 *A Chief Lady of Pomeiooc and Her Daughter*
Library of Congress, LC-USZ62-570.

◆ Figure 1.9 **John White, *Indians Dancing Around a Circle of Posts* (1590)**
©*The Trustees of the British Museum.*

were described as "three of the fayrest Virgins."[24] How else is the centrality of women recognized in this ritual? What do you make of the wide variety of costumes?

   While most of White's paintings focus on the Atlantic Coast Algonquians with whom he met and lived, a small part of his work focused on Aleutian Islanders. The British explorer Martin Frobisher sailed in search of a Northwest Passage to Asia in the 1570s, and landed in what is now Baffin Island, Northern Canada, between Greenland and Quebec Province. He brought back two captives with him, one man and one woman. White either sailed with Frobisher or met these Indians in London in 1577. In either case, White's attention to detail is once again evident. Figure 1.10 is that of a woman in a sealskin dress and distinctive high boots. Her face is tattooed, but what is most striking about the image is the baby's face visible inside her hood. Why did White paint yet another an image of Indian motherhood? What other similarities, if any, does this woman bear to the women near Roanoke that White painted a decade later?

Pocahontas of the Algonquian-speaking Powhatan people in Virginia is perhaps the most famous Native American woman (see p. 26.). Figure 1.11 represents the famous story of how she convinced her father, the powerful chief Powhatan, to

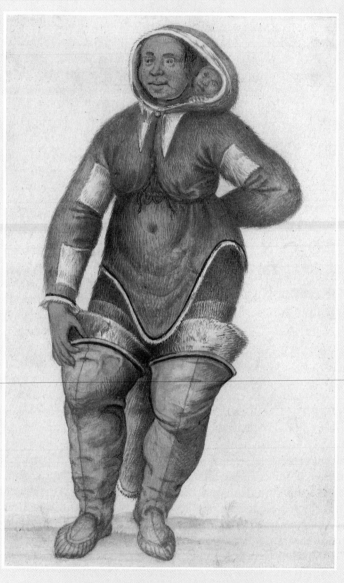

◆ Figure 1.10 **John White,** *Eskimo Woman* **(1577)**
©*The Trustees of the British Museum.*

King Powhatan *comands C. Smith to be slayne* his
daughter Pokahontas *beggs his life his thankfullness*
and how he Subiected 39 of their kings reade & histo

◆ Figure 1.11 *Pocahontas Convinces Her Father, Chief Powhatan, to Spare the Life of Captain John Smith,* from John Smith, *Generall Historie of Virginia* (1624)
© *Bettmann/CORBIS.*

spare the life of Captain John Smith. An unidentified illustrator prepared this image for Smith's account of his adventures, published in London in 1532. As Smith recounted it (writing about himself in the third person), "At last they brought him to Meronocomo, where was Powhatan their Emperor. Here more than two hundred of those grim Courtiers stood wondering at him, as he had beene a monster; . . . having feasted him after their best barbarous manner they could, a long consultation was held, but the conclusion was, two great stones were brought before Powhatan; then as many as could laid hands on him, dragged him to them, and thereon laid his head, and being ready with their clubs, to beate out his braines, Pocahontas the

Kings dearest daughter, when no intreaty could pre-vaile, got his head in her armes, and laid her owne upon his to save him from death."[25] What is Smith suggesting about Pocahontas and about himself by this story? What other possible interpretations of the events here depicted can you suggest?

Other images of Pocahontas come from her brief, celebrated trip to England, where she was presented as Native American royalty and as proof of the promise and success of the Jamestown settlement and of the eventual transplantation of English culture in the New World. Figure 1.12, a 1616 portrait painted shortly before her death, represents her as John Smith later described her: "a gracious lady" with a "very formall and civill . . . English manner."[26] The Virginia Company, which sponsored her trip and presumably commissioned the portrait, spent lavishly on her costume, with its rich lace and braid on her tapestry fabric dress. The hat was no doubt made of American beaver skins. What is the irony of picturing Pocahontas wearing this highly valued New World export? Why might Smith and others of the Virginia Company have sponsored this type of representation of Pocahontas? How does this portrait compare to that of the recently deceased English queen, Elizabeth, on page 24?

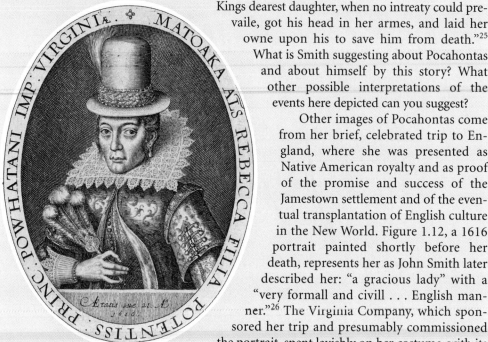

◆ **Figure 1.12** *Pocahontas* **(1616)**
National Portrait Gallery, Smithsonian Institution/Art Resource, New York.

QUESTIONS FOR ANALYSIS

1. How do we recapture the lives of people who left no written records? This visual essay features images of early Native American women and cautions that we must "read" these images carefully in using them to understand indigenous women's lives. What limitations do these images have as historical sources?

2. What commonalities do you find among the different representations here of Native American women? What differences?

3. One important characteristic of Native societies was the sexual division of labor. In what ways do these images depict women's economic participation in their communities?

DOCUMENT

African Women and the Slave Trade

EUROPEAN TRAFFICKING IN AFRICAN SLAVES began almost accidentally, in connection with Portuguese explorations of the west coast of Africa in search of gold and ivory. This 1442 account was recorded by the official archivist to the Portuguese royal family, Gomes Eannes de Azurara. It chronicles the adventures of various sea captains in the service of Prince Henry, nicknamed "the Navigator" for his leadership in exploring the seas, and also called "the Infant" (because he was son of the king). The Portuguese captains brought back blacks from the coast of Africa just east of the Cape Verde Islands and near the River Senegal. Their intent was as much to ransom them for African gold and other valuables as to enslave them in Portugal. As this account demonstrates, Europeans were simultaneously fascinated and repulsed by the looks and ways of these strange peoples. But their primary framework for understanding Africans was religion; thus, they referred to the captives as Moors (African Muslims) and believed that conversion to Catholicism could save and integrate them.

The first of the sea captains in service to the prince, Antam Goncalvez, had intended originally only to explore the African coast to the south of Cape Verde and to trade in gold and ivory with coastal Africans. In the process, he stumbled upon two Africans, one of whom was a woman, both already enslaved to the coastal Africans with whom he traded. In reference to the northern Africans who were still living in Portugal, he calls the woman, whom he captured, a Mooress, although he probably did not know her religious beliefs. He added the adjective "black" to distinguish her from lighter-skinned Berbers. Why might the other Africans have hesitated to save this one woman? What do you imagine was the Mooress's fate?

GOMES EANNES DE AZURARA
The Discovery and Conquest of Guinea 1441–1448 (1453)

CHAPTER XII

But when he had accomplished his voyage, as far as concerned the chief part of his orders, Antam Goncalvez . . . spoke to [his crew] in this wise: ". . . O How fair a thing it would be if we, who have come to this land for a cargo of such petty merchandise, were to meet with the good luck to bring the first captives before the face of our Prince." . . . As soon as it was night Antam Goncalvez chose nine men who seemed to him most fitted for the undertaking, and made his voyage with them as he had before determined. And, as they were going on their way, they saw a black Mooress come along (who was slave of those on the hill), and . . .

Antam Goncalvez bade them go at her; for if (he said) they scorned that encounter, it might make

SOURCE: Gomes Eannes de Azurara, *The Discovery and Conquest of Guinea 1441–1448*, trans. C. Raymond Beazley and Edgar Prestage (London: Hakluyt Society, 1896), pp. 40–43, 46, 66, 81–84, 110–111, 214–218, 258–260.

their foes pluck up courage against them. . . . [F]ollowing his will, they seized the Mooress. And those on the hill had a mind to come to the rescue, but when they perceived our people ready to receive them, they not only retreated to their former position, but departed elsewhere, turning their backs to their enemies.

L ANDING AT THE SAME PLACE, a second Portuguese captain asked to be allowed to conduct a second raid, as the following account indicates. How was his purpose different from that of Goncalvez?

CHAPTER XIII

. . . Although you are carrying off these two captives, and by their means . . . [Prince Henry of Portugal] may come to know something about this folk, yet that doth not prevent what is still better, namely, for us to carry off many more; for, besides the knowledge which the Lord [Henry] . . . will gain by their means, profit will also accrue to him by their service or ransom.

F OLLOWING GONCALVEZ'S RETURN, Prince Henry issued a formal commercial license for other Portuguese to trade with coastal Africans for slaves. The following selection describes how Lancarote de Freitas organized a much larger expedition. De Freitas was based farther south on the African coast, in Lagos (now Nigeria), which was just developing as a Portuguese trading post. He describes a swift slave raid carried out by his men against a community of Africans (again called Moors). How might his emphasis on the disarray of the Africans and their abandonment of family ties have affected his readers?

CHAPTER XIX

. . . They saw that the Moors, with their women and children, were already coming as quickly as they could out of their dwellings because they had caught sight of their enemies [the Portuguese]. They [the raiders], shouting out "St. James," "St. George," "Portugal," at once attacked them, killing and taking all they could. Then might you see mothers forsaking their children, and husbands their wives, each striving to escape as best he could. Some drowned themselves in the water; others thought to escape by hiding under their huts; others stowed their children among the sea-weed, where our men found them afterwards, hoping they would thus escape notice.

AFTER TWO OTHER SLAVING FORAYS, de Freitas brought more than two hundred captured Africans south to the trading post at Lagos. How do you account for the mixture of repulsion and sympathy that the author evidences, especially for the blackest of the captives? What do this and the previous selection tell you about the kin relations of the Africans captured? How does the author render the captives' spiritual beliefs?

CHAPTER XXV

. . . The seamen began to make ready their boats, and to take out those captives, and carry them on shore, as they were commanded. . . . were some white enough, fair to look upon, and well proportioned; others were less white like mulattoes; others again were as black as Ethiops, and so ugly, both in features and in body, as almost to appear (to those who saw them) the images of a lower hemisphere. But what heart could be so hard as not to be pierced with piteous feeling to see that company? For some kept their heads low and their faces bathed in tears, looking one upon another; others stood groaning very dolorously, looking up to the height of heaven, fixing their eyes upon it, crying out loudly, as if asking help of the Father of Nature; . . . to increase their sufferings still more, . . . was it needful to part fathers from sons, husbands from wives, brothers from brothers. No respect was shewn either to friends or relations, but each fell where his lot took him . . . [T]he mothers clasped their other children in their arms, and threw themselves flat on the ground with them; receiving blows with little pity for their own flesh, if only they might not be torn from them.

CHAPTER XXVI

. . . The sorrow of those captives was for the present very great. . . . [I]t chanced that among the prisoners the father often remained in Lagos, while the mother was taken to Lisbon, and the children to another part (in which partition their sorrow doubled the first grief).

BACK IN PORTUGAL, the Africans were further distributed. What does the following passage reveal of the terms of African slavery as it was first practiced in Portugal? The author seems to suggest that, unlike the Islamic Moors with whom he was familiar, these Africans had much more flexible beliefs and were open to Christian ideas. Why and how does Christianity apparently rescue them from their enslaved condition? Why might Portuguese women have wanted female slaves?

But from this time forth they began to acquire some knowledge of our country; . . . For as our people did not find them hardened in the belief of the other Moors; and saw how they came in unto the law of Christ with a good will; they made no difference between them and their free servants, born in our own country; . . . Yea, and some widows of good family who bought some of these female slaves, either adopted them or left them a portion of their estate by will; so that in the future they married right well; treating them as entirely free. Suffice it that I never saw one of these slaves put in irons like other captives, and scarcely any one who did not turn Christian and was not very gently treated.

THE TEXT THEN RETURNS TO the initial two captives that Goncalvez had seized. One of them convinced his captors that he was of African royal blood and could be returned and ransomed for a much larger group of Africans, drawn from the slaves of his own people. The ransom process included an unusual incident involving African women and their sexual desire for potential male slaves. What does the Portuguese chronicler's version tell us about his own assumptions about African women and female sexuality? How might his own prejudices have influenced his observations, for example, about the women's nakedness? We cannot really know whether the African women were actually intent on taking men as sexual slaves or whether they were engaged in some sort of performance meant to show their power or embarrass the Portuguese and better their side's exchange in the ransom. The author calls this "deceit." What other possibilities might explain the women's behavior?

CHAPTER XXXV

. . . And, after settling the matter of hostages, Antam Goncalvez received two Moors as security; and he on his side gave two others of those that he had with him. And those two . . . were taken to the tents of the Moors, where was a very great number of Moorish women, and those among the best of that land. . . . And the Moorish women, looking upon those two hostages, thought to try them, shewing a very great desire of lying with them; and those who thought themselves best favoured shewed themselves right willingly as naked as when they first came out of the bellies of their mothers, and so made them other signs sufficiently unchaste. . . . [T]he women nevertheless persevered in their unchaste purpose, making them signs of great security [indicating they would be safe], and asking them, as could be understood by their gestures, that they should perform what they sought. But whether this was attempted with deceit, or whether it was only the wickedness of their nature that urged them to this, let it be the business of each one to settle as he thinks best.

THE NEXT SELECTION FOLLOWS another slaving expedition by the energetic de Freitas, to the island of Arguin, somewhat north of Goncalvez's first landing. The Portuguese later built a fort there, which served as a way station and departure point for African slaves to be shipped across the Atlantic. Here we have another extraordinary incident featuring an African woman. Were the captors surprised by her resistance and, if so, why? What do you make of their coldness to her fate?

CHAPTER LXXI

And so the two, pursuing their voyage, came to the Isle of Arguim[.] . . . [T]heir booty was much diminished, for they captured no more than nine persons. . . . And since women are usually stubborn, one woman of that company began to take it in conceipt to refuse to walk, throwing herself on the ground and letting herself be dragged along by the hair and the legs, having no pity on herself; and her over-great stubbornness compelled our men to leave her there, bound, intending to return for her another day. . . . So remained the Mooress with her foolish stubborness, strongly bound in that wood, wherein I believe she would meet with a troublous death, for those who escaped thence, being frightened by the first encounter, would not return that way very soon.

THIS FINAL SELECTION PROVIDES the account of yet another African woman resisting her enslavement. How did the Portuguese slavers exploit African family bonds even while denigrating them? What else do we learn both about the prejudices of the Europeans and the lives and experiences of the Africans?

CHAPTER LXXXVII

Alvaro Fernandez returned again to the land of the Negroes[.] . . . And when the ship had been provisioned, they made their voyage straight to Cape Verde[.] . . . And so journeying along the sea coast, in a few days they went on shore again, and came upon a village, and its inhabitants issued forth like men who showed they had a will to defend their houses[.] . . . And Alvaro Fernandez seeing him, and judging him to be the leader of the band, went stoutly at him, and gave him such a great wound with his lance that he fell down dead[.] . . . Now the Guineas, perceiving that man to be dead, paused from their fighting, and it appeared to our men to be neither the time nor the place to withdraw them from that fear. But rather they returned to their ship and on the next day landed a little way distant from there, where they espied some of the wives of those Guineas walking. And it seemeth that they were going nigh to a creek collecting shell-fish, and they captured one of them, who would be as much as thirty years of age, with a son of hers who would be of about two, and also a young girl of fourteen years, who had well-formed limbs and also a favourable presence for a Guinea; but the strength of the woman was much to be marvelled at, for not one of the three men who came upon her but would have had a great labour in attempting to get her to the boat. And so one of our men, seeing the delay they were making, fearing which it might be that some of the dwellers of the land would come upon them, conceived it well to take her son from her and to carry him to the boat; and love of the child compelled the mother to follow after it, without great pressure on the part of the two who were bringing her.

QUESTIONS FOR ANALYSIS

1. How, according to these passages, did the Portuguese treat African men and women differently? What could account for these differences?

2. How was the slavery you read about here different from the racially based system that evolved in the Americas? In what ways might the enslaved Africans have escaped permanent servitude while under Portuguese control?

3. How did enslavement shatter the family bonds of Africans? What did the absence of family mean especially for individual women once they were captured?

4. What details of the story are missing from the Portuguese accounts? How might more information alter the meaning of the events here described?

NOTES

1. Mary P. Ryan, *Mysteries of Sex: Tracing Women and Men through American History* (Chapel Hill: University of North Carolina Press, 2006), 21.

2. Karen Kupperman, "International at the Creation," in Thomas Bender, ed., *Rethinking American History in a Global Age* (Berkeley: University of California Press, 2002), 105.

3. Judith K. Brown, "Economic Organization and the Position of Women among the Iroquois," *Ethnohistory* 17, nos. 3–4 (Summer–Fall 1970): 159.

4. Champlain, Samuel de. *The Works of Samuel de Champlain*. 6 vols. Ed. by H. P. Biggar (Toronto: The Champlain Society, 1922–1936), 136–37.

5. Judith K. Brown, "Economic Organization and the Position of Women among the Iroquois," 153.

6. Ibid., 153.

7. Richard White, *The Middle Ground: Indians, Empires, and Republics in the Great Lakes Region, 1650–1815* (Cambridge: Cambridge University Press, 1991), 63.

8. Ramón A. Gutiérrez, *When Jesus Came, the Corn Mothers Went Away: Marriage, Sexuality, and Power in New Mexico, 1500–1846* (Stanford: Stanford University Press, 1991), 34.

9. James Axtell, ed., *The Indian Peoples of Eastern America: A Documentary History of the Sexes* (New York: Oxford University Press, 1981), 142.

10. William Monter, "Protestant Wives, Catholic Saints, and the Devil's Handmaid," in Renate Bridenthal and Claudia Koonz, eds., *Becoming Visible: Women in European History* (Boston: Houghton Mifflin, 1977), 207.

11. John Huxtable Elliott, *Empires of the Atlantic World: Britain and Spain in America 1492–1830* (New Haven: Yale University Press, 2007), 64.

12. Carmen Tafolla, "La Malinche," in Tey Diana Rebolledo and Eliana Rivero, eds., *Infinite Divisions: An Anthology of Chicana Literature* (Tucson: University of Arizona Press, 1993), 198–99.

13. Susan Migden Socolow, *The Women of Colonial Latin America* (Cambridge: Cambridge University Press, 2000), 181–82.

14. Clara Sue Kidwell, "Indian Women as Cultural Mediators," *Ethnohistory* 39, no. 2 (Spring 1992): 97.

15. Jennifer Lyle Morgan, *Laboring Women: Reproduction and Gender in New World Slavery* (Philadelphia: University of Pennsylvania Press, 2004), 27.

16. Elliott, *Empires of the Atlantic World*, 100.

17. David Brion Davis, *Inhuman Bondage: The Rise and Fall of Slavery in the New World* (Oxford: Oxford University Press, 2006), 108.

18. P. D. Curtin, *The Rise and Fall of the Plantation Complex: Essays in Atlantic History* (Cambridge: Cambridge University Press, 1998), 109.

19. Neal Salisbury, "The Indians' Old World: Native Americans and the Coming of Europeans," in Peter C. Mancall and James H. Merrell, eds., *American Encounters: Natives and Newcomers from European Contact to Indian Removal, 1500–1850* (New York: Routledge, 2000), 7.

20. Father Joseph-François Lafitau, *Customs of the American Indians Compared with the Customs of Primitive Times,* ed. and trans. William N. Fenton and Elizabeth L. Moore (1724; Toronto: Champlain Society, 1977), 2:8.

21. Thomas Harriot, *A Briefe and True Report of the New Found Land of Virginia,* reprint of the 1590 De Bry edition (New York: Dover, 1972), 50.

22. John White, *The First Colony,* reprinted in *The Roanoke Voyages, 1584–1590,* Vol. I (London: The Hakluyt Society, 1955), 430.

23. Ibid., 428.

24. Paul Hulton, *America, 1585: The Complete Drawings of John White* (Chapel Hill: University of North Carolina Press, 1984), 114.

25. Captain John Smith, *The Generall Historie of Virginia, New England & the Summer Isles, Together with the True Travels, Adventures and Observations, and a Sea Grammar—Volume I* (1607), Library of Congress, American Memory, "The Capital and the Bay: Narratives of Washington and the Chesapeake Bay Region, ca. 1600–1925," http://memory.loc.gov/cgibin/query/r?ammem/lhbcb:@field(DOCID+@lit(lhbcb0262adiv12)) (accessed April 18, 2004).

26. Karen Ordahl Kupperman, *Indians and English: Facing Off in Early America* (Ithaca, NY: Cornell University Press, 2000), 199.

SUGGESTED REFERENCES

Early American History   Historical literature on the global context of early American history is a growing field. Thomas Bender has edited a fine introductory collection on the globalization of American history, *Rethinking American History in a Global Age* (2002), which includes several articles on early American history. One of the most interesting of the new studies to put U.S. national origins in a wider context is J. H. Elliott, *Empires of the Atlantic World: Britain and Spain in America, 1492–1830* (2006). David Brion Davis has published a magisterial overview of the history of slavery, *Inhuman Bondage: The Rise and Fall of Slavery in the New World* (2006). There is, as yet, no single text that deals with women's experiences from a variety of angles, but each of the topics here considered—Native American cultures, European arrivals, and the origins of transatlantic slavery—are developing a rich literature of gender.

Native American Women   There is a considerable and growing literature on Native American women and gender. For a gendered approach to archaeology, see Karen Olsen Bruhns and Karen E. Stothert, *Women in Ancient America* (1999). In *The Indian Peoples of Eastern America: A Documentary History of the Sexes* (1981), James Axtell offers primary documents with introductions. On the Iroquois, see Eleanor Leacock's pioneering account, in her introduction to the 1972 republication of Frederick Engels's Marxist classic, *The Origin of the Family, Private Property, and the State, in the Light of the Researches of Lewis Henry Morgan.* Also see Judith

K. Brown, "Economic Organization and the Position of Women among the Iroquois," *Ethnohistory* 17, nos. 3–4 (Summer–Fall 1970): 151–67, and Daniel K. Richter, *The Ordeal of the Longhouse: The Peoples of the Iroquois League in the Era of European Colonization* (1992). Theda Perdue's *Cherokee Women: Gender and Culture Change 1700–1835* (1998) is a classic.

Spanish America   Susan Migden Socolow, *The Women of Colonial Latin America* (2000), examines women in the first two centuries of Spanish America. Also see *Women in the Crucible of Conquest: The Gendered Genesis of Spanish American Society, 1500–1600* by Karen Vieira Powers (2005). The pioneering work on the sexual interactions between Spanish invaders and women of the Pueblo peoples is Ramón A. Gutiérrez's *When Jesus Came, the Corn Mothers Went Away: Marriage, Sexuality, and Power in New Mexico, 1500–1846* (1991). The controversy that this book generated among contemporary Pueblo peoples is lucidly discussed in *American Ethnologist* 21, no. 4 (1994). Mary P. Ryan, *Mysteries of Sex: Tracing Women and Men through American History* (2006), offers a very original analysis of the gender contact surrounding early Spanish America.

Early British Settlement   The five hundredth anniversary of Jamestown produced a reexamination of the Smith/Pocahontas/Rolfe relationship. See Camilla Townsend, *Pocahontas and the Powhatan Dilemma* (2004), and the exciting biography by Native American scholar Paula Gunn Allen, *Pocahontas: Medicine Woman, Spy, Entrepreneur, Diplomat* (2004).

The Atlantic Slave Trade   The gendered dimensions of the Atlantic slave trade in its first two centuries are also receiving considerable attention, much of it from economic historians who use sophisticated "cliometrics" (historical statistics) to arrive at more reliable numbers for the Africans who were forcibly transported. An important tool in this work is an extraordinary collection of the original sources documenting slave shipments throughout the long history of the trade: David Eltis, Stephen D. Behrendt, David Richardson, and Herbert S. Klein, eds., *The Trans-Atlantic Slave Trade: A Database on CD-ROM* (2000). Claire C. Robertson and Martin A. Klein, eds., *Women and Slavery in Africa* (1983), includes important articles by Herbert S. Klein and John Thornton on the demography of the African slave trade. Jennifer Lyle Morgan, *Laboring Women: Reproduction and Gender in New World Slavery* (2004), provides a provocative analysis of European male expectations and observations about both Amerindian and African women's bodies.

For selected Web sites, please visit the *Through Women's Eyes* book companion site at bedfordstmartins.com/duboisdumenil.

2

Colonial Worlds

1607–1750

I N 1690, LIKE MANY OTHER COLONISTS ON THE NEW England frontier, Hannah Swarton's community was raided by Indians, angered at the incursions on their lands. The Abenaki warriors, following the practices of their people, took the surviving men, women, and children back to their home villages as captives, there to be adopted, kept as slaves, or ransomed. Swarton's children were taken from her, and she was given as a slave to an Abenaki family. For the next eight months, she lived and traveled and ate and dressed as a Native woman. She was hungry, cold, exhausted, and terrified of being killed. Arriving in French Canada, her Indian master sold Swarton to local Catholics, who dressed her in European clothes, gave her a bed to sleep in, and fed her relatively well. But now that Swarton's outer self was saved, she felt that her inner self was endangered. As a Protestant, Swarton had been taught to view Catholics as papists, or people who mindlessly followed the pope, and to view Catholic practices and beliefs such as the veneration of Mary and the saints as idolatry. Now Swarton was pressured to convert to Catholicism: "[T]he Lady, my mistress, the nuns, the priests, the friars, and the rest set upon me with all the strength of argument they could." Yet she held on to her Protestant faith for four long years, until intercolonial negotiations permitted her to return to New England.[1]

Hannah Swarton's story, which we know because the renowned Puritan cleric Cotton Mather published it to teach the power of faith, shows modern readers that North America was home to a wide range of cultures and societies, close geographically yet far apart in lifeways and expectations for women. These different peoples, not just "Europeans" and "Indians" but French, English, Dutch, Spanish, Pueblo, Iroquois, Huron, Shawnees, Cherokees, and Ojibwas, just to name a few, knew each other as neighbors, trading partners, allies, and enemies. Women rarely fought, but they were caught up in these conflicts. Hannah Swarton was unusual in crossing not just one boundary but two, the first between English and Indian America and the second between Indian and French America. Her experience, first as a free woman and then as a captive and slave, reminds us that slavery in North America took many forms before it became synonymous with African origins. Her religious devotion and her family attachments link her to other women whose stories reveal the history of seventeenth- and early eighteenth-century North America through women's eyes.

SOUTHERN BRITISH COLONIES

Although colonists came from many European nations, the English dominated the eastern seaboard region, which eventually formed the political foundation of the United States as the thirteen English colonies. English cultural values were particularly influential in shaping early American assumptions concerning women's proper place. The male-headed family was the primary unit of society. Women's work was expected to be confined to household production, even though prevailing notions concerning the sexual division of labor were not always met, particularly among the poor. Both Protestant religious values and English law, especially as it related to property, reinforced women's subordination to men.

Ideas about women's roles framed the experiences of the Englishwomen who came as settlers to Britain's southern colonies as well as the African women who came bound as slaves. But the special circumstances of the New World also powerfully shaped migrant women's lives. The chronic shortage of marriageable (read English) women put them under irresistible pressure to marry quickly but also gave them some leverage in choosing a husband. The economic goals that dominated the plantation societies of the South not only created potential class conflict among whites but also led to the institution of a new form of slavery and the evolution of a distinct African American culture.

British Women in the South

As noted in Chapter 1, the English finally succeeded in establishing a permanent beachhead in North America at Jamestown in 1607 (see Map 2.1). Crucial decisions affecting the Virginia colony came initially from the Virginia Company of London, whose merchant directors hoped that they would reap a fortune from

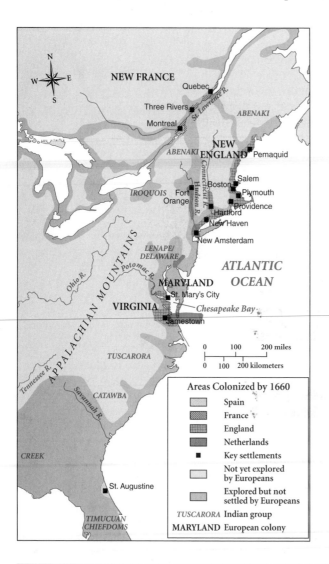

◆ **Map 2.1 Eastern North America, 1650**
Of the four European nations that had permanent colonies along the eastern seaboard of North America in 1650, only England had substantial numbers of colonists. Approximately twenty-five thousand British subjects lived in New England, and another fifteen thousand lived in the Chesapeake region. Europeans in the interior, particularly Dutch and French fur traders, established diplomatic relationships with Indian peoples, bringing with them European trade goods and diseases.

trade with Native Americans. Their economic hopes for Virginia shifted in 1613, when the colonists began raising tobacco in mass quantities for the European market (see p. 64). Along with other marketable commodities, such as rice and indigo, tobacco was crucial to the economies of the other southern British colonies: Maryland (1634), the Carolinas (1663), and Georgia (1732).

Once they shifted to these marketable crops, merchants who sought to exploit the potential wealth of North America needed a steady supply of laborers to make their ventures successful. A population explosion in England and rising levels of poverty facilitated the recruitment of thousands willing to make the hazardous journey across the Atlantic. The first settlers were overwhelmingly male. To redress this imbalance, in 1620 and 1621 the Virginia Company imported approximately 150 "tobacco brides" — "respectable" young women whose passages were paid for with 120 pounds of tobacco by men eager to acquire wives who could serve not only as sexual partners but also as another pair of agricultural hands. The disappearance of most of these women from historical records suggests that many died, some from disease and starvation in the hardship years of 1622–1623, others in the 1622 uprising of Powhatan's brother Opechecanough. Thus the imported brides made hardly a dent in improving the balance between the sexes. Women continued to immigrate in small numbers compared to men (in 1635, only 14 percent of the 2,010 settlers arriving from London were women), and the lack of marriageable women was a constant complaint among English men. Maryland, founded in 1634 to provide refuge for Catholics, had an even greater disproportion of men to women: in the colony's first decade, men outnumbered women by 6 to 1. In Maryland and Virginia, it was not until after 1700, when male immigration had slowed and subsequent American-born generations began to reproduce, that the sex ratio came into balance.

Even so, mortality rates remained exceptionally high in the Chesapeake region throughout the seventeenth century as a result of harsh conditions and diseases such as malaria and dysentery. Men's average life span was forty-eight years; women's was thirty-nine. (The hazards of childbirth caused the disparity; women who survived their childbearing years lived much longer than men.) The death of a spouse, usually an older husband, often cut marriages short; in Maryland, for example, only one in three couples could expect their marriage to last ten years. Widows, especially with inherited wealth from first husbands, remarried quickly, creating complicated households of stepsisters and stepbrothers.

The circumstances of the Chesapeake colonies made it difficult to reestablish as strong a patriarchal system as the one that flourished in England. The many children who came to adulthood with just one living parent had unusual freedom from parental oversight in their marriage choices. In the scattered homesteads of the southern colonies, with little communal oversight given to young couples, premarital sex was probably common. The availability of land and the uncertainty of life induced many Chesapeake fathers to leave land to their daughters as well as to their sons.

Married women, however, generally were just as subordinate to their husbands as in England. Under the English common law of coverture, which the

Chesapeake colonies followed, a married woman became a *feme covert* (meaning her legal identity was absorbed into that of her husband). Naming practices by which married women took their husbands' family names embodied this system. Without any separate legal identity, married women could not sue or be sued, hold public office, or vote. Their husbands had legal control over their property, their children, and even their bodies. When a married woman was brought before the court for an offense, her husband was held responsible. Further, given that a wife's sexual services were the property of her husband, he could be found guilty if she committed the crime of adultery.

Upon her husband's death a widow did receive a portion—a dower right, which was at least one-third of the estate—for the duration of her lifetime. Those few women who remained single or who remained widowed had the status of *feme sole*, which gave them some individual rights before the law. Chesapeake widows also had decent opportunities to improve their circumstances by remarrying well. Husbands often left their wives more than the accustomed one-third dower rights—perhaps because they were so uncertain that their children would live to adulthood—and even made wives executors of their estates. Thus, astute women could amass wealth and achieve a degree of economic autonomy. Elizabeth Digges, the widow of the former governor of Virginia, had an estate valued at 1,100 pounds, which was the largest in York County.

The most famous Chesapeake woman who acted independently was not a widow, but someone who never married. Margaret Brent, a well-connected English Catholic, came to Maryland in 1638. Both she and her sister Mary acquired substantial landholdings that they managed independently. Margaret Brent actively exercised her *feme sole* rights, making contracts, appearing in court to reclaim debts, and conducting her business freely. Her business acumen, her status as a large landholder and English gentlewoman, and the fact that she was not burdened by a husband with political entanglements led the governor of Maryland, Lord Calvert, to name her as his executor. When Calvert died in 1647, Maryland had recently experienced a local rebellion, and the troops that had put it down had yet to be paid. The responsibility of bringing order to the colony fell to Brent. The Maryland assembly resolved that "the colony was safer in her hands than any man's in the Province. . . . [S]he rather deserves favor and thanks from your honour for her so much concerning for the public safety."[2] Despite this show of trust and respect, the assembly refused in 1647 to honor Brent's novel demand that she be given two votes in the assembly, one based on her role as landowner and another on her role as representative of her male clients. Although Brent's story illustrates the fluid circumstances in the seventeenth-century Chesapeake colonies that allowed women to have unusual economic power—and in rare cases even limited political power—it is clearly an exceptional one.

In contrast to Brent, the vast majority of the early white immigrants to the Chesapeake—male and female—came as indentured servants. In Virginia and Maryland, and later in the Carolinas and Georgia, a system of "bound" labor predominated. Impoverished young people, seeking opportunities unavailable in Europe, bound themselves via a legal document (an indenture) to masters for fixed periods of time—usually between four and seven years—exchanging their labor for their passage to the colonies. In general, a white indentured servant cost about half as much as a black slave. Recognizing the importance of women in creating a stable colony, the Virginia Company eagerly recruited young women by using propaganda that assured them that they would be treated well and would find it easy to marry at the conclusion of their service. Although the company also promised that indentured women would not be "put into the ground to worke, but occupie such domestique imployments and housewifery as in England," this was often not the case.[3]

As many as three-quarters of the women who migrated to the Chesapeake colonies in the seventeenth century were indentured. Despite the promises of the colonies' promoters, indentured women servants found life harsh (see box, "The Trappan'd Maiden: or, The Distressed Damsel"). They carried out their responsibilities for food preparation and housekeeping in meager circumstances in small dwellings. In the early years, the zeal to produce a cash crop overrode the English sensibilities about proper gender roles. Instead of concentrating on domestic production, women servants often were sent into the tobacco fields—planting seedlings, hoeing, weeding, and, at harvest, stripping and processing the leaves for market.

Other conditions of their servitude added to the hardships of indentured women. Prohibited from marrying while servants, they were subject to sexual exploitation. When they became pregnant—and an estimated 20 percent of indentured women did—they were punished with a public whipping and a fine. Those unable to pay the fine had their time of servitude extended, usually by one to two years. A servant who claimed that her master was the father of her child was not released from service, for fear that if a "woman got with child by her master should be freed from that service it might probably induce such loose persons to lay all their bastards to their masters."[4] Rather, a pregnant servant's indenture was transferred to a new master, who paid the county for her services.

Because of the indenture system, most young white women who came to the Chesapeake colonies married relatively late, at age twenty-four or twenty-five. Marriage helped to mark a woman's freedom from bound labor, but it did not necessarily lighten her load. Some women married "up"—and found themselves the mistress of servants—but others married men less well off than their former masters. Until the legal codification of perpetual slavery for Africans in the later 1600s, many of them married enslaved African men. In addition to the responsibilities of childbirth and child care, in poorer families wives worked in the fields. In middling families, women conducted business and trade in their husbands' absences. Wives' contributions to the household economy were valued, but as elsewhere in the English world, married women lived highly circumscribed lives.

Discontent among indentured servants, female as well as male, played a major role in Bacon's Rebellion. In 1676, a rebel faction of the Virginia colony's elite, led by Nathaniel Bacon, recruited white indentured servants and African slaves to protest the high-handed rule of the royal governor. These men protested the governor's control over land and trade. They also argued that his policies shielding the lands of Native Americans from seizure and sale interfered with colonial men's ability to establish their own economic independence. They especially resented

The Trappan'd Maiden: or, The Distressed Damsel

This traditional ballad about the girl who "was cunningly Trappan'd" and "sent to Virginny from England, Where she doth Harship undergo" may or may not have actually been composed by a woman servant, but its lyrics capture the harsh quality of countless indentured women's lives. Note that instead of the customary young woman's lament of betrayal by a lover, this maiden's betrayer is an employer. Folk materials like this ballad form an important resource for historians in the attempt to reconstruct the lives of ordinary people who rarely left written records behind.

Give ear unto a Maid, that lately was betray'd,
And sent into Virginny, O:
In brief I shall declare, what I have suffer'd there,
When that I was weary, weary, weary, weary, O.

[Since] that first I came to this Land of Fame,
Which is called Virginny, O,
The Axe and the Hoe have wrought my overthrow,
When that I was weary, weary, weary, weary, O.

Five years served I, under Master Guy,
In the land of Virginny, O,
Which made me for to know sorrow, grief and woe,
When that I was weary, weary, weary, weary, O.

When my Dame says "Go" then I must do so,
In the land of Virginny, O;
When she sits at Meat, then I have none to eat,
When that I am weary, weary, weary, weary, O. . . .

the shortage of English women to marry. Women also joined the ranks of protesters. Sarah Drummond, the wife of one of Bacon's closest advisers, famously defied royal authority by declaring, "I fear the power of England no more than a broken straw."[5] After six months of hostilities, authorities in London constrained the local governor and allowed greater mobility to the lower ranks of free white men.

Although the rebels had forced an unprecedented crisis in Virginia affairs, the resolution of the rebellion taught the ruling powers of the colony how to quell cross-class conflicts among Englishmen and thus stabilize their own leadership. The colony's rulers went to great lengths to forestall any future alliance between white servants and black slaves, and they made it easier for land-hungry whites to seize treaty-protected territory from Native Americans.

If my Dame says "Go!" I dare not say no,
In the Land of Virginny, O;
The Water from the Spring, upon my head I bring,
When that I am weary, weary, weary, weary, O.

When the Mill doth stand, I'm ready at command,
In the Land of Virginny, O;
The Water for to make, which makes my heart to ake,
When that I am weary, weary, weary, weary, O.

When the Child doth cry, I must sing "By-a-by!"
In the Land of Virginny, O;
No rest that I can have, whilst I am here a Slave,
When that I am weary, weary, weary, weary, O.

A thousand woes beside, that I do here abide,
In the Land of Virginny, O;
In misery I spend my time that hath no end,
When that I am weary, weary, weary, weary, O.

Then let Maids beware, all by my ill-fare,
In the Land of Virginny, O;
Be sure to stay at home, for if you do here come,
You all will be weary, weary, weary, weary, O.

But if it be my chance, Homewards to advance,
From the Land of Virginny, O;
If that I, once more, land on English Shore,
I'll no more be weary, weary, weary, weary, O.

SOURCE: Charles Harding Firth, ed., *An American Garland: Being a Collection of Ballads Relating to America, 1563–1759* (Oxford: Blackwell, 1915), 251–53.

At the same time, economic and political power remained in the hands of large plantation owners, who continued to acquire not only the best land but also more and more slaves. They began to build large, elegant mansions for themselves, conspicuously displaying their wealth and social prominence. Women of the planter class, aided by a large retinue of slaves for household tasks, were able to devote time to such leisurely pursuits as studying French, playing music, writing letters, and doing needlework. Wealthy women also began to participate in a growing consumer economy, importing gowns, china, silver, and furniture. Privileged white women's attention to hospitality and fashion, as well as to domesticity and maternal duties, eventually became essential elements in the ideal of the genteel lady that reinforced southern patriarchal culture.

◆ Curing and Drying Tobacco

This image of tobacco processing depicts a common aspect of women's work in the early Chesapeake colonies, the laborious process of growing and harvesting tobacco. This image shows African men and women and white colonial women all working together. Five slaves in the background, including a child and two women, hang tobacco leaves to dry. The white women were probably indentured servants. One strips the cured leaves while the other packs them. Tobacco required nearly constant attention, so even though work changed with the season, there was always more than enough to do. *Culver Pictures.*

African Women

Whether plantation mistresses or wives of yeomen, white women in the southern colonies were inextricably tied up with slavery. Until the mid-seventeenth century, relatively few Africans had been imported into North America, and the historical records on them are spotty. One of the first African women was "Mary," who arrived

◆ **Henrietta Johnston,** *Portrait of Marie Peronneau Bacot,* **c. 1716**

Henrietta Johnston was the first portrait artist known to be working in the southern colonies and the first colonial artist to work in pastels. She arrived in 1708 in Charles Town, South Carolina, as the wife of an Anglican clergyman. Her American paintings are mostly of French Protestants (Huguenots), who were not welcome in New France and found homes and prosperity in South Carolina. Like all of her portraits of women, this painting depicts an elegant, beautifully coiffed member of the city's elite. Johnston herself did not enjoy such luxury. She used her artistic skill to help support her large family. Like less illustrious women at this time, she bartered her work for goods or skills. In this case, the sitter was the step-daughter of the physician who cared for Johnston's sickly husband and probably took the painting in payment. *The Metropolitan Museum of Art, Gift of Mrs. J. Insley Blair, 1947 (47.103.23) Image © Metropolitan Museum of Art.*

in Virginia in 1622 and ended up at the same plantation as "Antonio a Negro." Eventually the two won their freedom, married, adopted the surname Johnson, and became modest landowners, even owning slaves. The couple's experience points to an important fact about early African servitude: initially the system was a fluid one that allowed some blacks opportunities for freedom and created a small nucleus of free blacks in the region. By the end of the seventeenth century, however, chattel slavery had become an inescapable status for those of African descent.

The harshness of African women's American existence began when they were kidnapped or sold into the Atlantic slave trade, which had passed from the Iberians to the Dutch and the English (see p. 32). Of those captured in Africa, 10 to 20 percent died in transit, a figure that was no respecter of gender. In contrast to the sixteenth-century slave trade, by the mid-seventeenth century, the numbers and percentages of women being bought, shipped, and sold increased significantly. Of the estimated 215,000 Africans who arrived in the Americas as slaves between 1663 and 1714, some 39 percent were female.[6]

Begun as an institution that did not differ completely from the indentured servitude of poor white immigrants, slavery became a lifelong and inherited status starting in the middle of the seventeenth century. Scholars have pointed out that African slave women were particularly crucial to this shift. Virginia's laws reveal the steps by which perpetual slavery was institutionalized. A 1643 law placed a tax on the labor of African women, putting them in the same category as paid male (European and African) labor. White women were exempt from this tax, under the assumption that whatever work they might do in the fields was temporary and would eventually give way to their return to domestic concerns. By making a sharp distinction between black women's and white women's labor, the law thus contributed to the view of Africans as fundamentally distinct from Europeans. Eventually, the increased use of African men and women in the fields allowed the reinstitution of traditional English gender roles for white women. By 1722, Virginian William Beverly could write that "slaves of both sexes are employed together in tilling and manuring the ground" while "a white woman is rarely or never put to work in the ground."[7]

This first law distinguishing between black and white women was followed by others. Particularly important was the 1662 law that made bondage an inherited condition, derived only from the mother. Enslavement now extended beyond an individual's lifetime and was passed to offspring through the female parent, a major break with traditional English patrilineage. Reversion to matrilineage increased slave women's vulnerability to rape, even though the 1662 law imposed stiff penalties on whites who had sexual intercourse with blacks. Sexual relations between white female servants and black male slaves, which had once been quite common, were now deemed illegal. By contrast, sexual relations between white men and black women were largely ignored by the law. Indeed, should a master get his slave pregnant, the child's birth only added to his wealth in slaves. Laws that centered on women and their bodies illustrate the intersection of gender, sexuality, and reproduction in differentiating between free and enslaved, white and black.

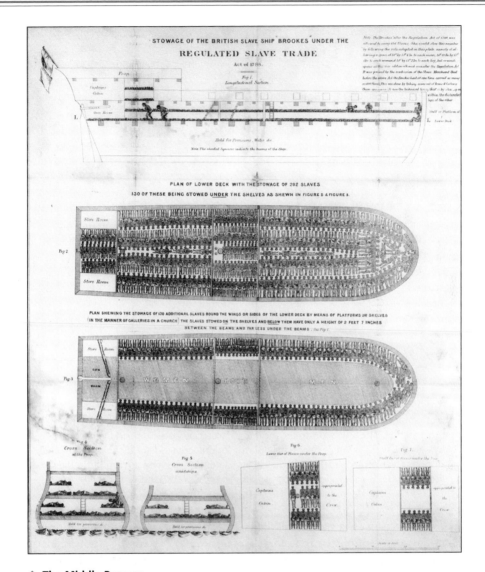

◆ The Middle Passage

In the horrific "middle passage" across the Atlantic, men were packed into the stultifying holds while women, posing less likelihood of mutiny, were held between decks. There they were vulnerable to crew members' sexual attacks. This image, of the British slave ship *Brookes*, which carried more than four hundred slaves, was circulated by antislavery groups first in England and then in America to increase opposition to slavery. *Library of Congress.*

◆ *Virginian Luxuries*

This early nineteenth-century painting by an unknown artist was hidden on the back of another painting. The title is key to the meaning. The term *luxuries* satirically links slave-holders' sexual exploitation of their female slaves with their beating of the male (and female) slaves. Both practices are equated in their violence and their perverse attraction for the slave-holding class. *Abby Aldrich Rockefeller Folk Art Collection, Colonial Williamsburg Foundation.*

Most African slaves were initially sent to the Chesapeake Bay colonies of Maryland and Virginia. In 1650 there were only 300 enslaved Africans in all of Virginia; by 1700 there were 13,000, and by 1750 there were 150,000. The majority of these slaves cultivated and processed tobacco. Tobacco could be raised on small farms as well as on large plantations; thus, slaveholding was widespread in the Chesapeake region. On small farms white and black, master and slave, and male and female worked together to bring in a crop, with African women performing both field work and domestic tasks, including spinning and weaving. On the great plantations, by contrast, all the labor of most slaves, women and men alike, went to cultivating tobacco; only a minority, again men as well as women, worked in domestic and personal service. Women's production in field work was notable. The records of planter Robert Parnafee indicate that the value of his female slaves' tobacco crop was 1,140 pounds, a figure nearly equal to his male slaves' production.

Because of the initially skewed sex ratio, the low fertility rates of African immigrant women, and above all the practice inherited from the West Indies of working slaves to death, Africans living in North America did not have enough children to offset their deaths until the 1720s, the result of better nutrition and declining disease rates. Even so, the hard labor and poor living conditions meant that African women's fertility rates remained lower than those of English women. The gradual creation of family units among North American slaves changed not only the history of the slave institution but also the lives of African Americans. For women, the birth and survival of their children was a powerfully mixed blessing, as surviving children could be and were often sold away from their mothers.

By the early eighteenth century, second- and third-generation slaves were forming a composite African American culture, adapted from multiple African origins but also including both English and Christian elements, in a process known as syncretism. Slaves whose parents and grandparents spoke different languages began to evolve a pidgin language, a mixture of English and African words. While many African religious practices continued, African Americans also incorporated African elements into Christianity as it spread among them in the middle of the eighteenth century. Women seem to have been especially responsible for transferring and adapting medicines, foods, and some religious practices. For example, they led shout-and-response dances and made quilts following African patterns of decoration.

In addition to the development of a syncretic African American culture, communities of free blacks began to develop throughout the South and its border regions as small numbers were freed by their masters or bought their own freedom. By one estimate, in some Virginia counties in the 1660s, free blacks made up as much as one-third of the black population.[8] Overall, a disproportionate number of free black colonial households were headed by women, reflecting African traditions of matrilocality as well as the legal restrictions that made it difficult for marriages with black women to be recognized as legitimate. The intensification and growth of slavery affected free blacks for the worse. They were, in the words of one historian, "an anomaly in a society committed to racial slavery,"[9] and their very presence was taken as incitement to slave rebellion. Denied the rights of free persons, black men could not vote or carry guns. Despite the efforts of the legislature, however, some white servant women continued to bear children by African American fathers. These interracial relationships were the major factor in the increase of the free African American population well into the eighteenth century.[10]

A substantial proportion of the early African population of North America was reimported from the British colonies of the Caribbean. This was particularly true of the Carolinas, which began virtually as a colony of the wealthy sugar island of Barbados. One of the earliest slave women in the Carolinas—we know her only as "Sara"—came in 1678, with no family of her own, accompanying her master for reasons about which we can only speculate. In South Carolina, slave importation was so dramatic after 1700 that Africans formed a majority of the population. "A fruitful woman . . . is very much valued by planters, and a numberous Issue esteemed the greatest Riches in this country," an observer wrote in 1737.[11]

Women were particularly involved in the Carolinas' two major export crops, one of which was the indigo plant, the source of a valuable blue-black textile dye. The other, rice, was South Carolina's most important and valuable product, in large part because African women had useful knowledge about its cultivation (see Figure 2.4, p. 108). They used African techniques for processing the rice, but with a critical difference. Women in Africa had spent a small part of their day pounding rice for their families; African women in America spent whole long days shelling rice for distant markets.

After two centuries of English colonization, tobacco, indigo, and rice plantations which were sustained by slave labor had created a distinctive economy and culture in the Chesapeake and Carolinas. Slaves could be found elsewhere in North America, too—an active African slave trade helped define port cities such as New York, Boston, and Newport, for example—but outside the southern British colonies, slavery did not constitute the primary source of labor or wealth.

NORTHERN BRITISH COLONIES

Despite their common English origins, the colonies of New England differed dramatically from the Chesapeake and Carolina settlements. Although climate and geography accounted for some of the differences—the land there did not offer possibilities for commercially oriented agriculture—at the center of the distinctive quality of New England was religion.

The people who founded the colonies of Plymouth (1620), Massachusetts Bay (1630), Connecticut (1635), and New Hampshire (1638) were Puritans, dissenters from the established Church of England. Puritans believed that the Anglican church, despite the English Reformation, retained too many vestiges of Catholicism. They wanted a more thorough reform of Christian worship and particularly objected to the hierarchical structures of Anglicanism. This notion of decentralizing religious collectivity was linked to a belief in the family as the "little commonwealth," the seed of orderly and virtuous community. Puritans, as the name suggests, were particularly intent on reversing what they saw as the moral degeneracy around them in England.

Puritanism acknowledged women's spiritual equality with men. Nonetheless, both the little commonwealth of the family and the greater one of the community were male-headed and women's role in Puritan society was definitely subordinate. The contradiction between Puritanism's religious radicalism and its social conservatism helps to account for some of the contradictions in women's experience in the northern colonies. While the majority accepted and lived the Puritan "goodwife" ideal, a minority followed the word of God into unconventional behaviors or were accused—as witches—of female responsibility gone horribly awry.

Subject to religious persecution and inspired by the idea of creating a harmonious Christian commonwealth in the New World— what Puritan leader John Winthrop described as "a city on a hill" that would be a model for all peoples—

nearly fifty thousand Puritans arrived in North America between 1620 and 1640. Dedicating themselves to a righteous and disciplined life based on a covenant with God, they established a society in which church and state intertwined, giving the religious and moral values of Puritanism the force of law. Whereas in the South commercial agriculture and slavery were the defining factors shaping women's lives, in New England religion served as the major force constructing gender roles and framing women's experiences. In a different way, the Quaker religion shaped the lives of women in the settlement of the Pennsylvania colony.

The Puritan Search for Order: The Family and the Law

In contrast to virtually all other groups of Europeans who settled on the North American continent, the Puritans did not send men alone: nearly three-quarters of Puritan migrants to New England came in family groups that included wives and daughters. Puritan notions of marriage combined mutuality and hierarchy. Husband and wife had reciprocal responsibilities, were enjoined to recognize their mutual dependence, and were charged with creating social order and community virtue together through their domestic conduct. As one historian puts it, they were "study mates and fellow travelers on the road to salvation."[12] At the same time, male headship characterized their families and wives were clearly secondary to their husbands. Indeed, female deference to male authority was the Puritans' model for humanity's relation to God.

New England women married early and had an astonishingly high childbirth rate, considerably more than women in England or the Chesapeake colonies. First-generation Plymouth women bore an average of 7.8 children, the majority of whom lived to adulthood. Within Puritan ideology, the family stood as a lynch-pin of social order, a value that was magnified by the frontier conditions of the New World. Although Puritans encouraged love and respect within the family, each person's role was clearly delineated by gender and age. So crucial was the family unit to social order that single adults were required to live with a family to ensure their righteous behavior.

Religion also shaped New England laws governing marriage and women's status. The Massachusetts colonies followed the English principle of *feme covert*. However, Puritans, in keeping with Protestant Reformation theology, viewed marriage as a civil contract rather than as a religious sacrament; thus they permitted divorce, offering women more legal options than they had in England. Nonetheless, remarriage was rarely allowed and women were still legally subordinate. A woman might be released from marriage to a husband who abandoned his family completely, but while married, she had to obey her husband's decisions, even if those decisions included abusive behavior.

The Puritan moral code, at least in the early years of settlement, punished both men and women—though not equally—for sexual crimes such as intercourse outside of marriage. As long as the couple married, premarital pregnancy was not harshly condemned. In the absence of marriage, however, a woman giving birth outside of marriage was pressured to name the father so that she and

◆ **Sarah Bradstreet's "Adam and Eve" Sampler**
The first American examples of needlework samplers were simple ones that contained rows
of letters and numbers and were made by young girls as part of their training in housewifery. By the end of the seventeenth century in New England, however, a distinctive female
art form—needlepoint "fancy" work—became widespread among more prosperous women
and was often taught in schools for girls that emphasized such skills as drawing and embroidery. In eighteenth-century Boston a school of needlepoint emerged that featured a popular
religious topic, Adam and Eve in the Garden of Eden. This example, created by Sarah
Bradstreet in 1754, indicates the way in which young women began to move beyond plain
needlework to needlepoint by including artwork in their designs and using fine embroidery
yarn. *Courtesy of Historic Deerfield, Inc. Photograph by Amanda Merullo.*

the child would not become burdens on the community but would be supported by the baby's father. Further, according to Puritan law, a liaison between a married man and an unmarried woman was a less serious offense than that between a married woman and an unmarried man. The former crime was deemed "fornication," while the latter was given the much more serious label of "adultery," As Puritan William Gouge put it, a woman's crime created "greater infamy before men, worse disturbance of the family, more mistaking of legitimate, or illegitimate children."[13] Similarly, the rape of a married woman was regarded, in the words of one historian, as "not the offense against the woman but the offense against her husband."[14]

[handwritten: fornication vs adultry]

Women's subordination to men was evident throughout Puritan society. Although the New England colonies mandated that all children be taught to read so that they could study the Scriptures (and women did have a high literacy rate), few girls attended school. Not surprisingly, few women wrote diaries or books. (See Documents, "By and About Colonial Women," pp. 88–102.) Of the 911 books produced in seventeenth-century New England, only 4 were by women. Of these, the most famous was Anne Bradstreet's *Several Poems Compiled with Great Variety of Wit and Learning* (1678). Bradstreet's brother, the pastor Thomas Parker, wrote to Bradstreet, "Your printing of a Book, beyond the custom of your sex, doth rankly smell."[15] Perhaps in response, Bradstreet wryly noted in one of her poems:

> I am obnoxious to each carping tongue,
> Who says my hand a needle better fits;
> A Poets pen all scorn I should thus wrong,
> for such despite they cast on female wits.[16]

[handwritten: ♡ anne Bradstreet]

Mary Rowlandson's *A True History of the Captivity and Restoration of Mrs. Mary Rowlandson* (1677) was also one of the most important books authored by a North America woman. Rowlandson, who had emigrated from England in 1639, wrote powerfully about her captivity and enslavement during the brutal colonist/Indian conflict known as King Philip's War. (King Philip was the colonists' name for the Wampanoag leader Metacom.) During this conflict, which coincided with Bacon's rebellion in Virginia and reflected the Indians' growing desperation at the hands of whites, one thousand white colonists and three thousand Nipmucs, Wampanoags, and Narragansetts were killed. Half the towns of Massachusetts were attacked, including Lancaster, where Rowlandson and her minister husband lived. Rowlandson's tale of her captivity includes her interactions with her mistress, Weetamoo, Metacom's sister-in-law, and a powerful woman in her own right. Among other things, Rowlandson survived by sewing shirts and stockings for her Indian captors, who appreciated her skill with a needle. Eventually she was ransomed by Massachusetts authorities. When the conflict ended, both Metacom and Weetamoo were killed, and their families sold into slavery in the West Indies. King Philip's war was a watershed in the history of New England. In the aftermath of the war, Native American survivors looked for safety by adopting English customs while others joined distant relatives in Canada or west of the Hudson River.

Trial of Anne Hutchinson

This excerpt from the published transcript of the 1637 trial of Anne Hutchinson (1591–1643) before a panel of Massachusetts Bay Colony judges headed up by Governor John Winthrop can only begin to suggest the theological intricacies of the interrogation. Hutchinson's religious crimes were several. Not only did she act in the male role of a religious teacher, but she compounded this crime by ministering to men as well as women. She was further accused of preaching various doctrines contrary to Puritan teaching. Not reflected in this excerpt is an intricate debate between Hutchinson and Winthrop about whether she diverged from the Protestant belief in salvation by God's grace to advocate the Catholic doctrine of salvation by "work," that is, human effort. As this excerpt indicates, Winthrop finally concluded that her central error, and one that could not be tolerated, was that she believed that God spoke directly to her and not through the intermediary of properly appointed (and male) ministers.

GOV.: Why do you keep such a meeting at your house as you do every week upon a set day? . . .

MRS. H.: I conceive there lyes a clear rule in Titus [Titus 11:3–5], that the elder women should instruct the young and then I must have a time wherein I must do it. . . . If any come to my house to be instructed in the ways of God what rule have I to put them away?

GOV.: But suppose that a hundred men come unto you to be instructed will you forbear to instruct them? . . .

MRS. H.: No, Sir, for my ground is they are men. . . .

Part of what made Rowlandson's narrative so successful was a horrified fascination with the details of a white woman's sojourn among people the colonists viewed as savages. Rowlandson's survival and rescue were also seen as a sign of God's blessing on the Puritan community, and she herself expressed the meaning of her ordeal in the context of faith: "The Lord hath shewn me the vanity of these outward things . . . that they are but a shadow, a blast, a bubble, and things of no continuance. That we must rely upon God himself, and our whole dependence must be upon him."[17]

While Puritan leaders valued Rowlandson for her pious example, they drew clear rules to discipline women who presumed to offer their own doctrinal interpretations. Even though Puritan women shared with men the right to be members of the church once they satisfactorily testified to their salvation, the clergy and other male community leaders periodically punished or banished heretical women who challenged male authority.

GOV.: You must shew your rule to receive them.

MRS. H.: I have done it.

GOV.: I deny it because I have brought more arguments than you have.

MRS. H.: I say, to me it is a rule. . . .

GOV.: . . . We must therefore . . . restrain you from maintaining this course. . . . We are your judges, and not you ours and we must compel you to it. . . .

MRS. H.: It is one thing for me to come before a public magistracy and there to speak what they would have me to speak and another when a man comes to me in a way of friendship privately there is a difference in that. . . . If you condemn me for speaking what in my conscience I know to be truth I must commit myself to the Lord.

MR. NOWEL (ASSISTANT TO THE COURT): How do you know that that was the spirit?

MRS. H.: How did Abraham know that it was God that bid him offer his son . . . ? . . . So me by an immediate revelation. . . .

DEP. GOV.: How! An immediate revelation. . . .

MRS. H.: By the voice of his own spirit to my soul. . . .

GOV.: The ground work of her revelations is the immediate revelation of the spirit and not by the ministry of the word, and this is the means by which she has very much abused the country that they shall look for revelations and are not bound to the ministry of the Word but God will teach them by immediate revelations and this hath been the ground of all these tumult and troubles. . . . [T]he sentence of the court you hear is that you are banished from out of our jurisdiction as being a woman not fit for our society. . . .

Disorderly Women

In the 1630s, Massachusetts leaders faced a major controversy regarding both religious orthodoxy and gender assumptions: the case of Anne Hutchinson. Hutchinson, a midwife, arrived in the colony with her merchant husband in 1634 and began her religious proselytizing among women only. She believed that people were "saved" by a direct and sudden infusion of God's spirit and contended that the Puritan ministers were preaching that salvation came from earthly obedience to Puritan laws. Her provocation went even deeper than her theological notions; she also contested the status of women in the Puritan religious world, if only by her assertion of religious authority. Hutchinson began holding informal religious meetings in her home that included both men and women. Although male leaders worried that her radical religious views were heretical and posed a threat to the colony, the formal accusation brought against her dealt with her behavior as a woman: the charge was that she had "rather been a Husband than a Wife and a preacher than a Hearer; and a Magistrate than a Subject."[18] Trial records indicate

unwomenlike / Behavior

that Hutchinson ably defended both her religious ideas and her right as a woman to expound upon them. However, after days of unrelenting interrogation, she made the mistake of openly claiming to have received direct revelation from God. The Puritan magistrates used this statement as evidence that she was "delusional." Excommunicated and banished, she moved first to Rhode Island, established in 1636 as a haven for the growing number of refugees from Massachusetts orthodoxy, before finally settling in New York (see box, "Trial of Anne Hutchinson").

The Hutchinson controversy represented not just a theological position that attracted men and women but also an undercurrent of female rebelliousness that community leaders felt compelled to repress. In the aftermath of Hutchinson's trial, churches began to drop the requirement that women make their conversion statements publicly. Instead they could relay their experience to their ministers who, in turn, would convey their words to the congregation. Moreover, one historian has found that during this crisis the percentage of female defendants brought before the courts rose significantly. Either women were becoming more assertive or the magistrates were becoming more determined to discipline them.

The most dramatic kind of disorderly act associated with women was witchcraft. Of the 344 people accused of being witches in the colonial period, 80 percent were female; of the men accused, half were relatives of accused women. Two major witch hunts occurred in New England: one during the period 1647–1663, in which seventy-nine people were accused and fifteen hanged, and an even larger episode in 1692, in Salem, Massachusetts, in which over two hundred were accused and nineteen were hanged.

Witchcraft was a complex crime. Sometimes women associated with heresy were charged with being Satan's servants. Many of Anne Hutchinson's critics, for example, hinted that she was a witch. For others, it was less their religious positions than their *maleficia*, or malicious actions against their neighbors, that brought such women to trial. Did milk sour, an animal die, a child take sick? Did a midwife assist at—or perhaps cause—a deformed birth? Did young girls have fits and see an unpopular village woman in spirit form? Did men believe themselves sexually ravaged by a neighbor woman with supernatural powers?

The finger often pointed at an older, poor, and powerless woman. She might have a reputation for being argumentative, discontented, or prideful. She might also be suspected of causing abortion, committing infanticide, or, if she were a midwife, using her healing power for ill instead of good. Another major category of witches—more evident in the Salem cases—were those with some measure of authority or prestige. For example, a widow engaged in a dispute with her husband's heirs over property rights was a likely candidate for suspicion. Indeed, as the frenzy escalated in Salem, some elite men and women were accused by young women who claimed the witches had "possessed" them. The young women's accusations gave them an unprecedented opportunity to influence community affairs and to exercise a degree of power, thus complicating the gendered dimensions of the incidents. Indeed, the clergy and the magistrates quickly lost control of the situation and ceased to support the prosecutions. Eventually, the governor of Massachusetts interceded and brought the trials to a halt in 1692.

What accounts for these tumultuous outbursts of witchcraft accusations? Most historians believe that societal tensions laid the groundwork. Many Salem residents were refugees from violent Indian wars on the southern Maine frontier. Their prominence in the Salem cases suggests a link between the community's susceptibility to believing in the malevolent power of witches among them (and those witches' ability, for example, to aid the "heathen" Indians in massacring the Christian colonists) and the insecurities of living near the frontier at a time of heightened Indian resistance to colonial encroachment. In addition, by the 1690s the stability of New England's Puritan order was being eroded by the growth of trade, an influx of immigrants, and the inroads of secularism and materialism. These tensions were compounded by a rise in population that put pressure on available land, which in turn created intergenerational tensions as young people chafed at the older generation's control of family property. While these anxieties help to explain the dynamics of witchcraft accusations, they do not fully explain why the witch hunts had such a strong gendered component. Whatever the source of the frenzy, the accused women had seemingly violated their prescribed gender roles.

Women's Work and Consumption Patterns

Only a small minority of women were involved in the dramatic events connected to mid- to late-seventeenth-century witch hunts or religious dissent. Most New England women led ordinary, work-filled lives. Wealthier women's labor was less physically demanding than poorer or rural women's, but all women's work was valued for its contribution to the family economy. The division of labor followed English patterns: men's duties concentrated outside the home in farming, fishing, or trade; women's duties centered within the home around food preparation, childbearing, and childrearing. Goodwives, as hardworking married women were called, tended domestic animals and vegetable gardens, and fashioned meals with the few cooking utensils available. They produced their own candles, soap, thread, cloth, and clothing.

Women created networks of female friends and relatives to help with their tasks. Since few women were mistresses of all necessary household trades, they usually bartered among themselves for necessities, especially in more remote areas where women's lives were harder and their time more constrained. Women trained their own daughters in wifely responsibilities and often took in daughters of neighbors to apprentice them in exchange for their household labor. And for another form of distinctly female labor — childbirth — women came together in close communion, often spending days at a prospective mother's home, giving practical assistance and emotional comfort during a time when almost one in ten New England women died during childbirth or of related complications.

Midwives were central figures in the New England world of women; their existence demonstrates that women could and did engage in work beyond their own homes. They generally were highly respected and often tended to other ailments with herbal remedies. Their assistance was rewarded with pa...

◆ Puritan Gravestone Art

New England's early eighteenth-century gravestones silently record the dangers of childbirth in colonial America. One contemporary estimate was that one-third of all full-term babies died before the age of five. Pregnant women also risked death. This gravestone, from New-buryport, Massachusetts, records the 1708 death of Mary Bailey, wife of John, whose death at age twenty-four strongly suggests death during childbirth. The image at the top of the stone is meant to embody the soul of the departed. *Farber Gravestone Collection, American Antiquarian Society.*

kind — chickens, eggs, cloth, sugar, and so on — or with coin from more prosperous citizens. Occasionally other women, too, moved outside the sexual division of labor. If her husband was away hunting, serving in the militia, or trading, a wife could conduct family business or represent her husband in legal matters. Widows, who as *femes sole* could act on their own, ran taverns, inns, or printing establishments. Many took pride in their abilities to manage their estates. Bostonian Ann

Pollard reported that "[by my] own proper gettings by my Labour and Industry [the estate of my husband] is Considerably Advanced and bettered."[19]

As the colonies' commerce increased, mercantile cities such as New York, Philadelphia, Boston, and Charleston grew in size and importance. At the same time, King William's War (1689–1697) and Queen Anne's War (1702–1713), European conflicts that also played out in the American colonial empires, created a dramatic rise in widows, who with their children often moved to urban centers like Boston, where widows represented 16 percent of the population by 1725. Poorer town women, encouraged to work by community leaders eager to keep them off the charity rolls, found employment as seamstresses and in other trades that drew on their wifely skills. Shopkeeping was another avenue for urban women, and historians estimate that between 1740 and 1775, more than ninety Boston women operated commercial enterprises.

In addition to urban/rural distinctions, other divisions were growing in New England. Approximately 3 percent of workingwomen in eighteenth-century New England were African slaves. In the cities, they worked as domestic servants and contributed to the leisure of their white mistresses, usually the wives of merchants, professionals, and craftsmen. For these prosperous women and their daughters, increased free time contributed to changes in their daily lives. Some took up activities like fancy needlework (see p. 72) that demonstrated their genteel feminine skills. Well-to-do women increasingly bought what they needed instead of making it themselves, and imported goods were especially popular. Boston milliner and merchant Elizabeth Murray offered satin gloves, ebony fans, and ermine muffs. Although this kind of opulence was unusual, it pointed to the emergence of a consumer culture in urban areas.

This consumer culture was part of a broad pattern of economic change evident in New England life, especially after 1700. High childbirth rates and immigration from numerous nations meant that the population of the four New England colonies (Massachusetts, Connecticut, Rhode Island, and New Hampshire) doubled every twenty-five years—in 1775 it was 345,000. As urban areas and commerce grew and class distinctions increased, men, increasingly focused on economic success, moved away from religion, leaving women to predominate in most churches; thus began a distinctive association of women with moral and spiritual matters that deepened over time (see pp. 147–51). Puritans' political control slipped as well, as the British Crown revoked the Massachusetts charter in 1684. In a new charter of 1692, the influence of the Puritan church was greatly reduced when property holding, not church membership, became the basis for freeman—and voting—status.

Some scholars argue that the breakdown of the Puritan commonwealth also eroded the power of the patriarchal family, giving women a greater degree of freedom. Certainly new prosperity and urban growth stimulated female education and opened increased economic opportunities for some women. Changes in church membership patterns gave women more voice in the religious sphere of life, but at a time when church influence was declining. Perhaps the most significant change toward the end of the colonial period in New England was the increased diversification in women's lives—the continued hard labor on the farms, the variety of work in the cities, the increased presence of female slaves as servants, and new goods for consumption for prosperous urban women. These patterns pointed to the segmentation of women's communities that would persist throughout the course of American history, in New England and beyond.

Dissenters from Dissenters: Women in Pennsylvania

Although the Puritans had come to North America to be able to practice their own religion free from persecution in England, they did not tolerate dissent in their own midst. Another group of dissenting English Protestants, the Quakers, who did not rely on an institutionalized clergy (and thus allowed for a much greater religious role for women), were banned in Massachusetts. Mary Dyer, a follower of Anne Hutchinson, was hanged in Boston in 1660 when she returned from exile as a Quaker. In 1681, Quaker William Penn received a charter from the British king giving him authority to establish a colony in the lands west of the Delaware River that had once been part of New Netherland. Pennsylvania was thus founded as a haven for the beleaguered Quakers.

Quaker women had no distinctive economic privileges, yet religious values made their society unusually egalitarian. George Fox, the seventeenth-century English founder of the sect, argued that before the "fall" that ousted Adam and Eve from Eden, men and women were "both meett helpes, and they was both to have Dominion over all that God made."[20] Fox's radical emphasis on equality between husband and wife was in keeping with Quaker ideas that criticized hierarchical relations in general. The Quakers believed that "the Inner Light of Christ" was available equally to all. This experience stressed the individual's direct relationship with God and de-emphasized ceremony and sermonizing. Among American Quakers, a number of women, such as Elizabeth Norris of Philadelphia, were noted for articulating the idea that women should not be subordinate to men. In contrast to the Puritan effort to suppress women's religious speech, Quaker women were often respected religious teachers, in part because religious ministry was not ordained or institutionalized among them.

Quaker institutions reflected women's high status. In Pennsylvania, women's local monthly groups sent representatives to quarterly meetings, which in turn sent representatives to the annual convocation in Philadelphia. Created "for the better management of the discipline and other affairs of the church more proper to be inspected by their sex," the meetings monitored family life in the community.[21] In particular, they forwarded petitions that determined whether a betrothed couple embraced appropriate Quaker values. By formalizing the responsibility of some Quaker matrons to monitor the behavior of other women, Quaker practice offered an additional degree of religious authority to women.

Pennsylvania Quakers' relation to African slavery was complex. On the one hand, British Quakers were among the first to develop a full fledged critique of slavery as a violation of God's law. On the other hand, the leadership of the Quaker community in Pennsylvania was made up of wealthy merchants, for whom traffic in slaves was an important element of their trade. As a result, about 20 to 30 percent of Pennsylvania's labor force before 1750 consisted of slaves and at least 10 percent of Philadelphia Quakers were slaveowners. A combination of religious objections and the migration of Germans and other immigrants to work as indentured servants in Pennsylvania's fertile farmlands led to a gradual decline in dependence on African slavery. Sometime after 1760, a slave woman named Margaret, already married to a free black man, secured her freedom; though in her forties, she began to have children, knowing they would be free. Her son James Forten became leader of the strongest free black community in British America.

OTHER EUROPES/OTHER AMERICAS

Despite the growing size and strength of the British colonies, the North American continent continued to be the site of other European nations' expansionist hopes, hopes which sometimes led to conflicts as great as the antagonisms between Europeans and Indians. Although both the Dutch and the British were Protestant nations, they were major commercial rivals, especially in the slave trade. Further, cultural differences went hand in hand with different economic purposes and gender patterns in colonial endeavors. For example, in North America, both the Spanish and the French kept their agricultural and settlement projects to a minimum, concentrating, especially in the French case, on trade. Thus their needs for female labor and family formation were considerably less and their toleration for marriages with Native Americans much greater.

New Netherland

The Dutch sojourn in North America was the briefest, lasting only from 1625 to 1674. The center of New Netherland was the port town of New Amsterdam (later New York City). In 1647, the stern reformer Peter Stuyvesant was brought in to administer the colony until the British took over in 1674.

Women's lives in New Netherland differed from those in the British colonies. Although both societies paid a great deal of attention to orderly families and proper domestic arrangements, Dutch women had more legal rights and economic authority. In contrast to the British concept of *feme covert,* Dutch women could choose a form of marriage in which women were considered their husband's partners and maintained their independent legal identities. Husband and wife viewed their possessions as community property and usually constructed a mutual will, in which each left the estate to the other, postponing the children's inheritance until both died. Married women could and did own property and manage their own businesses.

Margaret Hardenbroeck perfectly exemplified a New Netherland businesswoman. She immigrated to North America in 1659 and established herself as a successful trader who represented other merchants as well. When she married her first husband, she maintained her business and at his death became even wealthier.

◆ **Dutch Farm Family**
Martin Van Bergen of Leeds, New York, celebrated his prosperity by commissioning this painting of his farm in the Hudson River valley. The family's wealth is evident in the fine clothing the farmer and his wife (center) are wearing, the size of their home, and the presence of black slaves among their workers. Many Dutch farmers in the Hudson River valley prospered at the expense of slaves, whom they owned in much greater numbers than did their English neighbors. *Fenimore Art Museum, Cooperstown, New York.*

In her second marriage, the couple drew up a marriage contract that delineated her control over her own property and ensured that she would be able to continue her commercial activities. Husband and wife were highly successful traders and partners in their own shipping enterprise, often acting as each other's agent in business matters and in court.

In part because of the prominent role that the Dutch played in the slave trade, New Amsterdam was home to many enslaved Africans. Substantial numbers of slaves were shipped through the port and, in the 1660s, comprised 20 percent of the city's total population. African men worked on the wharves, and African women were domestic servants to wealthy families. (Stuyvesant himself owned forty slaves.) Concentrated in one city, slaves could develop explosive discontent, and there were at least two slave riots in New Amsterdam in the seventeenth century. In 1991, an excavation of an African burial ground in lower Manhattan unearthed the remains of a twenty-two-year-old woman with a musket ball lodged near her ribs, a likely casualty of one of these upheavals.[22]

New Amsterdam was also the home to some of the first Jews to arrive in North America. Many European Jews, expelled from Spain and Portugal, had migrated to the Netherlands. Some went on to Dutch colonies in the New World, where tolerance was considerably less. Among the first Jews to arrive in North America were twenty-three people, including six women and thirteen children, who had been driven out of another Dutch colony, Recife, Brazil, in 1654. Jews suffered under the haughty anti-Semitism of Peter Stuyvesant but were determined to remain and re-create their community. Miriam Israel Levy, the widow of one of the men in the original group, followed the Dutch practice of serving as executor of her husband's estate.[23] Even after the Dutch lost control of the colony to the British in 1674, Dutch Jews continued to migrate to New York, sometimes intermarrying with British colonists.

When the English conquered New Netherland, they decreed that Dutch inheritance laws could be sustained and Dutch contracts honored. However, as more English people settled in New York, they implemented English common law practices that circumscribed married women's property rights. Dutch women gradually became less visible in the public sphere. In Albany, for example, forty-six women were listed as traders before the British conquest, but by the turn of the eighteenth century, there were none. Women's names also became less prevalent in the rosters of skilled artisans and proprietors—brewers, bakers, and the like—and women were less likely to appear in court representing themselves or others. Margaret Hardenbroeck continued her business ventures, but when she bought land in New Jersey, her husband had to make the purchase for her. In 1710, the New York assembly passed a law that placed married women in the same legal category as minors and people of unsound mind. All these people presumably were not capable of acting on their own. Perhaps the reversal of women's property rights contributed to making New York the birth place of American women's fight for equal economic rights in the nineteenth century.

New France

New France was a large territory, covering almost as much of North America as the lands claimed by the British. Beginning in 1608 with the small settlement of Quebec, traders and missionaries spread south and west through the Great Lakes region and down the Mississippi, ultimately founding the city of New Orleans in 1718. Lightly populated and barely supported by the French Crown, New France was organized as a series of small communities closely linked to Indian villages. Although some farming took place, the major focus was trade, not agricultural settlement. Emigration from France was almost entirely made up of single men until between 1663 and 1673, when almost eight hundred marriageable women, known as *filles du roi* ("the king's daughters"), were shipped to Quebec; the families they formed with French men grew rapidly. Still, by 1700, the population amounted to less than 20 percent of British America's and included a substantial portion descended from the liaisons of French men and Native women.[24] Native wives of French traders along with the French religious women who worked to convert these *métis*, or mixed-race, families to Catholicism were important historical actors in the growth of New France.

The fur traders who moved into the upper Great Lakes and Illinois territories learned quickly that connection to a Native woman was the most important resource a French man could have on the frontier. Ojibwa, Huron, Illini, Missouri, and Osage women had excellent fur-preparation skills, could act as translators, and, most important, connected European traders to the Indian societies that provided them their wares. Native wives gave their European husbands, in the words of one historian, "an entrée into the cultures and communities of their own people. In this way, Indian women were the first important mediators of meaning between the cultures of two worlds."[25]

The practice of what the French called country marriage flourished in the late seventeenth century (see p. 23). Native women retained their relatively easy rights of divorce and the ability to retreat back into their families. At the same time, country marriages gave Native women more direct access to the trading goods and other resources coming into Indian lands from French traders.

By the eighteenth century, however, increasing numbers of these French/Native alliances were undertaken with the blessings of the church. Native women seem to have been more attracted to Catholicism than their menfolk were. Some historians see conversion as providing Native women with external resources as they became major conduits for the expansion of Catholicism into Native lands. Others argue that Catholic conversion, with its encouragement to female submission, destroyed these women's traditional sources of strength and independence. Either interpretation can be sustained by the experience of the Kaskaskia woman Aramapinchue, renamed Marie Rouensa. When her father urged her to marry a dissolute French trader in 1694, she was reluctant; already a convert, she turned to her priest, who supported her, telling her parents that "she alone was mistress" of her own life and decisions. In the end, Aramapinchue agreed to the marriage on the condition that her parents convert to Catholicism. Was this her assertion or her concession to the church's priorities?[26]

French Catholic women were permitted to participate in the work of saving the souls of American Indians. Particularly important in this regard were the Ursulines, a religious order with special commitment to the education of women. Marie de l'Incarnation, a woman with great energy and organizational gifts, came from Rouen, France, in 1639 to establish the first Ursuline community in New France. Although she was successful in establishing a community of Ursuline sisters in Quebec, she did not convert as many young Huron women as she had hoped would spread the faith among the Native population. The second Ursuline convent in North America was more successful in its educational mission. It opened in New Orleans in 1727, charged by French authorities with helping to

◆ Kateri Tekakwitha

Kateri Tekakwitha exemplified the attraction Catholicism held for many Native women. Daughter of an Algonquian mother and Mohawk father, Kateri arrived at a Jesuit mission near Montreal in 1677, already a convert. She developed a following of Native women who physically tortured themselves to demonstrate their faith. After her death in 1680, she became associated with miracles and healing, heightening the veneration she is still accorded today (she was beatified by Pope John Paul II in 1980). *Photo by Anne M. Scheuerman, Pittsford, New York.*

clean up the chronically disorderly and raucous port city. The girls who boarded at the convent school included Europeans, free blacks, enslaved Africans, and Indians. Marie Charlotte, a mulatto, was sent to the sisters by the terms of her dead father's will. An unnamed Osage young woman was also entrusted to the convent by her owner upon his death. Although distinctions of race and hierarchies of class certainly existed in the New Orleans Ursuline community, the sisters succeeded remarkably well in creating, in the words of its historian, "a shared femininity that cut across disparate geographic origins."[27]

New Spain

In 1608, the same year in which the French established Quebec City, the Spanish established Santa Fe in heart of Pueblo territory (see pp. 21–22) as a center for their soldiers, administrators, and merchants. Throughout the seventeenth century, tensions were building both among and between Natives and colonists. Priests and soldier/settlers had very different ideas about how to absorb Indians— as a tributary labor force or as converted Christians. The Pueblos' resentment over their economic and physical exploitation and the failure of the Spanish god to protect them from disease and abuse led to what became known as the Pueblo Revolt. In 1680, only a few years after both King Philip's War in New England and Bacon's Rebellion in Virginia, Pueblo peoples drove the Spanish out of New Mexico. In the aftermath, the revolt's leaders did all they could to rid the Pueblos of Christianity and return to the traditional religions exemplified by the corn mothers who had given birth to the world as they once knew it (see p. 8).

One of the most important areas of Native restoration was with respect to women, marriage, and gender roles. Spanish priests had sought to impose monogamous marriages on the Pueblos, angering Pueblo men and helping to spark the revolt. It is not clear to what extent Native women welcomed back their indigenous spiritual and sexual powers, nor is it known how much they missed the new kinds of protection that Catholicism and the Spanish military presence had offered them. After twelve years, colonial forces retook Santa Fe and killed or enslaved the Native rebels, including four hundred women and children. From this point on, Spanish control over the colony went largely uncontested. Indeed, in order to fend off the spread of French influence down the Mississippi, the Spanish moved east into what is now Texas. In 1718, a second Spanish capital was established in San Antonio, but the new city was in many ways more connected with French lands and populations in Louisiana than it was with Spain.

CONCLUSION: The Diversity of American Women

As diverse as the lives of North American women were in the seventeenth and eighteenth centuries, there were some commonalities. All women operated within a fairly rigid sexual division of labor, although the actual tasks assigned to them varied from culture to culture. Most women's roles included childbearing, childrearing, and food preparation. Within their communities, women tended to form strong bonds with other women in similar circumstances—whether grinding corn in the Pueblo communities, planting it in Iroquoia, bartering in female networks in New England, or forming supportive communities of slave women in the southern British colonies. With some exceptions, women shared an exclusion from direct political participation. They also shared the burdens—which varied widely—of adjusting to the new societies created by both contact and conflict in North America.

Despite these commonalities, the differences among women of this period were striking. Not only were there significant variations among Native American, African, and European women, there were also differences within each group. Native American women encompassed perhaps the richest cultural variety. But Africans as well represented various languages and cultural groups. Among European women, too, distinctions emerged. Between first- and second-generation settlers, there were major differences in quality of life, especially in the southern colonies. Beyond that, ethnic, religious, and regional differences proved powerful determinants of women's legal and economic circumstances. And by the mideighteenth century, class—both in growing cities and in the plantation regions of the South—had become as important as any other factor that shaped women's experiences.

Earlier generations of historians tended to see the colonial period as a monolithic one in which women's lives were static. Reading back from nineteenth-century middle-class gender roles, which relegated women firmly to the private world of the home, historians viewed the white colonial women's participation in a preindustrial household economy as empowering. A similar tendency to romanticize the hard life of Native American women contrasted their freedom and influence with the patriarchal structure within which European women lived. Although comparisons are perhaps inevitable, they can obscure the complexities of women's lives—both the diversity that characterized them and the points of common ground they shared. Such comparisons also deflect attention from the historical changes that shaped these women's lives: the conquest of Native Americans, the importation and enslavement of Africans, the massive migration of Europeans, and the economic and political maturation of the British colonies.

DOCUMENTS

By and About Colonial Women

LITTLE MATERIAL WRITTEN BY AMERICAN WOMEN in the seventeenth century is available to historians. Even in New England, where literacy was prized and most women were taught to read, relatively few women could write, as historians who have examined the signatures on deeds and other legal documents have discovered. In seventeenth-century New England, women produced only two of the fifty-seven surviving diaries from that period. More records exist from the mid-eighteenth century, when education opportunities for women expanded slightly. But for most of the period from 1600 to 1750, men wrote much of the material we rely on to learn about women's experiences. Even our knowledge of a famous and educated woman such as Anne Hutchinson comes from accounts written by men, such as ministers like John Cotton and John Winthrop.

MANUALS OF ADVICE

ONE CATEGORY OF MATERIAL written by men that gives us some insight into colonial women's lives is *prescriptive* literature—that is, works in which the authors prescribe, as opposed to describe, women's proper roles and actions. While these prescriptive writings do not tell us about how real women acted, they do reveal the expectations that society held for women and often suggest that male leaders were worried about women staying in their proper place. Puritan ministers paid special attention to the subject: between 1668 and 1735, clerics such as Cotton Mather produced approximately seventy-five printed sermons and tracts about women. The numerous published guides to housewifery were another major source of prescriptive notions.

In the seventeenth century, most of the reading material available to the colonists came from England and serves as a reminder that these first settlers were English in culture and values. One particularly popular guide was Gervase Markham's *Countrey Contentments* (1615), which was divided into two books, the first for men on such topics as hunting and the second, titled "The English Huswife," for women. Some of the advice for women focused on health remedies, such as advice for "obstructions of the liver" or for how "to increase a womans milk." "The Table," the major section of the book, provided recipes for "simple sallads" and an "excellent way to boil chickens." English colonists adapted old country recipes to new country foods, but they also learned from Native Americans how to prepare corn, which became a staple menu item north and south.

In addition to practical advice, Markham begins his treatise with a statement prescribing the ideal English housewife. As you read this prescription, look for the qualities of a good housewife that Markham thinks important.

GERVASE MARKHAM
Countrey Contentments (1615)

Having already in a summary of briefness passed through those outward parts of husbandry, which belong unto the perfect Husband-man, who is the father and master of the family, and whose offices and employments are ever for the most part abroad or removed from the house as in the field or yard: It is now meete that we defend in as orderly a method as we can to the office of our english Housewife, who is the mother and mistress of the family, and has her most general employments within the house; where from the general example of her virtues, and the most approved skilled of her knowledge, those of her family may both learn to serve God, and sustain man in that godly and profitable sort which is required at the hands of every true Christian.

First then to speak of the inward virtues of her mind; she ought, above all things, to be of an upright and sincere religion, and in the same both zealous and constant; giving, by her example, an incitement and spur unto all her family to pursue the same steps, and to utter forth by the instruction of her life those virtuous fruits of good living, which shall be pleasing both to God and his creatures; I do not mean that herein she should utter forth that violence of spirit which many of our (vainly accounted pure) women do, drawing a contempt upon the ordinary Ministry, and thinking nothing lawful but the fantasies of their own inventions, usurping to themselves a power of preaching and interpreting the holy word, to

which only they ought to be but hearers and believers, or at the most but modest persuaders, this is not the office either of good Housewife or good woman. But let our english Housewife be a godly, constant, and religious woman, learning from the worthy Preacher and her Husband those good examples which she shall with all careful diligence see exercised amongst her servants.

Next unto this sanctity and holiness of life, it is meete that our english Housewife be a woman of great modesty and temperance as well inwardly as outwardly; inwardly as in her behavior and carriage towards her Husband, wherein she shall shun all violence of rage, passion and humor, coveting less to direct than to be directed, appearing ever unto him pleasant, amiable, and delightful; and though occasion, mishaps or the misgovernance of his will may induce her to contrary thoughts, yet virtuously to suppress them, and with a mild sufferance rather to call him home from his error, then with the strength of anger to abate the least spark of evil, calling into her mind that evil and uncomely language is deformed though uttered even to servants, but most monstrous and ugly when it appears before the presence of a husband. . . .

To conclude, our english Housewife must be of chaste thought, stout courage, patient, untired, watchful, diligent, witty, pleasant, constant in friendship, full of good neighbor-hood, wise in discourse but not frequent therein, sharp and quick of speech, but not bitter or talkative, secret in her affairs, . . . and generally skillful in all the worthy knowledges which do belong to her vocation, of all, or most parts whereof I now intend to speak more largely.

SOURCE: Gervase Markham, *Countrey Contentments* (Amsterdam, 1615; repr., New York: De Capo Press, 1973), 1–4.

POETRY

O NE MAJOR BODY OF WORK written by a woman that historians can draw on is the poetry of Anne Dudley Bradstreet (1612–1672). Bradstreet came to Massachusetts in 1630 and eventually settled in Ipswich and later Andover. Well educated, she was an elite woman whose husband served as governor of the colony. Her first volume of verse, *The Tenth Muse, Lately Sprung Up in America* (1650), was also the first poetry volume produced by a colonist, and a highly successful one at that. Bradstreet's influential brother-in-law, John Woolbridge, arranged the London publication and explained in the introduction that it was "the work of a woman, honoured and esteemed where she lives, for . . . her exact diligence in her place, and discreet managing of her family occasions, and . . . these poems are but the fruit of some few hours, curtailed from her sleep and other refreshments."[28] This not-so-subtle assertion that Bradstreet's writing did not interfere with her wifely duties was to some extent borne out in the poetry itself. Bradstreet's many poems on daily life and family reveal a pious woman who enjoyed her role as wife and mother. But Bradstreet had a rebellious side as well. The very fact that she wrote and published her work set her outside the realm of women's proper sphere. And the content of much of her poetry criticized men who would limit women's intellectual endeavors.

The following extract of a poem about the late Queen Elizabeth of England (1533–1603) suggests Bradstreet's thoughts on women's capabilities.

ANNE BRADSTREET
In Honour of That High and Mighty Princess Queen Elizabeth of Happy Memory

Now say, have women worth? or have they none?
Or had they some, but with our Queen is't gone?
Nay masculines, you have thus taxed us long,
But she, though dead, will vindicate our wrong.
Let such as say our sex is void of reason
Know 'tis a slander now but once was treason.

But happy England which had such a queen;
Yea happy, happy, had those days still been.
But happiness lies in the higher sphere,
Then wonder not Eliza moves not here.
Full fraught with honour, riches and with days
She set, she set, like Titan in his rays.
No more shall rise or set so glorious sun
Until the heaven's great revolution,
If then new things their old forms shall retain,
Eliza shall rule Albion [Britain] once again.

SOURCE: Sandra M. Gilbert and Susan Gubar, comps., *The Norton Anthology of Literature by Women: The Tradition in English* (New York: Norton, 1985), 63–68.

LETTERS

L ETTERS, THOUGH RELATIVELY RARE, are another source for exploring early colonial women's experiences. The following examples offer insight into very diverse southern women's lives, that of the prosperous Eliza Lucas Pinckney and a desperate indentured servant, Elizabeth Sprig.

Eliza Lucas Pinckney (1722–1793), a South Carolinian woman, left numerous records detailing her life among her colony's elite. Daughter of a wealthy planter and invalid mother, Eliza Lucas ran the large household, supervised her father's estates in his lengthy absences, experimented with new crops, and was instrumental in introducing indigo to the region. She made good use of her father's legal library and not only represented her family in court but neighbors as well. Lucas married a much older man, the recently widowed Charles Pinckney, and became a devoted wife and energetic mother. At her husband's death, she again employed her business skills to run the complex estate of her family. Pinckney's letters and diaries reflect on the privileged life of an elite woman in the mid-eighteenth-century South, with slaves and servants at her disposal. As you read these letters, consider the factors in early South Carolinian life that shaped her opportunities and limits.

In the following passage from a letter to a Miss Bartlett, Pinckney is unusual in her concern for teaching her slaves to read, but typical of wealthy plantation women in how she spends her time.

ELIZA LUCAS PINCKNEY
To Miss Bartlett

In general then I rise at five o'Clock in the morning, read till Seven, then take a walk in the garden or field, see that the Servants are at their respective business, then to breakfast. The first hour after breakfast is spent at my musick, the next is constantly employed in recolecting something I have learned least for want of practise it should be quite lost, such as French and short hand. After that I devote the rest of the time till I dress for dinner to our little Polly and two black girls who I teach to read, and if I have my paps's approbation (my Mams I have got) I intend [them] for school mistres's for the rest of the Negroe children — another scheme you see. But to proceed, the first hour after dinner as the first after breakfast at musick, the rest of the afternoon in Needle work till candle light, and from that time to bed time read or write. 'Tis the fashion here to carry our work abroad with us so that having company, without they are great strangers, is no interruption to that affair; but I have particular matters for particular days, which is an interruption to mine. Mondays my musick Master is here. Tuesdays my friend Mrs. Chardon (about 3 mile distant) and I are constantly engaged to each other, she at our house one Tuesday — I at hers the next and this is one of the happiest days I spend at Woppoe. Thursday the whole day except what the necessary affairs of the family take up is spent in writing, either on the business of the plantations, or letters to my friends. Every other Fryday, if no company, we go a vizeting so that I go abroad once a week and no oftener.

SOURCE: *The Letterbook of Eliza Lucas Pinckney 1739–1762,* ed. Elise Pinckney (Columbia: University of South Carolina Press, 1997), 34, 35, 38.

Other letters of Pinckney show the energetic businesswoman at work. In the following excerpt from a 1740 letter to a friend, she explains her plans for one of her father's plantations, which she clearly considers her property.

Wont you laugh at me if I tell you I am so busey in providing for Posterity I hardly allow my self time to Eat or sleep and can but just snatch a minnet to write to you and a friend or two now. I am making a large plantation of Oaks which I look upon as my own property, whether my father gives me the land or not; and therefore I design many years hence when oaks are more valueable than they are now — which you know they will be when we come to build fleets. I intend, I say, 2 thirds of the produce of my oaks for a charity (I'll let you know my scheme another time) and other 3rd for those that shall have the trouble of putting my design in Execution. I sopose according to custom you will show this to your Uncle and Aunt. 'She is [a] good girls, says Mrs. Pinckney. 'She is never Idle and always means well.' 'Tell the little Visionary,' says your uncle, 'come to town and partake of some of the amusements suitable to her time of life.' Pray tell him I think these so, and what he may not think whims and projects may turn out well by and by. Out of many surely one may hitt.

In stark contrast to the lives of elite southern women like Pinckney were the lives of their servants. Details about the thousands of European women who came to the colonies as indentured servants in the seventeenth century are largely lost to historians because such women left few written records.

The following is a rare document, a letter written by a distressed servant in Maryland to her father. We cannot know what she had done to so displease her parent, but what does her letter indicate about the hardships facing indentured servants in America?

Elizabeth Sprigs

To Mr. John Sprigs White Smith in White Cross Street Near Cripple Gate London

Maryland Sept'r 22'd 1756.

Honred Father
My being for ever banished from your sight, will I hope pardon the Boldness I now take of troubling you with these, my long silence has been purely owing to my undutifullness to you, and well knowing I had offended in the highest Degree, put a tie to my tongue and pen, for fear I should be extinct from your good Graces and add a further Trouble to you, but too well knowing your care and tenderness for me so long as I retain my Duty to you, induced me once again to endeavour if possible, to kindle up that flame again. O Dear Father, belive what I am going to relate the words

of truth and sincerity, and Ballance my former bad Conduct [to] my sufferings here, and then I am sure you'll pitty your Destress[ed] Daughter, What we unfortunat English People suffer here is beyond the probability of you in England to Conceive, let it suffice that I one of the unhappy Number, am toiling almost Day and Night, and very often in the Horses druggery, with only this comfort that you Bitch you do not halfe enough, and then tied up and whipp'd to that Degree that you'd not serve an Annimal, scarce any thing but Indian Corn and Salt to eat and that even begrudged nay many Negroes are better used, almost naked no shoes nor stockings to wear, and the comfort after slaving dureing Masters pleasure, what rest we can get is to rap ourselves up in a Blanket and ly upon the Ground,; this is the deplorable Condition your poor Betty endures, and now I beg you have any Bowels of Compassion left show it by sending me some Relief, C[l]othing is the principal thing wanting, which if you should condiscend to, may easely send them to me by any of the ships bound to Baltimore Town Patapsco River Maryland, and give me leave to conclude in Duty to you and Uncles and Aunts, and Respect to all Friends

    Honred Father

    Your undutifull and Disobedient Child

SOURCE: Nancy Cott, ed., *Root of Bitterness: Documents of the Social History of American Women* (New York: E. P. Dutton, 1972), 89–90. Original Source: Isabel Calder, ed., *Colonial Captivities, Marches, and Journeys* (New York: Macmillan, 1935), 151–52. Reprinted by permission of Mrs. Alfred Howe Terry for the National Society of Colonial Dames of America in the State of Connecticut. Copyright 1935 by The Macmillan Co.

NEWSPAPER ADVERTISEMENTS

ANOTHER SOURCE THAT ALLOWS US to recapture women's voices are newspaper ads appearing in colonial publications. While men predominate among those offering services and goods for sale, as the eighteenth century wore on, women's names appeared with greater frequency.

What do the following ads suggest about the expansion of women's economic roles in urban colonial America?

Philadelphia Gazette, April 15, 1731

Elizabeth Gray, in Wallace's Alley, in Front Street near the sign of the Pewter Platter, in Philadelphia, washes and calendars [for?] any sort of linen cloth which hath received damage by salt water or otherwise and also table linens of damask and diaper, at a very reasonable rate.

Philadelphia Gazette, June 24, 1731

At Mary Gordon's shopkeeper in Front Street, is sold good Bohen Tea at 14 s. per pound by the single pound, and good Jamaican (?) pepper at 18 d.

August, 19, 1731. The widow Read, removed for the upper end of high street to the new printing office near the Market, continue to make and sell her well known ointment for the itch, with which she has cured abundance of people in and about this city for many years past. It is always effectual for that purpose, and never fails to perform the cure speedily. It also kills or drives away all sorts of Lice in once or twice using. It has no offensive smell; but rather a pleasant one; and may be used with the least apprehension of danger, even to a sucking infant, being perfectly innocent and safe. Price 2 s. a gallypot containing an ounce, which is sufficient to remove the most intolerable Itch, and render the skin clear and smooth. She also continues to make and sell her excellent family salve and ointment, for burns or scalds, (Price 15 an ounce) and several other sorts of ointments and salves as usual. At the same place may be had Lockyer's Pills at 3 d. a pill.

South Carolina Gazette, Charleston, October 22, 1744

This is to give Notice, to all Persons inclinable to put their Children to board, under the Care of the Subscriber [illegible], that she has noow Vacancies; where there is taught, as usual, Writing, and all sorts of fine Needle work. Masters likewise attend to teach Writing, Arithmetick, Dancing, and Musick, if required. Mary Hext.

ADVERTISEMENTS CONCERNING SERVANTS AND SLAVES called for the return of runaways or offered slaves for sale or slaves or servants for hire. What clues do the following ads give about slave women's experiences?

Virginia Gazette, Williamsburg, April 28 to May 5, 1738

RAN away on the 22d of February last, from Col. Richard Randolph's Quarter, in Amelia County, Four Negroes, viz. Sancho, a tall lusty fellow, about 25 Years of Age, cloathed with a Manx Cloth Wastecoat, white Plains Breeches, died Yellow, Plad Hose, and Hobb-nailed Shoes. Warwick, a middle-siz'd Fellow, thin Face, small Eyes, and a sneaking Look, cloathed as the other. Bella, a lusty likely Woman. Phebe, a small Woman, with Marks in her Face, cloathed as the other. Whoever takes up and secures the said Negroes, so that their Owner above mention'd may have them again, shall have Five Pistoles Reward, besides what the Law allows.

SOURCE: Thomas Costa, University of Virginia's College at Wise, "Virginia Runaways," http://etext.lib.virginia.edu/subjects/runaways/1730s.html (accessed May 31, 2004).

South Carolina Gazette, Charleston, December 23, 1745

To be hired out a home born Negro girl about thirteen or fourteen years of age who has been for some years past kept employed at her needle and is a handy waiting maid. Enquire at the Printer [illegible].

Boston Gazette, April 28, 1755

A likely Negro woman, about 25 years of age, has had the smallpox, and been in the country ten or twelve years, understands all household work, and will do either for town or country.

Boston Gazette, July 11, 1757

To be sold a strong, hearty Negro girl; and her son about a week old.

Boston Gazette, June 20, 1735

A white Servant Maids Time to be disposed of for about four years and a half; she is a Scotch woman that can do all sorts of Household Business and Knit, and thoroughly honest. Enquire of The Publisher.

LEGAL PROCEEDINGS

ALTHOUGH IN ENGLISH AND BRITISH COLONIAL LAW, married women as *femes covert* had no legal identity, women appear frequently in legal documents. Unmarried women and widows could act for themselves, and even some married women successfully petitioned the courts for *feme sole* rights in order to conduct a business — usually in the absence of their husbands. They sued and were sued, sold and bought property. Women appeared as beneficiaries or as servants and slaves in men's wills. Women were also brought to court as defendants, on trial for sexual offenses, slander, theft, infanticide, and witchcraft. With one exception, the will of Elizabeth Howland, the documents offered here are from courts in the Chesapeake region, but they have many similarities to those from other British colonies.

SLANDER AND THE COURTS

Slander cases were common throughout the colonies, revealing the way in which individuals in small communities placed great store on their reputations; when their neighbors engaged in gossip accusing them of inappropriate behavior, many victims turned to the court for satisfaction. In analyzing defamation cases from seventeenth-century Maryland, historian Mary Beth Norton has discovered that while women participated in only 19 percent of the colonies' civil cases, they appeared in over 50 percent of the slander cases.[29] Cases that men brought against their defamers tended to concern questions of business and honesty, while those by women focused on sexual irregularities, although witchcraft was another common accusation. While some women came to court to protect their reputations, others were summoned for having spread rumors. The repetition of names in the following cases testifies to how closely connected the settlers in Maryland were in the seventeenth century, but also suggests that some people had an affinity for both gossip and the courts.

What does women's gossiping indicate about their role in the community? What do the court cases suggest about privacy in colonial towns?

Michael Baisey's Wife (1654)

Richard Manship Sworne Saith that the wife of Peter Godson related . . . that Michael Baiseys wifes Eldest Son was not the Son of Anthony Rawlins her former husband, but She knew one at Maryland that was the father of him, but Named not the man, and that the Said Michael Baisey's wife was a whore and a Strumpett up and Down the Countrey, and Said that Thomas Ward of Kent tould her Soe.

Elizabeth Manship Sworne Saith the Same.

Margaret Herring Sworne Saith that the wife of Peter Godson affirmed that Anthony Rawlins Son was not his Son but the Son of another man at Maryland. . . .

Whereas Peter Godsons wife hath Slandered the wife of Michael Baisey & Saying She was a whore & a Strumpet up and Down the Countrey, It is ordered that the Said Godson's wife Shall be Committed into the Sheriffs hand untill She Shall find Security for the behaviour which the plft [plaintiff] is Satisfied with as he hath declared in Court. . . .

Whereas Mrs Godson was bound in a bond of Good behaviour from the 21st of October till the 5th of December towards the wife of Michael Baisey, and none appearing to renew the Said Bond, It is ordered that she be remitted from her Bond of Good behaviour.

Richard Manship's Wife (1654)

Bartho: Herringe aged forty yeares or thereabouts Sworne Saith, That Peter Godson and Richard Manship meeting in Yor Pettrs plantation, Richard Manship asked the Said Peter Godson

whether he would prove his wife a Witch, Peter Godson replyed take notice what I Say, I came to your house where your wife layd two Straws and the woman in a Jesting way Said they Say I am a witch, if I am a witch they Say I have not power to Skip over these two Strawes and bid the Said Peter Godson to Skip over them and about a day after the Said Godson Said he was Lame, and, thereupon would Maintaine his wife to be a witch

Bartho: Herringe . . .

John Killy aged twenty five yeares or thereabouts Sworne Sayth. That at the house of Phillip Hide, Richard Manship Said to Peter Godson you Said you would prove my wife a Witch, Peter Godson answered Gentlemen take Notice what I Say I will prove her a witch beare Witmess you that Stand by.

John Killey

—————————

SOURCE: *Archives of Maryland Judicial and Testamentary Business of the Provincial Court, 1649/50–1675*, ed. William Hand Browne (Baltimore, 1887), 10:399, 10:402, 10:403, 10:409.

Margarett Herringe aged twenty three or thereabouts Sworne Saith, That Rich: Manship asked Peter Godson if he would prove his wife a witch, and Peter desired them that were present to take Notice what he Said your wife tooke four Strawes and Said in the Name of Jesus Come over these Strawes, and upon this your wife is a witch and I will prove her one.

Whereas Peter Godson and his wife had defamed Richard Manship's wife in Saying She was a witch and Uttered other Slanderous Speeches agst her, which was Composed and Determined by the plft and defendant before mr Richard Preston, Soe as Peter Godson Should pay Charges of Warrants and Subpoenas in these Actions which Richard Manship desired may be Manifested in Court that the Said Peter Godson & his wife have acknowledged themselves Sorry for their Speeches & pay Charges.

WOMEN "JURORS"

Other court cases reveal the ways in which women could expand their limited public power. When women were accused of witchcraft, the court might ask a group of women, which usually included a midwife, to examine the defendant's body for telltale signs of witchcraft. They might also be called to duty in cases in which it was crucial to determine whether a woman had given birth.

In the following complex murder accusation, the court officially termed the group of women a "jury." What does the case suggest about women's access to authority in their communities?

Judith Catchpole (1656)

At a Generall Provinciall Court Held at

Putuxent September 22th

Present Capt William ffuller, m[r] John Pott Present

    m[r] Richard Preston: m[r] Michael Brooke

    m[r] Edward Lloyd

Whereas Judith Catchpole being brought before the Court upon Suspicion of Murdering a Child which She is accused to have brought forth, and denying the fact or that She ever had Child the Court hath ordered that a jury of able women be Impannelled and to give in their Verdict to the best of their judgment whether She the Said Judith hath ever had a Child

Or not . . .

The Names of the Jury of women Impannelled to Search the body of Judith Catchpole . . .

Rose Smith	mrs Cannady
mrs Belcher	mrs Bussey
mrs Chaplin	mrs Brooke
mrs Brooke	Elizabeth Claxton
mrs. Battin	Elizabeth Potter
	Dorothy Day

We the Jury of Women before named having according to our Charge and oath Searched the body of Judith Catchpole doe give in our Verdict that according to our best judgment that the Said Judith Catchpole hath not had any Child within the time Charged.

SOURCE: *Archives of Maryland Judicial and Testamentary Business of the Provincial Court, 1649/50–1675*, ed. William Hand Browne (Baltimore, 1887), 10:456–58.

Whereas Judith Catchpole Servant to William Dorrington of this Province of Maryland Was apprehended and brought before this Court upon Suspicion of Murthering a Child in her Voyage at Sea bound for this Province in the Ship Mary and ffrancis who Set forth of England upon her intended Voyage in or about october Last 1655 and arrived in this Province in or about January following, and her accuser being deceased and no murther appearing upon her Examination denying the fact; was Ordered that her body Should be Searcht by a Jury of able women, which being done the Said Jury returning their Verdict to this Court that they found that the Said Judith had not had any Child within the time Chargd And also it appearing to this Court by Severall Testimonies that the party accusing was not in Sound Mind, whereby it is Conceived the Said Judith Catchpole is not Inditable, The Court doth therefore order that upon the reasons aforesaid, that She the Said Judith Catchpole be acquitted of that Charge unless further Evidence appeare.

WIVES AND WIDOWS: PROPERTY SETTLEMENTS AND WILLS

Court records are a vital source of information about property holding. Through wills and property settlement documents, we can determine the range of goods that people owned and make distinctions between rich and poor; we can discover patterns of slave ownership and servant holding; and we can acquire some information about women's economic circumstances.

The following is a prenuptial settlement by Ralph Wormley, a wealthy man, on a widow, Mrs. Agatha Stubbings, whose first husband had been a successful merchant. How does it shed light on the economic advantages widows in early Virginia might have experienced? What clues does the reference to black "servaunts" give us about African Americans' circumstances in early Virginia?

Mrs. Agatha Stubbings (1645)

To All to whom these presents shall come I Ralph Warmley [sic] of the Parrish and County of Yorke in Virginia gentleman send Greeting etc. Knowe Yee, That I the sayde Ralph Wormley For and in consideration of the unfayned love and affection That I beare unto Mrs. Agatha Stubbings late the wife of Luke Stubbings of the County of Northampton gentleman deceased, And especially in Consideration of Matrimony intended presently (by gods grace) to bee solemnized betweene the sayde Ralph and the sayde Agatha doe by these presents give graunt confirme and endow, And by these presents have given graunted and in nature of a Free Joynture endowed unto Nathaniell Littleton Esquire and Phillip Taylor gentlemen . . . in trust For and on the behalfe of the sayde Agatha six Negro servaunts . . . Fower Negro men, and Two women, To say Sanio, and Susan his wife, and greate Tony, and his wife Dorothis, Tony the younger, and Will, Tenn Cowes, six Draught Oxen, two young Mares, two Feather Bedds and Furniture, sixe paire of sheetes of Holland, two Dyaper table cloathes, two dozen of Napkins and Cubboard Cloath to it, two dozen of Napkins, Twelve pewter dishes, one dammaske table cloath, one Dozen of Napkins and cubboard Cloath to it, To have and to hold, the said Recited promisses and every parte thereof, unto her the sayde Agatha, and the heyres [heirs] Lawfully ingendered between mee the said Ralph Wormley and shee the sayde Agatha whether Male or Female or both to bee equally devided after his decease Provided alwayes that the same and every parte thereof graunted as afore-

said shalbe and Remayne to the only use benifitt and behoofe of mee the said Ralph Wormley during my naturall Life, And in case I the said Ralph shall happen to depart this lyfe without issue begotten betweene mee the said Ralph and shee the said Agatha as aforesayde, Then the said demised promisses and every parte thereof with the proceeds and increase thereof shalbe and Remayne to the only use benifitt and behoofe of the sayde Agatha her heyres Executors or Administrators And For the true and reall performance of this deede and every parte and parcel thereof in manner and Forme aforesaid I the said Ralph Wormley doe bynde over unto the said Nathaniell Littleton Esquire and Phillip Taylor gentlemen the said Six Negroes and Six other Negroes, the sayde Tenn Cowes and other tenn Cowes, the sixe Oxen and other sixe Oxen, one plantation and houses whereon I now live scituate at Yorke aforesaid Conteyning Five hundred Acres more or lesse according to the purchase lately made by mee of Jefery Power to bee all Lyable and Responsable For the full Assurance of making good the abovesaid Joynture for the use of the said Agatha her heyres Executors or Administrators as aforesaid In Witnes whereof I the sayde Ralph Wormley have hereunto sett my hand and Scale the second day of this instant July Annoque Domini 1645.

Ralph Wormeley
The Seale

SOURCE: Susie M. Ames, ed., *County Court Records of Accomack-Northampton, Virginia 1640–1645* (Charlottesville: University Press of Virginia, 1973) 433–34.

Like Agatha Stubbings, Elizabeth (Tilley) Howland of Plymouth, Massachusetts, was also a widow. She died in the home of her daughter Lydia in December 1687. The 1672 will of her late husband, John Howland, left plots of land to his three sons, and to Elizabeth, "the use and benifitt of my now Dwelling house in Rockey nooke in the Township of Plymouth aforsaid, with the outhousing lands, . . . During her naturall life to Injoy make use of and Improve for her benifitt and Comfort."[30] He also made Elizabeth the executor of his estate. His six daughters received 20 shillings each. Elizabeth's 1686 will, reproduced here, offers many insights into her life, both spiritual and economic.

What kinds of goods does Howland leave to her descendants? What do they suggest about her class status? Is it significant that the only money she specifies is given to her eldest son? And that the only property she lists goes to the son of her eldest son? She itemizes a number of books in this document, yet she signs with her "mark," not a signature. What does this suggest about her education? Whom does she choose as her executors and why? Finally, why does Howland dedicate so much space to religious concerns in this will?

Elizabeth (Tilley) Howland (1686)

In ye Name of God Amen I Elizabeth Howland of Swanzey in ye County of Bristoll in ye Collony of Plymouth in New Engld being Seventy nine yeares of Age but of good & perfect memory thanks be to Allmighty God & calling to Remembrance ye uncertain Estate of this transitory Life & that all fflesh must Yeild unto Death when it shall please God to call Doe make constitute & ordaine & Declare This my last Will & Testament, in manner & forme following Revoking and Anulling by these prscnts all & every Testamt & Testamts Will & Wills heretofore by me made & declared either by Word or Writing And this to be taken only for my last Will & Testament & none other. And first being penitent & sorry from ye bottom of my heart for all my sinns past most humbly desiring forgivenesse for ye same I give & Committ my soule unto Allmighty God my Savior & redeemer in whome & by ye meritts of Jesus Christ I trust & believe assuredly to be saved & to have full remission & forgivenesse of all my sins & that my Soule wt my Body at the generall Day of Resurrection shall rise againe wt Joy & through ye meritts of Christs Death & passion possesse & inheritt ye Kingdome of heaven prepared for his Elect & Chosen & my Body to be buryed in such place where it shall please my Executrs hereafter named to appoint And now for ye settling my temporall Estate & such goodes Chattells & Debts as it hath pleased God far above my Deserts to be-

stow upon me I Do Dispose order & give ye same in manner & forme following (That is to say) First that after my funerall Expences & Debts paid wc I owe either of right or in Conscience to any manner of person or persons whatsoever in Convenient tyme after my Decease by my Execrs hereafter named I Give & bequeath unto my Eldest Son John Howland ye sum of five pounds to be paid out of my Estate & my Booke called Mr Tindale's Workes & also one pair of sheetes & one pr of pillowbeeres & one pr of Bedblanketts, Item I give unto my son Joseph Howland my Stillyards° & also one pr of sheetes & one pr of pillobeeres Item I give unto my son Jabez Howland my ffetherbed & boulster yt is in his Custody & also onc Rugg & two Blanketts yt belongeth to ye said Bed & also my great Iron pott & potthookes Item I give unto my son Isaack Howland my Booke called Willson on ye Romanes & one pr of sheetes & one paire of pillowbeeres & also my great Brasse Kettle already in his possession Item I give unto my Son in Law Mr James Browne my great Bible Item I give & bequeath unto my Daughter Lidia Browne my best ffeatherbed & Boulster two pillowes & three Blanketts & a green Rugg & my small Cupboard one pr of AndyIrons & my lesser brasse Kettle & my small Bible & my booke of mr Robbinsons Workes called Observations Divine & Morrall & allso my finest pr of Sheetes & my holland pillowbeeres, Item I give unto my Daughter Elisabeth Dickenson one pr of Sheetes & one pr of pillowbeeres & one Chest Item I give unto my

---

SOURCE: The Plymouth Colony Archive at the University of Virginia, http://etext.lib.virginia.edu/users/deetz/Plymouth/howlandwill.html (accessed April 2, 2004).

° Probably a weighing device.

Daughter Hannah Bosworth one pr of sheets & one pr of pillowbeeres, Item I give unto my Grand Daughter Elizabeth Bursley one paire of sheets and one paire of Pillowbeeres Item I give & bequeath unto my Grandson Nathaniel Howland (the son of Joseph Howland) and to the heires of his owne Body lawfully begotten for ever all that my Lott of Land with ye Meadow thereunto adjoyning & belonging lying in the Township of Duxbury neare Jones River bridge, Item I give unto my Grandson James Browne One Iron barr and on Iron Trammell now in his possession, Item I give unto my Grandson Jabez Browne one Chest Item I give unto my Grand Daughter Dorothy Browne my best Chest & my Warming pan Item I give unto my Grand Daughter Desire Cushman four Sheep, Item I give & bequeath my wearing clothes linnen and Woollen and all the rest of my Estate in mony Debts linnen or of what kind or nature or sort soever it may be unto my three Daughters Elisabeth Dickenson, Lidia Browne and Hannah Bosworth to be equally Devided amongst them, Item I make constitute and ordaine my loving Son in Law James Browne and my loving son Jabez Howland Executors of this my last Will and Testament, Item it is my Will & Charge to all my Children that they walke in ye Feare of ye Lord, and in Love and peace towards each other and endeavour the true performance of this my last Will & Testament In Witnesse whereof I the said Elizabeth Howland have hereunto sett my hand & seale this seventeenth Day of December Anno Dm one thousand six hundred Eighty & six.

The mark of Elisabeth **E H** Howland
Signed Sealed & Delivd
in ye prsence of us Wittnesses
Hugh Cole
Samuel Vyall
John Browne

LAWS ON WOMEN AND SLAVERY

Although slave women of this period left behind no written documents, references to them do appear in newspapers and in their owners' letters and diaries (see pp. 91–92). As the prenuptial settlement of Agatha Stubbings suggests, property inventories are another clue that historians use to determine something of slave women's environment. More impersonal, but vital to understanding slaves' experiences, are the laws that, taken together, created the system of perpetual slavery.

In the southern colonies, the laws that created boundaries between slave and free and black and white were added in a piecemeal fashion. One of the first legal distinctions between blacks and whites concerned the labor of women. Instead of taxing land, Virginia taxed planters according to the numbers of the laborers who worked in their tobacco fields.

In this first sentence of a 1643 statute designed to support the colony's ministers, the assembly refers specifically to taxing ("tithing") the labor of "negro women." Although white women worked in the tobacco fields, they are not mentioned here. What does the presence of black women and the absence of white women in this law suggest about the distinctions being made between the two?

Laws of Virginia (1643)

Be it further enacted and confirmed That there be tenn pounds of tob'o. per poll & a bushell of corne per poll paid to the ministers within the severall parishes of the collony for all tithable persons, that is to say, as well for all youths of sixteen years of age as upwards, as also for all negro women at the age of sixteen years.

SOURCE: William Waller Hening, ed., *The Statutes at Large, Being a Collection of All the Laws of Virginia* (Charlottesville: University Press of Virginia, 1969), I:242.

A N EVEN MORE DRAMATIC INDICATION of the hardening of lines between black and white is the short 1662 law that assigned the child of a black woman and a white man to the status of the mother. The statute also assigned penalties for interracial sex. The use of the term "christian" was common, to distinguish English people from Africans, who were considered heathens. What are the implications of this act for the institutionalization of slavery?

Laws of Virginia (1662)

WHEREAS some doubts have arisen whether children got by any Englishman upon a negro woman should be slave or free, Be it therefore enacted and declared by this present grand assembly, that all children borne in this country shalbe held bond or free only according to the condition of the mother. And that if any christian shall commit fornication with a negro man or woman, hee or shee soe offending shall pay double the fines imposed by the former act.

SOURCE: William Waller Hening, ed., *The Statutes at Large, Being a Collection of All the Laws of Virginia* (Charlottesville: University Press of Virginia, 1969), I:242. II:170.

QUESTIONS FOR ANALYSIS

1. What evidence do these documents offer about the diversity of women's experiences in colonial America? What are some of the hardships or challenges that women encountered? In what ways did women of this period seek control over their lives?

2. What do these documents suggest about societal expectations for white elite women's roles? About the roles of servants and slave women?

3. How do legal documents allow us to understand the experiences of women who left no personal writings behind? What insights can descriptions of property give about the social circumstances of colonial women? How do the court cases concerning slander and witchcraft portray women and expectations about their behavior?

VISUAL SOURCES

Material Culture

WOMEN'S LABOR WAS ESSENTIAL to the productivity and maintenance of early American societies. In the seventeenth and eighteenth centuries, virtually all women, regardless of ethnicity, class, region, or age, expected to labor hard and continuously. Further, the different work done by men and women was as much of a factor in defining gender as anything else. By the middle of the eighteenth century, only a tiny class of women—mistresses of southern slaveholding plantations—were characterized not by their work but by their lives of genteel leisure. In Puritan New England, by contrast, idleness aroused suspicion, and even women of considerable wealth prided themselves in their industriousness.

Yet, while almost all women worked in ways specific to their sex, what they did differed quite radically across cultures and regions. One of the themes in early European writing about Native American peoples was astonishment—and often horror—that Indian women seemed to have primary responsibility for systematic agriculture and the care of domestic animals, duties that were primarily male tasks in Europe. Europeans similarly commented on women's work among the African peoples who were brought to the Americas as slaves. But while European missionaries and educators sought to "civilize" Native women out of their agricultural habits, planters and slaveowners compelled African slave women to toil in their fields for the profit of their masters.

One way to understand the varieties of seventeenth- and early eighteenth-century American women's labor is to explore the written sources describing women's work. The approach of this essay, however, is to examine what historians call "material culture": the objects women owned and used and some of which were left to posterity. In museums and historic American homes, colonial women's domestic lives often are represented by costly, highly crafted items such as furniture and silver, which have been preserved as markers of their owners' wealth and genteel taste. Instead, this essay will concentrate on the more mundane aspects of material culture—the tools that women used in their daily routines and that point to their lives as productive rather than ornamental, filled with work rather than leisure.

The most obvious working implement used by European colonial women was the spinning wheel (Figure 2.1). Textile production in England was becoming increasingly industrialized by the late eighteenth century, but in New England it remained located in the home for much longer. Indeed, on the eve of the American Revolution, the family spinning wheel had become the icon of colonial political virtue in contrast to presumed British corruption and indolence. Not until the

◆ Figure 2.1 **Colonial Spinning Wheel**
American Textile History Museum, Lowell, Massachusetts 1993.83.1.

early nineteenth century did American textile production begin to leave the home and move into centralized workplaces (see pp. 197–99).

Textile production involves two basic processes: drawing out and spinning raw fibers into threads, and weaving those threads into fabric. In Europe, spinning had always been women's work, and it remained so in the British American colonies. Spinning was labor-intensive and is thus perhaps the best symbol for the necessity of separating women's and men's labor. Indeed, many terms for parts of the spinning wheel illustrate the female nature of the work—the "maidens" hold the bobbins, the "mother-of-all" holds the maidens, and the "distaff" holds fibers to be spun. By contrast, weaving had traditionally been men's work in England; however, not in New England, where women took over much of this process as well.

What do the size and structure of the wheel shown in Figure 2.1 suggest about colonial New England women's daily domestic labor? Why do you think historical museums feature spinning wheels so prominently? What do spinning wheels represent for American history and women's work?

Textile production was not limited to European women. Indeed, in virtually every indigenous American culture, women made crucial contributions to their communities with intricate mats and baskets woven from naturally growing plants. Unlike the Europeans, who wove cultivated cotton and linen thread into cloth, Native women did not use spindles or looms but instead twisted and wove fibers by hand. The baskets they made became the tools of their labor, as women carried baskets on their backs with daily foodstuffs. When the community packed up and moved, women carried possessions from place to place in the same baskets. Unlike the sturdy spinning wheel, woven products such as Indian baskets and English homespun were fragile and therefore few survive to the present day. Basket weaving continues to thrive among Native artisans, its purposes now including that of serving as souvenirs for tourists.

The tradition of the Rhode Island family that preserved and handed down the rare example of seventeenth century Indian women's basketry shown in Figure 2.2 sets it in the time of King Philip's War. According to family legend, the basket was traded for milk to an English colonist by an Algonquian woman.[31] Note the intricate geometric decoration incorporated into the basket. What does this tell us about role of basketry in native cultures over and above the functional? Why do you think the seventeenth-century colonial woman wanted the basket? Why was the native weaver willing to trade it for milk?

Besides textile production, another common element of women's work was food preparation. By cultivating and milling grain, Native American women provided fundamental nutrition for their communities. As we have seen, maize, or Indian corn, was especially associated by numerous Native American peoples with women's generative powers. Day after day, women performed the tedious and physically difficult tasks associated with corn production. Just as spinning and weaving were processes that women did constantly, so too was the shelling and hulling of corn.

◆ Figure 2.2 **Algonquian Basket (circa 1675)**
Courtesy of the Rhode Island Historical Society; Rhi X3 2660.

After the outer shell of the corn kernel had been removed, the next process was to break open the hull so that the grain at the center of the kernel could be prepared for cooking. In the Southwest, the corn-hulling process involved a slightly curved stone known as a metate, used together with a pounding instrument (see Figure 2.3). Although these corn-grinding stones were individual implements, women often worked in groups. As you try to imagine the innumerable poundings on the smooth surface of this metate stone, think about what the interactions among women might have been as they prepared cornmeal for their families and communities. Why were corn cultivation and processing exclusively female responsibilities?

African slave women also worked at cultivating and processing food. But unlike virtually all other female laborers in North America, they worked alongside

◆ Figure 2.3 **Metate (Grinding Stone)**
Courtesy of the Phoebe Apperson Hearst Museum of Anthropology and the Regents of the University of California, 1-4272, 1-4273.

African men. Even so, there is a distinctly women's view of early slave labor in that southern white slaveowners drew on the tools of African women's traditional work as agriculturists. African women's contributions to the technology of southern rice cultivation were particularly notable. They were skilled, for instance, in planting rice seeds in swampy lands, efficiently using their heels to make holes and then covering up the seeds that they dropped into them.

African women also were responsible for introducing methods for processing harvested rice. They usually did the backbreaking work of hulling and polishing the rice, pounding open the outer shell and then scouring out the inner germ. Their tools were fashioned according to those they remembered from Africa. Using a hollowed-out log and a pine branch, they pounded away in a method that required prolonged movement and tremendous strength. As one historian writes, "Mortar and pestle rice processing was an African technology. . . . Had slaves not introduced these methods in 1699 [and we might add, provided the raw labor power to employ them] colonists might have stepped up their search for workable animal- and water-powered mills."[32]

◆ Figure 2.4 **Hulling Rice in West Africa (*left*) and Georgia (*right*)**
Courtesy of Georgia Archives, Vanishing Georgia Collection, sap093.

Figure 2.4 contains two representations of the particular tools used to hull rice, one before and one after slavery. The engraving is an eighteenth-century depiction of women's work in West Africa. The photograph, dated 1925, is from the Georgia Sea Islands, where the legacy of preslavery African culture remained quite alive. What, if anything, seems to have changed about the methods or the workers who used these tools and performed this labor? How does this method of rice hulling compare to the tools for cornmeal preparation used by Native American women? What difference would it have made to a woman's relationship to her tools and labor that she was working not to feed her family and community, but to add to the profit of her employer?

Another material artifact of colonial woman's labor — the hearth — was built into the house itself. Here the raw foodstuffs were cooked over a constantly tended fire. In large plantation houses, where slave women did the kitchen labor, the kitchen was a building apart from the main house. But in New England and else-

◆ **Figure 2.5 New England Hearth**
Colonial Williamsburg.

where, the kitchen hearth was the center not only of settler women's domestic labor but of home life in general. The largest and sometimes only fireplace in the house, it provided a site for heat and sociability as well as for food preparation. "The central architectural feature of indoor space," writes a historian of women's domestic labor, "the kitchen fireplace dominated women's lives."[33]

The neat and nostalgic modern restoration of a colonial kitchen from the 1730s shown in Figure 2.5 challenges us to imagine the many forms of actual labor women did in and around their kitchen hearths. In most kitchens, for instance, pots were made of iron, which was heavy but inexpensive. The cook actually walked into the fireplace, which was quite deep, to stoke the coals, hang the pots, and remove the meat roasting in the fire. What other aspects of women's labor in and around the hearth is revealed in this picture? This particular colonial kitchen included an important improvement in the technology of the hearth: a swinging iron bar, which replaced a rope or piece of wood for the hanging of heavy pots. How did this ease women's work a bit? Notice also the small separate oven built into the side of the hearth, where women could bake bread with less risk of burning it. In what other ways might women's labor in the hearth have been made somewhat easier?

QUESTIONS FOR ANALYSIS

1. The Indian basket in Figure 2.2 was allegedly traded between a native and a white woman. How do the other tools of women's labor shown here link women of different cultures and communities to each other?

2. Both the spinning wheel (Figure 2.1) and the restored colonial kitchen (Figure 2.5) are staples of museums of early American culture and history. Why do you think that these artifacts of a "simpler" past appeal to museum goers?

3. What other artifacts of material culture might help us learn more about women's labor in this era?

VISUAL SOURCES

Depictions of "Family"
in Colonial America

IN THE VARIED CULTURES OF seventeenth- and eighteenth-century North America "family" meant different things—different groupings of people, different relations of affection, different hierarchies, and different implications for the larger society. One of the only characteristics that all these different meanings of "family" had in common was male dominance. Visual sources can convey relationships of power within the family in ways that written sources cannot.

The period explored in this chapter predates the sentimental ideal of the nuclear family that characterized nineteenth-century middle-class American society (see pp. 188–95). Nonetheless, family relations were, if anything, more crucial to daily life in the seventeenth and eighteenth centuries, because family was a system not only of emotions and kinship but of economics and production. While some of the family bonds illustrated here may seem unusual to modern Americans, they were nonetheless deeply felt and fundamental to the people who lived them.

Although family paintings were a luxury of the wealthy, American painters were struggling artisans more than they were purveyors of high culture. In these earlier years, we do not even know the names of the artists; scholars identify them by the families who patronized them rather than by their own reputations. Traveling from place to place and looking for commissions, American painters, unlike their British counterparts, were usually not formally trained.

One of the earliest family group paintings from colonial British America was the 1674 portrait of Elizabeth Clarke Freake (b. 1641) and child shown in Figure 2.6. By 1674, Freake had already borne six children, and although tradition identifies this baby as a girl, in fact infant boys and girls were dressed exactly alike, so it is difficult to distinguish them. This portrait is part of a series that includes a separate painting of the husband and father, Boston merchant John Freake. Painted as standing and facing toward his left, John Freake's portrait was probably meant to hang alongside that of his wife and child. John Freake died just a year after the painting was complete, and his widow—like so many other New England women—went on to remarry.

Art historians have discovered that this version of Elizabeth Freake and child was painted over an earlier painting done three years earlier. The major difference is that, in the later version, the mother's right arm is around her child, whereas in the earlier version, it was crossed in front of her chest. Why do you think, after three years, the painter was asked to make this change? What aspects of the

◆ Figure 2.6 **Elizabeth Freake and Child**
Worcester Art Museum, Worcester, Massachusetts, Gift of Mr. and Mrs. Albert W. Rice.

painting convey Elizabeth Freake's piety? What details suggest her wealth and social standing? How do these two dimensions come together in the overall portrait of mother and child?

Joint portraits of husband and wife from this period are very rare. Family portraits were meant to illustrate intergenerational family descent, not conjugal affection. Art historians are not sure who painted the example in Figure 2.7, but it is generally attributed to John Watson, a Scots immigrant who arrived in the colonies in 1714. A traveling artist in New Jersey, Pennsylvania, and New York, Watson is one of the first generation of painters working in America whose name is known to us. His style is much more refined than that of the anonymous painter of Elizabeth Freake and child in Figure 2.6.

Figure 2.7 records the alliance through marriage of two of the wealthiest Dutch American families in New York State, the Schuylers and the Wendells. Both

◆ **Figure 2.7 Johannes and Elsie Schuyler**
Collection of The New-York Historical Society, negative #1915.8.

were located in Albany and began to accumulate their wealth in the late seventeenth century through trade with the Mohawks and through extensive agricultural holdings. The husband, Johannes Schuyler, was an Albany merchant and later city mayor. The wife, Elsie Staats Wendell, also a member of a founding Dutch American family, was a decade older than her husband and already quite wealthy from her father and her first husband. A widow, she had given birth to nine children before she married Schuyler. Their first child was born eight months after their marriage and together they had three more. How do the details of this marriage help to explain the Schuylers' decision to commission a joint portrait? Notice that she chose to be pictured with papers and books in her hands; what might she be trying to indicate about her tastes and activities? What other aspects of this portrait signal the Schuylers' social status?

◆ Figure 2.8 **The Potter Family**
The Newport Historical Society (53.3).

We have no paintings of black families, slave or free, from the early eighteenth century. Indeed, African migrants were just beginning to live long enough to establish multigenerational kinship ties. However, some portraits of white families included a black domestic slave or servant among the family grouping.

The group portrait of the Potter Family of southern Rhode Island in Figure 2.8 was painted around 1740 by an unknown artist. The Newport Historical Society identifies the white male head of household as John Potter, a wealthy land- and slaveowner who later became a Quaker and freed his slaves. The Potters lived near Narragansett Bay, on one of several large plantations in the area whose land had been seized from Native people. Included in the picture are three unidentified women, no doubt Potter's wife, their daughter, and probably a collateral relative or friend of his wife. But what draws our modern attention is the young black boy holding a tea tray. Newport, Rhode Island, was the center of New England slave trading, and Potter was both a slave trader and slaveholder. Unlike most of Potter's slaves, who worked in the fields, this young child was likely a full-time domestic servant. How does the picture itself signal this information? Curiously, this slave child and Mr. Potter are portrayed as looking as directly at the viewer, while the three women look slightly away. Why might the painter have chosen to do this?

Why do you think that the Potters made the deliberate decision to include this child in the painting of their family grouping? The painting was permanently installed over the family's mantelpiece. How might it have affected master, mistress, and slave to see themselves together in the portrait day after day? Remember that the slave, in addition to being a worker, was also a marker of wealth: the Potters owned many. What else about the portrait suggests their wealth?

Figures 2.6, 2.7, and 2.8 are portraits of particular families, each with its own intentions, relationships, and personalities. All are products of Protestant New England and New Netherland societies, which revered domestic life and parent/child and husband/wife relations. Spanish America grew out of a very different religious and artistic tradition. Like the artists of Catholic Europe, most of its painters concentrated on religious themes. Undoubtedly the family they painted most frequently was Mary, Joseph, and the baby Jesus.

Castas paintings were a genre unique to New Spain, and represent a distinct pictorial approach to family relationships. *Castas* — in English, "castes" — refers to the intricate system, part racial and part economic, that constituted the social and political hierarchy of New Spain. Among English colonists, racial inequality was enforced by legal prohibitions against interracial marriage and a system in which only two racial identities were available: white and nonwhite. By contrast, in New Spain, interracial marriage within the church was encouraged, as a means to civilize, absorb, and ultimately eliminate nonwhite populations. This racial system, although different from the Protestant English one, was also hierarchical and white-dominated. The goal was to move up the racial scale, toward the apex of whiteness.

The *castas* system was a kind of taxonomy, or system of classification, and the paintings themselves contained indicators of that system. Most *castas* paintings consisted of sixteen different categories, painted on either a single canvas or separate canvases. The paintings depicted highly stylized categories rather than real people, and each family's racial composition was inscribed on the canvas. The artists painted their fantasy family groupings in beautiful colors and wearing exquisite clothes, so as to convey a sense of beauty, opulence, and wealth. Both as idealizations of interracial families and as depictions of New World wealth, the *castas* paintings were a kind of advertisement for the wonders and possibilities of New Spain. But scholars also suggest that the emphasis on hierarchical categorization indicates anxiety about the potential disorder of racial mixing and may have been "intended as reminders to the Spanish Crown that Mexico was still a rigidly structured society."[34]

The actual lives of interracial families, and their experience of racial inequality and hierarchy, bore little relationship to the depictions of the *castas* paintings. *Castas* were usually painted in the urban centers of Mexico City and Lima, but we can be confident that the images they purveyed and the system they represented would have been familiar on the northern borders of Mexico, among the colonists who came to Santa Fe and El Paso, for whom interracial liaisons and difficult living conditions were major factors of life.

The elaborate depiction of interracial combinations and offspring in Figures 2.9, 2.10, and 2.11, dated about 1715 and attributed to Juan Rodríguez Juárez, conveys the abstract and idealized quality of the *castas* genre. The two family combinations in Figures 2.9 and 2.10 are *español/India/mestizo* and *español/"negra"/ mulatto*. *India/mestizo* here means Christianized, urbanized people of mixed

◆ **Figure 2.9**
Mestizo Family
Courtesy of Breamore
House, Hampshire.

◆ **Figure 2.10**
Mulatto Family
Courtesy of Breamore
House, Hampshire.

◆ **Figure 2.11**
Indian Family
Courtesy of Breamore House, Hampshire.

Spanish and Indian descent. Note that in both these paintings, the man is European and white and the woman is not. Significantly, according to the *castas* system, Indian blood, in contrast to black blood, could be redeemed (Christianized and civilized) by admixture with Spanish blood. Figure 2.11 portrays an *India Barbara*, an Indian family unredeemed by any Spanish blood. What are the differences between the three images that suggest the hierarchical *castas* system? Why does each family unit consist only of mother, father, and child, rather than the much more diverse and numerous family units depicted in the Protestant portrait tradition?

QUESTIONS FOR ANALYSIS

1. In what different ways is male headship of family life depicted in these paintings?

2. What do these images tell us about women's roles in family relations?

3. What similarities and differences do you see among the women portrayed in these images?

NOTES

1. Cotton Mather, *A Narrative of Hannah Swarton Containing Wonderful Passages Relating to Her Captivity and Deliverance, in Puritans Among the Indians: Accounts of Captivity and Redemption, 1676–1724,* eds. Alden T. Vaughan and Edward W. Clark (Cambridge, MA: Belknap Press, 1981), 153.

2. *Proceedings of the General Assembly,* vol. 1 (January 1637/8–September 1664), 239. Archives of Maryland Online, http://www.mdarchives.state.md.us/megafile/msa/speccol/sc2900/sc2908/000001/000001/html/am1239.html (accessed August 5, 2004).

3. Paula A. Treckel, *To Comfort the Heart: Women in Seventeenth-Century America* (New York: Twayne, 1996), 37.

4. Carol Berkin and Leslie Horowitz, eds., *Women's Voices, Women's Lives: Documents in Early American History* (Boston: Northeastern University Press, 1998), 16.

5. Kathleen M. Brown, *Good Wives, Nasty Wenches, and Anxious Patriarchs* (Chapel Hill: University of North Carolina Press, 1996), 166.

6. David Eltis, *The Rise of African Slavery in the Americas* (Cambridge: Cambridge University Press, 2000), 196.

7. Peter Kolchin, *American Slavery, 1619–1877* (New York: Hill and Wang, 1993), 51.

8. Philip D. Morgan, *Slave Counterpoint: Black Culture in the Eighteenth-Century Chesapeake and Lowcountry* (Chapel Hill: University of North Carolina Press, 1998), 12.

9. Brown, *Good Wives, Nasty Wenches, and Anxious Patriarchs,* 214.

10. Paul Heinegg and Henry B. Hoff, "Freedom in the Archives: Free African Americans in Colonial America," *Common-Place* 5, no. 1 (October 2004), http://www.common-place.org.

11. Morgan, *Slave Counterpoint,* 100.

12. Laurel Thatcher Ulrich, *Good Wives: Image and Reality in the Lives of Women in Northern New England, 1650–1750* (New York: Oxford University Press, 1993), 115.

13. Treckel, *To Comfort the Heart,* 145.

14. Mary Beth Norton, *Founding Mothers and Fathers: Gendered Power and the Forming of American Society* (New York: Knopf, 1996), 351.

15. Lyle Koehler, *A Search for Power: The "Weaker Sex" in Seventeenth-Century New England* (Urbana: University of Illinois Press, 1980), 31.

16. Treckel, *To Comfort the Heart,* 105.

17. Mary Rowlandson, *The Sovereignty and Goodness of God: with Related Documents,* ed. Neal Salisbury (Boston: Bedford/St. Martin's, 1997), 112.

18. Norton, *Founding Mothers and Fathers,* 281.

19. Vivian Bruce Conger, "'If Widow, Both Housewife and Husband May Be': Widows' Testamentary Freedom in Colonial Massachusetts and Maryland," in Larry D. Eldridge, ed., *Women and Freedom in Early America* (New York: New York University Press, 1997), 249.

20. Karin A. Wulf, *Not All Wives: Women of Colonial Philadelphia* (Ithaca: Cornell University Press, 2000), 58.

21. Treckel, *To Comfort the Heart,* 175.

22. Michael L. Blakey, "The New York African Burial Ground Project: An Examination of Enslaved Lives, A Construction of Ancestral Ties," *Transforming Anthropology* 7, no. 1 (1998), http://www.huarchivesnet.howard.edu/0008huarnet/blakey1.htm (accessed October 19, 2007).

23. Leo Hershkowitz, "Original Inventories of Early New York Jews (1682–1763)," *American Jewish History* 90 (December 2002): 239–322.

24. Alan Taylor, *American Colonies* (New York: Viking, 2001), 368.

25. Clara Sue Kidwell, "Indian Women as Cultural Mediators," *Ethnohistory* 39, no. 2 (Spring 1992): 97.

26. Richard White, *The Middle Ground: Indians, Empires, and Republics in the Great Lakes Region, 1650–1815* (Cambridge: Cambridge University Press, 1991), 72.

27. Emily Clark, *Masterless Mistresses: The New Orleans Ursulines and the Development of a New World Society, 1727–1834* (Chapel Hill: University of North Carolina Press, 2007), 82.

28. Sandra M. Gilbert and Susan Gubar, comps., *The Norton Anthology of Literature by Women: The Tradition in English* (New York: Norton, 1985), 60.

29. Mary Beth Norton, "Gender and Defamation in Seventeenth-Century Maryland," *William and Mary Quarterly,* 3rd ser., 44 (January 1987): 4–5.

30. "The last will and testament of John Howland," Pilgrim Hall Museum, http://www.pilgrimhall.org/willjhowland.htm (accessed June 9, 2004).

31. Laurel Thatcher Ulrich, *The Age of Homespun: Objects and Stories in the Creation of an American Myth* (New York: Knopf, 2001), 41.

32. S. Max Edelson, *Plantation Enterprise in Colonial South Carolina* (Cambridge: Harvard University Press, 2006), 82.

33. Susan Strasser, *Never Done: A History of American Housework* (New York: Owl Books, 2000), 33.

34. Ilona Katzew, "Casta Painting: Identity and Social Stratification in Colonial Mexico," *Labertino* 1, nos. 1–2 (Fall 1997), http://www.gc.maricopa.edu/laberinto/fall1997/casta1997.htm (accessed November 16, 2007).

SUGGESTED REFERENCES

General Works   For a comprehensive overview of North American colonial history that goes beyond British America, see Alan Taylor, *American Colonies: The Settling of North America* (*The Penguin History of the United States,* Vol. 1) (2002); also see Peter Mancall and James H. Merrell, eds., *American Encounters: Natives and Newcomers from European Contact to Indian Removal, 1500–1850* (2007). For a comparative study of women's lives in New England and the Chesapeake colonies, see Mary Beth Norton, *Founding Mothers and Fathers: Gendered Power and the Forming of American Society* (1996). Sharon Block, *Rape and Sexual Power* (2006), creatively examines this understudied topic in all of British America. James Axtell, ed., *The Indian Peoples of Eastern America: A Documentary History of the Sexes* (1980), provides a rich interpretive and documentary collection.

Women in the Southern Colonies   An overview of women of the early South is Cynthia A. Kierner, *Beyond the Household: Women's Place in the Early South, 1700–1835* (1998). An important study that addresses a wide range of women is Kathleen M. Brown, *Good Wives, Nasty Wenches, and Anxious Patriarchs* (1996). Specialized studies that focus primarily on white women include Stephen Innes, ed., *Work and Labor in Early America* (1988); Gloria L. Main, *Tobacco Colony: Life in Early Maryland, 1650–1720* (1982); Mary Beth Norton, "Gender and Defamation in Seventeenth-Century Maryland," *William and Mary Quarterly* 3rd ser., 44 (January 1987); Darrett B. and Anita H. Rutman, *A Place in Time: Middlesex County, Virginia, 1650–1750* (1984); Terri L. Snyder, *Babbling Women: Disorderly Speech and the Law in Early Virginia* (2003); Lorena S. Walsh, "'Till Death Us Do Part': Marriage and Family in Seventeenth-Century Maryland," in Thad W. Tate and David L. Ammerman, eds., *The Chesapeake in the Seventeenth Century: Essays on Anglo-American Society* (1979). Julia Cherry Spruill's *Women's Life and Work in the Southern Colonies* (1938) remains a classic. On African women and slavery, see Philip D. Morgan, *Slave Counterpoint: Black Culture in the Eighteenth-Century Chesapeake and Lowcountry* (1998); Ira Berlin, *Many Thousands Gone: The First Two Centuries of Slavery in North America* (1998); David Barry Gaspar and Darlene Clark Hine, eds., *More Than Chattel: Black Women and Slavery in the Americas* (1996); Darlene Clark Hine, ed., *Black Women in American History: From Colonial Times through the Nineteenth Century* (1990); Allan Kulikoff, "The Beginnings of the Afro-American Family in Maryland," in Aubrey Land, Lois Green Carr, and Edward C. Papenfuse, eds., *Law, Society, and Politics in Early Maryland* (1977); Carole Shammas, "Black Women's Work and the Evolution of Plantation Society in Virginia," *Labor History* 26 (1985): 5–28; Peter H. Wood, *Black Majority: Negroes in Colonial South Carolina: From 1670 through the Stono Rebellion* (1974). On Native American women in the southern colonies, the leading study is Theda Perdue, *Cherokee Women: Gender and Cultural Change, 1700–1835* (1998).

Women in the Northern Colonies   Older works but still valuable starting points for the New England colonies are John Demos, *A Little Commonwealth: Family Life in Plymouth Colony* (1970), and Lyle Koehler, *A Search for Power: The "Weaker Sex" in Seventeenth-Century New England* (1980). On women and the law, see Cornelia Hughes Dayton, *Women before the Bar: Gender, Law, and Society in Connecticut, 1639–1789* (1995), and Marylynn Salmon, *Women and the Law of Property in Early America* (1986). The two major works on witchcraft are Carol F. Karlsen, *The Devil in the Shape of a Woman: Witchcraft in Colonial New England* (1987), and Mary Beth Norton, *In the Devil's Snare: The Salem Witchcraft Crisis of 1692* (2002). A study of women's household production is Laurel Thatcher Ulrich, *The Age of Homespun: Objects and Stories in the Creation of an American Myth* (2002). See also Laurel

Thatcher Ulrich's *Goodwives: Image and Reality in the Lives of Women in Northern New England* (1982). Midwifery is addressed in Rebecca Tannenbaum, *A Healer's Calling: Women and Medicine in Early New England* (2002), and the experiences of an urban tradeswoman are analyzed in Patricia Cleary, *Elizabeth Murray: A Woman's Pursuit of Independence in Eighteenth-Century America* (2000). Ann M. Little, *Abraham in Arms: War and Gender in Colonial New England* (2006), addresses warfare and captivity between New England and New France. Richard Godbeer, *Sexual Revolution in Early America* (2004), explores the complexity of Puritan attitudes toward sexuality and marriage. Several works address the experience of New England women who lived as captives in native societies, among them Teresa A. Toulouse, *The Captive's Position: Female Narrative, Male Identity, and Royal Authority in Colonial New England* (2006); and June Namias, *White Captives: Gender and Ethnicity on the American Frontier* (1993).

Other Europes/Other Americas   On New Netherland, see Linda Briggs Biemer, *Women and Property in Colonial New York: The Transition from Dutch to English Law, 1643–1727* (1983). Valuable articles include David E. Narrett, "Men's Wills and Women's Property Rights in Colonial New York," in Ronald Hoffman and Peter J. Albert, eds., *Women in the Age of the American Revolution* (1989). On Jews in New Netherland, see the first chapters of Beryl Lieff Benderly and Hasia R. Diner, *Her Works Praise Her: A History of Jewish Women in America from Colonial Times to the Present* (2003). On New France, Richard White's *The Middle Ground: Indians, Empires, and Republics in the Great Lakes Region, 1650–1815* (1991), is the place to start. Susan Sleeper-Smith, *Indian Women and French Men: Rethinking Cultural Encounter in the Western Great Lakes* (2001), and Karen Anderson, *Chain Her by One Foot: The Subjugation of Native Women in Seventeenth-Century New France* (1993), cover similar material from different points of view. Natalie Zemon Davis has brought her great insights into early modern women to New France in her portrait of Marie de l'Incarnation, in *Women on the Margins: Three Seventeenth-Century Lives* (1995). A more institutional history of the Ursulines can be found in Emily Clark, *Masterless Mistresses: The New Orleans Ursulines and the Development of a New World Society* (2007). Steve Aron's *American Confluence* (2005) examines the spread of New France south along the Mississippi. On New Spain, Ramón Gutiérrez's *When Jesus Came, the Corn Mothers Went Away, Marriage, Sexuality and Power in New Mexico, 1500–1846* (1991) remains the starting point for any inquiry into gender. Two new studies build on this work: James Brooks, *Captives and Cousins: Slavery, Kinship, and Community in the Southwest Borderlands* (2002), and Julianna Barr, *Peace Came in the Form of a Woman* (2007).

For selected Web sites, please visit the *Through Women's Eyes* book companion site at bedfordstmartins.com/duboisdumenil.

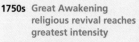

3

Mothers and Daughters of the Revolution

1750–1800

Y EARS AFTER THE AMERICAN REVOLUTION ENDED British colonial rule in 1783, Sarah Osborn applied for a widow's pension from the U.S. government. In her 1837 deposition, she described not only her husband's service as a soldier but also her contributions to the war effort. During one battle she took "her stand just back of the American tents, say about a mile from the town, and busied herself washing, mending, and cooking for the soldiers, in which she was assisted by the other females. . . . She heard the roar of the artillery for a number of days."[1] Osborn's account of life close to the fighting suggests a significant break from notions of women's traditional place at the hearth. But that she performed domestic work for her husband and his fellow soldiers also reveals that, even in the disruptive context of war, women's customary domestic roles prevailed. Osborn's experiences were hardly universal, yet her deposition underscores a crucial point. Even though the dramatic events of the second half of the eighteenth century centered on political and international concerns, which were customarily viewed as exclusively male terrain, women actively participated—although usually in distinctly gendered ways—in the American Revolution and the founding of the new nation.

Historians vigorously debate the long-term impact of the revolutionary crisis on women's lives. Some scholars argue that as white men enjoyed expanded legal and political rights during the postrevolutionary period, women's relative status declined. Others contend that women developed a new consciousness that led to their improved education and increased their opportunities to influence public life. These historians also point out that the religious revival of the period, the Great Awakening, similarly offered women a greater voice in the world beyond their homes. Neither scenario, however, neatly fits the experience of all women. This chapter emphasizes the ways in which women participated in the Revolution and traces the complex changes the revolutionary era brought to their lives. Although traditional expectations about women's roles were challenged, they were rarely overturned.

BACKGROUND TO REVOLUTION, 1754–1775

For two centuries North America was the site of contending colonial powers, with France, Spain, and England struggling with native peoples and each other to dominate the continent's land and resources. The transformation by which the region came to be controlled largely by Britain, and later the United States, was rooted in the French and Indian War of 1754–1763 and further consolidated by the American Revolution of 1776–1783. In the British colonies, women settlers on the frontier experienced the events leading up to the Revolution as part of an ongoing struggle over colonial freedom from British intervention. During the early years, colonists had enjoyed a high degree of freedom from British intrusion in their domestic affairs. But the French and Indian War, in which British and colonial troops conquered New France, brought dramatic changes. It was a costly war, and England insisted that the colonials pay their share through increased taxation, a burden that women, as consumers, often experienced firsthand. Moreover, the victory had opened up more land for British settlement: by the terms of the Treaty of Paris that ended the war, the French yielded their vast lands in North America to the British, who now claimed all the territory east of the Mississippi River (see Map 3.1). The war also drew in various Native American peoples, who sided and fought

1778	Mary Hays McCauley tends a cannon in the Battle of Monmouth, New Jersey
1780	General Washington orders strict control over women army followers
1780	Esther DeBerdt Reed and Sarah Franklin Bache organize Philadelphia women to support the troops
1780	Reed writes the broadside "Sentiments of an American Woman"
1780s–1807	Property-owning women allowed to vote in New Jersey
1781	British surrender at Yorktown, Virginia
1781	Articles of Confederation ratified
1781	Elizabeth Freeman ("Mum Bett") sues for her freedom in Massachusetts
1783	Treaty of Paris officially ends war
1783	Slavery banned in Massachusetts
1785	Jemima Wilkinson establishes a religious colony in New York
1787	Benjamin Rush's *Thoughts on Female Education* published
1788	U.S. Constitution adopted
1789	George Washington becomes first U.S. president
1790	Republican Motherhood ideal emerges
1790	Women's educational opportunities begin to expand outside the South
1790s	Second Great Awakening begins
1792	Mary Wollstonecraft's *A Vindication of the Rights of Woman* published in the United States
1793	The cotton gin invented
1793	Judith Sargent Murray's *Observations on Female Abilities* published
1796	John Adams elected president
1800	Thomas Jefferson elected president

◆ **Map 3.1 British Colonies in America, 1763**

Following the French and Indian War, the Treaty of Paris gave Britain control over all of New France east of the Mississippi and all of Spanish Florida. At the same time, Britain imposed the Proclamation Line of 1763, which prohibited white settlement west of the Appalachian Mountains. Subsequent legislation designated most of the western lands reserved for Indians. This western policy angered settlers hungry for land and land speculators eager to make a profit, and it contributed to the crisis in the British colonies that eventually led to the American Revolution.

with whichever European power they thought most likely to honor individual tribal claims to territory. Usually this was the French, who, unlike the British, had learned to live with Native Americans rather than drive them off their lands. The British victory imperiled Native Americans in part because they could no longer play off European powers against one another, and in part because of the avidness with which British colonists eyed the newly acquired territories.

The war accelerated emigration. Irish, Scots, Ulster Scots, Germans, and English peoples expanded the population of the British colonies, which counted almost 2 million settlers by 1765. Cities grew, but so did the population of the backcountry. Pressured for years by a scarcity of good, affordable land, settlers as well as land speculators coveted Native American lands along the frontier. The British, hoping to put an end to the recurring Indian wars, issued the Proclamation of 1763, which temporarily closed the land west of the Appalachians to settlement. Expansion-minded colonists resented (and often ignored) the proclamation line, thus fomenting conflict with Native Americans and creating tension between the colonies and the mother country.

The Growing Confrontation

Other British efforts to exert more control over the American colonies included a series of fiscal and administrative reforms that affected women primarily in their roles as household producers and consumers. The Revenue Act of 1764 (known as the Sugar Act) lowered duties on sugar but firmly established the means of enforcing their collection. Designed to defray the cost of keeping British troops in North America, the Sugar Act was followed by the 1765 Stamp Act, which required the use of embossed paper for legal documents and other printed matter. Forced to rescind the Stamp Act, the British Parliament in 1767 passed the Townshend Act, which included new duties on tea, coffee, and other items of household consumption, thus heightening women's political consciousness. At the same time, the British increased their bureaucratic presence in the colonies—the number of Crown officials doubled during this period—and sought to limit the autonomy of the colonies' governing assemblies.

As tensions between Britain and the colonists took center stage in the years after the French and Indian War, waves of social and economic problems roiled the colonies. Seaport towns and cities suffered an economic downturn after the war boom, and the colonists, especially those indebted to English creditors, became all the more resentful of British taxation. Hard times widened the gap between rich and poor in the colonies, deepening dissatisfaction. Extraordinary unrest in the back-country regions of the southern and middle colonies—where poor farmers went on rampages against Native Americans and resisted the authority of colonial elites on the seaboard—also promoted the desire for change. While perhaps resenting the wealthy colonial merchants and landed gentry who controlled so much of the economic and political life of the colonies, in some areas, especially the mid-Atlantic colonies, poor people diverted much of their anger toward British authority and its efforts to bring the American colonies more tightly into the imperial fold. Yet another social factor that paved the way for rebellion against imperial power was the Great Awakening, discussed later in this chapter (see pp. 147–51). This set of evangelical revivals, in which women were prominent participants, challenged traditional religion and promoted an egalitarianism that many scholars think fostered political unrest as well.

The onrushing crisis with England led some colonists to examine closely not only their relationship to the Crown but also their conceptions of the existing social order and government itself. Among educated elites, the ideas of the Enlightenment, especially of political philosophers such as John Locke, had a powerful impact. This European intellectual movement emphasized the rights of individuals, the role of reason, the promise of social progress, and the importance of the scientific method. In America, it contributed to the questioning of the British Crown's authority and to an appreciation for the rights of the individual.

The public debates occasioned by the British efforts to control the colonies more tightly were conducted almost exclusively by men. Although many addressed the questions of hierarchical structures within the British Empire and within the colonial governments, few questioned the hierarchy embedded in their gender system. Despite societal assumptions that the weighty considerations of government, diplomacy, and the economy were outside the realm of women's concerns, many women from diverse groups actively participated in the events surrounding the revolutionary conflict. But while many women found themselves acting in novel ways, for the most part their activities followed the traditional lines of household production and family obligation.

Liberty's Daughters: Women and the Emerging Crisis

When the colonists resisted the new taxes by boycotting British goods, women were necessarily involved. Where colonists had formerly relied on imported cloth, they now proposed to make their own cloth. Even though most textile production was women's work, initial reports of the substitution of homespun cloth for imported fabric often ignored women's contributions. In 1768, the *Providence Gazette* commended one man for the large quantities of cloth and yarn "spun in his own house," without reference to the women who were doing the work. But male patriots (as colonials who protested British domination were called) quickly realized their dependence on women's efforts, and northern newspaper reports of patriotic women's production of homespun cloth escalated.[2] In New England, spinning bees for manufacturing the yarn for homemade cloth were particularly popular. A group of twenty to forty young women, dressed in homespun and often observed by hundreds of spectators, would gather at a minister's home and there set to work spinning.[3]

Southern white women also produced homespun, but because they lived on farms and plantations often widely separated from one another, they rarely did so in the large groups typical in the North. Nor was there much publicity for their work, and indeed the southern press tended to criticize women for their extravagant taste in clothes and to suggest that men would have to persuade their wives to provide the necessary assistance.[4] Although free white women did provide assistance, masters of large plantations bought equipment and set groups of slave women to spinning. Robert Carter of Virginia had his overseer "sett a part, Ten black Females the most Expert spinners . . .—they to be Employed in Spinning, solely."[5] This method of using slaves to produce cloth continued through the Revolutionary War, allowing some slave women to acquire new skills.

While black slave women had little choice in the matter of assisting their masters in their boycotts against the British, free white women could and did see themselves as acting in a patriotic cause, and many called themselves "Liberty's Daughters." Their spinning bees may not have resulted in a large amount of cloth, but their efforts took on symbolic importance and reinforced their importance as consumers—or nonconsumers in the boycott. The spinning bees were, says one historian, "ideological showcases" that demonstrated women's contribution to the colonial struggle.[6]

Beyond producing homespun, women practiced all sorts of economies as they spurned a wide variety of British goods. Tea became the focus of boycotts in the early 1770s, especially after 1773, when the British instituted new regulations designed to undercut the colonials' illegal importation of non-British tea. Some women substituted herbal teas and coffee and engaged in collective efforts to encourage other women to do the same. In Edenton, North Carolina, fifty-one women acknowledged their "duty" to support the nonimportation resolutions passed by the First Continental Congress in 1774 (see Figure 3.7, p. 162). Women boycotters were roundly applauded in the press for their sacrifice. Presbyterian leader William Tennent III told women that "you have it in your power more than

WILLIAM JACKSON,

an IMPORTER; at the

BRAZEN HEAD,

North Side of the TOWN-HOUSE,

and Opposite the Town-Pump, in

Corn-hill, BOSTON.

It is desired that the SONS and
DAUGHTERS of LIBERTY,
would not buy any one thing of
him, for in so doing they will bring
Disgrace upon themselves, and their
Posterity, for ever and ever, AMEN.

◆ **Don't Buy British Goods**
In reaction to the Townshend Act (1767), which imposed taxes on glass, paper, paint, and imported tea to pay for the salaries of British royal officials in the colonies, outraged colonists in the major seaports began a boycott of British imports in 1768. This broadside, which would have been posted in public places, was aimed at merchants who refused to honor the boycott. The reference to "Daughters of Liberty" conveys how important women as consumers were to colonial resistance in the crisis years preceding the American Revolution. *Courtesy of the Massachusetts Historical Society.*

all your committees and Congresses, to strike the Stroke, and make the Hills and Plains of America clap their hands."[7] And even southern papers celebrated women's role in making the tea boycott successful. The *South Carolina Gazette* reported that in Charleston eminent women "engaged in a Promise . . . to reject, and totally renounce the baneful Herb," and proposed to "exert themselves in Defence of those Rights which God and Nature has bestowed on us."[8]

Articles attributed to women appeared in both northern and southern newspapers. Whether these were actually written by women or by men using female pseudonyms, they helped to legitimate the idea of women as authors with valuable insights to impart. Some women wrote poems denouncing tea drinking.[9] Others produced thoughtful essays, such as one that appeared in 1774 in the *Virginia Gazette*, published by Clementina Rind, explaining that "[m]uch, very much, depends on the public virtue the ladies will exert at this critical juncture," and concluding that American women "will be so far instrumental in bringing about a redress of the evils complained of, that history may be hereafter filled with their praises, and teach posterity to venerate their virtues."[10]

Despite the widespread sense that politics was not a woman's affair, participation in the boycotts and in the production of homespun did bring women to the margins of political action and encouraged them to see themselves as part of a larger American whole. Even someone as young as thirteen-year-old Anna Green Winslow wrote in her diary in 1771, "As I Am (as we say) a daughter of liberty, I chuse to wear as much of our own manufactory as possible."[11] Another young girl, Betsy Foote, recorded her daily labor at spinning and carding, and reported that she "felt Nationly into the bargain."[12] Women wrote of duty, of civic virtues, of freedom, and of sacrifice. However, despite the centrality of women's contributions to the success of the Americans' resistance, their efforts were extensions of their roles within the home—as goodwives and consumers—and, as such, the potential challenge to the gender order was minimized.

WOMEN AND THE FACE OF WAR, 1775–1783

Colonial resistance escalated from boycotts and protests to armed conflict in April 1775, when British troops marched on Lexington and Concord, Massachusetts, in an effort to put down the growing rebellion. Although colonial leaders did not issue the Declaration of Independence until July 1776 (see the Appendix, A-1), the Revolution had begun. A struggle between imperial Great Britain and its colonies, the American Revolution was also a civil war in which British subjects fought one another and former friends and neighbors became enemies. While many colonists tried to avoid taking sides, historians estimate that about one-fifth of the white population were loyalists (i.e., loyal to Britain and opposed to the Revolution), also called Tories by their enemies. Probably two-fifths were patriots, supporters of the Revolution. Native Americans and African Americans, too, became embroiled in the conflict on both sides of the fence. A wide spectrum of Americans, both male and female, thus faced profound disruptions and complex decisions.

Choosing Sides: Native American and African American Women

Native American communities confronted particularly weighty choices. In part because their experiences with land-grabbing settlers had been so negative, many nations opted to side with the British—who had made some efforts to control the colonists' encroachment into Indian territory—and they waged war against the patriots and their Indian allies throughout the backcountry. In many of the Indian nations, including the Iroquois and the Cherokee, women traditionally exerted significant influence over the decision to go to war; the causes were often linked to the desire to avenge deaths of loved ones killed by enemies. As Native Americans became enmeshed in European and American conflicts, the rationale for warfare shifted from kinship issues, and women's role may have diminished. Nonetheless, when some of the Iroquois peoples (the Mohawks, Cayugas, Senecas, and Onondagas, but not the Oneidas and Tuscaroras) decided to ally with the British, they announced that the "mothers also consented to it," and some well-known Native American women were highly visible in the war effort. Molly Brant, a Mohawk woman who for many years had been the consort of Sir William Johnson, a British official on the frontier, followed the path of many Native American

◆ **"First Blow for Liberty"**
The Battle of Concord and Lexington (April 1775) marked the beginning of the
Revolutionary War. Although this nineteenth-century engraving is a romanticized rendering
of the conflict, its depiction of women assisting fallen soldiers appropriately acknowledges
women's presence on the battlefields of the American Revolution, battlefields that were often
in their own towns and villages. *Culver Pictures.*

women who had married white men and then mediated between the two cultures
(see p. 23). After Johnson died, Brant returned to her people and enjoyed unusual
wealth and status. She so actively engaged in revolutionary-era diplomacy on the
side of the British that one officer claimed that her influence among her tribe was
"far superior to that of all their Chiefs put together."[13]

Black women's choices in the Revolution were of a completely different nature.
Although small communities of free blacks existed throughout the colonies, the
Revolution affected slaves far more profoundly. For example, scarcities of foodstuffs and clothing bore particularly hard on slaves, whose owners gave their needs
a low priority. However, wartime labor shortages and political circumstances gave
slaves more room for maneuvering in their relations with their masters. Southern
whites repeatedly complained about slaves' insolence and intractability.
Slaveowners were particularly worried about the prospects of insurrection and

flight, especially after November 1775, when Virginia's royal governor offered freedom to rebels' slaves who agreed to fight for the British. His goal was twofold: to acquire troops and laborers, and to pressure white slaveholders to stay within the loyalist fold. His offer led to a massive flight of slaves, including both men expecting to serve as soldiers and also women and children.

Throughout the war, slave men and women pondered their choice: Could they make it safely to the British lines? Would the British be true protectors? Would the British or the rebels win? An estimated fifty-five thousand southern slaves escaped during the Revolution. Some made their way to the British; others, like Mary Willing Byrd's slaves in Virginia, had the British come to them. When the British left after occupying Byrd's home, forty-nine slaves went with them. Many other slaves simply escaped, looking for freedom independent of the British. Those who went over to the British often did so in groups, frequently with family members. Historians estimate that one-third of those who fled were women, a much higher proportion of runaways than before the Revolution. With nearby British troops offering sanctuary, women with children were willing to take the risk.

Escape from an owner, however, did not mean escape from danger and hardship. Former slaves were forced to work for the British, often at the most disagreeable tasks. When the British occupied Philadelphia, for example, they formed a "Company of Black Pioneers." This group of seventy-two men, fifteen women, and eight children were to "assist in Cleaning the Streets and Removing all Newsiances being thrown into the Streets."[14] Living conditions were harsh. In the British camps, many former slaves succumbed to smallpox and other diseases. In 1781, the British general Alexander Leslie reported that "about 700 Negroes are come down the River in the Small Pox." In an eighteenth-century version of germ warfare, he decided to "distribute them about the Rebell Plantations."[15] This callous attitude toward the black men and women under his care underlines the fact that most British officers viewed the slaves seeking freedom as pawns in the imperial struggle. Despite the unsettled conditions of wartime, black men and women fought an uphill battle to escape to freedom and survive.

White Women: Pacifists, Tories, and Patriots

White women also had to make decisions about the war, but of a very different sort than those of black slave women. The war created a painful situation for Quaker women, whose pacifism was a tenet of their religion. Maintaining a neutral stance was difficult. Patriots were often suspicious of Quakers, and Quakers themselves clearly struggled with their political identity. Margaret Morris, a Quaker from New Jersey, was concerned about the welfare of soldiers on both sides, yet she was critical of the patriots' rowdy and aggressive efforts to capture loyalists and proudly recounted her success in hiding a friend from a group of armed men who appeared at her door. At the same time, she described General George Washington's troops as "our side."

American or British, patriot or Tory: Did a woman's political identity follow her husband's? To whom would the wife of a Tory man show allegiance? Women whose loyalist husbands had been exiled or who had gone to fight with the British were subject to ostracism. They sometimes found their land and personal goods plundered. State laws permitting the confiscation of land of known Tories differed slightly regarding the rights of the wife or widow of an "absentee." Massachusetts, for example, acknowledged her dower rights in the estate only if she had remained in the state and not followed her husband. Most generally, states presumed that a woman's allegiance followed her husband's, in accordance with the assumptions of *feme covert*. Significantly, most states did not require the loyalty oaths of women that they required of men, an indication that women were not viewed as political actors.

Not all women followed the allegiance of their husbands. A few took up the patriot cause despite their husbands' loyalty to the British Crown. Florence Cook of Charleston, South Carolina, attempted to regain her family's dispossessed property after the war. In her petition, she described herself as a "Sincere friend to her Country," who taught her daughter "the love of Liberty and this her Native Country." Jane Moffit of Albany, New York, was protected from expulsion despite her husband's political sentiments because, said city leaders, she "has always been esteemed a Friend to the American Cause."[16]

In case after case, decisions about the fate of wives were based on the assumption that wives could not act independently of their husbands, but they also reflected the reality that some women directly aided the loyalist cause. Many women who remained behind when their loyalist husbands left did serve as couriers and spies or in other ways assisted the British. In Albany, thirty-two women were brought to the attention of the New York State Commissioners for Detecting and Defeating Conspiracies in 1780. Some, like Lidia Currey and Rachael Ferguson, were jailed for hiding loyalists in their homes. Others smuggled messages to British troops. In Philadelphia, Margaret Hutchinson carried "Verbal Intelligence, of what, she had seen of their [the Rebels] different Movements" to British spies. While in absolute numbers such daring women were not numerous, they were considered so serious a threat that patriot committees of safety sought the help of "discreet Women, of Known attachment to the American Cause" to search for contraband and hidden letters on the persons of suspected female Tory couriers.[17]

Maintaining the Troops: The Women Who Served

Service to one's country during wartime often becomes a defining moment of citizenship. Sacrifices become emblems of civic virtue and worthiness. Since the ultimate signs of service are bearing arms and risking death, women's contributions are frequently less valued than men's. During the Revolution, few women actually fought in combat. But the exceptions are notable. In South Carolina, one woman joined her son-in-law to resist 150 British soldiers who were trying to destroy a cache of ammunition. Pennsylvanian Mary Hays McCauley, perhaps the inspiration for the legendary Molly Pitcher, routinely carried water to troops in battle. When her husband fell at the Battle of Monmouth, New Jersey, in 1778, she took his place, keeping a cannon loaded in the face of enemy fire, for which she later

SARAH OSBORN
Remembering the Revolution

In 1837, Sarah Osborn (1756–1858) submitted a deposition to obtain a pension based on her husband's Revolutionary War service as a commissary guard. The statement provides evidence that her husband had indeed served and that she had firsthand knowledge of the course of the war. At the same time, her deposition reveals her own active participation on the battlefield. Osborn received her pension. How does she describe her activities in the Battle of Yorktown?

Deponent [Osborn] took her stand just back of the American tents, say about a mile from the town, and busied herself washing, mending, and cooking for the soldiers, in which she was assisted by the other females; some men washed their own clothing. She heard the roar of the artillery for a number of days, and the last night the Americans threw up entrenchments, it was a misty, foggy night, rather wet but not rainy. Every soldier threw up for himself, as she understood, and she afterwards saw and went into the entrenchments. Deponent's said husband was there throwing up entrenchments, and deponent cooked and carried in beef, and bread, and coffee (in a gallon pot) to the soldiers in the entrenchment.

On one occasion when deponent was thus employed carrying in provisions, she met General Washington, who asked her if she "was not afraid of the cannonballs?"

She replied, "No, the bullets would not cheat the gallows," that "It would not do for the men to fight and starve too."

They dug entrenchments nearer and nearer to Yorktown every night or two till the last. While digging that, the enemy fired very heavy till

received a pension from the state of Pennsylvania "for services rendered in the revolutionary war." Deborah Sampson, later Gannett, was one of a handful of female cross-dressers in the Revolution. Donning men's clothing and enlisting as Robert Shurtleff in the Fourth Massachusetts Regiment, she served eighteen months from 1782 to 1783 and was wounded twice before her sex was discovered and she was discharged (see Figure 3.6, p. 160). Another woman attempted to enlist in 1778 at Elizabethtown, New Jersey. A suspicious officer required that she submit to a physical exam, and the following day, "ordered the Drums to beat her . . . Threw the Town with the whores march."[18]

More generally, women's role in the military was one they had historically taken in warfare: the so-called camp follower. Some who attached themselves to the patriots' Continental Army under George Washington's command were prostitutes, but more were soldiers' wives. While officers' wives did make protracted vis-

about nine o'clock next morning, then stopped, and the drums from the enemy beat excessively. . . .

The drums continued beating, and all at once the officers hurrahed and swung their hats, and deponent asked them, "What is the matter now?"

One of them replied, "Are not you soldier enough to know what it means?"

Deponent replied, "No."

Then they replied, "The British have surrendered."

Deponent, having provisions ready, carried the same down to the entrenchments that morning, and four of the soldiers whom she was in the habit of cooking for at their breakfasts.

Deponent stood on one side of the road and the American officers upon the other side when the British officers came out of the town and rode up to the American officers and delivered up [their swords, which the deponent] thinks were returned again and the British officers rode right on before the army who marched out beating and playing a melancholy tune, their drums covered with black handkerchiefs and their fifes with black ribbons tied around them, into an old field and there grounded their arms and then returned into town again to await their destiny. Deponent recollects seeing a great many American officers, some on horseback and some on foot, but cannot call them all by name. Washington, Lafayette, and Clinton were among the number.

SOURCE: John C. Dann, ed., *The Revolution Remembered: Eyewitness Accounts of the War for Independence* (Chicago: University of Chicago Press, 1980), 244–45.

its to encourage their husbands and to participate in entertainments, most women who followed the army were poor men's wives. Their presence may have signaled a patriotic fervor to aid the cause, but more probably it indicated their desire to attend to their husbands' welfare as well as their inability to function on their own financially. Camp followers, often with their children in tow, faced extraordinary challenges, risking disease, injury, and death. Living under primitive conditions with scanty provisions, some even gave birth in army camps.

But camp followers did provide valuable services. Some were "sutlers," merchants who sold provisions to the troops. More commonly women such as Sarah Osborn, whose story opens this chapter, did laundry or worked as cooks (see box, "Remembering the Revolution"). Women served as nurses, both in the fields and at the general hospitals for the sick and wounded where conditions were primitive. While male doctors and their assistants performed the skilled work, female nurses were assigned "to see that the close-stools or pots are emptied as soon as possible after they are used . . . they are to see that every patient, upon his admission into the Hospital is immediately washed with warm water, and that his face and hands are washed and head combed every morning."[19] The sexual division of labor relegated women to menial tasks, and no matter how important this work was, women's compensation was small.

Even though he recognized that these women were crucial to the maintenance of the army, Washington found them exasperating nuisances. He viewed them as "a clog upon every movement" and worried that the cost of their subsistence cut into the provisions of his soldiers. In 1780, at West Point, officers were required to "make the Strictest inspection into the Carractor of the women who Draw [rations] in their Corps and report on their honour and Artificers." Unmarried women would be sent away; married women could stay but would be required to work as laundresses at minimal wages. Women's ragtag presence with the troops also undercut the public image of a victorious army. In addition, Washington was offended by poor women's lack of gentility, their failure to be ladylike. When he prepared to lead the troops through the city of Philadelphia after the Battle of Germantown, he issued orders that "not a woman belonging to the army is to be seen with the troops on their march."[20]

Thus, although camp followers lived and worked in the very midst of war, drawing on a physical fortitude associated with male activities, they did not break down traditional expectations about women's proper role. Their presence with the army was for the most part a reflection of their dependence. Women continued to be controlled not only by their husbands but also by what one historian terms "that most male of institutions, the military."[21] Their activities were extensions of women's traditional household work. Although many undoubtedly took pride in their patriotic contributions, they did not exhibit a new sense of independence.

Some women did not follow the armies but did observe the fighting as it came to them. Occupying armies commandeered homes for quartering soldiers, and women frequently bore the brunt of their demands for food and firewood. In September 1777, Elizabeth Drinker, alone with her children in Philadelphia, found herself the unwilling hostess to a British officer: "Our officer mov'd his lodging from the bleu Chamber to the little front parlor, so that he has the two front parlors, a chamber up two pair of stairs for his bagge, and the Stable wholly to himself, besides the use of the kitchen."[22] Catherine Van Cortlandt, a Tory woman, wrote disparagingly to her husband about the patriot troops who commandeered her house in New Jersey: "They were the most disorderly of their species and their officers were from the dregs of the people." She complained that "the farmers are forbid to sell me provisions, and the millers to grind our grain. Our woods are cut down for the use of their army, and that which you bought and left corded near the river my servants are forbid to touch, though we are in the greatest distress for the want of it."[23] Women caught in the crossfire worried about their personal safety and that of their children. While reported rapes were infrequent, British soldiers were brutal on occasion. More commonly, women had to adjust to being alone and to handling the day-to-day affairs of running a farm or managing a business in a husband's prolonged absence. Their independent management proved to be one of their most significant roles in the revolutionary era.

A small group of patriot women, reminiscent of the Daughters of Liberty who had organized spinning bees in the early stages of the Revolution, carved out more public ways of participating in the war effort by raising funds for the beleaguered Continental Army. Following a discouraging defeat at Charleston in 1780, Esther DeBerdt Reed, the wife of the governor of Pennsylvania, and Sarah Franklin Bache, the daughter of Benjamin Franklin, organized the Ladies Association of Philadelphia to raise money for the troops. They urged prosperous women to go without luxuries to aid the cause and asked poorer women to offer what they could. In a powerfully worded broadside (see box, "Sentiments of an American Woman"), Reed outlined the rationale for the fund-raising and answered any challenge to its appropriateness: "[H]e cannot be a good citizen who will not applaud our efforts for the relief of the armies which defend our lives, our possessions, our liberty."[24]

The Pennsylvania women publicized their efforts and sent letters to women in other states, urging them to raise funds as well. In Virginia, the scattered nature of settlement made an exact duplication of Pennsylvania's door-to-door effort impossible, but Martha Wayles Jefferson, wife of Governor Thomas Jefferson, did encourage other Virginia women to raise funds (Martha herself was not in good health), describing it as an "opportunity of proving that they also participate on those virtuous feelings."[25] In most cases, the sums raised were modest. In New Jersey, women collected $15,488 in paper dollars, but because of high inflation, the money purchased only 380 pairs of stockings for the state's soldiers.

The distribution of the $300,000 that the Philadelphia women collected offers a revealing insight into perceptions of women's supporting role. Writing to Washington, Reed explained that the women did not want the money to go into a general fund that would provide soldiers "an article to which they are entitled from the public." Rather, the women hoped that their money—approximately $2 per soldier in hard currency—might be given directly to the soldiers. Washington demurred: the men might waste it on liquor, and having hard currency, when they were generally paid in paper money, might create discontent and exacerbate inflation. He declared that their "benevolent donation" should be used to provide men with shirts and requested further that the women make the shirts themselves. In the midst of the exchange, Reed died of dysentery, but Bache followed through with the project, eventually sending Washington 2,220 shirts. A French visitor to Bache's home reported that "on each shirt was the name of the married or unmarried lady who made it."[26]

For the most part, these women's efforts received favorable attention from men. The editor of the *Pennsylvania Packet* grandiosely proclaimed that "the women of every part of the globe are under obligations to those of America, for having shown that females are capable of the highest political virtue."[27] Yet however novel the Philadelphia women's plan may have been, Washington's response placed their efforts firmly in the realm of woman's more traditional sphere—of sewing for her family. The Philadelphia women's efforts may have been more overtly political than the service of poor women following the army, but in both cases women's contributions were constrained by traditional notions of women's roles. The link between women's patriotism and the domestic sphere was to be one of the principal ideological legacies of the Revolution.

ESTHER DeBERDT REED
Sentiments of an American Woman

In 1780, Esther DeBerdt Reed (1746–1780) and Sarah Franklin Bache (1743–1808) created the Ladies Association of Philadelphia. As Reed explained it in a broadside, "Sentiments of an American Woman," the purpose was to organize women to be "really useful" in supporting the revolutionary effort. How does she characterize women's usefulness in wartime?

On the commencement of actual war, the Women of America manifested a firm resolution to contribute as much as could depend on them, to the deliverance of their country. Animated by the purest patriotism, they are sensible of sorrow at this day, in not offering more than barren wishes for the success of so glorious a Revolution. They aspire to render themselves more really useful; and this sentiment is universal from the north to the south of the Thirteen United States. Our ambition is kindled by the same of those heroines of antiquity, who have rendered their sex illustrious, and have proved to the universe, that, if the weakness of our Constitution, if opinion and manners did not forbid us to march to glory by the same paths as the Men, we should at least equal, and sometimes surpass them in our love for the public good. I glory in all that which my sex has done great and commendable. I call to mind with enthusiasm and with admiration, all those acts of courage, of constancy and patriotism, which history has transmitted to us. . . . So many famous sieges where the Women have been seen forgetting the weakness of their sex, building new walls, digging trenches with their feeble hands, furnishing arms to their defenders, they themselves darting the missile weapons on the enemy, resigning the ornaments of their apparel, and their fortune, to fill the public treasury, and to hasten the deliverance of their country; burying themselves

REVOLUTIONARY LEGACIES

The patriots emerged victorious in 1781 when the British surrendered at Yorktown, Virginia. In that same year, the colonies, now states, ratified the Articles of Confederation, their first attempt at national governance. Weaknesses in that body led eventually to adoption of the U.S. Constitution in 1788 (see the Appendix, p. A-4) and the inauguration of George Washington as the new nation's first president in 1789. As a national government was being framed, the various states also wrote constitutions. The period was rich with debates about the nature of government and the rights of citizens, as Americans pondered the implications of their Revolution. What were the legacies of the Revolution for women? For

under its ruins, throwing themselves into the flames rather than submit to the disgrace of humiliation before a proud enemy.

Brave Americans, your disinterestedness, your courage, and your constancy will always be dear to America, as long as she shall preserve her virtue. . . . And shall we hesitate to evidence to you our gratitude? Shall we hesitate to wear a cloathing more simple; hair dressed less elegant, while at the price of this small privation, we shall deserve your benedictions. Who, amongst us, will not renounce with the highest pleasure, those vain ornaments, when she shall consider that the valiant defenders of America will be able to draw some advantage from the money which she may have laid out in these; that they will be better defended from the rigours of the seasons, that after their painful toils, they will receive some extraordinary and unexpected relief; that these presents will perhaps be valued by them at a greater price, when they will have it in their power to say: *This is the offering of the Ladies.* The time is arrived to display the same sentiments which animated us at the beginning of the Revolution, when we renounced the use of teas, however agreeable to our taste, rather than receive them from our persecutors; when we made it appear to them that we placed former necessaries in the rank of superfluities, when our liberty was interested; when our republican and laborious hands spun the flax, prepared the linen intended for the use of our soldiers; when exiles and fugitives we supported with courage all the evils which are the concomitants of war. Let us not lose a moment; let us be engaged to offer the homage of our gratitude at the altar of military valour, and you, our brave deliverers, while mercenary slaves combat to cause you to share with them, the irons with which they are loaded, receive with a free hand our offering, the purest which can be presented to your virtue,
By An AMERICAN WOMAN.

SOURCE: *Pennsylvania Magazine of History and Biography* XVIII (1894): 361–63.

many, war and revolution translated into hardship and poverty; for others, new opportunities emerged, but these were always constrained by prevailing assumptions about women's marginal role in public life.

A Changing World for Native American Women

How the Revolution affected the lives of Native American women is difficult to gauge, in part because historians have so little evidence about these women's experiences. Many nations, especially those that sided with Britain, suffered devastating losses in the war. American forces in New York invaded Iroquois territory in 1779,

◆ **Sarah Franklin Bache**
Together with Esther DeBerdt Reed, Sarah Franklin
Bache, the daughter of Benjamin Franklin, organized
the Ladies Association of Philadelphia to raise money
for General George Washington's troops. This group of
elite women raised $300,000, which was used to provide
2,200 shirts to the soldiers. Like many of her female
peers, Bache actively supported the colonial cause, but
in ways that did not sharply challenge conventional
expectations about appropriate feminine behavior. *The
Metropolitan Museum of Art, Catharine Lorillard Wolfe
Collection, Wolfe Fund, 1901 (01.20). Image © The Metropolitan
Museum of Art.*

burning forty towns and destroying crops. The Cherokees in the Appalachian region
to the south suffered a similar destruction. Native American men's preoccupation
with warfare and their role in diplomacy may have heightened their power within
their own communities, but it also increased women's responsibilities in maintaining their communities in the men's prolonged absences, and in the face of destruction, disease, and starvation.

In the postwar period, as the weakened Native Americans started to come
under the power of the new federal government, challenges to traditional gender
roles arose. Men acted as primary mediators between their nations and the newly
created American government. As men's roles took on magnified importance,

◆ Redefining Gender Roles among the Creeks

This early nineteenth-century painting features Creek Indians as U.S. agent Benjamin Hawkins introduces them to plows as a first step in Americanizing them. Hawkins focuses his attention on the men, placing his back to a woman who stands amid the foodstuffs she has produced. This stance represents white officials' and missionaries' goal of redefining gender roles among the Creek so that men would abandon hunting in exchange for farming, while women would give up their traditional role of raising crops to undertake domestic roles in the home. *Unidentified artist, circa 1805.* Benjamin Hawkins and the Creek Indians. *Oil on canvas, 35 ⅞ × 49 ⅞ inches. Greenville County Museum of Art, Greenville, SC. Gift of the Museum Association, Inc., with funds donated by Corporate Partners: Ernst and Young; Fluor Daniel; Director's Circle Members: Mr. and Mrs. Alester G. Furman III; Mr. and Mrs. M. Dexter Hagy; Thomas P. Hartness; Mr. and Mrs. E. Erwin Maddrey II; Mary M. Pearce; Mr. and Mrs. John Pellett Jr.; Mr. W. Thomas Smith; Mr. and Mrs. Edward H. Stall; Eleanor and Irvine Welling; Museum Antiques shows, 1989, 1990, 1991, Elliott, Davis and Company, CPAs, sponsor; Collector's Group 1990, 1991.*

women may have correspondingly lost influence in their communities. The government's efforts to encourage Native Americans' assimilation to white norms also disturbed traditional patterns. American leaders insisted that men give up hunting to become farmers and that Native American women become farmer's wives. In a letter to the Cherokees in 1796, President George Washington was explicit about his expectations. "You will easily add flax and cotton which you may dispose of to the White people; or have it made up by your own women into clothing for yourselves. Your wives and daughters can soon learn to spin and weave."[28] But if white Americans envisioned a family order in which women were subordinate, Cherokee women adapted to the new expectations in ways that maintained their traditional roles in the community. They continued their customary farming work, tended livestock, and took on the responsibilities of spinning and weaving. In contrast, men found it far more difficult to adjust to their changed circumstances. Deprived of hunting by the loss of their lands and depletion of furs, they were often idle and despairing. Overuse of alcohol also contributed to the exploitation of Native Americans and to unhappy domestic situations in which women were abused.

After the Revolution, Native Americans became the objects of missionary activity, especially during the Second Great Awakening of the early nineteenth century (see pp. 189–90).White missionaries sought not only to convert the natives but to "civilize" them, in part by urging them to adopt European notions of proper male and female behavior. Calls for change also came from within Indian nations. Handsome Lake, a Seneca religious prophet who had been influenced by the Quakers, called for major reforms for his people. He promoted a return to some of the old ways, especially in regard to religion. He condemned the abuse of alcohol and criticized men's physical mistreatment of their wives. At the same time, however, he urged that they follow the family patterns of whites: men should take up farming and women limit themselves to spinning and weaving. Privileging the nuclear family and the husband-wife relationship, he downplayed the older emphasis on kinship relations and was especially critical of the tribes' matrons. In the long run, assimilative pressures and a changed economic and political order undermined women's position among many Native American peoples, especially where men took on economic roles of increased importance to the community and their families. But that process was neither immediate nor universal.

African American Women: Freedom and Slavery

For African American women, the Revolution also left a complex, but completely different, legacy. At the end of the war, many slaves who had fled to the British to achieve their freedom were evacuated by ship from New York, Charleston, and Savannah. Of those who left from New York and whose sex is known, 42.3 percent were women, and apparently many had their children with them. Once on board, however, they faced still more problems. Some of these African Americans were sold again into slavery in the West Indies; others were shipped to Nova Scotia, where they eked out an existence in harsh conditions; and some ended up in another marginal environment, a new colony in Sierra Leone, West Africa.

For some African Americans who had not joined the British, the most important legacy of the Revolution was freedom. Even before the conflict, a small movement had supported manumission (owners granting slaves their freedom), primarily the result of the Quakers' growing revulsion against slavery. The ideological issues at the center of the Revolution, especially those concerning natural rights and liberty, encouraged some white Americans to examine the institution of slavery. Even for those with little humanitarian interest in slaves themselves, the incongruity of building a nation based on notions of liberty while maintaining chattel slavery was troublesome. More mundane concerns also promoted antislavery sentiment—white immigrant workers who were increasingly available and who were easily hired and fired became more attractive in the urban commercial culture of the North. Anxieties about slave insurrections during the war raised further questions about the slave system.

African Americans were active participants in the emancipation process, especially in Massachusetts. Mum Bett, later known as Elizabeth Freeman, was the slave of Colonel John Ashley in Sheffield, Massachusetts. (See Figure 3.4, p. 158). In 1781 she petitioned a Massachusetts county court for her freedom. Freeman's suit, combined with several others, led to the state court's 1783 decision that "there can be no such thing as perpetual servitude of a rational creature."[29] In other northern states, manumission came through legislation. Only Vermont, in 1777, provided for immediate emancipation. Elsewhere, the process was protracted. In Pennsylvania, unborn children of slaves would not be free until they were twenty-eight years old. Although each year more slaves became free in the North, one-fourth of northern blacks were still enslaved as late as 1810. This gradualism meant that slave women would continue to bear children who would be slaves until they were adults, but they could take some comfort in their children's future freedom.

The emancipation laws, as well as individual manumissions in the North and the Upper South and the migration of southern free blacks, created growing free black populations in the last years of the eighteenth century, especially in cities such as Philadelphia, Boston, and New York. Although a small number of these African Americans were able to carve out a modest success, constrained education and pervasive discrimination limited their opportunities. Most women worked at jobs similar to those that had occupied them when they were slaves—domestic work, washing, cooking, and child care. Some black women were proprietors, especially of boardinghouses, where they would have been important resources for the freed blacks migrating to the cities during this period. A handful of women were prominent enough to make a mark in the historical record. Lydia York, for example, petitioned the Philadelphia Abolition Society to assist her in indenturing her niece Hetty. Catherine Ferguson, an ex-slave who had purchased her own freedom, established a school for poor black and white children in New York in 1793. Another former slave, Eleanor Harris, became the first black teacher in Philadelphia.

As they worked at their jobs and cared for their families, many free black women participated in building up the network of black institutions, including churches and benevolent societies devoted to self-help efforts that had emerged by the turn of the century. Their role in these organizations, however, has remained largely obscured in the historical record. These free black institutions were a source of strength and pride for the community, but they also exemplified the segregated lives that African Americans lived in the North. Emancipation brought freedom for some black women and men, but within the constraints of a racial and economic hierarchy. The egalitarian promises implicit in revolutionary ideology were closed to African Americans.

In the South, these promises were even less in evidence. In the Upper South, there was a spate of individual manumissions, especially through the wills of slaveholders, and the free black population did expand significantly. But there was no widespread sentiment for dispensing with the institution altogether. Most

◆ **Women Slaves in the Tobacco Fields**
In 1798, architect Benjamin Henry Latrobe produced this image labeled "An overseer doing
his duty. Sketched from life near Fredricsburg." Latrobe apparently recognized the irony presented by the overseer, a white male in the employ of the plantation owner, standing idly on
a tree stump, his duty merely to watch the two women slaves hard at work hoeing in a
tobacco field. *The Maryland Historical Society, Baltimore, Maryland.*

slaveowners were not unduly troubled by the implications of a rhetoric of individual freedom and natural rights for their system of chattel labor. Indeed, slaveowners became more deeply entrenched in the institution after the war, especially
in the Deep South, where the 1793 invention of the cotton gin, which mechani-
cally removed the seed and hull from the cotton fiber, made the crop more productive and thus more profitable. This gave new impetus to the slave system,
which was also reinforced by increased importation of African slaves, a trade
explicitly permitted by the U.S. Constitution until 1808. The regional differences
in patterns of slavery grew after the Revolution, with slaves in the Deep South
more likely to maintain a more distinct African-based culture and to live in more
isolation from whites.

In the Chesapeake region, tobacco declined in importance and the region's
economy diversified, creating more varied jobs for slave populations. While some
women had developed textile skills during the revolutionary period, for the most
part the skilled slaves in the Upper South were men, trained as wagon makers, mill
workers, or builders. As some male slaves became artisans, women inherited more
of the disagreeable labor such as breaking new ground and collecting manure.

Slaves also became extremely important to the growing urban areas of the region, and women in particular were used in the tobacco factories of Petersburg and Richmond, Virginia. Women also served as domestic workers and participated in city markets, selling wares such as cakes, oysters, and garden produce, an occupation that gave them an unusual amount of liberty to move about the city.

Most slaves, however, enjoyed little personal freedom. This was particularly evident in the way in which slaveholders in the Upper South increasingly sought to reproduce the slave population, forcing some black women into sexual relations with men not of their own choosing. Others encouraged slaves to form families. Thomas Jefferson provided gifts for at least one couple on his Virginia plantation and explicitly commented on the value of a fertile female slave: "I consider a woman who brings a child every two years as more profitable than the best man on the farm."[30]

Despite their appreciation of female slaves as breeders, slaveowners throughout the South expected pregnant women to work well into their pregnancy and to return to their labors almost immediately after delivery. The hardships of being a mother under these conditions were magnified by the constant threat of separation. A white observer in Wilmington, North Carolina, in 1778 described the trauma he witnessed: "A wench clung to a little daughter, and implored, with the most agonizing supplication, that they might not be separated."[31] Children could be sold from their parents, and husbands from their wives, even in the households of paternalistic owners. The effects of financial reversals or the death of the master often rippled through the slave quarters, undercutting slaves' efforts to create a stable family life.

White Women: An Ambiguous Legacy

Just as the Revolution had mixed results for black women, its meaning for white women eludes easy generalizations. Many women faced enormous hardships. Petitions from widows and soldiers' wives provide eloquent evidence for the personal tragedies that came with war. Sarah Welsh's husband had died in 1780, but "being a destress widow not knowing how to or whom aplication was to be made . . . untill it was too late," she waited until 1791 to ask the government for his back pay.[32] Many wives of Tory men, too, found themselves in dire straits. After the war, they waged lengthy, and only rarely successful, legal battles to regain property seized when their husbands left to fight with the British. While some impoverished women could turn to friends, many others worked in the few avenues of employment offered to women, such as shopkeepers, teachers, innkeepers, servants, seamstresses, or milliners. By 1800, as the nation moved toward the first stages of industrialization and the "putting-out" industries (those industries focused on producing goods such as textiles, shoes, and straw bonnets) expanded, poorer women increasingly turned to doing piecework in their homes (see pp. 196–97). For more privileged educated women, war and revolution contributed to a changed conception of self, as many expanded their horizons beyond the narrow sphere of the hearth. Women whose husbands served in the army or in the new state or federal governments were left alone for extended periods. As women had been doing since the early colonial period, they became "deputy husbands," managing farms and businesses and often rising impressively to the new challenges.[33]

In the extant correspondence and diaries from this period, primarily from the wives of officers and politicians, a distinct pattern concerning women's roles as deputy husbands emerges. Men originally left detailed instructions, urging their wives to consult male kin or neighbors. Through time, many men began to trust their wives' judgment; New Yorker James Clinton, for example, commented to his wife, Mary, "I Can't give any Other Directions About Home more than what I have done but must Leave all to your good Management."[34] Women themselves often made pointed reference to their own competence, and some even ignored their husband's directions. The letters of the Bartletts of New Hampshire are particularly revealing of the transformation in consciousness the war brought to one woman. When Josiah Bartlett wrote his wife with instructions about "my out Door affairs," or "my farming business," she initially replied in kind, referring to "Your farming business." But eventually she began to use the word "our." Even more explicit in pointing out that male and female roles had become less sharply defined was Lucy Flucker Knox in New York, who wrote to her husband, Henry Knox, that she was "quite a woman of business," adding, "[I hope that in the future] you will not consider yourself as commander in chief of your own house—but be convinced that there is such a thing as equal command."[35]

Although few women challenged their subordinate position as overtly as Lucy Knox, the postwar years did see a significant questioning of white women's status in the home and, to some extent, in politics. Early in the revolutionary crisis women speaking about politics often made apologies, almost ritualistically accepting women's inferiority. In a June 1776 letter to a female friend, Elizabeth Feilde followed her comments on contemporary politics with the following self-deprecating remark: "No; I assure you it's a subject for which I have not either Talents or Inclination to enter upon."[36] But in the turmoil of rebellion and war, the apologies became less evident as astute women got caught up in the dramatic events unfolding before them. Eliza Wilkinson of South Carolina frankly resented men's claim that women had no business with politics, writing to a friend in 1782, "I won't have it thought that because we are the weaker sex as to bodily strength, my dear, we are capable of nothing more than minding the dairy, visiting the poultry-house, and all such domestic concerns. . . . They won't even allow us the liberty of thought, and that is all I want."[37]

As Wilkinson's term "liberty of thought" suggests, many women made overt connections between the ideology of the Revolution concerning natural rights, liberty, and equality and the position of women. Abigail Adams's admonition to her husband, John Adams, that the men drawing up the new government and its code of laws should "remember the ladies" is probably the most famous expression of the handful of elite women who hoped to see at least modest changes in women's status (see Figure 3.2, p. 155). The issue attracted a significant amount of attention in the decade after the Revolution. Following publication in the United States in 1792 of *A Vindication of the Rights of Women* by the English activist Mary Wollstonecraft, American magazines debated women's rights and roles. Some articles referred to marriage as a form of slavery. Others blamed women's limited education for women's vanity and superficiality.

Did the flurry of attention to women's rights in the postrevolutionary era lead to an improvement in white women's status? The states in the new nation were now free of British legal statutes and could theoretically construct laws in keeping with the new emphasis on protecting individual rights. Divorce law was one area in which women did benefit. British common law did not allow divorce, but now all states except South Carolina permitted it. Still, the procedure was difficult. In most states, divorce petitions required action by the state assembly. Courts in Pennsylvania and the four New England states could decree divorce. Causes offered for divorce changed over time, hinting at a slight shift in marital expectations. During most of the colonial period, women were far more likely than men to seek a divorce, usually doing so on the grounds of desertion. After the Revolution, the grounds women used expanded to include adultery, and more men began to seek divorce, usually for desertion. The changes were subtle ones, as one historian concedes: "All one can say, and perhaps it is enough, is that after the war women were physically moving out of their unhappy households, an action that, judging from the divorce literature, had been relatively uncommon before the war."[38]

In other legal matters, white women gained little. In many states, widows' rights to their dower was, if anything, eroded in the years after the Revolution. In addition, states maintained the British system of coverture, a major impediment to married women's autonomy. Women continued to be excluded from juries and from legal training and thus were excluded from the male political culture that centered at the courthouse.

Most significantly, women were denied the vote. Despite the revolutionary rhetoric of equality, the majority of the founding fathers believed that in a democratic republic only independent people should be permitted to vote, and independent people, by definition, owned property. Thus propertyless men and all women were excluded. In the case of women, however, exclusion was less a matter of property than of sex. Married or not, women were assumed to be dependent creatures by nature. The fleeting exception to this assumption was New Jersey, whose 1776 state constitution did not explicitly define the qualifications for voters, declaring only that "all inhabitants" who met certain property and residence requirements "shall be entitled to vote," thus technically permitting both white women and blacks to vote. In the 1780s, some property-holding women seized the initiative and voted in local elections. A 1796 statute specifically excluded black people of both sexes but reaffirmed white women's right to vote.[39]

By 1800, however, criticism of women as voters in New Jersey had mounted. Some concern was voiced about occasional voting by wives and daughters who lived at home (and were thus not independent) and by men without property. When an 1807 referendum election revealed extensive fraud, the legislature moved to tighten suffrage requirements. All women were excluded on the grounds that they were easily manipulated by men. But at the same time the state expanded suffrage to include propertyless white men and sons living at home, further emphasizing the different political stature of men and women.

The results in New Jersey lend credence to the conclusion that, while men gained as a result of the Revolution, white women actually lost ground. After 1800, as states granted universal white male suffrage, women's exclusion from suffrage defined their political dependence and inequality more sharply than ever before. But to define women's experience solely in terms of their formal political and legal roles obscures other significant factors that shaped their lives. For many women, the revolutionary years sparked a political consciousness, one that encouraged women to move outside their preoccupations of home and family. At the same time, improvements in white women's education — the substantial number of revolutionary women's diaries and letters indicate that more women had become fully literate — helped to broaden women's vision and open some opportunities.

The move for improved education for both men and women accelerated after the war — for practical as well as ideological reasons. As the new nation began the long process of industrialization, its more complex economy required literacy and other skills. Formal education became more necessary as print replaced oral traditions. Americans also believed that the new republic required an educated, enlightened citizenry. Thomas Jefferson understood that schools were now needed to "instruct the mass of our citizens in these their rights, interests and duties, as men and citizens."[40] For women, the interest in educational reform was linked to the civic good. Observers roundly criticized the type of education elite white women most often received. Beyond basic literacy, women were taught domestic skills and refinements meant to enhance their position in the marriage market. But what sort of wife and mother could such a poorly educated woman become? The image of flighty women concerned primarily with fashion and sentimental novels seemed especially out of step with the expectations of the new nation.

Critics who addressed the issue of women's education at length included Mercy Otis Warren (see Figure 3.1, p. 154), Judith Sargent Murray, and Dr. Benjamin Rush. Although they challenged conventional assumptions that more fully educating women would make them less feminine and more discontented with their lot, these critics rarely recommended that women be educated primarily to move beyond the domestic sphere. Most of the proponents of improved education for women articulated an ideology that historians have called Republican Motherhood, the idea that women had vital roles in educating their children for their duties as citizens. One notable advocate, Abigail Adams, wrote, "If we mean to have heroes, statesmen, and philosophers, we should have learned women. If as much depends as it is allowed upon the early education of youth and the first principles which are instilled take the deepest root great benefit must arise from the literary accomplishments in women."[41] In addition to this emphasis on children, the ideology of the postrevolutionary years stressed that women's enlightened and virtuous influence on their husbands could contribute mightily to civic culture and order. (See Documents: Education and Republican Motherhood, pp. 174–80.)

The new thinking about women's education bore some fruit. Not only did some states, like Massachusetts in 1789, institute free elementary public schooling for all children, but academies and boarding schools specifically designed for middle-class and elite women proliferated in the North and eventually appeared in the

South. Parents and educators expected that this enhanced education would, according to one historian, "allow women to instruct their sons in the principles of patriotism, to make their homes well-run havens of efficiency, to converse knowledgeably with their husbands on a variety of subjects, and to understand family finance."[42] Rather than discouraging women from domestic pursuits, education was expected to improve their chances for a suitable and happy marriage. But many of the women educated at the new academies apparently were inspired to move beyond the household sphere. Some became famous as writers, missionaries, or reformers, and a substantial number became teachers themselves, pursuing jobs that offered the earliest form of professional opportunity for American women. The ideology of Republican Motherhood and the educational reforms it inspired began a long process of expanded opportunities for women. Eventually women would demand opportunities to learn as much as, and even alongside, men.

WOMEN AND RELIGION: THE GREAT AWAKENING

In addition to education, religion was crucial in the new conception of white womanhood arising in the last half of the eighteenth century. Waves of religious revivalism had begun as early as the 1730s and 1740s, inspired by English minister George Whitefield's preaching tours throughout the English colonies. Known as the Great Awakening, these outpourings of evangelical fervor reached their greatest intensity between the 1750s and the 1770s, especially in the South, where revivalism touched both blacks and whites. Complex theological issues were involved, but the one essential ingredient was conversion—an immediate and ecstatic religious experience. The Great Awakening split established churches and created increasing numbers of converts to new denominations, such as the Baptists and the Methodists, whose evangelicalism emphasized an emotional spiritual rebirth. Evangelical worshippers gathered outside, in fields and pastures, where their religious joy could have physical expression; the converted were likely to shout and jump about. Evangelicalism validated the religious experience of ordinary people. In challenging religious authority and church hierarchy, it promoted a new egalitarianism with an appeal that cut across gender, class, race, and slave status.

White Women's Religious Fervor

For much of the eighteenth century, women in New England churches, for which we have the most information, outnumbered men. Historians suggest that as men became increasingly involved in the region's thriving trade and business, they lost interest in a religion that required submission and restraint. Women, in contrast, were accustomed to subordination. Moreover, repeated experiences with the dangers of childbirth heightened their concern with salvation and spiritual matters. The Great Awakening temporarily brought many men back to the churches. But even as it slightly diminished women's numerical majority in their congregations, its egalitarianism and challenge to traditional orthodoxy nonetheless offered

◆ **The Great Awakening**
English evangelical preacher George Whitefield traveled between the
colonies and Britain in the 1740s and 1750s, helping to ignite the Great
Awakening. This mid-eighteenth-century painting depicts Whitefield's
charismatic effect on his audience. Given how deeply engaged women
were in the Great Awakening, it is appropriate that the image highlights a
young woman. Her transfixed gaze and the light that shines on her reinforce the sense that she is experiencing spiritual illumination. *National
Portrait Gallery, London.*

women a greater voice in religious worship and church affairs than had been available to women previously, with the exception of Quaker meetings (see p. 80).

Most commonly, Christian women's voices were heard as they offered their
dramatic conversion narratives, accounts of how they came to experience Jesus
Christ in their souls. They also made their presence known by their physical manifestations of the spirit—they wept and cried out, they moved and flailed around.
A Massachusetts woman, Sarah Sparhawk, was so physically affected that she

seemed "unbounded, and like one deprived of her reason."[43] While some ministers welcomed this display as evidence for their power as preachers, others resented what they saw as a distraction from their religious message. Some also worried about the unseemliness of women's physical expression of conversion.

Two radical religious groups centered around charismatic women who broke dramatically with tradition. Jemima Wilkinson, a former Quaker, believed that she was the female incarnation of Christ and attracted a host of devoted followers, primarily in Rhode Island and Connecticut (see Figure 3.5, p. 159). Mother Ann Lee, a founder of the "Shaking Quakers," or more simply "Shakers" (so named for the ecstatic dances that were part of their worship), styled herself as a preacher and prophet. In different ways both of these remarkable women minimized their femaleness. Wilkinson dressed in male-style clothing and refused to answer to her female name, insisting that she be called the Public Universal Friend. Lee required celibacy not only for herself but also for her followers. This adamant denial of sexuality blocked the issue of gender from undercutting her religious leadership.

In newer congregations, such as northern Baptist churches, women could vote to elect deacons and even "exhort," or act as a lay preacher. One of the more radical groups, the Separates, or Strict Congregationalists, explicitly affirmed women in their "just Right . . . to speak openly in the Church."[44] In the South, only one group, the Separate Baptists, permitted women official roles, appointing them as deaconnesses and eldresses. A Baptist minister traveling in Virginia and the Carolinas in the early 1770s described the duties of the eldresses as "praying, and teaching at their [women's] separate assemblies; presiding there for maintenance of rules and government; consulting with sisters about matters of the church which concern them, and representing their sense thereof to the elders; attending at the unction of sick sisters; and at the baptism of women, that all may be done orderly."[45]

But none of the larger denominations accepted women as preachers equal to male ministers. In backcountry regions, some women may have been traveling preachers, but generally their roles, even in evangelical churches, were unofficial. Typically, they served as counselors. Women created informal religious groups, encouraging friends and families along the road to conversion. Sarah Osborn of Newport, Rhode Island (not the same Sarah Osborn who participated in the Revolutionary War), organized a young women's religious society in 1737 that met more or less continuously for fifty years. In the 1760s, she expanded her focus and on Sunday evenings taught a group of African Americans in her home. Osborn had to tread carefully, however. Like Anne Hutchinson a century earlier, she was criticized for usurping the role of male ministers. She was therefore careful to explain that "to avoid Moving beyond [her] Line" she did not "instruct" married men or teenaged boys. She even justified her outreach to black men and women by characterizing both as "no otherwise now then children tho for Stature Men and Women."[46] Despite her willingness to picture herself as staying within the confines of traditional women's roles—of teaching other women, black men, and children—Osborn resisted suggestions that she halt her activities, sharply asking one critic, "[Would you] advise me to shut up my Mouth and doors and creep into obscurity?"[47] Throughout her life, she continued to exert considerable influence within her congregation, an experience shared by many women in evangelical churches throughout the country.

By 1800, the ability of white women to be active in doctrinal disputes and matters of church discipline and procedures diminished. In northern Baptist churches, for example, women's public voices were increasingly silenced after the Revolution. As the Baptists matured as a religious denomination, a growing bureaucracy and a new emphasis on an educated ministry eroded women's position in favor of men. Establishing respectability for the church often meant controlling "disorderly" women. This shift in women's influence was accomplished despite the fact that women outnumbered men in the congregation almost two to one, yet another indication that the egalitarian spirit of the postrevolutionary era did not encompass white women.

This suppression of women's voices was not long-lived, however. Beginning around 1795, another series of revivals, loosely categorized as the Second Great Awakening, swept the nation in periodic waves, lasting through the 1830s. In the eighteenth century, women's role in evangelical religion paralleled their course in the public sphere, where the ideas formulated around Republican Motherhood articulated a civic role for patriotic women that was only partially realized. Yet both evangelical religion and Republican Motherhood formed an important rationale for women's expanding roles in a wide range of benevolent and reform associations, other areas of informal public space that white women claimed as their own in the nineteenth century.

African American Women's Religious Lives

The religious ferment that so powerfully affected white women also touched the lives of many African American women. Too little is known about early African American women's spiritual world to make many generalizations. But we do know that the Africans herded aboard the slave ships brought with them diverse religions, including Islam. Most West African groups believed in a supreme being, as well as a series of lesser divinities, and venerated their ancestors. They had a rich variety of rituals, especially those connected to birth and death. Women played significant roles in religious expression, often serving as healers, mediums, or priestesses.

Only slowly did slaves convert to Christianity. The missionary efforts of the Society for the Propagation of the Gospel, founded in 1701 in London with a major goal to convert enslaved Africans throughout British America, made little headway. Masters resisted efforts to proselytize among their slaves, in part because they used the perceived difference between civilized Christians and "savage pagans" to rationalize slavery. Slaves themselves apparently showed little interest in the religion of their masters. There were notable exceptions, such as Phillis Wheatley, a New England slave who became a noted poet. (See Documents: Phillis Wheatley, Poet and Slave, pp. 169–73, and Figure 3.3, p. 156.)

Yet during and after the Revolution, the Great Awakening had a broad impact on slave women's lives. A few evangelical churches explicitly condemned the institution of slavery, and some slaveholders, moved by the evangelical message, freed their slaves or, at the least, encouraged their slaves to become Christians. Evangelicals within the Methodist and Baptist churches, especially the Separate Baptists in the South, reached out to the poor and uneducated, generally welcoming black converts. Scholars suggest other factors that made the evangelical Protestantism attractive to black Americans. The evangelical emphasis on spontaneous conversion harmonized with West African beliefs that "the deity entered the body of the devotee and displaced his or her personality."[48] Southern slaves syncretized this new form of Protestantism with their traditional religion to create a distinctive religious style. In turn, African influences—especially dances and shouts typical of West African religious rituals—influenced the shape of white evangelicalism.

Like white women, black women were highly visible in revivals. A 1741 account told of a "Moorish" woman on a South Carolina plantation "singing a spiritual at the waters edge." This same "heathen woman," according to her sympathetic owner, had a few days earlier "attained a certain assurance of the forgiveness of sins and the mercy of God in Christ, and that she, along with others who love Christ, was shouting and jubilating because of this treasure." Another observer described a black Virginia woman in 1776 who "clapped her hands in an ecstasy of joy."[49] Historians suggest that since many small southern revivals started in the household, slave women's role in bringing others to the conversion experience may have been significant, replicating the white women's role of counselor: "Within this setting, women became the principal creators of an affective style of worship and of revival culture more generally."[50] Although black women were rarely permitted to be preachers in eighteenth-century evangelical churches, they were able to create a sphere of influence and power for themselves, roles that would assume even greater importance in the nineteenth century, when the majority of slaves had adopted Christianity.

CONCLUSION: To the Margins of Political Action

Whatever their social or racial group, women living on the eastern part of the continent in the late eighteenth century were affected by the imperial conflicts that eventually resulted in the founding of a new nation. Most women's activities were filtered through traditional expectations about their female roles: slave women tried to protect their children; Native Americans maintained villages while men were at war; elite ladies sewed shirts for George Washington's army; poor women cooked for soldiers. Yet despite these traditional trajectories—and despite the fundamentally male character of eighteenth-century diplomacy, politics, and warfare—women did exercise some choice in the revolutionary era. They acted politically when they decided to escape slavery by fleeing to the British, when they participated in their native councils' deliberations over alliances, or when they chose to be loyalists or patriots.

The revolutionary era's dramatic events affected women in widely varying ways. Slave women in the North benefited from gradual emancipation, while many in the South suffered from their owners' deepening commitment to the institution of slavery. Many Native American women saw their traditional roles erode under the pressures of assimilation, yet most scholars marvel at their resilience and adaptability. White women's positions became more limited in some respects, as white men's political rights expanded while women's remained static.

But if the Revolution did not prompt a deep-seated questioning of women's rights and roles, it did embody harbingers of change, especially for white women. The economic expansion of the new nation would lead to industrial development and an expanded presence of women in the paid workforce. The U.S. territorial expansion would not only promote western migration of white women and their families but also significantly affect Native Americans and slaves. In addition, revolutionary ideology, educational advancements, and the egalitarianism of the Great Awakening sowed the seeds for greater participation of middle-class and elite women in public life, not in politics per se, but in informal spheres of public spaces — churches, benevolent societies, and reform movements — which were to be such an important part of nineteenth-century American culture.

VISUAL SOURCES

Portraits of Revolutionary Women

B Y THE MIDDLE OF THE EIGHTEENTH CENTURY, portraiture flourished in America. Its success was in part a product of prosperous colonials' enthusiasm for consumer goods. Imported items—textiles, furniture, china, and books—filled their homes and served as marks of refinement. Paintings also were signs of status and taste. While artists like Charles Willson Peale, John Singleton Copley, and Benjamin West were fine painters, they owed some of their success to their ability to produce images that heightened their subjects' self-images. These men, as well as a large number of lesser painters, turned out portraits that adorned their owners' homes much like fine furnishings. This enthusiasm for portraiture produced a sizable number of images of women, many of whom were prominent in the revolutionary era.

The 1763 portrait by John Singleton Copley shown in Figure 3.1 makes Mercy Otis Warren's high status quite clear. She is dressed in a rich fabric with elegant trimmings. The picture also emphasizes her femininity. Contemporaries understood the nasturtiums entwined in her hands as symbols of fertility, and indeed she had given birth the year before she sat for this portrait and would have another child the following year.

Warren and her husband, James, a politician and prosperous merchant, lived with their five children in Boston. She was active in politics and had close ties to her colony's revolutionary leadership through her husband, her brother James Otis (also a political leader), and her friends John and Abigail Adams. In private letters, she ruminated about the propriety of women's participation in politics, writing to one friend in 1774 that she understood that the topic was "a subject . . . much out of the road of female attention." Yet, she continued, "as every domestic enjoyment depends on the decision of the mighty contest, who can be an unconcerned and silent spectator? not surely the fond mother, or the affectionate wife who trembles lest her dearest connections should fall victims of lawless power, or at least pour out the warm blood as a libation at the shrine of liberty."[51]

But Warren went far beyond the role of concerned and informed mother and wife, becoming famous for her pamphlets, poems, and plays, many of which are social satires or political commentaries. In plays such as *The Defeat* (1773) and *The Affrighted Officers* (1776), she castigated the pro-British local officials and loyalists. She also produced widely circulated poems celebrating revolutionary exploits such as the Boston Tea Party and exhorting women to uphold the boycotts against British goods. After the war, she published two major works. With *Poems, Dramatic and Miscellaneous* (1790), she became one of three American women to have published

◆ **Figure 3.1** **John Singleton Copley, *Mercy Otis Warren* (1763)**
*John Singleton Copley, American, 1738–1815. Mrs. James Warren (Mercy Otis), about 1763. Oil on canvas.
126.05 × 100 cm (49⅝ × 39½ in.). Museum of Fine Arts, Boston. Bequest of Winslow Warren, 31.212. Photograph © 2004 Museum of Fine Arts, Boston.*

a book of poems, joining Anne Bradstreet and Phillis Wheatley. Her 1805 *History of
the Rise, Progress and Termination of the American Revolution,* a monumental three-
volume work, reflected Warren's deep commitment to the cause of the Revolution
and her hope for America's future as a repository of republican virtue.

Consider Warren's bearing and pose in this portrait. What sort of personality
do they suggest? How does Copley reveal Warren as a woman of many accomplishments?

◆ Figure 3.2 *Abigail Adams* (1785, artist unknown)
Fenimore Art Museum, Cooperstown, New York.

The portrait shown in Figure 3.2 gives us a visual record of one of the most admired of American first ladies, Abigail Adams. Dating from 1785, it was painted in London, where her husband, John Adams, future president of the United States, was serving in a diplomatic capacity. Abigail Adams's charm and brilliance come down to us through her extensive correspondence. Her letters from the revolutionary era reveal the able way in which she managed her family's farm in Braintree, Massachusetts, while her husband attended to politics in Boston and Philadelphia.

But Adams was more than an impressive "deputy husband." Like other women of her day, she had not been formally schooled, but she had access to an excellent library and acquired a sophisticated education. In her extensive correspondence to John and to friends like Mercy Otis Warren, Adams commented extensively on pressing political questions of the day.

In contrast to Warren, Adams did not write for publication; she made her mark on public life through informal channels. She offered advice freely to her husband. In 1776, as John participated in the Continental Congress, Abigail urged the assembled men, "Remember the Ladies, and be more generous and favourable to them than your ancestors. Do not put such unlimited power into the hands of the Husbands. Remember all Men would be tyrants if they could. If perticuliar care and attention is not paid to the Ladies we are determined to foment a Rebelion, and will not hold ourselves bound by any Laws in which we have no voice, or Representation."[52] While some historians have used this passage to portray Abigail Adams as a staunch feminist, most agree that the comment was made partly in jest and that she did not envision radical challenges to the prevailing sexual hierarchy and, in particular, was not advocating women's political equality. However, Adams did feel that women should be given more protections in law and strongly advocated for women's improved education so as to meet the prevailing goals of Republican Motherhood.

How does this portrait indicate Abigail Adams's status as an elite woman? Had the artist been portraying an elite man involved in the politics of the era, how might the portrait be different? How does Adams's projected image differ from that of Mercy Otis Warren (Figure 3.1)?

Figure 3.3, a portrait of Phillis Wheatley (see Documents: Phillis Wheatley, Poet and Slave, pp. 169–73), was not intended as an ornament for her home or that of her masters. Rather, it was commissioned as the frontispiece for her book, *Poems on Various Subjects, Religious and Moral* (1773). Wheatley's owner had sent the poems to London bookseller Archibald Bell, who in turn had taken them to an antislavery noblewoman, the Countess of Huntington, to receive permission for Wheatley to dedicate the book to her, a common practice designed to enhance a book's prestige. Huntington, enthusiastic about the poems, apparently asked for reassurance that the author was "*real, without a deception.*" Perhaps to offer proof to future readers that Wheatley was indeed a black slave, the countess requested a picture of Wheatley for the frontispiece. The painting was executed by another slave, Scipio Moorhead, owned by a Boston minister, and sent to England for engraving. Wheatley appreciated Moorhead's talents as an artist and wrote the following poem to "SM. a young *African* painter":

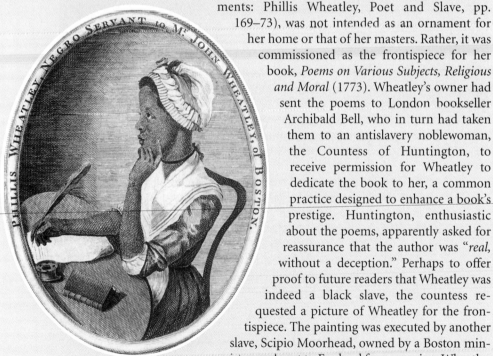

◆ Figure 3.3 **Scipio Moorhead,** *Phillis Wheatley* **(1773)**
Courtesy of the Massachusetts Historical Society.

To show the lab'ring bosom's deep intent,
and though in living characters to paint,
When first thy pencil did those beauties give,
And breathing figures learnt from thee to live,
How did those prospects give my soul delight,
A new creation rushing on my sight?
Still, wond'rous youth! each noble path pursue,
On deathless glories fix thine ardent view:
Still may the painter's and the poet's fire
To aid thy pencil, and thy verse conspire![53]

Why do you think Wheatley was so pleased by the portrait? Why do you suppose the painting includes the information that Wheatley was "servant to Mr. John Wheatley"?

Mum Bett, later Elizabeth Freeman, was born a slave, either in New York or Massachusetts, and eventually became the property of Colonel John Ashley of Sheffield, Massachusetts. In 1781, Mum Bett sued her master for her freedom. Her case, *Brom and Bett v. Ashley,* was one of several cases in Massachusetts that in 1783 led to the state supreme court's ruling that slavery was invalid in the state. Historians are not certain what circumstances led Mum Bett to her unusual course of action. One story, possibly apocryphal, indicates that she ran away from Ashley's home after receiving a blow from a heated shovel. A later account by novelist Catherine Sedgwick, the daughter of Freeman's lawyer Theodor Sedgwick, claimed that Freeman made her decision after hearing the Declaration of Independence (see the Appendix, p. A-1). It is also possible that she and her fellow slave Brom were chosen by prominent men interested in testing the constitutionality of slavery in Massachusetts. After her freedom, Mum Bett adopted the name Elizabeth Freeman and spent the rest of her life as a beloved paid servant to the Sedgwick family. When she died in 1829, Catherine Sedgwick's brother, Charles, wrote the following epitaph for her tombstone: "She was born a slave and remained a slave for nearly thirty years. She could neither read nor write, yet in her own sphere she had no superior nor equal. She neither wasted time nor property. She never violated a trust, nor failed to perform a duty. In every situation of domestic trial, she was the most efficient helper, and the tenderest friend. Good Mother, farewell."[54]

The watercolor portrait in Figure 3.4 was painted in 1811 by Susan Sedgwick, Catherine's sister-in-law. Freeman's dress is vivid blue, and she wears what is apparently a gold necklace around her neck. Why do you suppose the Sedgwick family made the effort (through the portrait and the poem) to document Freeman's life? What is the artist hoping to convey about Freeman in this portrait?

The turning point in Jemima Wilkinson's life came in October 1776 when she fell ill from a fever. When she recovered, she announced that she had died and been resurrected. She renamed herself Public Universal Friend and, as the text notes (see p. 149), became a charismatic evangelical preacher who emphasized the golden

◆ **Figure 3.4 Susan Anne Livingston Ridley Sedgwick, *Elizabeth Freeman ("Mum Bett")* (1811)**
Courtesy of the Massachusetts Historical Society.

rule of treating others as one wishes to be treated. Her followers had numerous congregations in Rhode Island and Connecticut; in 1785 they established a Friend's community in the frontier region of New York, where Wilkinson hoped they might be free from the worldly evils.

The portrait of Wilkinson at the age of sixty-three in Figure 3.5 was painted in 1816 by John L. D. Mathies, a self-taught artist living in the Guyanoga valley of

New York where Wilkinson lived at the end of her life. It gives us a glimpse of the self-styled prophetess. Wilkinson's insistence on obliterating her sex went beyond her refusal to answer to her name and her insistence that her followers avoid the feminine pronouns of "she" and "her" when referring to their leader. After hearing her preach in New Haven, Connecticut, one critical observer described her in 1787 as wearing "a light cloth Cloke with a Cape like a Man's—Purple Gown, long' sleeves to Wristbands—Mans shirt down to the Hands with neckband—purple handkerchief or Neckcloth tied around the neck like a man's—No Cap—Hair combed turned over & not long—wears a Watch—Man's Hat."[55]

How does Mathies present Wilkinson's gender in this portrait? Although Wilkinson's style of dress may have stemmed from her religious belief that she had died and been resurrected and thereby transcended her sex, why else might she have preferred male attire?

Deborah Sampson, whose portrait is in Figure 3.6, shared two things in common with Jemima Wilkinson. Like Wilkinson, she had been profoundly influenced by religious revivalism and became a Baptist in 1780. But her Middleborough, Massachusetts, church expelled her in 1780 for "dressing in men's clothes, and enlisting as a Soldier in the Army."[56] Sampson's cross-dressing may have dated to her days as an indentured servant, when she apparently sometimes performed farm labor, traditionally done by men, dressed in men's clothes.

At age eighteen, her period of indenture concluded, she became a masterless woman, an unusual status in the colonial era, having neither husband, father, nor a master to whom she was bound. This gave her rare freedom for a woman, and she moved from town to town, working sometimes as a teacher, sometimes as a weaver. Perhaps this freedom contributed to her startling course of action.

Beginning in 1782, for eighteen months, Sampson assumed men's clothing and the name Robert Shurtleff while she served as a soldier in the Fourth Massachusetts Regiment

◆ **Figure 3.5** *Jemima Wilkinson* **(1816)**
Courtesy of the Rhode Island Historical Society. RHi X3 1671.
Anonymous, from Memoir of Jemima Wilkinson, *1844. Lithograph.*

in the American Revolution. She was wounded twice before being discovered and honorably discharged. With the help of her friend Paul Revere, she later was successful in obtaining a small military pension from the U.S. Congress. Shortly after the war Sampson married and had three children. Then in 1802, she once again flouted convention by becoming a public lecturer. Dressed in a uniform and carrying a musket, she gave public talks about her military service and performed gun drills. Although she appeared at times apologetic for her "uncouth actions," she also

DEBORAH SAMPSON.

Published by H. Mann, 1797.

◆ **Figure 3.6 Joseph Stone, *Deborah Sampson* (1797)**
Special Collections and Archives, Charles E. Shain Library, Connecticut College.

pronounced, "I burst the tyrant bonds which held my sex in awe and clandestinely or by stealth, grasped an opportunity which custom and the world seemed to deny, as a natural privilege."[57]

Joseph Stone painted Sampson's portrait in 1797 under the commission of author Herman Mann, who used the imagery in the frontispiece of his book, *The Female Review: or Memoirs of an American Lady.* Mann interviewed Sampson for his book, although scholars argue that Mann invented many details to make for an even more dramatic story. He emphasized Sampson's desire for patriotic service but was careful not to dwell on her "masculine" qualities. He also took pains to stress her chastity, which "she had been taught to revere, even as dear as life itself."[58] Why do you think that Mann chose to feature a portrait depicting Sampson as a genteel young woman? How might this image of Sampson have fit with the contemporary call for Republican Motherhood? Based on what you have read, how do you think Sampson would have reacted to such an image?

QUESTIONS FOR ANALYSIS

1. How do the portraits presented here differ from one another? What factors might account for those differences?

2. How realistic are the portrayals of the women in these portraits? Are portrayals by professional artists more or less accurate, do you think, than the portrayals by amateur artists?

3. What roles do dress, props, and background play in defining the characteristics of the sitter?

Gendering Images of the Revolution

IN ADDITION TO THE REPRESENTATIONS OF American women contained in the portraits of the late eighteenth century are a variety of other images specifically connected to the American Revolution. Many of these—whether paintings or cartoons—had propagandistic purposes. Few portray actual women and instead render females as abstractions, often as icons of "Liberty."

◆ **Figure 3.7 "A Society of Patriotic Ladies" (1774)**
Library of Congress LC-USZ62-12711.

Englishmen on both sides of the Atlantic often ridiculed women's interest in fashion and represented them as weak-minded and frivolous. These negative stereotypes about women took on propagandistic value in Figure 3.7, a British cartoon, "A Society of Patriotic Ladies," created as a response to the fifty-one women of Edenton, North Carolina, who signed a pledge in 1774 to uphold the boycotts against British goods. By depicting fashionable women neglecting their children (note the child on the floor being licked by a dog) and acting in unfeminine ways (note the grotesque woman with the gavel), the cartoon devalues the boycott and American women at the same time.

Consider the choices of the cartoonist. Why do you think he decided to include a black servant in his drawing? Why did he depict the woman in the center being fondled by a man?

A number of images of women holding muskets circulated during the revolutionary era. Scholars think that the 1770 drawing in Figure 3.8 was modeled after a 1750 woodcut of Hannah Snell, an Englishwoman who had joined the British navy in 1745. Though *Miss Fanny's Maid* predates the outbreak of fighting, it coincides with the disruptive atmosphere of Boston in the 1770s. The American illustration was probably not intended to refer to a specific woman bearing arms; the story of cross-dressing Deborah Sampson (see p. 132) was not made public until 1781, for example. What do you think might have been the purpose of this image for revolutionary propagandists?

The tendency to depict women as abstractions was most evident in the widespread popularity of images of "Liberty." The convention of using a stylized woman to represent political virtues such as liberty or justice was a long-standing one in western European art, though, as one historian explains, "the female form [of liberty] does not refer to particular women, does not describe women as a group, and often does not even presume to evoke their natures."[59] Instead, this idealized image was intended to embody the principles for which men were fighting.

◆ **Figure 3.8** *Miss Fanny's Maid* **(1770)**
Courtesy, American Antiquarian Society.

◆ **Figure 3.9** **"Banner of Washington's Life Guard"** (date unknown)
Special Collections, John D. Rockefeller Jr. Library, Colonial Williamsburg Foundation.

Figure 3.9, "Banner of Washington's Life Guard," was used to represent a group of military men attached to General Washington. How do we know that this image is not of a real woman but is rather a symbol? What other symbols of the Revolution can you identify?

A more complex rendering of a female version of liberty appeared in the well-known painter Edward Savage's engraving "Liberty in the Form of the Goddess of Youth Giving Support to the Bald Eagle," created in 1796. In Figure 3.10, the youthful Liberty, clad in white with a garland of flowers, nourishes an eagle, who symbolizes the Republic. In the background is the flag of the union with a liberty cap. At the bottom right, lightning surrounds the British fleet in the Boston harbor. Crushed under Liberty's feet are symbols of the British monarchy: a key, a broken scepter, and the garter of a royal order. This version of Liberty was so popular that it was reproduced in many forms—including needlework—well into the nineteenth century. Why do you think Savage depicts Liberty as a "goddess of youth"? Why was the image so popular with Americans?

◆ Figure 3.10 **Edward Savage, "Liberty in the Form of the Goddess of Youth Giving Support to the Bald Eagle" (1796)**
Worcester Art Museum, Worcester, Massachusetts, gift of Mrs. Kingsmill Marrs.

◆ **Figure 3.11 Signpost for a Tavern (1777)**
Wadsworth Atheneum, Hartford. Bequest of Emma Bell King.

This type of image also appeared in commercial usage, as indicated in Figure 3.11, the signpost for a tavern in Bissell's Ferry, East Windsor, Connecticut. The sign was made originally in 1777 and then repainted in 1781 and 1801. Why would a tavern choose to feature a female icon of liberty? When the sign became worn, why do you think the tavern owners decided to repaint the original rather than create a new sign?

◆ **Figure 3.12** **Samuel Jennings,** *Liberty Displaying the Arts and Sciences* **(1792)**
The Library Company of Philadelphia.

A somewhat unusual depiction of a female Liberty had more radical political meaning than most versions. Figure 3.12 suggests the way in which revolutionary ideology ignited questions about women's and slaves' freedom. *Liberty Displaying the Arts and Sciences,* by Samuel Jennings (1792), was initially suggested by the artist himself to the Library Company of Philadelphia, an institution founded by Benjamin Franklin and others in 1731. The directors specifically asked Jennings to portray a tableau of "Liberty (with her Cap and proper Insignia) displaying the arts by some of the most striking Symbols of Painting, Architecture, Mechanics, Astronomy, &ca. whilst She appears in the attitude of placing on the top of a Pedestal, a pile of Books, lettered with, *Agriculture, Commerce, Philosophy & Catalogue of Philadelphia Library.*"[60] The directors, many of whom were active antislavery advocates, also requested the inclusion of African Americans and the symbolic broken chains. In the image, Liberty is offering a book to the grateful African Americans.

Examine the images associated with Liberty. What do they suggest? What did the library directors hope to convey in combining a depiction of Liberty, books, and freed slaves?

QUESTIONS FOR ANALYSIS

1. How do these diverse images of women contribute to our understanding of how gender shaped the experience of the American Revolution?

2. The images presented here have propagandistic purposes. If images of men had been used instead, how would they be different?

3. How can historians analyze these propagandistic images in the effort to reconstruct the actual experiences of women in the revolutionary era?

DOCUMENTS

Phillis Wheatley, Poet and Slave

EIGHTEENTH-CENTURY AMERICAN WOMEN left behind far more written material than those in the seventeenth century; we have diaries, letters, essays, and books to help us flesh out the lives of many women, especially educated white women. The experiences of individual black women are far more obscure in the historical record, with the important exception of poet Phillis Wheatley (c. 1753–1784). At age seven or eight, Wheatley, who was probably from the Gambia area of the West Coast of Africa, was brought to Boston as a slave. Her owners, John and Susannah Wheatley, were immediately impressed with her precociousness. "Without any Assistance from School Education, and by only what she was taught in the Family, she, in sixteen Months Times from her Arrival, attained the English Language, to which she was an utter Stranger before, to such a Degree, as to read any, the most difficult Parts of the Sacred Writings, to be the great Astonishment of all who heard her."[61] The Wheatleys, especially Susannah and her daughter Mary, took pride in their slave's learning but also in her quick and deeply felt conversion to Protestantism. Their own evangelical beliefs made them open to the notion of blacks' spiritual equality and led them to encourage Wheatley's religious and intellectual gifts.

Wheatley began writing poetry as early as 1765 and apparently published her first poem in 1767. By 1772, she had attempted, with the help of Susannah Wheatley and other sponsors, to publish a book of collected works in Boston. When that venture failed, she found a publisher in London and had the opportunity to accompany the son of her owner to London where she was able to complete the arrangements for *Poems on Various Subjects, Religious and Moral* (1773). At about the same time, her owners granted her freedom.

After the publication of her book, Wheatley continued to write, undeterred by her sadness at the deaths of her former owners, Susannah Wheatley in 1774 and John Wheatley in 1778, or by her own marriage in 1778 to a free black, John Peters. Her poems, such as one in honor of General George Washington, were published individually, but she failed to gain backing for her proposal, printed in the *Evening Post* and *General Advertiser* (1779), in which she described herself as a "female African" who sought subscriptions to print a second book of poems and letters to be dedicated to Benjamin Franklin. Other disappointments followed. Toward the end of her life she worked as a scrubwoman in a boardinghouse. Two of her children died, and she and her third baby died of complications in childbirth on December 8, 1784.

Because of the profoundly religious content of much of her work, Wheatley's poetry was warmly received by evangelical Protestants, both in England and in America. Apparently some slaveowners read Wheatley's poems to their slaves to encourage their conversion. Opponents of slavery also welcomed the poet's work, viewing her as proof of the humanity and capabilities of Africans.

LETTERS

TWENTY-TWO OF WHEATLEY'S LETTERS have survived. The first one, printed below, is to a black friend, Arbour Tanner, a servant to James Tanner in Newport, Rhode Island, who shared Wheatley's religious ardor. The letter refers to a frequent theme in the poet's work: the conversion of her fellow Africans. What is the purpose of Wheatley's letter to Tanner?

To Arbour Tanner

Boston May 19th 1772

Dear Sister

I rec'd your favour of February 6th for which I give you my sincere thanks, I greatly rejoice with you in that realizing view, and I hope experience, of the Saving change which you So emphatically describe. Happy were it for us if we could arrive to that evangelical Repentance, and the true holiness of heart which you mention. Inexpressibly happy Should we be could we have a due Sense of the Beauties and excellence of the Crucified Saviour. In his Crucifixion may be seen marvellous displays of Grace and Love, Sufficient to draw and invite us to the rich and endless treasures of his mercy, let us rejoice in and adore the wonders of God's infinite Love in bringing us from a land Semblant of darkness itself, and where the divine light of revelation (being obscur'd) is as darkness. Here, the knowledge of the true God and eternal life are made manifest;

But there, profound ignorance overshadows the Land, Your observation is true, namely that there was nothing in us to recommend us to God. Many of our fellow creatures are pass'd by, when the bowels of divine love expanded towards us. May this goodness & long Suffering of God lead us to unfeign'd repentance

It gives me very great pleasure to hear of so many of my Nation, Seeking with eagerness the way to true felicity, O may we all meet at length in that happy mansion. I hope the correspondence between us will continue, (my being much indispos'd this winter past was the reason of my not answering yours before now) which correspondence I hope may have the happy effect of improving our mutual friendship. Till we meet in the regions of consummate blessedness, let us endeavor by the assistance of divine grace, to live the life, and we Shall die the death of the Righteous. May this be our happy case and of those who are travelling to the region of Felicity is the earnest request of your affectionate

Friend & hum. Sert. Phillis Wheatley

SOURCE: Julian D. Mason Jr., ed., *The Poems of Phillis Wheatley* (Chapel Hill: University of North Carolina, 1989), 190.

THE FOLLOWING LETTER, to Rev. Samson Occom, a Mohegan Indian and Presbyterian minister, was published in the *Connecticut Gazette; and the Universal Intelligencer,* March 11, 1774, and widely reprinted. Written after Wheatley had gained freedom, it is her most critical statement about slavery. What is the essence of her criticism?

To Rev. Samson Occom

Rev'd and honor'd Sir,

I have this Day received your obliging kind Epistle, and am greatly satisfied with your Reasons respecting the Negroes, and think highly reasonable what you offer in Vindication of their natural Rights: Those that invade them cannot be insensible that the divine Light is chasing away the thick Darkness which broods over the Land of Africa; and the Chaos which has reign'd long, is converting into beautiful Order, and [r]eveals more and more clearly the glorious Dispensation of civil and religious Liberty, which are so insep[a]rably united, that there is little or no Enjoyment of one without the other. Otherwise, perhaps, the Israelites had been less solicitous for their Freedom from Egyptian slavery; I do not say they would have been contented without it, by no means, for in every human Breast, God has implanted a Principle which we call Love of Freedom; it is impatient of Oppression and pants for Deliverance; and by the Leave of our modern Egyptians I will assert, that the same Principle lives in us. God grant Deliverance in his own Way and Time and get him honour upon all those whose Avarice impels them to countenance and help forward the Calamities of their fellow Creatures. This desire not for their Hurt, but to convince them of the strange Absurdity of their Conduct whose Words and Actions are so diametrically opposite. How well the Cry for Liberty, and the reverse Disposition for the exercise of oppressive Power over others agree, — I humbly think it does not require the Penetration of a Philosopher to determine.

SOURCE: Mason, *Poems of Phillis Wheatley,* 203–4.

POEMS

OVER FIFTY OF WHEATLEY'S POEMS have survived. They encompass a wide range of topics, from elegies to thoughts "On Virtue," from religious commentaries to a patriotic ode to George Washington. Her references to Africa, Africans, and slavery are particularly interesting for the ways in which her poetry insists on the humanity of Africans and makes criticisms—sometimes veiled—of slavery.

On the surface, this 1772 poem seems to adopt white Christians' condescension toward pagan Africans, but what does the final line suggest?

On Being Brought from Africa to America

'Twas mercy brought me from my *Pagan* land,
Taught my benighted soul to understand
That there's a God, that there's a *Saviour* too:

Once I redemption neither sought nor knew.
Some view our sable race with scornful eye,
"Their colour is a diabolic die."
Remember, *Christians, Negroes,* black as Cain,
May be refin'd, and join th' angelic train.

SOURCE: Mason, *Poems of Phillis Wheatley,* 53.

THE FOLLOWING POEM, addressed to the British secretary of state for North America, was written in a period when tensions had eased—temporarily—between the colonies and the mother country, hence Wheatley's statement in the second stanza about grievances being addressed. The poem reveals not only her sensitivity to the political turmoil of the period but also her understanding of the parallels between the colonists' desire to resist British "enslavement" and her own people's experience of slavery. What does she seem to be asking Lord Dartmouth for in the final stanza?

To the Right Honourable William, Earl of Dartmouth, His Majesty's Principal Secretary of State for North America, &C.

HAIL, happy day when, smiling like the morn,
Fair *Freedom* rose *New-England* to adorn:
The northern clime beneath her genial ray,
Dartmouth, congratulates thy blissful sway:
Elate with hope her race no longer mourns,
Each soul expands, each grateful bosom burns,
While in thine hand with pleasure we behold
The silken reins, and *Freedom's* charms unfold.
Long lost to realms beneath the northern skies

She shines supreme, while hated *faction* dies:
Soon as appear'd the *Goddess* long desir'd,
Sick at the view, she languish'd and expir'd;
Thus from the splendors of the morning light
The owl in sadness seeks the caves of night.

No more, *America,* in mournful strain
Of wrongs, and grievance unredress'd complain,

No longer shalt thou dread the iron chain,
Which wanton *Tyranny* with lawless hand
Had made, and with it meant t' enslave the land.

Should you, my lord, while you peruse my song,
Wonder from whence my love of Freedom
        sprung,
Whence flow these wishes for the common good,
By feeling hearts alone best understood,
I, young in life, by seeming cruel fate
Was snatch'd from *Afric's* fancy'd happy seat:
What pangs excruciating must molest,
What sorrows labour in my parent's breast?
Steel'd was that soul and by no misery mov'd
That from a father seiz'd his babe belov'd:
Such, such my case. And can I then but pray
Others may never feel tyrannic sway?

For favours past, great Sir, our thanks are due,
And thee we ask thy favours to renew,

SOURCE: Mason, *Poems of Phillis Wheatley,* 82–83.

Since in thy pow'r, as in thy will before,
To sooth the griefs, which thou did'st once
    deplore.
May heav'nly grace the sacred sanction give
To all thy works, and thou for ever live
Not only on the wings of fleeting *Fame,*

Though praise immortal crowns the patriot's
    name,
But to conduct to heav'ns refulgent fane,
May fiery coursers sweep th' ethereal plain,
And bear thee upwards to that blest abode,
Where, like the prophet, thou shalt find thy God.

QUESTIONS FOR ANALYSIS

1. What do these selections of Wheatley's poems and letters reveal about the importance and role of religion in her life?

2. What are the grounds for her criticism of slavery?

3. How might opponents of slavery have used her poetry to criticize the institution?

DOCUMENTS

Education and Republican Motherhood

FOR MUCH OF THE COLONIAL PERIOD, women's opportunities for education were quite limited. A small number of slave women were instructed by benevolent owners, and some Native American women had access to missionary schools where the emphasis was on assimilation rather than education. White women had little formal schooling, and their training usually emphasized domestic skills with a smattering of reading and sums. By the time of the Revolution in New England, 90 percent of white men could write, while fewer than half of white women could.

The Revolution and its aftermath ushered in significant changes. Outside the South, where public schools were rare, primary public education for white women and men became more common. Women's opportunities for higher education—while not universally endorsed—also expanded. While some of the most famous schools, like Philadelphia's Young Ladies Academy, were in urban areas, educational entrepreneurs also established them in small towns such as Litchfield, Connecticut, where Sarah Pierce's school attracted young women from throughout the region, as well as from other states. The Bethlehem, Pennsylvania, Moravian Seminary had special appeal for parents eager to give their daughters a rigorous education; in addition to academic subjects, the school encouraged its students' industry and moral development. While the new schools still offered ornamental skills such as needlework and dancing, they emphasized academic subjects such as history, grammar, geography, logic, and philosophy.

The post-Revolution improvement in white women's education was in part a product of the efforts of reformers, who eagerly promoted the idea that in a republic, all citizens needed education to contribute to the general public good. In keeping with the ideas associated with Republican Motherhood (see p. 146), supporters of women's education argued that mothers needed to be well educated to prepare their children, especially their sons, for their duties as citizens. Advocates also emphasized the importance of women's influence on their husbands. While a number of people participated in the call for expanded opportunities, including Mercy Otis Warren and Sarah Pierce, two of the most significant, whose writings are reproduced here, were Dr. Benjamin Rush and Judith Sargent Murray.

"A PECULIAR MODE OF EDUCATION"

BENJAMIN RUSH SIGNED the Declaration of Independence and was the preeminent physician and medical teacher of the revolutionary era. His essay *Thoughts upon Female Education* reflects both increased expectations as well as the limits to new ideas about women's education. The curriculum he promoted included geography, bookkeeping, reading, and arithmetic and omitted the traditional female accomplishment of needlework. But he did not recommend that women study advanced mathematics, natural philosophy, or Latin or Greek, subjects that remained hallmarks of educated men. Rush and most other reformers emphasized the utilitarian potential of an academic curriculum for women. Although Rush lectured to both men at the College of Philadelphia and women at the Philadelphia Young Ladies Academy on natural philosophy, his presentation for the latter—"Lectures, Containing the Application of the Principles of Natural Philosophy, and Chemistry to Domestic and Culinary Purposes"—was tailored to their perceived future roles. Still, Rush's views were progressive for his time, when many people felt that too much learning might "unsex" a woman and make her unfeminine.

The following selection is from an essay based on a speech Rush gave to the Board of Visitors of the Young Ladies Academy of Philadelphia in 1787. As you read, take note of Rush's major justifications for educating women.

Benjamin Rush
Thoughts upon Female Education (1787)

There are several circumstances in the situation, employments and duties of women in America which require a peculiar mode of education.

I. The early marriages of our women, by contracting the time allowed for education, renders it necessary to contract its plan and to confine it chiefly to the more useful branches of literature.

II. The state of property in America renders it necessary for the greatest part of our citizens to employ themselves in different occupations for the advancement of their fortunes. This cannot be done without the assistance of the female members of the community. They must be the stewards and guardians of their husbands' property. That education, therefore, will be most proper for our women which teaches them to discharge the

SOURCE: Frederick Rudolph, ed., *Essays on Education in the Early Republic* (Cambridge: Belknap Press of Harvard University Press, 1965), 27–40.

dutics of those offices with the most success and reputation.

III. From the numerous avocations to which a professional life exposes gentlemen in America from their families, a principal share of the instruction of children naturally devolves upon the women. It becomes us therefore to prepare them, by a suitable education, for the discharge of this most important duty of mothers.

IV. The equal share that every citizen has in the liberty and the possible share he may have in the government of our country make it necessary that our ladies should be qualified to a certain degree, by a peculiar and suitable education, to concur in instructing their sons in the principles of liberty and government.

V. In Great Britain the business of servants is a regular occupation, but in America this humble station is the usual retreat of unexpected indigence; hence the servants in this country possess less knowledge and subordination than are required from them; and hence our ladies are obliged to attend more to the private affairs of their families than ladies generally do of the same rank in Great Britain. "They are good servants," said an American lady of distinguished merit . . . in a letter to a favorite daughter, "who will do well with good looking after." This circumstance should have great influence upon the nature and extent of female education in America.

[Rush proceeds to discuss the most important "branches of literature most essential for a young lady in this country," in which he emphasizes "a knowledge of the English language," "the writing of a fair and legible hand," "some knowledge of figures and bookkeeping," so that she "may assist her husband with this knowledge," "an acquaintance with geography and some instruction in chronology [history]," vocal music and dancing, "the reading of history, travels, poetry, and moral essays," and the "regular instruction in the Christian religion."]

A philosopher once said, "let me make all the ballads of a country and I care not who makes its laws." He might with more propriety have said, let the ladies of a country be educated properly, and they will not only make and administer its laws, but form its manners and character. It would require a lively imagination to describe, or even to comprehend the happiness of a country where knowledge and virtue were generally diffused among the female sex. . . .

The influence of female education would be still more extensive and useful in domestic life. The obligations of gentlemen to qualify themselves by knowledge and industry to discharge the duties of benevolence would be increased by marriage; and the patriot—the hero—and the legislator would find the sweetest reward of their toils in the approbation and applause of their wives. Children would discover the marks of maternal prudence and wisdom in every station of life, for it has been remarked that there have been few great or good men who have not been blessed with wife and prudent mothers.

"ALL THAT INDEPENDENCE WHICH IS PROPER TO HUMANITY"

ALTHOUGH JUDITH SARGENT MURRAY (1751–1820), the daughter of a distinguished and wealthy Gloucester, Massachusetts, family, also believed in the tenets of Republican Motherhood, she was far more radical than Rush in her approach to women's capabilities and needs. Murray's parents denied her the opportunity for the extensive education that they provided for her brother, but she was a voracious reader of both American and European writers. A contemporary of the Englishwomen historian Catharine Macaulay and women's rights activist Mary Wollstonecraft, Murray was an early American proponent of women's rights and an accomplished writer. Intensely religious, she had left the Puritan fold for Universalism, a far more egalitarian faith that encouraged her to challenge traditional authority. Already influenced by her religion, as well as her frustration over her limited schooling, Murray was further energized by the ideas swirling around the American Revolution that led her to articulate her belief in men's and women's mental and spiritual equality. As she contemplated the themes of liberty, equality, and independence, she struggled with her own dependence.

After she was widowed in 1787, her second marriage in 1788, like her first, provided little financial security, and she was highly conscious of the legal and financial constraints on women. It is not surprising, then, that many of her essays call for an education that would help women to be self-reliant and even self-supporting. She pointed out that she would want her daughters to be taught "industry and order." They "should be enabled to procure for themselves the necessaries of life; independence should be placed within their grasp."[62] Unlike reformers such as Rush who saw women's education primarily as a tool for promoting the family and the public good, Murray understood it as something contributing to women's independence, to a reverence of self. But she shared with more conventional reformers the assumption that most women would marry and have children and that women's improved education would make them better wives and virtuous Republican Mothers.

The essay excerpted here contains Murray's most radical statements concerning women's capabilities. It is the final installment of a four-part series, "Observations on Female Abilities," and highlights the accomplishments of two women. Why do you think Murray chose those women? How do you account for the seeming shift in tone and argument in the last two paragraphs?

Judith Sargent Murray
Observations of Female Abilities (1798)

We take leave to repeat, that we are not desirous to array THE SEX in martial habiliments;° we do not wish to enlist our women as soldiers; and we request it may be remembered, that we only contend for the *capabilities* of the female mind to become possessed of any attainment within the reach of *masculine exertion*. We have produced our witnesses; their depositions have been heard: the cause is before the public; we await their verdict; and, as we entertain all possible veneration for the respectable jury, we shall not dare to appeal from their decision.

But while we do homage to the women of other times, we feel happy that nature is no less bountiful to the females of the present day. We cannot, indeed, obtain a list of the names that have done honour to their Sex, and to humanity during the period now under observation: The lustre of those minds, still enveloped in a veil of mortality, is necessarily muffled and obscure: but the curtain will be thrown back, and posterity will contemplate, with admiration, their manifold perfections. . . . Nor is America destitute of females, whose abilities and improvements give them an indisputable claim to immortality. It is a fact, established beyond all controversy, that we are indebted for the discovery of our country, to female enterprize, decision and generosity. The great Columbus, after having in vain solicited the aid of Genoa, France, England, Portugal, and Spain—after having combated, for a period of eight years, with every objection that a want of knowledge could propose, found, at last, his only resource in the penetration and magnanimity of Isabella of Spain, who furnished the equipment,

°Characteristic garments or furnishings.

SOURCE: Sheila L. Skemp, ed., *Judith Sargent Murray: A Brief Biography with Documents* (Boston: Bedford, 1998), 145–49.

and raised the sums necessary to defray the expenses on the sale of her own jewels; and while we conceive an action, so honourable to THE SEX, hath not been sufficiently applauded, we trust, that the equality of the female intellect to that of their brethren, who have so long usurped an unmanly and unfounded superiority, will never, in this younger world, be left without a witness. We cannot ascertain the number of ingenious women, who at present adorn our country. In the shade of solitude they perhaps cultivate their own minds, and superintend the education of their children. Our day, we know, is only dawning—But when we contemplate a Warren [Mercy Otis Warren—see Figure 3.1, p. 154], a Philenia [Sarah Wentworth Morton, poet and novelist], &c. &c. we gratefully acknowledge, that genius and application, even in the female line, already gild, with effulgent radiance, our blest Aurora.

But women are calculated to shine in other characters than those adverted to, in the preceding Essays; and with proper attention to their education and subsequent habits, they might easily attain that independence, for which a [Mary] Wollstonecraft hath so energetically contended; the term, *helpless widow,* might be rendered as unfrequent and inapplicable as that of *helpless widower;* and although we should undoubtedly continue to mourn the dissolution of wedded amity, yet we should derive consolation from the knowledge, that the infant train had still a remaining prop, and that a mother could assist as well as weep over her offspring.

That women have a talent—a talent which, duly cultivated, would confer that independence, which is demonstrably of incalculable utility, every attentive observer will confess. THE SEX should be taught to depend on their own efforts, for the procurement of an establishment in life. The chance of a matrimonial coadjutor, is no more than a probable contingency; and if they were early accustomed to regard this *uncertain* event with suitable *indifference* they would make elections with that deliberation, which would be calculated to give a more rational prospect of tranquility. All this we have repeatedly asserted, and all this we do invariably believe. To neglect polishing a gem, or obstinately to refuse bringing into action a treasure in our possession, when we might thus accumulate a handsome interest, is surely egregiously absurd, and the height of folly. *The united efforts of male and female* might rescue many a family from destruction, which, notwithstanding the efforts of its *individual* head, is now involved in all the calamities attendant on a dissipated fortune and augmenting debts. It is not possible to educate children in a manner which will render them *too beneficial* to society; and the more we multiply aids to a family, the greater will be the security, that its individuals will not be thrown a burden on the public.

An instance of *female capability* this moment occurs to memory. In the State of Massachusetts, in a small town, some miles from the metropolis, resides a woman, who hath made astonishing improvements in agriculture. Her mind, in the early part of her life, was but penuriously cultivated, and she grew up almost wholly uneducated: But being suffered, during her childhood, to rove at large among her native fields, her limbs expanded, and she acquired a height of stature above the common size; her mind also became invigorated; and her understanding snatched sufficient information to produce a consciousness of the injury she sustained in the want of those aids, which should have been furnished in the beginning of her years. She however applied herself diligently to remedy the evil, and soon made great proficiency in writing, and in arithmetic. She reads every thing she could procure; but the impressions adventitiously made on her infant mind still obtained the ascendancy. A few rough acres constituted her patrimonial inheritance; these she has brought into a state of high cultivation; their productions are every year both useful and ornamental; she is mistress of agricolation, and is at once a botanist and a florist. The most approved authors in the English language, on these subjects, are in her hands, and she studies them with industry and success.

She has obtained such considerable knowledge in the nature of soils, the precise manure which they require and their particular adaptation to the various fruits of the earth, that she is become the oracle of all the farmers in her vicinity and when laying out, or appropriating their grounds they uniformly submit them to her inspection. Her gardens are the resort of all strangers who happen to visit her village; and she is particularly remarkable for a growth of trees, from which, gentlemen, solicitous to enrich their fruitgardens, or ornament their parterres, are in the habit of supplying themselves; and those trees are, to their ingenious cultivator, a considerable income. Carefully attentive to her nursery, she knows when to transplant and when to prune; and she perfectly understands the various methods of inoculating and ingrafting. In short, she is a complete *husbandwoman,* and she has, besides, acquired a vast stock of general knowledge while her judgment has attained such a degree of maturity, as to justify the confidence of the villagers, who are accustomed to consult her on every perplexing emergency.

In the constant use of exercise, she is not corpulent, and she is extremely active, and wonderfully athletic. Instances almost incredible, are produced of her strength. Indeed, it is not surprising that she is the idol and standing theme of the village, since, with all her uncommon qualifications, she combines a tenderness of disposition not to be exceeded. Her extensive acquaintance with herbs, contributes to render her a skilful and truly valuable nurse; and the world never produced a more affectionate attentive or faithful woman: Yet, while she feelingly sympathizes with every invalid, she is not herself subject to imaginary complaints; nor does she easily yield to real illness. . . .

Although far advanced in years, without a matrimonial connexion, yet, constantly engaged in useful and interesting pursuits, she manifests not that peevishness and discontent, so frequently attendant on *old maids;* she realizes all that independence which is proper to humanity; and she knows how to set a just value on the blessings she enjoys.

From my treasury of facts, I produce a second instance, equally in point. I have seen letters, written by a lady, an inhabitant of St. Sebastian (a Spanish emporium), that breathed the true spirit of commerce, and evinced the writer to possess all the integrity, punctuality and dispatch, which are such capital requisites in the mercantile career. This lady is at the head of a firm, of which herself and daughters make up the individuals—Her name is *Birmingham.* She is, I imagine, well known to the commercial part of the United States. She was left a widow in the infancy of her children, who were numerous: and she immediately adopted the most vigorous measures for their emolument. Being a woman of a magnanimous mind, she devoted her sons to the profession of arms; and they were expeditiously disposed of, in a way the best calculated to bring them acquainted with the art of war. Her daughters were educated for business; and, arriving at womanhood, they have long since established themselves into a capital trading-house, of which, as has been observed, their respectable mother is the head. She is, in the hours of business, invariably to be found in her counting-house; there she takes her morning repast; her daughters act as clerks (and they are adepts in their office), regularly preparing the papers and letters, which pass in order under her inspection. She signs herself, in all accounts and letters, *Widow Birmingham;* and this is the address by which she is designated. I have conversed with one of our captains, who has often negociated with her the disposal of large and valuable cargoes. Her consignments, I am told, are to a great amount; and one of the principal merchants in the town of Boston asserts, that he receives from no house in Europe more satisfactory returns. Upright in their dealings, and unwearied in their application, these ladies possess a right to prosperity; and we trust that their circumstances are as easy, as their conduct is meritorious.

"Would you, good Mr. Gleaner, station us in the counting-house?" No, my fair country-women, except circumstances unavoidably pointed the way. Again I say, I do but hold up to your view, the *capability* of your Sex; thus stimulating you to cultivate your talents, to endeavour to acquire general knowledge, and to aim at making your-selves so far acquainted with some particular branch of business, as that it may, if occasion requires, assist in establishing you above that kind of dependence, against which the freeborn mind so naturally revolts. Far be it from me, to wish to unsex you—I am desirous of preserving, by all means, those amiable traits that are considered as characteristic—I reverence the modesty and gentleness of your dispositions—I would not an-nihilate a single virtue; but I would assiduously augment the faithfulness and affection of your bosoms. An elegant panegyrist of your Sex, hath assigned you the superiority in the feelings of the heart; and I cannot more emphatically conclude my subject, than in his beautifully pathetic lan-guage:

"The pleasures of women must arise from their virtues. It is by the cradle of their children, and in viewing the smiles of their daughters, or the sports of their sons, that mothers find their happiness. Where are the powerful emotions of nature? Where is the sentiment, at once sublime and pathetic, that carries every feeling to excess? Is it to be found in the frosty indifference, and the sour severity of some fathers? No—but in the warm and affectionate bosom of a *mother*. It is she, who, by an impulse as quick as involuntary, rushes into the flood to preserve a boy, whose imprudence had betrayed him into the waves—It is she, who, in the middle of a conflagration, throws herself across the flames to save a sleeping infant—It is she, who, with dishevelled locks, pale and distracted, embraces with transport, the body of a dead child, pressing its cold lips to her's, as if she would reanimate, by her tears and her caresses, the insensible clay. These great expres-sions of nature—these heart-rending emotions, which fill us at once with wonder, compassion and terror, always have belonged, and always will belong, only to Women. They possess, in those moments, an inexpressible something, which car-ries them beyond themselves; and they seem to discover to us new souls, above the standard of humanity."

QUESTIONS FOR ANALYSIS

1. What do Rush and Murray see as the benefits of female education? How does the proper education of females differ from that of males?

2. What do Rush and Murray assume about the abilities of females?

3. How do Rush's and Murray's ideas accord with the ideas associated with Republican Motherhood?

NOTES

1. Mary Beth Norton and Ruth M. Alexander, eds., *Major Problems in American Women's History,* 2nd ed. (Lexington, MA: D.C. Heath, 1996), 81.

2. Mary Beth Norton, *Liberty's Daughters: The Revolutionary Experience of American Women, 1750–1800* (Boston: Little, Brown, 1980), 166.

3. Ibid., 167.

4. Cynthia Kierner, *Beyond the Household: Women's Place in the Early South, 1700–1835* (Ithaca, NY: Cornell University Press, 1998), 75.

5. Norton, *Liberty's Daughters,* 164.

6. Ibid., 168.

7. Ibid., 159.

8. Kierner, *Beyond the Household,* 80–81.

9. Norton, *Liberty's Daughters,* 159.

10. *Virginia Gazette,* September 15, 1774.

11. Marylynn Salmon, *The Limits of Independence: American Women, 1760–1800* (New York: Oxford University Press, 1994), 58.

12. Norton, *Liberty's Daughters,* 169.

13. Colin G. Calloway, *First Peoples: A Documentary Survey of American Indian History* (Boston: Bedford/St. Martin's, 2004), 159

14. Benjamin Quarles, *The Negro in the American Revolution* (Chapel Hill: University of North Carolina Press, 1961), 135.

15. Ibid., 142.

16. Linda K. Kerber, *Women of the Republic: Intellect and Ideology in Revolutionary America* (Chapel Hill: University of North Carolina Press, 1980), 52.

17. Ibid., 54.

18. Holly A. Mayer, *Belonging to the Army: Camp Followers and Community during the American Revolution* (Columbia: University of South Carolina Press, 1996), 20.

19. Kerber, *Women of the Republic,* 59.

20. Ibid., 57.

21. Mayer, *Belonging to the Army,* 124.

22. Kerber, *Women of the Republic,* 64.

23. Catherine Van Cortlandt, "Secret Correspondence of a Loyalist Wife," in Robert Marcus and David Burner, eds., *America Firsthand,* 4th ed. (Boston: Bedford, 1997), 2:109–11.

24. Norton, *Liberty's Daughters,* 80.

25. Ibid., 184.

26. Ibid., 187.

27. Ibid., 194.

28. Theda Perdue, *Cherokee Women: Gender and Culture Change, 1700–1835* (Lincoln: University of Nebraska Press, 1998), 111.

29. Peter Kolchin, *American Slavery, 1619–1877* (New York: Hill and Wang, 1993), 78.

30. Salmon, *Limits of Independence,* 111.

31. Jeffrey J. Crow, *The Black Experience in Revolutionary North Carolina* (Raleigh: North Carolina Department of Cultural Resources, 1977), 17.

32. Kierner, *Beyond the Household,* 99.

33. Barbara E. Lacey, "Women in the Era of the American Revolution: The Case of Norwich, Connecticut," *New England Quarterly* 53 (December 1980): 539.

34. Norton, *Liberty's Daughters,* 216.

35. Ibid., 223–24.

36. Ibid., 171.

37. Ibid., 188–89.

38. Kerber, *Women of the Republic,* 163–64.

39. Linda Grant De Pauw, *Founding Mothers: Women in America in the Revolutionary Era* (Boston: Houghton Mifflin, 1975), 100.

40. Salmon, *Limits of Independence,* 82.

41. De Pauw, *Founding Mothers,* 211.

42. Norton, *Liberty's Daughters,* 287.

43. Catherine A. Brekus, *Strangers and Pilgrims: Female Preaching America, 1740–1845* (Chapel Hill: University of North Carolina Press, 1998), 47.

44. Ibid., 49.

45. Ibid., 63–64.

46. Norton, *Liberty's Daughters,* 130.

47. Ibid., 130.

48. Sylvia R. Frey and Betty Wood, *Come Shouting to Zion: African-American Protestantism in the American South and British Caribbean to 1830* (Chapel Hill: University of North Carolina Press, 1998), 13.

49. Ibid., 110–11.

50. Ibid., 109.

51. Kerber, *Women of the Republic,* 83–84.

52. Nancy Neims Parks, "Abigail Adams," in John A. Garraty and Mark C. Carnes, eds., *American National Biography* (New York: Oxford University Press, 1999), 1:64.

53. Sidney Kaplan and Emma Nogrady Kaplan, *The Black Presence in the Era of the American Revolution,* rev. ed. (Amherst: University of Massachusetts Press, 1989), 181.

54. Bethany K. Dumas, "Elizabeth Freeman," in John A. Garraty and Mark C. Carnes, eds., *American National Biography* (New York: Oxford University Press, 1999), 8:440.

55. Brekus, *Strangers and Pilgrims,* 87.

56. Alfred F. Young, *Masquerade: The Life and Times of Deborah Sampson, Continental Soldier* (New York: Vintage, 2004), 80.

57. Julie Wheelwright, *Amazons and Military Maids: Women Who Dressed as Men in Pursuit of Life, Liberty, and Happiness* (London: Pandora, 1989), 133.

58. Sarah Purcell, *Sealed with Blood: War, Sacrifice, and Memory in Revolutionary America* (Philadelphia: University of Pennsylvania Press, 2002), 117.

59. Marina Warner, *Monuments and Maidens: The Allegory of the Female Form* (New York: Atheneum, 1985), 12.

60. Edwin Wolf II and Marie Elena Korey, *Quarter of a Millennium: The Library Company of Philadelphia 1731–1981* (Philadelphia: The Company, 1981), 79.

61. Daniel C. Littlefield, *Revolutionary Citizens: African Americans, 1776–1804* (New York: Oxford University Press, 1997), 14.

62. Kerber, *Women of the Republic,* 205.

SUGGESTED REFERENCES

General Works In *The Limits of Independence: American Women, 1760–1800* (1994), Marylynn Salmon provides a brief overview of the revolutionary era, and in *Revolutionary Mothers: Women in the Struggle for American Independence* (2005), Carol Berkin focuses specifically on the revolution. Crucial scholarly works are Linda K. Kerber, *Women of the Republic: Intellect and Ideology in Revolutionary America* (1980), and Mary Beth Norton, *Liberty's Daughters: The Revolutionary Experience of American Women, 1750–1800* (1980). For a review essay, see Jan E. Lewis, "A Revolution for Whom? Women in the Era of the American Revolution," in Nancy A. Hewitt, ed., *A Companion to Women's History* (2002), 83–99.

Women and the American Revolution Analyses of women's contributions to the colonists' efforts to resist British expanded control over the colonies are found in Linda Grant De Pauw, *Four Traditions: Women of New York during the American Revolution* (1974), and Cynthia Kierner, *Beyond the Household: Women's Place in the Early South, 1700–1835* (1998), as well as in the Salmon and Norton studies. The best sources on Native Americans are Colin G. Calloway, *The American Revolution in Indian Country* (1995), and "New England Algonquins in the American Revolution," in *Algonkians of New England: Past and Present,* Dublin Seminar for New England Folklife Annual Proceedings 1991, 51–165. On African American women and the Revolution, see Jeffrey J. Crow, *The Black Experience in Revolutionary North Carolina* (1977); Jeffrey J. Crow and Larry E. Tise, eds., *The Southern Experience in the American Revolution* (1978); Jacqueline Jones, *Labor of Love, Labor of Sorrow: Black Women, Work and the Family, from Slavery to the Present* (1985); Sidney Kaplan and Emma Nogrady Kaplan, *The Black Presence in the Era of the American Revolution* (1989); Cynthia Kierner, *Beyond the Household: Women's Place in the Early South, 1700–1835* (1998); Mary Beth Norton, "The Fate of Some Black Loyalists of the American Revolution," *Journal of Negro History* 58 (1973): 402–26; and Benjamin Quarles, *The Negro in the American Revolution* (1961; repr. 1996). On Phillis

Wheatley, see Charles W. Akers, "'Our Modern Egyptians': Phillis Wheatley and the Whig Campaign against Slavery in Revolutionary Boston," *Journal of Negro History* 60 (1975): 397–410, and Sondra O'Neale, "Slave's Subtle War: Phillis Wheatley's Use of Biblical Myth and Symbol," *Early American Literature* 21 (1986), 144–59.

Studies that focus primarily on white women's experience in the Revolution include Sally Smith Booth, *The Women of '76* (1973); Linda Grant De Pauw and Conover Hunt, *"Remember the Ladies": Women in America, 1750–1815* (1976); Mary Beth Norton, "What an Alarming Crisis Is This: Southern Women and the American Revolution," in Jeffrey J. Crow and Larry E. Tise, eds., *The Southern Experience in the American Revolution* (1978); and Alfred F. Young, "The Women of Boston: 'Persons of Consequence' in the Making of the American Revolution, 1765–76," in Harriet B. Applewhite and Darline G. Levy, eds., *Women and Politics in the Age of the Democratic Revolution* (1990). Two accounts of individual women provide insight into the problems conflicting loyalties created. See Patricia Cleary, *Elizabeth Murray: A Woman's Pursuit of Independence in Eighteenth-Century America* (2000), and John W. Jackson, *Margaret Morris: Her Journal with Biographical Sketch and Notes* (1949). On camp followers, see Holly A. Mayer, *Belonging to the Army: Camp Followers and Community during the American Revolution* (1996). For the story of Deborah Sampson, see Alfred F. Young, *Masquerade: The Life and Times of Deborah Sampson, Continental Soldier* (2004).

Revolutionary Legacies for Women   On revolutionary legacies for Native Americans, see Colin G. Calloway, *The American Revolution in Indian Country* (1995), and Theda Perdue, *Cherokee Women: Gender and Culture Change, 1700–1835* (1998). Other studies that do not address the Revolution specifically but provide valuable insights are Daniel R. Mandell, "Shifting Boundaries of Race and Ethnicity: Indian-Black Intermarriage in Southern New England, 1760–1880," *Journal of American History* 85 (1998): 466–501, and Margaret Connell Szasz, "'Poor Richard' Meets the Native American: Schooling for Young Indian Women in Eighteenth-Century Connecticut," *Pacific Historical Review* 49 (1980): 215–35. For African Americans, see Ira Berlin, *Many Thousands Gone: The First Two Centuries of Slavery in North America* (1998); Ira Berlin and Ronald Hoffman, eds., *Slavery and Freedom in the Age of the American Revolution* (1983); Gary B. Nash and Jean R. Soderlund, *Freedom by Degrees: Emancipation in Pennsylvania and Its Aftermath* (1991); Shane White, *Somewhat More Independent: The End of Slavery in New York City, 1770–1810* (1991); T. Stephen Whitman, *The Price of Freedom: Slavery and Manumission in Baltimore and Early National Maryland* (1997); Betty Wood, *Gender, Race, and Rank in a Revolutionary Age* (2000); and Arthur Zilversmith, "Quok Walker, Mumbet, and the Abolition of Slavery in Massachusetts," *William and Mary Quarterly* 25 (1968): 614–24.

There is an extensive literature that addresses the impact of revolutionary ideology on American women. See essays in Madelon Cheek, "'An Inestimable Prize,' Educating Women in the New Republic: The Writings of Judith Sargent Murray," *Journal of Thought* 20 (1985): 250–62; Joan R. Gundersen, "Independence, Citizenship, and the American Revolution," *Signs* 13 (1987): 59–77; R. M. Janes, "On the Reception of Mary Wollstonecraft's *A Vindication of the Rights of Woman*," *Journal of the History of Ideas* 39 (1978): 293–302; Mark E. Kann, *The Gendering of American Politics: Founding Mothers, Founding Fathers, and Political Patriarchy* (1997); Mary Kelley, "'Vindicating the Equality of Female Intellect': Women and Authority in the Early Republic," *Prospects* 17 (1992): 1–28; Linda K. Kerber, *No Constitutional Right to Be Ladies: Women and the Obligation of Citizenship* (1998); Jan Lewis, "The Republican Wife: Virtue and Seduction in the Early Republic," *William and Mary Quarterly*, 3rd ser., 44 (1987): 689–721; Margaret A. Nash, "Rethinking Republican Motherhood: Benjamin Rush and the Young Ladies' Academy of Philadelphia," *Journal of the Early Republic* 17 (1997): 171–91; Sheila L. Skemp, ed., *Judith Sargent Murray: A Brief Biography with Documents* (1998); and Rosemarie Zagarri, "Morals, Manners, and the Republican Woman," *American Quarterly* 44 (June 1992): 192–215. On women and divorce, see Norma Basch, *Framing American Divorce: From the Revolutionary Generation to the Victorians* (1999), and for New Jersey suffrage, see Judith Apter Klinghoffer and Lois Elkis, "'The Petticoat Electors': Women's Suffrage in New Jersey, 1776–1807," *Journal of the Early Republic* 12 (1992): 159–93.

Women in the Great Awakening   On women in the Great Awakening, see Catherine A. Brekus, *Strangers and Pilgrims: Female Preaching America, 1740–1845* (1998); Susan Juster, *Disorderly Women: Sexual Politics and Evangelicism in Revolutionary New England* (1994); and Stephen J. Stein, *The Shaker Experience in America: A History of the United Society of Believers* (1992). On African American women in particular, see Sylvia R. Frey and Betty Wood, *Come Shouting to Zion: African-American Protestantism in the American South and British Caribbean to 1830* (1998); Albert G. Raboteau, *Slave Religion: The "Invisible Institution" in the Antebellum South* (1978); and Mechal Sobel, *The World They Made Together: Black and White Values in Eighteenth-Century Virginia* (1987).

For selected Web sites, please visit the *Through Women's Eyes* book companion site at bedfordstmartins.com/duboisdumenil.

4

Pedestal, Loom, and Auction Block

1800–1860

Lucy Larcom spent her teenage years as a mill worker in the new factory town of Lowell, Massachusetts, on the Merrimack River. In 1835, at the age of eleven, she had moved to Lowell with her widowed mother, who had taken a job as manager of one of the company-owned boardinghouses to support herself and her children. For Lucy, working in the textile factory, a "rather select industrial school for young people," was the formative experience of her life, and she carried the memory into her future career as a poet and writer.[1] She loved doing work that was significant to the larger society and wrote of "the pleasure we found in making new acquaintances among our workmates." But in later years she became uneasy with the condescension of those who called themselves ladies toward her humble past as a factory girl. "It is the first duty of every woman to recognize the mutual bond of universal womanhood," Larcom wrote in her memoirs. "Let her ask herself whether she would like to hear herself or her sister spoken of as a shopgirl or a factory-girl or a servant-girl, if necessity had compelled her for a time to be employed."[2]

Larcom's experiences embodied two of the three crucial elements shaping the lives of women in the United States during the first half of the nineteenth century. First she subscribed to the influential ideology of womanhood, home life, and gender relations that treated women as fundamentally different from men; this ideology placed women on a pedestal, simultaneously elevated and isolated by their special domestic role. Second, Larcom was participating in the first wave of American industrialization, a process that dramatically redirected the young nation's economy and created new dimensions of wealth and poverty, levels of production and consumption, and ways of life. Historians tend to identify these two elements with two different and emerging classes — domestic ideology with the middle class, industrialization with the working class — but through the eyes of women like Lucy Larcom, it is possible to see that they were mutually influential.

The very cotton fibers that mill girls like Larcom spun and wove indicate the third major element considered in this chapter: slavery. By the nineteenth century, slavery was a regional social and economic system but one with profound national implications. Slavery was of incomparable importance to American women in the antebellum (pre–Civil War) years, not only to those who lived by or profited from unfree labor but also to those who dedicated themselves to ending slavery and, ultimately, to all who would endure the devastating conflict fought over it.

THE IDEOLOGY OF TRUE WOMANHOOD

Lucy Larcom's concern with the implications of her factory years for her character as a woman reflects a powerful ideology of gender roles that historians have variously labeled "the cult of true womanhood," "the ideology of separate spheres," or simply "domesticity." This system of ideas, which took hold in the early years of the nineteenth century just as the United States was coming into its own as an independent nation, treated men and women as complete and absolute opposites, with almost no common human traits that transcended the differences of gender. The ideology of true womanhood also saw the larger society as carved into complementary but mutually exclusive "spheres" of public and private concerns, work and home life, politics and family. "In no country has such constant care been taken as in America to trace two clearly distinct lines of action for the two sexes," declared Alexis de Tocqueville, the great French observer of American culture in the 1830s. "American women never manage the outward concerns of the family, or conduct a business, or take a part in political life; nor are they, on the other hand, ever compelled to perform the rough labor of the fields, or to make any of those laborious exertions, which demand the exertion of physical strength. No families are so poor, as to form an exception to this rule."[3]

The experience of innumerable women in antebellum America — the slave women of the South, the mill girls of the North, the impoverished widows of the new cities, the rising number of female immigrants, even the hardworking farm wives — contradicted these assertions. Yet no aspect of this complex reality seemed to interfere with the widespread conviction that this gender ideology was "true." The challenge of understanding American women's history in the first half of the nineteenth century is to reconcile the extraordinary hegemony — that is, breadth and power — of the ideology of separate spheres with the wide variety of American women's lives in these years, many of which tell a very different story.

Christian Motherhood

An ideology as culturally widespread as that of true womanhood is difficult to reduce to a set of beliefs, but several basic concepts do stand out. First and foremost, proponents situated true women in an exclusively domestic realm of home, family, and childrearing. They did not consider housewifery and childrearing as work but as an effortless expression of women's feminine natures. Action and leadership were reserved for man; inspiration and assistance were woman's province. The home over which women presided was not merely a residence or a collection of people but, to use a popular phrase, "a haven in a heartless world," where men could find solace from a grueling public existence. "The perfection of womanhood . . . is the wife and mother, the center of the family, that magnet that draws man to the domestic altar, that makes him a civilized being, a social Christian," proclaimed the popular women's magazine *Godey's Lady's Book* in 1860. "The wife is truly the light of the home."[4]

At the core of the idea of woman's sphere was motherhood. This basic contention was present in late eighteenth-century rhetoric about the importance of Republican Motherhood to the success of the American democratic experiment (see p. 146). In stark contrast to the self-serving individualism expected of men and rewarded by economic advancement in the larger world, proponents of true womanhood described motherhood as a wholly selfless activity built around service to others. Oddly enough, given the importance that American political culture placed on independence of character, maternal selflessness was seen as the very source of national well-being, training, citizens of the new nation to be virtuous, concerned with the larger good, and yet industrious and self-disciplined. Even women without children could bestow their motherly instincts on society's unloved and ignored unfortunates. "Woman's great mission is to train immature, weak and ignorant creatures, to obey the laws of God," preached author and domestic ideologue Catharine Beecher in one of her many treatises on true womanhood, "first in the family, then in the school, then in the neighborhood, then in the nation, then in the world."[5] Beecher herself was unmarried and childless (see box, "The Peculiar Responsibilities of the American Woman").

Women's expansive maternity was thought to make them natural teachers and underlay the feminization of this profession in the early nineteenth century. Whereas in the eighteenth century, teaching was seen as a fundamentally male vocation, by the nineteenth century women were increasingly regarded as best suited to instruct the young, and primary school teaching became an overwhelmingly female occupation. Especially in New England, public education was becoming widespread, and young Yankee women, literate but less expensive to hire than men, supplied the teachers. By one estimate, one-quarter of all women born in New England between 1825 and 1860 were schoolteachers at some point in their lives.[6]

Women's motherly vocation had a deeply religious dimension. True womanhood was a fervently Protestant notion, which gave a redemptive power to female devotion and selfless sacrifice. The true woman functioned as Christ's representative in daily life, and the domestic environment over which she presided served as a sort of sacred territory, where evil and worldly influences could be cleansed away. Beecher insisted that "the preparation of young ministers for the duties of the church does not surpass in importance the training of the minister of the nursery and school-room."[7]

The special identification of women with Christian piety was firmly established by a new wave of religious revivals that swept through American society in the late eighteenth and early nineteenth centuries. Beginning in the frontier communities of Ohio, Kentucky, and Indiana, the Second Great Awakening moved east by the 1810s and 1820s. Western New York was known as the "burned-over district" because of the zealous religiosity that swept through it in these years. Conveyed by preachers inspired by personal spiritual conviction rather than theological training, religious fervor especially thrived outside large cities. In the South, blacks and whites were drawn together in similar extended revivals. A cultural phenomenon with many different sources, the Second Great Awakening was a reaction both to the political preoccupations of the revolutionary period and to swift changes in the American economic system. This religious revivalism also had a populist element, as it bypassed established clerical authority in favor of more direct spiritual experience among the broad mass of the American people. New forms of Protestant worship, especially in Baptist and Methodist congregations, were evangelical, stressing personal conversion and commitment to rooting out sin in this world.

Religious enthusiasm and activism gave women, who were the majority of converts in these revivals, an arena for individual expression and social recognition that they were denied in secular politics. To establish their reputations as effective religious leaders, popular evangelical preachers relied on their female followers. Catharine Beecher's father, Lyman, and her brother, Henry Ward, were two such evangelical ministers. As for Catharine herself, she was never able to experience a full personal conversion and always doubted the depth of her religious

CATHARINE BEECHER
The Peculiar Responsibilities of the American Woman

In the first chapter of A Treatise on Domestic Economy *(1841), a book devoted to the details of childrearing and homemaking, author and domestic ideologue Catharine Beecher (1800–1878) elaborates her theory of American democracy and women's place in it. She insists that women's inclusion in the American promise of equality completely compatible with the subordination that she believed was divinely ordained in wives' relations to their husbands. More than a half century after the American Revolution, she shifted the grand political purposes served by women's special domestic role from the establishment of a stable nation to the spread of American Protestant ideals to the entire world.*

In this Country, it is established, both by opinion and by practice, that woman has an equal interest in all social and civil concerns; and that no domestic, civil, or political, institution, is right, which sacrifices her interest to promote that of the other sex. But in order to secure her the more firmly in all these privileges, it is decided, that, in the domestic relation, she take a subordinate station, and that, in civil and political concerns, her interests be intrusted to the other sex, without her taking any part in voting, or in making and administering laws. . . . In matters pertaining to the education of their children, in the selection and support of a clergy-

conviction. Nonetheless, the career she was able to build for herself as an authority on proper Christian womanhood was much assisted by the association of the Beecher name with evangelical piety.

Women's reputation for deeper religious sentiment was closely related to the assumption that the true woman was inherently uninterested in sexual expression, that she was "pure." The notion of woman's natural sexual innocence was a relatively modern concept. In traditional European Christian culture, women had been considered more dangerously sexual than men. The belief in women's basic "passionlessness," as one historian has named it, was a new idea that, in the context of the time, served to raise women's stature.[8] In the hierarchical nineteenth-century Protestant worldview, woman was less tied to humanity's animal nature than man was, and this lifted her closer to the divine. Sexual appetite in the female was virtually unimaginable.[9] These assumptions made the presence of prostitutes profoundly disturbing to nineteenth-century moralists. If women were as lustful as men, there would be no one to control and contain sexual desire. As Dr. William Sanger wrote in his pathbreaking 1860 study of prostitution in New York City,

man, in all benevolent enterprises, and in all questions relating to morals or manners, they have a superior influence. In such concerns, it would be impossible to carry a point, contrary to their judgement and feelings; while an enterprise, sustained by them, will seldom fail of success.

If those who are bewailing themselves over the fancied wrongs and injuries of women in this Nation, could only see things as they are, they would know, that . . . there is nothing reasonable, which American women would unite in asking, that would not readily be bestowed. . . . To us [Americans] is committed the grand, the responsible privilege, of exhibiting to the world, the beneficent influences of Christianity. . . . But the part to be enacted by American women, in this great moral enterprise, is the point to which special attention should here be directed. . . . The proper education of a man decides the welfare of an individual; but educate a woman, and the interests of the whole family are secured. . . .

The woman, who is rearing a family of children; the woman, who labors in the schoolroom; the woman, who, in her retired chamber, earns, with her needle, the mite, which contributes to the intellectual and moral elevation of her Country; even the humble domestic, whose example and influence may be moulding and forming young minds, while her faithful services sustain a prosperous domestic state;—each and all may be animated by the consciousness, that they are agents in accomplishing the greatest work that ever was committed to human responsibility.

SOURCE: Catharine Beecher, *A Treatise on Domestic Economy* (New York: Marsh, Capen, Lyon, and Webb, 1841), ch. 1.

"Were it otherwise, and the passions in both sexes equal, illegitimacy and prostitution would be far more rife in our midst than at present."[10] (See Documents: Prostitution in New York City, 1858, pp. 220–24.)

Starting in the 1820s, pious women expanded their religious expression beyond churchgoing to participation in a wide variety of voluntary organizations that promoted the spiritual and moral uplift of the poor and unsaved. Some of these female benevolent associations sponsored missionary efforts to bring the blessings of Christianity to unbelievers at home and abroad. By the 1830s, an extensive network of Protestant women's organizations was sending money to church missions throughout Asia and Africa. A handful of adventuresome women went to preach the gospel abroad, mostly as wives of male missionaries. Ann Hasseltine Judson, who served with her husband in the 1820s in Rangoon, Burma, was the first American woman missionary in Asia. Closer to home, female missionaries brought Christian solace to the American urban poor. Pious middle-class women joined their ministers in "friendly visiting" to preach the word of Christ to society's downtrodden and outcast.

Time, Midnight.   *Place*, not very far from the Academy of Music.
SERIOUS YOUNG LADY. "Ah! Fanny, *you* coming from the Opera!   How long have you been *gay?*"

◆ New York City Prostitutes

Whether the number of prostitutes rose dramatically in the mid-nineteenth century, as many observers charged, in large cities they were certainly more visible and thus more disturbing to the middle-class public. Prostitutes and their clients commonly frequented the "third tier" of theaters, which was informally reserved for them. As this contemporary cartoon indicates, they could even be found at the most elegant theaters. The joke in this cartoon refers to the difficulty of distinguishing between prostitutes and reputable women of fashion. The term "gay" referred to prostitution, not homosexuality, in the nineteenth century. *Culver Pictures.*

A Middle-Class Ideology

Despite the wide range of those who subscribed to its tenets, the ideology of true womanhood was a thoroughly middle-class social ethic. Certainly, the assumption that a woman should be insulated from economic demands to concentrate on creating a stable and peaceful home environment presumed she was married to a man able to support her as a dependent wife. The middle-class wife in turn was responsible for what Beecher characterized as "the regular and correct apportionment of expenses that makes a family truly comfortable."[11] The idealized true woman, presiding over a virtuous family life, was a crucial staple of the way Americans contrasted themselves with European aristocratic society. Adherence to the ideology of true womanhood also helped people of the middle classes to distinguish themselves from those they regarded as their social and economic inferiors. In their charitable activities among the poor, true women preached the gospel of separate sexual spheres and female domesticity, convinced that the absence of these family values, rather than economic forces, was what made poor people poor.

These ideas reflected changing conditions in middle-class American women's lives. The birthrate for the average American-born white woman fell from 6 in 1800 to 4.9 in 1850, in part because economic modernization meant that children were less important as extra hands to help support the family and more likely to be a financial drain. Also, technological developments—for example, the new cast-iron stove, which was easier and safer than open-hearth cooking (see Figure 2.5, p. 109)—were just beginning to ease women's household burdens. As the industrial production of cloth accelerated, women no longer had to spin and weave at home, although they still cut and sewed their family's clothes. Depending on their husbands' incomes, middle-class women might be able to hire servants to help with their labors. Even so, the middle-class housewife did plenty of work herself. Despite technological developments, leisure time was a privilege for only the very richest women. Laundry, the most burdensome of domestic obligations, remained a difficult weekly chore.

The doctrine of domesticity was elaborated by ministers in sermons and physicians in popular health books. But women themselves did much of the work of spreading these ideas. The half century in which this rigid ideology of gender flourished was also the period in which writing by women first found a mass audience among middle-class women. Lydia Sigourney, a beloved woman's poet; Mrs. E. D. E. N. Southworth, popular author of numerous sentimental novels; and Sarah Josepha Hale, editor of the influential women's magazine *Godey's Lady's*

◆ **Lilly Martin Spencer, *Washerwoman* (1854)**
Lilly Martin Spencer, an immigrant from France, was virtually the only woman in antebellum America to make a living as a painter. Despite her efforts at painting grander historical subjects, her domestic paintings were so popular that she concentrated on this genre. Her subjects included both domestic sentiments and domestic labor. She used her own servant as a model, and her paintings demonstrate an intimate knowledge of the actual labor involved in maintaining a household, as in this unusual painting of laundering. The same servant/model appears in other Spencer paintings, always robust and smiling. Spencer's own domestic life was unconventional: she had thirteen children, of whom seven survived; but with her husband's assent, she served as the family breadwinner while he tended to the household duties. *Hood Museum of Art, Dartmouth College, Hanover, New Hampshire; purchased through a gift from Florence B. Moore in memory of her husband, Lansing P. Moore, Class of 1937.*

Book (150,000 subscribers in 1860) all built successful careers elaborating the ideology of true womanhood. (See Visual Sources: *Godey's Lady's Book*, pp. 232–39.) In her influential and much reprinted *Treatise on Domestic Economy* (1841), Catharine Beecher taught that woman's sphere was a noble "profession," equal in importance and challenge to any of the tasks assigned to men. Her younger half sister, Harriet Beecher Stowe, relied heavily on the ideas of woman's sphere in her book *Uncle Tom's Cabin* (1851), which became the most widely read American novel ever written.

In the judgment of such women, the tremendous respect paid to woman's lofty state was one of the distinguishing glories of nineteenth-century America. While proponents of true womanhood insisted that woman's sphere differed from man's, they regarded it as of equal importance to society and worthy of respect. Lucy Larcom put it this way: "God made no mistake in her [woman's] creation. He sent her into the world full of power and will to be a *helper*. . . . She is here to make this great house of humanity a habitable and a beautiful place, without and within, a true home for every one of his children."[12]

The many women of the nineteenth century who energetically subscribed to the ideas of true womanhood were not brainwashed victims of a male ideological conspiracy. Private writings of middle-class women from this period, letters and diaries notably, show women embracing these ideas and using them to give purpose to their lives. Not only could the true woman claim authority over the household and childrearing, but the widespread belief in her special moral vocation legitimated certain kinds of activity outside the domestic sphere. Despite its middle-class character, the doctrine of true womanhood was strikingly widespread throughout antebellum American society. Almost the only women during this period who openly challenged its tenets were the women's rights radicals (see pp. 274–79).

Domesticity in a Market Age

By fervently insisting that women had to be insulated from the striving and bustle of the outside world, the advocates of true womanhood were implicitly responding to the impact of larger economic pressures on women's lives. The ideology of separate spheres and women's sheltered domesticity notwithstanding, women's history during this period can be understood only in the context of the burgeoning market economy. The development and growth of a cash-based market-oriented economy—as opposed to one in which people mostly produced goods for their own immediate use—reaches back to the very beginnings of American history and forward into the twentieth century. But early nineteenth-century America is rightly seen as the time in which the fundamental shift toward market-oriented production took place.

The spread of market relations had particular implications for women. In preindustrial society, men's work as well as women's was considered fundamentally domestic. Both sexes worked within and for the household, not for trade on the open market. By the eighteenth century, this was already changing as commercial transactions were growing in significance. Especially within urban areas, various household goods—soap and candles, for example, or processed foods like flour and spices—were available for purchase. By the early nineteenth century, households needed to acquire more and more cash to buy market goods to fill the needs of daily life. Acquiring this money became men's obligation.

With the rise of the market economy, much of men's work moved outside the home, and women alone did work in the domestic realm for direct use. Because work was increasingly regarded as what happened outside the home, done by men and compensated for by money, what women did in the home was becoming invisible as productive labor. From this perspective, the lavish attention the proponents of true womanhood paid to the moral significance of woman's domestic sphere might be seen as ideological compensation for the decline in its economic value.

Industrial depressions, which affected the entire society and not just the lower rungs of wage earners, were becoming a regular, seemingly inescapable characteristic of industrial society, the bust that inevitably followed the boom. In 1837, the U.S. economy, which had been growing by leaps and bounds, violently contracted, and prices dropped precipitously, banks collapsed, and wages fell by as much as a third. The Panic of 1837, as it was called for the response of investor and wage earner alike, was an early and formative experience in the life of the future women's rights leader Susan B. Anthony, whose father lost his grain mill business in that year.

Despite waning recognition of women's role in economic production, popular nineteenth-century ideology assumed that in the household women could counteract some of the more disturbing aspects of economic expansion. A woman's household management skills and emotional steadiness were supposed to be crucial in helping her family weather the shifting financial winds that were such an unnerving aspect of the new economy. "When we observe the frequent revolutions from poverty to affluence and then from extravagance to ruin, that are continually taking place around us," wrote Mrs. A. J. Graves in her popular handbook *Woman in America* (1841), "and their calamitous effects upon families brought up in luxury and idleness, have we not reason to fear that our 'homes of order and peace' are rapidly disappearing?"[13] Seen this way, the proper conduct of woman's sphere virtually became a matter of economic survival.

WOMEN AND WAGE EARNING

As Mrs. Graves's admonition indicates, the depiction of woman's sphere as unconnected to the striving and bustle of the outside world is misleading. Indeed, women felt the pressures of a cash-based, market economy in many ways. Some women found methods to earn cash remuneration for their labors. Others found ways to make money from within their households—for instance, by selling extra butter or eggs. Barely visible to a society focused on its own capacity for productive prosperity, impoverished urban women, widowed or deserted by men, scrounged or begged for pennies to buy shelter, food, and warmth.

Of all women's intersections with the cash economy and the forces of the market revolution, none was more important for women's history than the employment of young New England women like Lucy Larcom as factory operatives at the power-driven spindles and looms of the newly established American textile industry. Though their numbers were small, these young women constituted the first emergence of the female wage labor force (see the Appendix, p. A-37).

From Market Revolution to Industrial Revolution

To understand the experiences of early nineteenth-century women factory workers, we must place them in the setting of the era's industrial transformations. The growth of a market economy encouraged the centralization and acceleration of the production of goods. This industrializing process was gradual and uneven, a fact that becomes especially clear when we focus on the distinct contribution of women workers. For a long time after industrialization began, people continued to produce goods at home, even as their control over what they made and their share of its value were seriously eroded. In this transitional form of manufacture for market, male entrepreneurs, or factors, purchased the raw materials for production and distributed them to workers in their homes, then paid for the finished goods and sold them to customers. Workers no longer received the full cash value of what they had produced since the factor also made money from the process. In essence, the workers were receiving a wage for their labor instead of being paid for their products, which were no longer theirs to sell. Their labor was increasingly considered only a part, not the entirety, of the production process.

Shoemaking is a particularly interesting example, both because its transition to full industrialization was prolonged and because women and men underwent this transition at different rates. Making shoes for sale was already an established activity by the early nineteenth century, especially in cities north of Boston, notably Lynn, Massachusetts. At first, shoes were manufactured in home-based workshops in which the male head of the household was the master artisan and his wife, children, and apprentices worked under his direction. Starting in the 1820s and 1830s, a new class of shoemaking entrepreneurs brought male shoemakers, who specialized in cutting and sewing soles, to a centralized site, while women continued to sew the shoes' uppers and linings at home. By the 1840s and 1850s, women's labor was being directed and paid for by the entrepreneurs. It was not until later in the nineteenth century, after the Civil War, that women's part in shoe production moved into factories.

Clothing manufacture remained in a similar "outwork" phase for a long time. Women working at home produced most of the clothing manufactured for sale in the antebellum period. By 1860, there were sixteen thousand seamstresses in New York City alone.[14] Industrialization ravaged many of these mid-nineteenth-century poor women and their families. The manufacture of clothing did not begin to shift into factories until after the Civil War—and well into the twentieth century the workshop form of production continued to thrive, in sweatshops (see p. 339). Other industries that relied on women outworkers included straw-hat making and bookbinding. Limited to their homes by childrearing responsibilities, married women remained home-based industrial outworkers much longer than men or unmarried women. The more exclusively female that outwork became, the more poorly it paid.

Manufacturing could be said to be fully industrialized only when it shifted to a separate, centralized location, the factory, at which point home and work were fully separated. There the entrepreneurs could introduce more expensive machinery and supervise labor more closely, both intended to maximize their profits. Factories and the machines within them were the manufacturers' contribution to the process, the "capital" that gave them control and ownership over the product of the workers.

Male artisans, no longer the masters of their family workshops, experienced the shift to the factory as absolute decline; for women the shift of manufacturing to outside the home offered a more mixed experience. Factory ownership was entirely in the hands of men, and women, whose secondary status had already been established in home manufacturing, earned a much lower wage than men for tasks that were inevitably considered less skilled. Yet women's turn to factory labor also gave them the chance to earn wages as individuals, and at times to experience a taste of personal freedom. As Lucy Larcom explained, young women like herself "were clearing away a few weeds from the overgrown track of independent labor for other women."[15]

The Mill Girls of Lowell

By the 1820s textile production, one of the most important of America's early industries—and certainly the most female dominated—was decisively shifting in the direction of factory labor. If the impoverished "tailoresses" working out of their dark urban garrets stood for the depredations of industrial capital toward women, the factory girls of the textile industry came to represent the better possibilities that wage labor might offer women. And "girls" they were—unmarried, many in their teens. (See Visual Sources: Early Photographs of Factory Operatives and Slave Women, pp. 240–47.) Though they were only a tiny percentage of women—as of 1840, only 2.25 percent[16]—these first female factory workers understood themselves, and were understood by others in their society, as opening up new vistas of personal independence and economic contribution for their sex.

The story of the first women factory workers began in the American textile industry during and immediately after the War of 1812. At the beginning of the nineteenth century, Americans bought wool, linen, and cotton cloth manufactured in the textile factories of Great Britain. The war with England interrupted the transatlantic trade in factory-made cloth, creating an irresistible opportunity for wealthy New England merchants, who had heretofore made their money by importing British textiles, to invest in American-based industry. In 1814 in Waltham, Massachusetts, a group of local merchants opened the first American factory to house all aspects of textile production under one roof. In an early and daring example of industrial espionage, they had spirited out of England designs for water-driven machinery for both spinning and weaving. The investors enjoyed quick and substantial profits, and in 1823 the same group of venture capitalists opened a much larger operation twenty-three miles away, on Merrimack River farmland north of Boston. The new factory town, named after the leading figure in the merchant capital group, Francis Cabot Lowell, soon became synonymous with the energetic American textile industry and with the young women who provided its labor force.

Previously, in England and in earlier, unsuccessful efforts at factory textile production in the United States, whole families who would otherwise be destitute were the workers: Children worked the spinning machines and looms. This impoverished working population gave factory production a bad name, best captured by British poet William Blake's terrifying 1804 image of the "dark satanic mills" soiling "England's green and pleasant land."[17] Textile factories were regarded as poorhouses designed for keeping indigent people from disrupting society. Given the predominance of farming in the United States, this type of labor force was not as available to aspiring American textile industrialists. But an alternative had been identified as early as the 1790s by President George Washington's secretary of the treasury, Alexander Hamilton, an early promoter of American industrial production. Hamilton advocated hiring the unmarried daughters of farming families, who could move in and out of industrial production without becoming a permanent and impoverished wage labor force like that which haunted England. By laboring for wages in textile factories, these young women could for a time help provide their families with the cash that they increasingly required. The fact that the spinning of fiber for cloth had been the traditional work of women in the preindustrial household (especially unmarried women, hence the term "spinster") provided an additional argument for turning to a female labor force.

To the delight of New England textile capitalists, girls from Yankee farm families took to factory labor in the 1820s and early 1830s with great enthusiasm. Earning an individual wage offered them a degree of personal independence that was very attractive to these young women. Many were eager to work in the factories, despite thirteen-hour days, six-day workweeks, and wages of $1 to $2 per week.[18] "I regard it as one of the privileges of my youth that I was permitted to grow up among these active, interesting girls," Lucy Larcom wrote in her memoirs, "whose lives were not mere echoes of other lives, but had principles and purposes distinctly their own."[19] Even though they saved their wages and sent as much as possible to their families, the mill girls occasionally spent some of their earnings on themselves; for this they were regarded by contemporaries as spoiled and self-indulgent. And although their workdays were extraordinarily long and the labor much more unrelenting than that to which they were accustomed, they reveled in the small amounts of time they had for themselves in the evenings.

Larcom's reminiscences detail the lessons she and her sister attended, the writing they did, and the friendships they made. Factory girls at Lowell and elsewhere even formed female benevolent societies, as did their more middle-class counterparts.

One problem, however, stood in the way of the success of this solution to the problem of factory labor: Where were the young women workers to live? Given the scale of the labor force required by the large new factories and the decentralized character of the New England population, young women would have to be brought from their homes to distant factories. Parents were reluctant to allow their daughters to be so far from home and away from family supervision. Factory work for women, probably because it had been so dreadfully underpaid in England, was suspected of being an avenue to prostitution. The manufacturers' solution to both the housing and moral supervision dilemmas was to build boardinghouses for their young workers and to link work and living arrangements in a paternalistic approach to industrial production. Four to six young women shared each bedroom, and their behavior was closely supervised. The boardinghouses, and the camaraderie among young women that flourished there, added to the allure of factory labor. To the farm girls of New England, this was greater cosmopolitanism than they had ever known.

For about a decade, the city of Lowell and the Lowell system (as the employment of young farm girls as factory workers was called) were among the glories of the new American nation. Visitors came from Europe to see and sing the praises of the moral rectitude and industry of the women workers in this new type of factory production, free of the corruptions of the old world. "They were healthy in appearance, many of them remarkably so," Charles Dickens wrote after a visit in 1842, "and had the manners and deportment of young women; not of degraded brutes of burden."[20] The dignity and probity of the Lowell girls were crucial elements in the optimism that temporarily thrived regarding the possibilities of a genuinely democratic American version of industrial factory production, in which all could profit from the new levels of wealth. "The experiment at Lowell had shown that independent and intelligent workers invariably give their own character to their occupation," Larcom proudly wrote.[21] Young women workers wrote stories, essays, and poems about their experience at the factories for their own literary journal, the *Lowell Offering*, to put their uprightness and their intelligence on display. Larcom began her career as a writer this way. Factory owners, not insensitive to the propaganda value of such efforts, underwrote the magazine, paid the editor's salary, and distributed issues widely.

The End of the Lowell Idyll

Eventually, however, economic pressures took their toll on Lowell's great promise, at least for the workers. Declining prices for cotton and wool and investors' expectations of high returns led factory owners to slash wages. Within the first decade, wages were cut twice. The factory owners counted on the womanly demeanor of their employees to lead them to accept the cuts. But they were wrong. In 1834 and 1836, in response to lower wages, Lowell girls "turned out" — conducted

REGULATIONS

TO BE OBSERVED BY ALL PERSONS EMPLOYED IN THE FACTORIES OF THE

MIDDLESEX COMPANY.

The overseers are to be punctually in their rooms at the starting of the mill, and not to be absent unnecessarily during working hours. They are to see that all those employed in their rooms are in their places in due season. They may grant leave of absence to those employed under them, when there are spare hands in the room to supply their places; otherwise they are not to grant leave of absence, except in cases of absolute necessity. Every overseer must be the last to leave the room at night, and must see that the lights are all properly extinguished, and that there is no fire in the room. No overseer should leave his room in the evening while the mill is running, except in case of absolute necessity.

All persons in the employ of the Middlesex Company are required to observe the regulations of the overseer of the room where they are employed. They are not to be absent from their work, without his consent, except in case of sickness, and then they are to send him word of the cause of their absence.

They are to board in one of the boarding-houses belonging to the Company, unless otherwise permitted by the agent or superintendent, and conform to the regulations of the house where they board. They are to give information at the counting-room of the place where they board when they begin; and also give notice whenever they change their boarding place.

The Company will not employ any one who is habitually absent from public worship on the Sabbath, or whose habits are not regular and correct.

All persons entering into the employment of the Company are considered as engaged for twelve months; and those who leave sooner will not receive a regular discharge.

All persons intending to leave the employment of the Company are to give two weeks' notice of their intention to their overseer; and their engagement is not considered as fulfilled unless they comply with this regulation.

Smoking within the factory yards will in no case be permitted.

The pay-roll will be made up to the end of every month, and the payment made in the course of the following week.

These regulations are considered a part of the contract with persons entering into the employment of the MIDDLESEX COMPANY.

Samuel Lawrence, *Agent.*

Lowell, July 1, 1846.

Joel Taylor, Printer, Courier Office.

◆ Regulations, Middlesex Company (1846)

All of the Lowell companies required their young women workers to observe rules governing not only their activities in the factories but also their lives outside the mills. Most striking are the requirements that workers live in company-run boardinghouses and regularly attend church. No doubt the smoking prohibition applies to the male workers, mostly weavers, in the factory. *Center for Lowell History, Lowell, Massachusetts.*

◆ **Winslow Homer,** *The Morning Bell* **(1873)**
Boston-born Winslow Homer (1836–1910) was one of the most popular painters in the
nineteenth century. Among his subjects were the New England mill girls of the 1830s.
Homer worked from imagination rather than memory, recalling an industrial past in which
textile mills were small and set in the countryside. Yet the title of the image, *The Morning
Bell*, highlights the factory bell announcing the early morning call to labor. A poem of the
same name, published alongside Homer's image in *Harper's Magazine*, described the "heavy
factory bell" and those whose "weary feet obey its call . . . while others reap the sunshine of
their toil." *Corbis.*

spontaneous strikes—and in the process began to question notions of womanhood that forbade such demonstrations of individual and group assertion. They
repudiated the deference and subordination expected of them on the grounds of
their sex and championed, instead, their dignity and independence as proud
"daughters of freemen." One young striker, Harriet Hanson, who went on to
become a leader in the woman suffrage movement, remembered that the strike
"was the first time a woman had spoken in public in Lowell, and the event caused
surprise and consternation among her audience."[22] But the Panic of 1837, which
triggered contraction of the entire industrial economy, doomed the efforts of the
women operatives to act collectively, defend their jobs, and preserve the level of
their wages. Workers were laid off and mills shut down. Young girls went back to
their farm families to wait out the economic downturn.

When the economy revived and the mills resumed full production, workers
were expected to increase their pace, tend more machines, and produce more
cloth. Production levels rose, but wages did not. Moral concerns were giving way

to the bottom line. In the 1840s, Lowell's women workers joined with male workers in other Massachusetts factories in petitioning the state legislature to establish a ten-hour legal limit to their workdays as a way to resist work pressure and keep up levels of employment. This turn to the political system to redress group grievance was part of the larger democratic spirit of the period. It is especially striking to find women engaged in these methods at a time when politics was regarded as thoroughly outside of woman's sphere. Indeed, the legislative petitions of the women textile workers of the 1840s are an important indicator that women were beginning to imagine themselves part of the political process. But for precisely this reason, because women lacked whatever voting power male workers could muster, they were unable to secure any gains by their legislative petitions.

Conditions of factory labor were changing in other ways as well, most notably in the composition of the labor force. The Lowell system had been devised in the context of a shortage of workers willing to take factory jobs. By the 1840s, however, immigrants were providing an ever-growing labor pool for industrial employment. Coming to the United States in large numbers, they poured into the

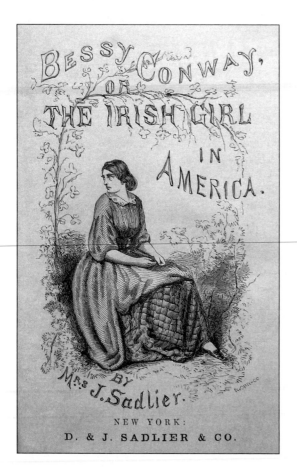

◆ Irish Immigration

Mary Anne Madden Sadlier, the author of the first American-written novel about an Irish immigrant woman, herself left Ireland in 1844. Living first in Montreal, she and her husband, James Sadlier, a book and magazine publisher, moved to New York City in 1860. Her novel *Bessy Conway, or The Irish Girl in America* (1861) modified the domestic focus of true womanhood ideology for a Catholic audience and blamed instead Protestant values and prejudices for the poverty and social ills that the Irish experienced in the United States. *John J. Burns Library, Boston College.*

wage labor force. America's first major wave of immigration included Germans, French, Canadians, and British, but the Irish were both the largest and the most economically desperate of all the new arrivals. Starting in 1845, a terrible blight on the potato crop that was the staple of the Irish diet, exacerbated by the harsh policies of England toward its oldest colony, threw the population into starvation conditions and compelled well over a million Irish men and women to emigrate to the United States. The textile capitalists, no longer pressured by labor shortages to make factory employment seem morally uplifting, paid low wages to and enforced harsh working conditions on these new immigrant workers, who soon constituted the majority of mill laborers.

Part of the initial attraction that native-born farm girls had for capitalists was the knowledge that they would eventually marry and return to their families and farms, and therefore their factory labor would be only a brief episode in their lives. The dreaded old world fate of becoming a permanently degraded and dependent wage labor class went instead to the Irish Catholic immigrants, who by 1860 were well over half of the workers in the industry. Immigrant men now worked the looms and immigrant women the spindles. The high moral character of the factory operatives—their womanly demeanor and hunger for self-improvement that were once the boast of the industry—was no more. Wage earning was increasingly seen as undermining respectable femininity. Workingwomen and true women were going their separate ways.

At the Bottom of the Wage Economy

Tremendous prejudice was directed at the Irish in the early years of industrialization, in no small part because they were becoming so thoroughly identified with wage labor. The Irish were one of the very few immigrant groups in American history in which the number of women roughly equaled that of men. Those who did not work in factories labored as domestic servants. In preindustrial America, the housewife had turned to young neighbors or kin as "helps" in her domestic obligations. Lucy Larcom worked for her sister in this traditional capacity whenever the downturns in factory conditions were too much for her. But in industrializing America, especially as the numbers of Irish immigrants grew, mistress and maid were becoming separated by a much greater cultural and economic gap and losing their sense of common task and purpose. In 1852, Elizabeth Cady Stanton, founding mother of the American women's rights movement (see pp. 274–79), complained of the "two undeveloped Hibernians in my kitchen" whose ignorance of modern household procedures she felt powerless to remedy.[23] The industrious, Protestant, Yankee middle-class housewife saw the Catholic Irish "girls" she hired to cook and clean and do laundry as dirty, ignorant, and immoral.

The divide between native-born middle-class mistress and immigrant wage-earning maid could almost be said to define class distinctions among women. Complaints about the difficulty of finding or keeping "good help" was a staple of middle-class female culture (see Figure 4.5, p. 237). Some women organized benevolent societies to place needy girls as workers in their own homes. However, the objects of their charity rarely regarded domestic service as a privilege. Domestic servants' habits of working erratically, changing employers often, and presenting a sullen demeanor were means of protesting a form of employment they did not like and that was not respected in democratic America, where the deference expected in personal service already had given it a bad name. Their employers could never understand why, even when wages were competitive, their domestic servants did their best to switch to factory employment. There, though the workday was long and the labor hard, a factory job ended with the dismissal bell when a young woman's time became her own.

At the very bottom of the economic ladder, beneath even the lower rungs of domestic service, were the urban poor. America had long had its poor people, but this destitute class was new, as it included able-bodied people willing but unable to find work that would support themselves and their families. The most desperate of the urban poor were the women with children but without men (or, more precisely, without access to the higher wages a man could earn). Such women were seen on the streets of the cities, begging for pennies or scavenging for wood or coal. These poor urban women were the absolute antithesis of true womanhood. The rooms in which they lived could hardly be called homes: they were not furnished, clean, or private. Unschooled and unsupervised, their children went into the streets or worked for a pittance to help support their families. Housework was especially difficult for poor urban women: they carried water for laundry or coal for warmth or small amounts of food for dinner up steps into tiny tenement apartments or down into cellar spaces (where twenty-nine thousand lived in New York City as of 1850).[24] After each downturn of the industrial economy, the numbers of urban poor swelled.

The Society for the Relief of Poor Widows, formed in New York City in 1799, was the first charity organized by women for women.[25] The charitable ladies did not provide outright cash or employment, instead dispensing spiritual and moral ministrations along with occasional food, coal, and clothing. In such exchanges, just as in the relationship between mistress and maid, middle-class and poor women met each other across the class divide, probably struck more with what separated them than with what they allegedly shared by virtue of their common gender.

WOMEN AND SLAVERY

Perhaps the greatest irony embedded in the dynamic beginnings of industrial capitalism is the degree to which it rested on a very different social and economic system that also thrived in early nineteenth-century America: chattel slavery. By 1800, as states from New England to Pennsylvania and Delaware abolished slavery, the institution had become identified exclusively with the South. Even so, a great deal linked the North with the South. The gigantic cotton crop grown by slave labor was the raw material of New England's textile industry. Among the greatest advocates of American democracy were numerous southern slaveholders, including four of this country's first five presidents. And at many levels, the regions shared a national culture. Their citizens read the same books and magazines, worshipped in the same Protestant denominations, and voted for the same political parties. Southern white women followed many essentials of the cult of domesticity. But underlying these similarities were fundamental differences, signifying a conflict between regions that eventually led to civil war.

The absence in the South of the wage relationship between producer and capitalist lay at the heart of these sectional differences. There were great profits accumulated in the South, and much of what was produced there was intended for sale. But the workers of the system were not paid any wages for their labor. They were *chattel* slaves, the value of whose current and future labor, along with the land they worked, constituted the wealth of their owners. Like the factory buildings and machines that produced wealth in the Northeast, they were capital; but they were also human beings.

Far more than even the most impoverished, degraded wage worker in the North, slaves were forbidden the basic elements of personal freedom—to live with their own families, to move about, to be educated, to marry and raise children—not to mention the loftier rights of citizenship. The slaves were traded as valuable commodities, objects of a legal commerce that was recognized by the laws of all the southern states and protected by the careful wording of the U.S. Constitution. Indeed, the Constitution, in permitting legislation ending the transatlantic slave trade after 1808 and relegating control over the institution of slavery entirely to the states, laid the foundation for an enormous commerce in slaves within the United States. The profitable, vigorous internal market in slaves touched the lives of virtually all African American persons, for each man and woman experienced either being sold, the fear of being sold, or the heartrending knowledge of a loved one being sold. The auction block loomed over all.

Plantation Patriarchy

Slave ownership in the nineteenth century was increasingly concentrated in the hands of fewer and fewer whites, although percentages varied across regions. Only an estimated 25 percent of southern white families owned any slaves in 1860; of these, only a small minority owned enough to qualify for elite status and significant political and economic power. On these great slave plantations, the large concentrations of land and labor formed the core of southern slave society (see Map 4.1). There, slaves were organized into large work gangs in which they raised the cotton, rice, sugar, and tobacco that made the South wealthy. These plantations were not only the economic core but the social, political, and cultural centers of slave society. In general, the nineteenth-century slave South did not develop the dynamic civil society that flourished in the North. The growth of an industrial economy and of a wage labor class was limited to a few urban centers, such as Richmond and Atlanta. With the sole exception of party politics, which wealthy men dominated, public life did not thrive. As a result, plantation women's lives varied dramatically from those of northern women.

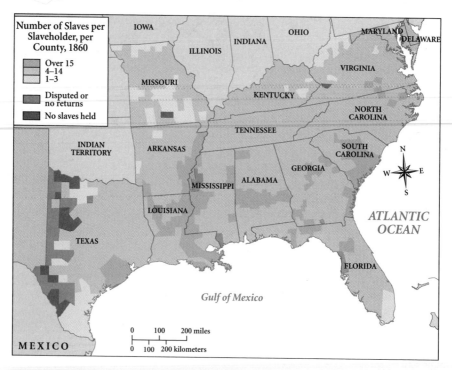

◆ Map 4.1 **Number of Slaves per Slaveholder, per County, 1860**
The cotton boom shifted enslaved African Americans to the lower and western South. In 1790, most slaves lived and worked on the tobacco plantations of the Chesapeake and in the rice and indigo areas of South Carolina. By 1860, the centers of slavery lay along the Mississippi River and in an arc of fertile cotton land sweeping from Mississippi through Georgia.

To begin with, family life was different. The ideological distinction between public and private, work and family—much touted in the North—did not really exist on the great plantations. The plantation was residence and workplace simultaneously, and the white male head of household presided over both. Instead of the mutually exclusive but allegedly equal gender roles dictated by the northern culture of domesticity, slave society was proudly patriarchal, with men's social and political power derived from their leadership in the home. Wealthy white southern men were fiercely jealous of the honor of their women and their families, and they were notorious for their willingness to resort to violence to avenge any perceived slights against them. Female deference to male authority was considered a virtue, and any moral superiority that women could claim gave them no social or political authority. Inasmuch as wealthy women left the daily tasks of childrearing to their slaves, maternity was neither revered nor sentimentalized.

Owners regarded slave men and women not just as workers but as permanent children—amusing, guileless, but lacking in judgment and authority. By this obfuscating ideology, the plantation community was treated as a single large family, with master-parents and slave-children, bound by devotion and reciprocal obligations of service and protection. One white woman, writing about her father's plantation, truly believed that "the family servants, inherited for generations, had come to be regarded with great affection. . . . The bond between master and servant was, in many cases, felt to be as sacred and close as the tie of blood."[26] When slavery was abolished, masters and mistresses were often astounded to discover the degree of hostility their former slaves felt toward them.

Plantation patriarchy was a gender and family system, but one organized around racial difference and inequality. The structures and inequalities of race, much like those of gender, were so omnipresent as to seem natural and God-given. "Black" equaled "slave" and was understood as the opposite not only of "white" but of "free." In contrast to this belief, it is important to recognize that by 1830 there were a third of a million black people in the United States who were nominally free, half of them living in the South. The lives of these people and their claims to free status were deeply compromised by the power of slavery and racial inequality. In the South they were kept out of certain occupations, forbidden to carry firearms, denied the right to assembly, and required to have passes to travel from county to county. Even in the North, where a small black urban middle class emerged in Philadelphia, New York, and Boston, most free blacks occupied the lowest ranks of wage labor as common laborers, dock workers, and, among women, domestic servants.

Despite slave society's insistence that the racial divide was absolute, the line that separated "black" from "white" was constantly being breached. Masters could—and certainly did—compel slave women to have sexual relations with them. When a slave woman gave birth to her master's child, how was the racial divide on which slave patriarchy was premised be maintained? The legal answer was that the child followed the status of the mother, a slave because her female parent was a slave. This simple legal answer to a complex set of social relations hidden within slave society had enormous implications for the lives of southern women, black and white. While slavery is usually considered a system for organizing labor and producing profit, it was also a way of organizing and restraining sexual and reproductive relations, of controlling which sexual encounters produced legitimate children. In other words, managing race necessitated managing gender and sexuality.

Plantation Mistresses

The link between racial inequality and gender ideals is evident in the effusive literary and rhetorical praise devoted to the southern white feminine ideal. Elite white women in plantation society were elevated to a lofty pedestal that was the ideological inverse of the auction block on which slave women's fate was sealed. As in the North, white women were supposed to be selfless, pure, pious, and possessed of great, if subtle, influence over husbands and sons. But the difference in the South was that white women's purity was defined in contrast to the condition of black slave women.

◆ **Charlotte Forten Grimké**
As a member of the tiny antebellum black middle class, Charlotte Forten (later Grimké) combined belief in the ideals of true womanhood and political and social activism on behalf of her race. She was born in 1837 into a relatively prosperous and politically active family in Philadelphia and was educated in Salem, Massachusetts. During the Civil War, she traveled to Union-controlled islands off the coast of South Carolina to teach emancipated slaves and kept a fascinating diary of her experience there. She married Francis Grimké, whose father and former owner was the brother of white abolitionists Sarah and Angelina Grimké. *Photographs and Prints Division, Schomburg Center for Research in Black Culture, The New York Public Library, Astor, Lenox, and Tilden Foundations.*

As slavery came under more and more open criticism from northern opponents during the nineteenth century, rhetorical devotion to elite white women's leisure and culture, to the preservation of their beauty and their sexual innocence, and to their protection from all distress and labor intensified. The message seemed to be that the purity of elite white womanhood, rather than the enslavement of black people, was the core value of southern society. "We behold," proclaimed southern writer Thomas Dew, "the marked efficiency of slavery on the conditions of woman — we find her at once elevated, clothed with all her charms, mingling with and directing the society to which she belongs, no longer the slave, but the equal and the idol of man."[27] For the most part, women of the slaveholding class also held to the opinion that a lady's life on a southern plantation was a great privilege. Any greater political and economic rights for white women were "but a piece of negro emancipation," declared Louisa McCord, daughter of an important South Carolina slaveholder and politician, in 1852.[28] She was sure that women like herself wanted no part of such a movement.

Whereas in the North, womanly virtues were meant to be universal, in the South, they were proudly exclusionary, applicable only to the few, a mark of the natural superiority of the elite and their right to own and command the labor of others. While the northern true woman was praised for her industrious domesticity, in the South a real lady was not allowed to sully herself or risk her charms with any actual labor, which was the mark of the slave. Leisure was especially the privilege of the unmarried young woman of the slaveholding class, who was not only spared any household obligations but also relieved of even the most intimate of responsibilities — dressing herself, for instance — by the presence of personal slaves. "Surrounded with them from infancy, they form a part of the landscape of a Southern woman's life," one woman recalled of her servants long after slavery had ended. "They watch our cradles; they are the companions of our sports; it is they who aid our bridal decorations; and they wrap us in our shrouds."[29]

Once a woman married, however, she took on managerial responsibility for the household. Unlike their husbands, who hired overseers to manage slaves in the fields, plantation mistresses themselves oversaw the labor of the household slaves and the feeding, clothing, and doctoring of the entire labor force. One admittedly unusual plantation mistress, who insisted that she was more put upon than privileged by the ownership of slaves, recalled that when she heard the news of the Emancipation Proclamation, she exclaimed, "Thank heaven! I too shall be free at last!"[30]

Because slavery was a labor system in which there were no positive incentives for hard work, the management of workers relied almost entirely on threats and punishments, including beatings. Within the household, the discipline of slaves was the responsibility of the mistress. The association of allegedly delicate womanhood with brutal violence was a disturbing aspect of the slave system, even to its most passionate adherents. Opponents of slavery played endlessly on this theme to indicate the fundamental corruption of the system, which reached even to the women of slaveholding families. "There are *female tyrants* too, who are prompt to lay their complaints of misconduct before their husbands, brothers, and sons, and to urge them to commit acts of violence against their helpless slaves," wrote Angelina Grimké, daughter of a powerful southern slaveowner, who left the South in 1829 to fight against the system (see pp. 271–73). "Other mistresses who cannot bear that their delicate ears should be pained by the screams of the poor sufferers, write an order to the master of the Charleston workhouse . . . to render the stroke of the whip or the blow of the paddle more certain to produce cuts and wounds."[31]

In the South, as in the North, marriage for free women legally prohibited them from the privileges of property ownership. Changing this practice was one of the initial goals of the American women's rights movement, within which southern white women, committed to the plantation patriarchy, were notoriously absent. Thus it is ironic that the first states to liberalize property laws for married women were southern — Mississippi (in 1839) and Arkansas (in 1840) — in order to protect the inheritance of slave ownership. Far more than middle-class northern women, elite southern women were expected to bring dowries — wealth packages — into their marriages, and it was not uncommon for a young woman to bring into her new home slaves from her parents' plantation. This was one of the many ways in which slaves were separated from their own families. To protect their daughters — and the family property that had been transferred with them—against spendthrift husbands, southern patriarchs modified married women's property laws to allow wives to retain title to inherited property. The first married women's property law to be reformed in the North in response to pressure from women's rights activists was in 1848 in New York State.

In all other ways, however, the slave system made for more severe constraints on free women than in the North. The rhetorical weight that rested on elite white women's purity meant that women's public activities were extremely limited. Unlike northern women, respectable southern white women had no means of earning money. Women who remained unmarried faced futures as marginal members in the households of their married kin. Whatever education existed for young women was oriented to the ornamental graces rather than more serious subjects. The sorts of benevolent societies that northern middle-class women formed to care for the indigent and poor did not exist in the South, although plantation mistresses, defensive about whether they were sufficiently benevolent, frequently claimed that the care and feeding of their own slaves constituted an equivalent moral responsibility.

For the most part, slaveholding women and men did not regard themselves as heading up a brutal and inhumane system. On the contrary, they were convinced that the society over which they presided, which elevated them to lives of such enviable grace and culture, was the best of all possible worlds, certainly better than the lives led by money-grubbing capitalists and degraded wage workers in the North. They regarded their slaves as well treated compared to the northern wage earners, whom they believed were ignored and eventually abandoned, their welfare of no concern to bosses who wanted only to exploit their labor and then dispose of them. "How enviable were our solidarity as a people, our prosperity and the moral qualities that are characteristic of the South," one southern matron mourned many years after the Civil War. Even in retrospect, she believed that white southerners' "love of home, their chivalrous respect for women, their courage, their delicate sense of honour, their constancy . . . [all] are things by which the more mercurial people of the North may take a lesson."[32]

Non-Elite White Women

While the power of southern society lay in the hands of the plantation elite, the majority of whites were not large slaveholders. Indeed, close to three-quarters of all white families owned no slaves and relied on their own labor, occasionally hiring a slave or two from a neighbor. Even the great majority of those who did own slaves were working farmers themselves, living and laboring alongside the few slaves they owned. These small farmers are often called yeomen, a British term signifying the nonnoble agricultural classes. The slave system would not have worked without the active support of the many white people who did not profit a great deal from it. Non-elite white men patrolled the roads for runaway slaves, voted in favor of aggressively proslavery state governments, and served as overseers and skilled craftsmen on the great plantations.

Women on the small farms and modest households of the South had much less interaction with planter culture than did their husbands. There was no common women's culture that linked them to plantation mistresses—another difference with the North. Indeed, the class gap between elite and non-elite whites was clearest when it came to women's roles. While elite women lived lives of leisure in their grand plantation houses, women of the yeoman class worked very hard both outside and inside their small homes. They continued to produce goods mainly for their own family's consumption, for instance, spinning and wearing homespun long after northern farm women were purchasing factory-made cloth. They sold a smaller portion of their produce for cash than those in the North. About the only thing that took such non-elite southern women away from their homes and farms was church. And even there, they lacked the numerous voluntary activities and associations that Protestant women formed in the North in pursuit of moral uplift.

Although southern yeomen had few or no slaves over whom to establish their patriarchal authority, they did have wives. Thus female subordination was prized in this sector of southern society. If the difference between the lives of non-elite and elite women was one of the most pronounced distinctions among southern whites, the ethic of male headship bonded white men across class boundaries. "As masters of dependents, even if only, or perhaps if especially, of wives and children," one historian observes, "every freeman was bound to defend his household, his property, against invasion."[33]

Slave Women

When we recall de Tocqueville's confident assertion in 1830 that American women were so privileged and honored that they "never labor in the fields," we begin to see the degree to which the slave women of the South were not only ignored in all the sweeping generalizations of true womanhood but also excluded from the category of "woman" altogether. Ninety percent of the slave women of the South labored in the cotton, sugar, tobacco, and rice fields that generated the region's wealth. Plantation patriarchy extolled an image of slaves who provided personal and domestic service in their own households (see Figures 4.11 and 4.12, pp. 245 and 246), but these were a small minority. It was the giant mass of agricultural slaves on whom the power of the planter class rested.

Nowhere in early nineteenth-century America was labor less separated by gender than in the fields of the plantation South. Slave women and men hoed and planted and reaped alongside each other in gangs that worked from sunup to sundown. For purposes of accounting and sale, women were regarded as partial "hands," but the lore of the plantation is full of stories of individual women famous for their strength and ability to work as hard as any man. A former slave named Ophelia Settle Egypt remembered that her mother "could do anything. She cooked, washed, ironed, spun, nursed, and labored in the field. She made as good a field hand as she did a cook." Egypt recalled, with some pride, that her mother could "outwork any nigger in the country. I'd bet my life on that."[34] On the larger

MARY BOYKIN CHESNUT
Slavery a Curse to Any Land

The diary kept by the South Carolina slave mistress Mary Boykin Chesnut (1823–1886) has long been regarded as a major source for insights into the minds of southern slaveholders. More recently, historians have explored Chesnut's views on the position of the women of this class. In writing about the hidden but extensive sexual relations between slaveholding men and their female slaves, she is far more resentful than sympathetic to slave women.

March 14, 1861: I wonder if it be a sin to think slavery a curse to any land. . . . [W]e live surrounded by prostitutes. An abandoned woman is sent out of any decent house elsewhere. Who thinks any worse of a Negro or Mulatto woman for being a thing we can't name. God forgive us, but ours is a monstrous system & wrong & iniquity. Perhaps the rest of the world is as bad. This is only what I see: like the patriarchs of old, our men live all in one house with their wives & their concubines, & the Mulattos one sees in every family exactly resemble the white children — & every lady tells you who is the father of all the Mulatto children in everybody's household, but those in her own, she seems to think drop from the clouds or pretends so to think — . . . . My disgust sometimes is boiling over — . . . . Thank God for my countrywomen — alas for the men! No worse than men everywhere, but the lower their mistresses, the more degraded they must be.

SOURCE: Mary Boykin Chesnut, *A Diary from Dixie* (1905; Boston: Houghton Mifflin, 1949), 21.

plantations, where some specialization of labor was possible, slave men practiced skills such as blacksmithing and carpentering while individual women might gain reputations as slave midwives, but overall, the demands of slave labor made little distinction by sex. Even among household slaves, estimated at about 10 percent of the labor force of the South, men served as personal valets, as butlers, and occasionally even as nursemaids for their owners' young sons.

In other ways, however, slave women's lives were distinguished from those of slave men. The vulnerabilities of their sex were exploited when they were beaten. Numerous stories record that slave women's skirts were raised over their heads before whippings, to humiliate them and perhaps to make their physical sufferings greater. Only a woman in the late stages of pregnancy might be spared the worst whippings, and only then to protect her baby, who, when born, would be worth a great deal to the slaveowner. Similarly, after giving birth, women were suspended from field labor just briefly. Northern visitors commented frequently on the sight of an old slave woman bringing infants to the fields so that their young mothers could nurse them quickly and return to work. When beatings failed to discipline female slaves who resisted their masters' control, sale was an even greater threat, especially if it meant separating a woman from her child. A runaway slave named Mrs. James Stewart told the story of a Maryland woman who was punished for resisting her master in all these ways: after beating her, the master controlled her by "taking away her clothes and locking them up. . . . He kept her at work with only what she could pick up to tie on her for decency. He took away her child which had just begun to walk. . . . He waited [to whip her] until she was confined [pregnant]."[35]

As chattels rather than persons with rights, slaves were not permitted legally binding marriage contracts, which might interfere with the master's right to buy and sell them away from their husbands or wives. Nonetheless, men and women under slavery went to great lengths to sustain conjugal and parental relationships. Frequently, such bonds linked women and men who belonged to different masters. In these so-called abroad marriages, it usually fell to the man to visit his wife and children. Often traveling at night to visit his family, without his master's knowledge or permission, the abroad husband risked being whipped or even sold away. (See Documents: Two Slave Love Stories, pp. 225–31.) Slaves had their own ritual for solemnizing their marriages, by together "jumping the broom." Masters might attend such ceremonies and even amuse themselves by providing for elaborate slave weddings that mimicked their own. But everyone understood that the bottom line was the slave's status as property, not her emotional attachment to another slave. When the Civil War ended slavery in the South, many African

◆ **Mary Boykin Chesnut (1847)**
Mary Boykin Chesnut is one of the few individual women of the plantation class who is known to historians. This rare, early photograph was taken in 1847, soon after she married James Chesnut, an up-and-coming South Carolina politician. Mary was only seventeen at the time. Both she and James came from families that owned numerous slaves. Living in her mother-in-law's home, Mary had much time for observation, conversation, and writing. Perhaps it is possible to see in her face the unflinching intelligence that made her the most important chronicler of domestic relations in the slave South. *Mulberry Plantation, Camden, South Carolina.*

HARRIET JACOBS
Trials of Girlhood

Harriet Jacobs (1813–1897) was born a slave in North Carolina. From the age of twelve, she was sexually harassed by an older white man who wanted her as his concubine. After a decade, she escaped from his home, but because of her attachment to her children, she stayed nearby, hidden in the cramped attic room of relatives. There she remained for seven years until she and her daughter finally fled the South. So extraordinary was Jacobs's story that its legitimacy was long doubted, but recent historians have substantiated virtually everything about her story, including her authorship.

I now entered on my fifteenth year—a sad epoch in the life of a slave girl. My master began to whisper foul words in my ear. Young as I was, I could not remain ignorant of their import. I tried to treat them with indifference or contempt. . . . He was a crafty man, and resorted to many means to accomplish his purposes. Sometimes he had stormy, terrific ways, that made his victims tremble; sometimes he assumed a gentleness that he thought must surely subdue. Of the two, I preferred his stormy moods, although they left me trembling. He tried his utmost to corrupt the pure principles my grandmother had instilled. He peopled my young mind with unclean images, such as only a vile monster could think of. I turned from him with disgust and hatred. But he was my master. I was compelled to live under the same roof with him—where I saw a man forty

Americans showed extraordinary determination in traveling great distances to find spouses long lost to sale.

Motherhood also distinguished the lives of slave women from those of slave men. For slave women, childbearing was simultaneously the source of their greatest personal satisfaction and their greatest misery, because their children ultimately belonged to the master. Slave mothers had the immensely difficult task of teaching their children to survive their owners' power and at the same time to know their own worth as human beings. Many decades later, one woman remembered how her mother spoke to her daily about the cruelties of slavery. Still young enough to be treated as her owners' pet, the child did not believe her mother until the master announced that her mother was to be sold away. "I felt for the first time in my life that I had been abused," she recalled. "My mother had been right. Slavery was cruel, so very cruel."[36]

Most of the direct testimony about the power of the auction block to sever the relation between slave mothers and children comes from the perspective of the child, but there are hints that some women tried to terminate their pregnan-

years my senior daily violating the most sacred commandments of nature. He told me I was his property; that I must be subject to his will in all things. My soul revolted against the mean tyranny. But where could I turn for protection? No matter whether the slave girl be as black as ebony or as fair as her mistress. In either case, there is no shadow of law to protect her from insult, from violence, or even from death; all these are inflicted by fiends who bear the shape of men. The mistress, who ought to protect the helpless victim, has no other feelings towards her but those of jealousy and rage. The degradation, the wrongs, the vices, that grow out of slavery, are more than I can describe. They are greater than you would willingly believe. . . .

Even the little child, who is accustomed to wait on her mistress and her children, will learn, before she is twelve years old, why it is that her mistress hates such and such a one among the slaves. Perhaps the child's own mother is among those hated ones. She listens to violent outbreaks of jealous passion, and cannot help understanding what is the cause. She will become prematurely knowing in evil things. Soon she will learn to tremble when she hears her master's footfall. She will be compelled to realize that she is no longer a child. If God has bestowed beauty upon her, it will prove her greatest curse. That which commands admiration in the white woman only hastens the degradation of the female slave.

SOURCE: Harriet Jacobs, *Incidents in the Life of a Slave Girl: Seven Years Concealed* (Boston: published for the author, 1861), ch. 5.

cies or even kill their infants rather than give birth for slaveowners. We can never know the number of such women, but individual examples tell much. Margaret Garner, a Kentucky slave woman who escaped to Ohio in 1856, became the most notorious of these avenging mothers in the nineteenth century when she slit the throat of her youngest child in anticipation of her and her children being recaptured and sent back south. Known at the time as the Black Medea, she became the central figure of Toni Morrison's great modern slave tragedy *Beloved* (1987).

There was much suspicion at the time that Garner's master was also the father of her children. Sexual relations between masters and slave women were an open secret in the South, heartily denied by slaveowners and yet virtually endemic to the society. The light complexions and white features of numerous nineteenth-century slaves were eloquent testimony to this intimate connection between slave and master. Mary Boykin Chesnut, a member of South Carolina's slaveholding aristocracy, knew of this hidden reality. Her diaries are much quoted by historians for what they reveal about slave society's contradictions (see box, "Slavery a Curse to Any Land," p. 212).

BELOVED CHILDREN
Cherokee Women Petition the National Council

The expansion of chattel slavery and plantation agriculture into the lower South required the United States to assist its property-hungry citizens to take over the lands of the native peoples living there, including the Cherokees. In the early nineteenth century, the federal government negotiated a number of land cessions in treaties with southern tribes, including the Cherokees. In 1817, thirteen Cherokee women sent this petition to their own National Council to warn against the transfer of any more lands to white ownership. The Cherokee had already adapted their culture to American ways, in hopes that they be allowed to remain where they were and to live in peace with neighboring whites, aspirations that were encouraged by President James Monroe. The signers spoke for those women who had given up their traditional agricultural responsibilities in favor of American domestic tasks, such as making clothing. Nonetheless, their words indicate a continuing identification through their gender with the land: to sell it, they told the council, would be like "destroying your mothers." Among the signers was eighty-year-old Nancy Ward, whose high standing among her people harked back to an earlier age in which women shared political and social authority with men.

May 2, 1817
The Cherokee ladys now being present at the meeting of the chiefs and warriors in council have thought it their duty as mothers to address their beloved chiefs and warriors now assembled.

Our beloved children and head men of the Cherokee Nation, we address you warriors in council. We have raised all of you on the land which we now have, which God gave us to inhabit and raise provisions. We know that our country has once been extensive, but by repeated sales

While running afoul of Christian morality, masters' sexual exploitation of slave women was encouraged by everything else about the slave system: the master was the legal owner of the slave woman's sexuality and reproductive capacity along with her labor; any child born of a slave woman was also a slave, thus benefiting the master financially; and a slave woman could occasionally gain small favors for herself or her children through sexual relations with her master. In one of the best-known accounts of a master's sexual aggression toward a female slave, Harriet Jacobs described how, when she was only fifteen, her master began to insist that she have sex with him (see box, "Trials of Girlhood"). In the end, she thwarted her master's intentions but only by finding another older white man to

[it] has become circumscribed to a small track, and [we] never have thought it our duty to interfere in the disposition of it till now. If a father or mother was to sell all their lands which they had to depend on, which their children had to raise their living on, [it] would be indeed bad & [so would it] be removed to another country. We do not wish to go to an unknown country which we have understood some of our children wish to go over the Mississippi, but this act of our children would be like destroying your mothers.

Your mothers, your sisters ask and beg of you not to part with any more of our land. We say ours. You are our descendants; take pity on our request. But keep it for our growing children, for it was the good will of our creator to place us here, and you know our father, the great president, will not allow his white children to take our country away. Only keep your hands off of paper talks for it's our own country. For [if] it was not, they would not ask you to put your hands to paper, for it would be impossible to remove us all. For as soon as one child is raised, we have others in our arms, for such is our situation & [they] will consider our circumstance.

Therefore, children, don't part with any more of our lands but continue on it & enlarge your farms. Cultivate and raise corn & cotton and your mothers and sisters will make clothing for you which our father the president has recommended to us all. . . . Nancy Ward to her children: Warriors to take pity and listen to the talks of your sisters. Although I am very old yet [I] cannot but pity the situation in which you will here [sic] of their minds. I have great many grand children which [I] wish them to do well on our land.

Source: Presidential Papers Microfilm: Andrew Jackson (Washington, D.C., 1961, series 1, reel 22).

become her lover, a moral compromise for which she expressed deep shame for the rest of her life. Modern DNA analysis has strengthened suspicion that even Thomas Jefferson, author of the Declaration of Independence and third president of the United States, was implicated in the sexual and reproductive underside of slavery. The likelihood that he had a long sexual relationship with his slave Sally Hemings, starting when she was only fourteen and resulting in the birth of several children, suggests how commonplace were masters' appropriations of their female slaves' bodies. Modern efforts to render the Hemings-Jefferson relationship as a great interracial love story ignore the absolutely unrestrained white male power inherent in the structures of slavery.

The issue of deliberate breeding was an explosive one in the slave South. Opponents of slavery accused owners of encouraging and arranging pregnancies among their female slaves to produce more slaves to sell on the lucrative internal slave market. Evidence suggests that they were right. "Marsa used to sometimes pick our wives fo' us," former slave Charles Grandy recalled. "Marsa would stop de old niggertrader and buy you a woman. . . . All he wanted was a young healthy one who looked like she could have children, whether she was purty or ugly as sin."[37] Women of childbearing age who were described as "good breeders" brought a higher price on the auction block. The southern elite understandably resented the charges that they deliberately bred the slaves whom they claimed to protect, but the economic development of slavery in its last decades certainly points in this direction.

In the nineteenth century, slavery expanded into what was called the "new" or "lower" South (western Georgia, Florida, Alabama, Arkansas, Mississippi, Louisiana, and Texas). This move was greatly facilitated by a sustained, concerted effort of land-hungry whites, aided by the state governments of Georgia and the Carolinas, to push the Indian peoples of the Southeast — the Creek, Chickasaw, Choctaw, and especially Cherokee — off their extensive lands. The Cherokee in particular had tried to adapt to American society and resist land sales (see box, "Beloved Children"), and Cherokee women had learned the domestic tasks of housewifery. Cherokee leader Sequoyah had devised a written language, enabling the translation of the Christian Bible and the drafting of a political constitution. Some Cherokees even became slaveholders. But all of these efforts proved ineffective once Andrew Jackson, an old "Indian fighter," was elected president. Jackson pushed the Indian Removal Act of 1830 through Congress and then, ignoring Supreme Court decisions favoring Cherokee rights, sent federal troops to Georgia to execute it. In 1838, the Cherokee were forcibly driven into the newly established Indian Territory west of the Mississippi, across what the Cherokees called the "Trail of Tears." The new slave lands became the center of cotton and tobacco productivity. Meanwhile, in the older southern states of Virginia, Maryland, and the Carolinas, where soil had become exhausted and productivity slumped, slaves themselves became a kind of crop, a surplus to be sold.

Any hope that the bonds of gender might have crossed the boundaries of race and class was crushed by the burden that slave concubinage laid on southern society. Jealous or suspicious mistresses vented on their slaves the anger and rage they dared not express to their husbands. Harriet Jacobs feared her mistress every bit as much as she did her master. Female slaves who worked in the plantation house were at greatest risk, exposed day in and day out to the mistress's moods. Slave narratives frequently describe an impatient or intolerant mistress striking out at a cook or a nursemaid or even a slave child unable to handle an assigned task. In their diaries and letters, slaveowning white women recorded their secret fears of violent retribution from slaves. As Civil War was breaking out, Mary Boykin Chesnut wrote anxiously about the death of a cousin who, it was suspected, had been "murdered by her own people."[38] Although both black and white women suffered in the slave system, slave women knew they could expect no sympathy from their mistresses. The luxury and culture of the white southern woman were premised on the forced labor and sexual oppression of her slaves. Violence against and violations of slave women mocked southern deference to womanhood and female sexual purity. With only the rarest of exceptions, slavery turned black and white women against each other and set their interests and their perspectives in direct opposition.

CONCLUSION: True Womanhood and the Reality of Women's Lives

Perhaps at no other time in American history were the prescriptions for a proper domestic role for women more precise and widely agreed on than in antebellum America. Much of the young country's hope for stability and prosperity rested on the belief in a universally achievable middle-class family order, with the devoted, selfless wife and mother at the center.

As we shall see, some women were able to use the ideology of true womanhood to expand their sphere in subtle ways, but even so, this ideology was exceedingly rigid and limiting, ignoring the reality of women who led very different sorts of lives. Factory operatives were outside the boundaries of acceptable womanhood because they lived and worked in what *Godey's Lady's Book* editor Sarah Josepha Hale called "the accursed bank note world" that only men were supposed to occupy.[39] And slave women were deprived—absolutely—of the protection and privileges that were meant to compensate true women for their limited sphere. While the rhetoric of true womanhood seemed to place domestic women at the heart of American society, in reality the giant processes in which these other women were caught up—industrialization and slavery—were the dynamic forces shaping the young American nation and foreshadowing the trends and crises of its future.

DOCUMENT

Prostitution in New York City, 1858

As chief physician in the 1850s for the "lock hospital" to which New York City prostitutes were sent when they were arrested, Dr. William Sanger had both knowledge of and compassion for the women he attended. Hopeful that more accurate information about prostitution would help to eradicate the practice, he interviewed two thousand prostitutes, using a carefully drawn-up set of questions. He was determined to bring the facts of prostitution to light and to convey the prostitutes' experiences and thoughts more realistically. The originals of Sanger's interviews were destroyed in a fire the year after he gathered them, so his published report to the trustees of the New York Alms House provides the closest we have to a firsthand account from the prostitutes themselves. Interestingly, Sanger did no research into the men who were the prostitutes' clientele.

Sanger's sample, although not randomly selected, was large enough to allow for reliable generalizations. Among the generalizations Sanger's data allowed him to make were the following: most prostitutes were from fifteen to twenty years old; three-fifths were native born; among the immigrants, 60 percent were Irish; one-fifth were married; half had children; half were or had been domestic servants; half were afflicted with syphilis; the average length of life after entering prostitution was four years.

Sanger estimated that six thousand women were engaged in commercial sex in New York City, a number based on his careful survey of police records, lock hospitals, and known brothels. Others estimated much higher numbers. Even so, Sanger's estimates were distressing. As Sanger repeatedly insisted, they reflected not the inherent lack of virtue of the prostitutes but rather the relentless financial pressure on poor urban women. The effects of a sharp economic depression in 1857 are detected everywhere in the prostitutes' descriptions of their situations.

Sanger believed that women were too often blamed for prostitution; he wanted to show that they were the victims, both of men's callousness and their own lack of economic opportunity. Despite these reformist sentiments, however, Sanger held conventional notions of femininity. Indeed, he championed prostitutes because he was certain that most women would never of their own accord undertake a life of casual sex. Rather, he believed, they must have been deserted, seduced, driven by destitution, or forced into prostitution by some other extraordinary event over which they had no control. Underlying his compassion for those who were remorseful, the traces of a harsher set of judgments can be found. Thus Sanger's report can be read as evidence of middle-class attitudes toward female sexuality, as well as of prostitutes' own experience.

What follows is Sanger's summary and analysis of the two thousand answers given to one of his most revealing questions: "What are the causes of your becoming a prostitute?" As you read, think about how the personal stories that Sanger relates allow us to imagine a more complicated set of explanations for individual women's entry into prostitution than the categories he uses.

WILLIAM W. SANGER
The History of Prostitution: Its Extent, Causes, and Effects throughout the World (1858)

[Question:] *What are the causes of your becoming a prostitute? . . .*

Causes	Numbers
Inclination	513
Destitution	525
Seduced and abandoned	258
Drink, and the desire to drink	181
Ill-treatment of parents, relatives, or husbands	164
As an easy life	124
Bad company	84
Persuaded by prostitutes	71
Too idle to work	29
Violated	27
Seduced on board emigrant ships	16
Seduced in emigrant boarding houses	8
Total	2000

This question is probably the most important of the series, as the replies lay open to a considerable extent those hidden springs of evil which have hitherto been known only from their results. First in order stands the reply [which 513 respondents chose], "Inclination," which can only be understood as meaning a voluntary resort to prostitution in order to gratify the sexual passions. . . .

SOURCE: William W. Sanger, *The History of Prostitution: Its Extent, Causes, and Effects throughout the World* (New York: Medical Publishing, 1921), 488–522.

The force of desire can neither be denied nor disputed, but still in the bosoms of most females that force exists in a slumbering state until aroused by some outside influences. . . . In the male sex nature has provided a more susceptible organization than in females, apparently with the beneficent design of repressing those evils which must result from mutual appetite equally felt by both. In other words, man is the *aggressive* animal, so far as sexual desire is involved. Were it otherwise, and the passions in both sexes equal, illegitimacy and prostitution would be far more rife in our midst than at present.

Some few of the cases in which the reply "Inclination" was given are herewith submitted, with the explanation which accompanied each return. C. M.: while virtuous, this girl had visited dancehouses, where she became acquainted with prostitutes, who persuaded her that they led an easy, merry life; her inclination was the result of female persuasion. E. C. left her husband, and became a prostitute willingly, in order to obtain intoxicating liquors which had been refused her at home. E. R. was deserted by her husband because she drank to excess and became a prostitute in order to obtain liquor. . . . Enough has been quoted to prove that, in many of the cases, what is called willing prostitution is the sequel of some communication or circumstances which undermine the principles of virtue and arouse the latent passions.

Destitution is assigned as a reason in five hundred and twenty-five cases. In many of these it is unquestionably true that positive, actual want, the apparent and dreaded approach of starvation, was the real cause of degradation. . . .

During the progress of this investigation in one of the lower wards of the city, attention was drawn to a pale but interesting-looking girl, about seventeen years of age, from whose replies the following narrative is condensed, retaining her own words as nearly as possible.

"I have been leading this life from about the middle of last January (1856). It was absolute want that drove me to it. My sister, who was about three years older than I am, lived with me. She was deformed and crippled from a fall she had while a child, and could not do any hard work. . . . One very cold morning, just after I had been to the store, the landlord's agent called for some rent we owed, and told us that, if we could not pay it, we should have to move. The agent was a kind man, and gave us a little money to buy some coals. We did not know what we were to do, and were both crying about it, when the woman who keeps this house (where she was then living) came in and brought some sewing for us to do that day. She said that she had been recommended to us by a woman who lived in the same house, but I found out since that she had watched me, and only said this for an excuse. When the work was done I brought it home here. I had heard of such places before, but had never been inside one. I was very cold, and she made me sit down by the fire, and began to talk to me, saying how much better off I should be if I would come and live with her. . . .When I got home and saw my sister so sick as she was and wanting many little things that we had no money to buy, and no friends to help us to, my heart almost broke. However, I said nothing to her then. I laid awake all night thinking, and in the morning I made up my mind to come here. . . . I thought that, if I had been alone, I would sooner have starved, but I could not bear to see her suffering. She only lived a few weeks after I came here. I broke her heart. I do not like the life. I would do almost any thing to get out of it; but, now that I have *once done wrong*, I can not

get any one to give me work, and I must stop here unless I wish to be starved to death."

These details give some insight into the under-current of city life. The most prominent fact is that a large number of females, both operatives and domestics, earn so small wages that a temporary cessation of their business, or being a short time out of a situation, is sufficient to reduce them to absolute distress. Provident habits are useless in their cases; for, much as they may feel the necessity, *they have nothing to save,* and the very day that they encounter a reverse sees them penniless. The struggle a virtuous girl will wage against fate in such circumstances may be conceived: it is a literal battle for life, and in the result life is too often preserved only by the sacrifice of virtue. . . .

Moralists say that all human passions should be held in check by reason and virtue, and none can deny the truthfulness of the assertion. But while they apply the sentiment to the weaker party, who is the sufferer, would it not be advisable to recommend the same restraining influences to him who is the inflictor? No woman possessed of the smallest share of decency or the slightest appreciation of virtue would voluntarily surrender herself without some powerful motive, not pre-existent in herself, but imparted by her destroyer. Well aware of the world's opinion, she would not recklessly defy it, and precipitate herself into an abyss of degradation and shame unless some overruling influence had urged her forward. This motive and this influence, it is believed, may be uniformly traced to her weak but truly feminine dependence upon another's vows. . . . Thus there can be little doubt that, in most cases of seduction, female virtue is trustingly surrendered to the specious arguments and false promises of dishonorable men.

Men who, in the ordinary relations of life, would scruple to defraud their neighbors of a dollar, do not hesitate to rob a confiding woman of her chastity. They who, in a business point of view, would regard obtaining goods under false pretenses as an act to be visited with all the severity of the law, hesitate not to obtain by even viler fraud the surrender of woman's virtue to their fiendish lust. Is there no inconsistency in the social laws which condemn a swindler to the state prison *for his offenses,* and condemn a woman to perpetual infamy *for her wrongs*? Undoubtedly there are cases where the woman is the seducer, but these are so rare as to be hardly worth mentioning.

Seduction is a social wrong. Its entire consequences are not comprised in the injury inflicted on the woman, or the sense of perfidy oppressing the conscience of the man. Beyond the fact that she is, in the ordinary language of the day, ruined, the victim has endured an attack upon her principles which must materially affect her future life. The world may not know of her transgression, and, in consequence, public obloquy may not be added to her burden; but she is too painfully conscious of her fall, and every thought of her lacerated and bleeding heart is embittered with a sense of man's wrong and outrage. . . . It can not be a matter of surprise that, with this feeling of injustice and insult burning at her heart, her career should be one in which she becomes the aggressor, and man the victim; for it is certain that in this desire of revenge upon the sex for the falsehood of one will be found a cause of the increase of prostitution. . . .

In one of the most aristocratic houses of prostitution in New York was found the daughter of a merchant, a man of large property, residing in one of the Southern states. She was a beautiful girl, had received a superior education, spoke several languages fluently, and seemed keenly sensible of her degradation. Two years before this time she had been on a visit to some relations in Europe, and on her return voyage in one of her father's vessels, she was seduced by the captain, and became pregnant. He solemnly asserted that he would marry her as soon as they reached their port, but the ship had no sooner arrived than he left her. The poor girl's parents would not receive her back into their family, and she came to New York and prostituted herself for support. . . .

"Ill-treatment of parents, husbands, or relatives" is a prolific cause of prostitution, one hundred and sixty-four women assigning it as a reason for their fall. . . .

J. C.: "My father accused me of being a Prostitute when I was innocent. He would give me no clothes to wear. My mother was a confirmed drunkard and used to be away from home most of the time." Here we have a combination of horrors scarcely equaled in the field of romance. The unjust accusations of the father, and his conduct in not supplying his child with the actual necessaries of life, joined with the drunkenness of the mother, present such an accumulation of cruelty and vice that it would have been a miracle had the girl remained virtuous. It is to be presumed that no one will claim for this couple the performance of any one of the duties enjoined by their position. . . .

Great as are the duties and responsibilities of a father, they are equaled by those devolving upon a husband. He has to provide for the welfare of his wife besides caring for the interests of his children. . . . All married prostitutes can not be exonerated from the charge of guilt, yet the facts which will be hereafter quoted prove that many were driven to a life of shame by those who had solemnly sworn to protect and cherish them. . . .

C. H.: "I was married when I was seventeen years old, and have had three children. The two boys are living now; the girl is dead. My oldest boy is nearly five years old, and the other one is eighteen months. My husband is a sailor. We lived very comfortably till my last child was born, and then he began to drink very hard, and did not support me and I have not seen him or heard any thing about him for six months. After he left me I tried to keep my children by washing or going out to day's work, but I could not earn enough. I never could earn more than two or three dollars a week when I had work, which was not always. My father and mother died when I was a child. I had nobody to help me, and could not support my children, so I came to this place. My boys are now living in the city, and I support them with what I earn by prostitution. It was only to keep them that I came here." . . . In order to feed her helpless offspring she was forced to yield her honor; to prevent them suffering from the pains of hunger, she voluntarily chose to endure the pangs of a guilty conscience; to prolong their lives she periled her own. And at the time when this alternative was forced upon her, the husband was lavishing his money for intoxicating liquor. If she sinned — and this fact can not be denied, however charity may view it — it was the non-performance of his duty that urged, nay, positively forced her to sin. She must endure the punishment of her offenses, but, after reading her simple, heart-rending statement, let casuists decide what amount of condemnation will rest upon the man whose desertion compelled her to violate the law of chastity in order to support her children. . . .

Seventy-one women were persuaded by prostitutes to embrace a life of depravity. One of the most common modes by which this end is accomplished is to inveigle a girl into some house of prostitution as a servant, and this is frequently done through the medium of an intelligence office. . . . [At such establishments] servants who wish to obtain situations register their wants and pay a fee. . . .

Keepers of houses sometimes visit these offices themselves, but generally some unknown agent is employed, or, at times, one of the prostitutes is plainly dressed, and sent to register her name as wishing a situation, so as to be able to obtain admission into the waiting-room. There she enters into conversation with the other women, whom she uses all the art she possesses to induce to visit her employer. . . .

Some of the sources of prostitution have been thus examined. To expose them all would require a volume; but it is hoped that sufficient has been developed to induce observation and inquiry, and prompt action in the premises.

QUESTIONS FOR ANALYSIS

1. Why does Sanger think it highly unlikely that women ever are responsible for their entry into prostitution? Do you agree with him on this?

2. How does Sanger distinguish his approach to and opinions about prostitution from those he calls "moralists"?

3. Where do economic conditions show up in Sanger's account of the causes of prostitution?

DOCUMENTS

Two Slave Love Stories

MOST OF THE HISTORICAL TESTIMONY ABOUT SLAVERY comes from the writings of slaveowners, who understood little about the interior emotional lives of their slaves. By and large, they considered emotional bonds between slaves as insignificant, except when they hampered the master's power and control. Formal marriage was not possible between slaves, who could not make legally binding agreements between themselves that interfered with their masters' rights of ownership. And as Polly Shine, whose testimony appears here, explains, slaveowners actively interfered in the creation of such bonds: "They did not let us know very much about our people. . . . [T]hey took us away from our parents when we was real young so that when they got ready to trade us we would not put on too much demonstration or holler and take on so much."

But two kinds of sources, both represented here, reveal the slaves' own perspective on their condition: slave narratives and oral histories. In the decades leading up to the Civil War, people who had escaped from slavery wrote personal accounts of their experiences. Since slaves were forbidden to learn to read and write, some of these fugitives needed the help of sympathetic white listeners to record their stories and secure publication. Others had been secretly taught, either by compassionate owners or by other slaves, and were literate enough to write their own accounts. Rather than disinterested reports on slavery, these slave narratives were intended to provide northern white audiences with evidence of the system's fundamental inhumanity.

The most famous slave narrative was *The Narrative of the Life of Frederick Douglass,* first published in 1845 and subsequently revised and republished in many versions. Modern audiences are also familiar with Harriet Jacobs's *Incidents in the Life of a Slave Girl,* first published in 1861 (see box, "Trials of Girlhood," pp. 214–15). Douglass's account of slavery contributed to the antislavery cause by its heart-wrenching account of the young Frederick's forcible separation from his mother and his heroic path to freedom. Douglass's exceptionally articulate writing was itself powerful propaganda against the slave system, which denied the humanity, capacity, and individuality of slaves. Jacobs's narrative concentrated on the sexual assaults of her master and the cruelty and indifference to her suffering of her mistress. The themes of these two accounts—motherhood and chastity violated—were popular and effective in antebellum antislavery literature.

Interviews taken from former slaves, long after the system's eradication, provide a second kind of source for the direct experience of black people under slavery. In the 1930s, as part of the New Deal Works Project Administration (see p. 541), federally funded interviewers were sent throughout the South to record the memories of the last generation of black people to have lived under slavery, all of whom had been children at the time and were now almost eighty or older. Preserved only as typescripts (and in a few cases, as primitive tape recordings) for many years, the WPA oral histories were made available in published form in the 1960s.

As do the written slave narratives of the nineteenth century, these twentieth-century sources have many limitations. Most of the interviewers were white and many of the interviewees were probably deferential to or intimidated by them. Perhaps that is why Polly Shine begins her account with assurances that her masters were such "plumb good" owners. Certainly the details of her account tell a different story. In addition, in most cases interviewers wrote down the words of their informants after the interview was concluded, a process that introduced many errors and omissions. Furthermore, interviewers were expected to render the testimony in dialect, and the result probably reflects their expectations of how black people talked as much as the actual speech of the narrators.

Nonetheless, despite the problems of memory, transcription, and interviewer bias, the slave oral histories of the 1930s are extraordinary and crucial resources. The sheer number of people included—2,300 separate interviews in over forty volumes—constitutes a massive archive of insights into slavery as slaves experienced it; and the narrators, unlike the exceptional few who escaped and then rendered their tales into slave narratives before the Civil War, bring us much closer to the common experience of slavery.

WILLIAM AND ELLEN CRAFT

WILLIAM CRAFT'S ACCOUNT of his and his wife Ellen's escape differs from Douglass's and Jacobs's narratives in several respects. Refugees usually escaped slavery as individuals (like Douglass) or, more rarely, as a single parent with a child. The Crafts, however, fled together—Ellen posing as a young white slaveowner and William as "his" slave valet. The narrative itself focuses our attention on the deep marital attachment of these two people, as they together stole their way out of the South. The cooperation and trust between them and their sense that their fates must always be joined carried them through to freedom. Moreover, this narrative was produced without white assistance. William Craft waited twelve years after his escape before publishing his story in order to learn to write it on his own.

Although William narrates their tale, Ellen emerges as a clear and strong character. Her light complexion—both her father and grandfather were white (indeed, the owners of her mother and grandmother)—was the crucial factor that underlay their entire incredible plan. Ellen not only passed through the color line as white; she passed through the gender line as male. Indeed, each transgression necessitated the other: inasmuch as a white female lacked sufficient authority to travel across the South with a male slave, Ellen had to turn herself into a man.

And feeling that as a black slave she was deprived of the protections and privileges of white womanhood, she was willing to cross the line into manhood. William's decision to refer to Ellen as "he" and "my master" after the deception began makes the Crafts' narrative even more compelling. At the crucial moment in their escape, Ellen found within herself an unexpected boldness, as if she had become in truth that which she was masquerading as: someone with white male self-confidence and assertiveness.

As you read, consider what aspects of the slave system and assumptions about race and gender allowed the Crafts to thwart the system. What about the Crafts' story made it useful to the antislavery cause?

Running a Thousand Miles for Freedom; or, The Escape of William and Ellen Craft from Slavery (1860)

My wife's first master was her father, and her mother his slave, and the latter is still the slave of his widow.

Notwithstanding my wife being of African extraction on her mother's side, she is almost white — in fact, she is so nearly so that the tyrannical old lady to whom she first belonged became so annoyed, at finding her frequently mistaken for a child of the family, that she gave her when eleven years of age to a daughter, as a wedding present. This separated my wife from her mother, and also from several other dear friends. But the incessant cruelty of her old mistress made the change of owners or treatment so desirable, that she did not grumble much. . . . After puzzling our brains for years, we were reluctantly driven to the sad conclusion that it was almost impossible to escape slavery in Georgia, and travel 1,000 miles across the slave States. . . .

We were married, and prayed and toiled on till December, 1848, at which time (as I have stated) a plan suggested itself. . . .

Knowing that slaveholders have the privilege of taking their slaves to any part of the country they think proper, it occurred to me that, as my wife was nearly white, I might get her to disguise herself as an invalid gentleman, and assume to be my master, while I could attend as his slave, and that in this manner we might effect our escape. After I thought of the plan, I suggested it to my wife, but at first she shrank from the idea. She thought it was almost impossible for her to assume that disguise, and travel a distance of 1,000 miles across the slave States. However, on the other hand, she also thought of her condition. She saw that the laws under which we lived did not recognize her to be a woman, but a mere chattel, to be bought and sold, or otherwise dealt with as her owner might see fit. Therefore the more she contemplated her helpless condition, the more anxious she was to escape from it. . . .

Some of the best slaveholders will sometimes give their favourite slaves a few days' holiday at Christmas time; so, after no little amount of perseverance on my wife's part, she obtained a pass from her mistress, allowing her to be away for a few days. The cabinet-maker with whom I worked gave me a similar paper, but said that he needed my services very much, and wished me to return as soon as the time granted was up. . . .

On reaching my wife's cottage she handed me her pass, and I showed mine, but at that time neither of us were able to read them. . . .

SOURCE: William Craft, *Running a Thousand Miles for Freedom; or, The Escape of William and Ellen Craft from Slavery* (London: W. Tweedie, 1860).

However, at first, we were highly delighted at the idea of having gained permission to be absent for a few days; but when the thought flashed across my wife's mind that it was customary for travellers to register their names in the visitors' book at hotels, as well as in the clearance or Custom-house book at Charleston, South Carolina . . . our spirits droop[ed] within us.

So, while sitting in our little room upon the verge of despair, all at once my wife raised her head, and with a smile upon her face, which was a moment before bathed in tears, said, "I think I have it!" I asked what it was. She said, "I think I can make a poultice and bind up my right hand in a sling, and with propriety ask the officers to register my name for me." I thought that would do.

It then occurred to her that the smoothness of her face might betray her; so she decided to make another poultice, and put it in a white handkerchief to be worn under the chin, up the cheeks, and to tie over the head. This nearly hid the expression of the countenance, as well as the beardless chin. . . .

We sat up all night discussing the plan and making preparations. Just before the time arrived, in the morning, for us to leave, I cut off my wife's hair square at the back of the head, and got her to dress in the disguise and stand out on the floor. I found that she made a most respectable looking gentleman.

My wife had no ambition whatever to assume this disguise, and would not have done so had it been possible to have obtained our liberty by more simple means; but we knew it was not customary in the South for ladies to travel with male servants; and therefore, notwithstanding my wife's fair complexion, it would have been a very difficult task for her to have come off as a free white lady, with me as her slave; in fact, her not being able to write would have made this quite impossible. We knew that no public conveyance would take us, or any other slave, as a passenger, without our master's consent. . . .

We shook hands, said farewell, and started in different directions for the railway station. I took the nearest possible way to the train, for fear I should be recognized by someone, and got into the negro car in which I knew I should have to ride; but my *master* (as I will now call my wife) took a longer way round, and only arrived there with the bulk of the passengers. He obtained a ticket for himself and one for his slave to Savannah, the first port, which was about two hundred miles off. My master then had the luggage stowed away, and stepped into one of the best carriages. . . . [From Savannah they took train and boat to Baltimore.]

They are particularly watchful at Baltimore to prevent slaves from escaping into Pennsylvania, which is a free State. After I had seen my master into one of the best carriages, and was just about to step into mine, an officer, a full-blooded Yankee of the lower order, saw me. He came quickly up, and, tapping me on the shoulder, said in his unmistakable native twang, together with no little display of his authority, "Where are you going, boy?" "To Philadelphia, sir," I humbly replied. "Well, what are you going there for?" "I am travelling with my master, who is in the next carriage, sir." "Well, I calculate you had better get him out; and be mighty quick about it because the train will soon be starting. It is against my rules to let any man take a slave past here, unless he can satisfy them in the office that he has a right to take him along."

The officer then passed on and left me standing upon the platform, with my anxious heart apparently palpitating in the throat. At first I scarcely knew which way to turn. But it soon occurred to me that the good God, who had been with us thus far, would not forsake us at the eleventh hour. So with renewed hope I stepped into my master's carriage, to inform him of the difficulty. I found him sitting at the farther end, quite alone. As soon as he looked up and saw me, he smiled. I also tried to wear a cheerful countenance, in order to break the shock of the sad news. . . . [A]s there was no time to lose, I went up to him and asked him how he felt. He said "Much better," and that he thanked God we were getting on so nicely. I then said we were not getting on quite so well as we had anticipated. He anxiously and quickly asked what was the matter. I told him. He started as if struck by lightning, and exclaimed, "Good Heavens! William, is it possible that we are, after all, doomed to hopeless bondage?" I could say nothing, my heart was too full to speak, for at first I did not know what to do. However we knew it would never do to turn back. . . . So, after a few moments, I did all I could to encourage my companion, and we stepped out and made for the office: but how or where my master obtained sufficient courage to face the tyrants who had power to blast all we held dear, heaven only knows! . . . We felt that our very existence was at stake, and that we must either sink or swim. But, as God was our present and mighty helper in this as well as in all former trials, we were able to keep our heads up and press forwards.

On entering the room we found the principal man, to whom my master said, "Do you wish to see me, sir?" "Yes," said this eagle-eyed officer; and he added, "It is against our rules, sir, to allow any person to take a slave out of Baltimore into Philadelphia, unless he can satisfy us that he has a right to take him along." "Why is that?" asked my master, with more firmness than could be expected. "Because, sir," continued he, in a voice and manner that almost chilled our blood, "if we should suffer any gentleman to take a slave past here into Philadelphia; and should the gentleman with whom the slave might be travelling turn out not to be his rightful owner; and should the proper master come and prove that his slave escaped on our road, we shall have him to pay for; and, therefore, we cannot let any slave pass here without receiving security to show, and to satisfy us, that it is all right."

This conversation attracted the attention of the large number of bustling passengers . . . not because they thought we were slaves endeavouring to escape, but merely because they thought my master was a slaveholder and invalid gentleman, and therefore it was wrong to detain him. The officer, observing that the passengers sympathised with my master, asked him if he was not acquainted with some gentleman in Baltimore that he could get to endorse for him, to show that I was his property, and that he had a right to take me off. He said, "No"; and added, "I bought tickets in Charleston to pass us through to Philadelphia, and therefore you have no right to detain us here." "Well, sir," said the man, indignantly, "right or no right, we shan' let you go." These sharp words fell upon our anxious hearts like the crack of doom, and made us feel that hope only smiles to deceive.

For a few moments perfect silence prevailed. My master looked at me, and I at him, but neither of us dared to speak a word, for fear of making some blunder that would tend to our detection. . . .

We felt as though we had come into deep waters and were about being overwhelmed, and that the slightest mistake would clip asunder the last brittle thread of hope by which we were suspended, and let us down for ever into the dark and horrible pit of misery and degradation from which we were straining every nerve to escape. While our hearts were crying lustily unto Him who is ever ready and able to save, the conductor of the train that we had just left stepped in. The officer asked if we came by the train with him from Washington; he said we did, and left the room. Just then the bell rang for the train to leave; and had it been the sudden shock of an earthquake it could not have given us a greater thrill. The sound of the bell caused every eye to flash with apparent interest, and to be more steadily fixed upon us than before. But, as God would have it, the officer all at once thrust his fingers through his hair, and in a state of great agitation said, "I really don't know what to do; I calculate it is a right." He then told the clerk to run and tell the conductor to "let this gentleman and slave pass"; adding, "As he is not well, it is a pity to stop him here. We will let him go." My master thanked him, and stepped out and hobbled across the platform as quickly as possible. I tumbled him unceremoniously into one of the best carriages, and leaped into mine just as the train was gliding off towards our happy destination.

POLLY SHINE

WHEN POLLY SHINE WAS NINETY YEARS OLD, WPA interviewer B. E. Davis took down her story in Madisonville, Texas. Hers is one of the fuller WPA narratives. She was an only child, she explains, as her parents "had been put together or married when they was in their middle life." Most of her account, like that of the majority of the WPA narratives, is about the nature of the work slaves did and the conditions under which they lived. But as she dutifully answered the questions Davis most likely asked (they were omitted from the transcript)—Did you see slaves sold? How were slaves punished? Could you read? Did you go to church?—she also recalled a dramatic story of love between a man and a woman that almost thwarted the master's control over them. Shine was a teenager when slavery was abolished. This story, which may have been told to her by her parents, obviously made a powerful impression on her. It is a tale of both heroic and tragic passion. As you read, try to imagine the original interview. What can you tell of Shine and Davis's attitudes toward each other and to the story that she told?

WPA Interview (1938)

I was born in Shreveport, La. in 1848. My father's name was Jim Shine and mother's name was Jessie Shine. . . .

Well, Maser he was a jolly good man but strict. Mistress was a plum angel and their 3 children they was plum good. They were real good to their black people. Yes Maser he would whip the negro if he had to but not beat them up like some Masers would. . . .

Maser had about 100 acres in his plantation and about 35 or 40 slaves. He planted it all in cotton, corn and sugar cane. . . . Maser woke us every morning about 4 o'clock with a big bell, so'es we could get our morning work done, eat and be in the field at daylight or before and be ready to work. Well, no he never had no overseer, he done all that himself and he worked us till plum dark every day, we just quit long enough to eat our dinner at noon then right back to work.

That is we worked from sun to sun as we called it then. . . .

Yes, I have seen slaves sold and auctioned off. They made us wash and clean up real good first, then grease our hands and feet also our legs up to our knees and greased our neck, face and ears good so we would look real fat and slick. Then they would trot us out to and fro before our buyers and let them look us over real good. They felt of our legs, arms and so on before they would offer a price for us. We would be awful sad because we did not know what kind of Maser we were going to have, did'nt know but what he would be real mean to us or would take us plum out of the state where we never would see or hear of our people any more. . . .

Yes, I have seen a few slaves in chains because they would be so unruly that their Maser would have to put them in chains. We have one slave there on our plantation that Maser could not do anything with in the way of keeping him at home. When night come—he had him a girl that lived over on another plantation joining ours and that negro would go over there when Maser told him

SOURCE: Interview by B. E. Davis, February 1, 1938, in George P. Rawick, ed., *The American Slave: A Composite Autobiography,* ser. 2 (Texas Narratives Part 8) (Westport, CT: Greenwood Press, 1977), 9:3511–17.

to go to bed in his quarters, and just as soon as Maser got to bed he would get up and slip off over to see his girl and he would not come back to his quarters until just before daylight, then he would not be any account at all that day. So Maser he tried ever way to get along with that negro without putting him in chains, he whipped him and the patterrollers° they got hold of him several times but that did not do any good so he finely got him some chains, and put around that negroes legs and then he would get him a pole and hop around on, he would get over there some way to see his girl. They got to where they could get them chains off that negro and Maser he would not be out done so he fixed that negro a shed and bed close to a tree there on the plantation and chained his hands and feet to that tree so he could not slip off to see his girl. Of course that fixed the negro slave so he could not travel at night to see his girl, but still that did not do any good but Maser finely did put a stop to the negro

°Slang for "patrollers," white men who stopped slaves off their plantations to make sure that they were not escapees.

man running around at night, then his girl started. She would come over there to his shed and bed and they would lay around there, talk and go on all night, so that negro he would lose so much sleep that he still was not any account. Still they could not out do Maser. He put that negro up for sale and not one that lived there close by would not [sic] offer to buy him as they knew how he was, but there was a man that came in there from another state offered to buy him from Maser and he sold him, and when that negro found out that his Maser had sold him he began to beg him not to. He promised Maser if he would not sell him and take him away from his girl and would let him go . . . to see his girl once a week, he would stay at home and be a real good negro, as him and this girl had one child by now. But Maser would not listen to that negro as he had done had too much trouble with him and let the man have him. The man told him he could not go to see any girl where he was carrying him as there was not any girls there for him to slip off to see. That like to have killed that negro but it did not do any good.

QUESTIONS FOR ANALYSIS

1. How did the characters in these two accounts reject and resist the assumptions about black people fundamental to the slave system? On what personal resources did they draw to make their challenges?

2. Both of these stories were written after the fact: the Crafts' ten years following emancipation and Polly Shine's after about seven decades. Evaluate the role memory plays in these accounts, and consider the ways in which it distorts or possibly authenticates the narrators' experiences.

3. What do these stories tell about the forces shaping love and other intimate relations among black people under slavery?

Godey's Lady's Book

B Y 1850 GODEY'S LADY'S BOOK, with forty thousand subscribers, was the most widely circulated "ladies' magazine" in the United States. For $3 a year, readers from all over the country enjoyed a rich monthly collection of fiction, history (specializing in heroes and heroines of the American Revolution), poetry, and illustrations. Contributors to the magazine included well-known writers such as Nathaniel Hawthorne, who elsewhere bitterly castigated women writers as "that damned mob of scribbling women."[40] Lavish pictorial "embellishments," printed from full-page, specially commissioned steel engravings and hand-colored by the magazine's special staff of 150 female colorists (wage laborers, unlike most of the magazine's readers), lifted *Godey's* above the run-of-the-mill periodicals published for the literate female public. Subscribers treasured their issues, circulated them among friends, and preserved them in leather bindings. The magazine's large readership was testimony to the degree to which *Godey's* both reflected and affected the sympathies and values of its subscribers.

Godey's Lady's Book was edited by a woman and published by a man. Sarah Josepha Hale, a schoolteacher, mother, and widow from Boston, had turned to magazine editing to support herself and her children after the death of her husband in 1828. Like Catharine Beecher, she had pronounced views on the dignity and power of woman's distinct domestic sphere. In the aftermath of the Panic of 1837, she joined forces with a commercially minded publisher, Louis Godey, to become the editor of *Godey's Lady's Book.* Her concerns for feminine values were now combined with his eye for women's possibilities as consumers. The magazine's illustrations thus combined advertisements for the latest fashions (which readers took to their seamstresses to duplicate) with illustrations promoting the feminine ideal of selflessness, purity, and subtle maternal influence. Although the editor Hale was consistent in preaching this notion of women's redemptive, domestic influence throughout her career, her position became more defensive in the 1840s in reaction to the rising tide of the women's rights movement, which she thought dangerous both to women and to the nation (see pp. 274–79): "The elevation of the [female] sex will not consist in becoming like man, in doing man's work, or striving for the dominion of the world. The true woman . . . has a higher and holier vocation. She works in the elements of human nature."[41]

Through stories and images, *Godey's Lady's Book* preached a compelling if conservative doctrine of women's importance to the nation. In a society rapidly being transformed by economic growth and political upheaval, domestic women were expected to provide emotional and spiritual stability. They were to function,

◆ Figure 4.1 *The Constant, or the Anniversary Present* (1851)
Courtesy of the Houghton Library at Harvard University.

as Figure 4.1 advocates, as "the constant" to middle-class American family life. This drawing illustrated a story of a young wife whose quiet, steady love wordlessly convinced her wandering husband to join with her in embracing the healing "close communion of home life."[42] Note the woman's pose, at once submissive to her husband and protective of her children. This image was juxtaposed against another illustration warning women against being a flirtatious "coquette."

The ideology of true womanhood imbued motherhood with both secular and spiritual roles. *Godey's Lady's Book* considered mothers as crucial to preserving the memory of the American Revolution and to securing its legacy within a stable, peaceful, and permanent American nation. Mothers accomplished this task by raising the next generation of citizens. The citizen-child was usually figured as male. "How Can an American Woman Serve Her Country?" *Godey's* asked. The answer: "By early teaching her sons to consider a republic as the best form of government in the world."[43] Motherhood was also a religious obligation, as the visual

◆ Figure 4.2 *The Christian Mother* (1850)

General Research Division, The New York Public Library, Astor, Lenox, and Tilden Foundations.

reference to the Madonna and Child in Figure 4.2 makes quite clear. This equation—of American mother and mother of Christ—became more problematic as the midcentury influx of European Catholic immigrants (see pp. 202–04) put images of Mary off-limits to the overwhelmingly Protestant middle class. Consider how the spiritual and secular dimensions of nineteenth-century motherhood are reconciled in this image.

While preaching the virtues of motherhood and domesticity, female ideologues of middle-class femininity portrayed teaching as a natural profession for women, drawing as it did on maternal virtues and emotions. Hale wrote that "the

◆ Figure 4.3 ***The Teacher*** **(1844)**
Culver Pictures.

reports of common school education show that women are the *best* teachers," in response to which she sponsored a petition to Congress urging public support for women's teacher training.[44] Teaching had previously been the province of men and began changing into a woman's occupation only during the 1820s and 1830s. Outside of the South, public education, long considered essential to a virtuous citizenry, was expanding at a rapid rate. Inasmuch as female teachers were usually paid a third or less of what men were paid, the reasons for the shift were economic as well as ideological. Consider the similarity between the representation of woman as teacher (Figure 4.3) and as mother (Figure 4.2).

◆ Figure 4.4 *Purity* (1850)

Picture Collection, The Branch Libraries, The New York Public Library, Astor, Lenox, and Tilden Foundations.

Barbara Welter, the first modern historian to examine the ideology of true womanhood, identified its four basic elements as domesticity, piety, submission, and purity.[45] Purity of course referred to sexuality (not just experience but also desire), of which the true woman was expected to be innocent. In Figure 4.4, the feminine virtue of purity is illustrated at the same time it is used to advertise designs for fashionable wedding dresses. How do ideological and economic concerns come together in this image?

The middle-class character of the doctrine of domesticity was revealed in the frequent illustrations of the difficulties that the true woman had in hiring and

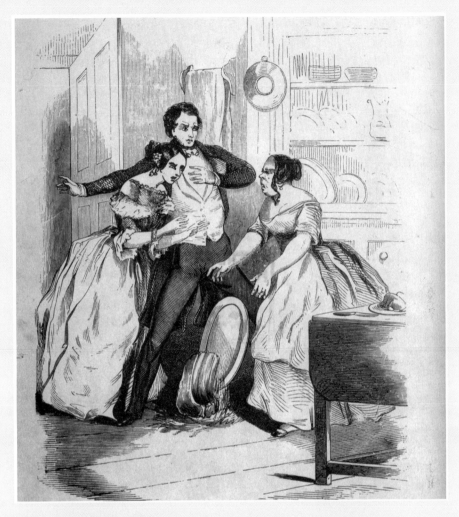

◆ Figure 4.5 **Cooks** (1852)
General Research Division, The New York Public Library, Astor, Lenox, and Tilden Foundations.

supervising household servants. Although—or because—the relation between
mistress and maid was one of the more distressing of the middle-class housewife's
domestic obligations, the stories and drawings about this dilemma were invariably humorous, with the incompetent and stupid housemaid or cook as the sure
butt of the joke. The very face and figure of the cook in Figure 4.5 indicate a
female quite different from the mistress (see Figure 7.7 on p. 443 for a late
nineteenth-century parallel). How is the mistress designated as a true woman
while the cook is not? What does the illustration suggest about the relationship of
husband and wife, as well as that of mistress and maid?

◆ Figure 4.6 *Shoe Shopping* (1848)
General Research Division, The New York Public Library, Astor, Lenox, and Tilden Foundations.

Although *Godey's Lady's Book* insisted on the distinction between woman's domestic sphere and man's worldly obligations, it hinted at the ways that economic realities and the larger society impinged on middle-class women's efforts to practice their home-based ideals. Although Hale preached women's special virtues as an antidote to the distressingly materialistic world outside the home, *Godey's* itself purveyed those same worldly values. The true woman was a frequent shopper, and in 1852 the magazine instituted a shopping service to assist its readers in the purchase of accessories and jewelry. Figure 4.6 portrays middle-class women leaving their cloistered homes for the pleasures and luxury of an elegant shoe emporium, presided over by a male clerk. Looking at this mid-nineteenth-century illustration, keep in mind the women workers far away who manufactured these shoes. Note also how shopping is portrayed as a recreational activity already at this early stage in market society.

QUESTIONS FOR ANALYSIS

1. Examine the expressions, demeanor, and dress of the women from the *Godey's* illustrations shown here. What do they have in common? Why do they show so little variety? How might women readers have regarded these images and tried to imitate them?

2. Look at the profiles of the true women from *Godey's*. Notice their tiny waists, the composure of their hands, the elegance of their bearing. How do these and other details reinforce the message that women are unfit for the public sphere?

3. Consider *Godey's* in light of fashion magazines you are familiar with today. What is the appeal of fashion magazines for women? How seriously do you take the lifestyle and the profiles modeled in the magazines you read? How can such sources be read critically to reveal something about contemporary times?

Early Photographs of Factory Operatives and Slave Women

Photography, invented in France in the 1830s, came to the United States in the 1840s. By 1850, commercial photographers were working in all the major cities. Compared to portrait painting, photography was quick and relatively inexpensive, exactly the modern form of artistic representation appropriate to a young, democratic nation. Perhaps also because so many Americans were on the move, they wanted these small, portable pictures of themselves to send to loved ones. In Massachusetts alone, there were four hundred photographic studios by 1855.[46] Nationwide the estimate is three thousand by 1860.[47] Pocket-size portraits could be had for a few dollars, and common folks, not just the well-to-do, were eager to purchase their likenesses. In 1853, the *New York Tribune* estimated that 3 million photographs were being made annually. Unfortunately, only a very few have survived.[48]

The earliest of these photographs are known as daguerreotypes, named for Louis Jacques Daguerre, the Frenchman who discovered the technology in 1837. The daguerreotypist created a positive image on a metal plate treated with mercury and exposed to light. The finished product was enclosed in a case to protect it from the light. In the United States, the technology gave way in the mid-1850s to simpler and less expensive processes: the tintype (which shortened the sitting time and reduced the cost) and the ambrotype (which used glass instead of metal for the photographic plate and produced a negative rather than a positive image).[49] By the early 1860s, photographers were learning how to make multiple positive prints on paper from negative glass plates. In the early studio photographs, sitters had to remain still for minutes, sometimes with their heads in braces to keep them still; not surprisingly, few smiled. The images that resulted were extremely fragile but also often stunning in their intimacy and delicacy. The sitters seem to look out at us over a century or more, inviting us to study them and detect their sentiments.

For modern students of history, who rely on images for a great deal of information, photographs are particularly satisfying as a source of historical documentation. In our eagerness to see precise, seemingly objective images of the past, however, it is important to realize that the objects of these early historical photographs are selective: some things — and people — were photographed relatively frequently and others not at all. To put it another way, we cannot see photos of everything about which we are curious, only of what previous generations wanted to be seen. Thus, in addition to the obvious visible information that these early photographs convey about the American past, they also document what versions and aspects of themselves nineteenth-century Americans wanted to preserve.

The images that follow—of female factory workers and of slaves—represent women living and working outside the dominant, middle-class ethic of mid-nineteenth-century true womanhood. Their existence prompts us to ask: who took care to preserve these images and why?

FACTORY OPERATIVES

Female textile factory operatives arranged to have their own photographs taken. They posed in their work clothes and held shuttles as symbols of their work as spinners and weavers of cloth. The tools signified that the sitter was a skilled worker, with valuable knowledge, experience, and ability. As these images indicate, the women were proud of their presence in and contribution to the burgeoning industrial economy of those years.

Workers often posed for these portraits in groups, which suggests that they thought of their labor as collective and of their coworkers as friends. For women, coworkers were often relatives as well; sisters and cousins followed their kin into the mills, took jobs that had been secured for them, and worked in the same room at the same task. Factory work was a new experience for most of these young women, and the presence of familiar faces may have eased their transition into a strange environment. Family relations were still crucial elements of their lives, even in the impersonal environment of the textile factory.

By 1860, textile factories and the women who worked in them were found throughout much of New England. The four young women shown in Figure 4.7

◆ Figure 4.7 **Four Women Mill Workers (1860)**
American Textile History Museum, Lowell, Massachusetts.

◆ Figure 4.8 **Two Women Mill Workers (1860)**
American Textile History Museum, Lowell, Massachusetts.
(Special thanks to Claire Sheridan for her help in researching this photograph.)

were photographed near Winthrop, Maine. The two Lowell weavers pictured in Figure 4.8 look enough alike to be sisters. By 1860, when both of these tintypes were taken, Irish newcomers were beginning to take over from Yankee workers in the textile industry, and these women may have been Irish-born. As you study the photographs presented in Figures 4.7 and 4.8, examine the poses, settings, and props. What do they suggest about these women's identities and perhaps even their thoughts? What do the photographs capture about these women's relationships?

The unusual collection of ambrotypes in Figure 4.9 was taken in 1854 in Manchester, New Hampshire, by a group of male and female employees of the Amoskeag Manufacturing Company and presented to the foreman who oversaw their labor. Although the men and women worked together in the carding room, preparing the raw cotton for the spinning process, they did different work. The men worked the carding machines, which began the process, while the women tended the drawing frames and double speeders, which turned the raw fibers into crude strands in preparation for spinning. Despite earning lower wages than the men, women who worked in the carding room were among the best paid of their sex. These subjects posed themselves as dignified, upstanding individuals, dressed in their best clothes for the camera's eye. What does the fact that men and women allowed themselves to be photographed together suggest about gender relations in factories? How do Figures 4.7, 4.8, and 4.9 represent the pride that early factory workers took in their position?

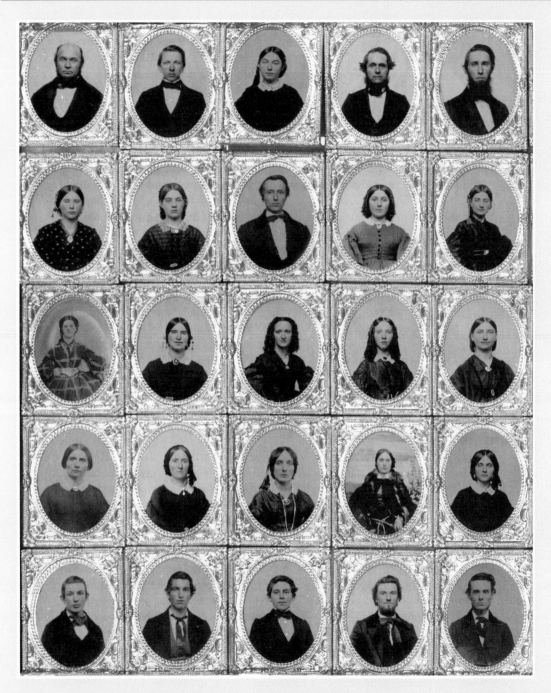

◆ Figure 4.9 **Amoskeag Manufacturing Company Workers (1854)**
Courtesy of the Manchester (N.H.) Historic Association.

SLAVE WOMEN

Unlike factory operatives, slaves did not choose to have their photographs taken. The following photographs of slave women come from two different sources. The first group is that of slave baby nurses, portrayed with their white charges or as part of a larger family group. The slaveholders who arranged for these photographs meant to convey that these black women, the "mammies" of southern nostalgic memory, were beloved, trusted servants to their families. Dissenting from opponents' portrayal of slaveholders as a violent, inhumane class, many regarded themselves as benevolent masters and mistresses who lived in harmony and intimacy with the slaves entrusted to their care.

◆ Figure 4.10 **The Hayward Family's Slave Louisa with Her Legal Owner (c. 1858)**
Missouri Historical Society, St. Louis.

From the perspective of the twenty-first century, nearly 150 years after the abolition of slavery, such photographs can tell a different story. These nineteenth-century black women look out at us with a humanity and individuality that slavery denied they had. Their expressions and poses suggest the complex, if controlled, meanings that their responsibilities to care for white children may have had for them. What appeared to be maternal love was actually unpaid labor. These photographs did not belong to them but to their masters. Where were their own children as they attended to those of their owners?

Of the numerous photographs of slave mammies, we know more about the individuals in Figure 4.10 than most. At a slave auction in New Orleans in 1858, the Hayward family bought the slave woman Louisa, age twenty-two, to serve as nursemaid. The tiny child in the photograph was her legal owner. Many decades later, after he had grown up, he gave the ambrotype to the Missouri Historical Society.[50] What does the fact that he so treasured this photograph tell you about the relations between slaves and masters? As you look into Louisa's eyes, try to recover what she was feeling when the photograph was taken.

By contrast, nothing is known about the family portrayed in Figure 4.11, although the photographer, Thomas Easterly of St. Louis, was well known. What is most striking about this 1850 family photograph is the absence of a white woman. We have to wonder what happened to her and what her absence means for the

◆ Figure 4.11 **Thomas Easterly, *Family with Their Slave Nurse* (c. 1850)**
Thomas Martin Easterly, Father, Daughters, and Nurse, *about 1850, daguerreotype. © The J. Paul Getty Museum, Los Angeles.*

black woman who is included. The slave mistress may have died, leaving the black woman to take over her domestic and childrearing duties. Could the man, like so many slave masters, have had his own sort of intimate relationship with the unnamed black woman whom he includes in his family portrait? Consider the affectionate grouping of the father and daughters and the physical isolation of the black woman. What does this composition suggest about this family? Again, what do you see in the face of the slave nurse?

In a different category from the photographs of domestic slaves are the images of freed slave women that northern photographers made in the context of the Civil War. Like the famous photographs that Mathew Brady took of battlefields

◆ Figure 4.12 **Timothy O'Sullivan, *Plantation in Beaufort, South Carolina* (1862)**
Library of Congress, LC-B8171-152-A.

and male soldiers, these images were meant to document the North's purposes in the war and the Union army's military conduct. Figure 4.12 shows a photograph taken in 1862 by Timothy O'Sullivan, a colleague of Brady's, on a plantation in Beaufort, South Carolina.

O'Sullivan was traveling with the Union army, which had seized and occupied the coastal Sea Islands of eastern Georgia and South Carolina early in the war. Their masters and overseers having fled, these black people continued to work the plantations where they lived but now under the supervision of northern officers, in anticipation of the relationship later formalized within the U.S. Army's Freedmen's Bureau (p. 332). O'Sullivan posed this picture of an entirely black, multigenerational family just freed from slavery. Contrast this image with Figures 4.10 and 4.11, the photographs taken by slaveholders to document their notions of the sentiments that bound slaves to white families. How does O'Sullivan's photograph give evidence to the bonds of love and kinship among black people that the cruelties of the plantation system ignored and threatened? Do you see anything different in the faces and postures of these black people?

QUESTIONS FOR ANALYSIS

1. Compare the attitudes and expressions of the factory operatives and the slave women, especially the slave "mammies." How does the fact that one group chose to photograph themselves while the others were photographed by their masters change the meaning of the photographs?

2. All of these early photographs show women defined by their labor. Does work, in any way, offer common ground between factory operatives and slaves? How are the women in these photographs different from the images in *Godey's Lady's Book* (Visual Sources, pp. 232–39) of middle-class "true women"? What do you think of the fact that the former were more likely to come down to us in photographs, while the images of the latter were preserved in illustrations and paintings?

3. Consider what photographs add to historical documentation. What can photographs, even at this early stage, tell us about women's history that other sorts of images cannot? Conversely, how should we analyze photographs to avoid the temptation of regarding them as transparent mirrors of a lost historical reality?

NOTES

1. Lucy Larcom, *A New England Girlhood: Outlined from Memory* (Boston: Houghton Mifflin, 1889), 222.

2. Ibid., 200.

3. Alexis de Tocqueville, *Democracy in America* (1841; repr., New York: Schocken Books, 1977), 6.

4. Harvey Green, *The Light of the Home: An Intimate View of the Lives of Women in Victorian America* (New York: Pantheon, 1983), 56.

5. Catharine Beecher, *Woman Suffrage and Woman's Profession* (Hartford: Brown & Gross, 1871), 175.

6. Nancy Cott, *The Bonds of Womanhood: "Woman's Sphere" in New England, 1780–1835* (2nd ed., New Haven: Yale University Press, 1997), 28.

7. Beecher, *Woman Suffrage and Woman's Profession,* 28.

8. Nancy Cott, "Passionlessness: An Interpretation of Victorian Sexual Ideology, 1790–1850," *Signs* 4 (1978): 219–36.

9. Ibid.

10. William Sanger, *The History of Prostitution: Its Extent, Causes, and Effects throughout the World* (New York: Medical Publishing, 1921), 488.

11. Catharine Beecher, *A Treatise on Domestic Economy* (1841; repr., New York: Schocken Books, 1978), 178.

12. Larcom, *New England Girlhood,* 198.

13. Mrs. A. J. Graves, *Woman in America: Being an Examination into the Moral and Intellectual Condition of American Female Society* (New York: Harper and Brothers, 1841), 58.

14. American Social History Project, *Who Built America? Working People and the Nation's Economy, Politics, Culture and Society* (New York: Pantheon Books, 1989), 1:249.

15. Larcom, *New England Girlhood,* 196.

16. Alice Kessler-Harris, *Out to Work: A History of Wage-Earning Women in the United States* (New York: Oxford University Press, 1982), 47.

17. "Jerusalem," in *William Blake: Selected Poems* (1804; repr., London: Bloomsbury Publishing Ltd., 2004), 114.

18. Cott, *Bonds of Womanhood,* 38.

19. Larcom, *New England Girlhood,* 196.

20. Charles Dickens, *American Notes* (London: Chapman and Hall, 1842), ch. 4.

21. Larcom, *New England Girlhood,* 146.

22. Harriet Hanson Robinson, *Loom and Spindle: Or Life among the Early Mill Girls* (New York: T. Y. Crowell, 1889), 83.

23. Elizabeth Cady Stanton to Paulina Wright Davis, December 6, 1852, in Ann D. Gordon, ed., *The Selected Papers of Elizabeth Cady Stanton and Susan B. Anthony: In the School of Anti-Slavery, 1840 to 1866* (New Brunswick: Rutgers University Press, 1997), 214.

24. Christine Stansell, *City of Women: Sex and Class in New York, 1789–1860* (New York: Alfred A. Knopf, 1986), 47.

25. Ibid., 14.

26. Susan Smedes, *Memorials of a Southern Planter* (Baltimore: Cushings and Bailey, 1887), 48.

27. Brenda E. Stevenson, *Life in Black and White: Family and Community in the Slave South* (New York: Oxford University Press, 1996), 42.

28. Stephanie McCurry, *Masters of Small Worlds: Yeoman Households, Gender Relations, and the Political Culture of the Antebellum South Carolina Low Country* (New York: Oxford University Press, 1995), 223.

29. Caroline Howard Gilman, *Recollections of a Southern Matron* (New York: Harper and Brothers, 1838), 94.

30. Caroline Elizabeth Merrick, *Old Times in Dixie Land: A Southern Matron's Memories* (New York: Grafton Press, 1901), 18.

31. Angelina Grimké, *An Appeal to the Women of the Nominally Free States* (1838), in Nancy Cott, ed., *Root of Bitterness: Documents of the Social History of American Women* (Boston: Northeastern University Press, 1986), 197.

32. Virginia Clay-Clopton, *A Belle of the Fifties: Memories of Mrs. Clay of Alabama: Covering Social and Political Life in Washington and the South* (New York: Doubleday, 1905), 212.

33. McCurry, *Masters of Small Worlds,* 260.

34. Gerda Lerner, ed., *Black Women in White America: A Documentary History* (New York: Vintage Books, 1992), 34–35.

35. Benjamin Drew, ed., *A North-side View of Slavery: The Refugee; or, The Narratives of Fugitive Slaves in Canada Related by Themselves* (Boston: J. P. Jewett and Co., 1856), 187.

36. Lerner, ed., *Black Women in White America,* 38.

37. Stevenson, *Life in Black and White,* 232.

38. Mary Boykin Chesnut, *A Diary from Dixie* (1905; Boston: Houghton Mifflin, 1949), 212.

39. Cott, *Bonds of Womanhood,* 68.

40. Susan Conrad, *Perish the Thought: Intellectual Women in Romantic America, 1830–1860* (Secaucus, NJ: Citadel Press, 1978), 20. See Nathaniel Hawthorne, "Witches: A Scene from Main Street," *Godey's Lady's Book* 42, no. 17 (1851): 192.

41. Sarah Josepha Hale, "Editors' Table," *Godey's Lady's Book* 42 (1851): 65.

42. Alice B. Neal, "The Constant, or the Anniversary Present," *Godey's Lady's Book* 42 (1851): 5.

43. Kate Berry, "How Can an American Woman Serve Her Country?" *Godey's Lady's Book* 43 (1851): 362.

44. Sarah Josepha Hale, "Editor's Table," *Godey's Lady's Book* 47 (1853): 554.

45. Barbara Welter, "The Cult of True Womanhood, 1820–1860," *American Quarterly* 18 (1966): 151–74.

46. John Wood, ed., *America and the Daguerreotype* (Iowa City: University of Iowa Press, 1991), 95.

47. Oliver Jensen et al., *An American Album* (New York: American Heritage Publishers, 1968), 21.

48. Ibid.

49. Kenneth E. Nelson, "A Thumbnail History of the Daguerreotype," Daguerreian Society, http://www.daguerre.org (accessed June 8, 2004).

50. Information from Duane Sneddeker, photographic curator, Missouri Historical Society.

SUGGESTED REFERENCES

True Womanhood   The term "true womanhood" was first introduced into historical studies by Barbara Welter in "The Cult of True Womanhood, 1820–1860," *American Quarterly* 18 (1966): 151–74. The two most important full-length studies of the cult of domesticity are Nancy Cott's study of New England middle-class women's lives and ideas, *The Bonds of Womanhood: "Woman's Sphere" in New England, 1780–1835,* 2nd ed. (1997), and Kathryn Kish Sklar's intellectual biography of Catharine Beecher, *Catharine Beecher: A Study in American Domesticity* (1976). An original and revealing local study is Mary Ryan's *Cradle of the Middle Class: The Family in Oneida County, 1780–1835* (1983). On the important editor of *Godey's Lady's Book,* see Ruth Finley, *The Lady of Godey's: Sarah Josepha Hale* (1974). Catharine Beecher's *A Treatise on Domestic Economy,* first published in 1841 and subsequently reissued numerous times, eventually in an 1869 version coauthored with Harriet Beecher Stowe and titled *The American Woman's Home* (reissued 2002), is invaluable for ideas on femininity and domesticity in this period. On the sexual dimension of true womanhood ideology, see Nancy Cott's article "Passionlessness: An Interpretation of Victorian Sexual Ideology, 1790–1850," *Signs* 4 (1978): 219–36.

Early Industrial Women Workers   The most comprehensive modern research into female mill workers at Lowell is found in the work of Thomas Dublin: *Women at Work: The Transformation of Work and Community in Lowell, Massachusetts, 1826–1860,* 2nd ed. (1993), and *Farm to Factory: Women's Letters, 1830–1860,* 2nd ed. (1993). An earlier but still very valuable study is Hannah Josephson, *The Golden Threads: New England's Mill Girls and Magnates* (1949). Jeanne Boydston examines the impact of early industrialization on women's household labor and family roles in *Home and Work: Housework, Wages, and the Ideology of Labor in the Early Republic* (1990). There is no full-length biography of Lucy Larcom, but Bernice Selden's *The Mill Girls: Lucy Larcom, Harriet Hanson Robinson, Sarah G. Bagley* (1983) considers the three best-known Lowell writers and activists. Larcom's autobiography, *A New England Girlhood: Outlined from Memory* (1889), remains well worth reading.

Mary Blewett concentrates on the shoe industry, where home work continued to play a major role for a long time, in *Men, Women, and Work: Class, Gender, and Protest in the New England Shoe Industry, 1780–1910* (1988), and *We Will Rise in Our Might: Workingwomen's Voices from Nineteenth-Century New England* (1991). Carol Turbin considers a uniquely female industry, collar making and laundering, in *Working Women of Collar City: Gender, Class, and Community in Troy, New York, 1864–1886* (1992). Christine Stansell investigates the lives of impoverished urban women and children in *City of Women: Sex and Class in New York, 1789–1860* (1986). Regarding prostitution in this early period, see Barbara Meil Hobson, *Uneasy Virtue: The Politics of Prostitution and the American Reform Tradition* (1990).

Women in Slave Society   To understand women in the slave South, various sources must be consulted. For women of the plantation class, the best study is Elizabeth Fox-Genovese, *Within the Plantation Household: Black and White Women of the Old South* (1988). Stephanie McCurry has written about the lives of poor white women in *Masters of Small Worlds: Yeoman Households, Gender Relations, and the Political Culture of the Antebellum South Carolina Low Country* (1995). Deborah Gray White has authored the first comprehensive study of slave women in *Ar'n't I a Woman: Female Slaves in the Plantation South,* rev. ed. (1999). Also see the relevant chapters in Jacqueline Jones, *Labor of Love, Labor of Sorrow: Black Women, Work, and the Family from Slavery to the Present* (1986). Brenda Stevenson considers all these groups in one Virginia county in *Life in Black and White: Family and Community in the Slave South* (1996). Suzanne Lebsock's *The Free Women of Petersburg: Status and Culture in a Southern Town, 1784–1860* (1984) investigates the understudied subject of property holding among women, white and black, in the slave South.

For selected Web sites, please visit the *Through Women's Eyes* book companion site at bedfordstmartins.com/duboisdumenil.

5

Shifting Boundaries

EXPANSION, REFORM, AND CIVIL WAR
1840–1865

T HE YEAR 1848 WAS A DECISIVE ONE IN THE HISTORY of the nation and its women. Mexico, on the losing side of a grueling war with the United States, had just signed the Treaty of Guadalupe Hidalgo and transferred 1.5 million square miles of land and thousands of human beings to U.S. sovereignty. The term "Manifest Destiny," coined a few years before, described the young nation's ambition to wrest much of the continent from its resident peoples, who, U.S. expansionists claimed, could not be trusted to exploit its potential riches. Responding to this crusade, tens of thousands of land-hungry American women and men crossed the central plains to settle on the Pacific Coast. Less than a year after the end of the Mexican War, the discovery of gold in California dramatically accelerated this migration.

The beginning of the American women's rights movement also dates from 1848. Female reformers had been engaged for several decades in efforts to reshape and perfect American society. As proponents of temperance and opponents of slavery, women had pushed at the boundaries of the so-called woman's sphere and moved into more public roles in these years. With the inauguration of the women's rights movement at the Seneca Falls Convention of 1848, they openly breached these boundaries, directing their utopian hopes and activist energies toward the freedom of women themselves.

Finally in 1848, the issue of slavery began to move into American party politics. Although Congress had been evading the issue of slavery for decades, in that year the first political party to oppose the expansion of slavery, the Free-Soil Party, was established, followed by the formation of the Republican Party six years later. On the basis of its antislavery platform, the Republican Party captured the presidency in 1860, prompting eleven southern slave states to secede and fracturing the nation. The resulting Civil War threw the lives of all women, Union and Confederate, white, black, and Native American, into upheaval for four deadly years.

In different ways, each of these historical processes was a kind of "movement." In this dynamic period in American history, when traditional social arrangements were being challenged and reformulated, when politics were confronting fundamental questions about the nature of American democracy and the future of the American nation, when the physical nation itself was breaking and remaking its borders, and when these vital sources of growth gave way to war and destruction and death, American women were on the move as well. Despite cultural conventions about their rootedness at home, American women struck out in all sorts of directions, playing a distinctive part in the nation's history and transforming themselves in the process.

AN EXPANDING NATION, 1843–1861

For a century before and a half century after 1848, continental expansion was a defining aspect of the American experience. Starting in the 1840s, however, the westward movement of American settlers entered a distinctive phase. In 1843, the Oregon Trail, an overland route across the Rocky Mountains, was mapped, and over the next two decades approximately 350,000 Americans crossed the continent, moving through the Indian lands of mid-America to reach the Pacific Coast. The migrants were mostly young American families: men charged with economic obligation and women with childbearing and childrearing responsibilities. Except for slaves brought by southerners, they were for the most part white and, given the costs of

1848	**First New York State Married Women's Property Act passed**
1848	**Seneca Falls Convention initiates women's rights movement**
1848	Free-Soil Party founded
1850	Compromise of 1850, including Fugitive Slave Law, passed
1850	California becomes a state
1850	**First National Women's Rights Convention held in Worcester, Massachusetts**
1851	**Susan B. Anthony and Elizabeth Cady Stanton's partnership begins**
1852	**New York Women's Temperance Society formed**
1852	**Harriet Beecher Stowe's *Uncle Tom's Cabin* published**
1854	Republican Party formed
1854	Congress passes Kansas-Nebraska Act; guerrilla war between pro- and antislavery advocates follows
1854	**Elizabeth Cady Stanton addresses New York legislature on women's rights**
1857	Supreme Court decides *Dred Scott v. Sandford*, rejecting possibility of black citizenship
1860	**Second New York State Married Women's Property Act passed**
1860	Republican candidate Abraham Lincoln elected president
1860– 1861	Southern states secede
1861	Civil War begins
1863	Emancipation Proclamation declares slaves in rebel territory free
1863	**Women's National Loyal League established**
1863	Battle of Gettysburg proves turning point in war
1863	Food riots in Richmond, Virginia, and draft riots in New York City erupt
1865	Robert E. Lee surrenders
1865	Lincoln assassinated
1865	Thirteenth Amendment ratified

the trek, from the middle ranks of society. When gold was discovered in California in 1848, the character and purposes of American migration changed. Hordes of eager, ambitious men — and a few women — rushed to California to realize their dreams of quick wealth rather than permanent settlement. The outbreak of the Civil War effectively curtailed the overland migration, and when expansion resumed, it took a different form, following the nation's new railroad system to concentrate on the great expanse of the trans-Mississippi plains (see pp. 397–403 and the map at the end of the book).

Throughout the period of migration along the Oregon Trail, women from the diverse cultures that met in the West came into conflict. Mexican women who lived in the Southwest were pushed aside as American women moved into their lands. Self-identified "respectable" women shunned prostitutes and female adventurers. Through it all, Indian women were relegated to the status of domestic servants, and by the outbreak of the Civil War, Mexican women were beginning to labor for American women in the same capacity. The conflicts between different groups of women were sometimes overt, sometimes implicit, but always more significant than the commonalities that the ideology of true womanhood claimed they shared.

Overland by Trail

Historians and American popular culture have long celebrated the selfless wives and pioneer mothers for their role on the Oregon Trail, and it is undoubtedly true that men alone could not have made the new claims of continental nationhood a reality. But what of the actual experience of the individual women who pulled up stakes, cooked and laundered out of their primitive wagons for half a year or longer, gave birth and tended children across more than two thousand miles? Men usually made the decision to move. In 1852, Martha Read wrote to her sister of her reluctance to emigrate from New York with her husband: "It looks like a great undertaking to me but Clifton was bound to go and I thought I would go rather than stay here alone with the children."[1] Other women undertook the crossing with the same eagerness as did their men. Looking west from the banks of the Missouri River that same year, Lydia Rudd wrote in her diary, "With good courage and not one sign of regret . . . [I] mounted my pony."[2] Individual families joined together in long lines ("trains") of thirty to two hundred covered wagons to share the effort and the danger of the trip. Many single men made the overland crossing, but few unmarried women did.

Occasionally, documents left by the migrants provide glimpses into the domestic tension that accompanied the difficult decision to uproot and migrate. A month into her 1848 trip to Oregon Territory, Keturah Belknap recorded a quarrel she overheard in a nearby wagon between a husband and wife: "She wants to turn back and he won't, so she says she will go and leave him . . . with that crying baby." Then Belknap heard a "muffled cry and a heavy thud as if something was thrown against the wagon box." She heard the wife say, "Oh you've killed it," to which the husband responded that "he would give her more of the same."[3] In another of these rarely recorded incidents of desperate female resistance, one woman on the trail was so determined to turn back that she set the family's wagon on fire.[4]

Throughout the crossing, men and women had distinctive responsibilities. Men drove the wagons and tended the animals. Women fed their families, cared for their children, and did their best to "keep house" in a cramped wagon bumping its way across the country. As the months wore on and the horses and oxen weakened, women walked more often than they rode. Men's tasks were concentrated during the day; after the wagons stopped and the animals were tended, they could snatch a bit of time to relax. If decisions about direction or pace had to be made, the men met alone and made them. The women's workdays were effectively the reverse. They woke up earlier to prepare breakfast, cared for children as the train moved forward, and worked for many hours after the wagons stopped to prepare for the next day. On the Oregon Trail, everyone worked to the full limit of her or his capacities. Even so, the average woman's workday was several hours longer than that of a man.

Overlanders took care to bring with them some of the few household improvements American women had gained in settled areas by the mid-nineteenth century, such as industrially spun cloth, prepared flour, and soap. Other modern inventions—iron stoves, for example—could not be carried easily, returning women to the domestic conditions of their mothers' and grandmothers' generations. On the rare days when the wagon train stopped, many women did laundry, pounding the dirt out of clothes in cold running streams. Often women begged men to stop the train to observe the Sabbath, but instead of resting, women caught up on their work.

In certain situations, women had to help the men drive the wagons or tend the stock. Rather than seize the chance to show that they could do a man's job, they were frequently reluctant to undertake new and difficult obligations on top of their regular work, clinging to the ideas of true womanhood as a way to preserve dignity on the trail. As Catherine Haun's party crossed the daunting mountain range to Oregon, she described how she joined in to keep the wagons from plunging uncontrollably back and forth. She complained bitterly, not so much that the work was difficult as that it was "unladylike." Whatever the conditions, however, she always had time for "tatting, knitting, crocheting, exchanging recepes [sic] . . . or swapping food," activities that "kept us in practice of feminine occupations and diversions."[5]

Women had exclusive responsibility for children on the trip. Since the average period between births for white women in 1850 was twenty-nine months, it is reasonable to assume that many, perhaps most, women were either pregnant or nursing and caring for infants in the wagons. Pregnancy was not discussed publicly, although "confinement" was not possible on a wagon train. Often the only way that a historian reading a woman's letters or diary can detect a pregnancy is through the woman's references to "getting sick," followed soon afterward by mention of a new child. "Still in camp, washing and overhauling the wagons," Amelia Stewart Knight wrote in her 1853 trail diary. "Got my washing and cooking done and started on again . . . (here I was sick all night, caused by my washing and

◆ An American Family Arrives in California

Artist William S. Jewett titled this painting, completed in 1850, *The Promised Land*. It commemorates the 1846 arrival of the Andrew Jackson Grayson family of Missouri to California. Jewett, also a newcomer to California, discovered that he could make a better living by painting than by panning for gold. Each of the family members indicates a different aspect of American settlement of the Far West. Mr. Grayson wears the buckskin clothes, adapted from Indian dress, that mark him as a pioneering westerner. His son wears a fanciful robe to signify his future rule over all that his father surveys. And what of Mrs. Grayson? How has the artist used her to represent not the danger and hard work of the overland crossing but the middle-class domestic family culture by which the migrants sought to Americanize the West? By picturing a time before the upheaval unleashed by the 1848 gold rush, this painting reminds us of another kind of dream that California embodied for emigrating Americans. *William S. Jewett,* The Promised Land—The Grayson Family, *1850, oil on canvas, 50¼ × 64 inches, Terra Foundation for the Arts, Daniel J. Terra Collection, 1999.70; photograph courtesy of Terra Foundation for the Arts Chicago.*

working too hard).” Within two weeks, just as their trip ended, she gave birth to her eighth child. She had been pregnant but had not referred directly to it for the entire six-month trip west.[6]

In contrast to the infrequent references to birth, deaths, especially of children, were amply described. On her way to Oregon in 1862, Jane Gould Tortillott wrote about overtaking a particularly ill-fated wagon train. “There was a woman died in this train yesterday," she wrote. "She left six children, one of them only two day's [*sic*] old." Three days later, they passed the train. "They had just buried the babe of the woman who died days ago, and were just digging a grave for another woman who was run over. . . . She lived twenty-four hours, she gave birth to a child a short time before she died. The child was buried with her."[7] Older children were also at risk since their busy mothers could not always supervise them. There are numerous stories of children falling under and being crushed by the wheels of a moving wagon. While her mother was caring for a new baby, according to Catherine Sager, "[I got] the hem of my dress caught on an axle-handle, precipitating me under the wheels both of which passed over me, badly crushing my left leg."[8]

As the number of overlanders rose, more and more graves marked the trail. Lydia Rudd, who had begun her trip west so optimistically, within weeks was counting the graves she passed. Many migrants died of cholera, a swift-moving infectious disease that killed by severe dehydration. The disease had come with European immigrants in the mid-nineteenth century, and the overland migrants brought it with them as they traveled west. Sarah Royce wrote in her diary about the death of a man in her group: "Soon terrible spasms convulsed him. . . . Medicine was administered which afforded some relief . . . but nothing availed and in two or three hours the man expired." After the body was buried and the wagons were cleansed, Royce could only wait. "Who would go next?"[9]

Women's relief at having arrived at their destination in Oregon or Washington or California was quickly replaced by the realization that they still had to build homes and establish communities. Long after they had moved west, many continued to miss the lives and families they had left behind. Still, numerous memoirs written about the trail experience and diaries handed down to children and grandchildren attest to the pride that overlanders, women as much as men, took in pioneering American society in the Far West. These records speak of the sense of accomplishment that such settlers felt for their endurance and determination.

The Underside of Expansion: Native Women and Californianas

The mid-nineteenth-century ideologies of Manifest Destiny and of true womanhood came together to designate the women emigrants as agents of civilization, responsible for establishing a settled, propertied American family existence in the West. While individual women suffered during the crossing, their way of life, culture, and standards for womanhood eventually triumphed, and over time their willingness to move west was vindicated. The Native women and the resident Mexican citizens who were pushed violently out of the way as the United States overtook the continent experienced conquest and displacement instead. The process of American expansion set women against each other on the grounds of culture, race, and ethnicity.

Migrating overlanders crossed through Indian Territory in large numbers. Rather than appreciating the disruption and threat that they posed to Native peoples, emigrant women imagined that they were constantly at risk from the "red man." Over and over, trail accounts speak of Indian "attacks" that turn out to be something quite different. Hunger and illness were spreading among the Plains Indians, a consequence of encroaching American settlement. To alleviate their poverty, Indians requested or demanded food and money from the emigrants as they passed through their lands. In 1849, Sarah Royce's wagon train was stopped outside of Council Bluffs, Iowa, by Sioux who wanted payment of a toll. A tense encounter ensued, in which the American men brandished their weapons and declared that "the country we were traveling over belonged to the United States and that these red men had no right to stop us." Royce recorded "the expression of sullen disappointment, mingled with a half-defiant scowl" on the Indians' faces as the emigrants moved on.[10]

In and around the U.S. Army forts and trading posts that dotted the trail were Native women who had left their own people to live with white men in informal sexual and domestic unions but who had been abandoned when the men married white women. In some cases their Native communities did not allow them to return, so these women ended up on the edges of white culture, as domestic servants to women settlers or prostitutes to men, and were met with scorn as "black dirty squaws."[11] "Squaw" had originally been used by white people simply to mean

◆ **Sarah Winnemucca (c. 1883–1891)**
Sarah Winnemucca was born in 1844 to the Paiute tribe on the Nevada–California border. A champion for the rights of her people, she wrote the first autobiography of a Native American woman, *Life among the Piutes* (1883). At about the same time, she lectured to white audiences on the lives and sufferings of Native Americans. To satisfy her audiences' desire to see a "real" Indian, she wore this elaborately beaded deerskin dress over red leather leggings and Indian moccasins. Like the Grayson boy in the picture shown on page 256, she appears in regal dress. She was the daughter and granddaughter of Paiute leaders, and her crown was meant to reinforce her billing as "Princess" Winnemucca. She died in 1891, exhausted and frustrated in her efforts to get white America to treat her people fairly. *Nevada Historical Society.*

"Indian woman," but the word had come to hold exclusively negative connotations of sexual degradation and unrelenting, unrewarded, and unskilled female labor.

Compared to the numerous accounts from white women who feared Indians, few Native women left records of how they felt about white people. In her autobiography, Sarah Winnemucca, a Paiute from the eastern side of the Sierra Nevada, related her encounter with American emigrants who crossed into her people's lands when she was a small child. (See Documents: Cross-Cultural Encounters in California, 1848–1850, pp. 287–95.) The Paiutes had their own rumors that the white people "were killing everybody and eating them." The men of her father's band were away from camp and the women and children were gathering seeds when they realized that whites were approaching. The terrified women buried their children up to their necks in mud and then hid their faces with bushes. "Can any one imagine my feelings buried alive . . . ?" Winnemucca recalled. "With my heart throbbing and not daring to breathe, we lay there all day." Her parents rescued her later that night. Soon after, the band's winter supplies were burned by a party of white men, and their impoverishment began.[12]

Native peoples on the Pacific Coast suffered severe losses as Americans poured into their lands. California Indians were particularly devastated. Their traditional sources of food were destroyed by American settlement and agriculture. Outright violence cost many lives. In 1850 at Clear Lake in northern California, 130 Pomo Indians, including women and children, were massacred by a U.S. Army detachment. At times, young native girls were kidnapped into servitude, and some were undoubtedly raped by white settlers. Sarah Winnemucca remembered that her mother feared that her "young and very good-looking" sister was unsafe among white men, even those whom her grandfather considered friends. These assaults, along with the sexually transmitted diseases that American men brought with them, dramatically reduced Native women's fertility. The California Indian population, which had already been cut in half by disease and poverty in the years of Mexican rule, declined even more precipitously — from 150,000 to 30,000 — between 1850 and 1860.

When they reached California, Americans also encountered the Californios, descendents of the original Mexican colonists. Most of the first Mexican women who had come to California (Californianas) were the wives of soldiers and banished convicts, but far less is known about them than about the women of the small class of Mexican landholders, celebrated in both Mexican and American legend. Starting in the 1830s, American men who went to California made their way into Mexican society by marrying the women of these elite families. In 1841 Abel Stearns, an ambitious merchant from Massachusetts, married Arcadia Bandini, daughter of one of the largest landholders in California. Arcadia, who was fourteen when she married the forty-year-old Abel, outlived her husband; when she died in 1912, she was the richest woman in southern California.

Mexican law gave married women more control over their property than did U.S. law. This helped to account for the phenomenon of the Californiana *ranchera*, the older woman or widow who controlled her own property with strength and savvy. Maria Angustias de la Guerra Ord was such a woman. The daughter of the most prominent Californio in Santa Barbara, she presided over the elaborate home she shared with her husband, Manuel Cesarin. (See Documents: Cross-Cultural Encounters in California, 1848–1850, pp. 287–95.) Helen Hunt Jackson's popular 1880 novel, *Ramona: A Romance of the Old Southwest,* offered a fictional portrait of such a woman in Senora Morena, a Mexican widow who was consumed with hatred for the Americans for seizing her land and despoiling her culture. Allegedly Jackson modeled her heroine after Arcadia Bandini's sister, Ysadora.

Once California became a state in 1850, legislators sought to preserve some of the advantages that Mexican law provided married women, but gradually state courts and legislatures began to rewrite and reinterpret the laws of marital property to conform to the American standard, which favored husbands over wives. These legal shifts may have helped to accelerate the transfer of California lands from Mexican to American ownership in the 1850s and 1860s. As this happened, many Mexican women in California followed the path of Indian women into landlessness, domestic service, and poverty.

The Gold Rush

The combination of the discovery of gold in 1848 with the end of the Mexican War and the achievement of statehood in 1850 greatly accelerated the Americanization of California. The year before the discovery of gold, there were four thousand overland migrants; the year after, there were thirty thousand. Overlanders were joined by other gold-seekers who sailed around the southern tip of South America or crossed the wild Panamanian isthmus. Large numbers of miners came from Chile, Sonora Province in Mexico, and China. At the end of the war with Mexico, California had been populated by one hundred thousand Indians, perhaps a tenth as many Mexicans, and only a few thousand Americans. After the discovery of gold, it became one of the most cosmopolitan places on earth. Based on almost unlimited hopes for the quick achievement of fortune, California society was thoroughly cash-dependent; anything could be bought, and everything cost dearly.

Most of the gold-seekers were men. By one estimate, for every one hundred men in gold country, there were only three women.[13] Some of these women came with their husbands, either to share in the adventure or to fulfill a sense of conjugal duty. But some women longed to go west, to pursue their own adventurous dreams. In a letter to her mother soon after news broke of the discovery of gold, Susan B. Anthony, later one of the founders of the women's rights movement, wrote, "I wish I had about $100,000 of the precious dust. I would no longer be [a] School marm."[14] Anthony did not go, but there were women who did join the rush, some to work close to the mines and others to set up businesses in San Francisco or Sacramento and make their fortunes at a distance. One of the few African American women in gold-rush San Francisco was Mary Ellen Pleasant, who ran a boardinghouse and a restaurant from 1849 through 1855. "A smart woman can do very well in this country," one woman wrote to a friend back east. "It is the only country that I ever was in where a woman recev'd anything like a just compensation for work."[15]

Despite the economic unpredictability of gold-rush California, women continued to maintain class differences among themselves. Middle-class women tended to remain in San Francisco, where they could purchase furniture, solid houses, and the labor of servants, albeit for enormous sums. Louise Clappe was the rare example of a middle-class woman who lived in the goldfields. She came with her physician husband and set up housekeeping in a tiny cabin furnished with three chairs, several rough tables, a bed, and a trunk. Of the three other white women who made up female society there, one was Irish-born and earned the enormous sum of $100 a week doing laundry. Clappe, who missed having servants as much as she did the company of women of her own class, became one of her customers. "Since all women cannot be manglers," she wryly observed of the Irish woman's work washing and pressing her clothes, "the majority of the sex must be satisfied with simply being mangled."[16]

Most white women at the diggings were probably more like the unnamed laundress than like Clappe. While their husbands sought their fortunes at the mines, these women supported their families by feeding, housing, sewing, and laundering for the hordes of unmarried men who were willing to pay well for such services. When Luzena Wilson arrived in the boom town of Nevada City with her husband, she realized that women could make good money tending to the miners. She charged two hundred men $25 each a week for meals.[17] Mary Ballou, who ran a similar establishment, was astounded at the money she could make in California compared to how little women's labor was worth in the East. Even so, she concluded, "I would not advise any Lady to come out here and suffer the toil and fatigue that I have suffered for the sake of a little gold."[18]

Of all the women in gold-rush California, prostitutes have drawn the most attention from historians, much of it either romantic or salacious. "The first females to come were the vicious and unchaste," wrote Hubert Howe Bancroft, the state's first historian. "Flaunting in their gay attire, they were civilly treated by the men, few of whom, even of the most respectable and sedate, disdained to visit their houses."[19] This image of the gold-rush prostitute who was accorded the respectability in California denied to her elsewhere in American society is inaccurate. So, too, is the claim that sexual labor provided these women with wealth and independence. The glamorous whores of California legend were few and limited to San Francisco. Closer to the goldfields, the majority of prostitutes worked in seedy "crib hotels," where they had sex with many men for $1 or $2 per customer. All were at great risk for venereal disease, beatings, and early death.

The hierarchy of sex service in midcentury California reflected sharp racial and national distinctions, with white American and French women in the highest strata, and Mexicans, South Americans, and African Americans much lower. At the very bottom were the Chinese. By the late 1850s, approximately thirty-five thousand Chinese men had come as miners but had been forced by discriminatory laws into low-paid, unskilled labor. The much smaller numbers of immigrant Chinese women were found almost exclusively in prostitution, a situation that did not change until federal measures restricted Chinese immigration in 1882 (see p. 407). By 1860, approximately two thousand women had been kidnapped or purchased in China and sent to the United States, where they were resold for tremendous profits. Chinese prostitutes were held in virtual slave conditions. Their terms of indenture were repeatedly extended for all sorts of spurious reasons, and many did not outlive their terms. Should they somehow elude their captors and the Chinese syndicates that organized the trade, they had no place to turn. U.S. courts ruled that prostitutes who had run away were guilty of the crime of property theft (of themselves) and brought them back to their masters. A few Chinese prostitutes were able to marry Chinese laborers, but American law prohibited marriage to white American men.

Middle-class American women settlers expended little compassion on prostitutes. They were intent on distinguishing themselves from what they saw as the debased standards of womanhood brought in by the gold rush. Author and reformer Eliza Farnham, who had left New York for Santa Cruz to become an independent woman farmer just before gold was discovered, was a fervent advocate of the ideology of true womanhood and one of the "missionar[ies] of virtue, morality, happiness and peace" to the golden land of California. She had only contempt and pity for the very different sorts of women who were rushing in to live "a false life, derelict from noble self-respect and divine purity."[20] When a vigilante movement sprang up in the 1850s to drive out the gambling and prostitution that had become endemic in San Francisco, Farnham championed its violent methods in the name of establishing the higher morality that she identified with women like herself. (See Documents: Cross-Cultural Encounters in California, 1848–1850, pp. 287–95.)

ANTEBELLUM REFORM

The physical expansion of the United States, along with the economic transformation of early industrialization, generated a thriving spirit of moral and social activism from 1840 to the Civil War. Antebellum reformers pushed beyond established social and cultural norms in their attempts to improve, even perfect, both the individual and the society. The centers of this reform ferment were in New York and New England, as if the era's impatience with established boundaries took a metaphoric rather than physical form in that region. Initially rooted in deeply religious conviction, the antebellum reform movement eventually followed the lodestar of moral virtue to arrive at the deeply political issues of abolition and women's rights. Accordingly, reform activism was virtually nonexistent in the slave South.

Women played a notable role in antebellum reform. By one estimate, at any given time as many as 10 percent of adult women in the Northeast were active in benevolent and reforming societies in these years.[21] The influential ideology of true womanhood credited women with the selflessness necessary to counterbalance male individualism. Women's modest efforts on behalf of the community's welfare were thus compatible with domesticity and female respectability. But over time, women's dedication to moral and social causes led them beyond their home-bound roles and to the edges of woman's allotted sphere. In the case of women's rights, some women crossed over into new gender territory altogether.

Expanding Woman's Sphere: Maternal, Moral, and Temperance Reform

Following the intense wave of revivals in the late 1820s known as the Second Great Awakening (see pp. 189–90), women from an ever-wider swath of American society became involved in efforts to deepen and broaden the Protestant faith. Initially their role was to support male missionaries in bringing Christianity to the unconverted at home and abroad. For the most part, they deferred to male clergy and kept to their place, but the fervor of their faith inspired some to venture into new territory, figuratively and literally. In 1836, for instance, Narcissa Whitman and Eliza Spaulding traveled with their minister husbands to Oregon Territory by wagon, probably the first American women to do so, to convert the Nez Perce and Cayuse Indians.

Even in these supportive roles, however, pious women began to form their own organizations dedicated to aspects of their religious duty. They formed mothers' societies to protect the virtue of their children from the rampant immorality they perceived in a society in social and economic flux. These organizations published magazines to advise mothers and established and administered orphanages and Sunday religious schools. By emphasizing the Christian exercise of maternal responsibility, their members wielded their maternal role to expand social authority for their sex. Pious women also formed moral reform societies to combat the upsurge of drink, prostitution, and other forms of what they called "vice." By the early 1840s there were four hundred female moral reform societies in New England and New York. Moral reform enthusiasm was expansive enough to cross boundaries of race and class. Women of the tiny African American middle class formed their own societies to encourage standards of sexual decorum and family respectability in the free black community. The Lynn, Massachusetts, branch brought together artisans' wives and unmarried seamstresses to guard against the prostitution that they feared would take root in factory towns.

Moral reform societies were particularly concerned with the increase in casual sexuality among young women impoverished by the economic forces of rapid industrialization. Female moral reformers raised money to send ministers to save the souls of those women who had already "fallen" and campaigned to exclude from upstanding society "persons of either sex known to be licentious."[22] Eventually they became bolder and reached out directly to prostitutes, despite the threat that such actions posed to their own womanly respectability. Because they considered sexual excess as fundamentally male and regarded all women, even prostitutes, as its victims, they felt that sexual immorality represented sin in its most distinctly male form. To be sure, if prostitutes were not sufficiently penitent, they lost their claim to Christian women's sympathy. Nonetheless, women's moral reform activism deepened many middle-class women's gender consciousness and expanded their sense of common womanhood, thus helping to lay the foundations for the later women's rights movement.

Women's religiously motivated social activism in the mid-nineteenth century reached its height in the temperance movement. Americans were heavy drinkers in these years, but the temperance fervor focused on more than alcohol abuse. In an era of rapid and disorienting economic growth, the lack of self-restraint expressed through drunkenness provided a convenient explanation for why so many people suffered dramatic downward social mobility. The gospel of temperance promised that if a man could just control his impulses, subdue his appetites, and redirect his energies, his family might survive and even prosper through economic shifts. No reform movement was more widely supported in the 1840s and 1850s.

Although drunkenness was considered (not quite accurately) to be an exclusively male vice, images of its female victims—the suffering wives and children of irresponsible drunkards—figured prominently in anti-alcohol propaganda. Not content to remain mere symbols for the tragedies that "King Alcohol" wreaked, women became active proponents of temperate living. They began to form their own Daughters of Temperance societies to challenge both the morality and the legality of commerce in alcohol. When New York women activists created a women's temperance society in 1852, five hundred women attended the convention.

Like the moral reform associations, women's temperance organizations incubated the expression of female discontent with middle-class family life and marital practices. Temperance activism allowed women to criticize men for their failure to live up to the marital bargain, by which wives would subordinate themselves to their husbands so long as the men were reliable breadwinners and even-handed patriarchs. Numerous female activists began their reform careers within the temperance movement, among them Susan B. Anthony, the women's rights pioneer, and Frances Ellen Watkins Harper, the most prominent midcentury African American woman writer and speaker. After the Civil War, women's temperance activism continued to grow until it led to the most important women's organization of the Gilded Age, the Woman's Christian Temperance Union (see pp. 352–53).

Exploring New Territory: Radical Reform in Family and Sexual Life

As women's enthusiasm for moral reform and temperance suggests, family and sexual life were important concerns of antebellum female reformers. The private nuclear family that was so central to the middle-class cult of domesticity was also a locale for domestic violence, sexual abuse, and female disempowerment. Some antebellum reformers called for more radical changes in women's sexual and reproductive lives and for the establishment of alternative social systems not based on the private family.

Women's menstrual, reproductive, and sexual complaints made them eager advocates and consumers of health reform. Unwilling to rely on the questionable diagnoses of regular physicians, health activists developed alternative therapeutic regimes to increase bodily vitality. They made use of natural, non-invasive methods and urged avoiding too much sensual stimulation as unhealthy. The "water cure," a system that emphasized cold-water baths and loose clothing, offered comfort to women worn out from too many and too frequent pregnancies. A program developed by reformer Sylvester Graham stressed the benefits of cold, unspiced foods (from which we inherited the Graham cracker) and promised to remedy sexual as well as digestive complaints.

Mary Gove Nichols, an outspoken critic of the sexual abuses hidden within marital life, advocated both the Graham and water-cure systems. Through the 1840s, she spoke forcefully and wrote explicitly about women's physical frustrations and sufferings in marriage. Insistent that "a healthy and loving woman is impelled to material union" — that is, sexual intercourse — "as surely, often as strongly as man," she declared that "the apathy of the sexual instinct in woman is caused by the enslaved and unhealthy condition in which she lives."[23] Few nineteenth-century women ever encountered such direct speech about female sexuality as did Nichols's readers and audiences. Paulina Wright, who went on to be a leader in the women's rights movement, was also a women's health lecturer. She used a female manikin to teach women about their sexual and reproductive anatomy.

Radical reformers of sexuality and the family could be found as residents of the many communitarian experiments that sprang up in the 1830s and 1840s. These intentional communities posed a range of challenges to conventional notions of marriage and the family. The Shakers occupied one end of the continuum, prohibiting all sexual relations, even within marriage. Men and women lived and worshipped in separate but conjoined communities, coming together to dance and sing their religious ecstasies. Obviously unable to enlarge their numbers by biological reproduction, Shakers took in orphans, apprentices, and individuals in flight from unhappy families, including destitute widows. In the 1830s, an estimated six thousand Shakers lived in nineteen communities throughout the country. Their celibate way of life and the alternative they offered to the private, patriarchal family strongly appealed to women, particularly inasmuch as their founder and chief saint was a woman. "Mother" Ann Lee had emigrated in the 1770s from England, where she had suffered marital rape and domestic abuse. She taught that God was both male and female, and that marriage was based on the subjugation of women and thus violated divine law.

On the other end of the continuum, the Oneida community sanctified extramarital sexuality. Moved by deep dissatisfaction with his own marriage, in 1848 John Humphrey Noyes founded a community in Oneida, near Syracuse, New York. Its members owned property collectively and raised children communally, but the collectivization of sexual relations was the source of the community's greatest notoriety. Both men and women were sexually active but foreswore monogamy, lest they substitute attachment to an individual for the exclusive love of God. They also practiced a strict contraceptive regime that required men to withhold ejaculation through prolonged sexual intercourse. Despite the Oneidans' sexual radicalism, they were deeply Christian and justified all their practices in biblical terms. The collectivization of housework, the availability of different sexual partners, male responsibility for contraception, and what might fairly be called the institutionalization of foreplay offered women at Oneida alternatives available nowhere else. Yet Noyes's insistence on retaining authority over all community life (including assigning sexual partners) also gave Oneida a deeply patriarchal air. Nonetheless, the Oneida community survived into the 1880s.

The Church of Jesus Christ of Latter-day Saints, commonly known as the Mormons, was the most historically significant of these intentional antebellum communities. It is also difficult to assess through the eyes of women, because the estimations of insiders and outsiders were so different with respect to women's status in it. Founded in 1830 in Palmyra, New York, nine years later the Mormons numbered fifteen thousand. The group migrated several times, eventually forming a cooperative community in Nauvoo, Illinois. Responding to rumors that Mormon leaders had multiple wives, non-Mormons drove them out, and starting in 1847, the community trekked farther west to Utah. There, polygamy became an open practice, a sign of special divinity. In 1870, in response to federal pressure against polygamy, the Utah Territory enfranchised its women to indicate their power and stature. When Elizabeth Cady Stanton, the great philosopher of nineteenth-century women's rights who had her own critique of marriage, traveled to Salt Lake City in 1871, she reported that "the Mormon women, like all others, stoutly defended their religion, yet they are no more satisfied [with their marriage practices] than any other sect."[24] The Mormons held to the practice of polygamy until 1896, when they formally rejected it in order for Utah to be admitted as a state.

While the Shakers, the Oneidans, and the Mormons were inspired by radical Christian notions of human perfectibility, there were other communal experiments based on more secular, indeed socialist, ideas. The most famous was Brook Farm, founded in Roxbury, Massachusetts, in 1841 by members of the Boston-based intellectual circle known as the Transcendentalists. For its brief existence, Brook Farm combined high culture and cooperative labor. Although young Georgiana Kirby, recently arrived from England, was not one of the luminaries of the experiment, she enthused, "[T]he very air seemed to hold more exhilarating qualities than any I had breathed before."[25] Margaret Fuller was the most prominent woman associated with Brook Farm, which she visited frequently as she was writing the first full-length feminist treatise in American history, *Woman in the Nineteenth Century* (see box, "What Woman Needs").

Crossing Political Boundaries: Abolitionism

Of all the forms of antebellum social activism, the movement to abolish chattel slavery had the most profound impact on American history, contributing significantly to the social and political tensions leading to the Civil War. Like temperance and moral reform, abolitionism arose out of a deep religious conviction that slaveholding was a sin that the truly God-fearing had the obligation to eliminate.

MARGARET FULLER
What Woman Needs

Margaret Fuller (1810–1850) was the most prominent woman intellectual in antebellum America. In 1844, she wrote an article on the conflict between women's possibilities and their assigned roles. A year later she published a longer version as Woman in the Nineteenth Century. *Less overtly political than other women's rights activists, she was nonetheless widely admired by them for her ideas and teachings.*

Without attaching importance, in themselves, to the changes demanded by the champions of woman, we hail them as signs of the times. We would have every path laid open to woman as freely as to man. Were this done and a slight temporary fermentation allowed to subside, we should see crystallizations more pure and of more various beauty. . . .

[T]hen and only then will mankind be ripe for this, when inward and outward freedom for woman as much as for man shall be acknowledged as a right, not yielded as a concession. . . . If the negro be a soul, if the woman be a soul, appareled in flesh, to one Master only are they accountable. There is but one law for souls, and if there is to be an interpreter of it, he must come not as man, or son of man, but as son of God.

Were thought and feeling once so far elevated that man should esteem himself the brother and friend, but nowise the lord and tutor of woman, were he really bound with her in equal worship, arrangements as to function and employment would be of no consequence. What woman needs is not as woman to act or rule, but as nature to grow, as an intellect to discern, as a soul to live freely and unimpeded, to unfold such powers as were given her when we left our common home.

SOURCE: Bell Gale Chevigny, *The Woman and the Myth: Margaret Fuller's Life and Writings,* rev. ed. (Boston: Northeastern UP, 1997), 248.

"Let but each *woman* in the land do a Christian woman's duty," implored the Boston Female Anti-Slavery Society in 1836, "and the result cannot fail to be [the slave's] instant, peaceful, unconditional deliverance."[26] But unlike other reform movements, abolitionism brought its proponents, women along with men, into open conflict with America's basic political and religious institutions.

The call for immediate, uncompensated abolition of slavery and full civil rights for black people first came from the free black community, which by 1820 numbered over a quarter of a million. Many free blacks were kin to enslaved people, whom they struggled to purchase or smuggle into freedom through the Underground Railroad, the elaborate system of escape routes they developed to aid

MARIA STEWART
On Religion and Morality

Maria W. Stewart (1803–1879) was the first American-born woman to speak in public before a mixed audience of men and women. In all her writings and speeches (as in this 1831 article published in the Liberator*), she urged the free black community of Boston, of which she was a member, to practice self-help, to become educated, and to work for the uplift of all, but especially black women, from lives of degrading toil. By speaking explicitly as a woman for the entire black community, she initiated the tradition of black women's activism in America. After two years of speaking and writing, she became discouraged by the resistance to her message by both whites and some black men and left Boston. She continued to serve her community, albeit less publicly.*

I was born in Hartford, Connecticut, in 1803; was left an orphan at five years of age; was bound out in a clergyman's family; had the seeds of piety and virtue early sown in my mind; but was deprived of the advantages of education, though my soul thirsted for knowledge. . . . [I]n 1826, was married to James W. Stewart; was left a widow in 1829; was, as I humbly hope and trust, brought to the knowledge of the truth, as it is in Jesus, in 1830. . . .

From the moment I experienced the change, I felt a strong desire, with the help and assistance of God, to devote the remainder of my days to piety and virtue, and now possess that spirit of independence, that, were I called upon, I would willingly sacrifice my life for the cause of God and my brethren.

All the nations of the earth are crying out for Liberty and Equality. Away, away with tyranny and oppression! And shall Africa's sons be silent any longer? . . .

I am of a strong opinion, that the day on which we unite, heart and soul, and turn our attention to knowledge and improvement, that day the hissing and reproach among the nations of the earth against us will cease. And even those who now point at us with the finger of scorn, will

fleeing slaves. African American women aided the cause of abolitionism in other ways as well. In 1831, Maria Stewart, a black domestic servant from Connecticut, became the first American woman to criticize slavery publicly before mixed audiences of women and men (see box, "On Religion and Morality").

Black men and women who had experienced slavery directly also challenged the institution. Frederick Douglass escaped slavery in Maryland in 1838 to become

aid and befriend us. It is of no use for us to sit with our hands folded, hanging our heads like bulrushes, lamenting our wretched condition; but let us make a mighty effort, and arise; and if no one will promote or respect us, let us promote and respect ourselves. . . .

Why cannot we do something to distinguish ourselves, and contribute some of our hard earnings that would reflect honor upon our memories, and cause our children to arise and call us blessed? Shall it any longer be said of the daughters of Africa, they have no ambition, they have no force? By no means. Let every female heart become united, and let us raise a fund ourselves; and at the end of one year and a half, we might be able to lay the corner-stone for the building of a High School, that the higher branches of knowledge might be enjoyed by us; and God would raise us up, and enough to aid us in our laudable designs. . . .

How long shall the fair daughters of Africa be compelled to bury their minds and talents beneath a load of iron pots and kettles? Until union, knowledge and love begin to flow among us. How long shall a mean set of men flatter us with their smiles, and enrich themselves with our hard earnings; their wives' fingers sparkling with rings, and they themselves laughing at our folly? Until we begin to promote and patronize each other. Shall we be a by-word among the nations any longer? Shall they laugh us to scorn forever? . . . We have never had an opportunity of displaying our talents; therefore the world thinks we know nothing. And we have been possessed of by far too mean and cowardly a disposition, though I highly disapprove of an insolent or impertinent one. Do you ask the disposition I would have you possess? Possess the spirit of independence. The Americans do, and why should not you? Possess the spirit of men, bold and enterprising, fearless and undaunted. Sue for your rights and privileges. . . . That day we, as a people, hearken unto the voice of the Lord our God, and walk in his ways and ordinances, and become distinguished for our ease, elegance and grace, combined with other virtues, that day the Lord will raise us up, and enough to aid and befriend us, and we shall begin to flourish.

SOURCE: Maria Stewart, from "Religion and the Pure Principles of Morality, The Sure Foundation on Which We Must Build," the *Liberator*, October 1831.

an internationally renowned advocate of freedom for his people. Sojourner Truth was born in New York in 1797 as Isabella Baumfree, a slave before the institution was abolished in that state. After her emancipation, she spent several years in a religious community in New York City, dropped her slave name, and rechristened herself Sojourner Truth to signify her self-chosen vocation as an itinerant preacher and prophet. Starting in 1846, she also became an abolitionist lecturer, traveling as far west as Kansas. Unlike most other black abolitionists, Truth did not present a respectable, middle-class face to the world. She spoke and acted like the woman she was—unlettered, emotionally intense, opinionated, and forthright. In her dialect and style, she made a tremendous impact, especially on white audiences. Author Harriet Beecher Stowe praised "her wonderful physical vigor, her great heaving sea of emotion, her power of spiritual conception, her quick penetration, and her boundless energy," and wondered what such a woman might have been and done had she not been born into slavery.[27]

Knowing that their numbers and influence were insufficient to uproot slavery, African American abolitionists sought sympathetic white allies, beginning with William Lloyd Garrison. From 1831 until 1865, Garrison edited the abolitionist newspaper the *Liberator*. Women were always a substantial proportion of Garrison's followers. His radical principles, universalist notions of human dignity, and personal appreciation for women's discontent with their sphere made him a trusted leader. Elizabeth Cady Stanton—not one to bestow praise on men lightly—wrote of him: "I have always regarded Garrison as the great missionary of the gospel of Jesus to this guilty nation, for he has waged uncompromising warfare with the deadly sins of both Church and State. My own experience is, no doubt, that of many others. . . . [A] few bold strokes from the hammer of his truth and I was free!"[28]

♦ **Frances Ellen Watkins Harper**
Frances Ellen Watkins Harper was a teacher, lecturer, social activist, and poet. Although a free person from birth, she and her family fled their southern hometown of Baltimore after the 1850 passage of the Fugitive Slave Law, which put even free African Americans at risk for seizure as runaway slaves. She was the first African American woman to work for the American Anti-Slavery Society (see pp. 272–73). Following the Civil War, she worked on behalf of the southern freedpeople and continued her political and literary efforts through the end of the century. *Library of Congress, LC-USZ62-118946.*

In 1833 Garrison founded the American Anti-Slavery Society, which was committed to the immediate, uncompensated abolition of slavery. Its membership was racially integrated, although the majority of its members were white. At first, men led the organization and women took supporting roles. Lucretia Mott, an influential Quaker who went on to become the leader of female abolitionists, attended the founding meeting of the American Anti-Slavery Society, but neither she nor any other women were listed as members. "I do not think it occurred to any one of us at the time, that there should be propriety in our signing the [founding] document," she later wrote.[29]

Accordingly, women abolitionists, white and black, organized separate auxiliary female societies. In the Philadelphia Female Anti-Slavery Society, formed also in 1833, black women were 10 percent of its members and an even higher proportion of its officers.[30] Among the most prominent were Charlotte Forten (grandmother of the better-known Charlotte Forten Grimké; see p. 208); Forten's daughters, Margaretta, Sarah Louise, and Harriet; and Grace and Sarah Douglass (not related to Frederick). Despite greater wealth and education than the overwhelming majority of African Americans, these women were no strangers to racial prejudice. In 1838, when a nationwide meeting of women abolitionists was held in Philadelphia, a mob, infuriated by witnessing black and white women meeting together, attacked them and burned down Pennsylvania Hall, the building they had just dedicated to the abolitionist movement.

Female abolitionists' willingness to go beyond the limits of female propriety to defeat slavery, combined with their increasing realization that free women, white as well as black, experienced barriers to full personhood like those faced by slaves, pushed many of them in the direction of women's rights. Sarah and Angelina Grimké led the way. Born into a wealthy and politically prominent slaveholding

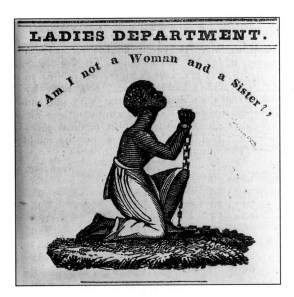

◆ **Am I Not a Woman and a Sister?**
This image, widely used in antislavery literature, expresses the complex sentiments that underlay women's abolitionist activism. The rhetorical question "Am I Not a Woman and a Sister?" challenges the fundamental premise of chattel slavery that the slave woman was mere property. Instead, she is portrayed as sister to the free woman, a member of the same human family. At the same time, the image emphasizes the inequality of the two, as the female slave is pictured as a powerless supplicant, waiting on the actions of the abolitionist woman to reach down and lift her up from her chains. This version appeared on the special pages for women in William Lloyd Garrison's abolitionist newspaper, the *Liberator*. *By permission of the Houghton Library, Harvard University.*

SARAH GRIMKÉ
On the Traditions of Men

Sarah Grimké (1792–1873) and her sister Angelina were slaveowners turned abolitionists. Their attacks on slavery brought them tremendous criticism from the organized clergy of Massachusetts, which issued a "Pastoral Letter" accusing the sisters of stepping outside of the sphere God had assigned their sex. Sarah's defense of women's equal right (and obligation) to uproot slavery was published in 1838 in a series of abolitionist and feminist essays entitled Letters on the Equality of the Sexes and the Condition of Women.

The Lord Jesus defines the duties of his follower in his Sermon on the Mount. . . . I follow him through all his precepts, and find him giving the same directions to women as to men, never even referring to the distinction now so strenuously insisted upon between masculine and feminine virtues: this is one of the anti-christian "traditions of men" which are taught instead of the "commandments of God." Men and women were CREATED EQUAL; they are both moral and accountable beings; and whatever is *right* for man to do, is *right* for woman.

SOURCE: Elizabeth Ann Bartlett et al., eds., *Sarah Grimké: Letters on the Equality of the Sexes and Other Essays* (New Haven: Yale UP, 1988), 38.

family in South Carolina, in 1829 the sisters fled to Philadelphia, where they became Quakers and abolitionists. Driven by their deep conviction of slavery's profound sinfulness, in 1836 they followed Maria Stewart's lead and preached against slavery to "promiscuous" (mixed) audiences of men and women, providing shockingly detailed descriptions of the sexual corruptions of slavery. The Massachusetts General Association of Congregationalist clergy publicly reprimanded them: "We appreciate the unostentatious prayers and efforts of woman in advancing the cause of religion at home and abroad . . . but when she assumes the place and tone of man as a public reformer, . . . her character becomes unnatural. . . .We especially deplore the intimate acquaintance and promiscuous conversation of females with regard to things which ought not to be named."[31] The sisters neither admitted error nor retreated. Instead, they insisted that it was not man's place but God's to assign woman's sphere (see box, "On the Traditions of Men").

The Grimkés' courageous defense of their equal rights as moral beings and social activists produced a split in the abolitionist movement over the role of women. One wing, led by Garrison, moved to include women as full and equal participants in the work of converting white Americans to realize the moral necessity of abolishing slavery. After 1840, women served as officers and paid organizers of the American Anti-Slavery Society. A second wing, which included among its leaders Frederick Douglass, insisted that the issue of women's equality needed to be kept separate from that of abolition. The non-Garrisonians moved in the direction of more pragmatic, political methods, including the formation of political parties against slavery. These two issues—separating abolition from women's rights and moving beyond moral to political methods—were connected. Women, who were identified with moral purity and who lacked political rights, had little to offer a more political approach to abolitionism, at least until they began to make claims for suffrage.

The surfacing of political methods within abolitionism reflected the dramatic democratization of electoral politics in this period. By 1840, virtually all adult white men, regardless of wealth, had the right to vote. White men of all ranks followed elections closely, boasted proudly of their partisan inclinations, and contended openly for the candidates of their choice. Historians have labeled this expansion of political involvement "Jacksonianism" because the Democratic Party, formed in 1828 to nominate Andrew Jackson for the presidency, was its first institutional embodiment, followed in 1834 by the formation of the Whig Party. While in 1824 only 30 percent of adult white men went to the polls, 80 percent did so in 1840. Free black men lost political rights in these years and, by 1860, were enfranchised in only four states—Maine, Massachusetts, New Hampshire, and Vermont.

Nor were women included in the Jacksonian expansion of the franchise. On the contrary, the right to vote was becoming the distinguishing characteristic of white American manhood. Yet, as the reformist spirit of the age began to spill over into politics, women were drawn into the excitement of electoral contests. They participated in political discussions and championed candidates and parties. When they felt compelled to formally register their political opinion on an issue, they turned to the only mechanism allowed to them: petitioning their legislators. As early as 1830, non-Indian women petitioned the U.S. government to halt the violent removal of the Cherokees from their own lands. Women also petitioned their state legislatures to ban the sale of alcohol and to make men's seduction of women a punishable crime.

Women abolitionists conducted the most controversial of these petition campaigns. Starting in the 1830s, they began to gather thousands of signatures on petitions to Congress to ban slavery in the territories and in Washington, D.C., and to end slave trade from state to state. "Let us know no rest til we have done our utmost to . . . obtain the testimony of every woman . . . against the horrible Slave-traffic," they declared.[32] In 1836, Congress passed a "gag rule" to table all petitions on slavery without discussion, but abolitionist women only intensified their efforts (see Map 5.1). Their congressional champion, John Quincy Adams (who had become a Massachusetts congressman after a single term as president) defended the movement of women beyond the boundaries of woman's sphere into the male world of politics: "Every thing which relates to peace and relates to war, or to any other of the great interests of society, is a political subject," he declared. "Are women to have no opinions or actions on subjects relating to the general welfare?"[33]

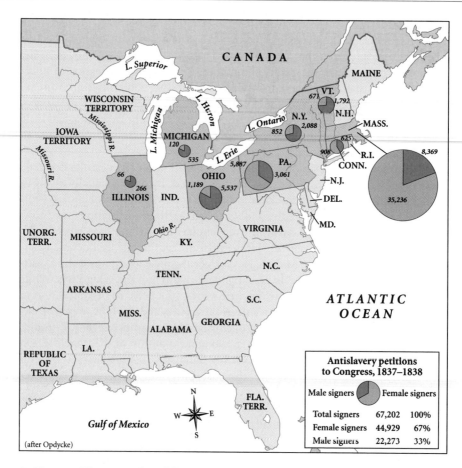

◆ Map 5.1 **Women and Antislavery, 1837–1838**
In the late eighteenth and early nineteenth centuries, most legislative petitions from women came from individuals, for instance to legally dissolve their marriages. In the 1830s, when women began to petition collectively on behalf of pressing political issues, the tone of their petitions became less supplicating and more assertive. Men and women usually submitted separate petitions on behalf of common goals. This map indicates the geographically concentrated character of women's antislavery activism. Their petitions to the U.S. Congress accelerated the interregional tensions and national crisis over slavery, leading twenty-three years later to the Civil War.

Entering New Territory: Women's Rights

Starting in the 1840s, all of these developments—moral reform and temperance, circulating petitions against slavery, the Grimkés' defense of their equal right to champion slaves—led many women reformers into women's rights. But unlike other activists, advocates of women's rights openly challenged the basic premise of true womanhood—that women were fundamentally selfless—and insisted that women had the same claim on individual rights to life, liberty, property, and happiness as men.

First articulated in 1792 by the English radical Mary Wollstonecraft, the doctrine of women's rights was brought to the United States in the 1820s by Frances Wright, a Scotswoman who gained great notoriety by her radical pronouncements on democracy, education, marriage, and labor. The threat that Wright's ideas represented to notions of respectable Christian womanhood can be appreciated by Catharine Beecher's horrified description of her: "There she stands, with brazen front and brawny arms, attacking the safeguards of all that is venerable and sacred in religion, all that is safe and wise in law, all that is pure and lovely in domestic virtue."[34] For several years, any woman who publicly advocated radical ideas was derisively called a "Fanny Wright woman."

For women's rights to grow from a set of ideas associated with one maligned individual into a reform movement took several decades. Changing state laws that deprived married women of all independent property rights was an early goal. These laws treated wives as nonpersons before the law, on the grounds that they were dependents on and subordinates to their husbands' authority. This pervasive Anglo-American legal principle was called "coverture," a term signifying the notion that marriage buried (or "covered") the wife's selfhood in that of the husband (see pp. 59–60). A law to undo coverture by granting married women the same rights to earnings and property as single women and all men was introduced into the New York State legislature in 1836 by Elisha Hertell. Hertell was assisted by Ernestine Rose, a Jewish immigrant who had fled an arranged marriage in Poland, married a man of her own choosing, and settled in New York City to become a leader in the "free-thinking" (atheistic) community. Despite great effort, however, Rose was able to gather only a handful of women's names on a petition supporting Hertell's bill.

By the 1840s, two other women joined Rose to work on behalf of married women's economic rights. One was Paulina Wright (later Davis), the activist who had started her career as a women's health educator. The other was Elizabeth Cady Stanton, destined to become the greatest women's rights thinker of the nineteenth century. (See Documents: Elizabeth Cady Stanton, Writing in the *Lily* and *Una*, pp. 296–303.) Born into a wealthy and politically conservative New York family, Elizabeth Cady possessed great intelligence and high spirits that consistently led her afoul of the boundaries of woman's sphere. Her father, Daniel Cady, was a prominent lawyer and a judge, and although she could never hope to follow in his footsteps, she read law informally in his office. As a young woman, she was deeply influenced by her cousin, the abolitionist Gerrit Smith. In his home, a stop on the Underground Railroad, she met fugitive slaves. She also met her future husband, the charismatic abolitionist orator Henry Stanton. In 1840, despite her father's opposition, Elizabeth and Henry married. When Henry introduced his new bride to Sarah and Angelina Grimké, they noted that they "were very much pleased" with Elizabeth but wished "that Henry was better calculated to help mould such a mind."[35]

Elizabeth Cady Stanton soon found her mentor in Quaker and abolitionist leader Lucretia Mott. On her honeymoon in London in 1840, she met Mott at an international antislavery convention at which female delegates were confined behind an opaque curtain and barred from participating in formal discussions. Both women were incensed, but the thrill of meeting each other outweighed the insult. "The acquaintance of Mrs. Mott, who was a broad, liberal thinker on politics, religion, and all questions of reform, opened to me a new world of thought," Cady Stanton later recalled.[36] For the next several years, Mott instructed her young protégée in the principles of women's rights. Cady Stanton lobbied in the New York legislature for reform of married women's economic rights. In April 1848, the legislature passed a bill that gave wives control over inherited (but not earned) wealth.

By this time Cady Stanton was the mother of four boys and living in the small industrial town of Seneca Falls, New York. Her husband was often away working for the abolitionist cause. With Lucretia Mott as her teacher and Henry Stanton as her husband, Elizabeth Cady Stanton was perfectly situated to bridge the gap between the moral activist tradition of women reformers and the increasingly political focus within abolitionism. She was also eager for a dramatic change in her own life. "The general discontent I felt with woman's portion as wife, mother, housekeeper, physician, and spiritual guide," she wrote, "the wearied, anxious look of the majority of women impressed me with a strong feeling that some active measures should be taken to right the wrongs of society in general, and of women in particular."[37] In July 1848, Cady Stanton, Mott, Mott's sister Martha Coffin Wright, and two other local female abolitionists called a public meeting in a local church to discuss "the social, civil and religious condition of Woman." Of the approximately three hundred women and men who attended, one-third, including a large contingent of Quakers, endorsed a manifesto entitled "Declarations of Sentiments and Resolutions," which, in part, rewrote the Declaration of Independence to declare that "all men *and women* are created equal" (emphasis added).[38]

The Seneca Falls manifesto went on to list eighteen instances of "repeated injuries and usurpations on the part of man toward woman." (See the Appendix, p. A-18 for the complete text.) Women were denied access to professions, trades, and education, their rights in marriage and motherhood, their self-confidence and their moral equality before God. The most controversial resolution asserted women's equal right to vote. To abolitionist purists, however, resort to the ballot represented participation in a fundamentally corrupt system. Yet more and more issues about which women cared — including temperance and abolition — were being debated and resolved within the electoral arena. And, as Cady Stanton repeatedly insisted, all the other changes needed in women's condition would ultimately require women's ability to affect the law. Frederick Douglass, living nearby in Rochester, was the only man in the room who could not vote, and he supported the suffrage resolution eloquently. After debate, the delegates passed it.

In the years after the Seneca Falls Convention, the women's rights movement grew energetically but haphazardly. Lucy Stone, the first U.S. woman to receive a bachelor's degree and a traveling lecturer on abolition and women's rights,

◆ "Bloomer Costumes or Woman's Emancipation"

The heavy skirts worn by middle-class women in the mid-nineteenth century were awkward and confining. In the 1850s, women's rights advocates adopted an alternative costume, which featured loose trousers under a shortened skirt. Named after Amelia Bloomer, a Seneca Falls neighbor of Elizabeth Cady Stanton who championed the outfit in the pages of the *Una* (see Documents: Elizabeth Cady Stanton Writing in the *Lily* and *Una*, pp. 296–303), the "reform dress" was actually first developed by the women of the Oneida community. Bloomers were widely lampooned, as in this cartoon, which links them to male accessories and behaviors. Those who tried the bloomer costume reluctantly gave it up when it brought them so much unwanted attention that they were more rather than less restricted in their freedom of movement. *National Museum of American History, Smithsonian Institution, neg. #49741-B.*

inspired many women to join the ranks. Women learned about the new movement from friends and relatives. In 1851, Susan B. Anthony, living in nearby Rochester, met Cady Stanton and the two women immediately formed a working friendship that lasted sixty years. Women brought women's rights ideas with them as they migrated west. In 1850 California emigrants Eliza Farnham and Georgiana Bruce debated women's rights as side by side they plowed their Santa Cruz farm.

Throughout the 1850s, women's rights advocates met in conventions to share ideas, recruit new adherents, and fortify themselves for future efforts. At one such meeting, in 1851 in Akron, Ohio, abolitionist Sojourner Truth delivered a women's rights speech that has come down through the years as a forceful case for a new standard of womanhood expansive enough to include women like her (see box, "I Am as Strong as Any Man").

Gradually, these pioneering activists began to reform the laws that denied women, especially wives, their rights, especially their economic rights. Cady Stanton and Anthony conducted the most successful of these campaigns in New York State. Cady Stanton, confined by her growing brood of children, wrote the speeches and petitions from her Seneca Falls home. In these years, she spoke in

---

SOJOURNER TRUTH
I Am as Strong as Any Man

The most oft-cited version of Sojourner Truth's eloquent 1851 women's rights speech was published by a white activist, Frances D. Gage, twelve years after it was delivered. Recently, historian Nell Painter has drawn attention to a version of the speech published in the Anti-Slavery Bugle *at the time Truth made her remarks. In this presumably more accurate version, Truth (c. 1797–1883) makes her important argument for women's rights on the basis of her own experience of black womanhood but without the southern dialect, the "Ain't I a woman" refrain, or the lament for her children lost to slavery, all of which Gage attributed to her.*

I am a woman's rights [woman]. I have as much muscle as any man, and can do as much work as any man. I have plowed and reaped and husked and chopped and mowed, and can any man do more than that? I have heard much about the sexes being equal; I can carry as much as any man, and can eat as much too, if I can get it. I am as strong as any man that is now. . . .

I can't read, but I can hear. I have heard the Bible and have learned that Eve caused man to sin. Well, if woman upset the world, do give her a chance to set it right side up again. The Lady has spoken about Jesus, how he never spurned woman from him, and she was right. When Lazarus died, Mary and Martha came to him with faith and love and besought him to raise their brother. And Jesus wept and Lazarus came forth. And how came Jesus into the world? Through God who created him and the woman who bore him. Man, where was your part?

SOURCE: Marius Robinson, *The Anti-Slavery Bugle*, June 21, 1851, reprinted in Nell Irvin Painter, *Sojourner Truth: A Life, a Symbol* (New York: Norton, 1996).

public only once, in 1854, before the members of the New York legislature. Anthony, freer as an unmarried woman, traveled through the state to collect signed petitions on behalf of women's civil and political rights. Women's rights reformers also confronted cultural practices that, along with laws, constrained women.

In 1860, the New York State legislature finally passed a bill that gave wives the rights to own and sell their own property, to control their own wages, and to claim rights over their children upon separation or divorce. Cady Stanton was ready to move on to a campaign to liberalize divorce laws, but this was too much even for women's rights radicals. Moreover, by this point, political conflicts over slavery between North and South had reached such a level of intensity that, like other Americans, women's rights activists were thoroughly preoccupied with the fate of the Union.

CIVIL WAR, 1861–1865

Ever since the northern states had ended slavery early in the nineteenth century, national political leaders had tried to render the practice an exclusively southern problem. In 1820, Congress had crafted the Missouri Compromise, which drew a line across the territories of the Louisiana Purchase at the southern border of the new slave state of Missouri and declared that no further slave states (with the exception of Missouri itself) could be established north of it. The goal was to keep the number of slave and nonslave states equal so as to give neither side an advantage in the Senate. Despite the petitions of abolitionist women, the two major parties, the Democrats and the Whigs, cooperated in keeping debate over slavery out of national politics. But continuing western expansion, especially the acquisition of lands from Mexico that lay outside the Louisiana Territory, eroded this fragile political balance.

In 1850, congressional leaders crafted a second compromise. California would enter the Union as a nonslave state, in exchange for which special federal commissioners would be appointed with the power to return people charged with being runaway slaves to those who claimed to be their masters. Escaping to the North would no longer mean freedom, as it had for Frederick Douglass or Ellen and William Craft (see Documents: Two Slave Love Stories, pp. 225–31). Slave-catching was now effectively federalized under the Fugitive Slave Law. What southerners regarded as proper federal protection of their property rights, northerners regarded as evidence that an ambitious slave power was taking over the country. From this point forward, the expansion of slavery became an increasingly explosive national political issue, culminating in the secession of South Carolina in December 1860 and the beginning of the Civil War in April 1861.

Just as the Civil War pitted brother against brother, women, too, were intensely divided in their loyalties, with the difference, of course, that women were barred from both the ballot box and the battlefield. But as in all civil wars, the home front was impossible to separate from the battle front. Women on both sides actively supported their causes and their armies. A small but surprising number participated directly, either on the battlefield or in the politics that shaped the changing purposes for which the war was fought. All women were affected by the war — its passions, victories, devastations, and deaths.

Women and the Impending Crisis

As the political conflict over slavery intensified, women were drawn into the growing crisis. Most famously, Harriet Beecher Stowe wrote *Uncle Tom's Cabin* to dramatize the dangers facing the escaping slave under the new federal law (see box, "Reflections on *Uncle Tom's Cabin*"). By far the most popular American novel ever written, the story of the slave Eliza fleeing slave-catchers to save her child was avidly read when it first appeared in installments in an antislavery newspaper in 1851 to 1852. Inspired by Stowe's book, Harriet Jacobs, who had actually escaped from slavery twelve years before, determined to write her own story. *Incidents in the Life of a Slave Girl: Written by Herself* was published in 1861, with the help of white abolitionist Lydia Maria Child.

Throughout the political events of the 1850s, women's involvement was everywhere. In 1854, the Republican Party was founded to oppose the expansion (though not the existence) of slavery, and it succeeded in bringing the issue squarely into the center of national politics. The party's 1856 presidential nominee was U.S. Senator John Frémont of California, one of the men who had originally surveyed the Oregon Trail. His wife, Jessie Benton Frémont, was the first wife of a presidential candidate to figure significantly in a national campaign. Daughter of U.S. Senator Thomas Hart Benton of Missouri, the young, attractive, and vivacious woman was considered a liberal influence on her husband. Campaign paraphernalia advertised Jessie as much as her husband. Although John Frémont was defeated by the Democratic candidate, James Buchanan, the Republicans succeeded in displacing the Whigs to become one of the two major national parties.

Then, in 1857, the Supreme Court ruled in favor of slavery in the momentous case *Dred Scott v. Sandford*. The case might more appropriately be called the Dred and Harriet Scott case since it involved not only Missouri slave Dred Scott but also his wife, Harriet. Together they sued their owner for their freedom and that of their two daughters. By being brought in 1834 into federal territory where slavery was not lawful, the Scotts argued, they had become free persons. A majority of the Supreme Court ruled against the Scotts. In addition, Chief Justice Roger B. Taney wrote an opinion that the entire legal framework dating back to the Missouri Compromise was unconstitutional because it violated slaveowners' property rights. The sons of the Scotts' original owner eventually bought their freedom, but the larger battle between pro- and antislavery forces for control of the federal government had been profoundly intensified by the decision.

The election of 1860 took place against the background of abolitionist John Brown's abortive guerrilla raid on the federal armory in Harpers Ferry, Virginia, which was intended (but failed) to start a general slave uprising. To southerners, the handful of black and white antislavery warriors under Brown's command constituted exactly the violent threat that they long had feared from abolitionists.

HARRIET BEECHER STOWE
Reflections on Uncle Tom's Cabin

Harriet Beecher Stowe (1811–1896) was the daughter, sister, and wife of influential Protestant ministers. Like her sister Catharine Beecher, (see pp. 188–91) she was a highly successful author, whose books elaborated the ideas of true womanhood. In 1849, her eighteen-month-old son died, an experience that informed her powerful antislavery novel, Uncle Tom's Cabin, *published in 1851–1852. In it, the slave heroine Eliza is threatened with the loss of her own child, through sale rather than death. Stowe's novel is widely credited with building popular antislavery sentiment, especially among women, in the North.*

For many years of her life, the author avoided all reading upon or allusion to the subject of slavery, considering it as too painful to be inquired into. . . . But, since the legislative act of 1850, when she heard, with perfect surprise and consternation, Christian and humane people actually recommending the remanding of escaped fugitives into slavery, as a duty binding on good citizens, . . . she could only think, These men and Christians cannot know what slavery is; if they did, such a question could never be open for discussion. . . . You, mothers of America, — you who have learned, by the cradles of your own children, to love and feel for all mankind, — by the sacred love you bear your child; . . . — I beseech you, pity the mother who has all your affections, and not one legal right to protect, guide, or educate, the child of her bosom! . . . If the mothers of the free states had all felt as they should, . . . the sons of the free states would not have connived at the extension of slavery, in our national body; the sons of the free states would not, as they do, trade the souls and bodies of men as an equivalent to money, in their mercantile dealings. There are multitudes of slaves temporarily owned, and sold again, by merchants in northern cities; and shall the whole guilt or obloquy of slavery fall only on the South?

SOURCE: Harriet Beecher Stowe, *Uncle Tom's Cabin* (1851–52; New York: Bantam Classics, 1982), 437–38.

Many northerners regarded Brown quite differently, as a martyr. "I thank you that you have been brave enough to reach out your hands to the crushed and blighted of my race," Frances Ellen Watkins Harper wrote to Brown as he awaited execution after his capture by federal forces. "I hope from your sad fate great good may arise to the cause of freedom."[39]

For president, the Republicans nominated former Illinois Congressman Abraham Lincoln, a moderate critic of slavery, hardly an abolitionist. Despite his moderation, his election was intolerable to the South because he was a Republican. But to many northerners, Lincoln's election was cause to celebrate. Twenty-one-year-old Frances Willard, who would go on to head the Woman's Christian Temperance Union in the 1870s, observed events from her Illinois home: "Under the present system I am not allowed to vote for [Lincoln], but I am as glad on account of this Republican triumph as any man who has exercised the elective franchise can be."[40]

By April 1861, eleven southern slave states had seceded from the Union to form the Confederate States of America. On April 13, South Carolina slaveholder Mary Chesnut watched as southern gunboats fired on U.S. ships that Lincoln had sent to provision federal Fort Sumter in Charleston harbor. She recorded her reaction upon learning that federal forces had surrendered to the Confederates: "[I] sprang out of bed and on my knees — prostrate — I prayed as I never prayed before."[41]

Chesnut understood that war had begun in earnest. North and South, men and boys rushed to enroll in their local regiments, and wives and mothers prepared to say good-bye. "Love for the old flag became a passion," wrote Mary Livermore from Illinois, "and women crocheted it prettily in silk, and wore it as a decoration on their bonnets and in their bosoms."[42] Both sides hoped for a brief war and a glorious victory but got instead a four-year conflict, the deadliest war in American history.

Women's Involvement in the War

Although formally excluded from enlistment and armed service, both Union and Confederate women were deeply involved in the war. Eager and patriotic, a minority found their way to the battlefields, as nurses, spies, and strategists; a few, disguised as men, even served as soldiers. (See Visual Sources: Women on the Civil War Battlefields, pp. 304–17.) Far more women participated at a distance. Because both armies were decentralized and almost entirely unprovisioned — except for munitions — by their respective governments, women volunteers were responsible for much of the clothing, feeding, and nursing of the soldiers. In the South this was done at a local level. Within a few months after the conflict had begun, Mary Ann Cobb, wife of a Confederate officer in Georgia, found herself charged with rounding up provisions for a company of eighty men, largely by going door-to-door among her neighbors.

In the North, where women had greater experience in running their own voluntary associations, soldiers' relief was better organized. Local societies were drawn together in a national organization known as the United States Sanitary Commission. Mary Livermore spent the war directing the Chicago branch. Her duties were manifold: "I . . . delivered public addresses to stimulate supplies and donations of money; . . . wrote letters by the thousand . . . ; made trips to the front with sanitary stores . . . ; brought back large numbers of invalid soldiers . . . ;

assisted to plan, organize, and conduct colossal [fund-raising] fairs . . . ; detailed women nurses . . . and accompanied them to their posts."[43] The experience turned Livermore and others like her into skilled, confident organization women, and after the war they used these experiences to build even more ambitious women's federations. On the basis of her experience organizing relief supplies for northern soldiers, Clara Barton went on to found the American division of the International Red Cross.

The labors of such women earned them elaborate praise. But for the average woman on either side of the conflict, these were not years of uplifting service or patriotic heroism so much as of prolonged suffering. Women struggled to support their families without the aid of husbands, sons, and brothers. Anna Howard Shaw, who later became one of America's leading suffragists, was a young woman living in rural Michigan in 1861: "I remember seeing a man ride up on horseback, shouting out Lincoln's demand for troops. . . . Before he had finished speaking the men on the [threshing] machine had leaped to the ground and rushed off to enlist, my brother Jack . . . among them. . . . The work in our community, if it was done at all, was done by despairing women whose hearts were with their men."[44]

Since the North lost much of its labor force to the fighting, the South, which relied on slave workers, initially had the advantage. Even so, most white southerners were small-scale subsistence farmers who relied almost entirely on their own labor rather than on that of slaves. With or without official leaves from the Confederate army, numerous southern soldiers responded to the entreaties of their wives to leave their posts, come home, and bring in the harvest. "Since your connection with the Confederate army, I have been prouder of you than ever before . . . ," one such woman wrote to her husband, "but before God, Edward, unless you come home we must die."[45] By the middle of the war, such seasonal desertions, conservatively estimated at more than one hundred thousand, as much as 10 percent of the Confederate forces, were a major strain on the South's capacity to fight.

As the conflict wore on, patriotism and optimism gave way to discontent on both sides. In the South, the situation was exacerbated by a Union naval blockade that led to food shortages and triple-digit inflation. In the spring of 1863, the women of Richmond rampaged through the streets protesting the high cost of food and demanding that they be able to buy bread and meat at the same prices as the Confederate armies. Three months later, New York City was paralyzed by mobs protesting passage of a federal Conscription Act that allowed wealthy men to buy themselves out of the draft for $300. Elizabeth Cady Stanton, who had just moved to the city with her three youngest children, found herself in the middle of the upheaval. She watched as one of her older sons was recognized by the rioters as "one of those three-hundred-dollar fellows." "You may imagine what I suffered in seeing him dragged off," she wrote to her cousin. "I was alone with the children expecting every moment to hear the wretches thundering at the front door. . . . I then prepared a speech, determined, if necessary, to go down at once, open the door and make an appeal to them as Americans and citizens of the Republic."[46] The mob changed direction, and she fled the city with her family.

Emancipation

While the South was fighting to preserve slavery and defend its sovereignty, the war aims of the North remained muddled. For more than a year, Lincoln insisted that his only goal was to end secession and restore the Union. The president was unwilling to declare opposition to slavery for fear that the border states of Kentucky, Missouri, Maryland, and Delaware, where slavery was legal, would leave the Union and join the Confederacy. The abolition of slavery became the Union's goal only after slaves themselves took action through a massive, prolonged process of what has been characterized as "self-emancipation." Like the slaves who for decades had run away, men and women in large numbers began to flee into the arms of the Union army, buoyed by news of northern victories and hoping that they would be freed. One woman described her escape onto a Union gunboat sailing down the Mississippi River. "We all give three times three cheers for the gunboat boys and three times three cheers for big Yankee sojers an three times three cheers for gov'ment," she recalled; "an I tell you every one of us, big and little, cheered loud and long and strong, an' made the old river just ring ag'in."[47] Union officers disagreed on how to respond to the masses of refugees. Those unsympathetic to the antislavery cause wanted to return them to their owners, but the army eventually decided on a policy of accepting them under the category of confiscated enemy property. Thousands of these human "contraband" provided crucial aid to the Union army as laborers, cooks, and servants. As many as forty thousand gathered in Washington, D.C., where Sojourner Truth, Harriet Jacobs, and others organized a freedmen's village.

As their numbers increased, Lincoln realized that the steady flight of the southern slave labor force offered an irresistible military advantage to the Union. Accordingly, he issued the Emancipation Proclamation, to take effect on January 1, 1863, which declared all slaves in rebel territory "forever free" and instructed the Union army and navy to "recognize and maintain the freedom of such persons." The status of slaves living in the Union border states and areas of the Confederacy already under Union control, however, was left untouched. Since the Union could not actually emancipate slaves in lands it did not control, the proclamation was meant only to encourage slaves in the renegade regions to abandon their masters and free themselves. Despite its limits, however, the Emancipation Proclamation finally made the Civil War a war against slavery.

Women's rights leaders Elizabeth Cady Stanton and Susan B. Anthony were determined to push Lincoln to enact a more comprehensive abolition policy. "If it be true that at this hour, the women of the South are more devoted to their cause than we to ours, the fact lies here," wrote Cady Stanton. "The women of the South know what their sons are fighting for. The women of the North do not."[48] Along with Lucy Stone and other women's rights activists, they formed the Women's National Loyal League to force Lincoln to adopt a broader emancipation policy. As abolitionist women had done thirty years before, they gathered signatures on petitions to Congress to "pass at the earliest practicable day an act emancipating all persons of African descent."[49] The league collected and submit-

◆ **Edmonia Lewis, *Forever Free* (1868)**
Edmonia Lewis's sculpture commemorates the Emancipation Proclamation. Born to a free black father and a Chippewa mother, Lewis felt her artistic ambitions ignited by the battle for black freedom. During the war, she sought support from Boston abolitionists and began her career by creating a medallion of John Brown and a bust of Robert Gould Shaw, the commander of the black Union regiment, the Massachusetts 54th. In 1865, she left the United States and joined a group of American women artists in Rome, but her subject matter remained concerned with issues of race, gender, and freedom. Completed in 1868, this sculpture features the classic abolitionist icon of the supplicant slave woman (see p. 271). In this case, however, the emancipating figure is a freedman. Both man and woman have broken their chains.
Howard University Gallery of Art, Washington, D.C.

ted to Congress 260,000 signatures, two-thirds of them from women. The first popular campaign ever conducted on behalf of a constitutional amendment, these efforts contributed significantly to the 1865 passage and ratification of the Thirteenth Amendment, which permanently abolished slavery throughout the United States (see Appendix, pp. A-13–A-14).

In 1863, after two years of grueling warfare, the military tide began to turn in the Union's favor. An important factor was the Union army's decision to permit African American men to fight. Close to two hundred thousand enlisted, providing a final burst of military energy as well as a manly model of black freedom. On July 4, 1863, the Union won a decisive battle at Vicksburg, Mississippi, just one day after its equally decisive victory at Gettysburg, Pennsylvania. Still, the war lasted two more years. In the autumn of 1864, General William Tecumseh Sherman marched the western division of the Union army across Georgia and South Carolina, determined to break the spirit of the rebellion by destroying everything of value as he went. At her plantation, Mary Chesnut found "every window was broken, every bell torn down, every piece of furniture destroyed, every door smashed in."[50]

Finally, on April 9, 1865, almost four years to the day after the attack on Fort Sumter, General Robert E. Lee, head of the Confederate army, surrendered. An ex-slave woman from South Carolina remembered, "[On] de fust day of freedom we was all sittin' roun' restin' an' tryin' to think what freedom meant an ev'ybody was quiet an' peaceful."[51] "The people poured into the streets, frenzied with gladness," wrote Mary Livermore, "until there seemed to be no men and women in Chicago, — only crazy, grown-up boys and girls." Then, five days later, Lincoln was assassinated. "From the height of this exultation," Livermore wrote, "the nation was swiftly precipitated to the very depths of despair." She continued, "Never was a month so crowded, with the conflicting emotions of exultation and despair, as was the month of April 1865."[52] Not all women saw it the same way. "Thank God, the wretch has gotten his just deserts," exulted a Confederate woman.[53]

CONCLUSION: Reshaping Boundaries, Redefining Womanhood

In the years from 1840 to 1865, the women of the United States had traveled a tremendous distance. They had taken a country across a continent. They had joined in a series of social movements to remake and reform American society. They had challenged slavery and undertaken systematic reform in their own status as women. They had begun to demand their inclusion in the democratization of American politics. And, along with men but in their own ways, they had joined in the fight over the character and existence of the Union, participating in the Civil War both on and off the battlefield.

Their experiences through these changes had by no means been the same. Some women had taken possession of new land, in the process displacing others from their homes of long standing. Some had challenged crucial elements of American society and culture and ended up challenging conventional notions of womanhood itself. And while some had defended and lost their right to own slaves, those who had been slaves became free women. Through all of this, however, American women had been deeply involved in these years of momentous national change and had been changed in the process. In the decades after the Civil War, in the victorious North and the struggling South, they began to enter more fully into public life, as workers and socially engaged citizens, in civic organizations and in colleges. Like 1848, 1865 was a decisive year in the history of the nation and of its women.

DOCUMENTS

Cross-Cultural Encounters in California, 1848–1850

Each of these selections focuses on the cross-cultural experience of women in California at the moment of statehood. Three groups of people—the Indians, the Californios (Mexican citizens who lived in California prior to American statehood), and the emigrants from the East (called Americans or Yankees by all concerned)—came upon each other with various combinations of curiosity, hospitality, alliance, exploitation, and violence. Starting in the late eighteenth century, the Californios thinly populated the Pacific Coast up to the San Francisco Bay. Coastal Natives became their laborers and servants. Inland and to the north, larger numbers of Indian peoples still lived the nomadic lives of their ancestors. The arrival of Yankee emigrants beginning in the mid-1840s brought rapid change. Within a few years, the Californios had lost control of the coastal lands, the lives of the Natives had been profoundly disrupted by illness and warfare and death, and California had become the thirty-first state of the United States.

SARAH WINNEMUCCA

Our first eyewitness to these encounters, Sarah Winnemucca, was born in 1844. Her name was then Thocmetony. Her people, later called Paiutes or Piutes (she thought as a corruption of "pine nuts," a crucial part of the tribe's diet), had for centuries moved back and forth between the area near what is now Reno, Nevada, and the eastern part of Oregon. Later she adopted the English name Sarah, and Winnemucca was the name of her father and paternal grandfather. Despite a fearful and violent initial exposure to white people, she lived among, married into, and cooperated with them for much of her adult life. She used her knowledge of American culture, her connections to influential U.S. figures, and her exceptional language skills to speak on behalf of her people as their conditions worsened. When she was forty years old, she wrote her autobiography.

Sarah's account is addressed to an American audience and is meant to give the Native side of the encounter between the two peoples. In this selection she describes her first meeting, at age six, with white people and the strong interest that her maternal grandfather, Captain Truckee, took in the Americans, alongside whom he fought during the Mexican War. Her account reveals how the American newcomers, like the Californios before them, were able to extract labor from the Paiutes. Hiram Scott and Jacob Bonsal, Americans who are featured prominently in her story, ran a business ferrying people over the San Joaquin River near Stockton, California. In this episode, Sarah's mother goes with her father to live and work with the Americans, while her husband, who is hostile to them, stays away. In the end, her mother's pleading with the Americans wins permission for Sarah and her family to return to their band.

As you read, consider what this selection reveals about Paiute family dynamics. In the disagreements in Sarah's family about whether to trust the Americans, who prevails and why? How are those family dynamics extended to include the Yankee newcomers, to whom Sarah's grandfather is so devoted, and with what consequences? Why is her mother so frightened for Sarah's sister, and what resources does she have to protect her? Finally, as a young child, what frightens Sarah about these strange people, and what attracts her to them?

I was born somewhere near 1844, but am not sure of the precise time. I was a very small child when the first white people came into our country. They came like a lion, yes, like a roaring lion, and have continued so ever since, and I have never forgotten their first coming. My people were scattered at that time over nearly all the territory now known as Nevada. My grandfather was chief of the entire Piute nation, and was camped near Humboldt Lake, with a small portion of his tribe, when a party . . . was seen coming. When the news was brought to my grandfather, he asked what they looked like? When told that they had hair on their faces, and were white, he jumped up and clasped his hands together, and cried aloud,

"My white brothers, my long-looked-for white brothers have come at last!". . . [T]he next spring the emigrants came as usual, and my father and grandfather and uncles, and many more went down on the Humboldt River on fishing excursions. While they were thus fishing, their white brothers came upon them and fired on them, and killed one of my uncles, and wounded another.

Nine more were wounded, and five died afterwards. My other uncle got well again, and is living yet. Oh, that was a fearful thing, indeed!

After all these things had happened, my grandfather still stood up for his white brothers. . . .

It was late that fall when my grandfather prevailed with his people to go with him to California. It was this time when my mother accompanied him. Everything had been got ready to start on our journey. My dear father [who was not friendly to the Americans] was to be left behind. How my poor mother begged to stay with her husband! . . .

At last we came to a very large encampment of white people, and they ran out of their wagons, or wood-houses, as we called them, and gathered round us. I was riding behind my brother. I was so afraid, I told him to put his robe over me, but he did not do so. I scratched him and bit him on his back, and then my poor grandfather rode up to the tents where they were, and he was asked to stay there all night with them. After grandpa had talked awhile, he said to his people that he would camp with his brothers. So he did. Oh, what nice things we all got from my grandpa's white brothers! Our men got red shirts, and our women got calico for dresses. Oh, what a pretty dress my sis-

SOURCE: Sarah Winnemucca Hopkins, *Life among the Piutes: Their Wrongs and Claims*, ed. Mrs. Horace Mann (1883; Reno: U Nevada P, 1994), 5–38.

ter got. I did not get anything, because I hid all the time. I was hiding under some robes. . . .

So I kept thinking over what [my grandfather] said to me about the good white people, and saying to myself, "I will make friends with them when we come into California." . . .

One of my grandpa's friends was named Scott, and the other Bonsal. . . . We stayed there some time. Then grandpa told us that he had taken charge of Mr. Scott's cattle and horses, and he was going to take them all up to the mountains to take care of them for his brothers. He . . . told his dear daughter that he wanted her two sons to take care of a few horses and cows that would be left. My mother began to cry, and said, "Oh, father, don't leave us here! My children might get sick, and there would be no one to speak for us; or something else might happen." He again said, "I don't think my brothers will do anything that is wrong to you and your children." Then my mother asked my grandfather if he would take my sister with him. My poor mother felt that her daughter was unsafe, for she was young and very good-looking. . . .

So my brothers took care of their horses and cows all winter, and they paid them well for their work. But oh, what trouble we had for a while! The men whom my grandpa called his brothers would come into our camp and ask my mother to give our sister to them. They would come in at night, and we would all scream and cry; but that would not stop them. My sister, and mother, and my uncles all cried and said, "Oh, why did we come? Oh, we shall surely all be killed some night." My uncles and brothers would not dare to say a word, for fear they would be shot down. So we used to go away every night after dark and hide, and come back to our camp every morning. One night we were getting ready to [leave the Scott house], and there came five men. . . . My uncles and my brothers made such a noise I don't know what happened; . . . I asked my mother if they had killed my sister. She said, "We are all safe here. Don't cry." . . . My poor sister! I ran to her, I saw tears in her eyes. I heard someone speak close

to my mother. I looked round and saw Mr. Scott holding the door open [to escape]. Mother said, "Children, come."

He went with us and pointed to our camp, and shook his head ["no"], and motioned to mother to go into a [separate] little house where they were cooking. He took my hand in his, and said the same words that I had learned, "Poor little girl." . . . Oh, what pretty things met my eyes. I was looking all over and I saw beautiful white cups, and every beautiful thing on something high and long, and around it some things that were red.

I said to my sister, "Do you know what those are?" for she had been to the house before with my brothers. She said, "That high thing is what they use when eating, and the white cups are what they drink hot water from, and the red thing you see is what they sit upon when they are eating." There was one now near us, and I thought if I could sit upon it I should be so happy! I said to my mother, "Can I sit on that one?" She said, "No, they would whip you." . . .

So I said no more. . . . Then the woman fixed five places and the men went out and brought in my brothers, and kept talking to them. . . . Brother said, "Mother, Mr. Scott wants us all to stay here. He says you and sister are to wash dishes, and learn all kinds of work. We are to stay here all the time and sleep upstairs, and the white woman is going to teach my sister how to sew. I think, dear mother, we had better stay, because grandpa said so, and our father Scott will take good care of us. . . ." All the time brother was talking, my mother and sister were crying. I did not cry for I wanted to stay so that I could sit in the beautiful red chairs. . . .

[My mother said to her sons,] "Oh, how can that bad man keep you from going [with me back to your father]? . . . Oh, if your father only knew how his children were suffering, I know he would kill that white man who tried to take your sister. I cannot see for my life why my father calls them his white brothers. They are not people. They have no thought, no mind, no love. They are beasts, or they would know I, a lone woman, am here with them. They tried to take my girl from me and abuse her before my eyes and yours too, and oh, you must go too."

"Oh, mother, here [Mr. Scott] comes!"

My mother got up. She held out her two hands to him, and cried out,—

"Oh, good father, don't keep my children from me. If you have a heart in you, give them back to me. Let me take them to their good father, where they can be cared for."

We all cried to see our poor mother pleading for us. Mother held on to him until he gave some signs of letting her sons go with her; then he nodded his head,—they might go.

ELIZA FARNHAM

T HE SECOND SELECTION was written by the New York–born author Eliza Farnham. Farnham arrived in California from Boston in 1849, just after the discovery of gold and right before statehood, about the same time that Sarah Winnemucca was encountering her first white people farther east. A thirty-two-year-old mother of two sons, Farnham had inherited land in the area of the Santa Cruz Mission from her recently deceased husband, who had been one of the first U.S. citizens in the area and had bought land there from the local Californio families.

Farnham's childhood was impoverished, but she succeeded in gaining an education and became a writer. Because her husband was away on the West Coast for much of their married life, she had the responsibility of supporting herself and her children, and she found ways to take advantage of the opportunities that were just beginning to open to women. She wrote *Life in Prairie Land* (1846), a popular account of her years on the Illinois frontier. Then she was employed as the first matron of women for the New York State prison at Sing Sing (now Ossining). There she gained a reputation for the courage to make humane reforms in the treatment of prisoners, but she was dismissed in 1848. At this point, she decided to go to California to take possession of the lands inherited from her husband. By the time she arrived in California, she was already something of a public figure.

Farnham held a distinctive set of ideas about womanhood, an idiosyncratic and crusading version of the doctrine of sexual spheres, quite different from that of the women's rights movement emerging at just this time. She did not advocate equality of the sexes or for women to join men in the public sphere, but she firmly rejected the idea that women should subordinate themselves to men. Her own life was marked by repeated acts of boldness and independence. In the context of American expansion, she contended that women had a special role to play in national life, based on their unique claim to moral leadership. Women could help the United States fulfill its national mission, its "Manifest Destiny," but only if they were allowed a broader scope for their distinctive talents. In California, she hoped that woman's superior moral influence could counter the rapacious, masculine spirit of the gold rush. "Believing that the presence of women would be one of the surest checks upon many of the evils that are apprehended," she determined to go there and help claim the area for the best—not the worst—of American nationhood.[54]

Farnham's first grand plan was to import Yankee women to serve as wives for the American men rushing into California. But when no other women took up her invitation, she went to California herself, traveling by ship around the tip of South America. Arriving in Santa Cruz, she moved into a crude one-room ranch house, which she optimistically renamed El Rancho La Libertad (Freedom Ranch). She began to farm potatoes and onions and plant fruit trees. Despite her best efforts, her agricultural experiment failed. She needed to hire male laborers, but most of the able-bodied men had left for the goldfields. Within a few years, she had married an abusive Irish immigrant, had secured one of the first divorces in the county, and had left the state.

Farnham's final plan was to write about her experiences in California, and in this, at last, she was successful. The following selection is from her memoir, *California, In-doors and Out* (1856). In this episode, she is returning from a trip to San Francisco and stays overnight at the *rancho* home of a Californio family near San Juan Bautista. There, the Castro family, an extended network that includes the "senior senor," his wife, his children, their cousins, and Indian servants, offers her hospitality.

As you read, consider how the Californios' way of life offends the "Yankee housewife" in Farnham. What about it does she appreciate? On what basis do she and the women of the household communicate and connect? What do you think she means by the sentence "No ungratified want or cankering ambition, shorn of the power to achieve, consumes them"? Does she mean to criticize the Americans as well as the Californios? How can the sense of Manifest Destiny that brought Americans to California be detected in Farnham's account?

Our weary horses did not get so well over the ground to-day. . . . An American had told us that we could find comfortable quarters at Castro's rancho, about eighteen miles further on, and thither we bent our way. It was nightfall before we reached the neighborhood he had indicated, and after dragging wearily on till it seemed as if neither of the animals could possible get over another mile, we descried a light which appeared to be twice that distance away and quite off the road. . . . [W]e learned that Castro's ranch was still two miles away, but that we could stay there for the night.

On the ground, under the corridor that ran along the old adobe building, two immense fires were blazing, around which were gathered twenty or thirty men and women, and several mules and horses. . . .

The Yankee housewife thinks, now, I ought to have been very comfortable; for the kitchen, in her land, is a bright, cheerful place to enter from the chilliness of a dark night. But this was not a Yankee kitchen. The apartment might have been eighteen by twenty-four feet, lighted only by a door in day time, and, at this hour, by the fitful blaze of the wood-fires, built upon a sort of brick range that ran across the end of the room. In the

SOURCE: Eliza Farnham, *California, In-doors and Out, or How We Farm, Mine, and Live Generally in the Golden State* (New York: Dix, Edwards, 1856; repr., Amsterdam: F. De Graaf, 1972), 123–31.

corner, at one end of this range, a dirty Indian girl was making tortillas — the bread of the country. She was kneading a large lump of dough upon a stone bench, slightly hollowed toward the centre, beside which stood a very ill-favored basin of water, into which she occasionally thrust her hands. . . .

At the other end of the range, a buxom merry-faced girl was superintending a pot of *caldo* [a heavy, hot soup], and another of *frijoles* [beans], with an apron before her so excessively dirty, that I involuntarily reached my hand out to stay it when it fell too near the cooking. Five or six other young women were sitting or standing about, and several more were passing in and out to other parts of the *casa* [house]. A merrier set could nowhere be found; they chatted to me in Spanish, and laughed if I failed to understand them. They laughed when they could not understand my English. They examined my riding-hat, habit, whip, rings, watch, pin — every thing, in short, their eyes could see, and put on whatever they could detach from my person, trying its effect with a critical and generally an approving eye. . . .

After what seemed an interminable delay, I was called to supper in a long, spacious room or hall, at the upper end of which stood two beds. The long table occupied one entire side near the wall. . . . When we were seated, the senior senor threw each a tortilla from a stack that was piled on the cloth near his plate, and, helping himself, signed to us to do likewise. The supper was delicious. The mercy of Providence, in the shape of a fasting stomach, enabled me to forget the filthy apron, and the long hair and suspicious-looking arms of the Indian girl, and I made ample amends for the fast that I had observed since morning. . . .

The supper was a far more palatable one than I believed it could be. The *caldo* was deliciously flavored; the tortillas very sweet and crisp; and everybody knows the *frijole* so well that praise of it would be quite superfluous. When we had supped, I retired again to the kitchen, and here I found all the young people taking their evening meal, quite informally, seated upon the earthen floor about the room. Two or three large toilet basins, placed in various parts, contained the food, from which each supplied his or her plate at will; and my cook, with the formidable apron, washing the dishes as they were handed to her; an operation which she performed in a very summary manner, by dashing a handful or two of water over the plate, tilted on the edge of the kettle, and, shocking to tell, wiping them on the very apron! . . .

The sleeping-apartment was in the second story, to which I mounted by a sort of ladder, constructed by tying bits of wood, upon two poles, with thongs of green hide, and placed against the sill of the door. The chamber was the entire size of the building, and was used as clothes, store-room, and granary. Two beds occupied the nearer end; wheat and barley the remote one, and sides of leather, old barrels, boxes, broken chairs, etc., the intermediate space. Zarapas [probably *serapes*, decorative blankets] of all styles were pendant from the roof, rafters, and walls. I objected to the door, as lacking all means of fastening, but my solicitude was promptly removed by the intelligence that six or eight persons were to share the apartment with me. I certainly did wish for a curtain of some sort; but my extreme weariness suggested that the curtain of irresistible sleep would divide me from all the world in a very few moments. The bed was not of the freshest, though everything upon it was snowy white; but my sleep was unbroken till the words, "the horses are ready, ma'am," sounded loudly in my ears next morning. With infinite difficulty, a pint bowl of water was obtained for my ablutions, and I soon descended equipped for departure. . . .

This, then, was a Spanish rancho and the manner of life in it. These people were the owners of a great estate here, and another up the coast, on which were hundreds, if not thousands, of horned cattle and horses. Not a drop of milk nor an ounce of butter could be had in their house. Their chief articles of food are beef and beans. Of the wheat grown on their lands they make a kind of coarse flour which they use in porridge. The tortilla can only be made of fine flour, which they have always imported, though occupying one of the finest wheat countries in the world. The simplicity of their external lives is quite in harmony with that of their natures. No ungratified want or cankering ambition, shorn of the power to achieve, consumes them, and though the same lack of material refinement in almost any other people would argue a positive coarseness which could not fail to distress a stranger, their whole manner, though familiar to a degree, is so evincive of kindness and respect, that there is nothing left to read or doubt as to their motives. They are a simple-hearted people, whose contentment flowed out in acts of continual hospitality and kindness to all who came to them before their peaceful dream of life was broken in upon by the frightful selfishness of the late emigration. It is difficult for us to imagine contentment in the idle, aimless life of these rancheros, or cheerfulness in the dark, dirty, naked houses they inhabit; but they have sufficed for them.

MARIA ANGUSTIAS DE LA GUERRA ORD

I N THE 1870s AND 1880s, Hubert Howe Bancroft, California's first major historian, recorded the memories, or *testimonios*, of those pre-statehood Californios who were still alive. Most of his aged narrators were men, but among the women he interviewed was Maria Angustias de la Guerra Ord. Through her father, she had been closely attached to the mission at San Juan Bautista, and the events described took place in that vicinity. This excerpt from her reminiscence describes her role in that part of the Mexican War that took place in California in the area between Los Angeles and Monterey.

Angustias de la Guerra Ord's *testimonio* has become a source of controversy among historians. As originally recorded in 1878, she declared, "*[L]a toma del pais no nos gusto nada a los californios, y menos a las mujeres.*" In 1956, this important sentence was mistranslated as "The conquest of California did not bother the Californios, least of all the women," and this mistranslation was subsequently much quoted. But later scholars corrected the translation to clarify that her actual opinion was in fact the opposite: "The conquest of California wasn't liked by the Californians, least of all the women."[55]

Angustias de la Guerra Ord's tale concerns an attempt by the Californio forces to kidnap the U.S. consul, Thomas Larkin. In the ensuing fray, José Antonio Chavez, one of the would-be kidnappers, was wounded. Ord's story involves Chavez's efforts to elude pursuit by the U.S. Army. The first person to give Chavez refuge was the Californiana wife of a Yankee, who disobeyed her husband to harbor her fugitive countryman. Then he fled to the house of a fellow soldier, and this man brought Chavez to the home of de la Guerra Ord.

As you read, consider how de la Guerra Ord insists on her domestic authority to the Yankees and how the U.S. officer indicates his military authority in response. Why is de la Guerra Ord motivated to help Chavez, and who do you think gets the better of the encounter, she or the Americans? Who is living in the de la Guerra Ord residence and why? How does this account illuminate the family relations in Rancho Castro that Eliza Farnham found so confusing?

I was in bed, having given birth to a baby girl a few days before. I was very astonished by what the soldier told me. He reported what had happened to Chavez, and for the love of God, to take him out of his house and hide him in mine. The words, "love of God," had great force and made me think. My husband was away at our Pajaro ranch. I decided to dress and though it was raining hard, to go to see my brothers, Pablo and Miguel, who were prisoners, to ask them what they thought I should do. Not having my husband there to consult with, I wanted to know their opinion. . . .

I was very angry with the Americans, because they had mistreated my brothers, holding them prisoners without cause or reason. I angrily told [Pablo] that if he thought that the Yankees believed they could find a person at will, I would hide him.

Finally I went to the soldier's house myself and consulted with Chavez about the means of getting him to my house as he couldn't walk because of the dislocation of his ankle. The son-in-law of the soldier was a Portuguese of small stature, and as Chavez was also small, the two together would make one man of large stature. The Portuguese carried Chavez sitting on his shoulders covered with a Spanish shawl and a felt hat which I had provided. Thus they passed through the guards of my Yankees and arrived at my house without being discovered. I had already returned to my house and gotten into bed, . . . I told no one my plan and nobody suspected anything.

During my husband's absence, Capt. Mariano Silva and his wife, Maria de la Torre, were living at my house. I informed them of the situation about Chavez. When he arrived he was confined in a room. No one but Capt. Silva and his wife, my daughter, Manuela, and I saw him. . . .

During the night, with a full moon, I heard a noise in my little garden. Some sheep I owned had

gotten in. I sent an Indian girl to tell the cook to get the sheep out. The girl only opened the door and saw the armed soldiers. She closed it and came to tell me. Then I spoke to Silva, telling him that I believed the Americans had surrounded my house. Then we heard a rap on the door, and I told Silva to go and see what they wanted. Then they told my servants that Chavez was hiding in a room because they were going to kill him. Silva's wife went to get [Chavez]. Meanwhile the Indian maids took off the blankets from the couch which had been put in my room. We put Chavez there by the garden so he could breathe easily, and as he was very slender, the whole space was stuffed with blankets so that it would be smooth. We put my baby, Carolina, to bed on top of him. Silva's wife got into my bed with me. . . .

[T]he Lieutenant and his people came into my bedroom without saying a word. He had a pistol in one hand and a candle in the other. He looked under my bed but found nothing. Then he came near me holding the pistol and candle to my face and said that he was hunting for a man who was said to be hidden in my house. I asked him if he had found him, and he said he had not. It pleased me greatly because I had not told them any lies. Then he said he was rather tired and that he regretted having had to bother me, because he supposed that I was rather frightened, and would like a chair to sit down. I answered that I was not frightened by anything and that he could go to his house to rest, because no one could rest in my room who was not a member of my family or a friend. He said good night and nothing more. . . . This military search and occupation of my house lasted from 10:00 P.M. until 2 or 3 in the morning.

Chavez came out of hiding and Silva's wife applied remedies to his foot. He said to me, "Madam, I am alive today because of you." To which I replied, "What I have done for you today, I would do tomorrow for an American if you unjustly attempted to do him wrong."

Chavez left 2 days later. He went from my house dressed as a woman. In the pines he mounted a horse and went to Santa Barbara.

SOURCE: Maria Angustias de la Guerra Ord, *Occurrences in Hispanic California*, trans. and ed. Francis Price and William Ellison (Washington, DC: Academic Press of American Franciscan History, 1956), 61–64.

QUESTIONS FOR ANALYSIS

1. Each of these three women writes about her combination of fear and curiosity regarding the strangers she encountered. About what is each curious? What are the different sources of their fear, and how does each exhibit or conceal her reaction?

2. What are the sources of strength on which Farnham, de la Guerra Ord, and the mother of Sarah Winnemucca each draw? How does the absence of men affect the way they act?

3. What role does the preparation and consumption of food play in these various cultural encounters? How is intercultural hospitality expressed? How important were manufactured goods from the East in the cross-cultural encounters of California in the late 1840s?

4. The Farnham and de la Guerra Ord episodes occurred quite close geographically at about the same time, in 1850. Can you imagine how de la Guerra Ord would have reacted to Farnham as a guest in her home and what Farnham might have thought of her?

D O C U M E N T S

Elizabeth Cady Stanton, Writing in the *Lily* and *Una*

M OST OF WHAT WE KNOW about the early campaign for women's rights comes from what its advocates said to each other at their meetings and to their political representatives in addresses to legislatures. But women's rights aimed to be a popular movement as well. Proponents spread ideas through magazines and newspapers that were shared from household to household. In the print medium, historians can detect the connection between women's rights ideas and the lives and concerns of a broader range of women.

Throughout the 1850s, Elizabeth Cady Stanton, well known for her role in initiating the woman's rights convention at Seneca Falls in 1848, wrote articles for the women's rights press. She was comfortable and prolific with her pen, and her popular writings were simultaneously accessible and passionate, humorous and serious. In addition, she was raising a large family of children through the 1850s (she had seven in total) and writing suited her more than traveling to women's rights meetings.

Stanton published the first three of these articles in the *Lily*, a monthly periodical published in her hometown of Seneca Falls under the editorship of Amelia Bloomer. Bloomer began her journalistic career by writing articles in a local newspaper edited by her lawyer husband. Her decision in 1849 to publish a women's reform monthly seems to have been her response to the 1848 Women's Rights Convention in Seneca Falls, which she attended. At its height, in 1851, the *Lily* was sent to four thousand subscribers a month. In addition to providing Stanton with a venue for her writings, Bloomer introduced Stanton to Susan B. Anthony, a Rochester, New York, teacher who worked with Bloomer in the temperance movement.

Anthony and others turned to the talented Stanton to author many of the manifestos and resolutions for the women's rights and woman suffrage movements. Stanton could express complicated ideas in accessible language for general audiences. Stanton began her lifelong career as a popular political writer with her writings for the *Lily*. She never wrote a single, sustained treatise on women's rights. Instead, she offered her readers powerful insights about women's status, possibilities, history, and future while linking those insights to contemporary events or daily preoccupations.

During the 1850s, Stanton integrated her own concerns with housekeeping and childrearing into her reform and political writings. As of 1850, she had three children, all boys. (Her first daughter was born in 1852.) Her two eldest sons, named after their father and maternal grandfather, respectively, were Henry and Daniel. Stanton combined their names into that of the fictional son, Henry Neil, in her six-part "Conversations with Mother" series. New York State was considering legislation requiring all citizens, not just parents of students, to pay school taxes. No doubt the influx of Irish immigrants, whose presence can be detected in Stanton's article, added to the controversy over this measure. How did Stanton both employ and transcend common assumptions about motherhood to discuss political issues? Instead of using her own name, she signed these articles "Sunflower." Why do you think she made this choice?

Henry Neil and His Mother Conversation No. 6

Henry. — "Well, Mother, last vacation we used to have long talks about temperance; now I have a great many questions to ask you about 'free schools,' and, to begin, do you think the State ought to educate all the children within its boundaries?"

Mother. — "Certainly I do."

Henry. — "What! build the school houses, pay the teachers, supply the fire wood, &c. &c. Why it would be a great expense to the State!"

Mother. — "No, Henry, it would be far cheaper for the State to educate its people, and thus make them intelligent and industrious, than to suffer them to grow up in ignorance and idleness. But before I answer you fully, let me ask you one or two questions. Suppose we take a little boy, separate him from his vicious companions and his accustomed haunts of idleness, for six or seven hours a day—place him in a well ventilated, well regulated school room, teach him to read, write and cypher, to speak politely and make a bow, will he not necessarily grow up a more respectable man, than if left, all his boyhood, the mere victim of idleness and vice?"

Henry. — "Yes, and what is true of one boy is true of all. I have no doubt that education makes men better citizens."

. . . Mother. — "Looking at this, then as a mere question of dollars and cents, — which do you suppose costs the most, to keep a boy in school say ten years, or to pay the expense of bringing him some dozen times before a police court for two or three years residence in a county jail, for the support of his wife and children in the poor house, for his confinement in the state prison some dozen years, and finally for the building of a gallows and all the expenses incurred by that civilized manner of finishing off a criminal. Rely upon it, it costs ten times as much to take care of a criminal, as it does to educate a child."

Henry. — "Does the State pay for all this?"

Mother. — "Yes, the State supports prisons, jails, houses of refuge, poor houses and poor people in their own houses—it supports standing armies, courts martial, and militia trainings. It supports rumsellers, gambling houses and brothels, and strange to say, people quietly submit to be taxed for all these evils, and yet grumble most dolorously about the school tax; at the same time no reasonable man pretends to say, that a good school system, so free that all who will may learn, is not productive of more good than any or all of these other 'institutions' put together."

. . . Henry. — "But do you think, mother, that parents generally care enough about education to send their children, even if schools were free?"

Mother. — "Oh! yes, there are no parents, however ignorant themselves, but desire education

SOURCE: "Henry Neil and His Mother Conversation No. 6," *The Lily*, July 1850, pp. 54–55. Thanks to the Stanton/Anthony Papers Project, Rutgers University, for the transcript and annotation of this article.

for their children. It is estimated by the Superintendent of Common Schools, from official returns procured for this express purpose, that the number of children annually excluded from the public schools, in consequence of the inability of their parents and guardians to meet the rate bills, imposed under the former law, was 50,000 in this state. Only think of it, 50,000 children willing to learn, thrust out of our district schools by state authority."

Henry. — "But do you think that those who have no children ought to be taxed for schools?"

Mother. — "Why not pay for educating a neighbor's child as well as for shutting up a neighbor's murderer?"

Henry. — "What you say seems right to me now, you have such a simple way of settling all points of right and wrong, that when I talk with you there never seems to be but one side to a question; but when I go down town and listen to the men arguing, and hear them tell about the law, the constitution, the opinions of the Judges of the Supreme Court, . . . I do get so befogged that I begin to think there is no such thing as absolute truth."

Mother. — "Well, Henry, note down the objections you hear against the free school system, and I will measure them all by the 'golden rule' and tell you what they are worth."

DESPITE ITS FLOWERY TITLE, the *Lily* was not afraid to tackle difficult subjects. Its primary concern was temperance (controlling and the consumption of alcohol) and prohibition (halting its sale). The temperance campaign reached new levels of intensity in 1850, as state after state considered passing laws banning the sale of liquor. The temperance reform was supported by many middle-class women in Stanton's home state of New York. Stanton's specialty was to draw women's attention to the deeper, more radical implications of their opposition to the liquor industry. In the following article, she moves from women's concerns with excessive drinking to the much more controversial issue of women's right to vote. How does she link these two issues?

Editorial

The time has been when [women] were very zealous in the cause, and believed they could effect much by circulating the [temperance] pledge, passing resolutions and sending petitions to the Legislature. — Simple souls! They knew not their own weakness nor the strength of the foe they would combat but a film has fallen from their eyes and the cobwebs of ignorance are being brushed from their understandings and they now realize that there is but one sure way of vanquishing the enemy and that they are denied the right of acting in that way. Many have grown weary and heartsick at the treachery and desertion of pretended friends, and are disgusted with the manner in which *men* conduct the warfare. Yet they know it is useless for *them* to take any action while the law sustains the traffic, and while they, like slaves and idiots, are forbidden a voice in the making of the laws. . . .

SOURCE: "Editorial," *The Lily*, October 1850, p. 77.

Not until she is regarded as a human being possessing the same wants and feelings, and endowed by her Creator with equal moral and intellectual capacities as man—not until her rights are fully recognized, and her voice listened to through the ballot box, and in Legislative halls, can woman do ought in a *public* way to stay the tide of drunkenness which is so fearfully increasing.

We mean not to say that she can do nothing for a temperance cause, or that she should remain indifferent and inactive while so many pitfalls of destructions are yawning to swallow up new victims, and to crush her beneath the weight of poverty and abuse, which are ever attendant upon the drunkard's path. She can do much by early instilling into the minds of her children a fear and hatred of the liquor traffic, and its agents. . . .

She should use everything in her power to induce the voters over whom she has influence to cast their ballots in a way that shall tell on this question—though here we can hope for little, for men are so wedded to "our party" that they care not what are the principles of its candidates. If women would do more than *this*, they must insist upon their rights, call conventions, make speeches, pass resolutions, and demand the right of expressing through the ballot box their abhorrence of the traffic, and their determination to hurl it from its strong hold.

I N ADDITION TO TEMPERANCE, the *Lily* also became identified—somewhat notoriously—with the issue of "dress reform." The rational redesign of women's clothing away from concerns of fleeting (and foreign) fashions and toward more realistic accommodation to women's bodies and daily activities fit well with Elizabeth Cady Stanton's concerns with healthy motherhood and efficient housekeeping. Stanton's cousin and closest friend, Elizabeth Smith Miller, is historically credited with adapting what was called "the Turkish costume"—calf-length pants overlaid with a loose tunic—to dress reform purposes. Stanton energetically took it up, and wrote about it. Despite her enthusiasm, after a few years Stanton tired of the effort of defending her clothes as a political choice and returned to more conventional dress choices. Eventually the Turkish costume became so identified with the *Lily*'s editor, Amelia Bloomer, that it became known as "the Bloomer," and the term later evolved to describe women's use of pants under their skirts. What does the dress reform issue tell us about the women's rights movement's social and cultural, as well as legal and political concerns?

Our Costume

Let the silk worm stay in its cocoon until its own wants compel it to throw it aside. Let every woman stay in her long petticoats, until she feels the necessity of a change; then no opposition, or trivial objections, will deter her; then she will not doubt or hesitate as to what she shall do; she will not heed the remarks of rude men and boys, and unmannerly women. Though I do not wish to convince any woman against her will, of the

SOURCE: "Our Costume," *The Lily*, April 1851, p. 31.

reasonableness of this change, yet I would answer some of the objections I have heard. Some say the Turkish costume is not graceful. Grant it. For parlor dolls, who loll on crimson velvet couches and study attitudes before tall mirrors—for those who have no part to perform in the great drama of life, for whose heads, hearts and hands, there is no work to do, the drapery is all well; let them hang it on thick and heavy as they please; though, to the highest artistic taste the human form is most beautiful, most graceful, wholly undraped and unadorned. . . . But for us, commonplace, everyday, working characters, who wash and iron, bake and brew, carry water and fat babies upstairs and down, bring potatoes, apples, and pans of milk from the cellar, run our own errands, through mud or snow; shovel paths, and work in the garden; why "the drapery" is quite too much—one might as well work with a ball and chain. Is being born a woman so criminal an offense, that we must be doomed to this everlasting bondage? "But," say some, "it is not the fashion!" Neither is it the fashion to be honest and virtuous, to lead simple, pure, and holy lives. The true, the earnest soul is always odd. . . . "But the men and boys laugh at us." That is a strong reason in its favor. It is good to be laughed at; the more ridicule you encounter the better. It strengthens and develops the character to stand alone. "What will the people say?" has been a powerful weapon, in crushing many generous impulses, high resolves, and noble deeds. Women are said to have excessive love of approbation; therefore must we cultivate indifference to the opinions of others, but be ever alive to their sufferings. Let the weal and the woe of humanity be everything to us, but their praise and their blame of no account.

I N 1853, AMELIA BLOOMER moved away from Seneca Falls and soon after ceased publishing the *Lily* altogether. That same year, a new periodical dedicated explicitly to women's rights made its appearance. *Una* was the project of Paulina Wright Davis, a married middle-class white woman. Childless, she threw herself into religious and moral causes, one of which, abolitionism, was the source of her growing radicalism. After the death of her husband, she became a health educator for women and an early proponent of legal reform granting wives independent property ownership. In 1850, she was the chief organizer for the first National Women's Rights Convention in Worcester, Massachusetts. *Una* was named after a character in Edmund Spenser's sixteenth-century epic poem *The Faerie Queene* who represented faith and purity in an ideal female form. By this time, its editor had shed her previous religious convictions and found conventional Protestantism intellectually indefensible and politically conservative.

With the *Lily* gone, Stanton turned to *Una* as a venue for her writings. The subject of the following article was a lightly fictionalized autobiography, *Ruth Hall*, by writer Fanny Fern. In addition to her strong endorsement of the case that the novel made for independent work and self-fulfillment for women, Stanton took issue with a critical review of the novel in an abolitionist newspaper, the *National Anti-Slavery Standard*. In her defense of Fern, Stanton anticipated a position she took more strongly after the Civil War, insisting that the case for women's emancipation was similar to and deserved as much sympathy and support as that of antislavery. How effective is she in making this connection?

Ruth Hall

Hardship and struggle always crush the weak and insignificant, but call forth and develop the true and noble soul. The great lesson taught in *Ruth Hall* is that God has given to woman sufficient brain and muscle to work out her own destiny unaided and alone. Her case, like ten thousand others, goes to prove the common notion that God made woman to depend on man, a romance and not a fact of every-day life.... Authors generally claim the privilege of writing about what they have seen and felt. Men have given us all their experience from Moses down to the last village newspaper; and how much that is palatable have they said of woman? And now that woman has seized the brush and brought forth on the canvas a few specimens of dwarfed and meager manhood, lo! What a furor of love and reverence has seized the world of editors and critics! ... This is but a beginning, gentlemen. If you do not wish us to paint you wolves, get you into lambs' clothing as quickly as possible....

Woman owes it to herself, to her sex, to the race, no longer to consent to and defend the refinements of degradation to which Christian woman is subject in the nineteenth century. We were sorry to see so severe a review of *Ruth Hall,* in an anti-slavery newspaper, as appeared in the "Anti-Slavery Standard." ... Read "Ruth Hall" as you would read the life of "Solomon Northup," a Frederick Douglass,—as you would listen to the poor slaves in our anti-slavery meetings. The story of cruel wrongs, suffered for weary days and years, finds sympathy in every breast.... Because a villain for

his own pleasure, has conferred on men the boon of existence, by what law, other than the Christian one—"Love your enemies"—am I bound to love and reverence him who has made my life a curse and a weariness, and who possesses in himself none of the Godlike qualities which command my veneration? We love our Heavenly Father, because he is just and good, and not because he is God. The blessed name of father does not belong to every man who merely begets a child. It takes love and kindness and sympathy to make a man my father. The law of affinity goes deeper than blood. What is it to me whether the man who robs me of my God-given rights, is a father, a brother, a husband, or a Southern slave-holder? Is my loss less because the blow is struck at the hearthstone? It is my privilege, in either case, to throw myself on the great heart of Humanity, and to plead my cause wherever I can find a court to listen. Resistance to tyrants is obedience to God. If the son is not taught at home, that there is a limit to his rights, he will never learn it elsewhere.

If woman had done her duty to her sires and sons, think you it would have taken them nearly one hundred years, after giving to the world a declaration of rights that made every king in Europe tremble beneath his crown, to see that a woman has a right to property she inherits, and to the wages she earns with her own hands? Pray, do not let the teaching come from the anti-slavery men, that there are spots on this green earth, where tyranny may vent itself unknown and unrebuked. What are the strokes, the paddle or the last, to the reined insults, with which man seeks to please or punish woman?

SOURCE: *"Ruth Hall," Una,* February 1855, pp. 29–30.

IN 1853, ANTOINETTE BROWN, born in 1825, became the first woman to be officially ordained as a minister in the United States. A graduate of Oberlin College and a close friend of activist Lucy Stone, she was also a supporter of women's rights and a regular speaker at its conventions. Like Elizabeth Cady Stanton, she married another political activist and bore seven children, though two died in infancy. Despite these similarities of lifestyle and general reform conviction, Stanton disagreed with Brown on some of the premises on which they based their women's rights arguments. In the spirit of open and sisterly disagreement practiced within women's rights circles, Elizabeth Stanton used the pages of *Una* to challenge Brown on an issue of perennial interest to proponents of women's equality: the similarity or difference of women and men. Stanton's eloquent statement in favor of the fundamental identity of the sexes represented her thinking in the 1850s. After the Civil War, Stanton followed the scientific thinking of the time to allow for greater differences of temperament—though not of rights—between the sexes. How effective is Stanton's argument about the identity of the sexes as a basis for women's equal rights?

Rev. Sydney Smith vs Rev. Antoinette L. Brown

"A great deal has been said of the original difference of capacity between men and women; as if women were more quick and men more judicious,—as if women were more remarkable for delicacy of association, and men for stronger powers of attention. All this we confess appears to us very fanciful. . . . "

Here is the opinion of the Rev. Sydney Smith, the distinguished English Essayist and Divine. To speak of a natural mental difference in the sexes, was an absurdity to him fifty years ago. To speak of their identity, is an absurdity to the Rev. Antoinette Brown in 1855. In her recent speech at Albany before a legislative committee, she said she would institute no comparison between men and women. "As well," she said, "you may ask which is the largest, a railroad or a steamboat; which is the longest, a boa constrictor or a day in June." Now I beg leave to differ entirely with Antoinette Brown. I think boys and girls, men and women can be compared. As moral and intellectual beings, does not all history prove them the same? There is no end to speculations or theories on any subject, and there is no way of combating visions

or shadows. But of those things of which the evidence of our senses attest, we may reason and judge. Well, then, to let pass that indescribable something, in which it is said that all men and women differ, and to come down to what we see, and hear, and feel, what have we?

Man eats and drinks and sleeps, and so does woman. He runs and walks, laughs and cries, feels joy and sorrow, pleasure and pain, and so does woman. He is religious, penitent, prayerful, dependent, and so is woman. He is courageous, bold, self-reliant, enduring, and so is woman. He is ambitious, loves glory, fame, power, and so does woman. He loves to think, reason, write, speak, debate, declaim, and so does woman. In fact what has man ever done that woman has not done also?—what does he like, that she does not like too? Are not our hopes and fears for time and eternity the same? What virtue or vice, what aspiration or appetite has ever crowned or clouded the glory of manhood, that we have not seen in woman too, its beauty or its blight? The physical differences we see between some men and women, produced by different employments, may also be seen between man and man. . . . Theory may say that if man and woman from the beginning were educated precisely alike, man would still be the larger, the stronger. When the experi-

SOURCE: "Rev. Sydney Smith vs Rev. Antoinette L. Brown," *Una*, 1855, pp. 69–70.

ment is fully made, it will be time enough to admit the assumption. But suppose we admit that man is physically larger than woman, what do you gain by the admission? Among the athletic, the muscular, the brawny, are by no means the great men in the best sense of that word, neither are they the strongest physically. . . .

Men and women are not so unlike in person either, but by skillful dressing the one may pass for the other. George Sand, the assumed name of the distinguished Madame Dudevant, has travelled incognito in man's attire through many countries and observed society in all its phases in Parisian life. There are many instances of men escaping from prison in woman's attire, undiscovered, and of women disguised as soldiers, fighting in the hottest of the battle, side by side with those they loved. In children's plays, boys and girls are constantly seen wrestling, running, climbing, comparing their strength and swiftness. I never heard it hinted in the play-ground or the school-room that boys and girls were not legitimate subjects of comparison. When a girl, I have gone many a time from our Academy gate to the belfry, snowball in hand, to punish a boy for washing my face. The girls in my native village, not only tried strength with boys in the play-ground, but we measured lances with them in the sciences, languages and mathematics. In studying Algebra and Geometry, in reading Virgil or the Greek Testament, I never found out the difference in the male and female mind. In those days there was no feminine way of extracting the cube root of x, y, z; no masculine ways of going through all the moods and tenses of the verbs Amo and Tupto.

We have had so much sentimental talk in all our woman's conventions, by the friends of the cause, about the male and female element, and by outsiders, on woman's sphere, her mission, her peculiar duties, &c, that I should like to have all this mysterious twaddle thoroughly explored; all these nice shades of differences fully revealed. It is not enough to assert that there always has been, is, and always will be a difference. The question, What is it?

QUESTIONS FOR ANALYSIS

1. To what other social reform causes was the antebellum women's rights movement connected and what impact did these links have on its advocates?

2. What are the differences between Stanton's writings in the *Lily* and *Una*? To what do you attribute these?

3. How does Stanton use the beliefs and concerns of less activist women to make her case for women's rights? Is she convincing? Why or why not?

Women on the Civil War Battlefields

THE BATTLEFIELD has not always been an exclusively male space. Wives and mothers of common soldiers came to cook, launder, and nurse the men of their families, while officers' wives were permitted social visits with their husbands. But women went to the scene of fighting for other reasons too. Political passions are no respecter of gender, and patriotism, dedication to cause, eagerness to be a part of historic events, and the simple desire for adventure brought women to the bloody heart of the Civil War.

The most common battlefield role of women was nurse — the "angel" of the battlefield who comforted wounded and dying soldiers, representing domestic tranquillity in the midst of armed conflict. Despite the desperate need for medical personnel to care for the enormous number of casualties, female nurses had to fight their own kinds of battles with male medical officers for the opportunity to serve. A much smaller number of women also served the Union and Confederate armies in less conventionally womanly ways, as spies, strategists, and even soldiers.

While the Civil War had a tremendous impact on women overall, generating aspirations for greater public responsibilities and more rights, those who had had direct battlefield experience found it difficult to have their particular contributions fully appreciated. Northern male veterans could count on an old-age army pension in recognition of their services, but only some of the women who served received anything, and even then they received less than men. African American women, whose dedication and need were particularly great, were especially undercompensated. Many of the images in this essay are taken from memoirs written by women who served on and around battlefields, who wrote to make sure that the historical record included their stories. They succeeded in permitting us to see the Civil War through women's eyes.

THE NURSES

An estimated ten thousand women served as nurses during the Civil War.[56] Nursing was not yet a profession requiring special training and would not become so until the turn of the twentieth century (see p. 457). At first, both military hospitals and battlefield infirmaries were run by male surgeons who had little to offer the wounded beyond the removal of a limb and whiskey to blunt the pain. Their assistants were also men, themselves often recuperating from battlefield injuries. Nursing under wartime conditions seemed too brutal for women, an unacceptable offense against their modesty.

Nonetheless, care of the sick and injured was traditionally a female skill, and women began to offer their services as soon as the first call for troops was issued. In the North, Dorothea Dix, already well known for her work to improve the treatment of the insane, persuaded Edwin Stanton, U.S. secretary of war, to appoint her as superintendent of nursing for the Union army. "All nurses are required to be plain looking women," Dix declared. "Their dresses must be brown or black with no bows, no curls, no jewelry and no hoop skirts."[57] Clothing had to be not only respectable but also functional in the gory environment of the military hospitals. Louisa May Alcott, unmarried and struggling to become a writer, was one of those Dix recruited. "I love nursing and *must* let out my pent-up energy in some new way," she wrote in the journal that became her first published book, *Hospital Sketches*. "I want new experiences and am sure to get 'em if I go."[58] In 1861 Congress authorized pay of $12 a month for the female nurses under Dix's supervision, about a third of what male nurses received.

In the regimental hospitals away from Washington, D.C., women whose relatives had been wounded or who felt moved to care for the troops convinced local medical staff to allow them to serve without army commission or pay. Mary Ann Bickerdyke of Illinois became a legend for her battlefield stamina and disregard for military hierarchy. Bickerdyke was a mother and widow in her midforties. She was a dedicated caregiver, moving from battlefield to battlefield, cooking and laundering as well as tending to the Union army wounded. Eventually, she was appointed field agent for the United States Sanitary Commission, which, despite its name, was not part of the government but rather a massive, largely female, volunteer organization that provided clothing and medical supplies to the Union army.

Like other nineteenth-century women with commanding personalities, Bickerdyke assumed the powerful female appellation of "Mother." In an environment that reserved official control for men, the title of "Mother" could be translated into informal public authority. Bickerdyke insisted that she had the right to be near the action and to tend to the troops as she saw fit, on the basis of selfless concern for "her" boys. Indeed, Mother Bickerdyke seems to have treated most of the military men with whom she came into contact, including surgeons and generals, as overgrown boys for whom she knew best. Like other such female figures with unusual public standing who called themselves Mother—such as the late nineteenth-century labor organizer Mother Jones—Bickerdyke used this reworked maternal ideal as a framework for venturing beyond the genteel middle-class role of true womanhood.

Bickerdyke saw much military action. She arrived in Vicksburg, Mississippi, in time for the city's surrender to General Ulysses S. Grant, and escorted home Union soldiers released from the notoriously brutal Confederate prison at Andersonville, Georgia. In 1864, she joined General William Tecumseh Sherman, with whom she claimed a special bond, for his devastating march across the heart of the South. At the end of the war, when Sherman and his troops paraded through

◆ **Figure 5.1 F. O. C. Darley, *Midnight on the Battlefield* (1890)**
Milstein Division of United States History, Local History, and Genealogy, The New York Public Library, Astor, Lenox, and Tilden Foundations.

Washington, D.C., to celebrate victory, Mother Bickerdyke rode in a place of honor. Then she slipped back into private life. In 1886, the army awarded her a pension of $25 a month.

Figure 5.1 depicts the initial episode of the Bickerdyke story, her role at the battle of Fort Donelson, Tennessee, site of an early Union victory. Bickerdyke achieved renown for her courage in remaining at the killing fields late at night, until she was absolutely sure that she had found all survivors. The illustration, a steel engraving, was commissioned for *My Story of the War*, an account of the wartime contribution of the women of the Sanitary Commission, written in 1889 by Mary Livermore. It pictures Bickerdyke as a female savior, alone in her attempt to sustain life in a field of death. How did the artist choose to idealize her? How does the use of light (and dark) suggest women's role on the battlefield?

Although the gender conventions of southern society were more restrictive, and less encouraging of the kind of public presence and demonstration of organizational talent that characterized women's nursing involvement with the Union cause, women provided hospital care for southern soldiers as well. They could be found in the mammoth military hospitals in the Confederate capital of Richmond and at temporary medical facilities close to the battlefields and near to their own homes and communities. Because records of the Confederacy, including lists and numbers of women who served as nurses, were destroyed in the Union seizure and burning of Richmond, it is impossible even to estimate their numbers.

White women showed their patriotic dedication to the Confederate cause by attending wounded soldiers' bedsides, talking them through their suffering and dying, reading to them, and writing letters to their families. The dirtier jobs — bathing wounds, cleaning up the bloody sites of surgery, preparing corpses — were often done by slave women brought along by their mistresses. Relatively early, in 1862, the Confederate Congress began paying women for their nursing services. Their wages ranged from $30 to $40 a month, figures that seem quite high until the wildly inflated currency of the Confederacy is taken into account. Wages were allotted even for slave women, although the money was no doubt paid to their masters and mistresses.

The painting depicted in Figure 5.2 is one of the few images we have of southern women acting as nurses for Confederate soldiers. The painting is not a portrait of a particular woman, but a generalized image of southern white womanhood devoted to the Confederate cause. The artist, William Ludwell Sheppard, served in the Army of Northern Virginia and began his career as an illustrator and watercolorist of the war from a romanticized, southern perspective. *In the Hospital* was painted in the first year of the war. What audience did Sheppard have in mind? If we could compare it with an image from 1863 or 1864, what might be different? What are the similarities and differences between this and the prior image, of Mother Bickerdyke ministering to a Union soldier? How did this image help to build what later became, as one historian puts it, "the legend of female sacrifice, . . . of Confederate women's unflinching loyalty"?[59]

Catholic nuns were the only group of women on the battlefield with any prior experience in caring for the wounded. Their selflessness and virtue were unassailable. For these reasons, they were more welcomed than other Civil War nurses by the male military establishment, an attitude that is particularly remarkable given the rampant anti-Catholic prejudice of the era. Civil War chronicler Mary Livermore, no admirer of "the monastic institutions of that [Catholic] church," nonetheless praised the Catholic nurses: "They gave themselves no airs of superiority or holiness, shirked no duty, sought no easy place, bred no mischief."[60] Livermore thought the sisters represented a model of organized public service that Protestant women would do well to follow. Dorothea Dix, on the other hand, resented the Catholic women, who were not under her supervision.

◆ Figure 5.2 **William Ludwell Sheppard, *In the Hospital* (1861)**
The Granger Collection, New York.

◆ Figure 5.3 **Sisters of Charity with Doctors and Soldiers, Satterlee Hospital, Philadelphia (c. 1863)**
Courtesy, Archives Daughters of Charity, Emmitsburg, Maryland.

Dedicated to the service of God and humanity rather than the victory of North or South, the sisters attended both Confederate and Union wounded. During the long Union siege of Vicksburg, the Sisters of Charity cared for Confederate soldiers and civilians alike. The same order provided nurses for the giant Satterlee Hospital in Philadelphia, which received many of the Union wounded from the war's deadliest battle, Gettysburg. Figure 5.3 shows most of the forty nuns who served at Satterlee. How did the nuns' religious habits solve the problems of uniform and functional clothing for nurses? While other Civil War nurses were portrayed individually, why and with what effect did these women appear as a group?

Most of the women valorized for their contributions to the war effort were white. Yet African American women, for whom the outcome was of the greatest importance, found their own way to the battlefields. Some were free black women from the North who went south to attend to the welfare of freed slaves living in areas occupied by the Union army. But others were themselves fugitives from slavery, who provided an important source of support labor for the northern war effort. These women served as cooks and laundresses for the Union troops and as servants for the officers. Although much of their labor was subservient, they were participating in an enterprise that would bring their people freedom, and this gave their labor new meaning.

◆ Figure 5.4 **Susie King Taylor**

Susie King Taylor is the rare example of a refugee from slavery whose name and wartime story we know. She was born near Savannah, Georgia, in 1848 to a fourteen-year-old slave mother. Her grandmother, who lived nearby, was free and taught Susie to read and write. In the spring of 1863, she fled with relatives to a South Carolina coastal island that was Union-occupied, where she secured her own freedom. There the Union army encouraged the refugees to undertake formal marriages, and Susie, fourteen at the time, wed Edward King.

Like other eager freed slaves, her husband enlisted in one of the special "colored" divisions of the Union army, and King went to the battlefield with him. She worked as a laundress but was also entrusted with cleaning and caring for the musketry. The privilege of holding and handling guns was one of the markers of freedom for freed male slaves and for Susie King as well. "I learned to handle a musket very well while in the regiment," she wrote, "and could shoot straight and often hit the target."[61] Primarily, however, she was a nurse and served in a segregated military hospital for black soldiers. She and the other black nurses received $10 a month, $2 less than white women.

After the war, King worked as a teacher and a domestic servant in Georgia until she was widowed. She then moved to Boston, where, in 1879, she married Russell Taylor. In 1902 she published *A Black Woman's Civil War Memoirs*. Of the more than one hundred extant Civil War reminiscences by women, hers is the only account by a former slave woman. Part of the impulse to publish her story may have been to clarify that her wartime service — and perhaps that of other freedwomen as well — went beyond that of a laundress. Figure 5.4 is the image she chose as the frontispiece for her book. Compare it to the Sisters of Charity photograph shown in Figure 5.3. How does King convey her sense of dignity and historic contribution to the war effort?

THE SPIES

By far, the most well-known African American woman on the battlefield was Harriet Tubman, renowned for her role as conductor on the Underground Railroad. Born a slave in Maryland about 1821, she ran away from her master in 1849 and returned numerous times, often disguised as a man, to rescue as many as seventy enslaved relatives and friends. When the war began, she came back from Canada, where she had gone to evade the Fugitive Slave Law, and made her way to the Union-occupied South Carolina coastal islands to offer her services. There, she functioned in virtually every role available to women in and around the fighting. She was a nurse, a liaison between the Union army and the many refugees from slavery, a spy, and a military strategist for Union coastal invasions into Georgia and South Carolina.

Tubman began her military service in the way that most women did, as a nurse, first to the former slaves and then to black troops along the Carolina coast. There is some indication that cures she learned as a slave made her especially valuable in this role. But it soon became clear that, as a black woman who could appear to be a common slave, she could move easily about the South, gathering information for the Union army. Union officers asked her to organize a corps from among the black male refugees to serve with her as military spies and scouts.

In 1863, on the basis of Tubman's reports, a regiment of 150 black Union soldiers sailed up South Carolina's Combahee River to cut the enemy's supply lines, seize or destroy foodstuffs, and encourage the desertion of the slave labor force of the plantations along the banks. Eight hundred black men and women — "thousands of dollars worth of property," according to a contemporary newspaper account — fled to the Union gunboats and were transferred to the freedmen's encampments on the occupied Sea Islands.[62] The raid was commemorated more than a century later when a group of black feminists from Massachusetts took as their name the Combahee River Collective (see p. 685).

Despite influential supporters, after the war Tubman was never able to secure the back pay or army pension that white women such as Mother Bickerdyke received. In 1867, her husband, John Tubman, was murdered by a white man, who was acquitted of the crime. She spent the rest of her life in Auburn, New York, struggling to raise money to support herself and an old-age home for ex-slaves that she established. Proceeds from her memoir, *Scenes in the Life of Harriet Tubman*, were her major source of income. Tubman was not literate, and so her oral reminiscences were recorded in book form by a neighbor and friend, Sarah H. Bradford. Figure 5.5, the book's frontispiece, is described as a woodcut likeness of Tubman in her "costume as scout." Like other women on the battlefield (see Figure 5.7), Tubman wore a combination of men's and women's clothing. The jacket may have been military issue. What about this outfit reconciles her femaleness with the largely male nature of the battlefield? What might have been the impact on her readers of showing this former slave woman posed in front of a military camp, carrying an ammunition pouch and a gun?

If Tubman's race allowed her to spy for the North, white southerner Rose O'Neal Greenhow's sex allowed her to spy for the South. In the Union capital of Washington, D.C., nearby southern sympathizers were able to conduct a brisk trade in military information. Some of these spies were women who made use of their sexual attractiveness to serve their cause. Greenhow, one of the best known, was described by a contemporary as possessed of "almost irresistible seductive powers."[63]

When the war broke out, Greenhow was a widow and mother in her mid-thirties. She was prominent in Washington, D.C., social circles and had connections to important congressmen, including her nephew Senator Stephen A. Douglas of Illinois. Committed to the Confederate cause and opposed to freedom for black people, she gathered political and military information helpful to the South from her numerous admirers and lovers, allegedly information that helped the Confederates win the first battle of Bull Run. Although constantly under suspicion, she avoided arrest by appealing to principles of gentlemanly chivalry shared by North and South alike.

◆ **Figure 5.5 Harriet Tubman**
© *Bettmann/Corbis.*

Eventually, however, Greenhow was arrested and sent to a special Washington prison reserved for enemy agents, many of them women. She was subsequently released to Virginia. The circumstances of her death, soon after, were as extraordinary as those of her life. In 1864 she was a passenger on a British boat running the Union naval blockade off the Carolina coast. Northern gunships fired, and Greenhow's lifeboat capsized. She was close to shore and would have made it to land except that she held on to her purse, which was heavy with gold, and therefore drowned.

The photograph in Figure 5.6 was taken by a member of the studio of renowned Civil War photographer Mathew Brady, when Greenhow was imprisoned. What comment does the photographer's artful posing make on Greenhow's

◆ Figure 5.6 **Rose O'Neal Greenhow in the Old Capitol Prison with Her Daughter (1862)**
Library of Congress LC-DIG-cwpbh-04849.

career as a Confederate spy? What do Greenhow's dress, pose, and the presence of her daughter suggest about her imprisonment at Union hands?

THE SOLDIERS

Although we will never know their numbers, hundreds of women, possibly more, fought on the battlefields of the Civil War. These women warriors fall into two categories: those who were known to be women at the time and those who passed themselves off as men. In the first category were the so-called daughters of the regiment. Often arriving in camp with their newly enlisted husbands, a few may have also been as motivated by the desire to see military action as by marital sentiment. After performing such womanly tasks as nursing, cooking, and laundering, occasionally these women took on the all-important job of carrying the regiment's flag (or standard) into battle. Soldiers, who were recruited at the local and state level, fought as much out of loyalty to their regiment as to the army or the nation, and the way their regimental colors were displayed represented their comradeship and military fervor. The standard bearer's job was to lead and encourage the troops, and women who undertook this role inspired tremendous devotion from their comrades.

Bridget Divers, known as "Michigan Bridget," was one of these regimental daughters. An Irish immigrant, she came to the First Michigan Calvary with her husband. Early in the war, her regiment was the object of a surprise attack, and the troops panicked. One of Divers's comrades remembered how she leaped to her feet, grabbed the flag, and yelled, "Go in Boys and bate [beat] Hell out of them."[64] Divers found army life so much to her liking that, after the war, she continued to serve with her husband in the western Indian conflicts.

As with other such women, the legends that accrued around Michigan Bridget emphasized her combination of manly bravery and female sympathy. Figure 5.7, a steel engraving commissioned, like that of Mary Ann Bickerdyke (Figure 5.1), by Mary Livermore for *My Story of the War*, portrays Divers bearing the U.S. flag in the midst of battle. Divers knew how to shoot, and Livermore approvingly wrote of her, "When a soldier fell she took his place, fighting in his stead with unquailing courage."[65] How and with what purpose does the artist position Divers with respect to the battle? Why might she have been pictured with a flag instead of the gun that she allegedly knew how to use? And why might the artist have chosen to show her carrying not the regimental colors but the U.S. flag?

"Of the three hundred and twenty-eight thousand Union soldiers who lie buried in national cemeteries," the editors of the *History of Woman Suffrage* (1881) wrote, ". . . hundreds are . . . women obliged by army regulation to fight in disguise."[66] "Passing women," as historians have come to label such women, fought in many wars, but they seem to have been particularly numerous in the U.S. Civil War. The Union army discovered and dismissed many women among its recruits, and the sex of others was not discovered until they were wounded or killed. Dur-

◆ Figure 5.7 **F. O. C. Darley, *A Woman in Battle—"Michigan Bridget" Carrying the Flag* (1888)**
Milstein Division of United States History, Local History, and Genealogy, The New York Public Library, Astor, Lenox, and Tilden Foundations.

ing the war, authorities' greatest fear was that women who had sneaked into the ranks would engage in immoral sexual activities with male soldiers. Stories of women who disguised themselves as men in order to fight continued to surface for many decades. In 1910, an Illinois Civil War pensioner who had gone by the name Albert Cashier was discovered to be a woman, declared insane, sentenced to an asylum, and forced to dress as a woman.[67] For a long time after the war, some passing women, like Cashier, lived as men. They worked in men's occupations and even married women, who invariably claimed to have believed their husbands to be men, which is hard to believe but impossible to dismiss.

◆ Figure 5.8 **Madam Velazquez in Female Attire (*left*) and Harry T. Buford, 1st Lieutenant, Independent Scouts, Confederate States Army (*right*)**
Documenting the American South (http://docsouth.unc.edu), The University of North Carolina at Chapel Hill Libraries. From Loreta Janeta Velazquez, The Woman in Battle: A Narrative of the Exploits, Adventures, and Travels of Madame Loreta Janeta Velazquez, Otherwise Known as Lieutenant Harry T. Buford, Confederate States Army *(Richmond: Dustin, Gilman & Co., 1876).*

With one exception, all of the well-known passing women of the Civil War era were Union soldiers. Loreta Velazquez, a Cuban immigrant, began her career in the Confederate army with her husband's support but maintained her masquerade even after he was killed. Using the name Harry T. Buford, Velazquez fought as an officer with several regiments and participated in the Confederate victory at the first battle of Bull Run. Although she was wounded, she escaped detection and continued to live a life of high adventure after the war.

In 1876, Velazquez wrote a popular and controversial memoir, *The Woman in Battle*, in which she described her lifelong habit of wearing men's clothes and the attraction that being able to make money like a man held for her. Her book included the illustrations shown in Figure 5.8 of her female and male personae. How did she depict herself as a woman, and what designated her visually as a man? Above all, what point might she have been seeking to make by demonstrating through illustrations that she could shift from role to role? How does her story begin to suggest what today is called the social construction of gender?

QUESTIONS FOR ANALYSIS

1. What are the similarities in the images of women who served as Civil War nurses? What attitudes toward women help explain these similarities?

2. Male soldiers are issued official uniforms to designate their rank and military affiliation. What similarities do you notice in Divers's and Tubman's outfits? How might this clothing have constituted a kind of informal uniform for women on the battlefield?

3. The Civil War was fought between two cultures as much as between two economic and political systems. Do you detect patterns in the images of northern versus southern women? What do these differences tell you about the gender dimensions of the North–South divide?

4. Taken as a group, do these images indicate that the women who participated directly in the war did more to maintain or to undermine standard gender roles?

NOTES

1. Martha S. Read to Lorinda Shelton, April 6, 1852, Norwich, New York, http://xroads.virginia.edu/~HYPER/HNS/domwest/read.html (accessed June 16, 2004).

2. Lillian Schlissel, ed., *Women's Diaries of the Westward Journey* (New York: Schocken Books, 1982), 188.

3. Cathy Luchetti, ed., *Women of the West* (St. George, Utah: Antelope Island Press, 1982), 145.

4. John Mack Faragher, *Women and Men on the Overland Trail* (New Haven: Yale University Press, 1979), 172.

5. Schlissel, *Women's Diaries of the Westward Journey*, 179–80.

6. Ibid., 214.

7. Ibid., 223.

8. Ibid., 39.

9. Sarah Royce, *A Frontier Lady*, excerpted in Ida Rae Egli, ed., *No Rooms of Their Own: Women Writers of Early California* (Berkeley: Heyday Books, 1992), 15.

10. Ibid., 13.

11. Glenda Riley, *A Place to Grow: Women in the American West* (Arlington Heights, IL: Harlan Davidson, 1982), 127.

12. Sarah Winnemucca Hopkins, *Life among the Piutes: Their Wrongs and Claims* (1883; repr., Bishop, CA: Sierra Media, 1969), 11.

13. J. S. Holliday, *The World Rushed In: The California Gold Rush Experience* (New York: Simon and Schuster, 1981), 164.

14. Susan B. Anthony to Mary Anthony, February 7, 1848, in Ann D. Gordon, ed., *The Selected Papers of Elizabeth Cady Stanton and Susan B. Anthony: In the School of Anti-Slavery, 1840–1866* (New Brunswick: Rutgers University Press, 1996), 134.

15. Anonymous to Catherine D. Oliver, 1850, in Edith Sparks, *Capital Instincts: Female Proprietors in San Francisco, 1850–1920* (Chapel Hill: University of North Carolina Press, 2006), 58.

16. Louise Clappe, *The Shirley Letters, Being Letters Written in 1851–1852 from the California Mines* (1922; repr., Santa Barbara: Peregrine, 1970), 36.

17. Schlissel, *Women's Diaries of the Westward Journey*, 6.

18. Christiane Fischer, ed., *Let Them Speak for Themselves: Women in the American West* (New York: E. P. Dutton, 1978), 43–45.

19. Holliday, *The World Rushed In*, 165.

20. Eliza W. Farnham, *California, In-doors and Out, or How We Farm, Mine, and Live Generally in the Golden State* (1856; repr., Amsterdam: F. De Graaf, 1972), 384.

21. Nancy Hewitt, *Women's Activism and Social Change: Rochester, New York, 1822–1872* (Ithaca: Cornell University Press, 1984), 40.

22. Constitution of the New-York Female Moral Reform Society, 1836, reprinted in Dawn Keetley and John Pettegrew, eds., *Public Women, Public Words: A Documentary History of American Feminism*, vol. 1, *Beginnings to 1900* (Madison, WI: Madison House, 1997), 129.

23. T. L. Nichols, M.D., and Mrs. Mary S. Gove Nichols, *Marriage: Its History, Character and Results; Its Sanctities and Its Profanities; Its Science and Its Facts* (New York: T. L. Nichols, 1854), 202.

24. Elizabeth Cady Stanton, *Eighty Years and More: Reminiscences, 1815–1897* (1898; repr., Boston: Northeastern University Press, 1993), 284.

25. Georgiana Bruce Kirby, *Years of Experience: An Autobiographical Narrative* (New York: G. P. Putnam's Sons, 1887), 99.

26. Boston Female Anti-Slavery Address, July 13, 1836, reprinted in *Our Mothers Before Us: Women and Democracy, 1789–1920* (Washington, DC: Foundation for the National Archives, 1998), 11–23.

27. Harriet Beecher Stowe, "Sojourner Truth: The Libyan Sibyl," *Atlantic Monthly*, April 1863, 473–81.

28. Elizabeth Cady Stanton, "Speech to the Anniversary of the American Anti-Slavery Society," *The Liberator*, May 18, 1860, 78.

29. Carolyn Williams, "The Female Antislavery Movement: Fighting Against Racial Prejudice and Promoting Women's Rights in Antebellum America," in Jean Fagan Yellin and John C. Van Horne, eds., *The Abolitionist Sisterhood: Women's Political Culture in Antebellum America* (Ithaca: Cornell University Press, 1994), 162.

30. Jean R. Soderlund, "Priorities and Power: The Philadelphia Female Anti-Slavery Society," in *The Abolitionist Sisterhood*, 73.

31. "Pastoral Letter of the Massachusetts Congregationalist Clergy," 1837, in Aileen Kraditor, ed., *Up from the Pedestal: Selected Writings in the History of American Feminism* (Chicago: Quadrangle Books, 1968), 51.

32. Boston Female Anti-Slavery Address, July 13, 1836, 11–23.

33. Quoted in Lori D. Ginzberg, *Women and the Work of Benevolence: Morality, Politics, and Class in the Nineteenth-Century United States* (New Haven: Yale University Press, 1990), 93.

34. Ibid., 26.

35. Angelina Grimké Weld to Gerrit and Anne Smith, June 18, 1840, in Gilbert Barnes and Dwight Dumond, eds., *Letters of Theodore Dwight Weld, Angelina Grimké Weld, and Sarah Grimké, 1822–1844* (New York: Appleton-Century, 1934), 2: 842.

36. Stanton, *Eighty Years and More*, 83.

37. Ibid., 147–48.

38. "Declarations of Sentiments and Resolutions, Seneca Falls Convention," 1848, reprinted in Kraditor, *Up from the Pedestal*, 183–89.

39. Frances Ellen Watkins Harper, letter to John Brown, November 25, 1859; reprinted in James Redpath, *Echoes of Harpers Ferry* (Boston: Thayer and Eldridge, 1860), 418–19.

40. Frances Willard, *Glimpses of Fifty Years: The Autobiography of an American Woman* (Chicago: H. J. Smith, 1889), 155.

41. Mary Chesnut, April 12, 1861, in C. Vann Woodward, ed., *Mary Chesnut's Civil War* (New Haven: Yale University Press, 1981), 46.

42. Mary Livermore, *My Story of the War* (Hartford: A. D. Worthington, 1898), 465.

43. Ibid., 472.

44. Anna Howard Shaw, with the collaboration of Elizabeth Jordan, *The Story of a Pioneer* (New York: Harpers Bros., 1915), 51.

45. Bell Irvin Wiley, *Confederate Women* (Westford, CT: Greenwood Press, 1975), 177.

46. Elizabeth Cady Stanton to Nancy Smith, July 20, 1863, in Theodore Stanton and Harriot Stanton Blatch, eds., *Elizabeth Cady Stanton as Revealed in Her Letters, Diary, and Reminiscences* (New York: Harper & Brothers, 1922), 95.

47. Dorothy Sterling, ed., *We Are Your Sisters: Black Women in the Nineteenth Century* (New York: W.W. Norton, 1984), 239.

48. Elizabeth Cady Stanton, "To the Women of the Republic," April 24, 1863, reprinted in *The Selected Papers of Elizabeth Cady Stanton and Susan B. Anthony: In the School of Anti-Slavery*, 483.

49. Elizabeth Cady Stanton, Susan B. Anthony, and Matilda J. Gage, eds., *History of Woman Suffrage* (Rochester, NY: Susan B. Anthony, 1881), 79.

50. Mary Chesnut, May 7, 1865, in *Mary Chesnut's Civil War*, 802.

51. Sterling, *We Are Your Sisters*, 244.

52. Livermore, *My Story of the War*, 469.

53. Cited in Marilyn Mayer Culpepper, *All Things Altered: Women in the Wake of Civil War and Reconstruction* (Jefferson, NC: McFarland, 2002), 23.

54. "California Association of American Women," circular, February 28, 1848, republished with *California, In-doors and Out*.

55. Angustias de la Guerra Ord, *Occurrences in Hispanic California*, trans. and ed. Francis Price and William Ellison (Washington, DC: Academic Press of American Franciscan History, 1956), 59. For the correction, see Rosaura Sánchez, *Telling Identities: The California "Testimonios"* (Minneapolis: University of Minnesota Press, 1995), 324.

56. Mary Denis Maher, *To Bind Up the Wounds: Catholic Sister Nurses in the U.S. Civil War* (New York: Greenwood Press, 1989), 51.

57. Ibid., 53.

58. Louisa May Alcott, *The Journals of Louisa May Alcott*, ed. Joel Myerson, Daniel Sheahy, and Madeleine B. Stern (Boston: Little, Brown, 1989), 110.

59. Drew Gilpin Faust, "Altars of Sacrifice: Confederate Women and the Narratives of War," *Journal of American History* 76 (1990): 1203.

60. Maher, *To Bind Up the Wounds*, 39.

61. Susie King Taylor, *A Black Woman's Civil War Memoirs: Reminiscences of My Life in Camp with the 33rd U.S. Colored Troops, Late 1st South Carolina Volunteers*, excerpted in *Growing Up Female in America: Ten Lives*, ed. Eve Merriam (New York: Dell, 1971), 195.

62. *Commonwealth*, July 10, 1863, cited in Earl Conrad, *Harriet Tubman* (Washington, DC: Associated Publishers, 1943), 169.

63. Elizabeth Leonard, *All the Daring of the Soldier: Women of the Civil War Armies* (New York: W. W. Norton, 1999), 94.

64. Ibid., 123.

65. Livermore, *My Story of the War*, 116.

66. Stanton, Anthony, and Gage, *History of Woman Suffrage*, 2:23.

67. Leonard, *All the Daring of a Soldier*, 188–89.

SUGGESTED REFERENCES

Women and the West　For general overviews on women and the West in this period, see Julie Roy Jeffrey, *Frontier Women: The Trans-Mississippi West, 1840–1880* (1979), and Glenda Riley, *Women and Indians on the Frontier* (1984). On the overland trail experience, see John Mack Faragher, *Women and Men on the Overland Trail* (1979). Lillian Schlissel has edited a major collection of overland trail diaries in *Women's Diaries of the Western Journey* (1992). For the impact of American migration on the California Indians, see Albert Hurtado, *Indian Survival on the California Frontier* (1987), and *Sex, Gender and Culture in California* (1999). On the Cherokee experience through women's eyes, see Theda Perdue, *Cherokee Women: Gender and Culture Change, 1700–1835* (1998). Gae Canfield has written a biography of Sarah Winnemucca, *Sarah Winnemucca of the Northern Paiutes* (1983). On Mexican California, see Ramón A. Gutiérrez and Richard J. Orsi, eds., *Contested Eden: California before the Gold Rush* (1997), and Rosaura Sánchez, *Telling Identities: The Californio "Testimonios"* (1995). On women and the California gold rush, see Joanne Levy, *They Saw the Elephant: Women in the California Gold Rush* (1990). Susan Lee Johnson offers a gendered history in *Roaring Camp: The Social World of the California Gold Rush* (2000). Important book-length primary sources concerning women in the West in this period include Louise Clappe, *The Shirley Letters from the California Mines, 1851–1852* (1998); Eliza Farnham, *California, In-doors and Out* (1972); and Sarah Winnemucca Hopkins, *Life among the Piutes: Their Wrongs and Claims* (1994).

Women and Reform Movements　For the roots of women's reform activism, see Ann Boylan, *The Origins of Women's Activism, New York, and Boston, 1797–1840* (2002); Keith Melder, *Beginnings of Sisterhood: The American Woman's Rights Movement, 1800–1850* (1977); Mary Ryan, *Cradle of the Middle Class: The Family in Oneida County, New York, 1790–1865* (1981); and Anne F. Scott, *Natural Allies: Women's Associations in American History* (1993). On female moral reform, see Barbara J. Berg, *The Remembered Gate: Origins of American Feminism, the Woman, and the City, 1800–1860* (1978), and Carroll Smith-Rosenberg, "Beauty, the Beast and the Militant Woman: A Case Study of Sex Roles and Social Stress in Jacksonian America," *American Quarterly* 23 (1971), 562–84. On temperance, see Barbara Epstein, *The Politics of Domesticity: Women, Evangelism, and Temperance in Nineteenth-Century America* (1981). Two studies on women and health reform are

Susan Cayleff, *Wash and Be Healed: The Water Cure Movement and Women's Health* (1987); and Jean L. Silver-Isenstadt, *Shameless: The Visionary Life of Mary Gove Nichols* (2002). On women and utopian communities, see Lawrence Foster, *Women, Family and Utopia: Communal Experiments of the Shakers, the Oneida Community, and the Mormons* (1991), and Louis J. Kern, *An Ordered Love: Sex Roles and Sexuality in Victorian Utopias — The Shakers, the Mormons, and the Oneida Community* (1981). On Margaret Fuller, see Charles Capper, *Margaret Fuller: An American Romantic Life*, 2 vols. (1992, 2007), and Bell Gale Chevigny, ed., *The Woman and the Myth: Margaret Fuller's Life and Writings* (1997).

Women and Abolitionism   There is much written on women and abolitionism, including Blanche Hersh, *The Slavery of Sex: Female Abolitionists in Nineteenth-Century America* (1978); Nancy Hewitt, *Women's Activism and Social Change, Rochester, New York, 1822–1872* (2001); Julie Roy Jeffrey, *The Great Silent Army of Abolitionism: Ordinary Women in the Antislavery Movement* (1998); Gerda Lerner, *The Grimké Sisters from South Carolina* (1967); Shirley Yee, *Black Women Abolitionists: A Study in Activism, 1828–1860* (1992); Jean Baker Yellin and John C. Van Horne, eds., *The Abolitionist Sisterhood: Women's Political Culture in Antebellum America* (1994); and Susan Zaeske, *Signatures of Citizenship: Petitioning, Antislavery, and Women's Political Identity* (2003). On Sojourner Truth, see Nell Painter, *Sojourner Truth: A Life, a Symbol* (1996). On women's rights, see Ellen Carol DuBois, *Feminism and Suffrage: The Emergence of an Independent Women's Movement in America, 1848–1869* (2003) and *Woman Suffrage, Women's Rights* (1998), and Nancy Isenberg, *Sex and Citizenship in Antebellum America* (1998). An important collection of hitherto unpublished sources for the period can be found in Ann D. Gordon, ed., *The Papers of Elizabeth Cady Stanton and Susan B. Anthony*, vol. 1, *In the School of Anti-Slavery* (1997). Elizabeth Cady Stanton's engaging autobiography, *Eighty Years and More: Reminiscences, 1815–1897* (2002), should also be consulted. Bonnie Anderson situates American women's rights in an international context in *Joyous Greetings: The First International Women's Movement, 1830–1860* (2000).

Women and the Civil War   On women's roles leading up to the Civil War, see Jean Baker, *Mary Todd Lincoln: A Biography* (1987), and Melanie Gustafson, *Women and the Republican Party, 1854–1900* (2001). On Harriet Beecher Stowe and *Uncle Tom's Cabin,* see Joan Hedrick, *Harriet Beecher Stowe: A Life* (1994), and Barbara Ann White, *The Beecher Sisters* (2003). On southern women during the war, see Laura Edwards, *Scarlett Doesn't Live Here Anymore: Southern Women in the Civil War Era* (2000); Drew Gilpin Faust, *Mothers of Invention: Women of the Slaveholding South in the American Civil War* (1998); and George Rable, *Civil Wars: Women and the Crisis of Southern Nationalism* (1989). For women in the North, important studies include Jeanie Attie, *Patriotic Toil: Northern Women and the American Civil War* (1998), and Lori Ginzberg, *Women and the Work of Benevolence: Morality, Politics, and Class in the Nineteenth-Century United States* (1990). Elizabeth Leonard, *All the Daring of the Soldier: Women of the Civil War Armies* (1999), covers both sides, including women as soldiers. Jane E. Schultz provides an excellent account of female nurses on both sides of the conflict in *Women at the Front: Hospital Workers in Civil War America* (2004). Sister Mary Denis Maher examines an understudied topic in *To Bind Up the Wounds: Catholic Sister Nurses in the U.S. Civil War* (1989). Two new biographies of Harriet Tubman are Catherine Clinton, *Harriet Tubman, The Road to Freedom* (2004), and Kate Clifford Larson, *Bound for the Promised Land: Harriet Tubman, Portrait of an American Hero* (2003).

For selected Web sites, please visit the *Through Women's Eyes* book companion site at bedfordstmartins.com/duboisdumenil.

6

Reconstructing Women's Lives North and South

1865–1900

IDA B. WELLS, MARY KENNEY, AND M. CAREY THOMAS were all daughters of the Civil War era. Wells was born in 1862 to Mississippi slaves; Kenney in 1864 to Irish immigrants in Hannibal, Missouri; and Thomas in 1857 to a wealthy Baltimore Quaker family. Despite these great differences in background, the unfolding of each woman's life illustrates the forces that affected American women's history in the years after the Civil War and, in turn, women's capacity to be forces in the making of American history.

Wells (later Wells-Barnett) was shaped by the violent struggles between former slaves seeking to realize their emancipation and white southerners seeking to retain their racial dominance. As a journalist, Wells exposed new, brutal methods of white supremacy, and her work sparked an organized women's movement among African Americans. Kenney (later O'Sullivan) was a lifelong wage earner who recognized that workers needed to act collectively rather than individually to improve their lives. A path-breaking female labor organizer, she helped form the Women's Trade Union League (WTUL) in 1903 (see pp. 458–59). Thomas, a self-proclaimed tomboy as a child who did not marry as an adult, became a pioneer of higher education for women. She was one of the first women to graduate from Cornell University and to receive a doctorate (in Switzerland), and she was the founding dean of Bryn Mawr College. In the post–Civil War (or postbellum) years, such individuals laid the basis for an era of extraordinary achievement by American women.

"Reconstruction" is the term used to describe the period of American history immediately after the Civil War, the revision of the U.S. Constitution to deal with the consequences of emancipation, the rebuilding of the South after the devastations of war, and the reconstitution of national unity after the trauma of sectional division. The formal period of Reconstruction lasted twelve years. It ended in 1877 when U.S. troops withdrew from the former Confederacy, leaving the South to work out its own troubled racial destiny without federal oversight and the North to concentrate on industrial development and economic growth.

The word "reconstruction" can also be used to cover a longer period, during which the U.S. economy was reconstituted entirely around industrial capitalism. The free labor ethic on which the Republican Party was founded evolved into a commitment to unbridled industrialization. The society's wealth, optimism, and productivity were not shared equally. On the contrary, the gap between rich and poor grew enormously during the postbellum years, producing great tension and violence between owners and workers. With chattel slavery eliminated, industrial society could no longer ignore its internal class divisions, and by the end of the century, conflict between labor and capital overtook the inequalities of race as the most overt challenge to national unity.

Women were reconstructing their lives in these years as well. In the defeated South, women emancipated from slavery grappled with the challenges and dangers of their tentative freedom, while their former mistresses sought to maintain the privileges of white supremacy under new conditions. In the North, a determined group of women sought equal political rights, and the woman suffrage movement came into its own. Industrial capitalism generated both a rapidly expanding female labor force and new leisure and wealth for middle- and upper-class women. Between 1865 and 1900, women's labor, the terms of appropriate womanhood within which women lived, and their scope for public action all expanded. By the end of the nineteenth century, the basis had been laid for an epoch of female assertion and accomplishment unparalleled in American history.

GENDER AND THE POSTWAR CONSTITUTIONAL AMENDMENTS

American history's first presidential assassination (Abraham Lincoln), followed quickly by its first presidential impeachment (Andrew Johnson), left the executive branch in shambles and the legislative branch in charge of national Reconstruction. Republicans controlled Congress, and former abolitionists, known as Radicals, controlled the Republican Party. To protect the North's victory and their party's control over Congress, the Radicals were determined to enfranchise the only population on whom the Republicans could depend in the defeated Confederacy—former slaves. In 1866, Radicals proposed an amendment to the U.S. Constitution to establish the citizenship of ex-slaves. The Fourteenth Amendment began with a simple, inclusive sentence: "All persons born or naturalized in the United States, and subject to the jurisdiction thereof, are citizens of the United States and of the State wherein they reside."

Leaders of the women's rights movement hoped to revise the Constitution and reconstruct democracy without distinction of either race *or* gender. Despite their best efforts, however, the ratification of the Fourteenth Amendment in 1868, followed by that of the Fifteenth Amendment in 1870, established black suffrage without reference to woman suffrage. Thwarted in Congress, these women turned to the U.S. Supreme Court to argue that women's political rights were included within the new constitutional definitions of national citizenship and political rights.

Their efforts failed. The only actual enfranchisement of women in the Reconstruction era occurred in the territories of Wyoming (1869) and Utah (1870), where a handful of legislators accorded women the vote in territorial and local elections. Even so, the campaign for women's enfranchisement changed and expanded, drawing new adherents from the Midwest and the Pacific Coast. The old alliance with abolitionists was shattered, and most efforts for women's equality were no longer linked to those for racial equality. The advocates of woman suffrage undertook a campaign that would require an additional half century and another constitutional amendment—the Nineteenth, ratified in 1920—to complete. (See pp. 488–89 and, for the complete text of all amendments to the U.S. Constitution, Appendix pp. A-12–A-17.)

Constitutionalizing Women's Rights

In 1865 and 1866, as Congress was considering how to word the Fourteenth Amendment, women's rights activists called for woman suffrage to be joined with black suffrage in a single constitutional act. Many northern women had fought for the end of slavery, so, in the memorable words of Elizabeth Cady Stanton, "Would it not be advisable, when the constitutional door is open, [for women to] avail ourselves of the strong arm and blue uniform of the black soldier to walk in by his side?"[1] To pursue this goal, Stanton, Anthony and others formed the American Equal Rights Association, dedicated to both black and woman suffrage. "We resolved to make common cause with the colored class—the only other disfranchised class," observed Lucy Stone, "and strike for equal rights for all."[2]

But Radicals in Congress contended that pursuing woman suffrage and black suffrage simultaneously would doom the latter, which was their priority. Accordingly, they wrote the second section of the Fourteenth Amendment, meant to encourage states to grant voting rights to former slaves, to apply only to "male inhabitants . . . twenty-one years of age and citizens of the United States." This was the first reference to gender in the U.S. Constitution. Woman suffragists petitioned Congress to get the wording changed, but abolitionist Wendell Phillips told them, "This hour belongs to the Negro," leaving Stanton to wonder impatiently if "the African race is composed entirely of males."[3]

Two years after the 1868 ratification of the Fourteenth Amendment, congressional Radicals wrote the Fifteenth Amendment to advance black suffrage more forcefully, explicitly forbidding disfranchisement on the grounds of "race, color or previous condition of servitude." Gender was not included, leading Stanton to charge that "all mankind will vote not because of intelligence, patriotism, property or white skin but because it is male, not female."[4]

The American Equal Rights Association collapsed, and in its wake, woman suffragists divided over whether to endorse the Fifteenth Amendment. To reconcile woman suffrage advocacy with the Radical Republican agenda, in 1869 Lucy Stone and her husband, Henry Ward Blackwell, organized the American Woman Suffrage Association. They focused on campaigns for suffrage at the state level and in 1870 inaugurated the *Woman's Journal*, a weekly newspaper published for the next fifty years. Elizabeth Cady Stanton and Susan B. Anthony took a different

◆ **Elizabeth Cady Stanton and Susan B. Anthony**
Taken in 1870, this is the earliest photograph of the most important partnership in the U.S. woman suffrage movement. Stanton and Anthony had already been collaborating for two decades, and would do so for another three. Stanton's rambunctious curls and Anthony's severe bun give some indication of their quite different yet compatible personalities. Despite their bond, there was a hint of inequality between them. Although Anthony was only five years younger, she addressed her friend as "Mrs. Stanton," while Stanton called her "Susan." © *Bettmann/Corbis.*

route. They broke with their former Radical Republican allies and formed the rival National Woman Suffrage Association (NWSA).

Of the two societies, the NWSA pursued the more aggressive, independent path. The organization's newspaper, defiantly named the *Revolution*, lasted only two years. It proclaimed on its masthead: "Women their rights and nothing less; men their rights and nothing more." NWSA gained political autonomy for the suffrage movement but at the cost of an important part of the women's rights legacy: attention to the interrelation of the hierarchies of race and gender. As the larger society left behind the concerns of the ex-slaves and of Radical Reconstruction, much of the woman suffrage movement did, too, envisioning women's emancipation largely in terms of white women.

A New Departure for Woman Suffrage

Once the new constitutional amendments had been ratified, the NWSA proposed an inventive, bold interpretation of them. The argument was both simple and profound: first, women were "persons" whose rights as national citizens were established by the first sentence of the Fourteenth Amendment; second, the right to vote was central to and inherent in national citizenship. Third, and most important, women's right to vote was thus already established and did not require any additional constitutional change.

This argument, which was called the New Departure, brought to prominence one of the most unusual advocates in the history of woman suffrage, Victoria Claflin Woodhull. Born into poverty, Woodhull made her way into the highest ranks of New York society, in large part by cultivating powerful men. Aided by a congressman friend and without the knowledge of other suffragists, in 1871 she presented the case for the New Departure before the Judiciary Committee of the U.S. House of Representatives. Within a year, however, Woodhull had become involved in a scandal over the alleged adultery of Henry Ward Beecher, powerful Brooklyn minister and brother of Catharine Beecher and Harriet Beecher Stowe (see pp. 188–89; 280–81). Under a new federal anti-obscenity law, the Comstock Act (named for Anthony Comstock, the "social purity" crusader who drafted the legislation), Woodhull was jailed for sending accounts of the scandal through the federal mails. Stanton, one of the few suffragists who steadfastly defended Woodhull, insisted, "We have already women enough sacrificed to this sentimental, hypocritical prating about purity. If this present woman be crucified, let men drive the spikes."[5] Woodhull avoided jail but dropped out of public life; she eventually moved to England, where she married a wealthy man, remade her reputation, and lived until 1927.

Independent of Woodhull, suffragists around the country pursued their voting rights on the basis of the New Departure theory that they needed only to take hold of the right to vote, which was already theirs. During the elections of 1871 and 1872, groups of women went to their local polling places, put forth their constitutional understanding to stunned election officials, and stepped forward to submit their votes. In Washington, D.C., the African American journalist Mary Ann Shadd Cary was able to register but not to vote. Susan B. Anthony convinced polling officials in her hometown of Rochester, New York, to let her vote. "Well I have been & gone & done it!!" she wrote exuberantly. "Positively voted the Republican ticket."[6] Two weeks later, she was arrested for violating a federal law meant to disfranchise former Confederates. Her trial was a spectacle from start to finish. The judge ordered the jury to find Anthony guilty, which it did, and the judge's final insult was to refuse to jail Anthony so as to keep her from appealing her verdict (see box, "Not One Is My Peer, All Are My Political Sovereigns").

The U.S. Supreme Court finally considered the suffragists' argument in 1875, in the case of Virginia Minor, of St. Louis, Missouri, who sued the official who

SUSAN B. ANTHONY
Not One Is My Peer, All Are My Political Sovereigns

Soon after voting in the 1872 presidential election, Susan B. Anthony (1820–1906) was arrested for violating federal law. She approached her trial, held in June 1873, as an opportunity to argue the injustice of denying women political equality. For weeks before, she lectured extensively on the constitutional basis of her decision to cast her ballot. At the trial, after being declared guilty, Anthony made a statement that her right to a jury trial was meaningless so long as she was tried by men who did not share her disfranchised condition.

All of my prosecutors, from the 8th ward corner grocery politician, who entered the complaint, to the United States Marshal, Commissioner, District Attorney, District Judge, your honor on the bench, not one is my peer, but each and all are my political sovereigns; . . . [I have been tried] by forms of law all made by men, interpreted by men, administered by men, in favor of men, and against women; . . . But, yesterday, the same man-made forms of law, declared it a crime . . . for you, or me, or any of us, to give a cup of cold water, a crust of bread, or a night's shelter to a panting fugitive as he was tracking his way to Canada. And every man or woman in whose veins coursed a drop of human sympathy violated that wicked law, reckless of consequences, and was justified in so doing. As then, the slaves who got their freedom must take it over, or under, or through the unjust forms of law, precisely so, now, must women, to get their right to a voice in this government, take it; and I have taken mine, and mean to take it at every possible opportunity.

SOURCE: Susan B. Anthony's response to Judge Hunt at her June 1873 trial, "Stanton and Anthony Papers Online Project," Rutgers University, http://ecssba.rutgers.edu/docs/sbatrial.html (accessed June 19, 2004).

had not allowed her to vote. In *Minor v. Happersett*, one of the most important rulings in the history of women's rights (see the Appendix, p. A-25), the Supreme Court ruled unanimously that, while Minor was indeed a citizen, voting was not a right but a privilege bestowed by the federal government as it saw fit. Not only did this decision strike the New Departure theory dead, but it also indicated that the Court was bent on narrowing the meaning of the Fourteenth and Fifteenth Amendments in general. Subsequently, the Court permitted more and more devices to deprive black men of their franchise and constitutional civil rights.

After the *Minor* decision, the NWSA began to advocate a separate constitutional amendment, modeled on the Fifteenth, to bar disfranchisement explicitly "on the grounds of sex." This was the wording that would eventually go into the Nineteenth Amendment (1920), but for the time being, the proposed amendment made little headway. In 1876, NWSA leaders, uninvited, forced their way into the national celebration in Philadelphia of the hundredth anniversary of the Declaration of Independence. "Our faith is firm and unwavering in the broad principles of human rights proclaimed in 1776, not only as abstract truths, but as the corner stones of a republic," they declared. "Yet we cannot forget, even in this glad hour, that while all men of every race, and clime, and condition, have been invested with the full rights of citizenship under our hospitable flag, all women still suffer the degradation of disfranchisement."[7]

WOMEN'S LIVES IN SOUTHERN RECONSTRUCTION AND REDEMPTION

Meanwhile, life in the defeated South was being reconstructed as well. No element of freedom came easily or automatically for the former slaves, and southern whites changed their lives and expectations reluctantly. Black women fought for control over their labor, their children, and their bodies. Elite white women sought new capacities and strengths to accommodate the loss of the labor and wealth that slaveowning had given them. White women from the middle and lower ranks remained poised between loyalties of race and the resentments of class.

By 1870, all the southern states had met the terms Congress mandated for readmission to the Union. After the removal of federal troops in 1877, white southerners, in a process known as Redemption, moved to reclaim political control and to reassert white superiority. The region's economy, still largely agricultural, slowly began to industrialize. The complex result of these post-Reconstruction social, political, and economic changes was known as the New South.

Black Women in the New South

After the defeat of the Confederacy, many freedwomen and freedmen stayed on with their masters for months because they did not know they had been freed or had nowhere to go. Some took to the road to find long-lost spouses and family members. Those who could not travel posted advertisements, such as this one in the *Anglo-African Magazine*: "Martha Ward Wishes information concerning her

◆ The Right to Marry

As disregard of slave marriages had been considered one of the fundamental immoralities of slavery, immediately after the Civil War the Freedmen's Bureau rushed to legalize marriages among freedpeople, who were eager to have their unions recognized. To indicate that slaves had been married in fact if not in law, bureau officials "solemnized" rather than authorized these marriages. In this engraving, an African American Bureau chaplain presides at a ceremony for two former slaves; the husband was serving in the U.S. Army. *© Corbis.*

sister, Rosetta McQuillan, who was sold from Norfolk, Va. About thirty years ago to a Frenchman in Mobile, Ala."[8]

The hard-won family reunions of the freed slaves did not always end happily. Some spouses had formed new unions. Laura Spicer, sold away from a Virginia plantation, was contacted by her husband three years after the war ended. He had since become attached to another woman and was deeply conflicted. "I do not know which I love best, you or Anna," he wrote to Spicer. "[T]ry and marry some good, smart man . . . and do it because you love me, and not because I think more of the wife I have got than I do of you."[9] Nor were parents always recognized by the children they had been forced to leave behind. "At firs' I was scared of her, 'cause I didn't know who she was," one child remembered of her mother. She put me in her lap an' she most' nigh cried when she seen de back o' my head . . . where de lice had been an' I had scratched em."[10]

In 1865, the U.S. Army, charged with occupying and governing the defeated Confederacy, organized a special division to deal with the former slaves. The Freedmen's Bureau provided temporary relief, oversaw their labor, and adjudicated disputes with former masters. It was the first systematic welfare effort of the U.S. government for an oppressed racial minority. One of its tasks was to ensure that freedpeople had rights over and to their own children. On returning to the Union, southern states had passed laws, known as black codes, to limit the freedoms of newly emancipated slaves. Apprenticeship laws provided for the indenture of black children into servitude regardless of the wishes of their parents. Black mothers and grandmothers fought especially hard against the black codes. "We were delighted when we heard that the Constitution set us free," Lucy Lee of Baltimore explained, "but God help us, our condition is bettered but little; free ourselves, [but] deprived of our children. . . . Give us our children and don't let them be raised in the ignorance we have [been]."[11]

The deepest desire of the freedpeople was to have their own family farms. However, Congress was unwilling to reapportion the southern lands that might have established genuine black self-sufficiency. A few former slaves became homesteaders on public lands in Florida, Kansas, Texas, and Alabama, and a handful were able to acquire substantial property. But the overwhelming majority found that they had to continue to work for others, largely as agricultural labor. The fundamental dilemma of Reconstruction for most ex-slaves centered on their returning to work for white people: On what terms? With what degree of personal freedom? And for what compensation?

One of the most subtle and complex aspects of this dilemma concerned the disposition of black women's labor. During slavery, women worked alongside men in the fields (see p. 211). Black women began to leave field work immediately after emancipation, much to the dismay of white landowners who knew women's importance to the agricultural labor force. Some observers reported that black men, eager to assert the rights of manhood over their families, were especially determined that their wives not work for whites. Black women, who discovered that any assertion of autonomy toward white employers might be punished as unacceptable "cheekiness," had their own reasons for withdrawing their labor.

To achieve even a small degree of independence from direct white oversight, three out of four black families ended up accepting an arrangement known as sharecropping. Working on small farms carved out of the holdings of landowners, sharecropping families kept only a portion of the crops they grew. There were no foremen to drive and beat them, and they could work together as families. But in bad times, the value of their yield did not equal the credit that white landowners had extended them to cover their expenses, and most ended up in permanent indebtedness.

The ex-slaves were more successful in realizing their desire for education. Even before the war ended, black and white women from the North had gone south to areas occupied by the Union army to begin teaching the black population. Throughout Reconstruction, freedpeople built their own schools, funded by the Freedmen's Bureau and northern missionary societies, to gain the basics of

◆ **Winslow Homer, *The Cotton Pickers* (1876)**
In 1876, as federal Reconstruction was drawing to a close, renowned Boston-born painter
Winslow Homer (1836–1910) went south to make sketches of African American women and
children, which in turn became the basis for a series of powerful paintings. In *The Cotton
Pickers*, Homer portrays African American women doing agricultural labor, which, along
with domestic service, constituted their major postwar occupation. If the content of black
women's labor stayed as it had under slavery, how might the meaning of that labor for them
have changed with emancipation? *Winslow Homer,* The Cotton Pickers, *1876, Los Angeles County
Museum of Art. Acquisition made possible through Museum Trustees: Robert O. Anderson, R. Stanton Avery,
B. Gerald Cantor, Edward W. Carter, Justin Dart, Charles E. Ducommon, Camilla Chandler Frost, Julian
Ganz Jr., Dr. Armand Hammer, Harry Lenart, Dr. Franklin D. Murphy, Joan Palevsky, Richard E.
Sherwood, Maynard J. Toll, and Hal B. Wallis. Photograph © 2005 Museum Associates/LACMA.*

literacy. Edmonia Highgate, the daughter of fugitive slaves, was one of the many
sympathetic women who taught in these schools. She was motivated by a sense of
racial solidarity to return to the South, and she worked among former slaves for
six years, until sheer exhaustion forced her to retire.[12]

Many of the colleges and universities that are now referred to as "historically
black" began during the era of Reconstruction. Unlike long-standing prestigious
white institutions, many of these institutions, for instance Howard University,
established in Washington, D.C., in 1867, were opened to women as well as to
men. In 1881, white multimillionaire John D. Rockefeller founded the Atlanta
Baptist Female Seminary, an all-female school that later became Spelman College.
While most of these institutions provided little more than a high school education throughout the nineteenth century, they nonetheless played a major role in
educating black leaders. They educated women who went on to become teachers

throughout the South. This fragile educational infrastructure helped to create a small southern black middle class in cities like Atlanta, Richmond, and New Orleans.

The right to vote awarded to ex-slave men by the Fourteenth and Fifteenth Amendments lay at the very core of ex-slaves' hopes for the future. During Reconstruction, freedmen's exercise of the ballot, protected by federal troops, helped to elect approximately two thousand black men to local, state, and national political office. Despite their own disfranchisement, black women understood the political franchise as a community rather than an individual right. They regularly attended political meetings and told men who had the vote how to use it. Southern white women, by contrast, regarded the enfranchisement of black men as yet another insult to their sex and their race.

White Women in the New South

At the end of the war, white women faced loss and defeat, not emancipation and hope for the future. Food shortages were compounded by the collapse of the economy. More than a quarter million southern white men died on Civil War battlefields, leaving one generation of widows and another that would never marry. Occupation by federal troops after the war deepened white southerners' feelings of humiliation. One historian argues that southern white women, who did not share men's sheer relief at getting off the battlefield, harbored greater resentment than southern white men toward the North.[13]

Elite white women felt the loss of their slaves acutely. If they wanted black men in their fields and black women in their kitchens, they had to concede to some of the freedpeople's new expectations for wages, personal autonomy, and respect. Elite white women began for the first time to cook and launder for themselves and their families. "We have most of the housework to do all the time," complained Amanda Worthington of Mississippi, "and . . . it does not make me like the Yankees any better."[14]

Non-elite white southerners were less affected by the withdrawal of slave labor, but because they lived much closer to the edge of subsistence, they suffered far more from the collapse of the economy and the physical devastation of the South. Economic pressures drove many into the same sharecropping arrangement and permanent indebtedness as ex-slaves. Poor southern white women and their children also provided the labor force for the textile mills that northerners and a new class of southern industrialists began building in the 1880s. Inasmuch as black people were not allowed to work in the mills, white women experienced textile work as a kind of racial privilege. Many poor white women believed as fervently as former plantation mistresses in the inviolability of racial hierarchies.

Even so, the collapse of the patriarchal slave system provided new opportunities for public life for those white women who chose to take them. Elite women became involved in the memorialization of the Confederacy. They raised funds, built monuments, and lionized the men who had fought for southern independence, all the while creating an expanded civic role for their sex. Poor farm women found their opportunities in the Grange, a social and educational movement that later fed into the rise of Populism (see pp. 412–14).With a very few exceptions, however, southern white women kept their distance from woman suffrage efforts, which reminded them all too much of the federal intervention to enfranchise their former slaves.

Racial Conflict in Slavery's Aftermath

Changes in gender and racial relations together generated considerable violence in the postwar South. Whites experienced African American autonomy as a profound threat. The Ku Klux Klan, founded in 1866 in Pulaski, Tennessee, terrorized freedpeople for asserting their new freedoms. Klan members sexually humiliated, raped, and murdered many freedwomen. In Henry County, Georgia, two Klansmen pinned down Rhoda Ann Childs; she told a congressional investigation in 1871, "[They] stretched my limbs as far apart as they could . . . [and] applied the Strap to my Private parts until fatigued into stopping, and I was more dead than alive." She was then raped with the barrel of a gun.[15]

Through such actions, white men were both punishing black men and attempting to reassert their slave-era control over black women's bodies. Black women were determined to defend themselves. An African American woman recalled that after the war her father vowed "never to allow his wife and daughters to be thrown in contact with Southern white men in their homes." Decades later, she felt the same: "There is no sacrifice I would not make . . . rather than allow my daughters to go in service where they would be thrown constantly in contact with Southern white men, for they consider the colored girl their special prey."[16] In an age when sexual propriety was still the essence of true womanhood, black women were determined to challenge the notion that they and the men of their race were sexually immoral.

Eventually, the region's hidden history of cross-racial sex took an even more deadly form. Whites charged that black men were sexual predators seeking access to white women. The irony, of course, was that under slavery, it was white men who had unrestricted sexual access to black women. Southern white women of all classes supported these charges against black men, and most northerners assumed that they were true. At the slightest suspicion of the merest disrespect to a white woman, black men could be accused of sexual aggression and lynched — killed (usually hanged) by mobs who ignored legal process to execute their own form of crude justice. Lynchings, often involving gruesome mutilation as well as murder, were popular events in the post-Reconstruction South, with white women and children attending amid a carnival-like atmosphere. In 1892, the high point of this practice, 160 African Americans were lynched.[17]

Ida B. Wells, an African American journalist from Memphis, Tennessee, inaugurated a campaign, eventually international in scope, to investigate and expose the false charges behind the epidemic of lynchings and to get leading white figures to condemn it. She recognized that allegations of black men's lewd behavior toward white women were closely related to assumptions of black women's sexual

◆ **Ida B. Wells with the Family of Thomas Moss**
In 1893, the date of this photograph, Ida B. Wells (standing left) was already an important figure for her courageous journalistic exposé of the lynchings of southern black men. She organized African American clubwomen to join her and challenged white reformers to speak out against this barbaric practice. With her are the widow and orphans of Thomas Moss, the Memphis shopkeeper whose murder inspired Wells's crusade. In 1895, Wells married Frederick Barnett, a Chicago newspaper publisher, and they raised four children. She remained a lifelong activist. *The University of Chicago Library, Special Collections Research Center, Ida B. Wells Papers.*

disreputability and contended that black women had a major role to play in challenging the system that led to lynchings. Her efforts helped to catalyze the organization of an African American women's reform movement. (See Documents: Ida B. Wells, "Race Woman," pp. 358–62.)

Southern blacks' efforts to claim their rights suffered many major setbacks in the late nineteenth century. One by one, all-white Democratic parties "redeemed" state governments from Republicanism and ended what they called "black rule," instituting devices to disfranchise black men, such as requiring voters to demonstrate literacy, to pay exorbitant poll taxes, or to prove that their grandfathers had been voters. By the beginning of the twentieth century, black voting had been virtually obliterated throughout the South.

Meanwhile, a new legal system of rigid racial separation in social relations was being put in place. Called Jim Crow, after a foolish minstrel character played by whites in black makeup, these laws and practices were a way to humiliate and intimidate black people. Legal segregation of the races had not been necessary under slavery, where black people had no rights, but now it became a way to reassert white domination. Recalling what enforced segregation felt like, a southern black woman wrote, "I never get used to it; it is new each time and stings and hurts more and more. It does not matter how good or wise my children may be; they are colored. . . . Everything is forgiven in the South but color."[18]

Segregation affected many things including education, public services, and public accommodations, but black women particularly resented Jim Crow regulations in public transportation. Wells began her career as a defender of her race in 1884 by suing the Tennessee railroad company that ejected her from a special "ladies" car and sent her instead to the "colored" car. Twelve years later, the Supreme Court considered a similar suit by Homer Plessy against a Louisiana railroad for its segregation policy. In *Plessy v. Ferguson* (1896), the Court characterized the entire Jim Crow regime as "separate but equal" and thus compatible with the Fourteenth Amendment's requirement of equality before the law. This constitutional defense of segregation survived for nearly sixty years. (See Appendix, p. A-26.)

FEMALE WAGE LABOR AND THE TRIUMPH OF INDUSTRIAL CAPITALISM

Industrial growth accelerated tremendously after the defeat of the slave system and the northern victory in the Civil War. Intense competition between industrialists and financial magnates gradually gave way to economic consolidation. By 1890, industries such as steel, railroads, coal mining, and meat production were dominated by a handful of large, powerful corporate entities. The mirror reflection of the growth of capital, the American working class also came into its own and organized to find ways to offset the power of its employers.

The growth of the female labor force was an important part of this development, although it flew in the face of the still-strong presumption that women belonged exclusively in their homes. Domestic service was the largest sector, but manufacturing labor by women, especially the industrial production of garments, with its distinctive and highly exploitative form of production, the sweatshop, was growing faster.

The dynamic growth of industrial society produced a level of class conflict in the last quarter of the nineteenth century as intense as any in American history. Starting in 1877, as the federal army retreated from the South and the first postwar depression receded, waves of protests by disgruntled workers shook the economy and drew a powerful and violent response from big business and government. Coming so soon after the Civil War, escalating class antagonism seemed to threaten national unity again, this time along economic rather than sectional lines. Women played a significant role in these upheavals and, in doing so, laid the groundwork for a female labor movement in the early twentieth century.

Women's Occupations after the Civil War

Between 1860 and 1890, the percentage of the nonagricultural wage labor force that was female increased from 10.2 to 17 percent (see Chart 6.1, Women and the Labor Force, 1800–1900). Since the population in these years increased enormously, the change in absolute numbers was even more dramatic: by 1890, 3.6 million women were working for pay in nonagricultural labor, more than twice the number in 1870. The average pay for women remained a third to a half of the pay for men. The great majority of white working women were young and unmarried. The outlines of black women's labor were somewhat different, remaining

◆ Chart 6.1 **Women and the Labor Force, 1800–1900**

Year	Percent of All Women in the Labor Force	Percent of the Labor Force That Is Female
1800	4.6	4.6
1810	7.9	9.4
1820	6.2	7.3
1830	6.4	7.4
1840	8.4	9.6
1850	10.1	10.8
1860	9.7	10.2
1870	13.7	14.8
1880	14.7	15.2
1890	18.2	17.0
1900	21.2	18.1

Sources: *W. Elliot Brownlee and Mary M. Brownlee,* Women in the American Economy: A Documentary History *(New Haven: Yale University Press, 1976).* Historical Statistics of the United States: Colonial Times to 1970, *Part 1, Bicentennial Edition, Bureau of the Census, U.S. Department of Commerce, 1975.* "Marital and Family Characteristics of Workers," *March 1983, U.S. Department of Labor.* Statistical Abstract of the United States, *Bureau of the Census, U.S. Department of Commerce, 1983 and 1992; Daphne Spain and Suzanne Bianchi,* Balancing Act *(New York: Russell Sage, 1996).*

largely agricultural until well into the twentieth century. Black women also were much more likely to work outside the home after marriage.

Much of what historians have written about working women of the nineteenth century, especially the numbers and statistics, is guesswork. Although women had been working for wages since the 1830s, it was not until 1890 that the U.S. census began to identify or count working women with any precision. After the Civil War, some states investigated female wage labor, framing their inquiries in moralistic terms. State labor bureaus paid a great deal of attention, for instance, to disproving the assertion that working women were inclined to prostitution. These statistical portraits were fleshed out by investigative reporting, usually by middle- or upper-class women, who went among the working classes to report on their conditions. (See Documents: The Woman Who Toils, pp. 363–68.)

Nonetheless, it is clear that, for white women, paid domestic work was on the decline. Domestic servants, who before the war were the majority of the white female labor force, constituted less than 30 percent by the end of the century. Working women had long been impatient with domestic service and left it whenever they could, usually for factory labor. After the Civil War, the end of slavery tainted personal service even more. Investigator Helen Campbell took testimony in the mid-1880s in New York City from women who had abandoned domestic service. "I hate the very words 'service' and 'servant,'" an Irish immigrant renegade from domestic labor explained. "We came to this country to better ourselves, and it's not bettering to have anybody ordering you around."[19]

As white women workers shifted out of domestic service, the percentage in manufacturing increased to 25 percent as of 1900. Women continued to work in the textile industry, and in the shoe industry women organized their own trade union, the Daughters of St. Crispin (named after the patron saint of their trade), but it survived only a few years. The biggest change in women's manufacturing labor was the rise of the garment industry, as the antebellum outwork system began to give way to more fully industrialized processes (see pp. 196–97).

The industrial manufacture of clothing depended on the invention of the sewing machine, one of the most consequential technological developments in U.S. women's history. The introduction of the sewing machine accelerated the subdivision of clothing production into discrete tasks. Thus a single worker no longer made an entire piece of clothing but instead spent her long days sewing sleeves or seams, incurring the physical and spiritual toll of endless, repetitive motion. Unlike the power looms and spindles of the textile mills, sewing machines did not need to be housed in massive factories but could be placed in numerous small shops. As sewing machines were also comparatively inexpensive, the cost of buying and maintaining them could be shifted to the workers themselves, who were charged rent or made to pay installments for them.

Profits in the garment industry came primarily from pushing the women workers to produce more for less pay. This system became designated as the "sweating" system, meaning that it required women workers to drive (or sweat) themselves to work ever harder. Women workers were usually paid for each piece completed, whereas men tended to be paid for time worked. Employers set a low piece rate, lowering it even further as women produced more. Often workers were charged for thread and fined for sewing errors. The work was highly seasonal, and periods of twelve-hour workdays alternated with bouts of unemployment. At the beginning of the Civil War, the average earnings of sewing women were $10 per week; by 1865, they were $5 per week.

Regardless of their ability or speed, women in the garment, textile, and shoe industries were generally considered unskilled workers, in part because they worked in a female-dominated industry, in part because they were easily replaced by other women, and in part because they learned their work on the job rather than through a formal apprenticeship. The higher pay associated with so-called skilled labor was reserved for trades that men dominated. A few women gained entrance to male-dominated trades, such as typesetting, where they earned up to $15 per week. Initially, women made their way into print shops by replacing male workers who were out on strike, but they were let go when the men came back to work. Eventually, the printers' union voted to admit women as equal members, only the second male trade union to do so.

In the 1870s, a new field began to open up for female wage earners: office work. Before 1860, the office environment had been totally male, filled by young men aspiring to careers in business or law. During the Civil War, young women began to replace men as government copyists and stenographers. The shift to female labor was accelerated by another crucial technological development, the typewriter. Women, with their smaller hands, were thought to be especially suited to typing. Office work required education and a command of the English language, adding to its prestige as an occupation for women. It also paid more than textile mills or garment sweatshops. Yet from the employers' perspective, hiring women rather than men to meet the growing demand for clerical labor constituted a considerable savings. By 1900, office work was still only 9 percent of the female labor force, but it was the fastest-growing sector, a harbinger of things to come in the twentieth-century female labor force (see the Appendix, p. A-39).

Who Were the Women Wage Earners?

Age and marital status were crucial elements in the structure of the female labor force. In 1890, three-quarters of white working women were unmarried. As a leading historian of working women puts it, "In the history of women's labor market experience in the United States the half century from about 1870 to 1920 was the era of single women."[20] Unlike working men, whose wages were supposed to provide for an entire family, these young women allegedly had no one but themselves to support. "Working girls" were expected to work for pay for only a few years, then marry and become dependent on the earnings of their husbands. This was the principle of the so-called family wage, which justified men's greater wages as much as it did women's lesser. Wage labor for women was meant to be an interlude between childhood and domestic dependence, while men expected to work throughout their adult lives.

The reality of working women's lives was considerably more complex. Approximately 10 to 15 percent of urban families were headed by single mothers

◆ The Invention of the Typewriter

A practical machine for mechanical writings—the typewriter—was devised just after the Civil War. Further changes were later made in the size of the machine and placement of the keyboard as well as the arrangement of the letters. This illustration from a manual on typewriting originally appeared with the caption "Operator sitting in correct position for rapid writing." From the beginning, women were envisioned as the major operators of this new technology. © *Corbis.*

and were acutely disadvantaged by the family wage system.[21] A working woman who was a wife and/or mother was considered at best an anomaly and at worst an indicator of family and social crisis. African American women wage earners were three times as likely as white women to be married, partly because their husbands' pay was so low and partly because many chose to work themselves rather than send their daughters into work situations where they would be vulnerable to sexual harassment from white men. In historical hindsight, African American women were pioneering the modern working women's pattern of combining wage labor and domestic responsibilities; but at the time, the high number of black working mothers was the object of much disparagement.

Most unmarried wage-earning women lived in their parents' homes, where, contrary to the ideal of the single male breadwinner, their earnings were crucial supplements to family support. However, perhaps as many as a third of single women wage earners lived outside of families. Carroll Wright, a pioneering labor statistician, reported in "The Working Girls of Boston" (1889), a Massachusetts Bureau of Statistics of Labor report, that in Massachusetts many young women workers were "obliged to leave their homes on account of bad treatment or conduct of [a] dissipated father or because they felt the need of work and not finding it at home, have come to [a large city]."[22] Philanthropists established charity boardinghouses to protect these so-called women adrift, who seemed vulnerable without parents or husbands to protect them. One of the major purposes of the Young Women's Christian Association (YWCA), formed soon after the Civil War, was to provide supervised housing for single, urban working women.

Responses to Working Women

Contemporaries' attempts to grapple with the growing female labor force contained a revealing contradiction. On the one hand, social observers contended that only women driven by sheer desperation should work outside the home. Other working women were taking work away from truly needy women and—even more disturbing—from male breadwinners. If young working women used any part of their pay to buy attractive clothing or go out with men, they were castigated for frivolity. "[Working girls] who want pin-money do work at a price impossible for the self-supporting worker, many married women coming under this head," observed journalist Helen Campbell.[23]

On the other hand, those women who were driven into wage labor by absolute necessity were so ill-paid, so unrelentingly exploited, as to constitute a major social tragedy. "All alike are starved, half clothed, overworked to a frightful degree," wrote the same Helen Campbell, "with neither time to learn some better method of earning a living, nor hope enough to spur them in any new path."[24] Sympathetic observers concluded that the only humane response was to remove young women from the labor force altogether. Wage-earning women were therefore criticized if they worked out of choice or pitied if they worked out of need. In either case, they seemed to be trespassing where they did not belong: in the wage labor force.

Set against middle-class social observers' steady chorus of criticism or lament, the lives and choices of working women hint at a different picture. Working girls objected to the constant supervision at philanthropic working girls' homes, stubbornly spent their wages as they pleased, engaged in recreational activities that were considered vulgar, occasionally continued to work even after they got married, and preferred their morally questionable factory jobs to the presumed safety of domestic service. Though they were criticized for taking jobs away from the truly deserving, many regarded themselves simply as women who liked to earn money, preferred the sociability of sharing work with others, chose the experience of manufacturing something new over endless domestic routine, and enjoyed their occasional moments of hard-earned personal freedom.

Class Conflict and Labor Organization

Women were part of all the dramatic strikes and labor conflicts of the late nineteenth century. During the nationwide rail strikes in 1877, in which workers protested layoffs and wage cuts, women were among the mobs that burned roundhouses and destroyed railroad cars. Women's involvement in such violent acts underlined the full fury of working-class resentment at the inequalities of wealth in postbellum America. "Women who are the wives and mothers of the [railroad] firemen," reported a Baltimore newspaper, "look famished and wild and declare for starvation rather than have their people work for the reduced wages."[25] President Rutherford B. Hayes sent federal forces, recently withdrawn from occupying the South, to suppress the riots. More than a hundred strikers were killed nationwide.

In the late 1870s, many angry workers joined the Knights of Labor, originally a secret society that became the largest labor organization of the nineteenth century. The Knights aimed to unite and elevate working people and to protect the country's democratic heritage from unrestrained capitalist growth. In 1881, the Knights, unlike most unions, admitted women (housewives as well as wage earners). At its peak, the Knights of Labor had 750,000 members, of whom some 10 percent were women. Its goal was to unite "the producing classes," regardless of industry or occupation or gender. Race was more complicated. In the South, the Knights admitted black workers in segregated local chapters, but in the West, the organization excluded Chinese men, whom it regarded as economic competitors rather than as fellow workers.

The Knights played a major role in the nationwide campaign to shorten the workday for wage earners to eight hours, a movement of obvious interest to women. On May 1, 1886, hundreds of thousands of workers from all over the country struck on behalf of the eight-hour day. At a related rally a few days later in Chicago's Haymarket Square, a bomb exploded, killing seven policemen. Although the bomb thrower was never identified, eight male labor leaders were charged with conspiracy to murder. Lucy Parsons, the wife of one of the accused, helped conduct their defense. An African American woman, Lucy had met her husband in Texas, where he had gone after the war to organize black voters for the

Republican Party. Defense efforts eventually won gubernatorial pardons for three of the accused men, although not in time to save Albert Parsons. The violence and repression unleashed by the Haymarket incident devastated the Knights of Labor. By 1890, it had ceased to play a significant role in American labor relations. The eight-hour workday would not be won for many decades.

After the collapse of the Knights, the future of organized labor was left to male-dominated trade unions and their umbrella organization, the American Federation of Labor (AFL), founded in 1886 by Samuel Gompers, a cigar maker from New York City. While the goal of the Knights was inclusive, to unify the producing classes, the purpose of AFL unions was exclusive, to protect the jobs of skilled and relatively well-paid labor from less-skilled, lower-paid workers. Most members of AFL unions regarded women workers as exactly this sort of threat: unskilled, underpaid workers who took men's jobs during strikes. Adapting the domestic ideal of true womanhood from the middle class, the AFL subscribed to the notion that women belonged in the home and that decent pay for a male worker was a wage sufficient to keep a wife out of the labor force.

Nonetheless, the late nineteenth-century labor movement did provide a few exceptional working women with the chance to begin speaking and acting on behalf of female wage earners. Leonora Barry and Mary Kenney were among the first women appointed by unions to organize other women workers. In 1886, the Knights of Labor designated Barry, a widowed Irish-born garment worker, to head its Woman's Department (see box, "Women in the Knights of Labor"). Although meeting with her might mean being fired, women workers around the country shared with Barry their complaints about wages and working conditions. Barry was their devoted advocate, but after two years, frustrated with the timidity of many working women and perhaps also with the limits of her support from the male leadership of the organization, she resigned her position.

Mary Kenney's trade was bookbinding. She joined an AFL union in Chicago and in 1891 was appointed the federation's first paid organizer for working women. She believed that working women should organize themselves but that they also needed the moral and financial support of middle- and upper-class women. The AFL was less committed to working women than the Knights, and Kenney was dismissed from her post after only six months. In the decades to come, many more female labor activists followed Barry and Kenney to play important roles in shaping women's history.

WOMEN OF THE LEISURED CLASSES

Paralleling the expansion of the American working class was the dramatic growth, both in numbers and wealth, of the middle and upper classes. For this reason, one of several terms used for the post-Reconstruction years is the Gilded Age. The term, first used by Mark Twain in a novel about economic and political corruption after the Civil War, captured both the riches and superficiality of the wealthier classes in the late nineteenth century. In the United States, with its proud

LEONORA BARRY
Women in the Knights of Labor

Leonora Barry (1849–1930) was one of the first female labor organizers. Her final report to the Knights of Labor expresses the ambivalence toward wage earning women that was so common in the late nineteenth century: they belonged at home but deserved equality in the labor force. In 1890, Barry, a widow when she began her assignment, resigned when she remarried.

I believe it was intended that man should be the breadwinner. But as that is impossible under present conditions, I believe women should have every opportunity to become proficient in whatever vocation they choose or find themselves best fitted for. When I took a position at [the Woman's Department's] head, I fondly hoped to weld together in organization a number of women as would be a power for good in the present, . . . I was too sanguine, . . . and I believe we now should . . . put more women in the field as Lecturers to tell women why they should organize as part of the industrial hive, rather than because they are women. There can be no separation or distinction of wage-workers on account of sex, and separate departments for their interests is a direct contradiction of this. . . . Therefore I recommend the abolition of the Woman's Department, believing as I now do that women should be Knights of Labor without distinction, and should have all the benefits that can be given to men — no more, no less.

SOURCE: Leonora Barry, Woman's Department, Knights of Labor, 1889, Report of the General Investigator, Proceedings of the General Assembly of the Knights of Labor, 1888.

middle-class ethic, the distinction between upper and middle class has always been hard to draw with precision, but in these years what was more important was the enormous and growing gap between those who lived comfortable, leisured lives and those who struggled with poverty. While the poor labored unceasingly, the upper class enjoyed unprecedented new wealth and influence, and the middle class imitated their values of material accumulation and display. For women of the leisured classes, the Gilded Age meant both new affluence and growing discontent with an exclusively domestic sphere.

New Sources of Wealth and Leisure

The tremendous economic growth of the post–Civil War era emanated from the railroads that wove together the nation and carried raw materials to factories and finished goods to customers. The great fortunes of the age were made especially

◆ **Mary Kenney O'Sullivan and Children**
Kenney left school at fourth grade, "as far," she said, "as any children of wage earners . . . was expected to go,"[26] and became a skilled bookbinder. A natural labor organizer, she was encouraged and supported by both clubwomen and male unionists. In 1894, she married labor activist John F. O'Sullivan and had four children (one of whom died), but within a decade she was widowed. She played a major role in the founding of the Women's Trade Union League in 1903 and, like Ida B. Wells-Barnett, remained an activist throughout her life. *The Schlesinger Library, Radcliffe Institute, Harvard University.*

in iron mining, steel manufacturing, and railroad building—and in financing these endeavors. New technologies, government subsidies, cutthroat competition, and the pressure on workers to work faster and more productively contributed to this development. Dominated by a few corporate giants, this wealth was distributed very unevenly; in 1890 an estimated 1 percent of the population controlled fully 25 percent of the country's wealth.[27] In New York City alone, the number of millionaires went from a few dozen in 1860 to several hundred in 1865. Indeed, many of the great American family fortunes were begun in the Gilded Age: John D. Rockefeller in oil, Cornelius Vanderbilt in railroads, J. P. Morgan in finance, and Andrew Carnegie in steel. One of the very few women to amass spectacular wealth on her own was Hetty Robinson Green. She began her financial career with a $10 million inheritance, which she multiplied tenfold through shrewd investment. Operating as she did in the man's world of high finance, her womanliness was suspect. The popular press played up her eccentricities, dubbing her "the witch of Wall Street" rather than one of the brilliant financiers of the epoch.

Wives of wealthy men faced no such criticism. On the contrary, they were regarded as the ultimate in womanly beauty and grace. In the world of the extremely wealthy, men's obligation was to amass money while women's was to display and spend it. Wealthy women were also responsible for the conduct of "society," a word that came to mean the comings and goings of the tiny upper class, as if the rest of the population faded into insignificance by contrast. In *The Theory of the Leisure Class* (1899), sociologist Thorstein Veblen astutely observed that upper-class women not only purchased expensive commodities but were themselves their husbands' most lavish and enviable possessions.

Shopping was a new and important role for leisure-class women in the postbellum years. Middle-class women, who previously had responsibility for a great deal of productive household labor, became active consumers. With the dramatic increase in the country's manufacturing capacity, their obligation was now to purchase rather than to produce, to spend rather than to economize. They flocked to the many department stores established in this period, grand palaces of commodities such as Marshall Field's in Chicago (founded in 1865), Macy's in New York (1866), Strawbridge and Clothiers in Philadelphia (1868), Hudson's in Detroit (1887), and May's in Denver (1888). They filled the elaborate interiors of their homes with furniture and decorative items. Even at a distance from the proliferating retail possibilities of the cities, mail order catalogs allowed rural women to look at, long for, and occasionally purchase the many commodities of the age.

Rising incomes lifted the burden of housekeeping off urban middle- and upper-class women in other ways. Cities laid water and sewer lines, but only in wealthy neighborhoods in which households could afford the fees; indoor plumbing and running water made housework easier for prosperous women. But the most important factor in easing the load of housekeeping for leisure-class women was undoubtedly the cheap labor of domestic servants. Despite constant complaints about the shortage of domestic help, middle-class families regarded having at least one or two paid domestic servants as a virtual necessity. The wealthy had small armies of them. Laundry, which required enormous energy and much time when done in an individual household, was sent out to commercial establishments, where poor and immigrant women pressed and folded sheets and linens in overheated steam rooms.

Another important factor in freeing middle- and upper-class women from domestic demands was the declining birthrate (see the Appendix, p. A-36). Between 1850 and 1890, the average number of live births for white, native-born

◆ **Rike-Kumler Co. Department Store, Dayton, Ohio**
Department store counters were one place where working- and leisure-class women met.
Neat dress, good English, and middle-class manners were job requirements, even though pay
was no better than for factory work. Customers like the woman being fitted for gloves in this
1893 photograph sat, but clerks stood all day, one of the conditions of their work to which
they most objected. © *Bettmann/Corbis.*

women fell from 5.42 to 3.87. African American birthrates were not recorded in
the federal census until several decades later, but by all impressionistic evidence,
they declined even more dramatically, as freedwomen took control of their lives
at the most intimate level. Ironically, birthrates declined in inverse proportion to
class status: the wealthiest, with money to spare, had proportionately fewer children than the very poor, whose earnings were stretched to the limit but who relied
on their children for income.

In understanding the many individual decisions that went into the declining
birthrate among leisure-class women, the explanation is not obvious. There were
no dramatic improvements in contraceptive technology or knowledge in these

years. On the contrary, traditional means of controlling pregnancy—early versions of condoms and diaphragms—were banned by new laws that defined them as obscene devices; even discussions aimed at limiting reproduction were forbidden. Following the Comstock Act of 1873, which outlawed the use of the U.S. mails for distributing information on controlling reproduction, twenty-four states criminalized the dissemination of contraceptive devices.

Rather, declining birthrates seem to have been both a cause and an effect of the expanding sphere of leisure-class women. Women's decisions to limit their pregnancies reflected a growing desire for personal satisfaction and social contribution beyond motherhood. Even though maternity remained the assumed destiny of womanhood, many women were coming to believe that they could choose when and how often to become pregnant. In advocating "voluntary motherhood," Harriot Stanton Blatch encouraged women to choose for themselves when to have sexual intercourse (see box, "Voluntary Motherhood"). Reformers like Blatch did not yet envision the separation of women's sexual activity from the possibility of pregnancy, but they did believe that women should have control over both. The very term "birth control" and the movement to advance it came later in the twentieth century (see pp. 480–81), but basic changes in female reproductive behavior were already under way.

As women's reproductive lives changed, so did their understanding of their sexuality. To be sure, many restrictive sexual assumptions remained in place. Some physicians still regarded strong sexual desire in women as a disease, which they treated by methods ranging from a diet of bland foods to surgical removal of the clitoris. But the heterosexual double standard—that men's sexual desire was uncontrollable and that women's was nonexistent—was beginning to come under fire. By the end of the century, even the conservative physician Elizabeth Blackwell was writing in carefully chosen language that "in healthy, loving women, uninjured by the too frequent lesions which result from childbirth, increasing physical satisfaction attaches to the ultimate physical expression of love."[28]

Lesbianism, in the modern sense of women openly and consistently expressing sexual desire for other women, had not yet been named but in these years many leisure-class women formed intense attachments with each other. These "homosocial" relationships, as modern historians have designated them, ranged from intense, lifelong friendships to relationships that were as emotionally charged, as beset by jealousy and possessiveness, and quite possibly as physically intimate, as any heterosexual love affair. Mary (Molly) Hallock and Helena De Kay were two such friends. They met in 1868 as art students in New York and wrote frequently and passionately to each other. When Helena announced that she was marrying New York publisher Richard Gilder, Molly angrily wrote to him: "Until you came along, sir, I believe she loved me almost as girls love their lovers."[29]

Most of what we know about such homosocial relations comes from leisure-class women, perhaps because they wrote more letters that were preserved and handed down to families and archivists than working-class women did. But surely some working-class women experienced similar passions. A set of letters between

HARRIOT STANTON BLATCH
Voluntary Motherhood

In this 1891 speech, Harriot Stanton Blatch (1856–1940), daughter of Elizabeth Cady Stanton (see pp. 275–78), brilliantly exploited the nineteenth-century belief that motherhood was woman's highest vocation in order to argue for women's rights to control whether and when they had children. Although she used the term "race" here to mean humanity, she was relying on the racial "science" of the period, which emphasized the biological dimension of human progress.

Men talk of the sacredness of motherhood, but judging from their acts it is the last thing that is held sacred in the human species . . . men in laws and customs have degraded the woman in her maternity. Motherhood is sacred—that is, voluntary motherhood; but the woman who bears unwelcome children is outraging every duty she owes the race. . . . Let women but understand the part unenforced maternity has played in the evolution of animal life, and their reason will guide them to the true path of race development. . . . [Women] should refuse to prostitute their creative powers, and so jeopardize the progress of the human race. Upon the mothers must rest in the last instance the development of any species.

SOURCE: Harriot Stanton Blatch, "Voluntary Motherhood," 1891, in Aileen S. Kraditor, comp., *Up from the Pedestal: Selected Writings in the History of American Feminism* (Chicago: Quadrangle Books, 1968), 167–75.

two African American women living in Connecticut during the 1860s offers the rare example of a cross-class homosocial relationship, moreover one that was strongly suggestive of physical intimacy. Rebecca Primus, a schoolteacher, and Addie Brown, a seamstress, domestic worker, and laundress, conducted what the historian of their bond calls "a self consciously sexual relationship" focused on breasts and their fondling.[30]

By the late nineteenth century, such intense bonds were coming under scrutiny from physicians. Recognizing the obvious erotic qualities of these intense same-sex relationships, neurologists sought to give them the dignity of scientific recognition, even as they characterized them as "unnatural" or "abnormal." Women-loving women who, in an earlier decade, would have believed unquestioningly in the asexual purity and innocence of their attachments, were beginning to read scientific writings about homosexuality and to wonder about the meaning and nature of their own feelings.

◆ **"Get Thee Behind Me, (Mrs.) Satan!"**
By 1872, when this cartoon appeared in *Harper's Weekly* magazine, suffragist Victoria Woodhull had gained considerable notoriety both for her dramatic pro-suffrage testimony before a congressional committee and for her bold critiques of sexual hypocrisy within the marriage relationship. Her proclamations and behavior won her the label of America's foremost "free lover." This image, created by the great nineteenth-century political cartoonist Thomas Nast, portrays her as the devil incarnate. He contrasts Woodhull to a heavily burdened drunkard's wife, who will be further weighted down by following her lead. *Library of Congress LC-USZ62-74994.*

The "Woman's Era"

Before the Civil War, women had formed charitable and religious societies and had worked together on behalf of temperance, abolition, and women's rights (see pp. 262–79). After the war, associational fervor among women was more diverse, secular, and independent of male oversight. Participation in Gilded Age women's societies provided numerous women with new opportunities for collective activity, intellectual growth, and public life. By the end of the nineteenth century, leisure-class women had almost totally commandeered nongovernmental civic life from men. Thus, another apt label for the post-Reconstruction years is the Woman's Era.

The women's club movement began in the Northeast just after the Civil War among white middle-class women. In 1868, New York City women writers formed a group they named Sorosis (a botanical term that suggested sisterhood) to protest their exclusion from an event held by male writers. Simultaneously, a group of Boston reformers led by Julia Ward Howe (author of "The Battle Hymn of the Republic") organized the New England Women's Club, dedicated to the cultivation of intellectual discussion and public authority for leisure-class women.

Despite their impeccable reputations, both groups were publicly lambasted for their unladylike behavior. "Woman is straying from her sphere," warned the *Boston Transcript*.[31]

Despite such criticisms, women's clubs thrived among those middle-aged married women whose childrearing years were behind them. The concerns of the women's club movement evolved from literary and cultural matters in the 1870s to local social service projects in the 1880s to regional and national federations for political influence in the 1890s. Many public institutions established in the Gilded Age—hospitals and orphanages as well as libraries and museums—were originally established by women's clubs. From the Northeast, the club movement spread to the West and then the South.

Clubs by their nature are exclusive institutions, and the sororal bonds of women's clubs reflected their tendency to draw together women of like background. In the larger cities, class differences distinguished elite women's clubs from those formed by wives of clerks and shopkeepers. Working women's clubs were rarely initiated by wage-earning women themselves but were likely to be uplift projects of middle- and upper-class clubwomen. Race and religion were especially important principles of association. German Jewish women and African American women organized separately from the mainstream women's club movement, which was largely white and Protestant. Generally, middle-class Jewish or African American women formed their own clubs both to assist poorer women and to cultivate their own skills and self-confidence.

The ethic of women's clubs was particularly compelling to African American women. They formed organizations not just to enlarge their horizons as women but to play their part in the enormous project of post-emancipation racial progress. "If we compare the present condition of the colored people of the South with their condition twenty-eight years ago," explained African American clubwoman Sarah J. Early in 1893, "we shall see how the organized efforts of their women have contributed to the elevation of the race and their marvelous achievement in so short a time."[32] By her estimate, there were five thousand "colored women's societies" with half a million members. Black women organized separately from white women because they were serving a different population with distinctive needs but also because they were usually refused admission into white women's clubs. Racism was alive and well in the women's club movement.

The relation of the Gilded Age women's club phenomenon to woman suffrage is complex. At first, white women who formed and joined clubs took care to distinguish themselves from the radicalism and notoriety associated with woman suffragists. Yet women's rights and woman suffrage were standard subjects for club discussion, and over time members came to accept the idea that women should have political tools to accomplish their public goals. Black clubwomen were less hesitant to embrace woman suffrage in light of their concerns over the disfranchisement of black men. Over time women's clubs incubated support for woman suffrage within a wide swath of the female middle class and prepared the way for the tremendous growth in the suffrage movement in the early twentieth century (see pp. 469–76).

The Woman's Christian Temperance Union

The largest women's organization of the Woman's Era was the Woman's Christian Temperance Union (WCTU). Following on women's temperance activities in the 1850s (see p. 264), the WCTU was formed in 1874 after a series of women's "crusades" in Ohio and New York that convinced local saloon owners to abandon the liquor trade. Initially focused on changing drinking behavior at the individual level, the organization soon challenged the liquor industry politically and undertook a wide range of public welfare projects such as prison reform, recreation and vocational training for young people, establishment of kindergartens, labor reform, and international peace. These projects and the ability of the WCTU to cultivate both organizational loyalty and individual growth among its members were characteristics it shared with women's clubs, but the WCTU was different in

◆ Frances Willard Learns to Ride a Bicycle

Frances Willard, president of the WCTU, combined sympathy with conventional Protestant middle-class women and an advanced understanding of women's untapped capacities. In 1895, "sighing for new worlds to conquer," she learned to ride a bicycle, one of the signature New Woman activities of the period. "Reducing the problem to actual figures," she methodically reported, "it took me about three months, with an average of fifteen minutes' practice daily, to learn, first, to pedal; second, to turn; third, to dismount; and fourth, to mount."[33] Willard, not yet sixty, died in 1898, after which the WCTU never regained its prominence or progressive vision. *Courtesy of the Frances E. Willard Memorial Library and Archives.*

crucial ways. On the one hand, it defined itself explicitly as Christian; on the other hand, it was racially more inclusive than the club movement. The writer Frances E. W. Harper (see p. 270) was one of several African American WCTU spokeswomen, and black women were welcomed into the organization, though in separate divisions. The WCTU's centers of strength were less urban and more western and midwestern than those of women's clubs.

Finally, unlike the women's club movement, the WCTU was to a large degree the product of a single and highly effective leader, Frances Willard. Willard was born in 1839 and raised on a farm in Ohio. She never married. Determined to serve "the class that I have always loved and that has loved me always—the girls of my native land and my times,"[34] at age thirty-four she became the first Dean of Women at Northwestern University. In 1879, she was elected president of the WCTU, rapidly increasing its membership, diversifying its purposes, and making it the most powerful women's organization in the country. Disciplined and diplomatic, she was able to take the WCTU to levels of political action and reform that the unwieldy mass of clubwomen could never reach. Notably, this included active advocacy of woman suffrage, which the WCTU formally and enthusiastically endorsed in 1884. "If we are ever to save the State," Willard declared, "we must enfranchise the sex . . . which is much more acclimatized to self-sacrifice for others. . . . Give us the vote, in order that we may help in purifying politics."[35]

Consolidating the Gilded Age Women's Movement

The endorsement of woman suffrage by the WCTU convinced Susan B. Anthony to encourage and draw together the pro-suffrage leanings developing within so many women's organizations. "Those active in great philanthropic enterprises," she insisted, "[will] sooner or later realize that so long as women are not acknowledged to be the political equals of men, their judgment on public questions will have but little weight."[36] Accordingly, in 1888, in honor of the fortieth anniversary of the Seneca Falls Convention, the National Woman Suffrage Association (NWSA) sponsored an International Congress of Women, attended by representatives of several European countries and many U.S. women's organizations. Out of this congress came an International Council of Women and a U.S. National Council of Women, both formed in 1893. Both organizations were so broadly inclusive of women's public and civic activities as to admit anti-suffrage groups, and much to Anthony's disappointment, neither served as the vehicle for advancing the prospects of woman suffrage.

Other overarching organizational structures were formed. In 1890, the NWSA and the American Woman Suffrage Association reconciled, forming the National American Woman Suffrage Association, which led the suffrage movement for the next thirty years. On the international level, U.S. suffragists joined with European colleagues to initiate the formation of an International Woman Suffrage Association in 1902. The associative impulse was constantly tending to greater and greater combination, amalgamating women in clubs, clubs in state federations, and state federations in national organizations. The vision shared by these federative efforts was of a unity of women so broad and ecumenical as to obliterate all differences between women. But the vision of all-inclusivity was a fantasy. For as women's social activism and public involvement grew, so did their ambitions and rivalries. Even as the National Council of Women was formed, the leaders of the venerable Sorosis club, who felt they should have been chosen to head this endeavor, set up a rival in the General Federation of Women's Clubs. Nor were federations any more racially inclusive than individual clubs. The General Federation of Women's Clubs refused to admit black women's clubs. In 1895, African American women's clubs federated separately as the National Association of Colored Women, and the next year the National Council of Jewish Women was formed.

The ambitious scope and unresolved divisions of "organized womanhood" were equally on display in Chicago in 1893 at the World's Columbian Exposition, America's first world's fair. The Board of Lady Managers, led by wealthy Chicagoan Bertha Palmer, received public funds to build and furnish a special Woman's Building. At the Congress of Representative Women, an elaborate weeklong event, more than eighty sessions addressed "all lines of thought connected with the progress of women." The promise of the Woman's Building was that "all organizations can come together with perfect freedom and entire harmony and discuss the problems presented, even from divergent points of view, with utmost friendliness."[37] But its conception, establishment, and management were rife with disagreement, power struggles, and frustrated ambitions. The Board of Lady Managers argued with Susan B. Anthony and Frances Willard about how prominent to make woman suffrage. Despite much rhetoric about the importance of women's work, wage-earning women were not invited to participate in the building's planning or to speak for themselves at the congresses. And the leadership of the Woman's Building was as white as its gleaming walls. African American women, proud of their achievements since emancipation, petitioned Palmer to include them in the planning and management—but to no end. Willing as always to speak uncomfortable truths to those in power, Ida B. Wells exposed racism at the fair in a pamphlet she coauthored with Frederick Douglass, *Reasons Why the Colored American Is Not in the World's Columbian Exposition* (1893). Women from indigenous cultures, including the American Eskimo, were "on display" on the fair's midway as exotics.

Looking to the Future

By 1890, a new, more modern culture was slowly gathering force under the complacent surface of late nineteenth-century America. The Gilded Age was organized around grand and opposing categories: home and work, black and white, capital and labor, virtue and vice, masculine and feminine. While nineteenth-century society subscribed to a rigid hierarchy of values and a firm belief in absolute truth, modernist convictions allowed for greater contingency and relativism in assessing people and ideas. The concept of morality, so crucial to nineteenth-century cultural judgment, was losing some of its coercive force, giving way to a greater emphasis on individuality, inner life, the free development of personality, and psychological variety.

◆ The Woman's Building

The Woman's Building was one of the most successful exhibits at the World's Columbian Exposition in Chicago in 1893. Everything about it demonstrated the variety and extent of women's achievements. The architect was twenty-two-year-old Sophia Hayden, and all the interior adornments were designed by women. Books written by women filled the library, and paintings by women lined the art gallery. This photograph shows the special organizational hall where the achievements of women in their various organizations and societies were on display. © *Corbis.*

An important sign of this cultural shift was the growing displacement of the ideal of the "true woman" by the image of the "New Woman," both in women's rights circles and in popular representations of femininity. For modern women of the late nineteenth century, true womanhood no longer seemed virtuous and industrious but idle and purposeless. New Women pushed against the boundaries of woman's sphere to participate in public life, whether by earning a wage, gaining an education, or performing community service. (See Visual Sources: The

Higher Education of Women in the Postbellum Years, pp. 369–78.) Their ethic emphasized "woman's work," a term that sometimes meant paid labor, sometimes public service, but always an alternative to exclusive domesticity.

Clubwoman and author Charlotte Perkins Gilman was the first great spokeswoman for the New Woman. Gilman went so far as to criticize the single family household and the exclusive dedication of women to motherhood. "With the larger socialization of the woman of today, the fitness for and accompanying desire for wider combination, more general interest, . . . more organized methods of work for larger ends," she wrote in her widely read *Women and Economics* (1898), "she feels more and more heavily the intensely personal limits of the more primitive home duties, interests, methods."[38] Gilman's writings emphasized a second element of the New Woman ethic, the importance of female individuation, of each woman realizing her distinctive talents, capacities, and personality. Individualism was a long-standing American value, but it had been traditionally reserved for men. Men were individuals with different abilities; women were members of a category with common characteristics. New Womanhood challenged this vision of contrasting masculinity and femininity and claimed the legacy of individualism for women.

At age seventy-seven, Elizabeth Cady Stanton stressed this dimension in her 1892 speech "The Solitude of Self," presented to a committee of the U.S. Congress and then to the National American Woman Suffrage Association. "The point I wish plainly to bring before you on this occasion," she began, "is the individuality of each human soul. . . . In discussing the rights of woman, we are to consider, first, what belongs to her as an individual, in a world of her own, the arbiter of her own destiny."[39] The speech was Stanton's swan song from suffrage leadership. Anthony's vision of a moderate, broad-based suffrage movement contrasted with Stanton's inclination to relentlessly challenge women's conventional values. A few years later, Stanton went so far as to lambaste the Bible for its misogyny. The greatest expression of her lifelong passion for individual women's freedom, "The Solitude of Self" looked forward to a future of women's efforts for emancipation that would be so different from the approach of the Woman's Era, so modern in its emphasis on the self and on psychological change, as to require a new name: feminism.

CONCLUSION: Toward a New Womanhood

The end of the Civil War ushered in a period of great conflict. Reconstruction sought to restore the Union and to replace sectionalism with a single sense of nationhood, but at its end in 1877 unity remained elusive for all Americans. Various terms for the post-Reconstruction era indicate its different aspects. In the South during Redemption, black and white women regarded each other over an embattled racial gulf, altered and intensified by emancipation. Meanwhile, in the America of the Gilded Age, a new divide had opened up between labor and capital. As the American economy became increasingly industrialized, the numbers and visibility of women wage earners grew, along with their determination to join in efforts to bring democracy to American class relations. For their part, middle- and upper-class women created what is called the Woman's Era as they pursued new opportunities in education, civic organization, and public authority.

Two other aspects of the changing face of America in the late nineteenth century are considered in Chapter 7: the massive immigration that underlay the growth, and much of the assertiveness, of the American working class; and the physical expansion and consolidation of the nation through the further incorporation of western lands. Women were important actors in the multifaceted political crisis in the 1890s, which brought together all of these phenomena—racial and class conflict, woman's expanding sphere, massive ethnic change, and the nation's physical expansion up to and beyond its borders. By 1900, women were poised on the brink of one of the most active and important eras in American history through women's eyes, the Progressive years.

D O C U M E N T S

Ida B. Wells, "Race Woman"

IN THE YEARS AFTER 1877, when the federal protections of Reconstruction ended and the freed black population of the South was left on its own to resist resurgent white supremacy, a generation of exceptional female African American leaders emerged. Of these, none was more extraordinary than Ida B. Wells. Born in 1862 in Mississippi, she was orphaned at the age of sixteen by a yellow fever epidemic. Determined to assume responsibility for her siblings and to keep her family together, she found work first as a teacher and then as a journalist. In 1889 in Memphis, she purchased part ownership of an African American newspaper, the *Free Speech*. Her goal was to expose and publicize the mistreatment of her people. In an age notable for its florid and euphemistic writing, Wells's style was straightforward and explicit. She was not afraid to use the word "rape" to describe the accusations against black men and the experiences of black women.

Wells was catapulted into the role that changed her life when an African American man she knew, Thomas Moss, was lynched by a Memphis mob in 1892 (see pp. 335–36). Although the practice of lynching had a long history elsewhere, in the South during this period, the accused were black and the mobs white. Wells concluded that Moss's "crime" had been the competition that his successful grocery business posed to whites. Over a hundred years later, we take for granted the connections that she was the first to make: between the postwar political and economic gains made by freed people and the brutal violence unleashed on them by resentful whites; and between the long history of sexual exploitation of black women during slavery and the inflammatory charges made after emancipation to justify lynching—that black men were sexual predators.

Perhaps the most remarkable element of Wells's analysis was her insistence that black and white people sometimes voluntarily chose to be each other's sexual partners. She was not particularly in favor of the practice. She was what was called in this period a "race woman," meaning that her concerns were less for integration than for the happiness and progress of African Americans. "A proper self-respect is expected of races as individuals," she later wrote, "We need more race love; the tie of racehood should bind us [through] . . . a more hearty appreciation of each other."[40] Nonetheless, she appreciated the difference between willing and coerced sexuality and defended the former while criticizing the latter. She understood that so long as interracial sex was concealed as a fact of southern life, black people would pay the deadly price.

Her investigations into the practice of lynching got her driven out of Memphis in 1892. This autobiographical account details the impact that her harrowing experience had on African American women in the North, who went on to form the National Association of Colored Women and to join in the work of exposing the true nature, extent, and causes of southern lynchings. Exiled from the South, she moved to Chicago, where in 1895 she married Frederick Barnett, also a journalist and activist, and continued to battle for justice for her race by working for greater political power for black people. She played an early role in organizing African American women to secure and use the right to vote. Her autobiography remained unfinished and unpublished until brought into print by her youngest child, Alfreda Duster, more than a century after her mother's birth.

As you read, consider what led Wells to undertake an expose of lynching and how doing so challenged the expectations of race and gender that she faced. What does Wells's analysis of the causes of and attitudes toward the lynching of African Americans reveal about the dynamics between whites and blacks several decades after the end of slavery?

IDA B. WELLS
Crusade for Justice: The Autobiography of Ida B. Wells (1970)

While I was thus carrying on the work of my newspaper, . . . there came the lynching in Memphis which changed the whole course of my life. . . .

Thomas Moss, Calvin McDowell, and Henry Stewart owned and operated a grocery store in a thickly populated suburb. . . . There was already a grocery owned and operated by a white man who hitherto had had a monopoly on the trade of this thickly populated colored suburb. Thomas's grocery changed all that, and he and his associates were made to feel that they were not welcome by the white grocer. . . .

One day some colored and white boys quarreled over a game of marbles and the colored boys got the better of the fight which followed. . . . Then the challenge was issued that the vanquished whites were coming on Saturday night to clean out [Thomas's] Colored People's Grocery Company. . . . Accordingly the grocery company armed

SOURCE: Alfreda M. Duster, ed., *Crusade for Justice: The Autobiography of Ida B. Wells* (Chicago: University of Chicago Press, 1970), 47–82.

several men and stationed them in the rear of the store on that fatal Saturday night, not to attack but repel a threatened attack. . . . The men stationed there had seen several white men stealing through the rear door and fired on them without a moment's pause. Three of these men were wounded, and others fled and gave the alarm. . . . Over a hundred colored men were dragged from their homes and put in jail on suspicion.

All day long on that fateful Sunday white men were permitted in the jail to look over the imprisoned black men. . . . The mob took out of their cells Thomas Moss, Calvin McDowell, and Henry Stewart, the three officials of the People's Grocery Company. They were loaded on a switch engine of the railroad which ran back of the jail, carried a mile north of the city limits, and horribly shot to death. One of the morning papers held back its edition in order to supply its readers with the details of that lynching. . . . The mob took possession of the People's Grocery Company, helping themselves to food and drink, and destroyed what they could not eat or steal. The

...d the place closed and a few days later ...ained of the stock was sold at auction. , with the aid of city and county authorities a the daily papers, that white grocer had indeed put an end to his rival Negro grocer as well as to his business. . . .

Like many another person who had read of lynchings in the South, I had accepted the idea meant to be conveyed—that although lynching was irregular and contrary to law and order, unreasoning anger over the terrible crime of rape led to the lynching; that perhaps the brute deserved death anyhow and the mob was justified in taking his life.

But Thomas Moss, Calvin McDowell and Henry Stewart had been lynched in Memphis, one of the leading cities of the South, in which no lynching had taken place before, with just as much brutality as other victims of the mob; and they had committed no crime against white women. This is what opened my eyes to what lynching really was. An excuse to get rid of Negroes who were acquiring wealth and property and thus keep the race terrorized and "keep the nigger down." I then began an investigation of every lynching I read about. I stumbled on the amazing record that every case of rape reported . . . became such only when it became public.

Many cases were like that of the lynching which happened in Tunica County, Mississippi. The Associated Press reporter said, "The big burly brute was lynched because he had raped the seven-year-old daughter of the sheriff." I visited the place afterward and saw the girl, who was a grown woman more than seventeen years old. She had been found in the lynched Negro's cabin by her father, who had led the mob against him in order to save his daughter's reputation. That Negro was a helper on the farm. . . .

It was with these and other stories in mind in that last week in May 1892 that I wrote the following editorial:

Eight Negroes lynched since last issue of the *Free Speech.* They were charged with killing white men and five with raping white women. Nobody in this section believes the old thread-bare lie that Negro men assault white women. If Southern white men are not careful they will overreach themselves and a conclusion will be drawn which will be very damaging to the moral reputation of their women.

This editorial furnished at last the excuse for doing what the white leaders of Memphis had long been wanting to do: put an end to the *Free Speech.* . . .

Having lost my paper, had a price put on my life, and been made an exile from home for hinting at the truth, I felt that I owed it to myself and to my race to tell the whole truth now that I was where I could do so freely. Accordingly, the fourth week in June, the *New York Age* had a seven-column article on the front page giving names, dates and places of many lynchings for alleged rape. This article showed conclusively that my editorial in the *Free Speech* was based on facts of illicit association between black men and white women.

Such relationships between white men and colored women were notorious, and had been as long as the two races had lived together in the South. . . . Many stories of the antebellum South were based upon such relationships. It has been frequently charged in narratives of slave times that these white fathers often sold their mulatto children into slavery. It was also well known that many other such white fathers and masters brought their mulatto and quadroon children to the North and gave them freedom and established homes for them, thus making them independent.

All my life I had known that such conditions were accepted as a matter of course. I found that this rape of helpless Negro girls and women, which began in slavery days, still continued without . . . hindrance, check or reproof from church, state, or press until there had been created this race within a race—and all designated by the inclusive term of "colored."

I also found that what the white man of the South practiced as all right for himself, he assumed to be unthinkable in white women. They could and did fall in love with the pretty mulatto and quadroon girls as well as black ones, but they professed an inability to imagine white women doing the same thing with Negro and mulatto men. Whenever they did so and were found out, the cry of rape was raised, and the lowest element of the white South was turned loose to wreak its fiendish cruelty on those too weak to help themselves....

The more I studied the situation, the more I was convinced that the Southerner had never gotten over his resentment that the Negro was no longer his plaything, his servant, and his source of income. The federal laws for Negro protection passed during Reconstruction had been made a mockery by the white South where it had not secured their repeal. This same white South had secured political control of its several states, and as soon as white southerners came into power they began to make playthings of Negro lives and property. This still seemed not enough "to keep the nigger down."

Here came lynch law to stifle Negro manhood which defended itself, and the burning alive of Negroes who were weak enough to accept favors from white women. The many unspeakable and unprintable tortures to which Negro rapists (?) [here Wells inserted a parenthetical question mark to indicate her skepticism of these charges] of white women were subjected were for the purpose of striking terror into the hearts of other Negroes who might be thinking of consorting with willing white women.

I found that in order to justify these horrible atrocities to the world, the Negro was branded as a race of rapists, who were especially after white women. I found that white men who had created a race of mulattoes by raping and consorting with Negro women were still doing so wherever they could; these same white men lynched, burned and tortured Negro men for doing the same thing with white women; even when the white women were willing victims.

That the entire race should be branded as moral monsters and despoilers of white womanhood and childhood was bound to rob us of all the friends we had and silence any protests that they might make for us. For all these reasons it seemed a stern duty to give the facts I had collected to the world....

About two months after my appearance in the columns in the *New York Age,* two colored women remarked on my revelations during a visit with each other and said they thought that the women of New York and Brooklyn should do something to show appreciation of my work and to protest the treatment which I had received.... A committee of two hundred and fifty women was appointed, and they stirred up sentiment throughout the two cities which culminated in a testimonial at Lyric Hall on 5 October 1892.

This testimonial was conceded by the oldest inhabitants to be the greatest demonstration ever attempted by race women for one of their number.... The leading colored women of Boston and Philadelphia had been invited to join in this demonstration, and they came, a brilliant array ... behind a lonely, homesick girl who was an exile because she had tried to defend the manhood of her race....

So many things came out of that wonderful testimonial.

First it was the beginning of the club movement among the colored women in this country. The women of New York and Brooklyn decided to continue that organization, which they called the Women's Loyal Union. These were the first strictly women's clubs organized in those cities. Mrs. Ruffin of Boston, who came over to that testimonial ... called a meeting of the women at her home to meet me, and they organized themselves into the Woman's Era Club of that city. Mrs. Ruffin had been a member of the foremost clubs among white women in Boston for years, but this was her first effort to form one among colored women....

Second, that testimonial was the beginning of public speaking for me. I have already said that I had not before made speeches, but invitations

Philadelphia, Wilmington, Delaware, Pennsylvania, and Washington, D.C. . . . Philadelphia . . . Miss Catherine Impey of Somerset, England, was visiting Quaker relatives of hers in the city and at the same time was trying to learn what she could about the color question in this country. She was the editor of *Anti-Caste,* a magazine published in England in behalf of the natives of India, and she was there-

fore interested in the treatment of darker races everywhere. . . . [Thus happened] the third great result of that wonderful testimonial in New York the previous month. Although we did not know it at the time, the interview between Miss Impey and myself resulted in an invitation to England and the beginning of the worldwide campaign against lynching.

QUESTIONS FOR ANALYSIS

1. What were the underlying tensions and larger conflicts that led to the lynching of Thomas Moss?

2. What was the prevailing opinion about lynching that Wells was determined to challenge?

3. What did Wells see as the relationship between the long history of white men raping black women and the charges raised against black men of raping white women?

4. How did Wells's campaign contribute to the consolidation of the organized African American women's movement?

DOCUMENTS

The Woman Who Toils

THE LIVES AND LABORS of wage-earning women and leisure-class women intersected in numerous ways in the late nineteenth century. Maids, cooks, nannies, and laundresses provided the labor that made possible the elaborate homes and active social lives of leisure-class women. Working women and their children were the objects of the charitable and philanthropic projects that middle- and upper-class women, aiming for a larger role in community affairs, organized in these years. Above all, working women provided the labor to manufacture the food, clothing, and luxuries that distinguished the rich from the poor. As the authors of *The Woman Who Toils* wrote to wealthy women, working women provided "the labour that must be done to satisfy your material demands."[41]

By the end of the century, working-class women were also the subject of professional women's journalistic and sociological investigations, of which *The Woman Who Toils: Being the Experiences of Two Ladies as Factory Girls* (1903) is a notable example. The authors, Bessie and Marie Van Vorst, were upper-class women. Marie was born a Van Vorst, and Bessie married into the family. Neither went to college. Both were educated instead in the manner preferred by the upper classes for their daughters, by private tutors and at female academies. After Bessie's husband, Marie's brother, died, the two women, both still in their thirties, undertook together to establish greater economic independence for themselves. They moved to Paris and cowrote a novel about an upper-class American woman abroad. Their next collaborative effort was *The Woman Who Toils*, a journalistic account of the lives of wage-earning women. As upper-class New Women aspiring to independence, they were motivated by both their growing awareness of the lives of working-class women and their own authorial ambitions.

To research the book, they returned to the United States, assumed fictional identities, and took a series of working-class jobs. Marie worked in a New England shoe factory and a southern textile mill. Bessie became the Irishwoman "Esther Kelly" and took a job in a pickling factory in Pittsburgh, where she went from eagerness to exhaustion in a few short days. Moving from job to job in the factory, Bessie explored how different it felt to work for a preset daily wage and to work for payment by the piece—an arrangement that led workers to drive themselves to work faster. A day in the male workers' dining room allowed her to compare manufacturing to domestic service labor.

Throughout Bessie's account, the distance she maintained from the women she wrote about is evident. She and her sister-in-law chose a subtitle to clarify that they were still "ladies" despite their brief stint as factory girls. The young men with whom their coworkers associated, the recreation they sought, and the clothes they wore seemed to them "vulgar." Like most reformers, they did not endorse wage labor for women with children, a point emphasized by President Theodore Roosevelt in his introduction to their book. Nonetheless, Bessie came to appreciate the generosity of her coworkers, the pleasures of collective work, and the "practical, progressive" democracy of working-class life. Above all, it was the sheer physical demands of doing the job, descriptions of which are among the best parts of the Pittsburgh pickling section of *The Woman Who Toils*, that seem to have broken through her shield of gentility and brought her a measure of closeness to the women workers about whom she wrote.

As you read this account of working in the pickle factory, identify what Bessie Van Vorst finds attractive about the jobs she does and the women who do them, and what she finds repellent. Consider the points at which her class prejudices emerge, and the points at which she gets beyond them.

MRS. JOHN (BESSIE) VAN VORST AND MARIE VAN VORST
The Woman Who Toils: Being the Experiences of Two Ladies as Factory Girls (1903)

"What will you do about your name?" "What will you do with your hair and your hands?" "How can you deceive people?" These are some of the questions I had been asked by my friends.

Before any one had cared or needed to know my name it was morning of the second day, and my assumed name seemed by that time the only one I had ever had. As to hair and hands, a half-day's work suffices for their undoing. And my disguise is so successful I have deceived not only others but myself. I have become with desperate reality a factory girl, alone, inexperienced, friendless. I am making $4.20 a week and spending $3 of this for board alone, and I dread not being strong enough to keep my job. I climb endless stairs, am given a white cap and an apron, and my life as a factory girl begins. I become part of the ceaseless, unrelenting mechanism kept in motion by the poor. . . .

My first task is an easy one; anybody could do it. On the stroke of seven my fingers fly. I place a lid of paper in a tin jar-top, over it a cork; this I press down with both hands, tossing the cover, when done, into a pan. In spite of myself I hurry; I cannot work fast enough—I outdo my companions. How can they be so slow? Every nerve, every muscle is offering some of its energy. Over in one corner the machinery for sealing the jars groans and roars; the mingled sounds of filling, washing, wiping, packing, comes to my eager ears as an accompaniment for the simple work assigned to me. One hour passes, two, three hours; I fit ten, twenty, fifty dozen caps, and still my energy keeps up. . . .

When I have fitted 110 dozen tin caps the forewoman comes and changes my job. She tells me to haul and load up some heavy crates with pickle jars. I am wheeling these back and forth when the twelve o'clock whistle blows. Up to that time the room has been one big dynamo, each girl a part of it. With the first moan of the noon signal the dynamo comes to life. It is hungry; it has friends and favourites—news to tell. We herd down to a big dining room and take our places, five hundred of us in all. The newspaper bundles are unfolded. The menu varies little: bread and

SOURCE: Mrs. John Van Vorst and Marie Van Vorst, *The Woman Who Toils: Being the Experiences of Two Ladies as Factory Girls* (New York: Doubleday, Page & Co, 1903), 21–58.

jam, cake and pickles, occasionally a sausage, a bit of cheese or a piece of stringy cold meat. In ten minutes the repast is over. The dynamo has been fed; there are twenty minutes of leisure spent in dancing, singing, resting, and conversing chiefly about young men and "sociables."

At 12:30 sharp the whistle draws back the life it has given. I return to my job. My shoulders are beginning to ache. My hands are stiff, my thumbs almost blistered. The enthusiasm I had felt is giving way to numbing weariness. I look at my companions now in amazement. How can they keep on so steadily, so swiftly? . . . New girls like myself who had worked briskly in the morning are beginning to loiter. Out of the washing-tins hands come up red and swollen, only to be plunged again into hot dirty water. Would the whistle never blow? . . . At last the whistle blows! In a swarm we report: we put on our things and get away into the cool night air. I have stood ten hours; I have fitted 1,300 corks; I have hauled and loaded 4,000 jars of pickles. My pay is seventy cents. . . .

For the two days following my first experience I am unable to resume work. Fatigue has swept through my body like a fever. Every bone and joint has a clamouring ache. . . .

The next day is Saturday. I feel a fresh excitement at going back to my job; the factory draws me toward it magnetically. I long to be in the hum and whir of the busy workroom. Two days of leisure without resources or amusement make clear to me how the sociability of factory life, the freedom from personal demands, the escape from self can prove a distraction to those who have no mental occupation, no money to spend on diversion. It is easier to submit to factory government which commands five hundred girls with one law valid for all, than to undergo the arbitrary discipline of parental authority. I speed across the snow-covered courtyard. In a moment my cap and apron are on and I am sent to report to the head forewoman. . . .

She wears her cap close against her head. Her front hair is rolled up in crimping-pins. She has false teeth and is a widow. Her pale, parched face shows what a great share of life has been taken by daily over-effort repeated during years. As she talks she touches my arm in a kindly fashion and looks at me with blue eyes that float about under weary lids. "You are only at the beginning," they seem to say. "Your youth and vigour are at full tide, but drop by drop they will be sapped from you, to swell the great flood of human effort that supplies the world's material needs. You will gain in experience," the weary lids flutter at me, "but you will pay *with your life* the living you make."

There is no variety in my morning's work. Next to me is a bright, pretty girl jamming chopped pickles into bottles.

"How long have you been here?" I ask, attracted by her capable appearance. She does her work easily and well.

"About five months."

"How much do you make?"

"From 90 cents to $1.05. I'm doing piece-work," she explains. "I get seven-eighths of a cent for every dozen bottles I fill. I have to fill eight dozen to make seven cents. . . ."

"Do you live at home?" I ask.

"Yes; I don't have to work. I don't pay no board. My father and my brothers supports me and my mother. But," and her eyes twinkle, "I couldn't have the clothes I do if I didn't work."

"Do you spend your money all on yourself?"

"Yes."

I am amazed at the cheerfulness of my companions. They complain of fatigue, of cold, but never at any time is there a suggestion of ill-humour. The suppressed animal spirits reassert themselves when the forewoman's back is turned. Companionship is the great stimulus. I am confident that without the . . . encouragement of example, it would be impossible to obtain as much from each individual girl as is obtained from them in groups of tens, fifties, hundreds working together.

When lunch is over we are set to scrubbing. Every table and stand, every inch of the factory floor must be scrubbed in the next four hours. . . .

The grumbling is general. There is but one opinion among the girls: it is not right that they should be made to do this work. They all echo the same resentment, but their complaints are made in whispers; not one has the courage to openly rebel. What, I wonder to myself, do the men do on scrubbing day. I try to picture one of them on his hands and knees in a sea of brown mud. It is impossible. The next time I go for a supply of soft soap in a department where the men are working I take a look at the masculine interpretation of house cleaning. One man is playing a hose on the floor and the rest are scrubbing the boards down with long-handled brooms and rubber mops.

"You take it easy," I say to the boss.

"I won't have no scrubbing in my place," he answers emphatically. "The first scrubbing day they says to me 'Get down on your hands and knees,' and I says — 'Just pay me my money, will you; I'm goin' home. What scrubbing can't be done with mops ain't going to be done by me.' The women wouldn't have to scrub, either, if they had enough spirit all of 'em to say so."

I determined to find out if possible, during my stay in the factory, what it is that clogs this mainspring of "spirit" in the women. . . .

After a Sunday of rest I arrive somewhat ahead of time on Monday morning, which leaves me a few moments for conversation with a piece-worker who is pasting labels on mustard jars. . . .

"I bet you can't guess how old I am."

I look at her. Her face and throat are wrinkled, her hands broad and scrawny; she is tall and has short skirts. What shall be my clue? If I judge by pleasure, "unborn" would be my answer; if by effort, then "a thousand years."

"Twenty," I hazard as a safe medium.

"Fourteen," she laughs. "I don't like it at home, the kids bother me so. Mamma's people are well-to-do. I'm working for my own pleasure."

"Indeed, I wish I was," says a new girl with a red waist. "We three girls supports mamma and runs the house. We have $13 rent to pay and a load of coal every month and groceries. It's no joke, I can tell you." . . .

Monday is a hard day. There is more complaining, more shirking, more gossip than in the middle of the week. Most of the girls have been to dances on Saturday night, to church on Sunday evening with some young man. Their conversation is vulgar and prosaic; there is nothing in the language they use that suggests an ideal or any conception of the abstract. . . . Here in the land of freedom, where no class line is rigid, the precious chance is not to serve but to live for oneself; not to watch a superior, but to find out by experience. The ideal plays no part, stern realities alone count, and thus we have a progressive, practical, independent people, the expression of whose personality is interesting not through their words but by their deeds.

When the Monday noon whistle blows I follow the hundreds down into the dining-room. . . . I am beginning to understand why the meager lunches of preserve-sandwiches and pickles more than satisfy the girls whom I was prepared to accuse of spending their money on gewgaws rather than on nourishment. It is fatigue that steals the appetite. I can hardly taste what I put in my mouth; the food sticks in my throat. . . . I did not want wholesome food, exhausted as I was. I craved sours and sweets, pickles, cakes, anything to excite my numbed taste. . . .

Accumulated weariness forces me to take a day off. When I return I am sent for in the corking-room. The forewoman lends me a blue gingham dress and tells me I am to do "piece"-work. There are three who work together at every corking-table. My two companions are a woman with goggles and a one-eyed boy. We are not a brilliant trio. The job consists in evening the vinegar in the bottles, driving the cork in, first with a machine, then with a hammer, letting out the air with a knife stuck under the cork, capping the corks, sealing the caps, counting and distributing the bottles. These operations are paid for at the rate of one-half a cent for the dozen bottles, which sum is divided among us. My two companions are earning a living, so I must work in dead earnest or take bread out of their mouths. . . .

There is a stimulus unsuspected in working to get a job done. Before this I had worked to make the time pass. Then no one took account of how much I did; the factory clock had a weighted pendulum; now ambition outdoes physical strength. The hours and my purpose are running a race together. But, hurry as I may, as we do, when twelve blows its signal we have corked only 210 dozen bottles! This is no more than day-work at seventy cents. With an ache in every muscle, I redouble my energy after lunch. The girl with the goggles looks at me blindly and says: "Ain't it just awful hard work? You can make good money, but you've got to hustle."

She is a forlorn specimen of humanity, ugly, old, dirty, condemned to the slow death of the over-worked. I am a green hand. I make mistakes; I have no experience in the fierce sustained effort of the bread-winners. Over and over I turn to her, over and over she is obliged to correct me. During the ten hours we work side by side not one murmur of impatience escapes her. When she sees that I am getting discouraged she calls out across the deafening din, "That's all right; you can't expect to learn in a day; just keep on steady." . . .

The oppressive monotony is one day varied by a summons to the men's dining-room. I go eagerly, glad of any change. . . . The dinner under preparation is for the men of the factory. There are two hundred of them. They are paid from $1.35 to $3 a day. Their wages begin upon the highest limit given to women. The dinner costs each man ten cents. The $20 paid in daily cover the expenses of the cook, two kitchen maids, and the dinner, which consists of meat, bread and butter, vegetables and coffee, sometimes soup, sometimes dessert. If this can pay for two hundred there is no reason why for five cents a hot meal of some kind could not be given to the women. They don't demand it, so they are left to make themselves ill on pickles and preserves. . . .

[In the dining room] I had ample opportunity to compare domestic service with factory work. We set the table for two hundred, and do a thousand miserable slavish tasks that must be begun again

the following day. At twelve the two hundred troop in, toil-worn and begrimed. They pass like locusts, leaving us sixteen hundred dirty dishes to wash up and wipe. This takes us four hours, and when we have finished the work stands ready to be done over the next morning with peculiar monotony. In the factory there is stimulus in feeling that the material which passes through one's hands will never be seen or heard of again. . . .

My first experience is drawing to a close. I have surmounted the discomforts of insufficient food, of dirt, a bed without sheets, the strain of hard manual labor. . . . In the factory where I worked men and women were employed for ten-hour days. The women's highest wages were lower than the men's lowest. Both were working as hard as they possibly could. The women were doing menial work, such as scrubbing, which the men refused to do. The men were properly fed at noon; the women satisfied themselves with cake and pickles. Why was this? It is of course impossible to generalize on a single factory. I can only relate the conclusions I drew from what I saw myself. The wages paid by employers, economists tell us, are fixed at the level of bare subsistence. This level and its accompanying conditions are determined by competition, by the nature and number of labourers taking part in the competition. In the masculine category I met but one class of competitor: the bread-winner. In the feminine category I found a variety of classes: the bread-winner, the semi-bread-winner, the woman who works for luxuries. This inevitably drags the wage level. The self-supporting girl is in competition with the child, with the girl who lives at home and makes a small contribution to the household expenses, and with the girl who is supported and who spends all her money on her clothes. It is this division of purpose which takes the "spirit" out of them as a class. There will be no strikes among them so long as the question of wages is not equally vital to them all. . . .

On the evening when I left the factory for the last time, I heard in the streets the usual cry of murders, accidents and suicides; the mental food of the overworked. It is Saturday night. I mingle with a crowd of labourers homeward bound, and with women and girls returning from a Saturday sale in the big shops. They hurry along delighted at the cheapness of a bargain, little dreaming of the human effort that has produced it, the cost of life and energy it represents. As they pass, they draw their skirts aside from us, the cooperators who enable them to have the luxuries they do; from us, the multitude who stand between them and the monster Toil that must be fed with human lives. Think of us, as we herd in the winter dawn; think of us as we bend over our task all the daylight without rest; think of us at the end of the day as we resume suffering and anxiety in homes of squalour and ugliness; think of us as we make our wretched try for merriment; think of us as we stand protectors between you and the labour that must be done to satisfy your material demands; think of us — be merciful.

QUESTIONS FOR ANALYSIS

1. What different sorts of women does Bessie Van Vorst meet in the factory, and how and why do their responses to their work vary?

2. Why does Van Vorst conclude that working women are passive in accepting their working conditions and unwilling to stand up for themselves in the way of working men? Do you think she is right?

3. How might the working women described in *The Woman Who Toils* have responded on reading the book? What accounts for your view?

4. In light of Van Vorst's final comments, how do you think her life and attitudes were changed by her experience as a factory girl?

VISUAL SOURCES

The Higher Education of Women in the Postbellum Years

WHENEVER WOMEN HAVE SOUGHT to improve their lives, almost invariably they have begun by aspiring to better education. "The neglected education of my fellow-creatures is the grand source of the misery I deplore," wrote British feminist Mary Wollstonecraft in 1792.[42] In the revolutionary era, grateful political leaders praised educated women for their role in mothering an enlightened (male) citizenry (see p. 146). Within fifty years, women were teachers in America's burgeoning system of public education. Even so, women continued to have far less access to education than men. Before the Civil War, women could rise no further than the high school level at all-female seminaries. Only Ohio's Oberlin College, an evangelical Protestant institution founded in 1833, admitted a few women to its regular baccalaureate course, most famously women's rights advocate Lucy Stone, who graduated in 1847. Even at Oberlin, however, most women students were educated in a special "ladies' program," with easier language and mathematics requirements than the baccalaureate course.

Two developments in the 1860s made higher education much more available to women. In 1862, the Morrill Land Grant Act provided federal lands to states and territories for the support of public institutions of higher education. While the act did not explicitly mention women, as one historian has explained, "taxpayers demanded that their daughters, as well as their sons, be admitted."[43] As coeducation spread, long-standing concerns that such easy association between the sexes would coarsen women students and distract men began to give way. The great land-grant universities established in the 1860s and early 1870s in Illinois, Nebraska, Kansas, Arkansas, Ohio, and California accepted women students. Public universities founded earlier—in Michigan, Indiana, Iowa, Missouri, and Wisconsin—changed their policies to admit women. Private universities such as Northwestern and the University of Chicago in Illinois, Stanford in California, and Tulane in Louisiana, and colleges such as Whitman in California, Colorado College, and Grinnell in Iowa, also followed the trend. By the end of the century, coeducational institutions granted college degrees to approximately four thousand women each year.

Because the land-grant universities were primarily in the Midwest and West, most coeducation occurred in these regions. The most important exception in the East was New York's Cornell University, which opened in 1868. Cornell, like virtually all other coeducational colleges and universities, nonetheless remained an institution shaped largely by the needs of men. Female students had to struggle

◆ Figure 6.1 **Chafing Dish Party, Cornell University (1904)**

to establish their own place, starting with where to live, since dormitories housed male students only. The establishment of sororities solved the problem in many state universities. At Cornell, benefactor Russell Sage donated a special women's building. Figure 6.1 is a 1904 photograph of Cornell women at a get-together called a "chafing dish party" in one of their rooms in Sage Hall. What do the activities, dress, and furnishings in the photograph indicate about these women's lives as college students? Consider also what the photograph suggests about the relations among women at a largely male institution.

After the Civil War, the establishment of all-women's colleges also increased women's opportunities for higher education. The first of these, Vassar College, opened in 1865, funded by a wealthy brewer from Poughkeepsie, New York, who wanted to create an educational institution "for young women which shall be to them, what Yale and Harvard are to young men."[44] Philanthropists endowed other all-female institutions, and by 1891 Smith and Wellesley colleges in Massachusetts, Bryn Mawr College outside Philadelphia, and Goucher College near Baltimore were graduating women with bachelor's degrees. (Mount Holyoke in Massachusetts, begun many years before as a female seminary, upgraded to college level in 1890.) These all-women institutions produced about sixteen hundred college graduates each year. Combining all-female and coeducational institutions, public and private, by 1890 women were approximately 40 percent of the total of college graduates—an extraordinary development in less than four decades.

There was much debate about whether women students received a better education and had a better collegiate experience at an all-women's college or at a coed-

◆ Figure 6.2 **Class in Zoology, Wellesley College (1883–1884)**
Courtesy of Wellesley College Archives, photo by Seaver.

ucational institution. To strengthen their claims to intellectual superiority, the top women's colleges were dedicated to providing a first-class education in the sciences, which were becoming increasingly important in modern higher education. The Wellesley College class pictured in Figure 6.2 is studying zoology. The students are examining a fish skeleton and a piece of coral to learn about animal physiology. This photograph, like so many photos of late nineteenth-century college women, is carefully posed. How does the deliberate positioning of the students convey the intellectual seriousness, intensity, and engagement of the scientific learning going on in this all-female classroom? Consider the simple and functional character of the students' clothes, especially compared to the elaborate and costly appearance of elite women engaged in less serious pursuits (see picture on p. 347).

Figure 6.2 also underscores the opportunities that all-female colleges in this period provided for the employment of educated women. Here, unlike in most coeducational schools, women could be professors and administrators. The zoology professor, the young woman seated at the center, is Mary Alice Wilcox, a graduate of Newnham College, the women's college of Britain's Cambridge University. Standing behind her and slightly to the right is Alice Freeman, the twenty-eight-year-old Wellesley College president. Freeman, an early graduate of the University of Michigan, was the first woman to head an institution of higher education in the United States. In 1886, she married Harvard professor George Herbert Palmer and resigned her position as college president. Why might women professors have been employed only at all-women's colleges? What difference do you think they made to women's experience of higher education? How might the youth of professors such as Wilcox and administrators such as Freeman have influenced the learning of these women students?

Concerns went beyond the intellectual. Did coeducation provide too many opportunities for undo familiarity between young unmarried men and women? Were women's colleges hotbeds for passionate female friendships? Anxiety that higher education would have a negative impact on women's health, in particular on their reproductive capacities, haunted the early years of women's higher education. In 1873 Dr. Edward Clarke published a controversial book, *Sex and Education,* in which he argued that higher education for women drained vital physical energy — literally blood — from the reproductive organs to the brain. Defenders of women's education rushed to challenge Clarke's argument that higher education endangered women's reproductive and maternal vocation. They undertook scientific studies of women college students to demonstrate that physical health and intellectual growth were not incompatible. Proponents of women's education were particularly anxious to prove that the menstruation of college girls was not disrupted by disciplined study.

To further counter the charge that higher education weakened women physically, but also to strengthen women's bodies as well as their minds, colleges added women's athletics and physical education to their curricula. Competition, however, was prohibited as unladylike, certainly between the sexes in coeducational institutions but even among the women themselves. Nonetheless, in the 1890s, soon after basketball was introduced among young men, a modified version of the game became the rage among college women. Figure 6.3 is a photograph of the team of the class of 1904 from Wells College, an all-women's college in Aurora, New York. In addition to their white-tie blouses the players are wearing loose, divided "bloomer" skirts. What in the photograph gives evidence of the physical freedom that sports brought to women's college experience? Why might the photographer have posed the team members with their hands folded, rather than in a more forceful representation of young women in action?

Black women faced extraordinary educational challenges. In the first years of emancipation, the overwhelming goal for ex-slaves was basic literacy. During Reconstruction, black educational institutions were founded, virtually all of them opened to women as well as men, but these schools provided secondary and vocational rather than baccalaureate education. Even the nation's premiere all-black college, Howard University, founded in Washington, D.C., in 1867, did not open its collegiate program until 1897 and did not graduate its first woman BA until 1901. In the same year, Atlanta's all-female Spelman College also granted its first BA degree (see pp. 332–34).

By 1900, an estimated 252 African American women held bachelor's degrees, but almost all had been granted by predominantly white institutions, one-quarter from Oberlin College alone. Committed to equal education by both race and gender, Oberlin had produced the very first black woman college graduate — Mary Jane Patterson — in 1862. Many of its black female graduates, including Mary Church Terrell and Anna Julia Cooper, went on to become leading spokeswomen for their race and their sex.

◆ Figure 6.3 **Basketball Team, Wells College (1904)**
Wells College Archives, Louis Jefferson Long Library, Aurora, New York.

In southern black educational institutions, the dramatic downturn in race re-lations in the 1880s and 1890s had a discouraging impact on higher education for African Americans. Instead of striving for academic equality with white colleges, they concentrated on preparing their students for skilled trades and manual voca-tions. This approach to higher education was preached by Booker T. Washington, the era's premiere African American educator. Figure 6.4 is a photograph of a his-tory class at Hampton Institute, a freedmen's school founded in 1868 in Virginia where Washington began his career, and a model for many similar institutions throughout the South. In a controversial experiment in interracial education, Hampton also began enrolling Native American students in 1878.

Freedpeople regarded the educational opportunities that Hampton and other such schools provided them as immense privileges. Speaking at the 1873 gradua-tion, Alice P. Davis, born a slave in North Carolina in 1852, praised Hampton Institute as her alma mater: "[A] mother indeed she has been to us, for she has given us more instruction in these three years than our dear but illiterate mothers ever could."[45] Nonetheless, such institutions, which were often overseen by white benefactors, maintained strict controls over their black students, to train them in the virtues of industriousness and self-discipline. The young women were pre-pared for jobs as teachers, but also as domestic servants and industrial workers.

In 1899, Hampton's white trustees hired America's first important female doc-umentary photographer, Frances Benjamin Johnston, who was white, to portray the students' educational progress. Her photographs were displayed at the Paris

◆ **Figure 6.4** **Class in American History, Hampton Institute (1899–1900)**
Library of Congress LC-USZ62-38149.

Exposition of 1900, where they were much praised for both their artistic achievement and their depiction of racial harmony. Figure 6.4, entitled "Class in American History," is an exceptionally rich image for the diversity of its subjects and the complexity of its content. A white female teacher stands among her female and male, African American and Native American, students. All are contemplating a Native American man in ceremonial dress. He can be likened in some way to the scientific specimens in Figure 6.2. Consider what the man himself might have been thinking as he was exhibited to the gaze of both the photographer and the history class. Historian Laura Wexler has unearthed the name of one of the students, the young Indian woman standing at the far right: she is Adele Quinney, a member of the Stockbridge tribe.[46] What lessons were she and the other students being taught about American history by the living exhibit of traditional Indian ways placed before them? What do their precise posing and uniform dress suggest about the discipline expected of Hampton students? Above all, what does this single image capture about the forces at work in late nineteenth-century American society?

During the post–Civil War years, many "normal colleges" were established to concentrate exclusively on the training of teachers. Such schools provided a briefer, less demanding program of study than baccalaureate courses. With less competitive standards for admission and lower costs, they educated a much larger number of women students. The first teacher training institution supported with public funds was founded in 1839 in Framingham, Massachusetts. Normal colleges also benefited from the 1862 Morrill Act and were an important avenue of upward mobility for working-class immigrants, African Americans, and other people of color.

Many of these institutions survived into the twentieth century and became full-fledged colleges and universities. Figure 6.5 is a photograph of a class at Washington, D.C.'s Normal College, established in 1873. Because Washington was a

◆ Figure 6.5 **Science Class, Washington, D.C., Normal College (1899)**
Library of Congress LC-USZ62-14684.

southern town, public education there was racially segregated, and the Normal College enrolled only white students. Washington's Myrtilla Miner Normal School, founded in 1851 and named after a heroic white woman educator of African American girls, enrolled only African American students. The two schools remained separate and segregated until 1955, one year after the Supreme Court found segregated education unconstitutional in the case of *Brown v. Board of Education* (see p. 611). Then they were merged into the District of Columbia Teachers College, now named the University of the District of Columbia.

As in Figure 6.2, the students in Figure 6.5 are studying science, once again illustrating the importance of this subject in meeting the ambitions that the leaders of women's higher education had to offer young women a modern and intellectually challenging education. And yet the kinds of teaching and learning that went on in an elite college such as Wellesley and a teacher training institution such as the Normal School were very different. The former had a far more educated faculty and resources of equipment and specimens that the latter lacked. Consider what other differences can be detected by comparing this photograph with Figure 6.2. Figure 6.5 also invites comparison with Figure 6.4 because both photographs were taken by Frances Johnston. How has Johnston positioned her subjects in this picture, compared to those at Hampton Institute? What educational message is this different staging meant to communicate?

Like teachers, doctors were trained in specialized medical colleges. For most of the nineteenth century, a bachelor's degree was not a prerequisite to study medicine in the United States. Instead, students studied medicine at special medical schools and in undergraduate medical departments of large universities. The first major obstacle that women faced was gaining admission into these all-male programs of medical education. Anxieties about coeducation were particularly intense over the prospect of women sitting beside men at lectures about the human body. But women's desire for medical education was strong. Medicine, unlike other professions such as law or the ministry, fit comfortably with women's traditional role as healers. In 1849, after applying to a dozen major medical schools, Elizabeth Blackwell broke this educational barrier by graduating from Geneva Medical College in rural upstate New York.

One remedy was the establishment of all-female medical colleges. The Boston Female Medical College was established in 1849 by Dr. Samuel Gregory, who wanted to train women to attend their own sex in childbirth. Dr. Elizabeth Blackwell founded the Women's Medical College of New York in 1868 to help other women follow her into the profession. Such all-female schools played a major role in educating women physicians, but as they lacked adequate clinical resources and opportunities, women continued to demand admission to men's medical colleges, where they were eventually accepted.

By 1890, women represented between 15 and 20 percent of all medical students. After 1890, the number of medical colleges shrank, even as their standards rose. Educationally, the crucial change came in 1893 when the Johns Hopkins University in Baltimore established the first postgraduate medical course in the United States. A group of women, led by Mary Garrett, close friend of Bryn Mawr College dean

◆ Figure 6.6 **Graduating Class, Medical College of Syracuse University (1876)**
Prints & Photographs Department/Moorland-Spingarn Research Center, Howard University.

M. Carey Thomas, donated $500,000 to the new postgraduate medical college on the condition that women be admitted along with men. Overall, however, women began to lose access to medical education after 1890, and the percentage of women in most medical schools dropped by half or more by the turn of the century.

Figure 6.6 is a photograph of the 1876 class of the Medical College of Syracuse University, which in 1872 absorbed the resources of Geneva Medical College, Elizabeth Blackwell's alma mater. This medical class was impressively diverse, not only because four of the students were women but because one of them was

African American. Sarah Loguen (after marriage, Fraser) was the daughter of a fugitive slave who became an abolitionist. After graduation, she practiced medicine in Washington, D.C. Notice that the men look much more directly at the photographer than the women, several of whom look down or away. Does this photograph provide any hints about how the male students regarded their female colleagues or how the women felt about their presence in the medical classroom?

QUESTIONS FOR ANALYSIS

1. Nineteenth-century women's higher education proceeded along two parallel lines: the struggle for coeducation and the establishment of all-women's institutions. What were the advantages and disadvantages of each approach?

2. In what way did the motivations for and rewards of higher education differ for white and African American women?

3. How did the growth of higher education for women relate to other major postbellum developments in women's history discussed in this chapter?

Alice Austen:
Gilded Age Photographer

THE PHOTOGRAPHS OF Alice Austen document in a remarkable way two dimensions of the lives of middle- and upper-class women in the Gilded Age: the elaborate patterns of recreation that their wealth allowed them, and the challenges they began to make to established gender conventions. In other words, Austen recorded the society she saw both as a leisure-class woman and as a New Woman.

Austen was born in 1866 to a comfortable middle-class family that had moved away from the crowds and bustle of New York City for Staten Island, then a rural suburb. The conventional appearance of the Austen family hid the disturbing conditions of Alice's birth: her father deserted her mother when she was born, and Alice was raised with no knowledge of this man, not even his name. Nonetheless, Alice was by all accounts a happy and curious child in a family of adults that doted on her. She did not go to college, but attended a private high school for girls. By her late teens, her life was focused not on education or occupation, but on recreation. Although there were many young men in her circle of friends, she never married, later commenting that she was "too good to get married . . . too good at sports, too good at photography, too good at mechanical skills."[47] She chose instead to spend her life with another unmarried woman, Gertrude Tate, whom she met in 1899.

Austen made herself into a skilled photographer. Her seafaring uncle presented her with her first camera when she was only ten, and taking pictures became the center of her life. She made more than five thousand photographs in her lifetime, beginning with the heavy chemically coated glass negatives used in the 1880s and ending with the much simpler roll film of the Kodak era. She took extraordinary care to set up her photographs and position her sitters, and did all the difficult work of developing and printing herself.

Yet, for all her commitment, dedication, and lifelong involvement with photography, Austen was an amateur, meaning she did not make her living with her camera. She published one tiny book of pictures of Manhattan street life, and she was paid for only a handful of other photographs. Even when her fortunes declined, it never occurred to her to turn to her photography to support herself. During the Depression of the 1930s, she mortgaged and then lost ownership of the house in which she had been raised. She and Gertrude sold their belongings and scraped together a living, but by 1950, she was officially declared a pauper and remanded to the New York City Farm Colony on Staten Island. Months before

379

she died, she and her photographs were rediscovered by a young photographic historian named Oliver Jensen, who was researching a book later published as *The Revolt of American Women* (1952).

Figure 6.7, taken in 1886, is one of the earliest of Austen's images to have survived. Austen took pictures of her friends doing gymnastics and on bicycles as well as at tennis. Austen is the formally dressed young woman on the left. Instead of relaxing from playing tennis, as her friends were, Austen was busy setting up her picture, arranging the sitters' positions, making sure the light was perfect, and using a remote device to pull the shutter and take the picture—with herself in it. The others sat still for the exposure, but there is just a hint of movement in Austen. Under the racket to the lower left lay the cable by which Austen worked the shutter. In later pictures, she was able to better conceal the device. Why do you think that the faces of the young men and women in the photo are so open and their gaze at the camera so direct? Compare the expressions and poses of the

◆ Figure 6.7 **Alice Austen, Playing Tennis (1886)**
Alice Austen Collection, Staten Island Historical Society.

◆ Figure 6.8 **Alice Austen and Her Cousin (1894)**
Alice Austen Collection, Staten Island Historical Society.

women in this photograph to those in Figure 6.6. What do you suppose accounts for the differences in the two photos?

Figure 6.8, taken several years later, shows a more conventional scene of young people's leisure: Austen and her male cousin dressed up for the Annual Charity Ball at a local club. Austen was again the photographer, this time probably using a delayed-action shutter. The picture, taken in her family's parlor, features some of the elaborate furniture that filled Victorian homes. As an elderly woman looking at this photo, Austen described both figures as "looking as though we were shot out of a gun."[48] She remembered that she was concerned that the picture turn out well, but what other things might have been on her mind? How do this photograph and the relations between the figures compare to the scene in Figure 6.7?

The picture in Figure 6.9, of Austen and two of her friends dressed up as men, has become one of Austen's most famous photos. Like the Mexican artist Frida Kahlo, Austen became far better known and celebrated after her death than during her life. This photo, in the context of Austen's decision not to marry but to live her life with another woman, made her a historical icon for modern feminists

◆ Figure 6.9 **Alice Austen and Friends Dress Up as Men (1891)**
Alice Austen Collection, Staten Island Historical Society.

and lesbians. "Maybe we were better looking men than women," Austen quipped many years later when she was shown the photograph.[49] How did the three girls make themselves look like men, and how successful were they? Austen is the standing figure holding the cigarette. Compare the look on her face in this picture with that in Figures 6.7 and 6.8. What do you think the joke here is?

In Figure 6.10, there is another masquerade going on, this time with actual masks. Twenty-five-year-old Austen, on the right, and her best friend at the time, Trude Eccleston, have literally let down their hair. The photograph is taken inside Eccleston's bedchamber, in the house of her father, an Episcopalian minister. The women, normally held to the rules of respectability in their public lives, recorded themselves in private playing with elements of female disreputability. What else besides the bedchamber setting suggests openly sexual women, perhaps even prostitutes? Compare this image with Figure 6.9. Which photograph represents a more daring leap of self-presentation and identity?

Eventually, Austen began to take her camera beyond the confines of her suburban friends and family. Her only published photographs were those she took in the late 1890s in Manhattan. She took photos of the leisure-class districts uptown, featuring the transom cabs and trolleys that carried shoppers and tourists around

◆ Figure 6.10 **Alice Austen and Trude Eccleston Let Down Their Hair (1891)**
Alice Austen Collection, Staten Island Historical Society.

the city. However, the photos of people in Manhattan almost all concern those who lived downtown, in the working-class districts of the city. Most of them were probably immigrants.

Austen's pictures of New York City were taken at the same time that sociologists and social reformers were focusing on the plight of impoverished immigrants, but she did not intend her pictures to generate special sympathy or concern in the viewer. (See, for example, Visual Sources: Jacob Riis's Photographs of Immigrant Girls and Women, pp. 434–40.) Indeed, given her individualistic and leisure-class outlook, Austen may have been drawn by the vitality and individuality of her

◆ **Figure 6.11 Alice Austen, *Hester Street, Egg Stand* (1895)**
Alice Austen Collection, Staten Island Historical Society.

immigrant subjects. Figure 6.11 was taken on Hester Street, the central shopping area of the Jewish Lower East Side. One woman is selling eggs, and the other may have been buying them. What do you think the smiling woman was thinking of the photographer, and what might Austen have been thinking about her? How does this picture compare with those that Jacob Riis took of New York immigrants at about the same time?

QUESTIONS FOR ANALYSIS

1. How do the photographs that Alice Austen took compare to those of the professional photographer Frances Benjamin Johnston, her contemporary, in Figures 6.4 and 6.5?

2. What was it about the camera that encouraged Austen and other women of her class to express their individual perspectives through photography?

3. What impact do these photographs have on your understanding of gender roles of American society in the late nineteenth century?

NOTES

1. Elizabeth Cady Stanton, "This Is the Negro's Hour," *National Anti-Slavery Standard*, November 26, 1865, reprinted in Elizabeth Cady Stanton, Susan B. Anthony, and Matilda J. Gage, eds., *History of Woman Suffrage* (Rochester, NY: Susan B. Anthony, 1881), 2:94.

2. Ellen Carol DuBois, *Feminism and Suffrage: The Emergence of an Independent Women's Movement in America, 1848–1869* (Ithaca: Cornell University Press, 1999), 63.

3. Ibid., 60.

4. Ibid., 175.

5. Elizabeth Cady Stanton to Lucretia Mott, April 1, 1872, in Theodore Stanton and Harriot Stanton Blatch, eds., *Elizabeth Cady Stanton as Revealed in Her Letters, Diary and Reminiscences* (New York: Harper and Brothers, 1922), 137.

6. Susan B. Anthony to Elizabeth Cady Stanton, November 5, 1872, Ida H. Harper Collection, Huntington Library, San Marino, CA.

7. Stanton, Anthony, and Gage, *History of Woman Suffrage*, 3:31.

8. Dorothy Sterling, ed., *We Are Your Sisters: Black Women in the Nineteenth Century* (New York: Norton, 1984), 313.

9. Lucy Chase to unknown correspondent, 1868, American Antiquarian Society, Worcester, Massachusetts, excerpted in Nancy Woloch, ed., *Early American Women: A Documentary History, 1600–1900* (Belmont, CA: Wadsworth, 1992), 401.

10. Sterling, *We Are Your Sisters*, 311.

11. Ibid., 314.

12. Ibid., 293–305.

13. Marilyn Mayer Culpepper, *All Things Altered: Women in the Wake of Civil War and Reconstruction* (Jefferson, NC: McFarland, 2002), 135.

14. Ibid., 123.

15. Tera W. Hunter, *To 'Joy My Freedom: Southern Black Women's Lives and Labors after the Civil War* (Cambridge: Harvard University Press, 1997), 33.

16. "The Race Problem: An Autobiography: A Southern Colored Woman," *The Independent* 56 (1904): 586–89.

17. Arthur F. Raper, *The Tragedy of Lynching* (Chapel Hill: University of North Carolina Press, 1933), 13–14.

18. "The Race Problem," 586–89.

19. Nancy Cott et al., eds., *Root of Bitterness: Documents of the Social History of American Women*, 2nd ed. (Boston: Northeastern University Press, 1996), 360.

20. Claudia Goldin, "The Work and Wages of Single Women: 1870 to 1920," National Bureau of Economic Research Working Paper, No. WO375, 1979, 1.

21. Linda Gordon, *The Great Arizona Orphan Abduction* (Cambridge, MA: Harvard University Press, 1999), 8.

22. Nancy Cott, ed., *Root of Bitterness: Documents of the Social History of American Women,* First Edition (Boston: Northeastern University Press, 1986), 319.

23. Helen Campbell, *Women Wage-Earners: Their Past, Their Present, and Their Future* (Boston: Roberts Brothers, 1893), 190.

24. Ibid., 191.

25. Quoted in Barbara Wertheimer, *We Were There: The Story of Working Women in America* (New York: Pantheon Books, 1977), 178.

26. Mary Kenney O'Sullivan, unpublished autobiography, Schlesinger Library, Harvard University, Cambridge, MA.

27. Gary B. Nash et al., *The American People: Creating a Nation and a Society*, brief 5th ed. (New York: Addison Wesley Longman, 2000), 481.

28. Elizabeth Blackwell, "On Sexual Passion in Men and Women," 1894, reprinted in Cott et al., *Root of Bitterness* (1986), 302.

29. Women's historians first encountered the De Kay/Hallock romance in Carroll Smith-Rosenberg's pathbreaking essay, "The Female World of Love and Ritual: Relations between Women in Nineteenth Century America," which can be found in her collection of essays, *Disorderly Conduct: Visions of Gender in Victorian America* (New York: Oxford University Press, 1985), 53–76. Their relationship also formed the basis of Wallace Stegner's Pulitzer Prize–winning 1971 novel, *Angle of Repose*. Winslow Homer is thought to have been infatuated with De Kay, and painted a lovely, haunting portrait of her "in repose." Hallock became an important writer and illustrator of the West (see p. 401). The quote is from Smith-Rosenberg, p. 57.

30. Karen Hansen, "'No Kisses Is Like Yours': An Erotic Friendship between Two African-American Women during the Mid-Nineteenth Century," *Gender History* 7 (1995): 153.

31. Karen Blair, *The Clubwoman as Feminist: True Womanhood Redefined, 1868–1914* (New York: Holmes and Meier, 1980), 34.

32. Sarah J. Early, "The Organized Efforts of the Colored Women of the South to Improve Their Condition," 1893, reprinted in Dawn Keetley and John Pettegrew, eds., *Public Women, Public Words*, vol. 1 (Madison, WI: Madison House, 1997), 316.

33. Frances E. Willard, *How I Learned to Ride the Bicycle: Reflections of an Influential 19th Century Woman*, ed. Carol O'Hare (1895; repr., Sunnyvale, CA: Fair Oaks, 1991), 17, 75.

34. Mary Earhart, *Frances Willard: From Prayers to Politics* (Chicago: University of Chicago Press, 1944), 93.

35. Suzanne Marilley, *Woman Suffrage and the Origins of Liberal Feminism in the United States, 1820–1920* (Cambridge, MA: Harvard University Press, 1996), 128–29.

36. Ellen Carol DuBois, ed., *The Elizabeth Cady Stanton–Susan B. Anthony Reader: Correspondence, Writings, Speeches*, rev. ed. (Boston: Northeastern University Press, 1992), 176.

37. Ellen Henrotin to May Wright Sewall, in Jeanne Madeline Weimann, *The Fair Women* (Chicago: Academy Chicago, 1981), 529.

38. Charlotte Perkins Gilman, *Women and Economics: A Study of the Economic Relation between Men and Women as a Factor in Social Evolution* (Boston: Small, Maynard & Company, 1898), 156.

39. Elizabeth Cady Stanton, "The Solitude of Self," 1892, http://historymatters .gmu.edu/d/5315 (accessed December 13, 2007).

40. Patricia Schechter, *Ida B. Wells-Barnett and American Reform, 1880–1930* (Chapel Hill: University of North Carolina Press, 2001), 62–63.

41. Mrs. John Van Vorst and Marie Van Vorst, *The Woman Who Toils: Being the Experiences of Two Ladies as Factory Girls* (New York: Doubleday, Page & Co., 1903), 58.

42. Alice Rossi, ed., *The Feminist Papers from Adams to de Beauvoir* (Boston: Northeastern University Press, 1988), 40.

43. Rosalind Rosenberg, "The Limits of Access," in John Mack Faragher and Florence Howe, eds., *Women and Higher Education: Essays from the Mount Holyoke College Sesquicentennial Symposia* (New York: Norton, 1988), 110.

44. Helen Lefkowitz Horowitz, *Alma Mater: Design and Experience in Women's Colleges from Their Nineteenth-Century Beginnings to the 1930s* (New York: Knopf, 1984), 29.

45. M. F. (Mary Frances) Armstrong, *Hampton and Its Students, by Two of Its Teachers, Mrs. M. F. Armstrong and Helen W. Ludlow* (New York: G. P. Putnam, 1874), 89–90.

46. Laura Wexler, *Tender Violence: Domestic Visions in an Age of U.S. Imperialism* (Chapel Hill: University of North Carolina Press, 2000), 168.

47. Ann Novotny, *Alice's World: The Life and Photography of an American Original, Alice Austen, 1866–1952* (Old Greenwich, CT: Chatham Press, 1976), 60.

48. Ibid., 51.

49. Ibid., 50.

SUGGESTED REFERENCES

General Works   A general introduction to women's history in the period from 1865 to 1900 is Eleanor Flexner, *Century of Struggle: The Woman's Rights Movement in the United States* (1975), which is still the best overall history of women's rights in the United States. The equivalent work on black women's history is Paula Giddings, *When and Where I Enter: The Impact of Black Women on Race and Sex in America* (1984), a pioneering synthesis of black women's history after slavery. Alice Kessler Harris's magisterial history of working women, *Out to Work: A History of Wage-Earning Women in the United States* (1982), gives excellent coverage to this period. A general history of sexuality that treats the nineteenth century is Estelle B. Freedman and John D'Emilio, *Intimate Matters: A History of Sexuality* (1997).

Woman Suffrage   For more on the woman suffrage movement in the postbellum era, Ellen Carol DuBois, *Feminism and Suffrage: The Emergence of an Independent Women's Movement in the United States, 1848–1869* (1978), focuses on the struggle over the Fourteenth and Fifteenth Amendments; DuBois, *Women's Rights, Woman Suffrage* (1998), considers the New Departure period. Ann D. Gordon, ed., *The*

Selected Papers of Elizabeth Cady Stanton and Susan B. Anthony, Vol. II, Against an Aristocracy of Sex, 1866–1873 (2000), is a compilation of the important writings of the two suffrage leaders over this period. See Barbara Goldsmith's biography of Victoria Woodhull, *Other Powers: The Age of Suffrage, Spiritualism, and the Scandalous Victoria Woodhull* (1998). Helen L. Horowitz, *Rereading Sex: Battles over Sexual Knowledge and Suppression in Nineteenth-Century America* (2002), is comprehensive.

Black Women in the South   For further research on African American women in the era of Reconstruction and Redemption, Tera W. Hunter's *To 'Joy My Freedom: Southern Black Women's Lives and Labors after the Civil War* (1997) focuses on black women in Atlanta. Evelyn Brooks Higginbotham, *Righteous Discontent: The Women's Movement in the Black Baptist Church, 1880–1920* (1993), examines the roots of the southern black middle class. Deborah G. White, *Too Heavy a Load: Black Women in Defense of Themselves, 1894–1994* (1994), analyzes the black women's club movement. Two recent biographies of antilynching crusader Ida B. Wells are Patricia Schechter, *Ida B. Wells-Barnett and American Reform, 1880–1930* (2001), and Linda McMurry, *To Keep the Waters Troubled: The Life of Ida B. Wells* (1998).

White Women in the South   The pioneering work on white women in the postbellum South is Anne Firor Scott, *The Southern Lady from Pedestal to Politics, 1830–1930* (1970). Marilyn Mayer Culpepper, *All Things Altered: Women in the Wake of Civil War and Reconstruction* (2002), provides many firsthand accounts of white women in the period. Dolores Janiewski, *Sisterhood Denied: Race, Gender, and Class in a New South Community* (1985), examines non-elite southern white women, especially as they moved into industrial labor. Laura Edwards, *Gendered Strife and Confusion: The Political Culture of Reconstruction* (1992), examines challenges raised to southern patriarchy by black and white women after the Civil War. Martha Hodes, *Black Men, White Women* (1994), examines the history of interracial sex in the South. Glenda E. Gilmore, *Gender and Jim Crow: Women and the Politics of White Supremacy in North Carolina, 1896–1920* (1996), focuses on late nineteenth-century insurgent racism.

Working Women in the North   For additional reading on women and work, Barbara Wertheimer, *We Were There: The Story of Working Women in America* (1977), provides a survey of women's work and labor activism, emphasizing but not limited to wage earners. Mary Blewett, *We Will Rise in Our Might: Workingwomen's Voices from Nineteenth-Century New England* (1991), weaves together primary sources into a historical overview of women workers, as does Rosalyn Baxandall and Linda Gordon, eds., *America's Working Women: A Documentary History, 1600 to the Present* (revised ed., 1995). Mary Blewett, *Men, Women, and Work: Class, Gender, and Protest in the New England Shoe Industry, 1780–1910* (1988), examines nineteenth-century working women in a single industry. So does Susan Levine, *Labor's True Woman: Carpet Weavers, Industrialization, and Labor Reform in the Gilded Age* (1984), which also examines women in the Knights of Labor. Marjorie

Davies, *Woman's Place Is at the Typewriter: Office Work and Office Workers, 1870–1930* (1981), examines the shift from male to female office workers. Joanne Meyerowitz, *Women Adrift: Independent Wage Earners in Chicago, 1880–1930* (1988), concerns the lives of working women who did not live in families. Alice Henry, *The Trade Union Woman* (1915), remains a basic resource for the history of women in the labor movement, as does Philip Foner, *Women and the American Labor Movement: From Colonial Times to the Eve of World War I* (1971). Kathleen Nutter, *The Necessity of Organization: Mary Kenney O'Sullivan and Trade Unionism for Women, 1892–1912* (2000), is a biography of the first woman organizer in the AFL.

Leisure-Class Women in the North   Upper-class women in the Gilded Age are discussed in Maureen Montgomery, *Displaying Women: Spectacles of Leisure in Edith Wharton's New York* (1998). The pathologies of shopping are analyzed in Elaine Abelson, *When Ladies Go A-Thieving: Middle-Class Shoplifters in the Victorian Department Store* (1989). Barbara Solomon, *In the Company of Educated Women: A History of Women and Higher Education in America* (1985), is a comprehensive history of women's higher education; Helen Horowitz, *Alma Mater: Design and Experience in Women's Colleges from Their Nineteenth-Century Beginnings to the 1930s* (1984), focuses on the all-female colleges. Sarah Deutsch, *Women and the City: Gender, Space, and Power in Boston, 1870–1940* (2000), examines women's activism and class relations in Boston, and Maureen Flanagan, *Seeing with Their Hearts: Chicago Women and the Vision of the Good City, 1871–1933* (2002), covers similar territory in Chicago. Anne Firor Scott, *Natural Allies: Women's Associations in American History* (1991), is a comprehensive study of women's associations. Karen Blair, *The Clubwoman as Feminist: True Womanhood Redefined, 1868–1914* (1980), is the first scholarly study of the women's club movement. The WCTU is the subject of Ruth Bordin, *Women and Temperance: The Quest for Power and Liberty, 1873–1900* (1990). The starting point for the history of women's romantic friendships is Lillian Faderman's *Surpassing the Love of Men: Romantic Friendship and Love between Women from the Renaissance to the Present* (1994). Also see Martha Vicinus, *Intimate Friends: Women who Loved Women, 1778–1928* (2004), and Lisa Duggan, *Sapphic Slashers: Sex, Violence and American Modernity* (2000). On the photography of Alice Austen, see Ann Novotny, *Alice Austen: The Life and Times of an American Original* (1976), and Laura Wexler, *Tender Violence: Domestic Visions in an Age of U.S. Imperialism* (1999).

For selected Web sites, please visit the *Through Women's Eyes* book companion site at bedfordstmartins.com/duboisdumenil.

7

Women in an Expanding Nation

CONSOLIDATION OF THE WEST, MASS IMMIGRATION, AND THE CRISIS OF THE 1890S

TWENTY-THREE-YEAR-OLD SHIGE KUSHIDA arrived in San Francisco in 1892. American influences had already reached her in Japan. She was Protestant, western-oriented, and one of the first women who dared to speak in Meiji, Japan, before a mixed audience of men and women. She intended to get an education in the United States and return to her home country, but her experience, like that of so many other immigrants, did not go according to plan. Instead of studying, she married another Japanese Christian and settled in Oakland. There she raised her children and became a leader of the Issei (first-generation Japanese American) community. She saw to it that her daughters got the education she did not.[1]

The life of Shige Kushida Togasaki illustrates two grand historical processes that were reshaping American society at the end of the nineteenth century. First, the United States was beginning an unprecedented wave of immigration, which brought with it tremendous social challenges and national transformations. Second, the western part of the continent was being consolidated into the American nation. The frontier—in the sense of a westward-moving line of American settlement—was entering its final stages and, according to the 1890 census, coming to a close. Western settlement, which seems like a quintessentially American phenomenon, and mass immigration, which brought the nation into greater interaction with the rest of the world, shared important links. Both involved enormous movements of people across oceans and continents, bringing different cultures into contact and sometimes into conflict. Both involved efforts to "Americanize," sometimes violently, different cultures into the national mainstream. Both developments were motivated at the individual level by hopes for better lives, greater prosperity, and more personal freedom. And yet both processes dashed hopes as much as they realized them, among the immigrant poor and especially among the Native Americans pushed aside by continuing westward expansion.

Mass immigration and the consolidation of the West together helped to set the stage for a major economic and political crisis in the 1890s, as discontented immigrants, farmers, and wage workers found ways to challenge what they saw as a failure of America's democratic promise, notably the unequal distribution of America's new wealth and the unwillingness of the two established political parties to offer any vision of a better social and political path. The resolution of the crisis in favor of corporate power and the established political parties prepared the way for America's first forays abroad as an imperial power.

In all these developments — western consolidation, mass immigration, the political and economic crises of the 1890s, and the beginnings of American imperialism — women were involved, active, influential, and, as a result, changed. In the great movements of people into and through American society in the late nineteenth century, men initially predominated, but women soon followed. When they did, families were formed and temporary population shifts became permanent new communities. By the early twentieth century, American women's participation in the radical challenges of the 1890s, along with their support for or criticism of their country's ventures abroad, had made them a significant new force in U.S. political life.

CONSOLIDATING THE WEST

American settlement reached the Pacific Coast before the Civil War, but the continent's broad heartland remained largely Indian territory. This changed in the last decades of the nineteenth century as white settlement and expansion

1890	Federal census declares that frontier line is "closed"
1891	**Queen Liliuokalani becomes monarch of nation of Hawaii**
1892	Immigrant receiving station established at Ellis Island in New York City harbor
1892	People's Party formed in St. Louis
1893	Illinois Factory and Workshop Inspection Act passed
1893	Frederick Jackson Turner delivers paper, "The Significance of the Frontier in American History"
1893	**Colorado women win equal voting rights with men**
1893– 1894	National economic depression
1894	Pullman strike and national railroad disruption
1896	**Idaho women enfranchised**
1896	Populist Party collapses as William McKinley defeats William Jennings Bryan for president
1896	**Mary Harris ("Mother") Jones's fame as labor agitator begins**
1898	United States goes to war against Spain in Cuba
1898	United States annexes Hawaii
1899– 1902	United States fights Filipino independence movement
1900	**Zitkala-Ša's autobiographical writings begin to appear in the *Atlantic Monthly***
1903	President Theodore Roosevelt speaks out against "race suicide"
1907	U.S. and Japanese governments issue "Gentlemen's Agreement" to limit Japanese immigration
1910	Mexican Revolution spurs immigration to the United States
1910	Angel Island immigrant receiving station established in San Francisco Bay

overtook the Great Plains. The tremendous postbellum growth in industrial capitalism traced in Chapter 6 had as one of its major consequences the steady integration of the entire continent into the national economy. The growth of the cross-continental railroad system constituted the infrastructure for a booming national market that could provide eager consumers throughout the country with the beef and wheat and lumber produced in abundance in the broad expanse of the trans-Mississippi West.

These western lands were consolidated as part of the American nation through two main processes, which were distinguished as much by their gender practices as by anything else. Large numbers of single men and a few women went west to realize quick profits or find jobs in the region's mines and on its cattle ranges. This form of American expansion has long been celebrated as the "Wild West" in national legend and popular culture. But there was also a "Family West" in which settlers domesticated the prairies of America's heartland. Women and women's labor were as fundamental to this West as men and men's labor were to the other.

Native Women in the West

Despite their differences, both kinds of westerners shared a basic premise: Indians would have to be removed to make way for the new settlers, for their economic ambitions, and for what they regarded as their superior civilization. Here, the U.S. Army, fresh from its victory over the Confederacy, was crucial. After 1865, federal forces moved with full strength against the western tribes to wrest control of the Great Plains and open these huge interior expanses to white settlement. Native American raids against encroaching white settlers provoked military retaliation in an escalating series of wars that wore away at Native unity and resources. There were occasional Indian victories, most famously the 1876 Battle of the Little Big Horn in Montana, in which assembled Lakota Sioux warriors annihilated the U.S. Seventh Cavalry commanded by George A. Custer. The army was able to keep Native peoples in a state of constant defense, wearing away at their ability to resist.

Bands of Native Americans who resisted pacification were regarded as "hostiles" who could be killed with impunity by Americans. Made up not only of male warriors but also of women and children, they moved constantly to elude pursuing troops. One of the last such groups was Geronimo's band of Warm Springs Apache. His female lieutenant, Lozen, exemplified the Native American practice of allowing exceptional individuals to cross the gender divide. Lozen never married, was skilled in tracking the enemy, and performed the spiritual and military duties of a true warrior. Her brother called her "strong as a man, braver than most, and cunning in strategy."[2] For almost a decade, she helped her people evade and attack the U.S. Army, until the Apaches finally surrendered in southern New Mexico in 1886.

The massacre at Wounded Knee Creek in South Dakota in the winter of 1890 is often cited as the tragic end to the so-called Indian Wars. Following their defeat at the Little Big Horn, army troops had relentlessly pursued the Lakota Sioux.

Deeply dispirited, the Lakotas began to practice a new religion, the Ghost Dance, which promised restoration of their traditional lands and lives. Male and female dancers alike wore special robes, said to be designed by a woman, that they believed would protect them against bullets fired by white people. Believing that the Ghost Dance signaled a new organized insurgency, skittish soldiers fired on a camp of mostly unarmed native people, killing many hundred. "Women with little children on their backs" were gunned down, one white witness to the Wounded Knee massacre recalled, and it was many days before their frozen bodies could be retrieved and buried in a mass grave.[3]

Assaults against the Plains Indians took forms other than outright military conflict. By the 1880s, hunters and soldiers with new high-powered rifles had decimated the buffalo herds that were the material basis of Plains Indians' traditional way of life. The Plains peoples were thus vulnerable to forced relocations on government reservations of the sort that had been pioneered in the 1850s among Pacific Coast tribes (see Map 7.1). Allegedly designed to protect Indians from aggressive white settlers, these reservations instead became "virtual prisons."[4] Unable to support themselves by either farming or hunting, reservation Indians were dependent on food and clothing doled out by federal agents, who often embezzled as much as they dispensed. Instead of their traditional role in gathering and preparing food, Indian women were relegated to standing in long lines, waiting for rations that frequently did not come.

After serving the U.S. Army as translator and scout, Sarah Winnemucca became a crusader against the reservation system (see pp. 258–59). Her people, the Paiute, had been grossly exploited by the government agent who administered their Nevada reservation and who refused to dispense stores allocated to them. They were then relocated to a reservation in Washington Territory, where they lived uneasily among other Native peoples. Winnemucca traveled from California to Massachusetts to describe the sufferings of her people to white audiences, and even met with President Rutherford B. Hayes, but to no avail.

In conjunction with establishing reservations, U.S. policy coerced Native children into government-run boarding schools to be forcibly reeducated in the values and ways of dominant American culture. By the 1890s, several thousand children per year were removed from their parents' control and sent to schools where they were made to stop dressing, speaking, thinking, and believing "like Indians." Half the students were girls, whose forcible reeducation was regarded as crucial to the cultural transformation of the Native population. All too frequently, Native girls' assimilation into American culture consisted of training in menial occupations and in American standards of domesticity, which they learned as servants in the homes of nearby white families.

The goal of such programs was to save the child by destroying the Indian, but the transformations sought were elusive. Evidence of repeated and harsh punishments testifies to the refusal of girls as well as boys to give up their Indian ways. One elderly Indian woman recalled later, "Two of our girls ran away . . . but they got caught. They tied their legs up, tied their hands behind their backs, put them in the middle of the hallway so that if they fell asleep or something, the matron

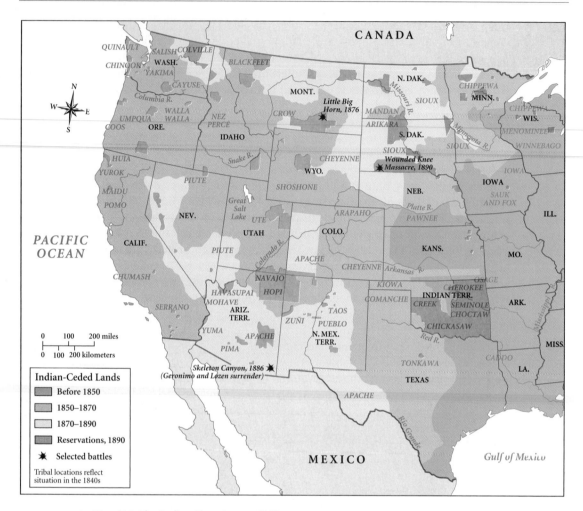

◆ **Map 7.1 The Indian Frontier, to 1890**
As settlers pushed westward after the Civil War, Native Americans put up bitter resistance
but ultimately to no avail. Over a period of decades, they ceded most of their lands to the
federal government. By 1890, they were confined to scattered reservations where the most
they could expect was an impoverished and alien way of life. *Map reproduced courtesy of Colin
Calloway.*

would hear them and she'd get out there and whip them and make them stand up
again."[5] Parents and tribal leaders protested the brutality of this coercive Americanization, but they could not stop it.

Some Native American women, however, were able to acquire English literacy and other useful skills in the boarding school system. They worked in reservation agencies and became teachers. A few, such as the Yankton Sioux writer
Gertrude Simmons Bonnin and the Omaha sisters Susan and Susette La Flesche,

became public advocates for their people. Sponsored by the white women of the Woman's National Indian Association to attend the Women's Medical College of Pennsylvania, Susan La Flesche graduated in 1889 to become the first white-trained Native woman physician. She served her people for many years, both as a doctor and as a political leader. Susette La Flesche was a writer and speaker on behalf of Indian causes. She helped to convert several influential white women to the cause of Indian reform, including Helen Hunt Jackson, author of the influential exposé of government mistreatment of Native peoples, *A Century of Dishonor* (see box, "A Century of Dishonor"). Bonnin became a writer and activist for Native American causes (see Documents: Zitkala-Ša: Indian Girlhood and Education, pp. 422–26).

Protests against the corruptions of the reservation system led in 1887 to congressional passage of the Dawes Severalty Act, which divided reservation lands into allotments for individual Native families, the remaining acreage to be sold to non-Indians. Allotment was meant as a reform alternative to demeaning reservation existence, but the way the system played out by no means ended Native peoples' misery. Where land was not very fertile, Native American families could not support themselves; and where the land could be productively farmed, whites

◆ **Before and After Americanization**
These "before-and-after" pictures of Indian children at government-run boarding schools were common in the late nineteenth century and were sometimes sent to philanthropic donors to illustrate the schools' success in Americanizing Indians (see also Figure 6.4, p. 374). Within a little more than a year, these three girls sat on chairs, not the floor, and had lost their blankets and braids, but they retained their sad faces. The book on the lap of Sarah Walker, the girl on the right in the "after" photograph, was meant to indicate her literacy, but we cannot know whether she had really learned how to read. © *2008 PFHC. Peabody Museum.* 2004.24.30439A; 2004.24.30440A.

HELEN HUNT JACKSON
A Century of Dishonor

Published five years after the nation's centennial, Helen Hunt Jackson's A Century of Dishonor *(1881) documents how U.S. Native American policy violated America's promise of liberty and freedom. The book helped catalyze public awareness of the corruptions and cruelties of the reservation system. Three years later, Jackson (1830–1885) drew on some of the same material for her popular California novel,* Ramona *(see p. 260).*

[W]e may hold nations to standards of justice and good faith as we hold men . . . [and that] a nation that steals and lies and breaks promises will be no more respected or unpunished than a man who steals and lies and breaks promises. . . . The history of the United States Government's repeated violations of faith with the Indians thus convicts us, as a nation, not only of having outraged the principles of justice, which are the basis of international law; and of having laid ourselves open to the accusation of both cruelty and perfidy; but of having made ourselves liable to all punishments which follow upon such sins — to arbitrary punishment at the hands of any civilized nation who might see fit to call us to account, and to that more certain natural punishment which, sooner or later, as surely comes from evil-doing as harvests come from sown seed.

To prove all this it is only necessary to study the history of any one of the Indian tribes. I propose to give in the following chapters merely outline sketches of the history of a few of them, not entering more into details than is necessary to show the repeated broken faith of the United States Government toward them. A full history of the wrongs they have suffered at the hands of the authorities, military and civil, and also of the citizens of this country, it would take years to write and volumes to hold. . . .

So long as there remains on our frontier one square mile of land occupied by a weak and helpless owner, there will be a strong and unscrupulous frontiersman ready to seize it, and a weak and unscrupulous politician, who can be hired for a vote or for money, to back him.

The only thing that can stay this is a mighty outspoken sentiment and purpose of the great body of the people. Right sentiment and right purpose in a Senator here and there, and a Representative here and there, are little more than straws which make momentary eddies, but do not obstruct the tide.

SOURCE: Helen Hunt Jackson, *A Century of Dishonor: A Sketch of the United States Government's Dealings with Some of the Indian Tribes* (New York: Harper and Brothers, 1881), 29–31.

managed to gain control. The allotment program also deepened the dependency of Indian women on their men, following the pattern of white society. In contrast to communal landholding and farming practices, the allotment program meant that women who chose to divorce their husbands risked the loss of economic resources under the control of male heads of household. A group of Hopi women vainly protested to the Bureau of Indian Affairs in 1894. "The family, the dwelling house and the field are inseparable" they wrote, "because the woman is the heart of these, and they rest with her."[6]

The Family West

As Native American control over the West weakened, American settlement across the vast continent continued apace. The passage of the Homestead Act in 1862 granted 160 acres to individuals willing to cultivate and "improve" the land. The railroads, themselves beneficiaries of federal largesse, also sold land to settlers to establish towns along their routes. Through this process, the broad central plains—from Minnesota to Montana to Oklahoma—were settled and Americanized. By the early twentieth century, one-quarter of the U.S. population lived west of the Mississippi.

This population was diverse. After Reconstruction, a small but steady stream of African American families was drawn west by the hope of independent farming. In all-black towns, such as Nicodemus, Kansas, and Langston, Oklahoma, African American women found ways to support their families that were less demeaning than working as domestic servants for white people. In Boley, Oklahoma, Lulu Smith started a dressmaking business; other women ran boarding-houses, catering services, and general stores.[7] European immigrants played a large role in western settlement, especially in the northern territories. In the late nineteenth century, in the period of mass immigration, one out of every two western settlers was foreign-born. The Homestead Act allowed land grants to immigrants who intended to become citizens. They, too, formed their own communities where they could live and speak and farm as they had in their home countries.

Meanwhile, in villages throughout New Mexico, Arizona, and southern California, Spanish-speaking women continued to live much as their mothers and grandmothers had. They maintained adobe homes and cultivated small plots, while the men in their families were increasingly drawn away to work in the mines, on the railroads, or on the commercial farms and ranches run by whites (known as Anglos). Ironically, while these Hispanic women were regarded by Anglo society as backward, they enjoyed considerable authority in their own communities. Local practices favored female property owning, and when widowed, women in these Hispanic enclaves preferred to head their own households rather than remarry. As the extension of the railroads brought national market pressures and a cash economy closer, however, the need for money became greater. Many of these women lost their distinctive advantages and followed their husbands into paid labor, as domestics in Anglo towns or agricultural wage laborers in Anglo fields.

◆ **San Juan Fiesta**

Many Spanish-speaking residents of the Southwest maintained their traditional village life into the late nineteenth century, even as their land and economic position were being lost to Anglo incursion. Religious holidays and life passages such as baptisms and marriages were extremely important, not just for the family but for the entire community. Women did the work of putting on these lavish events—the cooking and the making of fine clothes and also the fund-raising that made the occasions possible. This family fiesta in San Juan, a southern California town centered on its thriving mission-era church, took place about 1880. *Courtesy of the Autry National Center/Southwest Museum, Los Angeles, p.13250.*

Despite many differences, all these communities throughout the family-based West relied on women's unpaid labor, in striking contrast to the emphasis on middle-class female leisure and working-class female wage labor in the more urbanized parts of American society. Western women cooked, did laundry, and made clothes without benefit of many of the technological improvements available in more industrialized areas. While their husbands cultivated specialized commercial crops, the wives cared for animals and grew food for the family table. One Arizona woman described her morning chores: "[G]et up, turn out my chickens, draw a pail of water, . . . make a fire, put potatoes to cook, then brush and sweep half inch of dust off floor, feed three litters of chickens, then mix biscuits, get breakfast, milk, besides work in the house, and this morning had to go half mile after calves." She also contributed to her family's unending need for cash by churning twenty-four pounds of butter in four days. "Quit with a headache," she wrote in her diary. "Done too much work."[8]

Some women were inspired to try homesteading on their own. Perhaps as many as 15 percent of late nineteenth-century American homesteads were at some point controlled by women. Unmarried women who controlled their own

◆ Immigrants in the Great Plains

As with the growth of American industry, the settling of the Great Plains required immigrant labor and determination. The Homestead Act of 1862 made immigrants intending to become citizens eligible for federal land grants. Scandinavians were particularly drawn to homesteading. This Norwegian immigrant to Minnesota, Beret Olesdater Hagebak, sits alone in front of a small house made of sod, the most common building material available on the treeless plains. Her picture captures the difficult experience of immigrant farm women, who suffered both the cultural disorientation of immigration and the isolation of Plains farm life. *Photo by H. J. Chalmers, Minnesota Historical Society.*

homesteads combined two of the most irresistible resources for male settlers, land and female labor, and were besieged by marriage proposals. As one young Oklahoma woman wrote, as soon as she was awarded a claim, men started to court her: "The letters began pouring in—men wanting to marry me, men all the way from twenty-one to seventy-five."[9]

Western farm women did their homemaking in an environment where homes had to be built from scratch. On the plains, after spending the first few months living in temporary shelters, settler families would move into huts made of sod, the top layer of soil so dense with the roots of prairie grass that it could be cut into bricks. Women sprinkled their dirt walls and floors with water to keep down the dust, and decorated their unlikely homes as lavishly as they could, eager to banish the discomfort of being surrounded by dirt. Westering was an ongoing process; as families frequently moved and resettled on more promising land, it was left to the women to repeat the work of creating—both physically and emotionally—new home environments.

Of all the burdens for women settlers on the Great Plains, drudgery and loneliness seem to have been the worst, especially in the years when towns were still being established. Unlike their husbands, women rarely left the homestead—slaves, as some put it, to the cookstove and the washtub. Ignored when she complained that she "never got to go nowhere, or see anybody . . . or [do] anything but work," one Oklahoma woman packed up the children and fled. Overtaken by a wind and ice storm, she almost froze to death and ended up back at the homestead, disabled for life.[10]

The 1867 organization of the National Grange (the full title was the Order of the Patrons of Husbandry) helped to overcome women's isolation on the prairies. By the mid-1870s, three-quarters of the farmers of Kansas had joined.[11] Based on the premise that farm families had to cooperate to succeed against the corporate power of railroad and other monopolies, the Grange established farmer-run stores and grain elevators and promoted laws against unfair railroad rates. It also sponsored social and cultural events that enriched local community life and were of special importance to women, who played a prominent role in the Grange. Local chapters were required to have nine female members for every thirteen male members, and women served as officers and delegates to the national meetings. The sense of community that the Grange created prepared the way for more overtly political expressions of agricultural discontent, including the Farmers' Alliance in the late 1880s and the Populist movement of the 1890s (see pp. 411–13).

The "Wild West"

Alongside the families drawn by the promise of land and economic self-sufficiency were other westerners pursuing riskier schemes for getting rich. Both groups Americanized the West, but in different ways. While family settlement imported the American social and cultural values of industriousness and domesticity, these other westerners brought with them industrial capitalism, wage labor, and subor-

◆ On the Way to the Dance

Mary Hallock, the well-known late nineteenth-century artist and writer, got her start in New York literary circles, through her friendships with Helena De Kay and publisher George Gilder. In 1876, she married mining engineer Arthur Foote and spent all but the very last years of her long life in the West. She wrote and drew extensively out of these experiences, adapting the romantic conventions of Victorian literature to the excitement and exotic qualities of western life. This illustration accompanied a short story, written by Foote, provocatively entitled "The Rapture of Hetty." This image reinterprets the rituals of courtship where the wide open spaces of the West, rather than the flimsy buildings, dominate the landscape. How does Hallock's heroine subtly diverge from images of young women in the East? *From* The Century, *December 1891; courtesy of the Huntington Library, San Marino, CA.*

dination to growing corporate power. Despite their status as icons of individual freedom, the colorful cowboys of the cattle range and the grizzled miners of the gold and silver strikes were wage laborers and therefore suffered from wage dependence as much as industrial workers in New York and Chicago.

The contrasts between the Wild West and the Family West are particularly clear in terms of the radically different gender practices on which they rested. In the mines and cattle ranges, women wage earners were rare. Annie Oakley's riding and roping skills made her a featured player in Buffalo Bill Cody's Wild West Show in the 1890s, but cowgirls were a staple only in the Wild West of popular culture. The rapidly expanding female labor force found elsewhere in America existed in the West only in the largest cities, such as Denver, San Francisco, and Seattle.

There were other sorts of women in the Wild West, however. At first, most were prostitutes. Like the miners and cowboys who were their customers, they were black and white, English- and Spanish-speaking, native- and foreign-born. Initially, many of these women worked for themselves, as what one historian calls "proprietor prostitutes."[12] A few were able to earn or marry their way into respectable society. Others bought or rented brothels, hired other women, and became successful, if disreputable, businesswomen. In 1890, in Helena, Montana, one of the most prosperous real estate entrepreneurs was an Irish-born former prostitute, "Chicago Joe." But for most, prostitution was a thoroughly losing proposition. Two-thirds of prostitutes died young of sexually transmitted diseases, botched abortions, alcohol abuse, suicide, or homicide. As in other western businesses, the initial period of entrepreneurial exuberance was replaced by consolidated ownership. By the early twentieth century, men — pimps, landlords, and police — enjoyed most of the profits from western prostitution.

More respectable women — some rich, most poor — gradually began to move to western centers of industry. The wives of western mine owners lived in expensive, elegant homes, hired servants, and imported luxuries. The determination of a few to use their husbands' fortunes on behalf of their own social and philanthropic ambitions was legendary. Phoebe Appleton Hearst, whose husband got rich in the mines of California and Nevada, was a major benefactor of the University of California at Berkeley. Margaret (Molly) Tobin Brown, the daughter of Irish Catholic immigrants, married one of the rare individual prospectors to become wealthy off the mines. She bought and refurnished an elegant Denver mansion, hired tutors to teach her the ways of the upper class, and became a generous civic donor. In 1912, she survived the sinking of the ill-fated *Titanic*, earning herself the nickname of "Unsinkable Molly Brown."

At the other end of the class scale, wage-earning miners and cowboys also formed families. The immigrant copper miners of Anaconda, Montana, married the young Irish women who worked as domestic servants for their bosses or as waitresses in the local hotels. Mexican miners in Colorado brought their wives north to live with them and settled permanently in the United States. These working-class wives rarely took jobs outside the home, although they did earn money by feeding and housing single male miners, cowboys, and lumberjacks.

Western housewives lived with the constant fear of losing their husbands to violent death on the range or in the mines. Recognizing that unions would fight to raise wages and make working conditions safer, they were strong supporters of organized labor. They formed union auxiliaries that were very active during the militant strikes that rocked the region. In Cripple Creek, Colorado, miners' wives were involved in 1893 when the radical Western Federation of Miners won higher wages and in 1904 when the state militia drove union activists out of town. By far the most prominent female labor activist in the region was the legendary Irish-born Mary Harris ("Mother") Jones, who began her career as an organizer for miners' unions in the late 1890s. Mother Jones focused her attention on the miners—her "boys"—but she also understood the power of miners' wives and organized them into "mop and broom brigades" that were an effective tool against strikebreakers. Referring to one of the family dynasties most identified with corporate greed, Jones declared: "God Almighty made women and the Rockefeller gang of thieves made the ladies."[13]

Jones's contempt for female gentility notwithstanding, western working-class wives were as careful as women of the leisure classes to maintain a distinction between their own status as respectable women and the status of the disreputable women who had preceded them. Family life was gradually displacing the world of the dance halls and brothels. Respectable women took care not to live in the same areas as "fast" women. "If the world of work was divided into laborers and employers," writes one historian of the western female experience, "the world of women was divided into good women and bad."[14]

LATE NINETEENTH-CENTURY IMMIGRATION

While Americans were moving westward in the late nineteenth century, immigrants were pouring into the country, 27 million in the half century after 1880. These numbers dwarfed pre–Civil War immigration (see pp. 202–04). Five million came from Italy and an equal number from Germany, as well as 2 million Eastern European Jews, 1 million Polish Catholics, and 1 million Scandinavians. A small but growing number of Asians and Mexicans also came to the United States in these years. By 1910, Asians constituted 2 percent of all arriving immigrants. Numbers of Mexican immigrants are harder to determine. Until 1924, when the U.S. Border Patrol was established, the Mexican-U.S. border was virtually unregulated, and those crossing back and forth melded into already existing Spanish-speaking communities. This massive immigration turned the United States into an ethnically and religiously diverse people, no longer preponderantly English and Protestant but now broadly European, with a growing minority of resident Asians and Mexicans.

The gender patterns of these immigrations were complex. Among Slavic, Greek, and Italian immigrants, more men than women came to the United States. However, many men came as temporary workers and returned eventually to their homelands. As they did, and as more women came to marry those who remained, sex ratios tended to even out. Some groups, notably Eastern European Jews and new Irish immigrants, initially came in more gender-balanced numbers. Eventually, women constituted between 30 and 40 percent of all immigrants (see the Appendix, p. A-40) in these years.

The Decision to Immigrate

Women decided to leave their homelands and come to the United States for many reasons, some of which they shared with men. Faced with poverty, limited opportunity, and rigid class structures at home, families dispatched members to work in the United States and send money back. The booming U.S. economy had an insatiable need for workers in its factories, mines, and kitchens, and it lured men and women alike with its promises of high wages and easy prosperity. "This was the time . . . when America was known to foreigners as the land where you'd get rich," remembered Pauline Newman, who arrived from Lithuania in 1901. "There's gold on the sidewalk! All you have to do is pick it up."[15] Political persecution also pushed people out of their homelands. Jews began emigrating in large numbers in the 1880s to escape growing anti-Semitism in Eastern Europe, especially the violent, deadly riots called pogroms. Similarly, the upheavals that culminated in the Mexican Revolution of 1910 drove men and women north.

Young women also had their own distinctive reasons for emigrating. Many were drawn by the reputation that the United States was developing as a society that welcomed independence for women. A common story for young women of all groups involved fleeing from an overbearing, patriarchal father and from the threat of an arranged marriage. That was why Emma Goldman fled Russia in 1885. Upon arriving in the United States, she began a life of political activism that eventually made her the most notorious radical in the United States (see box, "Living My Life").

Other women came to the United States as wives or to become wives, to join husbands who had migrated before them or to complete marriages arranged in the old country. The Japanese government encouraged male immigrants to send back to Japan for women to marry. These women in turn sent letters and photographs to their potential husbands. This was a modern version of a traditional Japanese practice, but *shaskin kekkon* (literally, "photograph marriages") were regarded by Americans as akin to prostitution and still another indication of the allegedly low morals of Asians. Similar arrangements were common among European immigrants. Rachel Kahn came from Ukraine to North Dakota in 1894 to marry a Russian immigrant farmer with whom she had only exchanged pictures.[16]

Some women undoubtedly migrated for reasons so personal and painful that they were hidden from public view. Unmarried women who had become pregnant might flee or be sent away so that the scandal could be more easily hidden. The father of Lucja Krajulis's child would not marry her but sent her instead to the United States, where she was shuttled about among fellow Lithuanians.[17] During the 1910 Mexican Revolution, women in the countryside were raped by armed marauders, and crossing the border provided them escape from their shame.

The Immigrant's Journey

Having decided to move to the United States, immigrant women had many obstacles to negotiate. Passage in the steerage class of a transoceanic steamship in 1900 cost the modern equivalent of $400. It took ten to twenty days to cross from Italy to New York and twice as long from Japan to San Francisco, during which time passengers slept in cramped, unhealthy conditions below deck. One can only imagine the experience of pregnant women or mothers of infants. Photos of arriving immigrants show dazed women, with babies held tightly in their arms and older children clinging to their skirts.

EMMA GOLDMAN
Living My Life

Emma Goldman (1869–1940) was raised by an overbearing father and an uninterested stepmother. She was already interested in radical politics before she left Russia in 1885 to follow her sister Helena to become a garment worker in Rochester, New York. Within a few years she had become deeply involved with the anarchist movement. Her autobiography, Living My Life *(1931), is one of the most widely read life stories in American women's history.*

Helena also hated to leave me behind. She knew of the bitter friction that existed between Father and me. She offered to pay my fare, but Father would not consent to my going. I pleaded, begged, wept. Finally I threatened to jump into the Neva [River], whereupon he yielded. Equipped with twenty-five roubles — all that the old man would give me — I left without regrets. Since my earliest recollection, home had been stifling, my father's presence terrifying. . . . [Father] had tried desperately to marry me off at the age of fifteen. I had protested, begging to be permitted to continue my studies. In his frenzy he threw my French grammar into the fire, shouting: "Girls do not have to learn much! All a Jewish daughter needs to know is how to prepare gefüllte fish, cut noodles fine, and give the man plenty of children." I would not listen to his schemes; I wanted to study, to know life, to travel. Besides, I never would marry for anything but love, I stoutly maintained. It was really to escape my father's plans for me that I had insisted on going to America.

SOURCE: Emma Goldman, *Living My Life* (1931; New York: Courier Dover Publications, 1970), 1:11.

In 1892, the first federal receiving station for immigrants was established on Ellis Island in New York City harbor. The majority of immigrants were passed through quickly, although individuals judged "unfit" for admission could be isolated, confined, and eventually deported. Asian women were more likely to be kept for long periods at Angel Island, the equivalent site established in San Francisco Bay in 1910. Assumed to be sexually immoral, they were detained until they could establish their respectability by answering endless questions (for which they had carefully prepared) about themselves and the men they planned to marry. "Had I known it was like this," a thirty-year-old Chinese mother recalled, "I never would have wanted to come."[18]

Young European women in transit were regarded as sexually vulnerable rather than sexually immoral. Stories circulated of unaccompanied and disoriented immigrant girls tricked or forced into prostitution. This phenomenon was known at the time as "white slavery," a term that invoked memories of chattel (black) slavery. Feared as an international conspiracy to waylay and prostitute young women, white slavery was a major focus for anxieties about women and immigration. The actual extent of the practice is unknown.

Many immigrants kept on moving beyond their point of arrival in the United States, following friends or family or rumors of work. By the turn of the century, the populations of large midwestern cities such as Chicago and Milwaukee were preponderantly foreign-born. Numerous mining towns of the West were dense with immigrants as well. Many immigrants, wishing to retain something of their familiar homeland, preferred to live among people from their own village or region, but this could leave them ignorant of much about their new surroundings. Reformer Jane Addams told the poignant story of an Italian woman who had never seen roses in the few blocks of Chicago that she knew, thought they grew only in Italy, and feared that she would never enjoy their beauty again.[19]

Reception of the Immigrants

The United States' pride in its status as a nation of immigrants is embodied in New York harbor's Statue of Liberty, a giant female figure presented to the United States by the people of France in 1885 to represent the two countries' common embrace of liberty. The poem inscribed on the statue's base was written by Emma Lazarus, a descendant of Sephardic Jews who had arrived in the mid-seventeenth century. The words she wrote welcome the world's oppressed, those "huddled masses yearning to breathe free, / The wretched refuse of your teeming shore." But Lazarus's sentiment was not the norm. In the late nineteenth century, most native-born Americans regarded the incoming masses as disturbingly different aliens who could never assimilate.

Anti-immigrant legislation initially targeted Asians. The Page Law of 1875, the very first federal legislation meant to discourage immigration, was directed at Chinese women, on the assumption that most were prostitutes. In 1882, Congress passed a more comprehensive law, the Chinese Exclusion Act, which banned further immigration of Chinese laborers and their families. The few women who could prove that they were the wives or daughters of Chinese merchants already living in the United States were exempted. Once Chinese immigration had virtually ceased, Japanese workers began to come to the United States, but by the 1890s, anti-Asian sentiment on the West Coast had surfaced against them as well. In 1907, in the so-called Gentlemen's Agreement, the U.S. and Japanese governments agreed to restrict further immigration.

Laws against European immigrants, who were far more central to the U.S. economy, were not passed until 1921 and 1924, when highly restrictive national quotas were established, remaining in place until 1965 (see p. 761). Even before these laws, European immigrants were the targets of considerable prejudice and resentment. Degrading ethnic stereotypes were widely circulated as innocently amusing. (See Visual Sources: Women in the Cartoons of *Puck* Magazine, pp. 441–48.) Southern and Eastern European immigrants were seen as peoples whose strangeness and

State of California,
CITY AND COUNTY OF SAN FRANCISCO.

Chin Lung, a resident of San Francisco, being duly sworn according to law, deposes and says that he is a member of the firm of Sing Kee & Company No. 808 Sacramento Street in said City:

That his wife Leung Yee was a resident of this City for 5 or 6 years, and that she left this City per Steamship "*Belgic*" sailing for Hong Kong on the ____ day of October 1889.

That his daughter, Ah Kum, was born in San Francisco at No. 613 Dupont Street, in 1885, and left San Francisco with her mother in October 1889. *Chin Lung*

Subscribed and sworn to before me, this 1st day of *May* A.D. 1892.

F. B. Hoyt.
NOTARY PUBLIC.

◆ A Document of Chinese Immigration

Through diligent research, historian Judy Yung uncovered this sworn testimony given by her great-grandfather of her great-grandmother's immigration to the United States in 1892. She found that there were several strategic lies embedded within the document. First, his wife Leung Yee had not lived in the United States previously but was immigrating for the first time in 1892. Second, the daughter that she claimed on this document was in fact a young servant of the family. Such deceits were necessary—and common—to circumvent the prohibitions of the Chinese Exclusion Act of 1882. *File 12017/37232 for Leong Shee, Chinese Departure Application Case Files, 1912–1943, San Francisco District Office, Immigration and Naturalization Service, Record Group 85, National Archives and Records Administration—Pacific Region, San Bruno, CA.*

difference were fundamental, physical, and ineradicable. Religion was a major concern. The hundreds of thousands of Jews who arrived from Eastern Europe after 1880 were the first major group of non-Christians to settle in the United States. Even Catholics were regarded by American Protestants as so emotional and superstitious as barely to be fellow believers in Christ. Their devotion to a foreign pope was the source of much suspicion. Anti-Semitic and anti-Catholic attitudes abounded even among otherwise liberal-minded Americans. Susan B. Anthony could not understand by what logic "these Italians come over with the idea that they must be paid as much as intelligent white men."[20]

Americans were especially wary of immigrant gender relations, regarding their own attitudes as modern and those of the newcomers as Old World and patriarchal. They were particularly uneasy with the reproductive behavior of immigrant women. While the birthrates of native-born women had been falling for some time (see pp. 346–48), immigrant families were large. In 1903, President Theodore Roosevelt, concerned that immigrants' higher birthrates were overtaking those of native-born Americans, charged middle-class women who were working or going to college instead of having babies with responsibility for what he called "race suicide." "If the women do not recognize that the greatest thing for any woman is to be a good wife and mother," he declared in the introduction to *The Woman Who Toils* (see pp. 363–68), "why, that nation has cause to be alarmed about its future."[21] After some time in the United States, however, immigrant women started to want smaller families, too. Margaret Sanger, herself the daughter of Irish immigrants, founded the American birth control movement in the 1910s as a response to immigrant women's pleas for reliable ways to prevent unwanted pregnancy (see pp. 480–81).

Starting about 1910, settlement houses and other civic institutions initiated deliberate Americanization campaigns to assimilate immigrants into mainstream U.S. culture. While these programs did not regard immigrants as permanently alien to American society, they did look on their languages, religions, and cultural practices as foreign. Women's household routines were a particular object for reform, as were practices such as arranged marriages that seemed to violate American standards of family life. These Americanization programs became harsher during World War I, when nativism became much stronger and immigrants' patriotism was questioned.

Immigrant Daughters

Immigrant mothers and daughters confronted America very differently. Low wages made it difficult for immigrant men to meet the American standard of being the sole support of their families. Secondary wage earners were usually teenage children, not wives. Just as their families needed their earnings, the expanding labor force needed immigrant daughters' labor. Young girls were plunged immediately into the booming American economy, while their mothers remained largely homebound.

Young immigrant women predominated in the two largest categories of female wage labor, domestic labor and factory work. German, Polish, and Mexican girls met the late nineteenth-century middle-class demand for servants. By contrast, Italian parents did not want their daughters to work as servants in strange households and preferred that they take jobs where other family members could oversee their activities, such as in seasonal fruit picking.

Young immigrant women were also drawn into factory work, making their greatest contribution to the garment industry. The mass production of clothes in the United States could not have occurred without their labor. By 1890, one out of three garment workers was a woman, and most of those women were immigrants. Some — Russian Jews, Japanese, Italians — had worked in clothing factories in their home countries. New York and Chicago were the centers of the ready-made clothing industry in the United States, but garment factories filled with immigrant workers could be found throughout the country, from El Paso to San Francisco to Baltimore. Paid by the piece and pushed to work ever more quickly, young women earned low wages and risked occupational injuries. Sexual harassment was an additional problem for young immigrant women factory workers, as it was hard not to yield to the foremen who controlled their jobs.

Most of these young women workers lived with parents or other relatives, where intergenerational relations could be very tense. More than their brothers, girls were expected to turn over most of their wages to their parents. Mothers needed the money for household expenses, but daughters longed to spend some of their earnings on themselves. Disagreements did not end there. Daughters wanted to dress in the modern style, while mothers wanted them to look and behave like respectable girls in the old country. Battles could be even more intense with fathers. No one resisted Old World patriarchy more intensely than its daughters. The Russian Jewish novelist Anzia Yezierska wrote often of this theme. "Should I let him crush me as he crushed [my sisters]?" a character in her 1925 novel, *Bread Givers*, said of her father. "No. This is America. Where children are people. . . . It's a new life now. In America, women don't need men to boss them."[22]

Immigrant Wives and Mothers

While unmarried immigrant women were more likely to be wage earners than native-born women, the opposite was true of their mothers — very few of whom worked outside their homes. This behavior was not simply a carryover of Old World standards; Eastern European Jewish wives, for instance, had traditionally been shopkeepers or market vendors. Given the family wage system in the United States, however, adult immigrant women had difficulty finding paid work. Immigrant wives were nonetheless expected to contribute to the family economy. Because of the numbers of single male immigrants and the preference of many groups for living among people from their own country, boarding was very common among immigrants. Middle-class observers, who regarded familial privacy as sacred, condemned the immigrant practice of boarders living within families. Immigrants recognized the tensions but regarded them more tolerantly, and stories of liaisons between amorous boarders and discontented housewives were a source of much amusement in immigrant culture.

Women's housekeeping and childrearing tasks were daunting, both because of poverty and the surrounding alien culture. In densely populated cities, apartments were crowded and residents still relied on backyard wells and outdoor privies, augmented by public baths. Children playing on busy city streets required added supervision. Women hauled water up flights of stairs, purchased coal and wood for fuel, and fought a constant battle against ash and soot. Photographer Jacob Riis did pioneering work documenting these conditions. (See Visual Sources: Jacob Riis's Photographs of Immigrant Girls and Women, pp. 434–40.) Even so, American observers were frequently astonished at the levels of cleanliness immigrant women were able to maintain. While middle-class women dealt with their domestic obligations by hiring immigrant servants, immigrant women had no choice but to do their own scrubbing and ironing.

Immigrant mothers had responsibility for preserving customary ways against the tremendous forces working to Americanize them and their families. They continued to cook traditional foods and observe religious obligations, while their husbands and children entered into the American economic mainstream to make the family's living. As practices that were ancient and reflexive became deliberate and problematic, it fell to women to defend and perpetuate the old ways, thus laying the basis for what would eventually become American ethnic identity. Such practices constituted implicit resistance to the forces of Americanization and cultural homogenization. For the time being, however, such immigrant mothers were dismissed by their children as old-fashioned and quaint, their skills and knowledge irrelevant to the new world that their daughters mastered with such verve. Once again, Jane Addams subtly captured the emotional tenor of this role reversal in her description of the dilemma of immigrant women in search of runaway children in Chicago: "It is as if they did not know how to search for their children without the assistance of the children themselves."[23]

Despite these obstacles, adult immigrant women helped to construct lasting ethnic communities. In the mining town of Anaconda, Montana, Irish women, struggling to meet their family needs, nonetheless raised money to build St. Patrick's Catholic Church in 1888. This story was repeated in the immigrant neighborhoods within which the American Catholic church developed. Occasionally, immigrant wives' community activism took a political turn, as in 1902, when New York City Jewish women demonstrated against the rising cost of meat in the city's kosher markets. Like native-born middle-class women, late nineteenth-century immigrant women formed and joined associations, but for different reasons. They had been drawn to the United States by the promise of greater freedom, if not for themselves, then for their children. But they were learning that to realize that promise, they had to find ways to work together.

CENTURY'S END: CHALLENGES, CONFLICT, AND IMPERIAL VENTURES

For many of the women who immigrated to the United States or who migrated across the continent, the American dream remained elusive. Their frustrated hopes helped to fuel a dramatic crisis at century's end. The national economy, which had gone through a series of boom and bust cycles since the beginnings of industrialization in the 1830s, experienced its greatest economic crisis yet in 1893, as overextension of the railroad system, decline in gold reserves, and international collapse in agricultural prices set off a long, deep economic contraction that kept layoffs high, wages low, and economic growth stalled for four years. In the cities, the newest immigrants bore the brunt of massive unemployment and deep family disruption. In the agricultural heartland, crops could not be sold at a profit, and family farms failed. Factory workers and farmers were not natural allies; they were not even particularly sympathetic to each other. Nonetheless, the two groups moved together to confront the wealthy strata that ruled a complacent nation. The turmoil of the 1890s unleashed an unprecedented wave of industrial strikes and raised the prospects for a political movement, Populism, that mounted the first systematic challenge to entrenched political power since the rise of the Republican Party in the 1850s.

In the hotly contested presidential contest of 1896, the pro-business Republican candidate William McKinley defeated the Democratic-Populist nominee William Jennings Bryan, ending for the time being these challenges to entrenched power. In the wake of their victory, corporate leaders and Republican politicians brought the United States to join European nations in the race to acquire overseas colonies.

Women were active everywhere in the crises of the 1890s. They were the victims of desperate economic conditions, ardent supporters of strikes, spokeswomen for political challenges, and supporters and opponents of the new imperial ventures. In two especially important ways—winning the first victories for woman suffrage in the West and establishing settlement houses to assist urban immigrants—the decade brought American women to a new level of political prominence.

Rural Protest, Populism, and the Battle for Woman Suffrage

The years after Reconstruction were difficult for American farmers. With the dream of economic independence and self-sufficiency receding, farming families were driven into debt by the pressures of falling prices and rising costs. Culturally, rural Americans also felt that they were losing ground—and often their children—to the magnet of city life. The powerful railroad corporations that set rates for transporting their crops were a particular target of farmers' anger. "It is an undeniable fact that the condition of the farmer and their poor drudging wives is every year becoming more intolerable," Minnesotan Mary Travis complained in 1880. "We are robbed and crowded to the wall on every side, our crop [is] taken for whatever the middlemen are of a mind to give us, and we are obligated to give them whatever they have the force to ask for their goods or go without, and all this means so . . . much toil, and less help for the farmer's wife."[24]

The Grange led the way in the 1880s to the Farmers' Alliances. While continuing to encourage community life, the alliances emphasized the formation of farmers' buying and selling cooperatives to circumvent the powers of the banks and railroads. The Southern Alliance movement, which began in Texas in 1877, was particularly strong. In it, non-elite southern white women began to take a visible, public role. Southern black farmers organized separate Colored Farmers' Alliances, approximately half of whose 750,000 members were women. African American sharecroppers, who were trapped in debt because they had to acquire their supplies from their landlords at exorbitant credit rates, were particularly attracted to cooperatives. The People's Grocery in Memphis, the lynching of whose owner in 1892 catapulted Ida B. Wells into her reform career (see pp. 335–36), was probably one such cooperative enterprise.

By 1892, Farmers' Alliances in the Midwest came together with the Southern Alliance to form a new political party, ambitiously named the People's Party and commonly known as the Populists. Women were active in its meteoric life. Frances Willard, an important figure at the founding convention in St. Louis, brought the large and powerful Woman's Christian Temperance Union (WCTU) with her into the new effort. Several of the Populists' most successful organizers were also women. Kansan Mary Elizabeth Lease, daughter of Irish immigrants, was the fieriest of these radical female orators. "You wonder, perhaps, at the zeal and enthusiasm of the Western women in this reform movement," Lease proclaimed at the founding convention. "We endured hardships, dangers and privations, hours of loneliness, fear and sorrow; [w]e helped our loved ones to make the prairie blossom . . . yet after all our years of toil and privations, dangers and hardship upon the Western frontier, monopoly is taking our homes from us."[25]

The Populist insurgency lasted only four years, but it left an enduring mark on the history of women's rights. In the Reconstruction years, suffragists had fought for political rights via the U.S. Constitution (see pp. 326–27). During the 1890s, while national politics remained inhospitable to reform, the focus for woman suffrage, as for other democratic reforms, shifted to the state level. In several western states, the Populists endorsed woman suffrage, giving it new life.

The most important of these campaigns occurred in 1893, when the women of Colorado's suffrage societies, labor union auxiliaries, WCTU chapters, and Knights of Labor locals joined together to convince male voters to enfranchise them. In contrast to the violent, widespread class conflict in the western mining industry, the advocates of woman suffrage were proud of their ability to "work unitedly and well" for a common goal.[26] Middle- and upper-class women contributed money to hold giant women's rallies. Their respectability offset the charge that prostitutes' votes would further corrupt the world of politics. Suffragists linked their cause to struggling farmers and wage earners and asked for the vote as a tool against the entrenched power of railroads and mining corporations. "The money question has power to reach into the most sheltered home and bring want and desolation," Lease proclaimed. "Women have not invaded politics; politics have invaded the home."[27] Although suffragists had appealed to all parties, Populist support was crucial to victory. "There is less prejudice against and a stronger belief in equal rights in the newer communities," wrote suffrage journalist Ellis Meredith of this western victory. "The pressure of hard times, culminating in the panic of 1893, undoubtedly contributed to the success of the Populist Party and to its influence the suffrage cause owes much."[28] Three years later, Idaho women won a similar victory by an even greater margin.

Campaigns were also waged in Kansas and California, but they failed because of partisan conflict. In Kansas in 1894, two out of three male voters voted against woman suffrage and, according to Populist suffragist Annie Diggs, "the grief and the disappointment of the Kansas women were indescribable."[29] In 1896, the issue was put before the men of California. Seventy-six-year-old Susan B. Anthony went to the state to work for suffrage. At first, all three political parties endorsed the referendum, and labor, Socialist, Spanish-language, and immigrant newspapers also came out in its favor. But when national Populist leaders decided to campaign in the presidential election that year solely on the issue of currency reform ("free silver"), the political situation changed dramatically. The Democratic Party joined with the Populists to advocate basing the nation's currency on silver as well as gold, and the two parties "fused" behind the presidential candidacy of the charismatic Nebraskan orator William Jennings Bryan. Woman suffrage became a liability, and the Populists ceased to agitate on its behalf. Republicans turned against it, and the California referendum was defeated 45 percent to 55 percent. "We feel defeated, and it doesn't feel good," Anthony told a newspaper reporter. "But we must save ourselves for other States. 'Truth crushed to earth will rise again.'"[30]

In the South, woman suffrage, which had been held back by its association with black suffrage and with the Reconstruction-era effort to subordinate states' rights to federal authority, also got its first sustained support in the Populist era. In 1888, Texan Ann Other defended woman suffrage against its critics in the pages of the *Southern Mercury*, a Populist newspaper. "Those men who could think less of a woman because she took a judicious interest in the laws of her country would not be worth the while to mourn over," she wrote.[31]

Eventually, however, southern Populism was felled by the racial divisions inherited from slavery and deepening racial inequality at century's end. The threat of electoral cooperation between angry black and white farmers gave the final impetus to the new system of segregation and disfranchisement known as Jim Crow (see pp. 336–37).When southern suffrage campaigns resurfaced again in the twentieth century, they did so in the context of this aggressive racism, arguing for white women's votes as a means for countering black men's votes.

Nationally, the election of Republican William McKinley in 1896 signaled the defeat of the Populist movement. For women, however, the party's brief career had enormous consequences. The women of Colorado and Idaho now had full voting rights, in federal as well as state elections. Woman suffrage had become a live political issue, and its center had shifted from the Northeast, where the movement had begun, farther west, where male voters identified it with a more democratic political system. Having driven the People's Party from the electoral arena, the Republican Party absorbed some of its reform agenda. After 1896, the issue of woman suffrage passed into the hands of the reform-minded wing of the Republican Party, along with other Populist concerns, such as the impact of economic growth on the poor and the need for government regulation of corporations. As with the Populists, women activists and reformers would prove to be numerous and influential among these newly designated "Progressives" (see pp. 462–69).

◆ **Early Women Voters in Colorado, 1907**
In 1893, the Populist-controlled legislature of Colorado called for a referendum to amend
the state constitution to enfranchise women voters, the first time that the issue had been put
before large numbers of male voters. Colorado was a booming state, the center of the mining
industry, home both to the owners of great fortunes and a large, militant working class. The
woman suffrage referendum won with a strong majority, passing in over three-quarters of
the counties. Women followed up their victory by voting in substantial numbers for state
and federal offices. The pride that they took in their new status as active, voting citizens, is
obvious in the faces and stances of these women, standing with male voters outside a Denver
polling place. *Denver Public Library; Z-8811.*

Class Conflict and the Pullman Strike of 1894

Just as Populism was reaching its high point in 1893, the national economy collapsed, thousands of businesses failed, and nearly a quarter of wage workers lost
their jobs. The nation's most severe depression to date exposed critical problems
and deep social rifts. Women suffered, both as out-of-work wage earners and as
wives of unemployed men. Federal and state governments, following the laissez
faire principle of nonintervention in the marketplace, offered no help. Private
charities provided a few paying jobs — street cleaning for men and sewing for
women — but their efforts were inadequate to the need. Across much of the coun-

try, the winter of 1893–94 was one of the coldest ever recorded. Rosa Cavalleri, a recent immigrant from Italy to Chicago, recalled waiting in a line for free food: "Us poor women were frozen to death."[32] The spread of disease under such conditions — smallpox and typhoid in Chicago, diphtheria in New York — showed the middle and upper classes that, in a complex, modern society, misery and want could not be confined to one class: poverty put entire communities at risk.

For a handful, the moment promised a new American revolution. Amid rising working-class discontent, twenty-four-year-old Emma Goldman found her calling as a radical agitator and orator. She was already under suspicion for her role in the attempted assassination of the chairman of the Carnegie Steel Corporation during a violent strike at its Homestead, Pennsylvania, plant in 1892. The next year she led a phalanx of unemployed women in New York City. An advocate of anarchism, the political philosophy that condemned all government as illegitimate authority, she challenged the crowd, "Do you not realize that the State is the worst enemy you have? . . . The State is the pillar of capitalism and it is ridiculous to expect any redress from it."[33] She was arrested, tried, and sentenced to a year in prison for "inciting to riot." In jail, Goldman learned the trade of midwifery and became an advocate of sexual and reproductive freedom for working-class women.

The most dramatic of the strikes against falling wages and massive layoffs began in May 1894 at the Pullman Railroad Car Company just south of Chicago. Company founder George Pullman was proud of his paternalistic policy of providing for all his workers' needs; but now, determined to maintain profits, Pullman refused to lower rents in the company-owned housing, where employees were expected to live despite their diminished pay packets. Pullman's policy drew wives as well as women workers into the conflict. "Holding their babies close for shields," the antistrike *Chicago Tribune* reported of a workers' demonstration, "the women still break past the patrol lines and go where no man dares to step."[34] As railroad workers nationwide shut down the railroad system rather than transport Pullman cars, pressure grew on the federal government to intervene. President Grover Cleveland sent six thousand federal troops to quell riots and occupy the rail yards in Chicago. By early July, the strike was broken.

The Settlement House Movement

The Pullman strike also affected the future of middle- and upper-class women by putting a new development in female social reform, the settlement house movement, on the historical map. Settlement houses were pioneered in England in the 1880s by male college graduates who chose to live among and serve the urban poor. By 1890, settlement houses were beginning to appear in the United States, with the important difference that most of their participants were middle- and upper-class women. The most influential settlement house was Hull House, established in Chicago in 1889 by Jane Addams. (See Documents: Jane Addams and the Charitable Relation, pp. 427–33.)

Soon Hull House was serving several thousand people per week. Kindergarten and after-school classes helped immigrant mothers with child care and encouraged the spread of American values and culture. In contrast to later, more coercive forms of Americanization, however, Hull House valued immigrants for their home cultures as well. Creatively struggling with the gulf between immigrant mothers and their Americanized children, Jane Addams established the Hull House Labor Museum, where parents could demonstrate and explain to their children their traditional craft skills and thus "build a bridge between European and American experiences in such wise as to give them both more meaning."[35] Rooms were made available for union meetings and political discussion clubs. Immigrants in the neighborhood attended concerts and enjoyed the use of a gymnasium. A separate residence, named the Jane Club in homage to Addams, provided an alternative to commercial boardinghouses for young wage-earning women away from their families. "Hull-House is meant to be the centre for all the work needed around it," a sympathetic observer explained, "not committed to one line of work, but open to all that leads the way to a higher life for the people."[36]

The Pullman strike gave new prominence and impetus to the women of Hull House, who suddenly found themselves in the midst of Chicago's violent class conflict. Jane Addams, who had a reputation as an effective conciliator, was appointed to a special arbitration committee, but its members were unable to find a way to resolve the strike. Meanwhile, Florence Kelley, another Hull House member, was developing a more direct, long-term response to the frustration and demands of working-class immigrant families. The daughter of a Republican congressman and herself a Cornell University graduate, Kelley shared Addams's privileged background but had moved further beyond the expectations of women of her class. While living in Germany, she had become a socialist and corresponded with Karl Marx's collaborator, Friedrich Engels, about the condition of the Chicago poor. In 1892, she wrote him, "The most visible work is [being done] at the present moment by a lot of women who are organizing trade unions of men and women."[37] Kelley had come to Hull House to get away from an abusive husband and so knew something of wives' dependency. She deserves much of the credit for moving Hull House, and with it the entire settlement movement, decisively in the direction of modern social welfare reform.

Kelley crafted a body of protective labor laws designed to shield working-class families from the worst impact of the wage labor system. In 1893, she and others submitted a bill to the Illinois state legislature to prohibit the employment of children, constrain home-based manufacturing, and establish an eight-hour workday for adult women workers. Offered as a legislative response to the growing social and economic crisis of the poor, the Illinois Factory and Workshop Inspection Act was passed about a year before the Pullman strike. Kelley was appointed chief factory inspector for the state, and empowered to search out and prosecute violations of the new laws. She and her deputy inspectors, including the trade union activist Mary Kenney (see pp. 458–59), drew the attention of reformers, the state government, and labor unions to the extent and abuses of the sweating system in Illinois and helped to initiate a nationwide campaign to improve conditions in the garment industry. Many states began to pass similar factory and tenement inspection laws.

◆ **Jane Addams Reading to Her Nephew**
Jane Addams built her life as a reformer around the traditional womanly virtues of care, nurturance, and concern for family life, expressed on a large, public stage. Although she never married or became a mother, she was often photographed with the immigrant children served by Hull House. In her personal life, she was a devoted aunt. Buried in this tender picture of Addams with her nephew Stanley Linn, taken around 1894, is a tragedy. In the summer of 1894, with the railroads on strike, Addams's sister Mary died before family members could reach her. Jane became the legal guardian for Mary's children. Her biographer, Victoria Brown, observes that the twin tragedies of the Pullman strike and her sister's death took a considerable toll on Addams, who looks older here than her thirty-four years. *University of Illinois at Chicago, University Library Jane Addams Memorial Collection (JAMC_000_0029_1703).*

Other provisions of the law were not so successful. Illinois garment manufacturers united in opposition to the eight-hour workday for women workers. In the bitter aftermath of the Pullman strike, the Illinois Supreme Court ruled in 1895 that limitations on the working hours of women were a violation of their individual freedom of contract, without "due process of law." Kelley's father had helped to write the Fourteenth Amendment, which had enshrined the principle of due process in the U.S. Constitution, and she railed against the 1895 decision as a perversion of this principle, making it into "an insuperable obstacle for the protection of women and children."[38] Ending child labor also proved extremely difficult, as immigrant parents resisted efforts to deprive their families of young wage earners. But Kelley had chosen her life's work—to find the political backing and constitutional basis for social welfare provisions that would aid working-class women and families.

Women-based settlement houses soon appeared in other immigrant-dense cities, among them the Henry Street Settlement in New York City, led by Lillian Wald; Neighborhood House in Dallas; and the Telegraph Hill Neighborhood Association in San Francisco. While many white settlement leaders personally believed in greater racial justice, they yielded to the prejudices of the era and practiced racial segregation in the institutions they established. In the South, middle-class African American women organized their own settlements, most notably Atlanta's Neighborhood

Union, organized in 1908 by clubwoman Lugenia Hope. In the North, all-black set-tlement houses were also organized. Ida B. Wells-Barnett set up the Negro Fellow-ship Association in a rented house on Chicago's south side. Hull House, which had experimented with a few black residents in the 1890s, switched in the twentieth cen-tury to encouraging and supporting a separate black settlement house, the Wendell Phillips House. Similar black-oriented settlement houses were Robert Gould Shaw House in Boston, Karamu House in Cleveland, and Lincoln House in New York City.

Epilogue to the Crisis: The Spanish-American War of 1898

In an atmosphere shaped by the crisis of the 1890s, the United States embarked on its first extracontinental imperialist efforts. Imperial advocates contended that the acquisition of overseas colonies could provide both new markets to revive the American economy and a military challenge to invigorate American manhood. In an influential paper entitled "The Significance of the Frontier in American His-tory," historian Frederick Jackson Turner considered the advantages of an impe-rial future for the United States. Mourning the end of an era in which the defin-ing national purpose was to conquer the American continent, and concerned that immigrants could not be fully Americanized in the absence of the frontier experi-ence, Turner suggested that overseas expansion might be a way for the United States to continue to pursue its Manifest Destiny and maintain its frontier spirit.

Turner made his remarks in 1893 at the World's Columbian Exposition in Chicago, the same exposition that featured the Woman's Building (see pp. 354–55). Throughout the fair, America's rising imperial aspirations were on display. The spa-tial organization of the grounds reflected the country's new ambitions for world leadership. At the center was the Court of Honor, where the United States wel-comed and joined the great nations of Europe. Meanwhile, on the riotous Midway Plaisance at the fair's periphery, belly-dancing Arabs, tribal Africans, and exotic Asians drew enormous crowds, fascinated and amused by the unprecedented spec-tacle of the world's strange variety of peoples. The implication was clear: the people on the Midway, albeit fascinating, were inferior, uncivilized, and backward and needed the stewardship of the United States and other advanced Christian nations.

Some of the earliest manifestations of this crusading sense of American national superiority had come from Protestant missionaries, among whom women were prominent. Since the 1830s, women with a strong religious vocation had been bringing American values and culture along with English language and Christian Bibles to the peoples of Asia and Africa. Women's overseas missionary efforts entered a new, more organized phase in 1883 when the Woman's Christian Temperance Union (WCTU) created a division to undertake international work. Mary Clement Leavitt, a former schoolteacher from New Hampshire, became the first of the WCTU's "round the world missionaries," traveling around the Pacific, from Hawaii to New Zealand and Australia to Burma, Madagascar, China, and India, to spread the ideas of temperance.

Some Asian women were able to use the resources and perspective of the WCTU missionaries to address their own problems as they understood them. In Japan, for instance, the WCTU's combined message of female purity and activism became the basis for an anticoncubinage movement, while the antiliquor arguments were initially ignored by women. Nonetheless, the assumption of American superiority and world leadership constituted a kind of "soft" imperialism. Frances Willard made the link explicit when she said, "Mrs. Leavitt has been to the women of Japan what U.S. naval and economic power has been to its commerce: an opening into the civilized world."[39]

Willard wrote those words in 1898, the year that the United States entered into its first explicitly imperial overseas war and acquired its first formal colonial possessions. The so-called Spanish-American War began in Cuba, which had long drawn American attention as a possible territorial acquisition. Cuban nationalists were showing signs of winning a prolonged insurgency against Spanish colonial control. In May, the United States joined the war on the side of the Cuban forces, ostensibly to avenge the destruction of the U.S.S. *Maine*, an American battleship blown up under suspicious circumstances in Havana harbor. (It was later determined that powder on the deck exploded, probably by accident.) Spain was quickly routed, but instead of supporting Cuban independence, the United States enforced a new type of foreign oversight on the island. While not making Cuba a formal colony, the Platt Amendment, passed by the U.S. Congress in 1902, gave the United States a supervisory role over Cuban affairs that it retained until 1934.

As Spanish imperial power collapsed further, the United States claimed as colonies other Spanish possessions, including Puerto Rico and Guam. U.S. forces found it most difficult to consolidate control over the rich prize of the Spanish Philippines, the gateway to trade across the Pacific and throughout Asia. An indigenous Filipino independence movement fought back against the Americans, who had come in 1898 to liberate and stayed to control. The Filipinos turned what at first appeared to be a quick U.S. victory into a long and deadly conflict, which U.S. forces brought to an end only in 1902 through considerable expenditure of life (see box, "Women of the Philippines"). Unlike Cuba, the Philippines became a formal U.S. colony and remained so until 1946.

Alongside the economic justification for imperial expansion in search of new markets, a restless, insecure, and aggressive masculinity played a significant role in America's decision to go to war. Rising New York politician Theodore Roosevelt thoroughly embodied this phenomenon. With the memory of Civil War death tolls receding, men like Roosevelt were eager to demonstrate a manliness they felt was being challenged by immigrant men and threatened by activist women. Newspapers encouraged popular support for intervention. In political cartoons, Americans were portrayed as the manly protectors of the Cuban people, who were regularly depicted as suffering women (see Figure 7.12, p. 447). These eager imperialists "regarded the war as an opportunity," says one historian, "to return the nation to a political order in which strong men governed and homebound women proved their patriotism by raising heroic sons."[40]

Most American women joined the clamor and supported intervention on what they believed was the side of the Cubans. Remembering female service in the Civil War, they raised funds for military hospitals. But when it came to the unprecedented taking of overseas colonies, opinion was much more divided. By

CLEMENCIA LOPEZ
Women of the Philippines

Clemencia Lopez and her husband, Sixto, were leading advocates of the cause of Philippine independence to the American people. She defended her people's dignity and sovereign rights in this 1902 address to the New England Woman Suffrage Association, many members of which were active in the Boston-based Anti-Imperialist League. Subsequently she became a student at Wellesley College, one of the first Filipinas to attend a U.S. college.

You will no doubt be surprised and pleased to learn that the condition of women in the Philippines is very different from that of the women of any country in the East, and that it differs very little from the general condition of the women of this country. Mentally, socially, and in almost all the relations of life, our women are regarded as the equals of our men. . . .

. . . [I]t would seem to me an excellent idea that American women should take part in any investigation that may be made in the Philippine Islands, and I believe they would attain better results than the men. Would it not also seem to you an excellent idea, since representation by our leading men has been refused us, that a number of representative women should come to this country, so that you might become better acquainted with us?

. . . You can do much to bring about the cessation of these horrors and cruelties which are today taking place in the Philippines, and to insist upon a more humane course. I do not believe that you can understand or imagine the miserable condition of the women of my country, or how real is their suffering. . . . [Y]ou ought to understand that we are only contending for the liberty of our country, just as you once fought for the same liberty for yours.

SOURCE: Clemencia Lopez, "Women of the Philippines," address to the New England Woman Suffrage Association, published in *Woman's Journal*, June 7, 1902.

nature a pacifist, Jane Addams recognized the threat that rising militarism posed to a more general spirit of reform. On the streets around Hull House, she observed, children were "playing war": "[I]n the violence characteristic of the age, they were 'slaying Spaniards.'"[41] Susan B. Anthony also opposed the war, while her longtime friend and political partner, Elizabeth Cady Stanton, took the opposite position and believed that colonization would civilize the Filipino people.

The annexation of Hawaii during the war illustrates other aspects of the many roles women played in the U.S. move toward empire. In 1891, Queen Liliuokalani became the reigning monarch of the sovereign nation of Hawaii. She had been educated by American Protestant missionaries, was a devout Congregationalist, spoke English, and was married to a white American. Wealthy American planters already had enormous economic power in Hawaii, but U.S. tariff policies put them at a disadvantage in selling their fruit and sugar, and they pressed for a formal U.S. takeover of the islands. Now that its monarch was a woman, they redoubled their claims that only annexation could assure Hawaii's stability and progress. The U.S. entry into the war against Spain created a political environment favorable to their aspirations, and in 1898 Congress voted to acquire Hawaii. Unlike Texas in 1845 and California in 1848, however, Hawaii did not become a state but was designated a colonial territory.

The response of U.S. suffragists was not to condemn this move, even though the deposed head of state was a woman, or to object that Congress was imposing a government on the islands instead of allowing its residents to organize their own. Rather, they protested Congress's intention to write a territorial constitution for the Hawaiians that confined political rights to men only. As one historian writes, suffragists "substituted a critique of imperialism with a critique of patriarchy, and in the process lent their tacit approval to America's colonial project."[42] Even when they seemed to defend the rights of women in the colonies, late nineteenth-century suffragists did so within a framework that assumed the superiority of American culture and their right, as white Americans, to play a role in the nation's expansive "civilizing" mission.

CONCLUSION: Nationhood and Womanhood on the Eve of a New Century

At the beginning of the twentieth century, most American women faced the new century with considerable optimism. Not so long before, their country had gone through a horrible Civil War, but now it had more than recovered. The settlement of the western half of the continental United States gave a sturdy new physicality to American claims of nationhood. The U.S. economy more than equaled that of England, Germany, and France combined. Many immigrants had taken great risks and come far to participate in this spectacular growth. Strong and confident, the United States, once a colony itself, ended the century by acquiring its own colonies. The country was on its way to becoming a world power.

As this new era of national development dawned, women's prospects looked especially promising. With the important exception of Native American women, most American women in 1900 were living more active, more public, more individualized, and more expansive lives than prior generations. As a group, they were prepared to make a major contribution to solving the problems that accompanied America's new prosperity and place in the world. In the coming era, they would achieve as much influence as in any period of U.S. history. Already the beneficiaries of American progress, they were about to become the mainstays of the Progressive era, in which America undertook the challenging task of both reforming and modernizing itself.

D O C U M E N T S

Zitkala-Ša: Indian Girlhood and Education

T HE NATIVE AMERICAN WRITER and activist known as Zitkala-Ša was born
Gertrude Simmons in 1876. That same year, the Lakota Sioux achieved a stirring but brief victory over the U.S. cavalry at Little Big Horn. Her own band of
Eastern Sioux, the Yanktons, had already been confined on a reservation in South
Dakota, in the process of which her sister and uncle had died and her family had
begun to disintegrate. At age eight, she overcame her grieving mother's reluctance
and traveled to a Quaker-run school for Native children in Wabash, Indiana. Her
three years there were deeply unhappy, after which she returned to the Yankton
Reservation. But she found that she was not satisfied by the paths set out for her
in either world, Native or white ("paleface" as she called it), and she began to
search for her own way between them.

She resumed her education at Earlham College, another Quaker institution,
and left her family again to teach at the most famous of the Indian colleges,
Carlisle Institute in Pennsylvania. There she was beginning to find her voice—as
orator and writer both—and sought ways to preserve and convey the experiences
of her people to a broader American audience. Her career as a writer began in
1900 with the publication in the *Atlantic Monthly* of a series of autobiographical
vignettes, excerpted below. To designate a kind of personal rebirth, she signed this
work with a name that was both new and traditional, Zitkala-Ša, meaning Red
Bird. She subsequently worked for the Bureau of Indian Affairs and married a
Sioux man, Raymond Bonnin. Her essays were republished as 1921 as *American
Indian Stories*. By this time, her interests and energies had shifted from the literary to the political. In 1911, she became one of the founders and leaders of the
Society of American Indians (see p. 469).

Written early in her career—while she was still in her mid-twenties—these
autobiographical writings powerfully convey the complex and contradictory
nature of the pulls and pushes on Native young people of her transitional generation. Can you detect any literary devices that she uses to enrich her account? As
you read this piece, consider how she portrays the attractions of the white world
as an innocent child might understand them versus the reactions of their parents,
who had already lost so much in the confrontation with white society. What turns
her from an eager adventurer into a resentful and resisting young rebel?

ZITKALA-ŠA
American Indian Stories (1921)

INDIAN CHILDHOOD: THE BIG RED APPLES

The first turning away from the easy, natural flow of my life occurred in an early spring. It was in my eighth year; in the month of March, I afterward learned. At this age I knew but one language, and that was my mother's native tongue.

From some of my playmates I heard that two paleface missionaries were in our village. They were from that class of white men who wore big hats and carried large hearts, they said. Running direct to my mother, I began to question her why these two strangers were among us. She told me, after I had teased much, that they had come to take away Indian boys and girls to the East. My mother did not seem to want me to talk about them. But in a day or two, I gleaned many wonderful stories from my playfellows concerning the strangers.

"Mother, my friend Judéwin is going home with the missionaries. She is going to a more beautiful country than ours; the palefaces told her so!" I said wistfully, wishing in my heart that I too might go. . . . With a sad, slow smile, she answered: "There! I knew you were wishing to go, because Judéwin has filled your ears with the white man's lies. Don't believe a word they say! Their words are sweet, but, my child, their deeds are bitter. You will cry for me, but they will not even soothe you. Stay with me, my little one! Your brother Dawée says that going East, away from your mother, is too hard an experience for his baby sister."

Thus my mother discouraged my curiosity about the lands beyond our eastern horizon; for it was not yet an ambition for Letters that was stirring me. But on the following day the missionaries did come to our very house. . . .

Judéwin had told me of the great tree where grew red, red apples; and how we could reach out our hands and pick all the red apples we could eat. I had never seen apple trees. I had never tasted more than a dozen red apples in my life; and when I heard of the orchards of the East, I was eager to roam among them. The missionaries smiled into my eyes and patted my head. I wondered how mother could say such hard words against them.

"Mother, ask them if little girls may have all the red apples they want, when they go East," I whispered aloud, in my excitement. The interpreter heard me, and answered: "Yes, little girl, the nice red apples are for those who pick them; and you will have a ride on the iron horse if you go with these good people."

I had never seen a train, and he knew it.

"Mother, I am going East! I like big red apples, and I want to ride on the iron horse! Mother, say yes!" I pleaded. . . . With this they left us. Alone with my mother, I yielded to my tears, and cried aloud, shaking my head so as not to hear what she was saying to me. This was the first time I had ever been so unwilling to give up my own desire that I refused to hearken to my mother's voice.

There was a solemn silence in our home that night. Before I went to bed I begged the Great Spirit to make my mother willing I should go with the missionaries.

The next morning came, and my mother called me to her side. "My daughter, do you still persist in wishing to leave your mother?" she asked.

"Oh, mother, it is not that I wish to leave you, but I want to see the wonderful Eastern land," I answered. . . . My brother Dawée came for mother's decision. I dropped my play, and crept close to my aunt.

"Yes, Dawée, my daughter, though she does not understand what it all means, is anxious to

SOURCE: Zitkala-Ša, *American Indian Stories* (1921; repr., Lincoln: University of Nebraska Press, 1985), 39–56.

go. She will need an education when she is grown, for then there will be fewer real Dakotas, and many more palefaces. This tearing her away, so young, from her mother is necessary, if I would have her an educated woman. The palefaces, who owe us a large debt for stolen lands, have begun to pay a tardy justice in offering some education to our children. But I know my daughter must suffer keenly in this experiment. For her sake, I dread to tell you my reply to the missionaries. Go, tell them that they may take my little daughter, and that the Great Spirit shall not fail to reward them according to their hearts."

Wrapped in my heavy blanket, I walked with my mother to the carriage that was soon to take us to the iron horse. I was happy. I met my playmates, who were also wearing their best thick blankets. We showed one another our new beaded moccasins, and the width of the belts that girdled our new dresses. Soon we were being drawn rapidly away by the white man's horses.

SCHOOL DAYS OF AN INDIAN GIRL: THE LAND OF RED APPLES

There were eight in our party of bronzed children who were going East with the missionaries. Among us were three young braves, two tall girls, and we three little ones, Judéwin, Thowin, and I.

We had been very impatient to start on our journey to the Red Apple Country, which, we were told, lay a little beyond the great circular horizon of the Western prairie. Under a sky of rosy apples we dreamt of roaming as freely and happily as we had chased the cloud shadows on the Dakota plains. We had anticipated much pleasure from a ride on the iron horse, but the throngs of staring palefaces disturbed and troubled us.

On the train, fair women, with tottering babies on each arm, stopped their haste and scrutinized the children of absent mothers. Large men, with heavy bundles in their hands, halted near by, and riveted their glassy blue eyes upon us.

I sank deep into the corner of my seat, for I resented being watched. Directly in front of me, children who were no larger than I hung themselves upon the backs of their seats, with their bold white faces toward me. Sometimes they took their forefingers out of their mouths and pointed at my moccasined feet. Their mothers, instead of reproving such rude curiosity, looked closely at me, and attracted their children's further notice to my blanket. This embarrassed me, and kept me constantly on the verge of tears. . . .

It was night when we reached the school grounds. The lights from the windows of the large buildings fell upon some of the icicled trees that stood beneath them. We were led toward an open door, where the brightness of the lights within flooded out over the heads of the excited palefaces who blocked the way. My body trembled more from fear than from the snow I trod upon.

Entering the house, I stood close against the wall. The strong glaring light in the large whitewashed room dazzled my eyes. The noisy hurrying of hard shoes upon a bare wooden floor increased the whirring in my ears. My only safety seemed to be in keeping next to the wall. As I was wondering in which direction to escape from all this confusion, two warm hands grasped me firmly, and in the same moment I was tossed high in midair. A rosy-cheeked paleface woman caught me in her arms. I was both frightened and insulted by such trifling. I stared into her eyes, wishing her to let me stand on my own feet, but she jumped me up and down with increasing enthusiasm. My mother had never made a plaything of her wee daughter. Remembering this I began to cry aloud. . . .

I had arrived in the wonderful land of rosy skies, but I was not happy, as I had thought I should be. My long travel and the bewildering sights had exhausted me. I fell asleep, heaving deep, tired sobs. My tears were left to dry themselves in streaks, because neither my aunt nor my mother was near to wipe them away.

SCHOOL DAYS OF AN INDIAN GIRL: THE CUTTING OF MY LONG HAIR

The first day in the land of apples was a bitter-cold one; for the snow still covered the ground, and the trees were bare. A large bell rang for breakfast, its loud metallic voice crashing through the belfry overhead and into our sensitive ears. . . . And though my spirit tore itself in struggling for its lost freedom, all was useless.

A paleface woman, with white hair, came up after us. We were placed in a line of girls who were marching into the dining room. These were Indian girls, in stiff shoes and closely clinging dresses. The small girls wore sleeved aprons and shingled hair. As I walked noiselessly in my soft moccasins, I felt like sinking to the floor, for my blanket had been stripped from my shoulders. I looked hard at the Indian girls, who seemed not to care that they were even more immodestly dressed than I, in their tightly fitting clothes. While we marched in, the boys entered at an opposite door. I watched for the three young braves who came in our party. I spied them in the rear ranks, looking as uncomfortable as I felt.

A small bell was tapped, and each of the pupils drew a chair from under the table. Supposing this act meant they were to be seated, I pulled out mine and at once slipped into it from one side. But when I turned my head, I saw that I was the only one seated, and all the rest at our table remained standing. Just as I began to rise, looking shyly around to see how chairs were to be used, a second bell was sounded. All were seated at last, and I had to crawl back into my chair again. I heard a man's voice at one end of the hall, and I looked around to see him. But all the others hung their heads over their plates. As I glanced at the long chain of tables, I caught the eyes of a paleface woman upon me. Immediately I dropped my eyes, wondering why I was so keenly watched by the strange woman. The man ceased his mutterings, and then a third bell was tapped. Every one picked up his knife and fork and began eating. I began crying instead, for by this time I was afraid to venture anything more.

But this eating by formula was not the hardest trial in that first day. Late in the morning, my friend Judéwin gave me a terrible warning. Judéwin knew a few words of English; and she had overheard the paleface woman talk about cutting our long, heavy hair. Our mothers had taught us that only unskilled warriors who were captured had their hair shingled by the enemy. Among our people, short hair was worn by mourners, and shingled hair by cowards!

We discussed our fate some moments, and when Judéwin said, "We have to submit, because they are strong," I rebelled. "No, I will not submit! I will struggle first!" I answered.

I watched my chance, and when no one noticed, I disappeared. I crept up the stairs as quietly as I could in my squeaking shoes,—my moccasins had been exchanged for shoes. . . . On my hands and knees I crawled under the bed, and cuddled myself in the dark corner.

From my hiding place I peered out, shuddering with fear whenever I heard footsteps near by. Though in the hall loud voices were calling my name, and I knew that even Judéwin was searching for me, I did not open my mouth to answer. Then the steps were quickened and the voices became excited. The sounds came nearer and nearer. Women and girls entered the room. I held my breath and watched them open closet doors and peep behind large trunks. Some one threw up the curtains, and the room was filled with sudden light. What caused them to stoop and look under the bed I do not know. I remember being dragged out, though I resisted by kicking and scratching wildly. In spite of myself, I was carried downstairs and tied fast in a chair.

I cried aloud, shaking my head all the while until I felt the cold blades of the scissors against my neck, and heard them gnaw off one of my thick braids. Then I lost my spirit. Since the day I was taken from my mother I had suffered extreme indignities. People had stared at me. I had been tossed about in the air like a wooden puppet. And now my long hair was shingled like a coward's! In my anguish I moaned for my mother, but no one came to comfort me. Not a soul reasoned quietly with me, as my own mother used to do; for now I was only one of many little animals driven by a herder.

QUESTIONS FOR ANALYSIS

1. How do Zitkala-Ša's encounters with white society compare to those of Sarah Winnemucca in the 1840s (see pp. 287–90)?

2. Compare the response of the author to the noise and regimentation of her school to the experiences of European immigrants arriving into bustling, industrial American cities.

3. One scholar has characterized the assimilationist education offered by well-meaning white "friends of the Indian" as a kind of "tender violence."[43] Given Zitkala-Ša's account, what do you think of this term?

D O C U M E N T S

Jane Addams and the Charitable Relation

J ANE ADDAMS (1860–1935) was the leader of the American settlement house movement. After graduating in 1882 from Rockford Seminary in Illinois, she went to Europe in search of a larger purpose for her life. Like other daughters of wealthy families, she was looking for an alternative to the leisured, homebound life of the sort in which Alice Austen reveled (see Visual Sources: Alice Austen: Gilded Age Photographer, pp. 379–84). Restless leisure-class women like Addams did not require paid labor, but they did need work of large social purpose and a place and community in which to live. Visiting London, Addams learned of a "settlement" project of male college graduates who lived among and served the urban poor. She returned to Illinois, determined to establish a similar community of female college graduates dedicated to social service. In 1889 Addams persuaded a wealthy woman to donate a Chicago mansion, originally built by the Hull family and now in the center of a crowded immigrant district, for her planned settlement.

The reform-minded women who joined Addams to live and work in Hull House combined a palpable sympathy with the urban poor and a determination to find a nonrevolutionary solution to the era's class and ethnic conflicts. In Addams's words, they were determined "to aid in the solution of the social and industrial problems which are engendered by the modern conditions of urban life."[44] Their focus was especially on the welfare of women and children. They learned that in hard times poor women suffered the consequences of a double dependency—on men who could not be breadwinners and on governments that were slow to accept public responsibility for social welfare needs.

Addams wrote the essay excerpted here, "The Subtle Problems of Charity," in 1899, only a few years after the 1893 depression and 1894 Pullman Strike, before the success of her pioneering work at Hull House was widely acknowledged. The essay demonstrates Addams's dual vocation of empirical social observer and passionate social reformer. She actively struggled with the "perplexities" that plagued the efforts of leisure-class women like herself to respond to the needs of impoverished immigrants. In a society still imbued with a rigid morality, Addams displayed an impressive ability to avoid ethical absolutes in her understanding of immigrants' lives and choices.

Addams sought to interpret the long history of what she calls "the charitable relation." In the early nineteenth century, wealthy benefactors made sure that their money went only to the "worthy" poor, so as to encourage charity recipients to become self-supporting participants in a competitive, market-driven society. But Addams believed that these philanthropists treated their clients "exclusively as factors in the industrial system." By contrast, she advocated a more humanitarian ethic of "brotherhood and equality." She approached the problem of charity in broader terms, concerned that American political democracy should develop a social dimension. Her primary concern was not whether an individual was "worthy" of charity but the creation of constructive bonds and mutual understanding between those who need aid and those in a position to give it.

Simultaneous with this shift in the charitable ethic, the gender of those who dispensed philanthropic aid was changing. The traditional philanthropic leader had been a man who had succeeded in the struggle for individual wealth and gave in accordance with the values he credited for his own rise in society. But by the late nineteenth century, charity giving had become the responsibility of leisure-class women who had no direct experience with money making. In 1899, Addams was unsettled about the contradiction between leisure-class women's ignorance of material realities and the control they exerted over the lives of the needy poor who looked to them for necessary aid.

Contradictory intellectual frameworks can be detected in Addams's thinking about her relationship to the new immigrants. The beneficiary of expanding opportunities for higher education for women, Addams subscribed to the modern principles of progress and social science, which she used to make sense of the dilemmas she and other settlement house activists faced. She relied on Darwinian notions of evolution to characterize the inevitable and desirable development of society from the lower stages and backward cultures represented by European immigrants to the higher stages and superior cultures of the American bourgeoisie. Yet at the same time, she also regarded the "primitiveness" of these immigrant families as more natural, more basic, and in some ways more fundamentally human than the ways of her own class and culture. She felt that women of the middle and upper classes had lost touch with fundamental human needs and experiences that were instinctively understood by immigrant women.

Addams's analysis of the dilemmas of philanthropy was not limited to the problems of the charity givers but included the ethical dilemmas faced by the immigrant recipients. She resisted treating the immigrant poor as either passive or morally pure, seeing them instead as people struggling with their own contradictory values. In her view the new immigrants, like the larger American society into which they had come, quickly learned to respect economic success more than human compassion. Thus they admired but expected little from those who had achieved material wealth while they were polite to but contemptuous of the "good . . . and kind-hearted" women of wealth on whom they depended for crucial charitable aid.

Addams's concern with the relations between parents and children is also evident in this essay. She tended to see settlement house workers in the role of parents, sometimes beneficent, sometimes uncomprehending, of the childlike immigrants. This family-based model of class relations helped female settlement house activists legitimate their efforts at expanding their social authority: Addams and women like herself saw themselves as public "mothers." But as this essay makes clear, Addams also had considerable empathy for immigrant children. Within a few years, she would become a leader in the fight to ban child labor as well as to pass laws and regulations intended to move mothers out of the labor force so that they could devote themselves entirely to the rearing of their children.

By 1910 Jane Addams was the acknowledged head of the settlement movement and a leader in American philanthropy. In Hull House, she created a modern, progressive venue to which reformers from all over the world came, from British social democrat Sidney Webb to Japanese feminist Ichikawa Fusae. At times, she was misunderstood by both the poor and the rich for her determination to negotiate between the warring classes of turn-of-the-century American society, but her approach was widely influential on women and men alike. An instinctive revulsion at militarism, first evident during the Filipino-American conflict of 1899–1902, combined with the internationalism that she embraced at the neighborhood level in her Hull House work, led her to become, later in her career, a leader of the women's international peace movement (see Chapter 7).

JANE ADDAMS
The Subtle Problems of Charity (1899)

Probably there is no relation in life which our democracy is changing more rapidly than the charitable relation, that relation which obtains between benefactor and beneficiary; at the same time, there is no point of contact in our modern experience which reveals more clearly the lack of that equality which democracy implies. We have reached the moment when democracy has made such inroads upon this relationship that the complacency of the old-fashioned charitable man is gone forever; while the very need and existence of charity deny us the consolation and freedom which democracy will at last give.

Formerly when it was believed that poverty was synonymous with vice and laziness, and that the prosperous man was the righteous man, charity was administered harshly with a good conscience; for the charitable agent really blamed the individual for his poverty, and the very fact of his own superior prosperity gave him a certain consciousness of superior morality. Since then we have learned to measure by other standards, and

the money-earning capacity, while still rewarded out of all proportion to any other, is not respected as exclusively as it was. . . .

Of the various struggles which a decade of residence in a settlement implies, none have made a more definite impression on my mind than the incredibly painful difficulties which involve both giver and recipient when one person asks charitable aid of another.

An attempt is made in this paper to show what are some of the perplexities which harass the mind of the charity worker; to trace them to ethical survivals which are held not only by the benefactor, but by the recipients of charity as well; and to suggest wherein these very perplexities may possibly be prophetic.

. . . The charity visitor, let us assume, is a young college woman, well-bred and openminded. When she visits the family assigned to her, she is embarrassed to find herself obliged to lay all the stress of her teaching and advice upon the industrial virtues, and to treat the members of the family almost exclusively as factors in the industrial system. She insists that they must work

SOURCE: *Atlantic Monthly*, February 1899, 163–78.

and be self-supporting; that the most dangerous of all situations is idleness; . . . [I]t often occurs to the mind of the sensitive visitor, whose conscience has been made tender by much talk of brotherhood and equality which she has heard at college, that she has no right to say these things; that she herself has never been self-supporting; that, whatever her virtues may be, they are not the industrial virtues; that her untrained hands are no more fitted to cope with actual conditions than are those of her broken-down family.

The grandmother of the charity visitor could have done the industrial preaching very well, because she did have the industrial virtues; if not skillful in weaving and spinning, she was yet mistress of other housewifely accomplishments. In a generation our experiences have changed — our views with them. . . .

A very little familiarity with the poor districts of any city is sufficient to show how primitive and frontier-like are the neighborly relations. There is the great willingness to lend or borrow anything, and each resident of a given tenement house knows the most intimate family affairs of all the others. The fact that the economic conditions of all alike is on the most precarious level makes the ready outflow of sympathy and material assistance the most natural thing in the world. There are numberless instances of heroic self-sacrifice quite unknown in the circles where greater economic advantages make that kind of intimate knowledge of one's neighbors impossible. . . .

The evolutionists tell us that the instinct to pity, the impulse to aid his fellows, served man at a very early period as a rude rule of right and wrong. There is no doubt that this rude rule still holds among many people with whom charitable agencies are brought into contact, and that their ideas of right and wrong are quite honestly outraged by the methods of these agencies. When they see the delay and caution with which relief is given, these do not appear to them conscientious scruples, but the cold and calculating action of the selfish man. This is not the aid that they are accustomed to receive from their neighbors. . . .

The only man they are accustomed to see whose intellectual perceptions are stronger than his tenderness of heart is the selfish and avaricious man, who is frankly "on the make." If the charity visitor is such a person, why does she pretend to like the poor? Why does she not go into business at once? . . . In the minds of the poor success does not ordinarily go with charity and kindheartedness, but rather with the opposite qualities. The rich landlord is he who collects with sternness; who accepts no excuse, and will have his own. There are moments of irritation and of real bitterness against him, but there is admiration, because he is rich and successful. . . . The charity visitor, just because she is a person who concerns herself with the poor, receives a touch of this good-natured and kindly contempt, sometimes real affection, but little genuine respect. . . .

When the agent or visitor appears among the poor, and they discover that under certain conditions food and rent and medical aid are dispensed from some unknown source, every man, woman and child is quick to learn what the conditions may be and to follow them. . . . The deception arises from a wondering inability to understand the ethical ideals which can require such impossible virtues, combined with a tradition that charity visitors do require them, and from an innocent desire to please. It is easy to trace the development of the mental suggestions thus received. The most serious effect upon the individual comes when dependence upon the charitable society is substituted for the natural outgoing of human love and sympathy, which, happily, we all possess in some degree. . . . The charity visitor has broken through the natural rule of giving, which in a primitive society is bounded only by the need of the recipient and the resources of the giver; and she gets herself into untold trouble when she is judged by the ethics of that primitive society.

The neighborhood understands the selfish rich people who stay in their own part of the town. . . . Such people do not bother themselves about the poor; they are like the rich landlords of the neighborhood experience. But this lady visitor, who pretends to be good to the poor, and certainly does talk as though she were kind-hearted, what does she come for, if she does not intend to give them things which so plainly are needed? The visitor says, sometimes, that in holding her poor family so hard to a standard of thrift she is really breaking down a rule for higher living which they formerly possessed; that saving, which seems quite commendable in a comfortable part of the town, appears almost criminal in a poorer quarter, where the next-door neighbor needs food, even if the children of the family do not. She feels the sordidness of constantly being obliged to urge the industrial view of life. . . . She says sometimes: "Why must I talk always on getting work and saving money, the things I know nothing about? . . ."

Because of this diversity in experience the visitor is continually surprised to find that the safest platitudes may be challenged. . . .

The subject of clothes, indeed, perplexes the visitor constantly, and the result of her reflections may be summed up something in this wise: The girl who has a definite social standing, who has been to a fashionable school or to a college, whose family live[s] in a house seen and known by all her friends and associates, can afford to be very simple or even shabby as to her clothes, if she likes. But the working girl, whose family lives in a tenement or moves from one small apartment to another, who has little social standing, and has to make her own place, knows full well how much habit and style of dress have to do with her position. Her income goes into her clothing out of all proportion to that which she spends upon other things. But if social advancement is her aim, it is the most sensible thing which she can do. She is judged largely by her clothes. . . .

Have we worked out our democracy in regard to clothes farther than in regard to anything else?

The charity visitor has been rightly brought up to consider it vulgar to spend much money upon clothes, to care so much for "appearances." . . . The poor naturally try to bridge the [class] difference by reproducing the street clothes which they have seen; they therefore imitate, sometimes in more showy and often in more trying colors, in cheap and flimsy material, in poor shoes and flippant hats, the extreme fashion of the well-to-do. They are striving to conform to a common standard which their democratic training presupposes belongs to us all. The charity visitor may regret that the Italian peasant woman has laid aside her picturesque kerchief, and substituted a cheap street hat. But it is easy to recognize the first attempt toward democratic expression.

The charity visitor is still more perplexed when she comes to consider such problems as those of early marriage and child labor. . . . She discovers how incorrigibly bourgeois her standards have been, and it takes but a little time to reach the conclusion that she cannot insist so strenuously upon the conventions of her own class, which fail to fit the bigger, more emotional, and freer lives of working people. . . .

The sense of prudence, the necessity for saving, can never come to a primitive, emotional man with the force of a conviction, but the necessity of providing for his children is a powerful incentive. He naturally regards his children as his savings-bank; he expects them to care for him when he gets old, and in some trades old age comes very early. . . . [A] tailor whom I know, a Socialist, always speaks of saving as a bourgeois virtue, one quite impossible to the genuine workingman. He supports a family, consisting of himself, a wife and three children, and his parents, on eight dollars a week. He insists that it would be criminal not to expend every penny of this amount upon food and shelter, and he expects his children later to take care of him. . . .

The struggle for existence, which is so much harsher among people near the edge of pauperism, sometimes leaves ugly marks on character, and the charity visitor finds the indirect results most mystifying. Parents who work hard and anticipate an old age when they can no longer earn, take care that their children shall expect to divide their wages with them from the very first. Such a parent, when successful, seizes the immature nervous system of the child and hypnotizes it, so to speak, into a habit of obedience, that the nerves and will may not depart from this control when the child is older. The charity visitor, whose family relation is lifted quite out of this, does not in the least understand the industrial foundation in this family despotism.

The head of a kindergarten training class once addressed a club of working-women, and spoke of the despotism which is often established over little children. . . . [O]ne [working woman] said, "Ah, of course, she [meaning the speaker] doesn't have to depend upon her children's wages. She can afford to be lax with them, because, even if they don't give money to her, she can get along without it." . . .

It is these subtle and elusive problems which, after all, the charity visitor finds most harassing. . . . The greatest difficulty is experienced when the two [ethical] standards come sharply together, and when an attempt is made at understanding and explanation. The difficulty of defining one's own ethical standpoint is at times insurmountable. . . .

A certain charity visitor is peculiarly appealed to by the weakness and pathos of forlorn old age. One of these poor old women was injured in a fire years ago. She has but the fragment of a hand left, and is grievously crippled in her feet. Through years of pain she had become addicted to opium. . . . Five years of tender care have done wonders for her. She lives in two neat little rooms, where with a thumb and two fingers she makes innumerable quilts, which she sells and gives away with the greatest delight. Her opium is regulated to a set amount taken each day. . . . [S]he was kept for two years in a suburb where the family of the charity visitor lived, and where she was nursed through several hazardous illnesses. . . . Her neighbors are constantly shocked by the fact that she is supported and comforted by "a charity lady," while at the same time she occasionally "rushes the growler,"° scolding at the boys lest they jar her in her tottering walk. The care of her has broken through even that second standard, which the neighborhood had learned to recognize as the

°Drinks alcohol.

standard of charitable societies, that only the "worthy poor" are to be helped. . . . In order to disarm them, and at the same time to explain what would otherwise seem loving-kindness so colossal as to be abnormal, she tells them that during her sojourn in the suburb she discovered an awful family secret, a horrible scandal connected with the long-suffering charity visitor; that it is in order to prevent the divulgence of this that the ministrations are continued. Some of her perplexed neighbors accept this explanation as simple and offering a solution of a vexed problem. . . .

Of what use is all this striving and perplexity? Has the experience any value? It is obviously genuine, for it induces an occasional charity visitor to live in a tenement house as simply as the other tenants do. It drives others to give up visiting the poor altogether, because, they claim, the situation is untenable . . . the young charity visitor who goes from a family living upon a most precarious industrial level to her own home in a prosperous part of the city, if she is sensitive at all, is never free from perplexities which our growing democracy forces upon her.

We sometimes say that our charity is too scientific, but we should doubtless be much more correct in our estimate if we said that it is not scientific enough. . . . There is no doubt that our development of charity methods has reached this pseudo-scientific and stilted stage. We have learned to condemn unthinking, ill-regulated kind-heartedness, and we take great pride in mere repression, much as the stern parent tells the visitor below how admirably he is rearing the child who is hysterically crying upstairs, and laying the foundation for future nervous disorders. The pseudo-scientific spirit, or rather the undeveloped stage of our philanthropy, is, perhaps, most clearly revealed in this tendency to lay stress on negative action. "Don't give," "don't break down self-respect," we are constantly told. We distrust the human impulse, and in its stead substitute dogmatic rules for conduct . . . we forget that the accumulation of knowledge and the holding of convictions must finally result in the application of that knowledge and those convictions to life itself, and the course which begins by activity, and an appeal to sympathies so severe that all the knowledge in the possession of the visitor is continually applied, has reasonably a greater chance for ultimate comprehension.

For most of the years during a decade of residence in a settlement, my mind was sore and depressed over the difficulties of the charitable relationship. The incessant clashing of ethical standards, which had been honestly gained from widely varying industrial experience, — the misunderstandings inevitable between people whose conventions and mode of life had been so totally unlike, — made it seem reasonable to say that nothing could be done until industrial conditions were made absolutely democratic. The position of a settlement, which attempts at one and the same time to declare its belief in this eventual, industrial democracy, and to labor toward that end, to maintain a standard of living, and to deal humanely and simply with those in actual want, often seems utterly untenable and preposterous. Recently, however, there has come to my mind the suggestion of a principle, that while the painful condition of administering charity is the inevitable discomfort of a transition into a more democratic relation, the perplexing experiences of the actual administration have a genuine value of their own. . . .

The Hebrew prophet made three requirements from those who would join the great forward-moving procession led by Jehovah. "To love mercy," and at the same time "to do justly," is the difficult task. To fulfill the first requirement alone is to fall into the error of indiscriminate giving, with all its disastrous results; to fulfill the second exclusively is to obtain the stern policy of withholding, and it results in such a dreary lack of sympathy and understanding that the establishment of justice is impossible. It may be that the combination of the two can never be attained save as we fulfill still the third requirement, "to walk humbly with God," which may mean to walk for many dreary miles beside the lowliest of his creatures, not even in peace of mind, that the companionship of the humble is popularly supposed to give, but rather with the pangs and misgivings to which the poor human understanding is subjected whenever it attempts to comprehend the meaning of life.

QUESTIONS FOR ANALYSIS

1. Early in this essay, Addams speaks of the conditions in "the poor districts of any city" as "frontier-like." What does she mean by this? What were the similarities between the "settlement" of the West and "settlement" houses?

2. What is the "diversity of experience" that Addams witnessed in her work with immigrants in the neighborhood around Hull House, and how did it contribute to the ethical complexities about which she wrote?

3. The longest incident in this article is the story of the troubled old immigrant woman who was befriended and rescued by a leisure-class woman and then lied to her neighbors about her benefactor's motives. What does the incident reveal about the ethical dilemmas faced by charity recipients and charity givers alike, and about the obstacles that class inequalities posed to the creation of bonds between them?

4. How did Addams's experience as a member of the pathbreaking generation of women college graduates affect her perspective as a settlement house volunteer?

Jacob Riis's Photographs of Immigrant Girls and Women

In the decade 1880–1890, more than 5 million immigrants came through the port of New York, and many remained in the city, swelling its population by 25 percent. By 1890 nearly half of the city's dwellings were classified as "tenements," overcrowded urban slums where vulnerable and desperately poor people were overcharged for filthy, cramped, and unsanitary lodgings.

This rise in immigration coincided with new forms of social documentation. Pioneering social scientists provided statistics on the growing industrial labor force, including the women who were entering the workplace in unprecedented numbers. Local and state health bureaus collected information on the epidemic diseases such as diphtheria, cholera, and tuberculosis that threatened family life in the burgeoning cities. And photographers created searing images of the horrible living and working conditions of newly arrived immigrants. These new methods of documentation, informed by a rising sense of public responsibility for improving social conditions and alleviating poverty, allow us to look back through the perspectives of those who did the documenting, into the lives of late nineteenth-century immigrant girls and women.

One of the first series of photographs of immigrant women and children in the United States was produced in the 1880s and 1890s by a man who was himself an immigrant. Jacob A. Riis arrived in New York City from Denmark in 1870. After more than a decade struggling to earn a living, he found regular work as a newspaperman. He began as a police reporter, writing in a male-oriented, journalistic genre that sensationalized the seamy side of "downtown" life. Riis's own impulses, however, were more humanitarian and allied him with urban reformers, many of whom were women. He worked closely with Josephine Shaw Lowell, who founded the Charity Organization Society of New York State in 1882. His particular focus was "the slum," by which he meant not only the dilapidated tenement homes of the poor but the larger urban environment in which they lived and worked. He was especially concerned with children, and through them the mothers of immigrant families.

Convinced that only photographs could convey the shocking reality of urban poverty, Riis included them in *How the Other Half Lives: Studies among the Tenements of New York* (1890), a pioneering work of sociology that is still mined by historians and scholars for the insights it provides into urban immigrant life, nineteenth-century attitudes toward poverty and ethnicity, and the visual conventions of early documentary photography. Though the majority of the photographs deal with male subjects—homeless street boys, male vagrants, and gang members—Riis also took pictures of women and girls that give us glimpses of their lives. In its frequent resort to sensational and melodramatic conventions, *How the Other Half Lives* reflects its author's roots in mass commercial journalism, but it also skillfully adopts strategies from literary realism and the emerging field of social science to convey a probing portrait of poverty and its consequences.

Consistent with the late nineteenth-century's preoccupation with ethnic and racial characteristics, *How the Other Half Lives* is organized like a guided tour for the middle-class reader through the ethnic geography of lower New York. Not surprisingly, it invokes both positive and negative stereotypes in its descriptions and illustrations. Riis, as a northwestern European immigrant, had clear ethnic biases, but his prejudices were tempered by empathy and the recognition that "we are all creatures of the conditions that surround us."[45] His goal was to call attention to the plight of the poor, not to castigate them for their poverty.

Chapter V of Riis's book, "The Italian in New York," focuses on those who, as recent arrivals, were "at the bottom" of the economic and social hierarchy.[46] The frequently reproduced photograph shown in Figure 7.1 depicts the wife and infant child of a "ragpicker"—one who barely made a living by picking through public

◆ Figure 7.1 **In the Home of an Italian Ragpicker: Jersey Street**
Museum of the City of New York, the Jacob A. Riis Collection.

rubbish cans and dumps for rags to sell—in their subterranean home. Riis developed the innovative technology used to make this photograph, a new chemical process that produced a "flash" bright enough to light up dark and windowless areas.

The pose of the Italian mother and her tightly swaddled child, as well as her mournful, upturned gaze, is reminiscent of religious paintings of the Madonna and Child in which the Virgin Mary's sad expression foreshadows the suffering that awaits her infant son. In the chapter that includes this photograph, Riis offers an extended report, complete with comparative statistics, on the high mortality rates of infants and children in this Italian neighborhood. What other explanations can be offered for her upward look?

Italian families, no matter how poor, frowned on wives and mothers working outside the home. While the room in Figure 7.1 is sparsely furnished, what do the few items we see and their arrangement tell us about this woman and her daily life? In the text accompanying this photograph, Riis describes the Italian immigrant as "picturesque, if not very tidy."[47] Does his photograph support this characterization? What overall impression does it convey about Italian immigrant mothers? Also in the text relating to this image is Riis's description of Italian men as "hotheaded . . . and lighthearted" and of Italian women as "faithful wives and devoted mothers."[48] Note the man's straw hat hanging high on the wall. What are the possible explanations for the man's absence?

In Figure 7.2, Riis continues his progression through New York City's ethnic neighborhoods to "Jewtown," an area settled by large numbers of Eastern European Jews and marked by exceptional population density and industrial activity.

◆ Figure 7.2 **Knee Pants at Forty-Five Cents a Dozen—A Ludlow Street Sweater's Shop**
Museum of the City of New York, the Jacob A. Riis Collection.

As Riis notes, "Life here means the hardest kind of work almost from the cradle."[49] The "sweater" mentioned in the title of the photograph was a subcontractor who supplied garments to a larger manufacturer and hired other immigrants to do the work, often in his own tenement apartment. The ruthless competition to deliver finished goods at the lowest possible price pressured the sweater to offer impossibly low wages and push (or "sweat") workers to their physical limits during a working day that "lengthened at both ends far into the night."[50] While Riis criticizes the "sweater's . . . merciless severity"[51] in exploiting his fellow Jews, he concedes "he is no worse than the conditions that created him."[52]

Unlike the photograph shown in Figure 7.1, this photo was not posed and has no carefully arranged central figure. It catches its subjects off guard, and the blurring of some of their features suggests frantic activity and movement. The sweater is the moving figure with his back to the camera. The teenage girls in this picture are "greenhorns," newly arrived immigrant workers. One man looks up briefly from his work, but the other seems unwilling to lose a minute's time despite the photographer's presence. Piles of boys' short pants waiting to be finished are heaped on the floor and furniture. What visual clues tell us that this workshop is also a residence? What else goes on in this room? In what ways is it different from the living space of the Italian mother in Figure 7.1?

In contrast to the serious detachment of the adults, the young girl turns to smile directly into the lens and casually touches to her lips the long-bladed scissors she is using to cut the garments. Does this suggest she has not yet been disciplined to keep up with the brutal pace of piecework? Maybe Riis regarded her direct gaze as somewhat immodest, a consequence of work conditions that placed unsupervised young girls amid grown men. Or did she simply find pleasure in having her picture taken? In his second book, *The Children of the Poor* (1892), Riis noted that in contrast to adults, who resisted and feared being photographed, children loved posing for the camera and had a "determination to be 'took' . . . in the most striking pose they could hastily devise."[53] What other possible meanings can be suggested for this unusual and striking image of a young working woman?

Employers justified the low wages paid to female workers, which were inadequate for self-support, as supplements to a family income anchored by an adult male wage. Riis was sharply aware of the special hardships facing the unmarried, poor working women who had to live on their own. In his chapter "The Working Girls of New York," he describes the exploitation and harsh conditions they endured, sprinkling his narrative with tragic stories of underpaid and exhausted women workers driven to suicide, prostitution, and premature death. Like so many other late nineteenth-century reformers, Riis thought the best solution to working women's suffering was to get them out of the labor force. If they remained in it, their lives were bound to be intolerable.

Figure 7.3 is an unusual photograph of two adult women, past the age when even poor immigrant women were expected to leave the labor force. They are not driven by a supervisor as are the workers in Figure 7.2, but neither do they enjoy the camaraderie of other workers. How does their living space compare with that in the previous two photographs? What does their dress suggest about them?

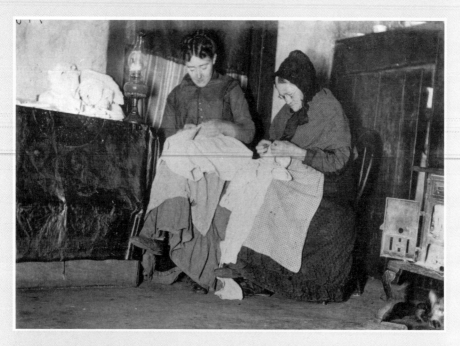

◆ **Figure 7.3 Sewing and Starving in an Elizabeth Street Attic**
Museum of the City of New York, the Jacob A. Riis Collection.

While we know little about these two women, the context of this photograph in *How the Other Half Lives* provides some help. Elsewhere in the narrative, Riis tells a heartrending story of two elderly sisters, the last of five siblings who had arrived from Ireland with their mother forty years before and who together made a scant living as lace embroiderers. When Riis encounters them, one of the sisters is crippled and the other, who had struggled to support them both, had recently been paralyzed in a fall. Now they were helpless and alone. How do the story, photograph, and title come together to reveal the conditions of aging women workers who had to support themselves through their own wage-earning capacities?

When wages were too low or unemployment too high, poor urban workers found themselves destitute and without shelter. Those who lacked even the pennies charged by commercial lodging houses ended up in overnight shelters in police stations. Of the half-million people seeking shelter in New York City in 1889, almost one-third sought refuge in makeshift facilities in police stations, and half of those were women. Riis knew firsthand about the filthy and dangerous conditions in the police station shelters. Recalling his own experience years before as a homeless vagrant in New York, he observed that "never was parody upon Christian charity more corrupting to human mind and soul than the frightful abomination of the police lodging-house."[54] He was particularly concerned when homeless women slept in the same room as men.

The photograph in Figure 7.4 was an illustration for an article Riis wrote for the *New York Tribune* in 1892, condemning the police station shelters. The West Forty-seventh Street police station was located in the aptly named Hell's Kitchen area of New York, and there is no doubt that Riis intended to shock readers with a graphic, unstaged photograph of women expelled from the domestic sphere, stripped of their dignity and privacy, eating and sleeping on filthy bare floors like animals. The extent of homelessness among women pointed to the collapse of working-class family life and indicated how deeply the combination of mass immigration, rapid urbanization, and economic collapse had rent the social fabric. Notice the details that reveal, perhaps unintentionally, how women manage to cooperate and care for their personal needs even under the harshest of circumstances. What do these details, and the facial expressions and postures of the women, reveal about social relations in this police station lodging room?

In *The Children of the Poor*, published originally as a series of articles in *Scribner's Magazine* in 1892, Riis turned his full attention to the group with whom he was most concerned, the children whose futures were being jeopardized by life in the tenements. Figure 7.5 is a rare individual portrait of an orphan, nine-year-old Katie, who attended the Fifty-second Street Industrial School, a charitable institution for indigent children. Although Katie did not earn wages, she was not spared hard work, for she cooked and cleaned for her three older working siblings. "In her person and work, she answered the question . . . why we hear so much about the

◆ Figure 7.4 **Police Station Lodgers: Women's Lodging Room in the West 47th Street Station**
Museum of the City of New York, the Jacob A. Riis Collection.

◆ **Figure 7.5 "I Scrubs": Katie Who Keeps House on West 49th Street**
Museum of the City of New York, the Jacob A. Riis Collection.

boys and so little about the girls," wrote Riis, "because the home claims their work earlier and to a much greater extent."[55] Consider Katie's clothing, posture, and expression. What do they suggest about her character and her prospects? In acknowledgment of Katie's contribution to her family's survival, Riis called Katie by the nickname often given to immigrant children who cared for younger siblings, "little mother." What does this tribute say about the economic role that mothers and other adult women played in the lives of poor families?

QUESTIONS FOR ANALYSIS

1. Riis clearly intended to shock comfortable Americans with his images of the slums. What might contemporaries have found most disturbing about his representations of immigrant women and girls?

2. Using Riis as an example, how would you evaluate the impact of documentary photography on middle-class America's reaction to poverty in the late nineteenth century? How do Riis's photographs of immigrants compare with the Alice Austen image on page 384?

3. Drawing on both Riis and Bessie Van Vorst (see Documents: The Woman Who Toils, pp. 363–68) as sources, in what ways did women's experience of poverty and underpaid labor in this period differ from that of men?

VISUAL SOURCES

Women in the Cartoons of *Puck* Magazine

B Y 1900 AMERICAN LITERACY in English had risen to about 90 percent of white Americans and 50 percent of African Americans. Among both groups women were more literate than men. America's high literacy rate helped create a market for low-cost, mass-market print media.

The late nineteenth-century reading public was particularly fond of illustrated magazines that mixed words and images, political commentary and humor. Chief among these was *Puck* magazine, launched in the 1870s by German immigrant Joseph Keppler. *Puck* and magazines like it offer useful glimpses into popular opinions and cultural attitudes of the period, including assumptions about gender. *Puck* was famous for its cartoons, which included both serious commentaries on political issues and lighthearted jokes about social and cultural matters. Both political and humorous cartoons frequently portrayed women—but in quite different ways.

The changing face and place of women in American society provided rich material for *Puck*'s humor. Many jokes in *Puck*'s cartoons rested on stereotypes of women, from the mannish middle-class suffragist to the backward female immigrant. *Puck*'s humorous treatment of late nineteenth-century women contrasted sharply with the magazine's frequent use of female figures in its didactic political cartoons. Here political abstractions in female form were as reverent and conventional as the images of immigrant and native-born women were overstated and ridiculous.

The 1892 cartoon strip in Figure 7.6 ridicules ethnic stereotypes, especially about gender relations. Pedro, an Italian immigrant, praises America for its promise of liberty and freedom, despite his uncomplaining, overburdened wife. Then, an Irish policeman berates Pedro for the treatment of his wife, even though his own wife works over a washtub. How is the reader to recognize Italian and Irish immigrants? Is it the men or the immigrant groups that are being stereotyped and ridiculed? What is the implication about the superiority of gender relations among native-born Americans?

The contrast between native-born and immigrant women, especially as employer and servant in the middle-class household, is featured in Figure 7.7, also published in *Puck* in 1892. The Irish maid was such a stock cartoon figure that she was always drawn the same way. Notice the similarity to the 1852 drawing in Figure 4.5 (p. 237). In this cartoon, however, the native-born employer, while beautiful and well dressed, is also being ridiculed. How does the cartoonist make fun of this woman? In what ways does the contrast between mistress and maid set up the joke? What does the cartoon's title mean, about the woman as well as about the rolling pin?

PEDRO.— Dis is de greata countra,
    De landa liberty
De placea to maka de mon.
    An' evera-t'inga free!

OFFICER McSWEENEY — Take oop thot great big boondle
    Or Oi'll take your haythen loife.
This is a land where ivery man
    Has got t' pertect his woife.

ISABELLA.— O Pedro! Pedro! don'ta swear,
    It maka me cry to see!
Whena we get past de corner,
    You giva de t'ings to me.

MRS. McSWEENEY.— It does me proud to hear yez say
    Yez tuk the poor gurl's par-r-rt.
But, Dinny dear, yez always had
    A koind, considerate hear-r-rt.

◆ **Figure 7.6 The Woman of It**

Collection of the New-York Historical Society, negative #76758d.

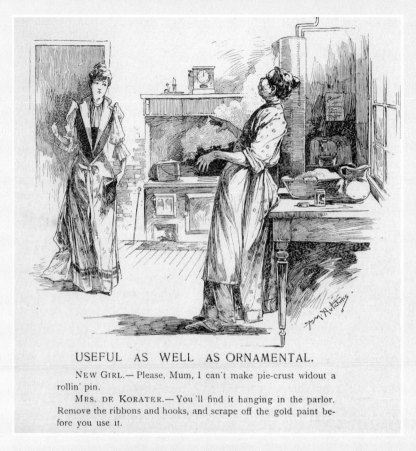

USEFUL AS WELL AS ORNAMENTAL.

NEW GIRL.— Please, Mum, I can't make pie-crust widout a rollin' pin.

MRS. DE KORATER.— You'll find it hanging in the parlor. Remove the ribbons and hooks, and scrape off the gold paint before you use it.

◆ Figure 7.7 **Useful as Well as Ornamental**
Collection of the New-York Historical Society, negative #76759d.

What does her name, "Mrs. de Korater," suggest about the role of middle-class women in America's consumer culture?

Puck also featured cartoons on women's demand for voting rights and entry into male-dominated professions. In Figure 7.8, a cartoon published in 1898, the woman away at her women's rights meeting sets up the joke. As far back as 1848, the great French cartoonist Honoré Daumier had used a similar image of a beleaguered husband, unmanned by the demands of childrearing in the absence of his wife, to warn of the chaos that public roles for women would bring to daily life. How does the cartoon subtly mock the absent woman's concerns with rights outside the household? How sympathetic is the cartoonist to the husband's hopes for a peaceful home and supportive wife? By changing the gender of the cradle-rocker from female to male, what does the cartoon suggest

IRONY.

For a quiet life he got him a wife; now, with patience more than human,
He tends the children and anxiously waits, each night, for the Coming Woman;
    For his wife o' nights on Woman's Rights declaims, with invectives hurled,
        That "The Hand That Rocks the Cradle is the Hand That Rules the World!"

◆ **Figure 7.8 Irony**
*Collection of the New-York Historical
Society, negative #76760d.*

WHAT WE ARE COMING TO.

THE TYPEWRITER.— Beg pardon! Did you say "My learned *sister* is mistaken —?"
THE LAWYER.— Yes; Miss Bigfee is the opposing counsel in this case.

◆ **Figure 7.9 What We Are
Coming To**
*Collection of the New-York Historical
Society, negative #76761d.*

about the old sentimental claim about maternal power: "The hand that rocks the cradle is the hand that rules the world"?

By the late nineteenth century, women were making gains into heretofore all-male professions such as medicine. The legal profession, however, remained determinedly male, making the notion of a woman lawyer a good way to make fun of women's changing roles and a fine source of pictorial amusement. Many of *Puck*'s visual jokes about women's new roles used the same stereotype as the female attorney in Figure 7.9, a caricature that bore a striking resemblance to Susan B. Anthony, the venerable leader of the nineteenth-century women's rights movement (see p. 327 for a photograph of Anthony). How is the woman lawyer portrayed as crossing the line into mannishness? Office work continued to be a male-dominated vocation, yet the cartoonist makes the male secretary look less than manly; how?

In contrast to the negative way middle-class women's ambitions for political and economic equality were usually rendered, the New Woman's increasing athleticism and physical vitality were attractive to illustrators, most famously Charles Dana Gibson. The 1900 *Puck* cartoon in Figure 7.10 owes a great deal to the new standard of feminine beauty represented by the strapping and beautiful "Gibson girl." What elements of the illustration make for an image of womanhood that

◆ Figure 7.10
**An Important
Point**
*Collection of the New-
York Historical Society,
negative #76762d.*

AN IMPORTANT POINT.
"I'm afraid we are a little slow yet."
"Possibly; but I'm sure we don't look slow!"

◆ **Figure 7.11 Unconscious of Their Doom**
Collection of the New-York Historical Society, negative #76763d.

was daringly sexy for the period? How does the dialogue between the two women undercut the visual portrayal of assertion and strength?

In the political cartoons so prominent in *Puck*, representations of actual women are rare, despite the growing involvement of women in politics. Instead, angels, goddesses, and madonnas are used as symbols for abstract concepts, such as national sovereignty or public virtue (see Visual Sources: Gendering Images of the Revolution, pp. 162 68). Ironically, cartoonists used women as symbols for the ideas and institutions of democratic political life from which actual women were excluded.

◆ Figure 7.12 **The Duty of the Hour: To Save Her Not Only from Spain but from a Worse Fate**
Culver Pictures.

Figure 7.11 features the powerful female figure "Columbia" to represent American democratic virtue and hope. Columbia was the female counterpart of Uncle Sam, who did not displace her as the personification of American nationhood until the 1920s. The dedication in 1885 of the Statue of Liberty gave Columbia new heft and importance. In this 1891 image she represents "human rights" as opposed to the "divine right" of monarchs, which she attacks by way of "education." What is the message about the future of American democracy as opposed to the outmoded European political order and its colonial minions? How does it benefit American democracy to be pictured as a woman?

Such uses of female imagery helped prepare the way for America to undertake its own imperial role by century's end. Mass media played a major role in stirring up popular enthusiasm for U.S. intervention in 1898 in the war between Cuba and Spain. The political cartoon in Figure 7.12 fuses visual and verbal clichés in support of Congress's declaration of war against Spain allegedly on Cuba's behalf. How does the cartoon play on the saying "Out of the frying-pan, into the fire"? How does the terrified dark-skinned young woman, who represents the national spirit of Cuba, contrast with the icon of Columbia in Figure 7.11? How does the female figure emphasize what many opinion makers saw as America's moral obligation to intervene on Cuba's behalf?

QUESTIONS FOR ANALYSIS

1. How do the *Puck* stereotypes of immigrant women compare to Jacob Riis's photographs of immigrant girls and women in Figures 7.1–7.5?

2. How does the symbolic use of female figures in late nineteenth-century political cartoons (Figures 7.11 and 7.12) contrast with the depictions of women in cartoons meant to amuse (Figures 7.6–7.10)?

3. How does the assumption that men should protect women function throughout these cartoons? Consider the stereotypes of immigrant women, the ridicule of native-born women entering public life, and the use of female representations to justify American imperial ambitions.

NOTES

1. Shige Kushida is mentioned in Mei Nakano, *Japanese American Women: Three Generations, 1890– 1990* (Berkeley: Mina Press, 1990). Our version of her life differs on the basis of information provided by Rumi Yasutake, Kobe University, author of *Transnational Women's Activism: The United States, Japan, and Japanese Immigrant Communities in California, 1859–1920* (New York: NYU Press, 2004).

2. Laura Jane Moore, "Lozen," in Theda Perdue, ed., *Sifters: Native American Women's Lives* (New York: Oxford University Press, 2001), 93.

3. Nelson Miles to George Baird, November 20, 1891, Baird Collection, Western Americana Collection, Beinecke Library, Yale University.

4. The term is from Alvin M. Josephy, *500 Nations: An Illustrated History of North American Indians* (New York: Knopf, 1994), 430.

5. Carolyn J. Marr, "Assimilation through Education: Indian Boarding Schools in the Pacific Northwest," http://content.lib.washington.edu/aipnw/marr.html (accessed June 28, 2004).

6. "A Man Plants the Fields of His Wife," in Ruth Barnes Moynihan, Cynthia Russett, and Laurie Crumpacker, eds., *Second to None: A Documentary History of American Women* (Lincoln: University of Nebraska Press, 1993), 2:82–83.

7. Linda Williams Reese, *Women of Oklahoma, 1890–1920* (Norman: University of Oklahoma Press, 1997), 152–53.

8. Diary of Lucy Hannah White Flake, excerpted in Joan M. Jensen, ed., *With These Hands: Women Working on the Land* (Old Westbury, NY: Feminist Press, 1981), 137–38.

9. Glenda Riley, *A Place to Grow: Women in the American West* (Arlington Heights: Harlan Davidson, 1992), 239.

10. Reese, *Women of Oklahoma*, 38.

11. Michael Lewis Goldberg, *An Army of Women: Gender and Politics in Gilded Age Kansas* (Baltimore: Johns Hopkins University Press, 1997), 40.

12. The term comes from Paula Petrik, *No Step Backward: Women and Family on the Rocky Mountain Mining Frontier, Helena, Montana, 1865–1900* (Helena: Montana Historical Society Press, 1987), 28.

13. Mother Mary Jones, *Autobiography of Mother Jones* (1925; repr., Chicago: C. H. Kerr, 1990), 204.

14. Elizabeth Jameson, "Imperfect Unions: Class and Gender in Cripple Creek, 1894–1904," in Milton Cantor and Bruce Laurie, eds., *Class, Sex, and the Woman Worker* (Westport: Greenwood Press, 1977), 171.

15. Joan Morrison and Charlotte Fox Zabusky, *American Mosaic: The Immigrant Experience in the Worlds of Those Who Lived It* (New York: E. P. Dutton, 1980), 9.

16. Linda Mack Schloff, *"And Prairie Dogs Weren't Kosher": Jewish Women in the Upper Midwest Since 1855* (St. Paul: Minnesota Historical Society Press, 1996), 28.

17. Edith Abbott, *Immigration: Select Documents and Case Records* (Chicago: University of Chicago Press, 1924), 719.

18. Him Mark Lai, Genny Lim, and Judy Yung, *Island: Poetry and History of Chinese Immigrants on Angel Island, 1910–1940* (San Francisco: San Francisco Study Center, 1980), 74.

19. Jane Addams, *Twenty Years at Hull-House,* edited with an introduction by Victoria Bissell Brown (1910; repr., Boston: Bedford/St. Martin's, 1999), 72.

20. Aileen Kraditor, *Ideas of the Woman Suffrage Movement, 1890–1920* (New York: Columbia University Press, 1965), 128.

21. Theodore Roosevelt, introduction to Mrs. John Van Vorst and Marie Van Vorst, *The Woman Who Toils: Being the Experiences of Two Ladies as Factory Girls* (New York: Doubleday, Page & Co., 1903), vii.

22. Anzia Yezierska, *Bread Givers* (1925; repr., New York: George Brazillier, 1975), 135.

23. Addams, *Twenty Years at Hull-House,* 166.

24. Ellen Carol DuBois, *The Elizabeth Cady Stanton–Susan B. Anthony Reader: Correspondence, Writings, Speeches,* rev. ed. (Boston: Northeastern University Press, 1992), 205.

25. Jensen, *With These Hands,* 157–58.

26. Susan B. Anthony and Ida H. Harper, eds., *History of Woman Suffrage* (Rochester, NY: Susan B. Anthony, 1902), 4:519.

27. Jensen, *With These Hands,* 147.

28. Ida H. Harper, ed., *History of Woman Suffrage* (New York: National American Woman Suffrage Association, 1922), 5:518.

29. Anthony and Harper, *History of Woman Suffrage,* 4:647.

30. "Women Keep Up Courage," *San Francisco Chronicle,* November 5, 1896. Thanks to Ann Gordon for the citation.

31. Marion K. Barthelme, ed., *Women in the Texas Populist Movement: Letters to the Southern Mercury* (College Station: Texas A&M Press, 1997), 111.

32. Moynihan, Russett, and Crumpacker, *Second to None,* 2:81.

33. Emma Goldman, *Living My Life,* ed. Richard and Anna Maria Drinnon (New York: New American Library, 1977), 122.

34. Kathryn Kish Sklar, *Florence Kelley and the Nation's Work* (New Haven: Yale University Press, 1995), 272.

35. Addams, *Twenty Years at Hull-House,* 156.

36. Alice Miller, "Hull House," *The Charities* (February 1892): 167–73.

37. Sklar, *Florence Kelley,* 215.

38. Ibid., 283.

39. Frances Willard, *The Autobiography of an American Woman, Glimpses of Fifty Years* (Chicago: Woman's Temperance Publishing Association, 1892), 431.

40. Kristin Hoganson, *Fighting for American Manhood: How Gender Politics Provoked the Spanish-American and Philippine-American Wars* (New Haven: Yale University Press, 1998), 11.

41. Allen Davis, *An American Heroine: The Life and Legend of Jane Addams* (New York: Oxford University Press, 1973), 140.

42. Allison Sneider, "Reconstruction, Expansion and Empire: The U.S. Woman Suffrage Movement and the Re-making of the National Political Community" (PhD dissertation, University of California–Los Angeles, 1999), 172.

43. Laura Wexler, *Tender Violence: Domestic Visions in an Age of U.S. Imperialism* (Chapel Hill: University of North Carolina Press, 2000).

44. Jane Addams, *Twenty Years at Hull-House*, 95.

45. Jacob A. Riis, *How the Other Half Lives: Studies among the Tenements of New York*, ed. David Leviatin (1890; repr. Boston: Bedford/St. Martin's, 1996), 61.

46. Ibid., 92.

47. Ibid., 91.

48. Ibid., 95.

49. Ibid., 129.

50. Ibid., 141.

51. Ibid., 140.

52. Ibid., 139.

53. Jacob A. Riis, *The Children of the Poor* (New York: Scribner's Sons, 1892), 82.

54. Jacob A. Riis, *The Making of an American* (New York: Macmillan, 1929), 150.

55. Riis, *Children of the Poor*, 80.

SUGGESTED REFERENCES

Women and Western Settlement   For an overall perspective on the consolidation of the West through the eyes of diverse groups of women, see the two excellent anthologies compiled by Susan Armitage and Elizabeth Jameson: *The Woman's West* (1987) and *Writing the Range: Race, Class, and Culture in the Women's West* (1997). Among many useful other books on this subject, see Glenda Riley, *A Place to Grow: Women in the American West* (1992); Ruth B. Moynihan, Susan Armitage, and Christiane Fischer Dichamp, eds., *So Much to Be Done: Women Settlers on the Mining and Ranching Frontier* (1990); and Julie Roy Jeffrey, *Frontier Women: The Trans-Mississippi West, 1840–1880* (1979). Linda Williams Reese, *Women of Oklahoma, 1890–1920* (1997), focuses on a single, interesting state. For two excellent local studies of women in the Wild West, see Marion Goldman, *Gold Diggers and Silver Miners: Prostitution and Social Life on the Comstock Lode* (1968), and Elizabeth Jameson, *All That Glitters: Class Conflict and Community in Cripple Creek* (1998). Two recent collections focus on Native American women in the West and cover a wide range of experiences: Theda Perdue, ed., *Sifters: Native American Women's Lives* (2001), and Nancy Shoemaker, ed., *Negotiators of Change: Historical Perspectives on Native*

American Women (1995). On the La Flesche sisters, see Norma Kidd, *Iron Eye's Family: The Children of Joseph La Flesche* (1969), and Benson Tong, *Susan La Flesche Picotte, MD: Omaha Indian Leader and Reformer* (1994). Helen Hunt Jackson's 1881 exposé, *A Century of Dishonor,* is still compelling. Valerie Mathes, *Helen Hunt Jackson and Her Indian Reform Legacy* (1997), also covers the formation of the Woman's National Indian Association.

On Mexican American women in the Southwest before the major waves of immigration in the twentieth century, see Sarah Deutsch, *No Separate Refuge: Culture, Class, and Gender on the Anglo-Hispanic Frontier in the American Southwest, 1880–1940* (1987), and Lisbeth Haas, *Conquests and Historical Identities in California, 1769–1836* (1995). Also, Linda Gordon's *The Great Arizona Orphan Abduction* (1999) examines ethnic and religious conflicts between Anglo and Hispanic women in southern Arizona.

Immigrant Women　The best general study on women and immigration is Donna Gabaccia, *The Other Side: Women, Gender, and Immigrant Life in the U.S., 1820–1990* (1994). Other general studies, concentrating mostly on European immigrants, include Katrina Irving, *Immigrant Mothers: Narratives of Race and Maternity, 1890–1925* (2000); Kristine Leach, *In Search of a Common Ground: Nineteenth and Twentieth Century Immigrant Women in America* (1995); and Doris Weatherford, *Foreign and Female: Immigrant Women in America, 1840–1930* (1986). For studies of women from particular groups, see the comparison of Italians and Eastern European Jews in Elizabeth Ewen, *Immigrant Women in the Land of Dollars: Life and Culture on the Lower East Side, 1890–1925* (1985), and Judith E. Smith, *Family Connections: A History of Italian and Jewish Immigrant Lives in Providence, Rhode Island, 1900–1940* (1985). Other studies of Jews include Susan Glenn, *Daughters of the Shtetl: Life and Labor in the Immigrant Generation* (1990), and Barbara Schreier, *Becoming American Women: Clothing and the American Jewish Experience* (1994). Linda Mack Schloff offers an unusual perspective in *"And Prairie Dogs Weren't Kosher": Jewish Women in the Upper Midwest since 1855* (1996). On Italian immigrant women, see Miriam Cohen, *Workshop to Office: Two Generations of Italian Women in New York City, 1900–1950* (1992), and Virginia Yans McLaughlin, *Family and Community: Italian Immigrants in Buffalo, 1880–1930* (1977). Hasia Diner considers Irish immigrant women in *Erin's Daughters in America: Irish Immigrant Women in the Nineteenth Century* (1983). Suzanne Sinke has researched an understudied group in *Dutch Immigrant Women in the United States* (2002).

For non-European immigrants, see *Chinese Women of America: A Pictorial History* (1986), *Unbound Feet: A Social History of Chinese Women in San Francisco* (1995), and *Unbound Voices: A Documentary History of Chinese Women in San Francisco* (1999), all by Judith Yung. See also Lucy Salyer, *Laws Harsh as Tigers: Chinese Immigrants and the Shaping of Modern Immigration Law* (1995). For Japanese women immigrants, see Mei Nakano, *Japanese American Women: Three Generations 1890–1990* (1990), and Evelyn Nakano Glenn, *Isssei, Nisei, War Bride: Three Generations of Japanese American Women in Domestic Service* (1986). On Mexican immigrant women, see Vicki Ruiz, *From Out of the Shadows: Mexican Women in Twentieth-Century America* (1998).

Women Reformers   On the history of women and the Populist revolt, see Rebecca Edwards, *Angels in the Machinery: Gender in American Party Politics from the Civil War to the Progressive Era* (1997), and Michael Lewis Goldberg, *An Army of Women: Gender and Politics in Gilded Age Kansas* (1997). For the western suffrage movement that Populism reinvigorated, see Rebecca Mcad, *How the Vote Was Won: Woman Suffrage in the Western United States, 1868–1914* (2004). For southern Populism, see Marion K. Barthelme, ed., *Women in the Texas Populist Movement: Letters to the Southern Mercury* (1997), and Julie Roy Jeffrey, "Women in the Southern Farmers' Alliance: A Reconstruction of the Role and Status of Women in the Late Nineteenth-Century South," *Feminist Studies* 3:1/2 (1975): 72–91.

On the Pullman strike from a women's perspective, see Janice Reiff, "A Modern Lear and His Daughters: Gender in the Model Town of Pullman," *Journal of Social History* 23 (1997): 316–41. For the leadership of Hull House women in this period, see Victoria Bissell Brown, *The Education of Jane Addams* (2004), and Kathryn Kish Sklar, *Florence Kelley and the Nation's Work* (1995). The best general studies of settlement houses are Allen F. Davis, *Spearheads for Reform: The Social Settlements and the Progressive Movement, 1890–1914* (1967) and Mina Carson, *Settlement Folk: Social Thought and the American Settlement Movement, 1885–1930* (1990). Kathryn Sklar, "Hull House in the 1890s: A Community of Women Reformers," *Signs* 10 (1985): 658–77, considers the personal dimension of Hull House for its women residents. Joan Waugh, *Unsentimental Reformer: The Life of Josephine Shaw Lowell* (1994), examines a leading woman reformer in New York in the 1893 depression. Elizabeth Lasch-Quinn considers racism and racial segregation in the settlement house movement in *Black Neighbors: Race and the Limits of Reform in the American Settlement House Movement, 1890–1945* (1993).

On the female missionary contribution, see Patricia Hill, *The World Their Household: The American Woman's Foreign Mission Movement and Cultural Transformation, 1870–1920* (1985); Patricia Grimshaw, *Paths of Duty: American Missionary Wives in Nineteenth-Century Hawaii* (1987); and Ian Tyrrell, *Woman's World/Woman's Empire: The Woman's Christian Temperance Union in International Perspective, 1880–1930* (1991). On gender and late nineteenth-century imperialism, see Kristin Hoganson, *Fighting for American Manhood: How Gender Politics Provoked the Spanish American and Philippine-American Wars* (1998); Gail Bederman, *Manliness and Civilization: A Cultural History of Gender and Race in the United States, 1880–1917* (1995); Alison Sneider, *Suffragists in an Imperial Age: U.S. Expansion and the Woman Question, 1870–1929* (2008); and Laura Wexler, *Tender Violence: Domestic Visions in an Age of U.S. Imperialism* (2000).

For selected Web sites, please visit the *Through Women's Eyes* book companion site at bedfordstmartins.com/duboisdumenil.

The Declaration of Independence

IN CONGRESS, JULY 4, 1776,
THE UNANIMOUS DECLARATION OF THE
THIRTEEN UNITED STATES OF AMERICA

When in the Course of human events, it becomes necessary for one people to dissolve the political bands which have connected them with another, and to assume among the Powers of the earth, the separate and equal station to which the Laws of Nature and of Nature's God entitle them, a decent respect to the opinions of mankind requires that they should declare the causes which impel them to the separation.

We hold these truths to be self-evident, that all men are created equal, that they are endowed by their Creator with certain unalienable rights, that among these are Life, Liberty, and the pursuit of Happiness. That to secure these rights, Governments are instituted among Men, deriving their just powers from the consent of the governed. That whenever any Form of Government becomes destructive of these ends, it is the Right of the People to alter or to abolish it, and to institute new Government, laying its foundation on such principles and organizing its powers in such form, as to them shall seem most likely to effect their Safety and Happiness. Prudence, indeed, will dictate that Governments long established should not be changed for light and transient causes; and accordingly all experience hath shown, that mankind are more disposed to suffer, while evils are sufferable, than to right themselves by abolishing the forms to which they are accustomed. But when a long train of abuses and usurpations, pursuing invariably the same Object evinces a de-

sign to reduce them under absolute Despotism, it is their right, it is their duty, to throw off such Government, and to provide new Guards for their future security. — Such has been the patient sufferance of these Colonies; and such is now the necessity which constrains them to alter their former Systems of Government. The history of the present King of Great Britain is a history of repeated injuries and usurpations, all having in direct object the establishment of an absolute Tyranny over these States. To prove this, let Facts be submitted to a candid world.

He has refused his Assent to Laws, the most wholesome and necessary for the public good.

He has forbidden his Governors to pass Laws of immediate and pressing importance, unless suspended in their operation till his Assent should be obtained; and, when so suspended, he has utterly neglected to attend to them.

He has refused to pass other Laws for the accommodation of large districts of people, unless those people would relinquish the right of Representation in the Legislature, a right inestimable to them and formidable to tyrants only.

He has called together legislative bodies at places unusual, uncomfortable, and distant from the depository of their public Records, for the sole purpose of fatiguing them into compliance with his measures.

He has dissolved Representative Houses repeatedly, for opposing with manly firmness his invasions on the rights of the people.

He has refused for a long time, after such dissolutions, to cause others to be elected; whereby the Legislative powers, incapable of Annihilation, have returned to the People at large for their exercise; the State remaining in the mean time exposed to all the dangers of invasion from without and convulsions within.

He has endeavoured to prevent the population of these States; for that purpose obstructing the Laws of Naturalization of Foreigners; refusing to pass others to encourage their migrations hither, and raising the conditions of new Appropriations of Lands.

He has obstructed the Administration of Justice, by refusing his Assent to Laws for establishing Judiciary powers.

He has made Judges dependent on his Will alone, for the tenure of their offices, and the amount and payment of their salaries.

He has erected a multitude of New Offices, and sent hither swarms of Officers to harass our People, and eat out their substance.

He has kept among us, in times of peace, Standing Armies without the Consent of our legislature.

He has combined with others to subject us to a jurisdiction foreign to our constitution, and unacknowledged by our laws; giving his Assent to their Acts of pretended Legislation:

For quartering large bodies of armed troops among us:

For protecting them, by a mock Trial, from Punishment for any Murders which they should commit on the Inhabitants of these States:

For cutting off our Trade with all parts of the world:

For imposing taxes on us without our Consent:

For depriving us, in many cases, of the benefits of Trial by jury:

For transporting us beyond Seas to be tried for pretended offences:

For abolishing the free System of English Laws in a neighbouring Province, establishing therein an Arbitrary government, and enlarging its Boundaries so as to render it at once an example and fit instrument for introducing the same absolute rule into these Colonies:

For taking away our Charters, abolishing our most valuable Laws, and altering fundamentally the Forms of our Governments:

For suspending our own Legislatures, and declaring themselves invested with Power to legislate for us in all cases whatsoever.

He has abdicated Government here, by declaring us out of his Protection and waging War against us.

He has plundered our seas, ravaged our Coasts, burnt our towns, and destroyed the lives of our people.

He is at this time transporting large armies of foreign mercenaries to compleat the works of death, desolation, and tyranny, already begun with circumstances of Cruelty & perfidy scarcely paralleled in the most barbarous ages, and totally unworthy the Head of a civilized nation.

He has constrained our fellow Citizens taken Captive on the high Seas to bear Arms against their Country, to become the executioners of their friends and Brethren, or to fall themselves by their Hands.

He has excited domestic insurrections amongst us, and has endeavoured to bring on the inhabitants of our frontiers, the merciless Indian Savages, whose known rule of warfare, is an undistinguished destruction of all ages, sexes, and conditions.

In every stage of these Oppressions We have Petitioned for Redress in the most humble terms: Our repeated Petitions have been answered only by repeated injury. A Prince, whose character is thus marked by every act which may define a Tyrant, is unfit to be the ruler of a free people.

Nor have We been wanting in attention to our British brethren. We have warned them from time to time of attempts by their legislature to extend an unwarrantable jurisdiction over us. We have reminded them of the circumstances of our emigration and settlement here. We have appealed to their native justice and magnanimity, and we have conjured them by the ties of our common kindred to disavow these usurpations, which, would inevitably interrupt our connections and correspondence. They too have been deaf to the voice of justice and of consanguinity. We must, therefore, acquiesce in the necessity, which denounces our Separation, and hold them, as we hold the rest of mankind, Enemies in War, in Peace Friends.

We, therefore, the Representatives of the United States of America, in General Congress, Assembled, appealing to the Supreme Judge of the world for the rectitude of our intentions, do, in the Name, and by Authority of the good People of these Colonies, solemnly publish and declare, That these United Colonies are, and of Right ought to be FREE AND INDEPENDENT STATES; that they are Absolved from all Allegiance to the British Crown, and that all political connection between them and the State of Great Britain, is and ought to be totally dissolved; and that as Free and Independent States, they have full Power to levy War, conclude Peace, contract Alliances, establish Commerce, and to do all other Acts and Things which Independent States may of right do. And for the support of this Declaration, with a firm reliance on the Protection of Divine Providence, we mutually pledge to each other our Lives, our Fortunes, and our sacred Honor.

John Hancock

Button Gwinnett	George Wythe	James Wilson	Josiah Bartlett
Lyman Hall	Richard Henry Lee	Geo. Ross	Wm. Whipple
Geo. Walton	Th. Jefferson	Caesar Rodney	Matthew Thornton
Wm. Hooper	Benja. Harrison	Geo. Read	Saml. Adams
Joseph Hewes	Thos. Nelson, Jr.	Thos. M'Kean	John Adams
John Penn	Francis Lightfoot Lee	Wm. Floyd	Robt. Treat Paine
Edward Rutledge	Carter Braxton	Phil. Livingston	Elbridge Gerry
Thos. Heyward, Junr.	Robt. Morris	Frans. Lewis	Step. Hopkins
Thomas Lynch, Junr.	Benjamin Rush	Lewis Morris	William Ellery
Arthur Middleton	Benja. Franklin	Richd. Stockton	Roger Sherman
Samuel Chase	John Morton	John Witherspoon	Sam'el Huntington
Wm. Paca	Geo. Clymer	Fras. Hopkinson	Wm. Williams
Thos. Stone	Jas. Smith	John Hart	Oliver Wolcott
Charles Carroll	Geo. Taylor	Abra. Clark	
of Carrollton			

The Constitution of the United States of America

AGREED TO BY PHILADELPHIA
CONVENTION, SEPTEMBER 17, 1787
IMPLEMENTED MARCH 4, 1789

We the People of the United States, in Order to form a more perfect Union, establish Justice, insure domestic Tranquility, provide for the common defence, promote the general Welfare, and secure the Blessings of Liberty to ourselves and our Posterity, do ordain and establish this Constitution for the United States of America.

ARTICLE I

Section 1.   All legislative Powers herein granted shall be vested in a Congress of the United States, which shall consist of a Senate and a House of Representatives.

Section 2.   The House of Representatives shall be composed of Members chosen every second Year by the People of the several States, and the Electors in each State shall have the Qualifications requisite for Electors of the most numerous Branch of the State Legislature.

No Person shall be a Representative who shall not have attained to the Age of twenty-five Years, and been seven Years a Citizen of the United States, and who shall not, when elected, be an Inhabitant of that State in which he shall be chosen.

Representatives and direct Taxes shall be apportioned among the several States which may be included within this Union, according to their respective Numbers, *which shall be determined by adding to the whole Number of free Persons, including those bound to Service for a Term of Years, and excluding Indians not taxed, three fifths of all other Persons.*[1] The actual Enumeration shall be made within three Years after the first Meeting of the Congress of the United States, and within every subsequent Term of ten Years, in such Manner as they shall by Law direct. The Number of Representatives shall not exceed one for every thirty Thousand, but each State shall have at Least one Representative; and *until such enumeration shall be made, the State of New Hampshire shall be entitled to chuse three, Massachusetts eight, Rhode Island and Providence Plantations one, Connecticut five, New-York six, New Jersey four, Pennsylvania eight, Delaware one, Maryland six, Virginia ten, North Carolina five, South Carolina five, and Georgia three.*

When vacancies happen in the Representation from any State, the Executive Authority thereof shall issue Writs of Election to fill such Vacancies.

The House of Representatives shall chuse their Speaker and other Officers; and shall have the sole Power of Impeachment.

Section 3.   The Senate of the United States shall be composed of two Senators from each State, *chosen by the Legislature thereof,*[2] for six Years; and each Senator shall have one Vote.

Note: The Constitution became effective March 4, 1789. Provisions in italics are no longer relevant or have been changed by constitutional amendment.

[1]Changed by Section 2 of the Fourteenth Amendment.
[2]Changed by Section 1 of the Seventeenth Amendment.

Immediately after they shall be assembled in Consequence of the first Election, they shall be divided as equally as may be into three Classes. The Seats of the Senators of the first Class shall be vacated at the Expiration of the second Year, of the second Class at the Expiration of the fourth Year, and of the third Class at the Expiration of the sixth Year, so that one-third may be chosen every second Year; and if Vacancies happen by Resignation, or otherwise, during the Recess of the Legislature of any State, the Executive thereof may make temporary Appointments until the next Meeting of the Legislature, which shall then fill such Vacancies.[3]

No person shall be a Senator who shall not have attained to the Age of thirty Years, and been nine Years a Citizen of the United States, and who shall not, when elected, be an Inhabitant of that State for which he shall be chosen.

The Vice President of the United States shall be President of the Senate, but shall have no Vote, unless they be equally divided.

The Senate shall chuse their other Officers, and also a President pro tempore, in the absence of the Vice President, or when he shall exercise the Office of President of the United States.

The Senate shall have the sole Power to try all Impeachments. When sitting for that Purpose, they shall be on Oath or Affirmation. When the President of the United States is tried, the Chief Justice shall preside: And no Person shall be convicted without the Concurrence of two thirds of the Members present.

Judgment in Cases of Impeachment shall not extend further than to removal from Office, and disqualification to hold and enjoy any Office of honor, Trust or Profit under the United States: but the Party convicted shall nevertheless be liable and subject to Indictment, Trial, Judgment and Punishment, according to Law.

Section 4. The Times, Places and Manner of holding Elections for Senators and Representatives, shall be prescribed in each State by the Legislature thereof; but the Congress may at any time by Law make or alter such Regulations, except as to the Places of Chusing Senators.

The Congress shall assemble at least once in every Year, and such Meeting *shall be on the first Monday in December, unless they shall by Law appoint a different Day.*[4]

Section 5. Each House shall be the Judge of the Elections, Returns and Qualifications of its own Members, and a Majority of each shall constitute a Quorum to do Business; but a smaller number may adjourn from day to day, and may be authorized to compel the Attendance of absent Members, in such Manner, and under such Penalties, as each House may provide.

Each House may determine the Rules of its Proceedings, punish its Members for disorderly Behavior, and, with the Concurrence of two thirds, expel a Member.

Each House shall keep a Journal of its Proceedings, and from time to time publish the same, excepting such Parts as may in their Judgment require Secrecy; and the Yeas and Nays of the Members of either House on any question shall, at the Desire of one-fifth of those Present, be entered on the Journal.

Neither House, during the Session of Congress, shall, without the Consent of the other, adjourn for more than three days, nor to any other Place than that in which the two Houses shall be sitting.

Section 6. The Senators and Representatives shall receive a Compensation for their Services, to be ascertained by Law, and paid out of the Treasury of the United States. They shall in all Cases, except Treason, Felony and Breach of the Peace, be privileged from Arrest during their Attendance at the Session of their respective Houses, and in going to and returning from the same; and for

---

[3]Changed by Clause 2 of the Seventeenth Amendment.

[4]Changed by Section 2 of the Twentieth Amendment.

any Speech or Debate in either House, they shall not be questioned in any other Place.

No Senator or Representative shall, during the Time for which he was elected, be appointed to any civil Office under the Authority of the United States, which shall have been created, or the Emoluments whereof shall have been increased, during such time; and no Person holding any Office under the United States, shall be a Member of either House during his Continuance in Office.

Section 7. All Bills for raising Revenue shall originate in the House of Representatives; but the Senate may propose or concur with Amendments as on other Bills.

Every Bill which shall have passed the House of Representatives and the Senate, shall, before it becomes a Law, be presented to the President of the United States; If he approve he shall sign it, but if not he shall return it, with his Objections to that House in which it shall have originated, who shall enter the Objections at large on their Journal, and proceed to reconsider it. If after such Reconsideration two thirds of that House shall agree to pass the Bill, it shall be sent, together with the Objections, to the other House, by which it shall likewise be reconsidered, and if approved by two thirds of that House, it shall become a Law. But in all such Cases the Votes of both Houses shall be determined by Yeas and Nays, and the Names of the Persons voting for and against the Bill shall be entered on the Journal of each House respectively. If any Bill shall not be returned by the President within ten Days (Sundays excepted) after it shall have been presented to him, the Same shall be a Law, in like Manner as if he had signed it, unless the Congress by their Adjournment prevent its Return, in which Case it shall not be a Law.

Every Order, Resolution, or Vote to which the Concurrence of the Senate and the House of Representatives may be necessary (except on a question of Adjournment) shall be presented to the President of the United States; and before the Same shall take Effect, shall be approved by him, or being disapproved by him, shall be repassed by two thirds of the Senate and House of Representatives, according to the Rules and Limitations prescribed in the Case of a Bill.

Section 8. The Congress shall have Power to lay and collect Taxes, Duties, Imposts and Excises, to pay the Debts and provide for the common Defence and general Welfare of the United States; but all Duties, Imposts and Excises shall be uniform throughout the United States;

To borrow money on the credit of the United States;

To regulate Commerce with foreign Nations, and among the several States, and with the Indian Tribes;

To establish an uniform Rule of Naturalization, and uniform Laws on the subject of Bankruptcies throughout the United States;

To coin Money, regulate the Value thereof, and of foreign Coin, and fix the Standard of Weights and Measures;

To provide for the Punishment of counterfeiting the Securities and current Coin of the United States;

To establish Post Offices and post Roads;

To promote the Progress of Science and useful Arts, by securing for limited Times to Authors and Inventors the exclusive Right to their respective Writings and Discoveries;

To constitute Tribunals inferior to the supreme Court;

To define and punish Piracies and Felonies committed on the high Seas, and Offenses against the Law of Nations;

To declare War, grant Letters of Marque and Reprisal, and make Rules concerning Captures on Land and Water;

To raise and support Armies, but no Appropriation of Money to that Use shall be for a longer Term than two Years;

To provide and maintain a Navy;

To make Rules for the Government and Regulation of the land and naval Forces;

To provide for calling forth the Militia to execute the Laws of the Union, suppress Insurrections and repel Invasions;

To provide for organizing, arming, and disciplining the Militia, and for governing such Part of them as may be employed in the Service of the United States, reserving to the States respectively, the Appointment of the Officers, and the Authority of training the Militia according to the discipline prescribed by Congress;

To exercise exclusive Legislation in all Cases whatsoever, over such District (not exceeding ten Miles square) as may, by Cession of particular States, and the acceptance of Congress, become the Seat of Government of the United States, and to exercise like Authority over all Places purchased by the Consent of the Legislature of the State in which the Same shall be, for the Erection of Forts, Magazines, Arsenals, dock-Yards, and other needful Buildings;—And

To make all Laws which shall be necessary and proper for carrying into Execution the foregoing Powers, and all other Powers vested by this Constitution in the Government of the United States, or in any Department or Officer thereof.

Section 9. The Migration or Importation of such Persons as any of the States now existing shall think proper to admit, shall not be prohibited by the Congress prior to the Year one thousand eight hundred and eight but a tax or duty may be imposed on such Importation, not exceeding ten dollars for each Person.

The privilege of the Writ of Habeas Corpus shall not be suspended, unless when in Cases of Rebellion or Invasion the public Safety may require it.

No Bill of Attainder or ex post facto Law shall be passed.

No capitation, or other direct, Tax shall be laid, unless in Proportion to the Census or Enumeration herein before directed to be taken.[5]

No Tax or Duty shall be laid on Articles exported from any State.

No Preference shall be given by any Regulation of Commerce or Revenue to the Ports of one State over those of another: nor shall Vessels bound to, or from, one State, be obliged to enter, clear, or pay Duties in another.

No Money shall be drawn from the Treasury, but in Consequence of Appropriations made by law; and a regular Statement and Account of the Receipts and Expenditures of all public Money shall be published from time to time.

No Title of Nobility shall be granted by the United States: And no Person holding any Office of Profit or Trust under them, shall, without the Consent of the Congress, accept of any present, Emolument, Office, or Title, of any kind whatever, from any King, Prince, or foreign State.

Section 10. No State shall enter into any Treaty, Alliance, or Confederation; grant Letters of Marque and Reprisal; coin Money; emit Bills of Credit; make any Thing but gold and silver Coin a Tender in Payment of Debts; pass any Bill of Attainder, ex post facto Law, or Law impairing the Obligation of Contracts, or grant any Title of Nobility.

No State shall, without the Consent of the Congress, lay any Imposts or Duties on Imports or Exports, except what may be absolutely necessary for executing its inspection Laws: and the net Produce of all Duties and Imposts, laid by any State on Imports or Exports, shall be for the Use of the Treasury of the United States; and all such Laws shall be subject to the Revision and Control of the Congress.

No State shall, without the Consent of the Congress, lay any duty of Tonnage, keep Troops, or Ships of War in time of Peace, enter into any Agreement or Compact with another State, or with a foreign Power, or engage in War, unless actually invaded, or in such imminent Danger as will not admit of delay.

Article II

Section 1. The executive Power shall be vested in a President of the United States of America. He

---

[5]Changed by the Sixteenth Amendment.

shall hold his Office during the Term of four Years, and, together with the Vice President, chosen for the same Term, be elected, as follows:

Each State shall appoint, in such Manner as the Legislature thereof may direct, a Number of Electors, equal to the whole Number of Senators and Representatives to which the State may be entitled in the Congress; but no Senator or Representative, or Person holding an Office of Trust or Profit under the United States, shall be appointed an Elector.

The Electors shall meet in their respective States, and vote by Ballot for two Persons, of whom one at least shall not be an Inhabitant of the same State with themselves. And they shall make a List of all the Persons voted for, and of the Number of Votes for each; which List they shall sign and certify, and transmit sealed to the Seat of the Government of the United States, directed to the President of the Senate. The President of the Senate shall, in the Presence of the Senate and House of Representatives, open all the Certificates, and the Votes shall then be counted. The Person having the greatest Number of Votes shall be the President, if such Number be a Majority of the whole Number of Electors appointed; and if there be more than one who have such Majority, and have an equal Number of Votes, then the House of Representatives shall immediately chuse by Ballot one of them for President; and if no Person have a Majority, then from the five highest on the List the said House shall in like Manner chuse the President. But in chusing the President, the Votes shall be taken by States, the Representation from each State having one Vote; a quorum for this Purpose shall consist of a Member or Members from two thirds of the States, and a Majority of all the States shall be necessary to a Choice. In every Case, after the Choice of the President, the Person having the greatest Number of Votes of the Electors shall be the Vice President. But if there should remain two or more who have equal Votes, the Senate shall chuse from them by Ballot the Vice President.[6]

The Congress may determine the Time of chusing the Electors, and the Day on which they shall give their Votes; which Day shall be the same throughout the United States.

No Person except a natural born Citizen, or a Citizen of the United States, at the time of the Adoption of this Constitution, shall be eligible to the Office of President; neither shall any Person be eligible to that Office who shall not have attained to the Age of thirty five Years, and been fourteen Years a Resident within the United States.

In Case of the Removal of the President from Office, or of his Death, Resignation, or Inability to discharge the Powers and Duties of the said Office, the same shall devolve on the Vice President, and the Congress may by Law provide for the Case of Removal, Death, Resignation, or Inability, both of the President and Vice President, declaring what Officer shall then act as President, and such Officer shall act accordingly, until the Disability be removed, or a President shall be elected.[7]

The President shall, at stated Times, receive for his Services a Compensation, which shall neither be increased nor diminished during the Period for which he shall have been elected, and he shall not receive within that Period any other Emolument from the United States, or any of them.

Before he enter on the Execution of his Office, he shall take the following Oath or Affirmation:—"I do solemnly swear (or affirm) that I will faithfully execute the Office of President of the United States, and will to the best of my Ability, preserve, protect and defend the Constitution of the United States."

Section 2.   The President shall be Commander in Chief of the Army and Navy of the United States, and of the Militia of the several States, when called into the actual Service of the United States; he may require the Opinion, in writing, of the principal Officer in each of the executive Departments, upon any Subject relating to the Duties of their respective Offices, and he shall have

[6]Superseded by the Twelfth Amendment.

[7]Modified by the Twenty-fifth Amendment.

Power to Grant Reprieves and Pardons for Offences against the United States, except in Cases of Impeachment.

He shall have Power, by and with the Advice and Consent of the Senate, to make Treaties, provided two thirds of the Senators present concur; and he shall nominate, and by and with the Advice and Consent of the Senate, shall appoint Ambassadors, other public Ministers and Consuls, Judges of the supreme Court, and all other Officers of the United States, whose Appointments are not herein otherwise provided for, and which shall be established by Law: but the Congress may by Law vest the Appointment of such inferior Officers, as they think proper, in the President alone, in the Courts of Law, or in the Heads of Departments.

The President shall have Power to fill up all Vacancies that may happen during the Recess of the Senate, by granting Commissions which shall expire at the End of their next Session.

Section 3. He shall from time to time give to the Congress Information of the State of the Union, and recommend to their Consideration such Measures as he shall judge necessary and expedient; he may, on extraordinary Occasions, convene both Houses, or either of them, and in Case of Disagreement between them, with Respect to the Time of Adjournment, he may adjourn them to such Time as he shall think proper; he shall receive Ambassadors and other public Ministers; he shall take Care that the Laws be faithfully executed, and shall Commission all the Officers of the United States.

Section 4. The President, Vice President and all civil Officers of the United States, shall be removed from Office on Impeachment for, and Conviction of, Treason, Bribery, or other high Crimes and Misdemeanors.

ARTICLE III

Section 1. The judicial Power of the United States, shall be vested in one supreme Court, and in such inferior Courts as the Congress may from time to time ordain and establish. The Judges, both of the supreme and inferior Courts, shall hold their Offices during good Behaviour, and shall, at stated Times, receive for their Services a Compensation, which shall not be diminished during their Continuance in Office.

Section 2. The judicial Power shall extend to all Cases, in Law and Equity, arising under this Constitution, the Laws of the United States, and Treaties made, or which shall be made, under their Authority;—to all Cases affecting Ambassadors, other public Ministers and Consuls;—to all Cases of admiralty and maritime Jurisdiction;—to Controversies to which the United States shall be a Party;—to Controversies between two or more States;—*between a State and Citizens of another State;*[8]—between Citizens of different States;—between Citizens of the same State claiming Lands under Grants of different States, and between a State, or the Citizens thereof, and foreign States, Citizens or Subjects.

In all Cases affecting Ambassadors, other public Ministers and Consuls, and those in which a State shall be Party, the supreme Court shall have original Jurisdiction. In all the other Cases before mentioned, the supreme Court shall have appellate Jurisdiction, both as to Law and Fact, with such Exceptions, and under such Regulations as the Congress shall make.

The trial of all Crimes, except in Cases of Impeachment, shall be by Jury; and such Trial shall be held in the State where said Crimes shall have been committed; but when not committed within any State, the Trial shall be at such Place or Places as the Congress may by Law have directed.

Section 3. Treason against the United States, shall consist only in levying War against them, or in adhering to their Enemies, giving them Aid and Comfort. No Person shall be convicted of Treason unless on the Testimony of two Witnesses to the same overt Act, or on Confession in open Court.

---

[8]Restricted by the Eleventh Amendment.

The Congress shall have Power to declare the Punishment of Treason, but no Attainder of Treason shall work Corruption of Blood, or Forefeiture except during the Life of the Person attainted.

ARTICLE IV

Section 1.   Full Faith and Credit shall be given in each State to the public Acts, Records, and judicial Proceedings of every other State. And the Congress may by general Laws prescribe the Manner in which such Acts, Records, and Proceedings shall be proved, and the Effect thereof.

Section 2.   The Citizens of each State shall be entitled to all Privileges and Immunities of Citizens in the several States.

A Person charged in any State with Treason, Felony, or other Crime, who shall flee from Justice, and be found in another State, shall on demand of the executive Authority of the State from which he fled, be delivered up, to be removed to the State having Jurisdiction of the Crime.

No Person held to Service or Labour in one State, under the Laws thereof, escaping into another, shall, in Consequence of any Law or Regulation therein, be discharged from such Service or Labour, but shall be delivered up on Claim of the Party to whom such Service or Labour may be due.[9]

Section 3.   New States may be admitted by the Congress into this Union; but no new State shall be formed or erected within the Jurisdiction of any other State; nor any State be formed by the Junction of two or more States, or parts of States, without the Consent of the Legislatures of the States concerned as well as of the Congress.

The Congress shall have Power to dispose of and make all needful Rules and Regulations respecting the Territory or other Property belonging to the United States; and nothing in this Constitution shall be so construed as to Prejudice any Claims of the United States, or of any particular State.

---

[9]Superseded by the Thirteenth Amendment.

Section 4.   The United States shall guarantee to every State in this Union a Republican Form of Government, and shall protect each of them against Invasion; and on Application of the Legislature, or of the Executive (when the Legislature cannot be convened) against domestic Violence.

ARTICLE V

The Congress, whenever two thirds of both Houses shall deem it necessary, shall propose Amendments to this Constitution, or, on the Application of the Legislatures of two thirds of the several States, shall call a Convention for proposing Amendments, which, in either Case, shall be valid to all Intents and Purposes, as Part of this Constitution, when ratified by the Legislatures of three fourths of the several States, or by Conventions in three fourths thereof, as the one or the other Mode of Ratification may be proposed by the Congress; Provided that no Amendment which may be made prior to the Year One thousand eight hundred and eight shall in any Manner affect the first and fourth Clauses in the Ninth Section of the first Article; and that no State, without its Consent, shall be deprived of its equal Suffrage in the Senate.

ARTICLE VI

All Debts contracted and Engagements entered into, before the Adoption of this Constitution, shall be as valid against the United States under this Constitution, as under the Confederation.

This Constitution, and the Laws of the United States which shall be made in Pursuance thereof; and all Treaties made, or which shall be made, under the Authority of the United States, shall be the supreme Law of the Land; and the Judges in every State shall be bound thereby, any Thing in the Constitution or Laws of any State to the Contrary notwithstanding.

The Senators and Representatives before mentioned, and the Members of the several State Legislatures, and all executive and judicial Officers, both of the United States and of the several

States, shall be bound by Oath or Affirmation, to support this Constitution; but no religious Test shall ever be required as a Qualification to any Office or public Trust under the United States.

ARTICLE VII

The Ratification of the Conventions of nine States shall be sufficient for the Establishment of this Constitution between the States so ratifying the Same.

Done in Convention by the Unanimous Consent of the States present the Seventeenth Day of September in the Year of our Lord one thousand seven hundred and Eighty seven and of the Independence of the United States of America the Twelfth. In Witness whereof We have hereunto subscribed our Names.

Go. Washington
President and deputy from Virginia

New Hampshire
John Langdon
Nicholas Gilman

Massachusetts
Nathaniel Gorham
Rufus King

Connecticut
Wm. Saml. Johnson
Roger Sherman

New York
Alexander Hamilton

New Jersey
Wil. Livingston
David Brearley
Wm. Paterson
Jona. Dayton

Pennsylvania
B. Franklin
Thomas Mifflin
Robt. Morris
Geo. Clymer
Thos. FitzSimons
Jared Ingersoll
James Wilson
Gouv. Morris

Delaware
Geo. Read
Gunning Bedford jun
John Dickinson
Richard Bassett
Jaco. Broom

Maryland
James McHenry
Dan. of St. Thos.
    Jenifer
Danl. Carroll

Virginia
John Blair
James Madison, Jr.

North Carolina
Wm. Blount
Richd. Dobbs
    Spaight
Hu Williamson

South Carolina
J. Rutledge
Charles Cotesworth
    Pinckney
Pierce Butler

Georgia
William Few
Abr. Baldwin

Amendments to the Constitution

AMENDMENT I [1791][1]

Congress shall make no law respecting an establishment of religion, or prohibiting the free exercise thereof; or abridging the freedom of speech,
or of the press; or the right of the people peace-
ably to assemble, and to petition the government
for a redress of grievances.

AMENDMENT II [1791]

A well-regulated militia being necessary to the security of a free State, the right of the people to
keep and bear arms shall not be infringed.

AMENDMENT III [1791]

No soldier shall, in time of peace, be quartered in
any house without the consent of the owner, nor
in time of war, but in a manner to be prescribed
by law.

AMENDMENT IV [1791]

The right of the people to be secure in their
persons, houses, papers, and effects, against
unreasonable searches and seizures, shall not be
violated, and no warrants shall issue but
upon probable cause, supported by oath or affirmation, and particularly describing the place to
be searched, and the persons or things to be
seized.

AMENDMENT V [1791]

No person shall be held to answer for a capital, or
otherwise infamous crime, unless on a present-
ment or indictment of a grand jury, except in
cases arising in the land or naval forces, or in the
militia, when in actual service in time of war or
public danger; nor shall any person be subject for
the same offence to be twice put in jeopardy of
life or limb; nor shall be compelled in any criminal case to be a witness against himself, nor be deprived of life, liberty, or property, without due
process of law; nor shall private property be taken
for public use without just compensation.

AMENDMENT VI [1791]

In all criminal prosecutions, the accused shall
enjoy the right to a speedy and public trial, by an
impartial jury of the State and district wherein
the crime shall have been committed, which district shall have been previously ascertained by
law, and to be informed of the nature and cause
of the accusation; to be confronted with the witnesses against him; to have compulsory process
for obtaining witnesses in his favor, and to have
the assistance of counsel for his defence.

AMENDMENT VII [1791]

In suits at common law, where the value in controversy shall exceed twenty dollars, the right of
trial by jury shall be preserved, and no fact tried
by a jury shall be otherwise reexamined in any
court of the United States, than according to the
rules of the common law.

---

[1]The dates in brackets indicate when the amendment was
ratified.

AMENDMENT VIII [1791]

Excessive bail shall not be required, nor excessive fines imposed, nor cruel and unusual punishments inflicted.

AMENDMENT IX [1791]

The enumeration in the Constitution, of certain rights, shall not be construed to deny or disparage others retained by the people.

AMENDMENT X [1791]

The powers not delegated to the United States by the Constitution, nor prohibited by it to the States, are reserved to the States respectively, or to the people.

AMENDMENT XI [1798]

The judicial power of the United States shall not be construed to extend to any suit in law or equity, commenced or prosecuted against one of the United States by citizens of another State, or by citizens or subjects of any foreign state.

AMENDMENT XII [1804]

The electors shall meet in their respective States, and vote by ballot for President and Vice-President, one of whom, at least, shall not be an inhabitant of the same State with themselves; they shall name in their ballots the person voted for as President, and in distinct ballots the person voted for as Vice-President, and they shall make distinct lists of all persons voted for as President, and of all persons voted for as Vice-President, and of the number of votes for each, which lists they shall sign and certify, and transmit sealed to the seat of government of the United States, directed to the President of the Senate;—the President of the Senate shall, in the presence of the Senate and House of Representatives, open all the certificates and the votes shall then be counted;—the person having the greatest number of votes for President shall be the President, if such number be a majority of the whole number of electors appointed; and if no person have such majority, then from the persons having the highest numbers not exceeding three on the list of those voted for as President, the House of Representatives shall choose immediately, by ballot, the President. But in choosing the President, the votes shall be taken by States, the representation from each State having one vote; a quorum for this purpose shall consist of a member or members from two-thirds of the States, and a majority of all the States shall be necessary to a choice. And if the House of Representatives shall not choose a President whenever the right of choice shall devolve upon them, before *the fourth day of March* next following, then the Vice-President shall act as President, as in the case of the death or other constitutional disability of the President.[2]

The person having the greatest number of votes as Vice-President shall be the Vice-President, if such number be a majority of the whole number of electors appointed; and if no person have a majority, then from the two highest numbers on the list the Senate shall choose the Vice-President; a quorum for the purpose shall consist of two-thirds of the whole number of Senators, and a majority of the whole number shall be necessary to a choice. But no person constitutionally ineligible to the office of President shall be eligible to that of Vice-President of the United States.

AMENDMENT XIII [1865]

Section 1. Neither slavery nor involuntary servitude, except as a punishment for crime whereof the party shall have been duly convicted, shall exist within the United States, or any place subject to their jurisdiction.

---

[2]Superseded by Section 3 of the Twentieth Amendment.

Section 2.   Congress shall have power to enforce this article by appropriate legislation.

AMENDMENT XIV [1868]

Section 1.   All persons born or naturalized in the United States, and subject to the jurisdiction thereof, are citizens of the United States and of the State wherein they reside. No State shall make or enforce any law which shall abridge the privileges or immunities of citizens of the United States; nor shall any State deprive any person of life, liberty, or property, without due process of law; nor deny to any person within its jurisdiction the equal protection of the laws.

Section 2.   Representatives shall be appointed among the several States according to their respective numbers, counting the whole number of persons in each State, excluding Indians not taxed. But when the right to vote at any election for the choice of electors for President and Vice-President of the United States, Representatives in Congress, the executive and judicial officers of a State, or the members of the legislature thereof, is denied to any of the male inhabitants of such State, being twenty-one years of age and citizens of the United States, or in any way abridged, except for participation in rebellion, or other crime, the basis of representation therein shall be reduced in the proportion which the number of such male citizens shall bear to the whole number of male citizens twenty-one years of age in such State.

Section 3.   No person shall be a Senator or Representative in Congress, or Elector of President and Vice-President, or hold any office, civil or military, under the United States, or under any State, who, having previously taken an oath, as a member of Congress, or as an officer of the United States, or as a member of any State legislature, or as an executive or judicial officer of any State, to support the Constitution of the United States, shall have engaged in insurrection or rebellion against the same, or given aid or comfort to the enemies thereof. Congress may, by a vote of two-thirds of each house, remove such disability.

Section 4.   The validity of the public debt of the United States, authorized by law, including debts incurred for payment of pensions and bounties for services in suppressing insurrection or rebellion, shall not be questioned. But neither the United States nor any State shall assume or pay any debt or obligation incurred in aid of insurrection or rebellion against the United States, or any claim for the loss or emancipation of any slave; but all such debts, obligations, and claims shall be held illegal and void.

Section 5.   The Congress shall have power to enforce, by appropriate legislation, the provisions of this article.

AMENDMENT XV [1870]

Section 1.   The right of citizens of the United States to vote shall not be denied or abridged by the United States or by any State on account of race, color, or previous condition of servitude.

Section 2.   The Congress shall have power to enforce this article by appropriate legislation.

AMENDMENT XVI [1913]

The Congress shall have power to lay and collect taxes on incomes, from whatever source derived, without apportionment among the several States, and without regard to any census or enumeration.

AMENDMENT XVII [1913]

Section 1.   The Senate of the United States shall be composed of two Senators from each State, elected by the people thereof, for six years; and each Senator shall have one vote. The electors in each State shall have the qualifications requisite for electors of [voters for] the most numerous branch of the State legislatures.

Section 2.   When vacancies happen in the representation of any State in the Senate, the executive authority of such State shall issue writs of election to fill such vacancies: Provided, that the Legislature of any State may empower the executive thereof to make temporary appointments until the people fill the vacancies by election as the Legislature may direct.

Section 3.   This amendment shall not be so construed as to affect the election or term of any Senator chosen before it becomes valid as part of the Constitution.

AMENDMENT XVIII
[1919; REPEALED 1933 BY AMENDMENT XXI]

Section 1.   After one year from the ratification of this article the manufacture, sale, or transportation of intoxicating liquors within, the importation thereof into, or the exportation thereof from the United States and all territory subject to the jurisdiction thereof, for beverage purposes, is hereby prohibited.

Section 2.   The Congress and the several States shall have concurrent power to enforce this article by appropriate legislation.

Section 3.   This article shall be inoperative unless it shall have been ratified as an amendment to the Constitution by the legislatures of the several States, as provided by the Constitution, within seven years from the date of the submission thereof to the States by the Congress.

AMENDMENT XIX [1920]

Section 1.   The right of citizens of the United States to vote shall not be denied or abridged by the United States or by any State on account of sex.

Section 2.   Congress shall have the power to enforce this article by appropriate legislation.

AMENDMENT XX [1933]

Section 1.   The terms of the President and Vice-President shall end at noon on the twentieth day of January, and the terms of Senators and Representatives at noon on the third day of January, of the years in which such terms would have ended if this article had not been ratified; and the terms of their successors shall then began.

Section 2.   The Congress shall assemble at least once in every year, and such meeting shall begin at noon on the third day of January, unless they shall by law appoint a different day.

Section 3.   If, at the time fixed for the beginning of the term of the President, the President-elect shall have died, the Vice-President-elect shall become President. If a President shall not have been chosen before the time fixed for the beginning of his term, or if the President-elect shall have failed to qualify, then the Vice-President-elect shall act as President until a President shall have qualified; and the Congress may by law provide for the case wherein neither a President-elect nor a Vice-President-elect shall have qualified, declaring who shall then act as President, or the manner in which one who is to act shall be selected, and such person shall act accordingly until a President or Vice-President shall have qualified.

Section 4.   The Congress may by law provide for the case of the death of any of the persons from whom the House of Representatives may choose a President whenever the right of choice shall have devolved upon them, and for the case of the death of any of the persons from whom the Senate may choose a Vice-President whenever the right of choice shall have devolved upon them.

Section 5.   Sections 1 and 2 shall take effect on the 15th day of October following the ratification of this article.

Section 6.   This article shall be inoperative unless it shall have been ratified as an amendment to the Constitution by the Legislatures of three-fourths of the several States within seven years from the date of its submission.

AMENDMENT XXI [1933]

Section 1. The eighteenth article of amendment to the Constitution of the United States is hereby repealed.

Section 2. The transportation or importation into any State, Territory, or Possession of the United States for delivery or use therein of intoxicating liquors, in violation of the laws thereof, is hereby prohibited.

Section 3. This article shall be inoperative unless it shall have been ratified as an amendment to the Constitution by conventions in the several States, as provided in the Constitution, within seven years from the date of the submission thereof to the States by the Congress.

AMENDMENT XXII [1951]

Section 1. No person shall be elected to the office of the President more than twice, and no person who has held the office of President, or acted as President, for more than two years of a term to which some other person was elected President shall be elected to the office of President more than once. But this article shall not apply to any person holding the office of President when this Article was proposed by the Congress, and shall not prevent any person who may be holding the office of President, or acting as President, during the term within which this Article becomes operative from holding the office of President or acting as President during the remainder of such term.

Section 2. This article shall be inoperative unless it shall have been ratified as an amendment to the Constitution by the legislatures of three-fourths of the several States within seven years

from the date of its submission to the States by the Congress.

AMENDMENT XXIII [1961]

Section 1. The District constituting the seat of Government of the United States shall appoint in such manner as the Congress may direct: A number of electors of President and Vice-President equal to the whole number of Senators and Representatives in Congress to which the District would be entitled if it were a State, but in no event more than the least populous State; they shall be in addition to those appointed by the States, but they shall be considered for the purposes of the election of President and Vice-President, to be electors appointed by a State; and they shall meet in the District and perform such duties as provided by the twelfth article of amendment.

Section 2. The Congress shall have the power to enforce this article by appropriate legislation.

AMENDMENT XXIV [1964]

Section 1. The right of citizens of the United States to vote in any primary or other election for President or Vice-President, for electors for President or Vice-President, or for Senator or Representative in Congress, shall not be denied or abridged by the United States or any State by reason of failure to pay any poll tax or other tax.

Section 2. The Congress shall have the power to enforce this article by appropriate legislation.

AMENDMENT XXV [1967]

Section 1. In case of the removal of the President from office or of his death or resignation, the Vice-President shall become President.

Section 2. Whenever there is a vacancy in the office of the Vice-President, the President shall nominate a Vice-President who shall take office upon confirmation by a majority vote of both Houses of Congress.

Section 3.   Whenever the President transmits to the President pro tempore of the Senate and the Speaker of the House of Representatives his written declaration that he is unable to discharge the powers and duties of his office, and until he transmits to them a written declaration to the contrary, such powers and duties shall be discharged by the Vice-President as Acting President.

Section 4.   Whenever the Vice-President and a majority of either the principal officers of the executive departments or of such other body as Congress may by law provide, transmit to the President pro tempore of the Senate and the Speaker of the House of Representatives their written declaration that the President is unable to discharge the powers and duties of his office, the Vice-President shall immediately assume the powers and duties of the office as Acting President.

Thereafter, when the President transmits to the President pro tempore of the Senate and the Speaker of the House of Representatives his written declaration that no inability exists, he shall resume the powers and duties of his office unless the Vice-President and a majority of either the principal officers of the executive department[s] or of such other body as Congress may by law provide, transmit within four days to the President pro tempore of the Senate and the Speaker

of the House of Representatives their written declaration that the President is unable to discharge the powers and duties of his office. Thereupon Congress shall decide the issue, assembling within forty-eight hours for that purpose if not in session. If the Congress, within twenty-one days after receipt of the latter written declaration, or, if Congress is not in session, within twenty-one days after Congress is required to assemble, determines by two-thirds vote of both Houses that the President is unable to discharge the powers and duties of his office, the Vice-President shall continue to discharge the same as Acting President; otherwise, the President shall resume the powers and duties of his office.

AMENDMENT **XXVI** [1971]

Section 1.   The right of citizens of the United States, who are eighteen years of age or older, to vote shall not be denied or abridged by the United States or by any State on account of age.

Section 2.   The Congress shall have power to enforce this article by appropriate legislation.

AMENDMENT **XXVII** [1992]

No law, varying the compensation for the services of the Senators and Representatives, shall take effect, until an election of Representatives shall have intervened.

Seneca Falls Declaration of Sentiments and Resolutions

IN 1848, ELIZABETH CADY STANTON, Lucretia Mott, and Martha Coffin Wright, among others, called a meeting in Stanton's hometown of Seneca Falls, New York, to discuss "the social, civil and religious condition of Woman." Over three hundred men and women attended, and one hundred signed a comprehensive document that detailed the discriminations women endured and demanded women's rights, most controversially the vote. "The Declaration of Sentiments" was forthrightly modeled on the Declaration of Independence (see p. A-1), which is telling evidence of the Seneca Falls signers' understanding that the liberties and rights promised by the American Revolution had not been extended to the female half of the population.

DECLARATION OF SENTIMENTS

When, in the course of human events, it becomes necessary for one portion of the family of man to assume among the people of the earth a position different from that which they have hitherto occupied, but one to which the laws of nature and of nature's God entitle them, a decent respect to the opinions of mankind requires that they should declare the causes that impel them to such a course.

We hold these truths to be self-evident: that all men and women are created equal; that they are endowed by their Creator with certain inalienable rights; that among these are life, liberty, and the pursuit of happiness; that to secure these rights governments are instituted, deriving their just powers from the consent of the governed.

Whenever any form of government becomes destructive of these ends, it is the right of those who suffer from it to refuse allegiance to it, and to insist upon the institution of a new government, laying its foundations on such principles, and organizing its powers in such form, as to them shall seem most likely to effect their safety and happiness. Prudence, indeed, will dictate that governments long established should not be changed for light and transient causes; and accordingly all experience hath shown that mankind are more disposed to suffer, while evils are sufferable, than to right themselves by abolishing the forms to which they were accustomed. But when a long train of abuses and usurpations, pursuing invariably the same object evinces a design to reduce them under absolute despotism, it is their duty to throw off such government, and to provide new guards for their future security. Such has been the patient sufferance of the women under this government, and such is now the necessity which constrains them to demand the equal station to which they are entitled.

SOURCE: Susan B. Anthony, Elizabeth Cady Stanton, and Matilda Joslyn Gage, eds., *History of Woman Suffrage* (Rochester, NY: S. B. Anthony, 1889).

The history of mankind is a history of repeated injuries and usurpations on the part of man toward woman, having in direct object the establishment of an absolute tyranny over her. To prove this, let facts be submitted to a candid world.

He has never permitted her to exercise her inalienable right to the elective franchise. He has compelled her to submit to laws, in the formation of which she had no voice. He has withheld from her rights which are given to the most ignorant and degraded men—both natives and foreigners.

Having deprived her of this first right of a citizen, the elective franchise, thereby leaving her without representation in the halls of legislation, he has opposed her on all sides.

He has made her, if married, in the eye of the law, civilly dead.

He has taken from her all right in property, even to the wages she earns.

He has made her, morally, an irresponsible being, as she can commit many crimes with impunity, provided they be done in the presence of her husband. In the covenant of marriage, she is compelled to promise obedience to her husband, he becoming, to all intents and purposes, her master—the law giving him power to deprive her of her liberty, and to administer chastisement.

He has so framed the laws of divorce, as to what shall be the proper causes, and in case of separation, to whom the guardianship of the children shall be given, as to be wholly regardless of the happiness of women—the law, in all cases, going upon a false supposition of the supremacy of man, and giving all power into his hands.

After depriving her of all rights as a married woman, if single, and the owner of property, he has taxed her to support a government which recognizes her only when her property can be made profitable to it.

He has monopolized nearly all the profitable employments, and from those she is permitted to follow, she receives but a scanty remuneration. He closes against her all the avenues to wealth and distinction which he considers most honorable to himself. As a teacher of theology, medicine, or law, she is not known.

He has denied her the facilities for obtaining a thorough education, all colleges being closed against her.

He allows her in Church, as well as State, but in a subordinate position, claiming Apostolic authority for her exclusion from the ministry, and, with some exceptions, from any public participation in the affairs of the Church.

He has created a false public sentiment by giving to the world a different code of morals for men and women, by which moral delinquencies which exclude women from society, are not only tolerated, but deemed of little account in man.

He has usurped the prerogative of Jehovah himself, claiming it as his right to assign for her a sphere of action, when that belongs to her conscience and to her God.

He has endeavored, in every way that he could, to destroy her confidence in her own powers, to lessen her self-respect, and to make her willing to lead a dependent and abject life.

Now, in view of this entire disfranchisement of one-half the people of this country, their social and religious degradation—in view of the unjust laws above mentioned, and because women do feel themselves aggrieved, oppressed, and fraudulently deprived of their most sacred rights, we insist that they have immediate admission to all the rights and privileges which belong to them as citizens of the United States.

In entering upon the great work before us, we anticipate no small amount of misconception, misrepresentation, and ridicule; but we shall use every instrumentality within our power to effect our object. We shall employ agents, circulate tracts, petition the State and National legislatures, and endeavor to enlist the pulpit and the press in our behalf. We hope this Convention will be followed by a series of Conventions embracing every part of the country.

RESOLUTIONS

WHEREAS, The great precept of nature is conceded to be, that "man shall pursue his own true and substantial happiness." [William] Blackstone in his *Commentaries* remarks, that this law of Nature being coequal with mankind, and dictated by God himself, is of course superior in obligation to any other. It is binding over all the globe, in all countries and at all times; no human laws are of any validity if contrary to this, and such of them as are valid, derive all their force, and all their validity, and all their authority, mediately and immediately, from this original; therefore,

Resolved, That such laws as conflict, in any way, with the true and substantial happiness of woman, are contrary to the great precept of nature and of no validity, for this is "superior in obligation to any other."

Resolved, That all laws which prevent woman from occupying such a station in society as her conscience shall dictate, or which place her in a position inferior to that of man, are contrary to the great precept of nature, and therefore of no force or authority.

Resolved, That woman is man's equal—was intended to be so by the Creator, and the highest good of the race demands that she should be recognized as such.

Resolved, That the women of this country ought to be enlightened in regard to the laws under which they live, that they may no longer publish their degradation by declaring themselves satisfied with their present position, nor their ignorance, by asserting that they have all the rights they want.

Resolved, That inasmuch as man, while claiming for himself intellectual superiority, does accord to woman moral superiority, it is preeminently his duty to encourage her to speak and teach, as she has an opportunity, in all religious assemblies.

Resolved, That the same amount of virtue, delicacy, and refinement of behavior that is required of woman in the social state, should also be required of man, and the same transgressions should be visited with equal severity on both man and woman.

Resolved, That the objection of indelicacy and impropriety, which is so often brought against woman when she addresses a public audience, comes with a very ill-grace from those who encourage, by their attendance, her appearance on the stage, in the concert, or in feats of the circus.

Resolved, That woman has too long rested satisfied in the circumscribed limits which corrupt customs and a perverted application of the Scriptures have marked out for her, and that it is time she should move in the enlarged sphere which her great Creator has assigned her.

Resolved, That it is the duty of the women of this country to secure to themselves their sacred right to the elective franchise.

Resolved, That the equality of human rights results necessarily from the fact of the identity of the race in capabilities and responsibilities.

Resolved, therefore, That, being invested by the Creator with the same capabilities, and the same consciousness of responsibility for their exercise, it is demonstrably the right and duty of woman, equally with man, to promote every righteous cause by every righteous means; and especially in regard to the great subjects of morals and religion, it is self-evidently her right to participate with her brother in teaching them, both in private and in public, by writing and by speaking, by any instrumentalities proper to be used, and in any assemblies proper to be held; and this being a self-evident truth growing out of the divinely implanted principles of human nature, any custom or authority adverse to it, whether modern or wearing the hoary sanction of antiquity, is to be regarded as a self-evident falsehood, and at war with mankind.

[Signers, in alphabetical order]

Caroline Barker
Eunice Barker
William G. Barker
Rachel D. Bonnel
   (Mitchell)
Joel D. Bunker
William Burroughs
E. W. Capron
Jacob P. Chamberlain
Elizabeth Conklin
Mary Conklin
P. A. Culvert
Cynthia Davis
Thomas Dell
William S. Dell
Elias J. Doty
Susan R. Doty
Frederick Douglass
Julia Ann Drake
Harriet Cady Eaton
Elisha Foote
Eunice Newton Foote
Mary Ann Frink
Cynthia Fuller
Experience Gibbs
Mary Gilbert

Lydia Gild
Sarah Hallowell
Mary H. Hallowell
Henry Hatley
Sarah Hoffman
Charles L. Hoskins
Jane C. Hunt
Richard P. Hunt
Margaret Jenkins
John Jones
Lucy Jones
Phebe King
Hannah J. Latham
Lovina Latham
Elizabeth Leslie
Eliza Martin
Mary Martin
Delia Mathews
Dorothy Mathews
Jacob Mathews
Elizabeth W. M'Clintock
Mary M'Clintock
Mary Ann M'Clintock
Thomas M'Clintock
Jonathan Metcalf
Nathan J. Milliken

Mary S. Mirror
Pheobe Mosher
Sarah A. Mosher
James Mott
Lucretia Mott
Lydia Mount
Catharine C. Paine
Rhoda Palmer
Saron Phillips
Sally Pitcher
Hannah Plant
Ann Porter
Amy Post
George W. Pryor
Margaret Pryor
Susan Quinn
Rebecca Race
Martha Ridley
Azaliah Schooley
Margaret Schooley
Deborah Scott
Antoinette E. Segur
Henry Seymour
Henry W. Seymour
Malvina Seymour
Catharine Shaw

Stephen Shear
Sarah Sisson
Robert Smallbridge
Elizabeth D. Smith
Sarah Smith
David Spalding
Lucy Spalding
Elizabeth Cady Stanton
Catharine F. Stebbins
Sophronia Taylor
Betsey Tewksbury
Samuel D. Tillman
Edward F. Underhill
Martha Underhill
Mary E. Vail
Isaac Van Tassel
Sarah Whitney
Maria E. Wilbur
Justin Williams
Sarah R. Woods
Charlotte Woodward
S. E. Woodworth
Martha C. Wright

Presidents of the United States

Years in Office	President	Party
1789–1797	George Washington	No party designation
1797–1801	John Adams	Federalist
1801–1809	Thomas Jefferson	Democratic-Republican
1809–1817	James Madison	Democratic-Republican
1817–1825	James Monroe	Democratic-Republican
1825–1829	John Quincy Adams	Democratic-Republican
1829–1837	Andrew Jackson	Democratic
1837–1841	Martin Van Buren	Democratic
1841	William H. Harrison	Whig
1841–1845	John Tyler	Whig
1845–1849	James K. Polk	Democratic
1849–1850	Zachary Taylor	Whig
1850–1853	Millard Fillmore	Whig
1853–1857	Franklin Pierce	Democratic
1857–1861	James Buchanan	Democratic
1861–1865	Abraham Lincoln	Republican
1865–1869	Andrew Johnson	Republican
1869–1877	Ulysses S. Grant	Republican
1877–1881	Rutherford B. Hayes	Republican
1881	James A. Garfield	Republican
1881–1885	Chester A. Arthur	Republican
1885–1889	Grover Cleveland	Democratic
1889–1893	Benjamin Harrison	Republican
1893–1897	Grover Cleveland	Democratic
1897–1901	William McKinley	Republican
1901–1909	Theodore Roosevelt	Republican
1909–1913	William H. Taft	Republican

1913–1921	Woodrow Wilson	Democratic
1921–1923	Warren G. Harding	Republican
1923–1929	Calvin Coolidge	Republican
1929–1933	Herbert C. Hoover	Republican
1933–1945	Franklin D. Roosevelt	Democratic
1945–1953	Harry S. Truman	Democratic
1953–1961	Dwight D. Eisenhower	Republican
1961–1963	John F. Kennedy	Democratic
1963–1969	Lyndon B. Johnson	Democratic
1969–1974	Richard M. Nixon	Republican
1974–1977	Gerald R. Ford	Republican
1977–1981	Jimmy Carter	Democratic
1981–1989	Ronald W. Reagan	Republican
1989–1993	George H. W. Bush	Republican
1993–2001	William Jefferson Clinton	Democratic
2001–2009	George W. Bush	Republican

Major U.S. Supreme Court Decisions Through Women's Eyes

THE FOLLOWING BRIEF EXCERPTS of Supreme Court decisions, carefully abridged from the full opinions delivered by the Court, have been selected for their particular importance to the history of women in the United States. Not all of them deal solely or primarily with gender discrimination. Those decisions concerning racism and the legacy of slavery, beginning with the 1856 *Dred Scott* case, have profound implications for women. Read one after another, these decisions give evidence of both the continuity of judicial reasoning and the dramatic shifts in judicial conclusions that have characterized the nation's highest court.

Dred Scott v. Sandford involved a slave couple who claimed they had gained freedom by virtue of residence for many years on free soil. The case took almost ten years to arrive before the Court, where a seven-to-two majority ruled that the Scotts remained slaves. In his last major opinion, Chief Justice Roger Taney not only dismissed the Scotts' claims, but he sought to intervene in the raging national political debate over slavery by declaring that any federal intervention in slavery, including the 1820 Missouri Compromise (which had banned slavery from the territories in which the Scotts had lived), was unconstitutional.

Dred Scott v. Sandford (1856)

It is difficult at this day to realize the state of public opinion in relation to that unfortunate race, which prevailed in the civilized and enlightened portions of the world at the time of the Declaration of Independence, and when the Constitution of the United States was framed and adopted. . . .

They had for more than a century before been regarded as beings of an inferior order, and altogether unfit to associate with the white race, either in social or political relations; and so far inferior, that they had no rights which the white man was bound to respect; and that the negro might justly and lawfully be reduced to slavery for his benefit. . . . We refer to these historical facts for the purpose of showing the fixed opinions concerning that race, upon which the statesmen of that day spoke and acted. It is necessary to do this, in order to determine whether the general terms used in the Constitution of the United States, as to the rights of man and the rights of the people, was intended to include them, or to give to them or their posterity the benefit of any of its provisions.

[T]he right of property in a slave is distinctly and expressly affirmed in the Constitution. . . . This is done in plain words—too plain to be misunderstood. And no word can be found in the Constitution which gives Congress a greater power over slave property, or which entitles property of that kind to less protection than property of any other description. . . .

Upon these considerations, it is the opinion of the court that the act of Congress which prohibited a citizen from holding and owning property of this kind in the territory of the United States north of the line therein mentioned, is not warranted by the Constitution, and is therefore void; and that neither Dred Scott himself, nor any of his family, were made free by being carried into this territory.

T HE FOURTEENTH AMENDMENT, which was designed to overturn the *Dred Scott* decision by defining national citizenship broadly enough to include the ex-slaves, became the constitutional basis for challenging both race and gender discrimination. Soon after its ratification in 1868, woman suffragists saw the amendment as a potential resource. The National Woman Suffrage Association contended that, inasmuch as women were citizens, their rights as voters were automatically secured. Accordingly, Virginia Minor tried to vote in her hometown of St. Louis, Missouri, and then sued the local election official who refused her ballot. Chief Justice Morrison Waite delivered the Court's unanimous opinion that although the Fourteenth Amendment did indeed grant women equal citizenship with men, it did not make them voters. His contention, that suffrage was not a civil right but a political privilege outside the amendment's intended scope, was underscored by the passage of the Fifteenth Amendment in 1870, which was addressed explicitly to voting. Waite's reasoning applied to all citizens, not just women. After the *Minor* decision, suffragists realized they needed a separate constitutional amendment to secure women's political rights.

Minor v. Happersett (1874)

The argument is, that as a woman, born or naturalized in the United States and subject to the jurisdiction thereof, is a citizen of the United States and of the State in which she resides, she has the right of suffrage as one of the privileges and immunities of her citizenship, which the State cannot by its laws or constitution abridge.

There is no doubt that women may be citizens. They are persons, and by the fourteenth amendment "all persons born or naturalized in the United States and subject to the jurisdiction thereof" are expressly declared to be "citizens of the United States and of the State wherein they reside." . . .

If the right of suffrage is one of the necessary privileges of a citizen of the United States, then the constitution and laws of Missouri confining it to men are in violation of the Constitution of the United States, as amended, and consequently void. . . . It is clear, . . . we think, that the Constitution has not added the right of suffrage to the privileges and immunities of citizenship as they existed at the time it was adopted.

It is true that the United States guarantees to every State a republican form of government. . . . No particular government is designated as republican, neither is the exact form to be guaranteed, in any manner especially designated. . . .

[I]t is certainly now too late to contend that a government is not republican, within the meaning of this guaranty in the Constitution, because women are not made voters.

INVOKING THE FOURTEENTH AMENDMENT three decades later, Homer Plessy argued that he had been denied equal protection of the law when a Louisiana statute forced him to travel in a separate all-black railroad car. By a vote of eight to one, the Court ruled against his claims and found the emerging system of state-sponsored racial segregation that was settling on the postslavery South to be fully constitutional. Writing for the majority, Justice Henry Brown argued that because a system of segregation affected both black and white, it was not discriminatory. The famous phrase by which this argument has come to be known—"separate but equal"—appears in the brave, dissenting opinion of Justice John Harlan. Note how the Court's ruling treats racial distinction and black inferiority as facts of nature that any legal decision must recognize.

Plessy v. Ferguson (1896)

A statute which implies merely a legal distinction between the white and colored races—a distinction which is founded in the color of the two races, and which must always exist so long as white men are distinguished from the other race by color—has no tendency to destroy the legal equality of the two races. . . .

The object of the [fourteenth] amendment was undoubtedly to enforce the absolute equality of the two races before the law, but, in the nature of things, it could not have been intended to abolish distinctions based upon color, or to enforce social, as distinguished from political, equality, or a commingling of the two races upon terms unsatisfactory to either. Laws permitting, and even requiring, their separation, in places where they are liable to be brought into contact, do not necessarily imply the inferiority of either race to the other. . . .

We consider the underlying fallacy of the plaintiff's argument to consist in the assumption that the enforced separation of the two races stamps the colored race with a badge of inferiority. If this be so, it is not by reason of anything found in the act, but solely because the colored race chooses to put that construction upon it. The argument necessarily assumes that if, as has been more than once the case, and is not unlikely to be so again, the colored race should become the dominant power in the state legislature, and should enact a law in precisely similar terms, it would thereby relegate the white race to an inferior position. We imagine that the white race, at least, would not acquiesce in this assumption. The argument also assumes that social prejudices may be overcome by legislation, and that equal rights cannot be secured to the negro except by an enforced commingling of the two races. We cannot accept this proposition. . . . Legislation is powerless to eradicate racial instincts, or to abolish distinctions based upon physical differences, and the attempt to do so can only result in accentuating the difficulties of the present situation.

IN *MULLER V. OREGON*, Curt Muller challenged the constitutionality of an Oregon law setting a maximum ten-hour working day for women employees. Starting in the 1880s, the Court had turned away from the Fourteenth Amendment's original purposes to emphasize its guarantee of the individual's right of contract in the workplace, free from state regulation. This reading made most laws setting limits on the working day unconstitutional. Arguing on behalf of Oregon, Louis Brandeis, lead counsel for the National Consumers' League, successfully pressed an argument for the law's constitutionality on the ground that it was directed only at women. Brandeis's argument circumvented the Fourteenth Amendment by contending that the federal government's constitutionally authorized police power, which permitted special regulations for the national good, allowed legislation to protect motherhood and through it "the [human] race." The Court ruled unanimously to uphold the Oregon law, with Justice David Brewer delivering the opinion. As in the *Plessy* decision, the Court held that physical difference and even inferiority are facts of nature that the law may accommodate and that are compatible with formal legal equality. Yet the decision here was hailed by many women reformers as a great victory. Brandeis was appointed to the Supreme Court in 1916, the first Jewish member of the Court.

Muller v. Oregon (1908)

We held in *Lochner v. New York* [1903] that a law providing that no laborer shall be required or permitted to work in bakeries more than sixty hours in a week or ten hours in a day was not as to men a legitimate exercise of the police power of the state, but an unreasonable, unnecessary, and arbitrary interference with the right and liberty of the individual to contract in relation to his labor, and as such was in conflict with, and void under, the Federal Constitution. That decision is invoked by plaintiff in error as decisive of the question before us. But this assumes that the difference between the sexes does not justify a different rule respecting a restriction of the hours of labor. . . .

That woman's physical structure and the performance of maternal functions place her at a disadvantage in the struggle for subsistence is obvious. This is especially true when the burdens of motherhood are upon her. Even when they are not, . . . continuance for a long time on her feet at work, repeating this from day to day, tends to injurious effects upon the body, and, as healthy mothers are essential to vigorous offspring, the physical well-being of woman becomes an object of public interest and care in order to preserve the strength and vigor of the race. . . .

Even though all restrictions on political, personal, and contractual rights were taken away, and [woman] stood, so far as statutes are concerned, upon an absolutely equal plane with [man], it would still be true that she is so constituted that she will rest upon and look to him for protection; that her physical structure and a proper discharge of her maternal functions—having in view not merely her own health, but the well-being of the race—justify legislation to protect her from the greed as well as the passion of man. The limitations which this statute places upon her contractual powers, upon her right to agree with her employer as to the time she shall labor, are not imposed solely for her benefit, but also largely for the benefit of all.

THE IRONY OF THE *MULLER* DECISION in favor of maximum hours laws to benefit women workers on the basis of their maternal dependency is underlined by the *Adkins* case, decided fifteen years later. *Adkins v. Children's Hospital* involved a congressionally authorized procedure for setting minimum wages for women workers in the District of Columbia. Writing for a five-to-three majority (Justice Brandeis had recused himself from the case), Justice George Sutherland found the maximum hours law unconstitutional on two major grounds. First, while minimum hours laws were constitutionally sanctioned public health measures, maximum wage laws were unacceptable restraints on free trade. Second, the ratification of the Nineteenth Amendment granting woman suffrage in the years since the *Muller* decision made protections of women on the basis of their need to be sheltered by men outdated. Thus, whereas in the earlier case the Court used an appeal to nature to sustain special labor laws that benefited women, in *Adkins,* the Court relied on an evolutionary approach to overturn such regulations.

Adkins v. Children's Hospital (1923)

In the *Muller* case, the validity of an Oregon statute, forbidding the employment of any female in certain industries more than ten hours during anyone day was upheld.... But the ancient inequality of the sexes, otherwise than physical, as suggested in the *Muller* case has continued "with diminishing intensity." In view of the great—not to say revolutionary—changes which have taken place since that utterance, in the contractual, political and civil status of women, culminating in the Nineteenth Amendment, it is not unreasonable to say that these differences have now come almost, if not quite, to the vanishing point....

[W]e cannot accept the doctrine that women of mature age, *sui juris* [able to act on their own behalf legally], require or may be subjected to restrictions upon their liberty of contract which could not lawfully be imposed in the case of men under similar circumstances. To do so would be to ignore all the implications to be drawn from the present day trend of legislation, as well as that of common thought and usage, by which woman is accorded emancipation from the old doctrine that she must be given special protection or be subjected to special restraint in her contractual and civil relationships.

I N THE WATERSHED CASE of *Brown v. Board of Education of Topeka,* the Supreme Court reversed its 1896 *Plessy v. Ferguson* decision to find state-sponsored racial segregation a violation of the Fourteenth Amendment guarantee of equal protection of the laws. The unanimous ruling was written by Earl Warren, newly appointed chief justice. Linda Brown was the plaintiff in one of several cases that the court consolidated, all of which challenged the constitutionality of racially segregated public schools. The case bears certain similarities to *Muller v. Oregon.* Both made use of sociological evidence, with *Brown* relying on research into the negative impact of segregation on young black children. Also as in *Muller,* the successful lead counsel in the *Brown* decision, NAACP lawyer Thurgood Marshall, ultimately was appointed to the Supreme Court, where he became the first African American justice.

Brown v. Board of Education of Topeka (1954)

The plaintiffs contend that segregated public schools are not "equal" and cannot be made "equal," and that hence they are deprived of the equal protection of the laws. . . .

Does segregation of children in public schools solely on the basis of race, even though the physical facilities and other "tangible" factors may be equal, deprive the children of the minority group of equal educational opportunities? We believe that it does. . . .

To separate them from others of similar age and qualifications solely because of their race generates a feeling of inferiority as to their status in the community that may affect their hearts and minds in a way unlikely ever to be undone. . . .

We conclude that, in the field of public education, the doctrine of "separate but equal" has no place. Separate educational facilities arc inherently unequal. . . .

Because these are class actions, because of the wide applicability of this decision, and because of the great variety of local conditions, the formulation of decrees in these cases presents problems of considerable complexity.

E STELLE GRISWOLD, executive director of the Planned Parenthood Federation of Connecticut, was arrested for providing a married couple with birth control instruction in violation of an 1879 state law forbidding any aid given "for the purpose of preventing conception." Writing for a seven-to-two majority, Justice William O. Douglas held the law unconstitutional, developing an innovative argument for the existence of a "zone of privacy" not specifically enumerated in the Constitution but found in the surrounding "penumbra" of specified rights. Note Douglas's lofty language about the nature of marriage.

Griswold v. Connecticut (1965)

This law . . . operates directly on an intimate relation of husband and wife and their physician's role in one aspect of that relation. . . .

[S]pecific guarantees in the Bill of Rights have penumbras, formed by emanations from those guarantees that help give them life and substance. . . . Various guarantees create zones of privacy. The right of association contained in the penumbra of the First Amendment is one, as we have seen. . . . The Ninth Amendment provides: "The enumeration in the Constitution, of certain rights, shall not be construed to deny or disparage others retained by the people." . . .

The present case, then, concerns a relationship lying within the zone of privacy created by several fundamental constitutional guarantees. And it concerns a law which, in forbidding the use of contraceptives rather than regulating their manufacture or sale, seeks to achieve its goals by means having a maximum destructive impact upon that relationship. Such a law cannot stand in light of the familiar principle, so often applied by this Court, that a "governmental purpose to control or prevent activities constitutionally subject to state regulation may not be achieved by means which sweep unnecessarily broadly and thereby invade the area of protected freedoms.". . .

We deal with a right of privacy older than the Bill of Rights—older than our political parties, older than our school system. Marriage is a coming together for better or for worse, hopefully enduring, and intimate to the degree of being sacred. It is an association that promotes a way of life, not causes; a harmony in living, not political faiths; a bilateral loyalty, not commercial or social projects.

L IKE THE *GRISWOLD* CASE two years earlier, *Loving v. Virginia* concerns the marriage relationship and government intrusion into it. Richard Loving was a white man who married Mildred Jeter, a black woman, in 1958 in Washington, D.C. When they moved to Virginia a year later, they were found guilty in state court of violating a 1924 Virginia law forbidding white people from marrying outside of their race, a crime known as "miscegenation." They appealed their conviction to the U.S. Supreme Court. Speaking for a unanimous Court, Chief Justice Earl Warren found this and similar laws in fifteen other states unconstitutional under the Fourteenth Amendment. The court's rejection of the argument that antimiscegenation laws were constitutionally acceptable because they rested equally on all races echoes the logic of its ruling in *Brown v. Board of Education,* in which intent to discriminate is crucial despite the superficially neutral language of the law.

Loving v. Virginia (1967)

This case presents a constitutional question never addressed by this Court: whether a statutory scheme adopted by the State of Virginia to prevent marriages between persons solely on the basis of racial classifications violates the Equal Protection and Due Process Clauses of the Fourteenth Amendment. . . .

In upholding the constitutionality of these provisions, . . . the state court concluded that the State's legitimate purposes were "to preserve the racial integrity of its citizens," and to prevent "the corruption of blood," "a mongrel breed of citizens," and "the obliteration of racial pride," obviously an endorsement of the doctrine of White Supremacy. . . . [T]he fact of equal application does not immunize the statute from the very heavy burden of justification which the Four-

teenth Amendment has traditionally required of state statutes drawn according to race. . . .

Over the years, this Court has consistently repudiated "distinctions between citizens solely because of their ancestry" as being "odious to a free people whose institutions are founded upon the doctrine of equality." At the very least, the Equal Protection Clause demands that racial classifications, especially suspect in criminal statutes, be subjected to the "most rigid scrutiny." . . .

Marriage is one of the "basic civil rights of man," fundamental to our very existence and survival. . . . Under our Constitution, the freedom to marry, or not marry, a person of another race resides with the individual and cannot be infringed by the State.

THE *REED V. REED* CASE involved the mother of a deceased child contesting an Idaho law mandating that preference be given to the father in designating an executor for a dead child's estate. Sally Reed's case was argued by then American Civil Liberties Union lawyer Ruth Bader Ginsburg. Ginsburg revived elements of the argument made in the 1874 *Minor* case, that the Fourteenth Amendment's guarantees of equal protection before the law applied in cases of discrimination against women. This time the Court accepted the argument. The unanimous opinion was written by Chief Justice Warren Burger. Like Brandeis and Marshall, Ginsburg was later a pathbreaking appointee to the Supreme Court, the second woman (after Sandra Day O'Connor) to serve.

Reed v. Reed (1971)

[W]e have concluded that the arbitrary preference established in favor of males by . . . the Idaho Code cannot stand in the face of the Fourteenth Amendment's command that no State deny the equal protection of the laws to any person within its jurisdiction.

In applying that clause, this Court has consistently recognized that the Fourteenth Amendment does not deny to States the power to treat different classes of persons in different ways. . . . The Equal Protection Clause of that amendment does, however, deny to States the power to legislate that different treatment be accorded to persons placed by a statute into different classes on the basis of criteria wholly unrelated to the objective of that statute. A classification must be reasonable, not arbitrary, and must rest upon some ground of difference having a fair and substantial relation to the object of the legislation, so that all persons similarly circumstanced shall be treated alike.

JANE ROE WAS THE PSEUDONYM of Norma McCorvey, an unmarried pregnant woman whose name headed up a class action suit challenging an 1879 Texas law criminalizing abortion. In *Roe v. Wade,* the Court ruled seven to two in Roe's favor. Justice Harry Blackmun wrote the lead opinion, relying on the concept of privacy developed in the *Griswold* case. His opinion included a detailed history of laws prohibiting abortion to show that these were of relatively recent vintage, an approach that contrasted with the antihistorical arguments of nineteenth-century cases such as *Dred Scott* and *Minor v. Happersett.* The *Roe* decision very carefully avoids declaring that a woman's right to abortion is absolute. The limits placed on women's choice—consultation with a physician, government interest in fetal life in the third trimester—opened the way for attempts to reinstitute limits on abortion.

Roe v. Wade (1973)

We forthwith acknowledge our awareness of the sensitive and emotional nature of the abortion controversy. . . . One's philosophy, one's experiences, one's exposure to the raw edges of human existence, one's religious training, one's attitudes toward life and family and their values, and the moral standards one establishes and seeks to observe, are all likely to influence and to color one's thinking and conclusions about abortion.

In addition, population growth, pollution, poverty, and racial overtones tend to complicate and not to simplify the problem. . . .

The Constitution does not explicitly mention any right of privacy. In a line of decisions, however, . . . the Court has recognized that a right of personal privacy, or a guarantee of certain areas or zones of privacy, does exist under the Constitution. . . .

This right of privacy . . . is broad enough to encompass a woman's decision whether or not to terminate her pregnancy. The detriment that the State would impose upon the pregnant woman by denying this choice altogether is apparent. Specific and direct harm medically diagnosable even in early pregnancy may be involved. Maternity, or additional offspring, may force upon the woman a distressful life and future.

Psychological harm may be imminent. Mental and physical health may be taxed by child care. There is also the distress, for all concerned, associated with the unwanted child, and there is the problem of bringing a child into a family already unable, psychologically and otherwise, to care for it. In other cases, as in this one, the additional difficulties and continuing stigma of unwed motherhood may be involved.

[A]ppellant [in this case Jane Roe] . . . [argues] that the woman's right is absolute and that she is entitled to terminate her pregnancy at whatever time, in whatever way, and for whatever reason she alone chooses. With this we do not agree. . . . [A] State may properly assert important interests in safeguarding health, in maintaining medical standards, and in protecting potential life. At some point in pregnancy, these respective interests become sufficiently compelling to sustain regulation of the factors that govern the abortion decision. The privacy right involved, therefore, cannot be said to be absolute. . . .

The appellee . . . argue[s] that the fetus is a "person" within the language and meaning of the Fourteenth Amendment. . . . If this suggestion of personhood is established, the appellant's case, of course, collapses, for the fetus' right to life would then be guaranteed specifically by the Amendment. . . .

The Constitution does not define "person" in so many words. . . . [T]he word "person," as used in the Fourteenth Amendment, does not include the unborn.

In view of all this, we do not agree that, by adopting one theory of life, Texas may override the rights of the pregnant woman that are at stake. We repeat, however, that the State does have an important and legitimate interest in preserving and protecting the health of the pregnant woman, . . . and that it has still *another* important and legitimate interest in protecting the potentiality of human life. . . .

With respect to the State's important and legitimate interest in the health of the mother, the "compelling" point, in the light of present medical knowledge, is at . . . the end of the first trimester. . . . [F]rom and after this point, a State may regulate the abortion procedure to the extent that the regulation reasonably relates to the preservation and protection of maternal health. Examples of permissible state regulation in this area are requirements as to the qualifications of the person who is to perform the abortion; as to the licensure of that person; as to the facility in which the procedure is to be performed. . . .

[T]he attending physician, in consultation with his patient, is free to determine, without regulation by the State, that, in his medical judgment, the patient's pregnancy should be terminated. If that decision is reached, the judgment may be effectuated by an abortion free of interference by the State.

With respect to the State's important and legitimate interest in potential life, the "compelling" point is at viability. This is so because the fetus then presumably has the capability of meaningful life outside the mother's womb. State regulation protective of fetal life after viability thus has both logical and biological justifications.

AFFIRMATIVE ACTION PROGRAMS were initially developed in the 1960s to aid African Americans to achieve greater educational and economic opportunity. President Richard Nixon urged them as a moderate response to the demands of militant civil rights activists. Nonetheless, these programs came under fire. In 1976, Allan Bakke, a white man, filed suit when his application for admission was rejected by the University of California at Davis Medical School. He argued that affirmative was the problem. His claim, based on the Fourteenth Amendment, became known as the "reverse discrimination" argument. The Court was sharply divided, four justices believing that Bakke was the victim of reverse discrimination, four justices believing that the Davis Medical School's affirmative action policy offered a reasonable approach to eradicating the effects of a long history of racial injustice. Justice Lewis Powell forged a five-to-four majority by writing an opinion that took both positions into account. An educational affirmative action plan premised on the goal of racial diversity could be constitutional if the system used was less rigid, less "quota"-like, than that of the Davis Medical School. The Court ordered Bakke admitted to the university's medical school.

University of California Regents v. Bakke (1978)

The Medical School of the University of California at Davis (hereinafter Davis) had two admissions programs for the entering class of 100 students — the regular admissions program and the special admissions program. . . . A separate committee, a majority of whom were members of minority groups, operated the special admissions program. The 1973 and 1974 application forms, respectively, asked candidates whether they wished to be considered as "economically and/or educationally disadvantaged" applicants and members of a "minority group" (blacks, Chicanos, Asians, American Indians). . . . Special candidates, however, did not have to meet the 2.5 grade point cutoff and were not ranked against candidates in the general admissions process. . . . Without passing on the state constitutional or federal statutory grounds the [lower] court held that petitioner's special admissions program violated the [Fourteenth Amendment] Equal Protection Clause. . . . Racial and ethnic classifications of any sort are inherently suspect and call for the most exacting judicial scrutiny. While the goal of achieving a diverse student body is sufficiently compelling to justify consideration of race in admissions decisions under some circumstances, petitioner's special admissions program, which forecloses consideration to persons like respondent, is unnecessary to the achievement of this compelling goal and therefore invalid under the Equal Protection Clause.

A SERIES OF CASES followed *Roe v. Wade* that both upheld and limited a woman's right to seek an abortion. The plaintiff in *Webster v. Reproductive Health Services* was attorney general for the State of Missouri, appealing a lower court ruling that found restrictions on a woman's right to abortion unconstitutional, including the requirement that a woman seeking a second- or third-trimester abortion must have a test to make sure that the fetus was not viable (could not live outside the womb). The lower court ruled that the law violated the Supreme Court's *Roe v. Wade* decision. The Supreme Court overturned this ruling. Chief Justice William Rehnquist wrote for the five-to-three majority that, while the *Roe* decision had recognized the state's obligation to protect potential life, it had been too rigid in establishing the point at which this became paramount. From Rehnquist's perspective, it was permissible for the state to act to favor childbirth even while preserving the woman's formal right to abortion.

Webster v. Reproductive Health Services (1989)

In *Roe v. Wade,* the Court recognized that the State has "important and legitimate" interests in protecting maternal health and in the potentiality of human life. During the second trimester, the State "may, if it chooses, regulate the abortion procedure in ways that are reasonably related to maternal health." . . .

[But] the rigid trimester analysis of the course of a pregnancy enunciated in *Roe* has resulted in . . . making constitutional law in this area a virtual Procrustean bed. . . . [T]he rigid *Roe* framework is hardly consistent with the notion of a Constitution cast in general terms, as ours is, and usually speaking in general principles, as ours does. . . .

[W]e do not see why the State's interest in protecting potential human life should come into existence only at the point of viability, and that there should therefore be a rigid line allowing state regulation after viability but prohibiting it before viability. . . . [W]e are satisfied that the requirement of these tests permissibly furthers the State's interest in protecting potential human life, and we therefore believe [the article] to be constitutional.

Both appellants and the United States as *amicus curiae* [filing a brief sympathetic to the parties that appealed the decision] have urged that we overrule our decision in *Roe v. Wade.* The facts of the present case, however, differ from those at issue in *Roe.* Here, Missouri has determined that viability is the point at which its interest in potential human life must be safeguarded. . . . This case therefore affords us no occasion to revisit the holding of *Roe.*

A P P E N D I X :
T A B L E S   A N D   C H A R T S

Table 1
Female Population of the United States by Race, 1790–2000

| | Number of Women | | | | Percent Distribution | | |
Year	Total	White	Black	Other Races	White	Black	Other Races
1790	n/a	1,556,572	n/a	n/a	n/a	n/a	n/a
1800	–	2,111,141	—	—	—	—	—
1810	–	2,873,943	—	—	—	—	—
1820	4,741,848	3,870,988	870,860	—	81.6	18.4	—
1830	6,333,531	5,171,165	1,162,366	—	81.6	18.4	—
1840	8,380,921	6,940,261	1,440,660	—	82.8	17.2	—
1850	11,354,216	9,526,666	1,827,550	—	83.9	16.1	—
1860	15,358,117	13,111,150	2,225,086	21,881	85.4	14.5	0.1
1870	19,064,806	16,560,289	2,486,746	17,771	86.9	13.0	0.1
1880	24,636,963	21,272,070	3,327,678	37,215	86.3	13.5	0.2
1890	30,710,613	26,830,879	3,753,073	126,661	87.4	12.2	0.4
1900	37,243,479	32,622,949	4,447,539	172,991	87.6	11.9	0.5
1910	44,727,298	39,579,044	4,942,228	206,026	88.5	11.0	0.5
1920	51,935,452	46,421,794	5,253,890	259,768	89.4	10.1	0.5
1930	60,807,176	54,404,615	6,035,789	366,772	89.5	9.9	0.6
1940	65,815,399	58,819,215	6,596,652	399,532	89.4	10.0	0.6
1950	76,139,192	67,894,638	7,744,182	500,372	89.2	10.2	0.7
1960	90,991,681	80,464,583	9,758,423	768,675	88.4	10.7	0.8
1970	104,299,734	91,027,988	11,831,973	1,439,773	87.3	11.3	1.4
1980	116,492,644	96,686,289	13,975,836	5,830,519	83.0	12.0	5.0
1990	127,470,455	102,210,190	15,815,909	9,444,356	80.2	12.4	7.4
2000	143,368,343	107,676,508	18,077,075	17,614,460	75.1	12.6	12.3

Source: Sandra Opdycke, *The Routledge Historical Atlas of Women in America* (New York: Routledge, 2000), p. 130; U.S. Census Bureau, *Statistical Abstract of the United States, 2001* (Washington: GPO, 2001).

Chart 1
U.S. Birthrate, 1820–2000

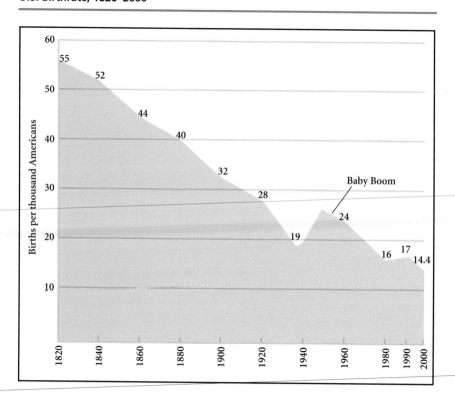

Source: Data from *Historical Statistics of the United States, Colonial Times to 1970* (1975); U.S. Census Bureau, *Statistical Abstract of the United States, 2001* (Washington: GPO, 2001).

Table 2
U.S. Women and Work, 1820–2000

Year	Percentage of Women in Paid Employment	Percentage of Paid Workers Who Are Women
1820	6.2	7.3
1830	6.4	7.4
1840	8.4	9.6
1850	10.1	10.8
1860	9.7	10.2
1870	13.7	14.8
1880	14.7	15.2
1890	18.2	17.0
1900	21.2	18.1
1910	24.8	20.0
1920	23.9	20.4
1930	24.4	21.9
1940	25.4	24.6
1950	29.1	27.8
1960	34.8	32.3
1970	43.3	38.0
1980	51.5	42.6
1990	57.4	45.2
2000	60.2	46.5

Source: U.S. Census Bureau, *Historical Statistics of the United States, Colonial Times to 1970* (Washington: GPO, 1975); *Statistical Abstract of the United States, 2002* (Washington: GPO, 2002).

Table 3
Percentage of Women in the U.S. Labor Force, by Family Status, 1890–2000

| | Total Female Labor Force | | | | Participation Rate in the Female Labor Force | | | |
Year	Single	Widowed/ Divorced	Married	Mothers*	Single	Widowed/ Divorced	Married	Mothers*
1890	68	18	14	—	41	30	5	—
1900	67	18	15	—	41	33	6	—
1910	61	15	24	—	48	35	11	—
1920	77†	—†	23	—	44†	—†	9	—
1930	54	17	29	—	46	34	12	—
1940	49	15	36	11	48	32	17	28
1950	32	16	52	26	51	36	25	33
1960	23	6	61	27	44	13	32	37
1970	22	14	63	38	53	46	41	43
1980	26	19	55	40	64	44	50	56
1990	26	20	54	39	67	47	58	67
2000	27	20	53	39	69	61	49	73

*Mothers of children under age eighteen.

†Single women counted with widows and divorced women.

Sources: Lynn Weiner, *From Working Girl to Working Mother: The Female Labor Force in the United States, 1820–1980* (Chapel Hill: University of North Carolina, 1985), 6; Bureau of Labor Statistics, "Labor Force Participation Rates of Women by Presence and Age of Children, March 1980–2000," http://www.bls.gov/opub/rtaw/pdf/table06.pdf (accessed August 13, 2004).

Table 4
Occupational Distribution (in Percentages) of Working Women Ages Fourteen Years and Older, 1900–2000

	1900	1910	1920	1930	1940	1950	1960	1970	1980	1990	2000
Professional, Technical, and Kindred Workers	8.2	9.6	11.7	13.8	12.8	12.2	12.5	15.2	13.6	18.5	21.8
Managers, Officials, and Proprietors	1.4	2.0	2.2	0.7	3.3	4.3	0.6	3.5	7.2	11.1	14.3
Clerical and Kindred Workers	4.0	9.2	18.7	20.9	21.5	27.4	29.1	34.2	33.6	27.8	23.5
Sales Workers	4.3	5.1	6.3	6.8	7.4	8.6	7.8	7.3	11.3	13.1	13.0
Craftsmen, Foremen, and Kindred Workers	1.4	1.4	1.2	1.0	1.1	0.5	1.2	1.8	2.4	2.2	2.2
Operatives and Kindred Workers	23.8	22.9	20.2	17.4	19.5	20.0	16.2	14.9	10.1	8.0	6.4
Laborers	2.6	1.4	2.3	1.5	1.1	0.9	0.6	1.0	2.0	0.5	0.4
Private Household Workers	28.7	24.0	15.7	17.8	18.1	8.9	7.9	3.8	1.3	1.0	1.3
Service Workers (Not Household)	6.7	8.4	8.1	9.7	11.3	12.6	13.5	16.5	17.8	16.8	16.4
Farmers and Farm Managers	5.8	3.7	3.2	0.4	1.2	0.7	0.5	0.2	0.3	0.3	0.3
Farm Laborers	13.1	12.0	10.3	6.0	2.8	2.9	1.2	0.6	0.6	0.7	0.4

Source: U.S. Census Bureau, *Historical Statistics of the United States,* Part 1, table D, 182–232; *Statistical Abstract of the United States, 1985* (Washington, D.C.: GPO, 1984), table 673; 1991 (Washington, D.C.: GPO, 1991), table 652; 2000 (Washington, D.C.: GPO, 2001), table 593; "Employed Persons by Major Occupation, Sex, Race, and Hispanic Origin, Annual Averages, 1983–2002," Current Population Survey, Bureau of Labor Statistics.

Note: Data beginning in 1990 are not directly comparable with data for earlier years because of the introduction of a new occupational classification system.

Table 5
Immigration to the United States, 1900–2006

Years	Female Immigrants to the United States	Total Immigrants to the United States
1900–1909	2,492,336	8,202,388
1910–1919	2,215,582	6,347,156
1920–1929	1,881,923	4,295,510
1930–1939	386,659	699,375
1940–1949	454,291	856,608
1950–1959	1,341,404	2,499,286
1960–1969	1,786,441	3,213,749
1970–1979	2,299,713	4,366,001
1980–1989	3,224,661	6,332,218
1990–1999	4,740,896	9,782,093
2000–2006	3,857,135	7,018,463

Source: U.S. Census Bureau, *Historical Statistics of the United States, Colonial Times to 1970* (Washington: GPO, 1975), Series C 102–114; U.S. Department of Justice, *1978 Statistical Yearbook of the Immigration and Naturalization Service* (Washington: GPO, 1978), table 10; *1984 Statistical Yearbook of the Immigration and Naturalization Service* (Washington: GPO, 1987), table I M M 4.1; *1988 Statistical Yearbook of the Immigration and Naturalization Service* (Washington: GPO, 1989), table 11; *1994 Statistical Yearbook of the Immigration and Naturalization Service* (Washington: GPO, 2002), table 1; *2003 Statistical Yearbook of the Immigration and Naturalizaton Service* (Washington: GPO, 2004), table 6; *2004 Statistical Yearbook of the Immigration and Naturalization Service* (Washington: GPO, 2005), table 7; *2005 Statistical Yearbook of the Immigration and Naturalization Service* (Washington: GPO, 2006), table 8; and *2006 Statistical Yearbook of the Immigration and Naturalization Service* (Washington: GPO, 2007), table 9.

Table 6
Women in the U.S. Congress, 1918–2008

Year	Number of Women Senate	House	Total	Percentage of Full Membership
1918	0	1	1	0.2
1922	1	3	4	0.8
1926	0	3	3	0.6
1930	0	9	9	1.7
1934	1	7	8	1.5
1938	2	6	8	1.5
1942	1	9	10	1.9
1946	0	11	11	2.1
1950	1	9	10	1.9
1954	2	11	13	2.4
1958	1	15	16	3.0
1962	2	18	20	3.8
1966	2	11	13	2.4
1970	1	10	11	2.1
1974	0	16	16	3.0
1978	2	18	20	3.7
1982	2	21	23	4.3
1986	2	23	25	4.7
1990	2	29	31	5.8
1994	7	47	54	10.1
1998	9	54	63	11.8
2000	9	57	66	13.0
2002	14	62	76	14.2
2004	14	60	74	13.8
2006	14	68	82	15.3
2008	16	71	87	16.3

Source: Sandra Opdycke, *The Routledge Historical Atlas of Women in America* (New York: Routledge, 2000), 133; Center for American Women and Politics, Rutgers University, http://www.rci.rutgers.edu/~cawp/Facts2.html (accessed on November 30, 2007).

Acknowledgments

Chapter 1

"On the Deaths of Caribbean Indians," from *The Devastation of the Indies* by Bartolomé de Las Casas. Reprinted with permission of Continuum International Book Publishing Group Ltd.

Map, "Major Trends of the Atlantic Slave Trade." From *The Atlantic Slave Trade: A Census* by Philip D. Curtin (1969). Reprinted with permission of the University of Wisconsin Press.

Chapter 2

"In Honour of That High and Mighty Princess Queen Elizabeth of Happy Memory," from *The Works of Anne Bradstreet*, edited by Jeannine Hensley. Used by permission of Harvard University Press. Copyright © by the President and Fellows of Harvard College.

"Letter to Miss Bartlett" and "Letter to a Friend, 1740" by Eliza Lucas Pinckney, from *The Letterbook of Eliza Lucas Pinckney 1739–1762*, ed. Elise Pinckney. Copyright © 1997, South Carolina Historical Society. Used with permission.

"1645 Prenuptial Settlement, re: Mrs. Agatha Stubbins, signed by Ralph Wormeley, the Seale." Susan M. Ames, ed., *County Court Records of Accomack-Northampton, Virginia, 1640–1645*. Copyright © 1973, University of Virginia Press. Used with permission of the publisher.

Chapter 3

"Letter to Arbour Tanner," "Letter to Reverend Samson Occom," "On Being Brought from Africa to America," and "To the Right Honorable William, Earl of Dartmouth." From *The Poems of Phillis Wheatley* edited and with an introduction by Julian D. Mason Jr. Copyright © 1966 by the University of North Carolina Press, renewed 1989. Used by permission of the publisher. www.uncpress.unc.edu.

Benjamin Rush, "Thoughts upon Female Education," from *Essays on Education in the Early Republic*, Frederick Rudolph, ed. Copyright © 1965 by the President and Fellows of Harvard College. Reprinted with permission of Harvard University Press.

Chapter 4

"Narrative of Polly Shine," Interview by B. E. Davis, from *The American Slave: A Composite Autobiography* by George P. Rawick, supplement, Series 2, Volume 9 (Texas Narratives Part 8). Copyright © 1977 by George P. Rawick. Reproduced with permission of Greenwood Publishing Group, Inc., Westport, CT.

Chapter 5

Excerpts from *Occurrences in Hispanic California*, by Maria Angustias de la Guerra Ord, translated by Francis Price and William Ellison. Copyright © 1956 Academy of American Franciscan History. Reprinted by courtesy of the Academy of American Franciscan History.

INDEX

A note about the index:
  Letters in parentheses following pages
  refer to:
    (b) for boxed excerpts
    (d) for documents
    (i) for text illustrations
    (v) for visual sources
    (m) for maps
    (c) for charts and graphs

Area ceded by the United States to Great Britain, 1818

Area ceded by Great Britain, 1818

WASHINGTON
Olympia

Columbia R.

Salem ★

OREGON COUNTRY
Agreement with Britain, 1846

OREGON

IDAHO

Boise ★

Helena ★

MONTANA

Missouri R.

NORTH DAKOTA

Bismarck ★

SOUTH DAKOTA

Pierre ★

Snake R.

WYOMING

LOUISIANA PURCHASE
From France, 1803

N. Platte R.

NEBRASKA

Sacramento R.

Carson City ★

Sacramento ★

NEVADA

San Joaquin R.

Salt Lake City ★

UTAH

MEXICAN CESSION
1848

Colorado R.

CALIFORNIA

Cheyenne ★

S. Platte R.

Platte R.

Denver ★

COLORADO

KANSAS

PACIFIC
OCEAN

ARIZONA

Phoenix ★

Santa Fe ★

NEW
MEXICO

TEXAS
Annexed, 1845

Red R.

TEXAS

ARCTIC OCEAN

RUSSIA

ALASKA
Purchased from Russia, 1867

Yukon R.

CANADA

GADSDEN PURCHASE
from Mexico, 1853

Bering
Sea

Gulf of
Alaska

Juneau ★

HAWAII
Annexed, 1898

Honolulu ★

PACIFIC
OCEAN

Rio Grande

MEXICO

| 0 | 250 | 500 miles |
| 0 | 250 | 500 kilometers |

| 0 | 50 | 100 miles |
| 0 | 50 | 100 kilometers |

Areas ceded by Britain, 1842
(Webster-Ashburton Treaty)

CANADA

St. Lawrence R.

MAINE

★ Augusta

VERMONT

Montpelier ★

Connecticut R.

Concord
★ N.H.

Lake Superior

Lake Ontario

NEW YORK

Albany ★

Boston
★

MASS.

Providence
★

RHODE
ISLAND

WISCONSIN

St. Paul
★

MINNESOTA

MICHIGAN

Lansing ★

Lake Michigan

Lake Huron

Lake Erie

PENN.

Hudson R.

Hartford
★

CONNECTICUT

Delaware R.

Trenton
★ ─ NEW JERSEY

Harrisburg
★

Susquehanna R.

★ Dover

─ DELAWARE

⊛ Annapolis

─ MARYLAND

WASHINGTON, D.C.

*Chesapeake
Bay*

Madison ★

IOWA

Des
★ Moines

INDIANA

OHIO

Columbus ★

ILLINOIS

Lincoln
★

Springfield
★

Indianapolis
★

WEST
VIRGINIA

Potomac R.

Charleston
★

James R.

Richmond
★

VIRGINIA

THE ORIGINAL THIRTEEN COLONIES

Topeka
★

Jefferson
★ City

MISSOURI

Missouri R.

Frankfort
★

KENTUCKY

Ohio R.

**Gained by treaty
with Britain, 1783**

Proclamation Line of 1763

NORTH
CAROLINA

Raleigh
★

Cape Fear R.

Cumberland R.

Nashville
★

TENNESSEE

Tennessee R.

ATLANTIC
OCEAN

Oklahoma
★ City

ARKANSAS

Arkansas R.

SOUTH
CAROLINA

Columbia
★

OKLAHOMA

Little
★ Rock

Mississippi R.

Atlanta
★

Savannah R.

ALABAMA

GEORGIA

0   150   300 miles

0   150   300 kilometers

MISSISSIPPI

Montgomery
★

Jackson
★

LOUISIANA

Tallahassee
★

FLORIDA

Austin
★

Baton
Rouge
★

**Areas taken
from Spain
in 1810, 1813**

**FLORIDA
Treaty with Spain,
1819**

Gulf of Mexico

BAHAMAS

U.S. Territories

ATLANTIC
OCEAN

San
Juan
★

**VIRGIN
ISLANDS**
*Acquired from
Denmark,
1916–1917*

PUERTO RICO
*Acquired from
Spain, 1898*

Caribbean Sea

0   50   100 miles

0   50   100 kilometers

CUBA

Book Companion Site for *Through Women's Eyes* at bedfordstmartins.com/duboisdumenil

The book companion site provides instructors and students with many resources for teaching and learning U.S. women's history.

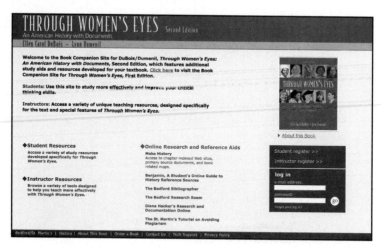

A **new** **Online Instructor's Resource Manual** features teaching tips and lecture suggestions, TV/film suggestions, ideas for term papers and other assignments, tips on working with visual sources, revised multiple-choice quizzes as well as exam questions, questions focused on in-text documents and visuals, and PowerPoint chapter outlines. Also available is a set of questions for use with i>clicker, a classroom response system.

A **revised** **Online Study Guide** for students includes annotated chapter outlines, note-taking outlines, identification terms, and chapter focus questions.

Make History contains a wealth of relevant chapter-by-chapter resources for classroom use or further research, including maps, images, primary documents, and links to historical Web sites.

Online Research and Reference Aids

- **Jules R. Benjamin's *A Student's Online Guide to History Reference Sources***
- ***The Bedford Bibliographer***
- ***The Bedford Research Room***
- **Diana Hacker's *Research and Documentation Online***
- ***The St. Martin's Tutorial on Avoiding Plagiarism* by Margaret Price**

For more information, please visit bedfordstmartins.com/duboisdumenil